1988

The Prentice-Hall Series in Marketing

PHILIP KOTLER, *Series Editor*

Abell/Hammond	*Strategic Market Planning: Problems and Analytical Approaches*
Corey	*Industrial Marketing: Cases and Concepts,* 3rd ed.
Green/Tull	*Research for Marketing Decisions,* 4th ed.
Keegan	*Multinational Marketing Management,* 3rd ed.
Russell/Verrill	*Otto Kleppner's Advertising Procedure,* 9th ed.
Kotler	*Marketing Management: Analysis, Planning, and Control,* 5th ed.
Kotler	*Principles of Marketing,* 3rd ed.
Kotler/Andreasen	*Strategic Marketing for Nonprofit Organizations,* 3rd ed.
Lovelock	*Services Marketing: Text, Cases, and Readings*
Myers/Massy/Greyser	*Marketing Research and Knowledge Development: An Assessment for Marketing Management*
Ray	*Advertising and Communication Management*
Stern/El-Ansary	*Marketing Channels,* 2nd ed.
Stern/Eovaldi	*Legal Aspects of Marketing Strategy: Antitrust and Consumer Protection Issues*
Urban/Hauser	*Design and Marketing of New Products*

STRATEGIC MARKETING FOR NONPROFIT ORGANIZATIONS

third edition

Philip Kotler

Northwestern University

Alan R. Andreasen

University of California at Los Angeles

PRENTICE-HALL, INC.

Englewood Cliffs, New Jersey 07632

Library of Congress Cataloging-in-Publication Data

Kotler, Philip.
    Strategic marketing for nonprofit organizations.

    Rev. ed. of: Marketing for nonprofit organizations /
Philip Kotler. 2nd ed. 1982.
    Includes index.
    1. Corporations, Nonprofit—Marketing.
2. Corporations, Nonprofit—United States—
Marketing—Case studies. I. Andreasen, Alan R.,
         II. Kotler, Philip. Marketing for
nonprofit organizations. III. Title.
HF5415.K6312 1987   658.8   86-25538

Editorial/production supervision and
  interior design: Laura Fillmore
Cover design: Diane Saxe
Cover illustration: Karen Goldsmith
Manufacturing buyer: Ed O'Dougherty

Previously published under the title of
  Marketing for Nonprofit Organizations.

Printed in the United States of America

10 9 8 7 6 5 4 3 2 1

ISBN 0-13-851205-1   01

PRENTICE-HALL INTERNATIONAL (UK) LIMITED, *London*
PRENTICE-HALL OF AUSTRALIA PTY. LIMITED, *Sydney*
PRENTICE-HALL CANADA INC., *Toronto*
PRENTICE-HALL HISPANOAMERICANA, S.A., *Mexico*
PRENTICE-HALL OF INDIA PRIVATE LIMITED, *New Delhi*
PRENTICE-HALL OF JAPAN, INC., *Tokyo*
PRENTICE-HALL OF SOUTHEAST ASIA PTE. LTD., *Singapore*
EDITORA PRENTICE-HALL DO BRASIL, LTDA., *Rio de Janeiro*

This book is dedicated to
MAURICE and BETTY KOTLER,
who provided my first introduction
to a nonprofit organization.
Philip Kotler

This book is dedicated to
JEAN MANNING,
whose love, encouragement, and insight
make all my work—as well as my life—
productive and joyful.
Alan R. Andreasen

Contents

9
Organizing for
Implementation
273

10
Leveraging Limited
Resources
301

11
Fundraising
321

III
DESIGNING THE
MARKETING MIX

12
Designing and Analyzing
Marketing Programs
351

13
Developing
New Offerings
377

14
Managing Offerings Over
the Life Cycle
396

IV
CONTROLLING
MARKETING STRATEGIES

22
Marketing Evaluation
and Control
616

Preface

This third edition of *Strategic Marketing for Nonprofit Organizations* comprises a major restructuring and extension of material that was pioneered in the first edition and modified in the second edition. This significant restructuring was brought about by—and in many ways gives concrete recognition to—the maturing of the field of nonprofit marketing. When the first edition of this book was being prepared, nonprofit marketing was just dimly recognized by a few scholars and a small number of innovative practitioners as able to make major contributions to resolving important social and economic problems.

The appearance of the second edition coincided with rapid growth in the acceptance and adaptation of marketing to fields such as postsecondary education, the arts, and health care. Still, the task facing authors of books such as this was very much one of introducing the concepts of marketing and showing those only marginally acquainted with—and sometimes vaguely hostile to—the promise of the new discipline how marketing might help achieve their organizational objectives. Much of the work continued to necessitate explaining and analogizing marketing so that those who did not yet see the potential could understand where marketing fit into their worlds and how it could have significant influences.

In 1987, this proselytizing effort is no longer necessary. The sectors of nonprofit marketing that recognized the potential of marketing at a very early stage, such as health care and higher education, are now at a point where the question is not whether one will use marketing but whether one will use it better than one's competitor or than one has in the past. Nonprofit marketing practitioners now comprise an experienced and sophisticated community. Even in fields relatively new to marketing, such as parks and recreation, library management, national social change programs, and state and local government administration, one increasingly finds specialists with formal training in marketing, considerable experience applying marketing in the private sector, or both.

For this audience and for the students who wish to someday join their ranks, the approach adopted in the first and second editions is no longer appropriate. If for no other reason than to exemplify the customer-centered precepts we are advocating in these volumes, we have chosen to change the text to make it more appropriate for the new audience of the latter half of the decade. This audience, we believe, needs to know not merely what marketing is and what it can do but, most important, how to do it well. This means knowing the most sophisticated and advanced tools and concepts the field has to offer and being able to use them on a day-to-day basis. This is the challenge accepted in the preparation of this third edition.

As was the case in the previous two editions, the major challenge of this book is to broaden and apply the conceptual system of marketing to the marketing problems of nonprofit organizations. These nonprofit organizations include a wide range of institutions and settings. Included are public sector organizations such as the National Cancer Institute, UCLA, Amtrak, the Peace Corps, and the U.S. Army as well as private nonprofits such as the American Cancer Society, Northwestern University, KCET public television, the National Education Association, the Chicago Symphony, and Cedars-Sinai Hospital. These organizations have two things in common. They seek to influence the behavior of one or more target audiences (just as profit-oriented firms do), and they do so not solely to benefit the organizations themselves but ultimately to benefit the members of the target audience, either individually or collectively, and thereby the society as a whole.

But why is a separate textbook needed for this context? Basic marketing texts cater primarily to the for-profit market. While recent editions of such texts inevitably have a chapter devoted to nonprofits, their focus is on marketing toothpaste, television, and fast-food restaurants. It requires special effort on the part of the nonprofit manager to see the relevance of the concepts presented in these texts to the nonprofit environment. One must bring to these texts an ability to generalize and see relationships between profit and nonprofit contexts, and this ability simply should not be required of a reader eager to learn and put into practice what marketing has to offer. This volume, like those before it, tries to provide an appropriate translation and introduction.

The book is divided into four basic parts reflecting the authors' orientation to the task of marketing in the nonprofit environment. In our view, marketing is at once a philosophy, a process of management, and a set of concepts and tools for carrying out the marketing management process. Thus, Part I of the book focuses on philosophy, what we characterize as "Developing a Customer Orientation." In Part I we discuss the environment the nonprofit manager faces, the philosophy that must be adopted, and the basic concepts that must be grasped to understand and segment critical target customer markets.

Part II then turns to the process. Here our emphasis is on strategic planning and organization. We outline the essence of this strategic orientation and show how marketing research, market measurement, and market forecasting can and must be used as the basic starting point of the strategic planning process. We show managers how to develop short- and long-range plans and then put in place the organization to carry them out. We conclude the section by describing approaches to the critical task all nonprofits face, that of leveraging limited resources through the use of volunteers, the assistance of other organizations, and effective fundraising.

Part III discusses a wide array of conceptual tools for carrying out detailed day-to-day and year-to-year tactics and programs. We begin by describing a set of tools to help the manager choose among alternative tactics and programs. We explain the major elements of the marketing mix, showing first how to develop new offerings and manage them over the "offer life cycle." We then outline the principal differences involved in marketing programs for products, services, and desirable social behaviors. We describe how to manage the various perceived costs involved in marketing exchanges and how to work through middlemen to achieve program effectiveness and efficiency. We introduce a number of basic concepts in the communication process and show how to use them in developing specific programs and tactics in advertising, sales promotion, public relations, and personal selling.

Part IV focuses on issues essential to all effective programs in the profit and nonprofit sectors. To learn from experience and to modify programs and tactics rapidly in response to changing marketing systems, the manager must institute well-conceived evaluation and control systems. It is only fitting that the book conclude with a section dealing with strategies for making the philosophy, process, and concepts we outlined in earlier sections self-renewing through effective evaluation and control systems.

Those who are familiar with the second edition will realize that this edition represents a significant revision and repositioning. Two new chapters, "The Marketing Philosophy" (Chapter 2) and "Formulating Communication Strategies for Influencing Behavior" (Chapter 18), have been added. The chapters "Understanding Customer Behavior" (Chapter 3), "Market Segmentation and Customer Targeting" (Chapter 4), "Marketing Research" (Chapter 6), "Managing Perceived Costs" (Chapter 16), and "Managing the Marketing Channel" (Chapter 17) have been substantially revised. Materials represented in several chapters in the second edition have been condensed in the chapters "Leveraging Limited Resources" (Chapter 10) and "Strategies for Products, Services, and Social Behaviors" (Chapter 15). In addition, a number of sections have been expanded, including those on such topics as the classification of nonprofit organizations, alternative organization forms, strategies for mature nonprofits, using various types of power to influence middlemen, direct mail and telephone marketing, and the use of marketing audits. All of these changes are consistent with the book's basic focus on strategic issues. As in earlier editions, each chapter begins with a vignette illustrating some of the major issues to be discussed in the chapter and concludes with a set of questions intended to provoke further discussion.

The first edition of this book was the result of a happy association with extremely creative and valued colleagues and students in the marketing department of the J. L. Kellogg Graduate School of Management at Northwestern University. The second edition benefited from dialogues with members of the marketing department: Bobby J. Calder, Richard M. Clewett, Jehoshua Eliashberg, Lakshmanan Krishnamurthi, Stephen A. LaTour, Sidney J. Levy, Trudy Kehret, Api Ruzdic, Louis W. Stern, Brian Sternthal, Alice M. Tybout, and Andris A. Zoltners. Excellent manuscript reviews of the second edition were provided by Professor Paul Bloom (University of Maryland); Professor Roberta N. Clarke (Boston University); and Professor Karen F. A. Fox (University of Santa Clara).

This third edition has benefited from the suggestions and reactions of many of those just named. Gratitude must also be expressed for insights and specific materials contributed by Jean Manning of Memel, Jacobs, Pierno, Gersh and Ellsworth, Los Angeles; William D. Novelli and Rachel Greenberg of Needham Porter Novelli, Washington; Terry Peigh of Foote Cone & Belding, Chicago; and Betty Ravenholt of The Futures Group, Washington. Exceptional care and effort were put into the preparation of the manuscript for this third edition by Lori Ramirez and her staff at UCLA's word processing center and by Irwin Powell.

STRATEGIC MARKETING FOR NONPROFIT ORGANIZATIONS

Marketing in the Nonprofit Environment

1. After a decade of declining enrollments and revenues, membership in the Boy Scouts of America rose 5.6 percent in 1982 over 1981, the largest increase in fourteen years. Its revenues rose to $1 million in profits annually. The BSA achieved this by changing its "product line" to fit its market. Scouts now learn computer skills to earn badges, and the Scouts' magazine, *Boys' Life,* now has an electronics column. Corporations sponsor hundreds of Scout posts. Explorer membership rose 21.3 percent in 1982, and a new product line extension, the "Tiger Cubs," has been established to market to those not yet old enough for Cub Scouts. The Tiger Cub program attracted 85,000 members in its first few months. A final contributor to the new profitability of the Scouts is their very successful merchandising of a broad line of products through wholly owned and franchised stores and mail order sales.[1]

2. In Albany, New York, the Albany Symphony Orchestra had accumulated a deficit of $108,000 by the mid-1970s. At that point a local businessman, Peter Kermain, decided that the Albany Symphony Orchestra had to choose a niche that gave it a special advantage in attracting audiences. He decided to mix into the typical Mozart and Beethoven program at each concert little-known contemporary works by living American composers. At the same time, to keep audiences in their seats the orchestra always included some popular classical works performed by popular soloists. The Albany Symphony's programming innovation resulted in a 67 percent increase in ticket sales in seven

years, the elimination of the orchestra's deficit, and an operating surplus in most years, a rarity among symphony orchestras.

Besides attracting new audiences, the orchestra's chosen niche created important advantages when it came to soliciting at funding agencies. In 1984, the Albany Symphony received $25,000 from the National Endowment for the Arts for general support and $17,000 to produce its first record. It also obtained $30,000 from Merrill Lynch, which presumably saw the American composers series as consistent with the firm's "Bullish on America" advertising themes.[2]

3. Since 1978, Carleton College, an excellent private four-year college in Northfield, Minnesota, has developed a well-planned marketing approach to student recruitment that has had significant payoffs. A survey the college conducted had shown that target high school students saw the college's location as too cold and isolated, the school itself as too "cerebral," and the library as too small. To counter these perceptions, Carleton updated the standard brochure by downplaying the cold weather, emphasizing the social and cultural attractions in nearby Minneapolis-St. Paul, and picturing the expansiveness of the library.

Buoyed by the success of this marketing innovation, Carleton conducted a further round of research, which indicated that there were significant regional differences in perceptions of the college and in students' major interests. Western students were found to be more interested than students from other regions in outdoor activities, and they were more "laid back" and informal in their approach to the classroom and campus life. By contrast, Eastern students were looking for a campus with academic prestige, whereas those in Minnesota felt that Carleton was too expensive for just a local college. As a result of these insights, Carleton decided to segment its target market and developed separate mailings for inquiring students from each of these key groups. Westerners were told about the lakes and outdoor recreation sites in nearby parts of Minnesota. Easterners were given much more information on Carleton's high educational standards and excellent teachers. And, finally, Minnesotans were given extensive information on financial aid and were told that Carleton was an institution with a decidedly national rather than just local reputation. As a result of these segmented messages, Carleton found that its mail response rate increased from 5.9 percent in 1978 to over 14 percent in 1980. Yearly applications rose from 1,470 to 1,875. Most crucially, the college remained financially solvent without being forced in any way to dilute its selection criteria.[3]

4. In a major contribution to solving world population problems, marketing helped distribute over 80 million condoms in Bangladesh in 1983 through 100,000 shops throughout the country. This was accomplished by a staff of 60 salespeople, 28 wholesalers, and a support staff of 160 selling condoms at about one-and-a-half cents each at retail. By contrast, 30,000 government workers in Bangladesh *give away* only half as

many condoms annually. An advisor to the private distribution program described the program as follows: "We're selling concepts and products the same as any other marketers except we're not making a profit. . . . We set the price high enough that it will represent something significant in the mind of the consumer, yet low enough so he can afford it, while allowing retailers an attractive margin. A local marketing/advertising firm is used to introduce the product, and package design and a brand name are selected in the same way Procter & Gamble would do it."[4] Similar "contraceptive social marketing" projects have now been developed in over a dozen countries. They have established conclusively the practicality and effectiveness of the kinds of strategies and tactics used in Bangladesh. Indeed, a $21 million social marketing program was funded by the U.S. Agency for International Development in 1984 largely because this agency has become a stronger believer in a marketing approach to this critical public health program.

5. In developing countries, about 340 million children under the age of five are at risk of dying each year due to diarrheal dehydration that results from infection and disease. Even when it is not fatal, dehydration can lead to severe malnutrition and eventually to stunted growth. Unfortunately, the condition is too often untreated, and sometimes the treatments that are provided actually magnify the problem. Mothers, for example, may withhold liquids or nourishment in the hope that this will stop the diarrhea, thereby depleting the child's supply of liquids and electrolytes. In a ten- to forty-pound human being, this depletion often proves fatal. It has recently been estimated that among young children in developing countries one diarrheal episode in 200 to 250 results in death.

Fortunately, we now know that simple rehydration with an inexpensive solution containing glucose, potassium, and salts (called oral rehydration therapy, or ORT) can virtually eliminate this major risk. Programs using social marketing techniques promoting ORT have had a major influence on the dehydration problem. To cite one example, in Alexandria, Egypt, in May of 1983, only 32 percent of adult women were aware of the dehydration problem and about 1.5 percent were aware that ORT was a potential solution. Barely 1 percent had ever used ORT at the time of this first study. After an intensive TV advertising and distribution campaign using advanced social marketing techniques, a second study in February, 1984, found that 87.2 percent of the women surveyed were aware of the dehydration problem, 87.4 percent of these women knew of ORT, and 36.2 percent had actually used it. Most significantly, diarrhea-related infant mortality rates dropped from 20 per 1,000 for those under one year of age and 26 per 1,000 for those one to five years old in 1982 to 4 per 1,000 for both age groups in 1983—a most dramatic and socially desirable outcome.[5]

Like products and services, ideas have life cycles. The idea of applying marketing to nonprofit organizations had its "birth" in a series of articles by Kotler and Levy,[6] Kotler and Zaltman,[7] and Shapiro[8] between 1969 and 1973. These articles argued that

> marketing is a pervasive societal activity that goes considerably beyond the selling of toothpaste, soap, and steel. Political contests remind us that candidates are marketed as well as soap; student recruitment in colleges reminds us that higher education is marketed; and fundraising reminds us that 'causes' are marketed.... [Yet no] attempt is made to examine whether the principles of 'good' marketing in traditional product areas are transferable to the marketing of services, persons, and ideas.[9]

In the years since the birth of this radical idea, a virtual stampede of marketing scholars and professionals has come forward to show that marketing principles are indeed of productive value to an expanding and amazingly diverse set of situations and organizations.

The growth period of this idea's life cycle has seen a dramatically steep rise in its acceptance. Driven partly by cost and competitive pressures and partly by the exciting promise marketing has to offer, practitioners in health care, education, and the arts rushed to embrace the new discipline and explore its possibilities. They were followed very shortly by the librarians, recreation specialists, politicians, and leaders of social service organizations and major charities. As this demand grew, so did the supply of scholars excited at the prospect of expanding the horizons of the discipline and testing the robustness of its concepts and tools. These scholars included both those inside academic marketing, such as the present authors and such people as Christopher Lovelock,[10] Charles Weinberg,[11] Michael Rothschild,[12] Paul Bloom,[13] Gerald Zaltman,[14] and numerous others, but also those outside the traditional field, such as Robin MacStravic in health care[15] and John Crompton in leisure and recreation.[16]

Today, the nonprofit marketing idea has clearly reached the maturity phase of its life cycle. The evidence is everywhere. Several general textbooks are now available,[17] as are text and trade books in specific subcategories such as the marketing of health care,[18] education,[19] social services,[20] and professional and social issues.[21] Specialized readers, conference proceedings, collections,[22] and casebooks[23] abound.

In addition to a growing array of articles on nonprofits in traditional and not-so-traditional journals, we now have the *Journal of Health Care Marketing,* the *Health Marketing Quarterly,* the *Praeger Series in Public and Nonprofit Sector Marketing,* the *Journal of Public Policy and Marketing, Healthmarketing, Hospital Public Relations,* the *Journal of Hospital Marketing,* the *Journal of Professional Services Marketing,* the *Journal of Marketing for Higher Education,* the *Journal of Marketing for Mental Health,* and the *Journal of Marketing/Management for Professionals*. Journals in such diverse fields as library science, art history, leisure studies, occupational therapy, and hospital management have joined the marketing bandwagon. To take just one example, in a recent review of library journals, Norman found eighty-seven articles, books, and monographs on some aspect of marketing.[24] Among the titles he found are "Marketing and Marketing Research: What the Library Manager Should Learn," *Journal of Library Administration* (Spring 1980); "The 'Marketization' of Libraries," *Library Journal* (1981); "Publicity and Promotion for Information Services in University Libraries," *Aslib Proceedings* (1974); and "Libraries: A Marketable Resource," *Canadian Library Journal* (1977).

In addition to this published output, courses in nonprofit marketing are now routinely demanded by MBA students at major universities as well as by swelling ranks of students from such diverse departments as health administration, public administration, arts administration, library science, law, social work, and leisure studies.

Major practitioner associations in nonprofit fields like the arts, health, and education now include interest groups specifically concerned with marketing. Virtually all such associations find that they must routinely schedule marketing presentations at their annual professional meetings, and from time to time they organize special miniconferences on various aspects of marketing theory and practice.

In the field, marketing specialists in nonprofit organizations are no longer a rarity. They no longer have to hide behind deceptive job titles like director of development, education coordinator, or patient liaison officer, nor is it necessary that they carry more conventional titles like public relations manager or advertising manager when their real job is marketing. Today, there are over 2,000 high-level marketing executives working in U.S. hospitals. A wide range of consulting organizations have sprung up in major centers, especially around Washington, D.C., to offer their services as marketing specialists in the nonprofit sector. To meet this new competition, the major traditional consulting firms have found that they must have special divisions or individuals dedicated to advising nonprofit marketing professionals.

Thus, after fifteen years of rapid growth, it is no longer necessary to market marketing to nonprofit managers or to convince marketing students and scholars that it is both feasible and legitimate to study this new and exciting application. What does this mean for nonprofit marketing education? First it means that today's textbooks, in contrast to earlier volumes, do not have to demonstrate in detail the diverse and sometimes unrecognized uses of marketing in a wide range of nonprofit, public sector, and individual contexts. It is no longer necessary to say in effect to readers, "I'll bet you didn't know that this was marketing or that you were doing marketing all along!" Nor is there a need to argue at length that most, if not all, nonprofit organizations would be better run and more successful if they did more marketing and did it better.

The basic goal for this book, then, is to provide a motivated audience of students and practitioners with the concepts, techniques, and illustrations needed to make them first-rate nonprofit marketing managers. The book, therefore, is decidedly not introductory in the sense of acquainting the naive reader with marketing and its possibilities and motivating him or her to begin to use marketing in the day-to-day management of a nonprofit organization. Instead, the book assumes that the reader is already motivated and knows a little about marketing and what it might do but wants to know how to actually carry out marketing programs more extensively and more effectively.

As will be demonstrated repeatedly in the chapters to follow, it is our view that a first-rate marketing manager is one who has acquired (1) an ingrained appreciation of the *philosophy* of marketing, (2) a comprehensive and practical *approach* to solving marketing problems, and (3) an *awareness and understanding* of some of the latest tools and techniques that can be used to make effective marketing decisions in specific areas. The book is organized around these objectives. Thus, the first two chapters in the first section are concerned with marketing philosophy as it applies to nonprofit organizations. The remainder of the present chapter, after a brief discussion of the potential contribution of marketing in the nonprofit sector, is devoted to carefully distinguishing nonprofit marketing from private sector, for-profit marketing. The attempt to clarify the meaning of "nonprofit" is not just an academic exercise. If there were not factors that were unique to the nonprofit context, there would be no point to a book like this; any of the many excellent general marketing texts would be perfectly satisfactory. But nonprofit marketing is not the same as for-profit marketing. The student and practitioner must appreciate the differences because they have major effects on what one can and cannot do as a marketing manager. We begin by considering the evolution of this new sector and the present significantly increased role for marketing.

Before proceeding, one definitional issue must be clarified. Some authors and several reporting agencies distinguish between two broad kinds of nonprofits. On the one hand, there are publicly owned government agencies like the U.S. Postal Service, the Office of Cancer Communications of the National Cancer Institute, and the British Railway System; on the other hand, there are nongovernmental or "third sector" nonprofits. Forms of ownership among the latter are very diverse; they range from corporations to cooperatives to individual enterprises. In our view, although nongovernmental and governmental nonprofits may differ in organizational form, they do not differ significantly in the unique marketing problems they face. Their differences from for-profit marketers are much more profound and are, indeed, the basis for this volume.

EVOLUTION OF NONPROFIT ORGANIZATIONS

Nelson Rosenbaum has proposed that since the American Revolution, the role of nonprofit organizations in society has evolved through four stages. The earliest stage conforms to what he terms a *voluntary/civic model*.[25] In Pilgrim times through the beginning of the present century, services that were not available from the government and were beyond the means of individual citizens were often provided by neighbors for each other. Thus, in those times—and in some rural areas and some fundamentalist religious communities today—citizens would band together to man the volunteer fire department or to help a needy family build a barn. Such a model was (and in some cases, still is) appropriate to a world with homogeneous interests, personal philosophies based on sharing, and a generally low level of economic welfare.

As the country prospered, the industrial revolution concentrated great wealth in the hands of a few families. Whether out of a sense of social responsibility or plain guilt, extremely rich families like the Morgans, Rockefellers, and Carnegies developed a pattern of what Rosenbaum calls *philanthropic patronage*. This patronage significantly benefited major U.S. educational and cultural institutions during the early part of this century.

Following the onset of the depression and the rapid growth of government-supported social institutions and programs, America turned in the 1940s and 1950s to a nonprofit model based on *rights and entitlements*. Many groups argued that they were entitled to at least partial support out of public taxation funds for their work, their institutions, or both, in part because they served the general social interest.

The final stage is the one in which we presently find ourselves—the *competitive/market* stage. In the earlier three stages, nonprofits relied for support on (1) individual willingness to share, (2) the generosity of the wealthy, or (3) the largess of federal, state, and municipal governments. Nonprofits have recognized that they can no longer rely on these traditional sources of support and must now be truly independent. This results in increasing attention to sound management principles, greater professionalism on the part of staff and managers, and more attention to generating a significant internal revenue base.

Three sets of factors in the nonprofit environment are driving the sector toward this new orientation.

1. *Changes in government spending patterns.* Recent shifts in public sentiment toward conservatism in social programs (vigorously supported by the Reagan administration), coupled with pressures for greater allocations to other budgetary sectors such as defense, have led to major cutbacks in discretionary social spending programs. Governmental aid to nonprofits fell 20 percent from 1981 to 1984. It now seems very likely that deficit reduction legislation passed in 1985 will accelerate this development. A second change in government

spending affecting nonprofits has been tighter control of costs in existing programs. This has been a particular problem for the health care sector.

2. *Changes in philanthropy.* A traditional method of filling the gap between nonprofit organizations' needs and government support, private sector donations, may not be adequate to the task, especially in certain sectors. Charitable giving by individuals as a percentage of per capita income fell from 1.99 to 1.84 percent between 1970 and 1980. On the other hand, business contributions to nonprofits rose from $.8 billion in 1970 to $2.7 billion in 1980. Still, the 1980 figure is well below the two percent of disposable income (that is, pretax earnings) that characterizes individual giving. Furthermore, foundation contributions rose only from $1.9 billion in 1970 to $2.4 billion in 1980, which, given inflation, is barely staying even.

3. *Changes in the economy.* Just when government and private sources of support are decreasing, forcing nonprofits to be more self-reliant, nonprofits find themselves increasingly attacked by for-profit firms in their own territories. Private organizations are now aggressively attacking various health care sectors, public transportation, and even prison management. This development means not only loss of revenue for nonprofits but increased competition for the personnel needed to effectively manage nonprofits.

GROWTH OF THE NONPROFIT SECTOR

The nonprofit sector is today surprisingly large. According to the IRS there were over 780,000 nongovernmental nonprofit entities in the United States as of June 30, 1983. Smith and Rosenbaum estimate that "the independent sector" (including institutions engaged in education and research, cultural activities, civic and social action, health services, human services, and religion) reported gross receipts to the IRS of $207.5 billion in 1979.[26] This figure is 8.8 percent of the U.S. gross national product. It represents significant growth from fiscal 1973, when receipts for the same set of organizations was only $73.5 billion, 5.6 percent of the GNP. Clearly, the independent nonprofit sector in the United States is growing much faster than the rest of the economy. These figures, as mentioned, do not even include nonprofit activities by government organizations.

The importance of the nonprofit sector is also shown in other figures. In 1980, private nonprofits employed 6.9 percent of all workers, up from 5.5 percent in 1960. The $50.2 billion in purchases by the nonprofit sector stimulated the indirect employment of an additional estimated 1.5 million workers. Between 1960 and 1975, the value of nonprofit plants and equipment grew at a rate of 13.4 percent per year, compared to 12.2 percent per year in the for-profit sector.

Nonprofits have different degrees of penetration in different industries. For example, nonprofits provide 20 percent of all hospital beds, where for-profit institutions provide 68 percent. Nonprofits also serve 41 percent of children in day-care centers, while for-profit institutions serve 51 percent. While for-profit companies collect 68 percent of the research and development grants, nonprofits collect 16 percent. And 20 percent of the post-secondary school revenues go to nonprofit organizations, while 34 percent go to for-profit companies.

The size of the nonprofit sector varies considerably by country, as does the role of government. Government and nongovernment nonprofit enterprises selling goods and services to the public in significant amounts employed 1.5 percent of the labor force in the United States in 1978. In the U. K. the figure was 8.1 percent; in Sweden, 8.2 percent; and in Austria, 13.7 percent.[27] In many countries, such as Sweden, there are virtually no private nonprofit organizations, whereas in the United States they are common.

RESOURCE GENERATION PROBLEMS

Although the independent sector is huge, its problems are substantial. According to Smith and Rosenbaum, the independent sector reported that it obtained only 50 percent of its revenues from internally generated income (that is, from marketed products and services).[28] This varies greatly by sub-sector, from 7 percent for religious organizations to 79 percent for education and research institutions. The unmet resource needs for these organizations are made up by private philanthropy (25 percent) and government support (25 percent).

Analysis within the subsectors further delineates the potential for marketing in specific narrower fields. A 1983 survey of nonprofit income sources carried out by the Rockefeller Foundation reported the average percentages of earned income for one group, arts organizations. Their results are given in Table 1-1.

Outside the arts field, the Rockefeller study found that colleges and universities generated only 52 percent of their own income, private and secondary schools 70 percent, zoos and aquariums 47 percent, and family service and child welfare organizations barely 14 percent.

Table 1-1

PERCENT OF INCOME THAT WAS EARNED BY SELECTED
NONPROFIT CATEGORIES, 1983

Organizations	% Income That Was Earned
121 Theaters	71
32 Major Symphonies	56
32 Regional Symphonies	55
91 Regional Ballet Companies	54
109 Opera Companies	48
64 Media Arts Centers	46
4,409 Museums	42

SOURCE: James C. Crimmins and Mary Kiel, *Enterprise in the Nonprofit Sector* (New York: The Rockefeller Brothers Fund, 1983), p. 141.

There are often more fundamental problems behind the revenue gaps. Consider the situation of the Catholic church. In 1966, as many as 55 percent of all adult Catholics under thirty years of age attended mass in a typical week. By 1975 the attendance rate had fallen to 39 percent. Other studies show strong discontent among American Catholics and a decline in the number of people who believe or practice the church's teaching. The growing alienation is attributed to the church's doctrinal rigidity and the increasing popularity of other organizations competing for people's time, interest, and loyalty. The impact on revenue generation is clear.

Education also has its problems. More than 170 private colleges have closed their doors since 1965 in the face of declining enrollment, dwindling endowments, and sharply rising costs. Some experts predict a further closing of anywhere between 10 and 30 percent of the nation's 3,000 colleges in the next decade as the number of college-age students shrinks 20 to 30 percent from today's level.[29]

Hospitals are also in trouble. In California, admissions to hospitals per 1,000 population were 134.8 in 1969 and 144.3 in 1974, but they were down to 124.8 in 1984. Similarly, patient days per 1,000 population fell from 995.6 in 1969 to 803.7 in 1984.[30] From 1976 to 1983, 329 hospitals permanently closed, a rate of more than 40 per year. An additional 500 may close before 1989, according to a recent study at Johns Hopkins University.[31] Among the reasons for the predicted accelerated rate of hospital closures are (1) government cuts in Medicaid and Medicare; (2) introduction of fixed payment schedules for diagnostically related groups of illnesses; (3) efforts by private insurers to discourage hospital use; (4) unemployment; and (5) growing competition. Ironically, the problem for smaller hospitals is exacerbated by the fact that as pressure increases to fill the revenue gap, larger hospitals are becoming more aggressive marketers, offering new services, forming neighborhood chain outlets, and reaching out to draw customers from greater distances to increase their occupancy rates.

DEFINING NONPROFIT MARKETING

The examples noted earlier of innovative marketing programs clearly indicate that marketing has a wide range of applications in nonprofit contexts. But it is also apparent that some of these applications are not very different from strategies and tactics one finds in profit-making organizations. Indeed, many governmental and nongovernmental nonprofits routinely carry on programs that are intended to be profit-making. They consciously sell products and services to bring in needed revenue. For some, such as theatres and symphonies selling individual tickets and subscriptions or hospitals "selling" surgery and convalescent care, generating this revenue is their primary business. For others, selling products and services is a secondary business designed to supplement a more basic social mission. This is the case of the Girl Scouts selling cookies, the Sierra Club selling calendars, the American Red Cross selling first-aid kits, and most museums selling a wide diversity of gift items, reproductions, and food and drinks. That these are not always trivial businesses is attested to by the fact that Girl Scout cookies comprise 10 percent of all cookies sold in the United States.

On the other hand, there are also *profit-making* organizations that carry out activities very much like those provided by nonprofit social service agencies. Allstate Insurance has mounted a substantial attitude-change project designed to secure public, government, and auto manufacturer support for air bags for automobiles. Reynolds Metals urges consumers to recycle cans, and the local gas company tells us about ways to *save* energy (not buy it!). The liquor industry promotes sensible drinking. Exxon sponsors programming on public television, and the 7-Eleven minimarket food chain and others are active in the annual muscular dystrophy charity drive. Many supermarkets and mail order firms help in the search for missing children.

And, if this were not confusing enough, there are now a number of quasi-governmental agencies like the postal service and Amtrak that appear to be neither traditional nonprofits nor profit-making organizations. As Lovelock points out, for example, the British Post Office became an independent corporation in 1961 and the U.S. Postal Service became an independent agency of the executive branch in 1971. These quasi-governmental organizations are often very large. For example, the British Railways Board holding company operates a passenger rail service, a freight rail service, a shipping firm, eleven harbors, a hovercraft company, a food service company (for trains and stations), a locomotive and rolling stock construction company, an international consulting firm, and a North American passenger sales business.[32]

Not all allocations of responsibilities between the private and public sectors in different countries are permanent, of course. In general, the trend has been to shift activities to the private sector (privatization). A recent move in that direction was the effort of the British government in the summer of 1984 to sell a 50.2 percent interest in British Telecommunications, the fourth largest telephone company in the world, to the public. Indeed, since 1979, the Thatcher government has sold off a number of small- to medium-sized businesses, including British Aerospace, the Sealink Cross-Channel Ferry Company, twenty-nine British Railways hotels, and the Jaguar Motor Car Division of state-owned British Leyland.

Finally, it must be noted that not all of the organizational alternatives available in the United States are possible in other countries of the world. In Thailand, for example, there is no legal entity like the U.S. nonprofit organization. As a consequence, Population Development Associates, a highly entrepreneurial rural developer and marketer of contraceptives, has been forced to set up a taxable enterprise but informally agree that any "profits" will be kept in the organization and not distributed to the nominal "stockholders."

CLASSIFICATION OF NONPROFIT ORGANIZATIONS

Since a welter of confusing organizational forms are doing "nonprofit marketing," it is essential that some definitions be established. A great many alternative definitions have been offered in recent years to distinguish "profits" from "nonprofits" and to separate various kinds of nonprofits from each other. Many authors suggest, as we have here, that the distinction between profits and nonprofits is not the only useful dichotomy, since even in the nonprofit sector there are public corporations like the postal service and state-run telephone and rail companies that are virtually indistinguishable from private corporations in their drive for sales and profits. Smith and Rosenbaum[33] suggest that *sources of funding* are a good basis for a typology, classifying organizations into those that are funded by (1) profit, (2) government revenues (taxes, grants, bonds, etc.), and (3) voluntary donations. Rados[34] suggests that within each area, a key distinction ought to be the organizational form of the venture (sole enterprise, association, corporation, partnership, or foundation). Fine,[35] on the other hand, emphasizes separating nonprofits and profits by the type of offering the organization is involved with (tangible products, services, or behavior changes).

Two authors propose a two-dimensional classification. Lovelock and Weinberg propose (after Smith and Rosenbaum) segregating public organizations in terms of their sources of financial support as well as by the extent of political control to which the organization is subject. They suggest that Amtrak and the U.S. Postal Service are examples of organizations under "tight political control," whereas British Railway and the U.K. post office are "largely independent of political control."[36]

A different kind of control is emphasized in Henry Hansmann's widely quoted partitioning of nonprofits according to two sets of characteristics. The first is whether the organization is *donative* or *commercial,* that is, whether it secures its revenues primarily from donations or from charges to users. The second is whether the organization is *mutual* or *entrepreneurial.*[37] Mutual organizations are primarily controlled by users, whereas entrepreneurial organizations are controlled by professional managers. For example, in the United States, the donative-mutual category would include many religions, local political organizations, and lobbying groups. The commercial-mutual category would include such groups as professional associations and nonprofit health or golf clubs. The donative-entrepreneurial category includes groups such as arts organizations, the Red Cross, and the Salvation Army. The commercial-entrepreneurial category would cover groups like nonprofit hospitals and contraceptive marketing programs.

A problem with many of these classification schemes is that they over-look the fact that nonprofit organizations often have different divisions that do different things, putting them simultaneously in different sectors of any typology. Thus, in Hansmann's classification scheme, the Los Angeles County Museum is donative-entrepreneurial with regard to amassing its collections yet commercial-entrepreneurial in its museum gift shop. Some hospitals are commercial-mutual in their outpatient services but donative-mutual in their candy striper patient services.

LEGAL DEFINITION AND THE PROBLEM OF UNRELATED INCOME

One very important classification dimension is the legal one. One may always ask whether the organization is, in fact, a legally defined nonprofit. Section 501 of the Internal Revenue Code grants tax-exempt status to twenty-three different categories of organizations. Thirty-nine percent are covered under Section 501(c)(3), which includes charitable, religious, scientific, and educational institutions. Section 501(c)(4) of the tax code includes civic leagues; section 501(c)(6), business leagues; and section 501(c)(7), social clubs.

It is essential that nonprofit managers obtain formal designation as nonprofits for their organizations since a great many benefits are available to such enterprises. For example, U.S. nonprofits receive the following special treatments or exemptions:

- Exemption from federal, state, and local income taxes.
- Exemption from local property taxes in most cases.
- Exemption from unemployment insurance payments in some areas.
- Lower bulk postage rates.
- Exemption from Robinson-Patman Act.
- Possible lower charges or none at all for federal services.
- Exemption from tort liability under common law.
- Hospitals and some other organizations can issue tax-exempt bonds.
- Charitable, educational, scientific, and certain other organizations can receive donations, gifts, and bequests that permit tax deductions for the giver.
- Access to donated space and air time from media.

Two rationales are typically offered for the special status of nonprofits. The most common is the "public goods" rationale, which argues that non-profits provide services such as health care, education, and basic research that would not be provided were it not for the tax subsidy offered by the government. The second rationale, called the "quality assurance" rationale, argues that nonprofits provide services in areas in which consumers are ordinarily ill-equipped to judge quality, such as health care and education. Having these services performed by tax-exempt nonprofits supposedly assures the public of quality and protection in situations where for-profit firms might charge excessive prices for inferior services.

In the past, government was relatively generous in granting special benefits to nonprofits. Ironically, however, the recent successes of marketing in the nonprofit sector have caused a major shift in federal thinking about nonprofits. In the past ten years many nonprofits have become extremely entrepreneurial, taking advantage of opportunities for direct revenue generation to supplement donative sources of funding. The Urban Institute estimates that about 10 percent of nonprofits now have some commercial enterprise.

In 1985, museum store sales reached $200 million. New York's Metropolitan Museum of Art now carries over 15,000 items, from an $18.50 Egyptian bas-relief to a $1,500 bronze copy of a Greek horse. Sales at the museum reached $34 million in 1985, an increase of 85 percent over 1981. Sales at Boston's Museum of Science, while more modest at $850,000, doubled over the same period. The Smithsonian has nine stores and a mail order business that generated $34.5 million in sales in 1985, up 29 percent over the previous year.[38]

These unrelated businesses need not involve only goods. Nonprofits have become excellent fund-raisers through the marketing of services. The "gala" is such a venture (see Exhibit 1-1). Other nonprofit ventures include the National Audubon Society leasing oil rights under its Louisiana gulf coast sanctuary and the Children's Television Workshop selling the rights to its Sesame Street characters to toy makers for a significant royalty.[39]

Although not all these ventures are successful (see Exhibit 1-2), they have led many in Washington to raise an alarm. These critics argue that the nonprofit sector, which was once dominated by donative organizations, is not only increasing its share of the GNP, but, more significantly, it is becoming dominated by "commercial nonprofits."[40] This new breed, it is argued, secures substantial portions of their income from the sale of goods and services. Further, such sales are mainly to those who can afford to pay, not to the poor and indigent whom the nonprofits were often granted their special status to serve. What's more, nonprofits have major unique competitive advantages in many sectors, including vocational schools, primary and secondary schools, nonprofit nursing homes, day-care centers, research laboratories, consulting organizations, automobile clubs, and educational testing services. A major concern is that in these industries, nonprofits represent unfair competition for for-profit firms, especially small businesses. Analysts have suggested that nonprofits have become major factors in industries like audiovisual supplies, analytical testing, and research services. Because existing for-profit firms cannot easily exit from these industries due to their large investments, the nonprofits have caused an oversupply of firms, a decline in prices, and lower returns on investment. In other industries, it is claimed that nonprofits can underprice competitors (for example, in securing gov-

EXHIBIT 1-1. The Met throws a gala

At the Metropolitan Opera's opening night festivities in September, 1985, Luciano Pavarotti performed *Tosca*. But then a select group of the bejeweled and black-tie audience stayed on at the opera house. They were guests at a dinner and fashion show that introduced Chanel's newest perfume, Coco. At the gala, twenty-five models emerged from a twelve-foot-tall bottle of Coco. For the right to reach the wealthy opera-goers, Chanel contributed $250,000 to the opera and financed the party. For the Met, too, the night was a success: According to the opera, Chanel's corporate largess helped it raise $1.2 million in a matter of hours.

If the entry of commerce into the long-sancrosanct halls of the arts has led to some criticism from purists, the opera's general manager says he sees it more realistically: In this new environment for nonprofits, he believes the needs of corporate sponsors must be taken into account.

"There certainly is a limit here, a question of how much of this is a good thing," said Bruce Crawford, whose financial savvy helped the Met reduce its deficit by about $6 million over the last two years. "But you have to be prepared to deliver to corporations. If they give you $400,000 or $500,000, they don't expect you to take the money and run. You've got to provide something that's beneficial to them in a marketing sense."

SOURCE: William Meyers, "The Nonprofits Drop the 'Non,'" Copyright © 1985 by the New York Times Company. Reprinted by permission.

ernment contracts) because of their significant tax and other cost advantages.

The reason nonprofits have "gotten away" with these "business" activities is that the IRS simply looks at the overall purpose of the organization, not at individual ventures, to define nonprofit status. In 1950, however, the Congress determined that nonprofits must pay taxes on proceeds of "unrelated" business activities. Thus, even when an organization has been designated a nonprofit, the government still pays very close attention to its individual activities. The government's position is that any revenue-generating activity that is *unrelated* to the organization's basic mission must be taxed as would a for-profit enterprise. Thus, a manager must clearly understand whether any present or proposed ventures for which marketing plans are to be developed will be officially classified by the IRS as unrelated business activities. The following conditions would lead to such a classification:

1. It must be a *trade or business;* that is, it must be designed to produce income from the sale of goods or services. This income production need not be for purposes of making a profit nor need it be undertaken by the nonprofit

EXHIBIT 1-2. The Children's Television Workshop misses a market

The Children's Television Workshop, which has been so successful in licensing its Sesame Street products, acknowledges that miscalculation and mismanagement recently caused it to stumble in the high tech area. C.T.W., believing that the computer revolution would take off and sustain a line of educational Sesame Street software for children, assembled an in-house staff of some fifty program developers three years ago and also introduced a children's computer magazine.

The project sailed smack into a collapsing market for personal computers, however, and C.T.W. lost close to $10 million from its ill-fated software activities betwen 1982 and 1985, its management said. C.T.W. dismissed the executive responsible for this fiasco and laid off virtually its entire software staff, merging the computer magazine into an existing one. Before this setback, C.T.W. had developed a host of electronic Sesame Street games and activities, and some thirty-three of them are now on the market, distributed by Apple, Atari, CBS, and Tandy. But today they bring in only 2 percent of C.T.W.'s revenues, far less than the organization had envisioned.

C.T.W. executives say they have learned painful lessons from the ill-conceived experience. They have since embarked on a new—and more cautious—business strategy.

"We engaged in much too rapid a buildup of staff and commitment before we had enough evidence on the sales and revenue side," says David V.B. Britt, C.T.W.'s executive vice-president, reflecting on his organization's software experiment. "We still have to look for revenue-generating activities if we want to sustain Sesame Street and other programs. But we are not going to be making major financial bets anymore. We are pulling back in and simplifying and streamlining our lines of business. We don't have the legs or financial staying power needed to see every investment through."

Of course, C.T.W. is continuing its successful licensing arrangements for Sesame Street products. It licenses some 1,600 items, ranging from a Big Bird battery-operated toothbrush to a Cookie Monster bulldozer, to thirty companies, including J.C. Penney and Hasbro. In all, revenues from all commercial endeavors came to $37.4 million in 1984, up from $29.8 million three years earlier.

SOURCE: William Meyers, "The Nonprofits Drop the 'Non.'" Copyright © 1985 by the New York Times Company. Reprinted by permission.

itself (that is, it may be through an affiliate). It must be *actively* pursued. On the other hand, interest, royalties, and dividend earnings are often exempt.

2. It must be *regularly carried on.* The standard of comparison here is the situation of for-profit businesses. Selling Girl Scout cookies, which is done only once a year, would be exempt. On the other hand, a seasonal venture such as Christmas tree sales that competes with seasonal for-profit businesses would qualify as "regularly carried on."

3. It must be *substantially unrelated* to the organization's exempt functions. Obviously, nonprofits will seek to define a venture as "related" if it can, but there must be a substantial, causal relationship. It is not enough that the proceeds are used to further tax-exempt programs.

Finally, certain activities of nonprofits have been defined categorically by Congress as tax-exempt. These include certain kinds of research, fund-raising functions, convenience services, trade shows, and bingo games.

Because the law in this area is changing rapidly and because nonprofits' marketing pressures on commercial ventures will grow, nonprofit managers should seek professional help if they are at all unsure about the classification of a particular venture. The American Red Cross, for example, received a ruling from the IRS that it did not have to pay taxes on its first-aid kits. According to the *New York Times,* however, Red Cross Project Director Mark Ambrose decided *not* to sell the kits in drug stores because "such an arrangement could raise a question of tax liability because the outlets [are] so clearly commercial."[41]

Above all, managers should be extremely careful that the amount of unrelated, taxable activity does not grow to comprise too large a percentage of overall revenue. Hopkins has suggested that if this percentage rises above 35 percent, the organization should be concerned that it may lose its overall tax-exempt status.[42] The IRS will permit virtually any kind of unrelated business but will be very attentive to the *total* quantity of such ventures.

THE NONPROFIT MANAGERIAL ENVIRONMENT

At this point it is necessary to ask why it is useful to classify the organizations at all? The obvious answer is a managerial one: Any taxonomy is useful for the purposes of nonprofit managers if it helps them make better decisions on how to run their enterprises. Legal classifications of organizations and their activities only specify what is possible for the nonprofit marketing manager. Other characteristics of nonprofit ventures significantly affect what the manager can and ought to do strategically. The important distinctions concern the nature of the organization's environment and the nature of the basic marketing activities the organization is engaged in.

NATURE OF THE ORGANIZATION'S ENVIRONMENT

Five key questions help define the organization's environment.

- Is the organization donative in whole or in part?
- Is the organization's performance likely to be subject to public scrutiny?
- Is marketing seen as undesirable from the standpoint of some or all members of the organization or its major sponsors or reviewers?
- Is the organization largely staffed by volunteers?
- Is performance judged largely by nonmarketing measures?

We shall consider each of these questions before turning to distinctions associated with the specific *activities* a nonprofit might perform.

Is the Organization Donative?   If the proposed activity or the organization as a whole is funded through private philanthropy or government grants, how one *can* market and *ought to* market is influenced in two major ways. First, outside funding agencies may establish restrictions on what can be done. In such cases, the least bothersome problem but nonetheless an important source of irritation is procedural restrictions that formally specify the steps to be taken, the forms to be filled out, the individuals with whom one must "touch base," or all three. To cite a typical example, many government contracts put a substantial hurdle before nonprofit marketers who wish to carry out research by requiring that questionnaires be approved by the Office of Management and Budget before being taken into the field.

More troublesome are outright restrictions on certain activities. Donors may require that a funded program target specific audiences, even though this may be an inefficient and ineffective use of the nonprofit's resources in the short run. They may proscribe certain media, prevent the hiring of particular specialist staff members, or require that some products be used where better choices are available elsewhere.

One problem of government sponsorship is that nonprofit marketers may not be allowed to choose the segments to which they will market. In some situations they may not be permitted to segment at all, as when the postal service must charge the same price for a first-class letter between any sender and receiver no matter what the costs of the service or the ability or willingness of either party to pay for the service.

In some cases, nonprofit marketers are required by sponsors to tackle segments that are very difficult to reach and influence in comparison with other segments on which limited resources might be more efficiently spent. Contraceptive marketing programs in many developing countries, for example, must be directed at consumers with low literacy and limited awareness of the birth control issue in villages where conventional distribution facilities are nonexistent or primitive. Agencies that would prefer in the short run to build marketing skills and develop a stable revenue base by marketing to more sophisticated—but still needy—urban target audiences are often effectively barred (or at least discouraged) from doing so by sponsoring agencies.

The second consequence of an organization's donative status is that the marketing task is doubled. Not only do marketers have to plan programs aimed at final consumers, they must also consciously plan strategies to insure continued—and preferably increased—outside support. This problem of having to market to multiple publics is not strictly unique to nonprofits. For-profit corporations must market to stockholders, investment specialists, regulatory agencies, town councils, and even labor unions. But in the private sector, these are typically relatively minor problems. Indeed, the interests of many of these secondary publics (for example, investors and town councils) are well served simply if the corporation's main customer marketing task is successful. More sales revenue means more profits, more jobs, more taxes. But it must be remembered that nonprofits get *50 percent* of their revenues from donations and grants. Support publics are therefore not at all minor concerns. Thus, nonprofits must arrange marketing strategies for *resource attraction* as well as *resource allocation.*

The problems of multipublic marketing will be taken up later in the book. At this point, it must be emphasized that marketing to multiple publics should, in fact, be a *marketing* activity. Too often, contacts with government agencies or major donors are left to the chief executive officer or chairman of the board with no input from the marketing staff.

Is There Public Scrutiny?   Nonprofits may find their marketing options severely restricted if they are subjected to constant public scrutiny. The kinds of problems that can occur are well illustrated by a 1980 situation involving the government of Canada. During the last years of the Trudeau administration, the Canadian government actively sought public support for its newly proposed constitution. To achieve this goal, the government decided to undertake a major advertising campaign at a cost of about $6 million. The campaign raised all sorts of questions about whether the government was doing "too much" marketing. Routine ads for agricultural products and job openings were quite acceptable, but government marketing of highly visible and controversial campaigns like that for the Constitution raised a number of public protests. Whereas it was estimated that federal government advertising in the United States cost about $146 million in 1979, in Canada, with one twentieth the population, total expenditures were higher at $160 million. This amounted to about $6.66 for each Canadian citizen, compared with $.65 per person in the United States. The U.S. federal government was the country's twenty-eighth largest advertiser, while in Canada it was the largest, up from seventeenth in 1969. The Canadian government's advertising expenditures, which now are three times those of the second largest advertiser, General Foods, have received extensive public criticism from both industry leaders and individual citizens. J. L. Foley, chairman of the Institute of Canadian Advertising, said that the growth in government advertising constitutes a threat to free speech, a waste of taxpayers' money and "a further emasculation of Parliament and parliamentary democracy." A reader of Toronto's *Globe and Mail* put it more simply. "Good government needs no advertising. It speaks for itself."[43]

The fact that a nonprofit organization is publicly accountable has other restrictive features. One consequence is that nonprofits feel they should ignore certain competitors or not compete with them. Bloom and Novelli distinguish between friendly and unfriendly competitors as follows:

> Social marketers must also be concerned about the impact of a type of competition that commercial marketers rarely face—the friendly competition pro-

vided by other social organizations fighting for the same cause. Thus, in developing a marketing plan for the smoking cessation program of the National Cancer Institute, it becomes necessary to consider the potential actions of the National Heart, Lung and Blood Institute, the U.S. Office of Smoking and Health, the American Cancer Society, the American Lung Association, the American Heart Association, and a host of others. Friendly competitors can help the social marketer in many ways, but they can also create fragmented efforts, funding problems, and other difficulties.[44]

Is Marketing Seen as Undesirable?   Over the years, marketing has had difficulty in gaining acceptance in a number of nonprofit organizations. One hindrance was the view that marketing really wasn't necessary. It was argued, for example, that good health does not need to be sold; that hospitals don't need to be marketed; that lawful behavior is simply a social requirement; and that one shouldn't have to advertise to drivers to get them not to speed.

Fortunately, the view that marketing is undesirable because it is unnecessary has faded away, in part because nonprofit managers and their supporters have learned the potential of marketing and in part because they have been starkly confronted with the *need* for it.

More vexing and more lasting is the sometimes not-so-subconscious opinion that at base marketing is *evil.* This opinion manifests itself in three views:

MARKETING IS SEEN AS WASTING THE PUBLIC'S MONEY.   As we have seen in the Canadian government case, a frequent criticism of marketing activities is that they are too expensive. In 1971, for example, the U.S. Army spent $10.7 million on advertising in a thirteen-week period in an effort to increase army enlistments, and this upset many people. Similarly, the U.S. Postal Service increased its cost of operations by establishing a marketing department within the postal service and giving it a large budget.[45] Many people carefully watch the marketing expenses of charitable organizations to make sure that they do not get out of line with the amount of money being raised.

Organizations, of course, should not add costs that do not produce an adequate return. Nonprofit organizations owe their publics an explanation of the benefits they are seeking to achieve through their marketing expenditures. They should not overspend and they should not underspend. At this stage, nonprofit organizations are more prone to underspend than to overspend on marketing. If the U.S. Army needs a certain number of recruits, $10 million spent on national television is probably the most efficient way to proceed. The issue should not be the absolute cost but the relative attraction cost per 1,000 new recruits. If the U.S. Postal Service needs to develop new and viable mail services for its users, its expenditure on marketing research, planning, testing, and promotion is proper if this expenditure is expected to yield a reasonable return.

MARKETING ACTIVITIES ARE SEEN AS INTRUSIVE. A second objection to marketing is that it often intrudes itself into people's personal lives. Marketing researchers go into homes and ask people about their likes and dislikes, their beliefs, their attitudes, their incomes, and other personal matters. A health clinic, for example, sent out researchers to study the fears of married men about vasectomies (male sterilization) in order to formulate a more effective information campaign on behalf of vasectomies. There is a widespread concern that if various government agencies started doing a lot of marketing research, the information might eventually be used against individual citizens or in mass propaganda. Citizens also dislike the fact that their tax money is being spent to do the research.

Ironically, marketing research is primarily carried on to learn the needs and wants of people and their attitude toward the organization's current products so that the organization can deliver greater satisfaction to its target publics. At the same time, organizations must show a sensitivity to the public's feelings for privacy.[46]

MARKETING IS SEEN AS MANIPULATIVE. A third criticism is that organizations will use marketing to manipulate the target market. Many smokers resent the antismoking ads put out by the American Cancer Society as trying to manipulate them through fear appeals. Some congressmen were upset with the report that the Interior Department planned to spend more money on a high-powered campaign to tout itself and "its photogenic boss."[47] Image ads by police departments are seen by some citizens as manipulative.

Administrators should be sensitive to the possible charge of manipulation when they implement a marketing program. In the majority of cases, the nonprofit organization is seeking some public good for which there is widespread consensus, and it is using proper means. In other cases, the charge of manipulation may be justified and such efforts, unless they are checked, will bring a "black eye" to the organization and to marketing.

These critiques are particularly acute in some segments of the nonprofit sector. In the personal health care industry, for example, there has until recently been a reluctance to use advertising, for two reasons. First, advertising is equated with "Madison Avenue gimmickry"; to advertise the hospital is ultimately to demean it. If it uses advertising, the hospital's reputation for quality will decline and physicians, believed to have an inherent repulsion for promotion of any type, will disassociate themselves from it. Second, advertising is viewed as unethical. This view suggests that advertising a hospital is tantamount to immorality, for it fosters the hospital's image as an institution that profits from the misery and misfortune of the ill and infirm.

These critiques may be generalized to all of marketing. A headline in *U.S. News and World Report* in 1985 asked, "Is 'Showbiz' Ruining America's Big Museums?" Joseph Veach Noble, director of the Museum of the City of New York, states the criticism: "This mercantile trend of our cultural institutions has been forced upon us, but it certainly isn't healthy. Aesthetic judgment must now take a back seat to whatever sells." Blockbuster shows produce excessive wear on facilities, divert money and personnel from work on the permanent collection, and alienate some regular museumgoers.[48]

Although these views are misguided, they do in large measure reflect the differing backgrounds of a great many of those with whom the professional marketer must work. It is a reality that not only creates tension, but may well restrict what the marketer is allowed to do. Such restrictions may include:

- Severely constraining budgets for advertising and marketing research.
- Requiring that media advertising time and space be donated, not paid for.
- Prohibiting or discouraging research into sensitive aspects of consumer thinking and behavior.
- Prohibiting certain promotion techniques, such as the use of fear appeals, humor, or "hard selling."
- Looking down on aggressive marketing as confirming the "negative image of marketing" and making future marketing more difficult.
- Promulgating internal "codes of ethics," as in medicine, accounting, and the law that severely hamper the range of acceptable marketing practices by the threat of removing accreditation or membership in an important professional group.

Is the Staff Primarily Volunteers?   A significant proportion of nonprofit organizations rely upon unpaid volunteers for clerical assistance, fundraising, stuffing envelopes, conducting tours, and even attracting other volunteers. Weisbrod has estimated that as of the mid-1970s, volunteers provided over 20 percent of nonprofits' labor resources.[49] This amounted to 6 billion hours of effort, the equivalent of 3 million full-time workers (4 percent of the U.S. labor force). This can create two types of problems for the nonprofit manager. First, the need for a steady influx of volunteers means that a third "public" is added to those to whom the manager must market. Programs must be designed to attract and retain paid personnel, while a watchful eye must be kept on possible ramifications of proposed programs on existing volunteers. Directors of blood donation programs who rely heavily on volunteers, for example, often find that plans for extending collection hours or expanding into new, marginal, and sometimes unsavory neighborhoods meet with strong resistance from the volunteer segment of their staff. Blood program managers have succeeded in these needed outreach efforts when they have first marketed the program and its benefits to the volunteers.

The second problem with volunteers involves day-to-day management. A universal complaint of managers who have to work with volunteers is that they are unreliable. One manager has what he calls a "rule of thirds" for volunteers. According to his experience, one-third of all volunteers will be highly motivated, eager to help out, and highly responsive to superiors' directions. At the other extreme is the third who seem to want little more than to tell their friends that they volunteered. They seldom appear at all for work. Their promises of assistance are rarely kept, and when they do appear, they resist directions to do anything they don't *really* feel like doing. The third in the middle is the group that can make or break the organization. The ability to effectively motivate and direct this group is the true test of a nonprofit manager's interpersonal skills. Although, as we shall outline in Chapter 10, many of the principal techniques of personnel management in the private sector can and ought to be applied in nonprofit organizations, the simple fact that a manager doesn't have the "carrot" of a salary or the "stick" of potential firing to use to motivate and direct the people needed to make the marketing program successful is often a crucial hindrance in carrying out an effective and fast-moving marketing program.

Is Performance Judged by Nonmarketing Standards?   Those who judge marketing performance in nonprofit organizations have often been trained in other disciplines and have only a crude appreciation of the realities of day-to-day management. This can seriously affect the kinds of marketing goals that are set for the nonprofit marketer.

Expectations for success, for example, can often be highly exaggerated. Those who evaluate nonprofit programs often want "everyone" to wear seat belts or to stop smoking or to give to their charity. As Peter Drucker notes, "To obtain its budget, [the nonprofit] needs the approval, or at least the acquiescence, of practically everybody who remotely could be considered a 'constituent.' Where a market share of 22 percent might be perfectly satisfactory to a business, a 'rejection' by 78 percent of its 'constituents' . . . would be fatal to a budget-based institution."[50]

A second problem with nonprofit marketing objectives is that accomplishments may be very difficult to detect because of their intangibility. How does one *know,* for example, that museum visits or symphony attendance have become more "educational" or that they "improve the quality of life in the community?" Yet these are often set as the marketing goals of nonprofit institutions. They are perfectly legitimate goals; they just present serious measurement problems. Unfortunately, the combination of that measurement difficulty and the glare of public accountability that faces many nonprofits leads managers too often to seek to achieve what is *measurable* rather than what is important. There is a serious danger, for example, that the nonprofit organization will become a budget maximizer. As Peter Drucker has noted:

> being paid out of a budget allocation changes what is meant by "performance" or "results." *"Results" in the budget-based institution means a larger budget. "Performance" is the ability to maintain or increase one's budget. . . .* Not to spend the budget to the hilt will only convince the budget-maker that the budget for the next fiscal period can safely be cut.[51] (Italics in original)

As we shall see, this is one of many distortions in planning and performance that the peculiar status of the nonprofit marketing task can give rise to.

In addition to the differences just described in organizational milieu, nonprofit marketers' options are often affected considerably by the things they are attempting to market. The major *organizational* mission of a church or a synagogue involves the promulgation of religious values, whereas the major organizational mission of museums involves cultural education. But some of the specific *activities* of these two institutions could be virtually identical from a marketing standpoint—both, for example, could be involved in promoting lotteries or reselling goods such as Christmas cards or posters. On the other hand, the *way* identical marketing activities are carried out may be affected by the type of organization. A church, for example, might feel it had to be relatively dignified in promoting its lottery or its Christmas cards; a museum might feel it should have a relatively "classy" promotion; a neighborhood youth group might feel that its image required a more casual, folksy style.

To further understand the peculiar opportunities and challenges facing the nonprofit manager, it is useful to classify the levels and types of activities such enterprises might undertake. Two bases for such a classification will be considered: (1) the type of demand, and (2) the nature of the exchange.

Type of Demand Problem.   Each marketing activity an organization undertakes is designed to ultimately affect the level of transactions that it has with its target audiences. At any point in time, the actual demand level may be below, equal to, or above the desired demand level. *Marketing management's task is to influence the level, timing, and character of demand in a way that will help the organization achieve its objectives.*

Demand may be in any one of eight states, and each presents a different marketing challenge:[52]

1. *Negative demand.* A market is said to be in a state of negative demand if a major part of the market dislikes the product and in fact may even pay a price to avoid it. People have a negative demand for vaccinations, dental work, vasectomies, and gall bladder operations. Employers feel a negative demand for ex-convicts and alcoholic employees. The marketing task is to analyze why the market dislikes the product and whether a marketing program can change the market's beliefs and attitudes through product redesign, lower prices, and more positive promotion.
2. *No demand.* Target consumers may be uninterested or indifferent to the product. Thus farmers may not be interested in a new farming method and college students may not be interested in taking foreign language courses. The marketing task is to find ways to connect the benefits of the product with the person's natural needs and interests.

3. *Latent demand.* A substantial number of consumers may share a strong desire for something that cannot be satisfied by any existing product or service. Thus there is a strong latent demand for nonharmful cigarettes, safer neighborhoods, and more fuel-efficient cars. The marketing task is to measure the size of the potential market and develop effective goods and services that would satisfy the demand.

4. *Falling demand.* Every organization, sooner or later, faces falling demand for one or more of its products. Churches have seen their membership decline, and private colleges have seen their applications fall. The marketer must analyze the causes of market decline and determine whether demand can be restimulated through finding new target markets, changing the product's features, or developing more effective communications. The marketing task is to reverse the declining demand through creative remarketing of the product.

5. *Irregular demand.* Many organizations face demand which varies on a seasonal, daily, or even hourly basis, causing problems of idle capacity or overworked capacity. In mass transit, much of the equipment is idle during the off-peak hours and insufficient during the peak travel hours. Museums are undervisited during weekdays and overcrowded during weekends. Hospital operating rooms are overbooked early in the week and underbooked toward the end of the week. The marketing task is to find ways to alter the time pattern of demand through flexible pricing, promotion, and other incentives.[53]

6. *Full demand.* Organizations face full demand when they are pleased with the amount of business they have. The marketing task is to maintain demand at its current level in the face of the ever-present possibility of changing consumer preferences and more vigorous competition. The organization must keep up its quality and continually measure consumer satisfaction to make sure that it is doing a good job.

7. *Overfull demand.* Some organizations face a demand level that is higher than they can or want to handle. Thus the Golden Gate Bridge carries more traffic than is safe; Yellowstone National Park is terribly overcrowded in the summertime; and the Picasso exhibit at the Museum of Modern Art attracted such crowds that visitors had to wait two hours in line to be admitted. The marketing task, called *demarketing,* requires finding ways to reduce the demand temporarily or permanently. General demarketing seeks to discourage overall demand and consists of such steps as raising prices and reducing promotion and service. Selective demarketing consists of trying to reduce the demand coming from those parts of the market that are less profitable or less in need of the service. Demarketing does not aim to destroy demand, but only to reduce its level.

8. *Unwholesome demand.* Products which are considered unwholesome will attract organized efforts to discourage their consumption. Unselling campaigns have been conducted against cigarettes, alcohol, hard drugs, handguns, X-rated movies, and large families. The marketing task is to get people who like something to give it up. Antiproduct marketers use such tools as fear communications, price hikes, and reduced availability to discourage consumption.

The Nature of the Exchange.   The market transaction that the nonprofit organization is trying to influence is most usefully conceived from a managerial standpoint as an *exchange.* Target audience members are asked to exchange something they value for something beneficial provided by the nonprofit organizations. As seen from the target consumer's perspective, he or she is being "asked" to incur costs or to make some sacrifices (that is, to give up something valuable) in return for some promised benefits. In the main, the kinds of costs consumers are usually asked to "pay" by nonprofit marketers are one of four types:

> 1. *Economic costs*—for example, to give up money or goods to a charity, or simply to buy a product or service.
> 2. *Sacrifices of old ideas, values, or views of the world*—for example, to give up believing that the world is flat, that women are inferior, that one is not getting senile, that one is not hooked on drugs, or that abortion is evil (or not evil).
> 3. *Sacrifices of old patterns of behavior*—for example, to start to wear seat belts or to let someone else meet some of your physical or psychological needs.
> 4. *Sacrifices of time and energy*—for example, to perform a voluntary service or give blood to a hospital or the Red Cross.

In return for these kinds of sacrifices, consumers in nonprofit enterprises receive benefits of three basic kinds: economic (both goods and services), social, and psychological. The combination of these kinds of sacrifices and benefits yield the matrix outlined in Table 1-2. Here we see that it is only the first two cells in the top left corner of the matrix that we typically identify as the domain of the profit sector—although, as we've noted, some nonprofits such as hospitals and schools promote these transactions as their primary objective. It is the other fourteen cells that are truly in the nonprofit domain, since *by definition* they cannot generate a profit. What does it mean to be responsible for transactions in these fourteen cells?

THE UNIQUENESS OF NONPROFIT MARKETING

In a landmark article, Michael Rothschild implicitly raised the question: What difference does it make *from a marketing management standpoint* to be involved in activities surrounding exchanges other than those where the consumer makes economic sacrifices for economic benefits? Rothchild asks, Why is it so hard to sell brotherhood like soap?[54] Among the answers that he and other authors have developed are the following:

> 1. There is usually very little good secondary data available to the nonprofit marketer about consumer characteristics, behaviors, media preferences, perceptions, attitudes, and the like compared to what is available in commercial markets. Although studies are sometimes available in the general social science literature, they seldom address key marketing issues.
> 2. Because the sacrifices consumers are asked to make often involve very central ego needs as well as attitudes and behaviors with respect to controversial or taboo topics, it is often very difficult to secure reliable research data from consumers to serve as the basis for marketing decisions. As Bloom and Novelli point out, "While people are generally willing to be interviewed about these topics, they are more likely to give inaccurate, self-serving, or socially desirable

Table 1-2

COST/BENEFIT MATRIX FOR THE PROFIT/NONPROFIT SECTORS

Costs	*Benefits*			
	A Product	*A Service*	*Social*	*Psychological*
Give Up Economic Assets	Buy a poster	Pay for surgery or an education	Donate to alma mater	Donate to charity
Give Up Old Ideas, Values, Opinions	Receive free Goodwill clothing	Support neighborhood vigilantes	Support Republicans	Oppose abortion
Give Up Old Behaviors, Undertake or Learn New Behaviors	Practice birth control and receive a radio	Undertake drug detoxification treatment	Go to geriatric group once a week	Wear seat belts
Give Up Time or Energy	Participate in a study and receive a coffeemaker	Attend a free concert	Volunteer for Junior League	Give blood

answers to such questions than to questions about cake mixes, soft drinks, or cereals."[55]

3. Very often consumers are being asked to make sacrifices where they are often largely indifferent about the issue. (For example, who really worried about water conservation or the effects of speeding on a country's energy consumption before we were told about it?). This means, as noted above, that marketers will have a serious development marketing problem, which can be extremely costly.

4. Consumers are often asked to make 180-degree shifts in attitudes or behaviors. In the private sector, a marketer simply tries to get consumers to value a product or service *more* than they used to (or at least more than they value competitors' offerings). Seldom does the marketer have a mandate to convert those who are *against* the product to favor it. Yet nonprofit marketers are asked to do this all the time. They must try to entice "macho men" into wearing seat belts, timid souls into giving blood or taking medication around which swirl rumors about devastating effects on sexual potency, or aging citizens to finally admit they are infirm or otherwise need assistance.

5. In the private sector it is often possible to modify an offering to better meet consumer needs and wants, but this is often difficult in the nonprofit sector. There is only one way to obtain blood, for example. Pills must be taken if one is to control high blood pressure. So many notes must be played by an organized set of musicians in order to perform Beethoven's Fifth Symphony. On the other hand, as will be noted in later chapters, the fact that some basic physical or behavioral aspect of the transaction cannot be changed does not mean that other elements of the marketing mix cannot. One can give blood in a great many different, often very attractive physical environments and social settings, for example. Most emphatically, even though the basic offering cannot be changed to meet consumers' needs and wants, other elements of the marketing mix (such as how the offering is described and promoted) can be very responsive to consumer needs and wants.

6. Because the issues with which nonprofits deal involve very complex behaviors and attitudes, especially in areas like health care or conservation, large amounts of information must be communicated to consumers. For example, to get consumers in developing countries to correctly and regularly use oral rehydration therapy (ORT) to keep their fragile offspring from dying from the loss of fluids and electrolytes during prolonged and severe bouts of diarrhea, they must learn (a) that dehydration *per se* is life-threatening for the child; (b) that ORT will solve the problem; (c) that the benefits of use exceed the costs; (d) that they must use it properly or else it will not be effective or, indeed, may cause more problems than it cures; and (e) that there are specific places where the salts can be obtained and that it will cost X units of the local currency.

7. Very often the benefits resulting from the sacrifice are not evident. If ORT is used properly and in time—that is, *before* the child becomes dehydrated—the mother will *not see* any benefits due to the action she took. A similar problem is faced by those trying to market high blood pressure control programs. High blood pressure is a health problem with no symptoms, and treatment with appropriate therapy does not result in immediately visible effects for its victims. As Rothschild points out, "In order to establish or maintain a behavior, there must be a positive reinforcer. . . . In many nonbusiness cases, neither positive nor negative reinforcements are perceivable."[56]

8. Another distinction in nonprofit marketing is that for some sacrifices, the benefits accrue to others and the individual making the sacrifice benefits little

or not at all. A case in point is the fifty-five-mile-per-hour speed limit. Drivers were asked to change their behavior in return for energy savings that would benefit the government, that would possibly keep prices for everyone down to some degree, and that would improve the bargaining position and perhaps the profits of U.S. oil companies. It is understandable that many drivers were not very responsive to marketing programs designed to get them to obey the new law.

9. Because many of the changes to be marketed involve intangible social and psychological benefits, it is often difficult to portray the offering in media presentations. Just how does one describe a symphony concert or the benefits of changed attitudes toward women or energy conservation? If a physical object is involved, its portrayal (for example, showing an orchestra or an army tank) simply does not capture the real benefits one is trying to communicate. Indeed, the product may simply carry the wrong connotations (for example, an orchestra in white tie and tails may connote an intimidating formal occasion; a tank may connote skill training that may not seem useful outside of an army setting).

SUMMARY

Marketing in public and nonprofit organizations is a radical management innovation that has finally reached a period of maturity after years of very rapid growth. Managers with marketing titles or clear marketing responsibilities abound in hospitals, arts institutions, schools and colleges, charities, and diverse government agencies. Responding to this mature climate, this book focuses on upgrading and systematizing marketing strategy formulation in nonprofit environments.

Upgrading marketing means developing (1) the proper philosophy of marketing, (2) a systematic approach to solving marketing problems, and (3) an awareness and understanding of key tools and techniques necessary for effective marketing management. Nonprofits are clearly in need of such help. Government support in many sectors is declining, private support is problematic, and competition is becoming more menacing. Fortunately, stories of successful applications of marketing to this environment are now common.

The starting point for a consideration of strategic marketing in nonprofit organizations is a clear perception and understanding of the unique environment in which they operate. Nonprofit organizations can be defined legally, but it is more crucial to understand the organization's environment and the specific marketing activities that constitute its mission. The major factors affecting the organization's environment are (1) whether it is a donative or commercial organization, (2) whether its performance is subject to public scrutiny, (3) whether marketing is perceived to be undesirable, (4) whether the organization is largely volunteer, and (5) whether marketing is judged by nonmarketing standards.

The missions of nonprofit organizations differ depending on the type of demand they seek to influence and the type of activity they are engaged in. Demand can be negative, latent, nonexistent, falling, irregular, full, overfull, or unwholesome. The organization's type of activity can be defined in terms of the key concept of exchange. On the one hand, target customers are asked to "pay" economic costs; sacrifice old ideas, values, and views of the world; sacrifice old patterns of behavior; or sacrifice time and energy. In return, they can expect products, services, social or psychological benefits, or some combination of these. Although nonprofits seek to influence exchanges of money for goods and services just like for-profit organizations, what makes them unique is their concentration on exchanges involving nonmonetary costs on the one hand and social and psychological benefits on the other. Influencing such exchanges requires different perspectives and modified techniques. Peculiarities of the present state of the nonprofit world make it hard to "sell brotherhood" like soap.

QUESTIONS

1. Nonprofits have many advantages in securing low-cost or free resources, special tax concessions, volunteer help, and free professional advice. Suggest how each of these special advantages can be a potential handicap for the nonprofit manager.

2. Many public relations directors and fundraising officers in nonprofit arts and charitable organizations argue that a new marketing director is unnecessary since they are already doing marketing. How would a chief executive officer counter such claims?

3. If you were the chief executive officer in question 2, how would you integrate public relations and fundraising with marketing in ways that would secure maximum cooperation from the existing personnel?

4. Give examples of the eight types of demand that a hospital marketing director might face.

5. In some countries, family planning programs are organized as independent nonprofits. Other programs are established as divisions of government ministries. What advantages and disadvantages would a marketing manager in the latter type of structure have in carrying out an effective program?

NOTES

1. John A. Byrne, "Prepared, At Last," *Forbes,* October 10, 1983, pp. 32–33.

2. Meg Cox, "Orchestra Thrives by Playing the Music People Didn't Want," *Wall Street Journal,* July 19, 1984, pp. 1–12.

3. "College Learns to Use the Fine Art of Marketing," *Wall Street Journal,* February 23, 1981.

4. Kevin Higgins, "Marketing Enables Population Control Group to Boost Results," *Marketing News,* October 14, 1983, p. 12.

5. Barbara Frost, *Social Marketing Oral Rehydration Therapy/Solution: A Workshop* (Washington, D.C.: Technologies for Primary Health Care Project, November 19, 1984).

6. Philip Kotler and Sidney J. Levy, "Broadening the Concept of Marketing," *Journal of Marketing,* January 1969, pp. 10–15.

7. Philip Kotler and Gerald Zaltman, "Social Marketing: An Approach to Planned Social Change," *Journal of Marketing,* July 1971, pp. 3–12.

8. Benson Shapiro, "Marketing for Nonprofit Organizations," *Harvard Business Review,* September-October 1973, p. 223–32.

9. Kotler and Levy, "Broadening the Concept of Marketing."

10. See, for example, Christopher H. Lovelock, "A Market Segmentation Approach to Transit Planning, Modeling and Management," in *Proceedings of the Sixteenth Annual Meeting of the Transportation Research Forum,* 1975, pp. 247–258.

11. See, for example, Charles Weinburg, "Marketing Mix Decision Rules for Nonprofit Organizations," in Jagdish Sheth, ed., *Research in Marketing,* vol. 3 (Greenwich, Conn.: JAI Press, 1980), pp. 191–234.

12. See, for example, Michael L. Rothschild, *An Incomplete Bibliography of Works Relating to Marketing for Public Sector and Nonprofit Organizations,* 3rd ed. (Madison, Wis.: Bureau of Business Research and Services, University of Wisconsin, 1981).

13. See, for example, Paul N. Bloom, "Evaluating Social Marketing Programs: Problems and Prospects," *1980 Educators Conference Proceedings* (Chicago: American Marketing Association).

14. Kotler and Zaltman, "Social Marketing."

15. Robin E. MacStravic, *Marketing Health Care* (Germantown, Md.: Aspen Systems Corporation, 1977).

16. See, for example, John L. Compton, "Public Services–To Charge or Not to Charge," *Business,* March-April 1980, pp. 31–38.

17. In addition to the first and second editions of the present volume, there are now the following: Christopher H. Lovelock and Charles B. Weinberg, *Marketing for Public and Nonprofit Managers* (New York: John Wiley, 1984); David Rados, *Marketing for Non-Profit Organizations* (Boston: Auburn House Publishing Company, 1981); and Armand Lauffer, *Strategic Marketing for Not-for-Profit Organizations* (New York: The Free Press, 1984).

18. Philip Kotler and Roberta N. Clarke, *Marketing for Health Care Organizations* (Englewood Cliffs, N.J.: Prentice-Hall, 1986).

19. Philip Kotler and Karen F. A. Fox, *Strategic Marketing for Educational Organizations* (Englewood Cliffs, N.J.: Prentice-Hall, 1985).

20. Richard K. Manoff, *Social Marketing* (New York: Praeger Publishers, 1985).

21. Seymour H. Fine, *The Marketing of Ideas and Social Issues* (New York, N.Y.: Praeger, 1981).

22. For example, Ralph M. Gaedeke, ed., *Marketing in Private and Public and Nonprofit Organizations: Perspectives and Illustrations* (Santa Monica, Calif.: Goodyear, 1977); Charles Lamb and O. C. Ferrell, eds., *Readings and Cases for Marketing for Nonprofit Organizations* (Englewood Cliffs, N.J.: Prentice-Hall); Michael P. Mokwa, William D. Dawson, and E. Arthur Priere, eds., *Marketing the Arts* (New York: Praeger Publishers, 1980); Michael P. Mokwa and Steven E. Permut, *Government Marketing* (New

York: Praeger Publishers, 1981); Philip D. Cooper, *Health Care Marketing: Issues and Trends* (Germantown, Md.: Aspen Systems Corporation, 1979).

23. Christopher H. Lovelock and Charles B. Weinberg, *Cases in Public and Nonprofit Marketing* (New York: John Wiley, 1984).

24. O. Gene Norman, "Marketing Libraries and Information Services: An Annotated Guide to the Literature," *Reference Services Review,* Spring 1982, pp. 69–80.

25. Nelson Rosenbaum, "The Competitive Market Model: Emerging Strategy for Nonprofits," *The Nonprofit Executive,* July 1984, pp. 4–5. See also Paul J. DiMaggio, "The Nonprofit Instrument and the Influence of the Marketplace on Policies in the Arts," in W. McNeil Lowry, ed., *The Arts and Public Policy in the United States* (Englewood Cliffs, N.J.: Prentice-Hall, 1984), pp. 57–99.

26. Bruce L. R. Smith and Nelson Rosenbaum, "The Fiscal Capacity of the Voluntary Sector," paper prepared for delivery at the Brookings Institution National Issues Seminar on "The Response of the Private Sector to Government Retrenchment," Washington, D.C., December 1981.

27. "The State of the Market," *The Economist,* December 30, 1978, p. 40; reprinted in Lovelock and Weinberg, *Cases,* p. 23.

28. Smith and Rosenbaum, "Fiscal Capacity."

29. See Humphrey Doerman, "The Future Market for College Education," *A Role for Marketing in College Admissions* (New York: College Entrance Examination Board, 1976), pp. 1–53.

30. S. J. Diamond, "Medicine Takes on New Look," *Los Angeles Times,* February 10, 1985.

31. Ronald Kotulak, "Hospitals, Facilities Across U.S. Threatened," *Chicago Tribune,* July 22, 1984, pp. 1, 12.

32. Christopher H. Lovelock, "An International Perspective on Public Sector Marketing," in Mokwa and Permut, *Government Marketing,* pp. 114–143.

33. Smith and Rosenbaum, "Fiscal Capacity."

34. Rados, *Marketing.*

35. Fine, *Marketing of Ideas.*

36. Lovelock and Weinberg, *Marketing for Public and Nonprofit Managers.*

37. Henry Hansmann, "The Role of Nonprofit Enterprises," *The Yale Law Journal,* April 1980, pp. 835–901.

38. "Mixing Class and Cash," *Time,* December 9, 1985, p. 56.

39. William Meyers, "The Nonprofits Drop the 'Non,'" *New York Times,* November 24, 1985, pp. F1, 2, 9.

40. *Unfair Competition by Nonprofit Organizations with Small Business: An Issue for the 1980s* (Washington, D.C.: Office of Advocacy, U.S. Small Business Administration, November 1983).

41. Meyers, "The Nonprofits," p. F9.

42. Bruce R. Hopkins, "The Tax Implications of Profit-Making Ventures," *The Grantsmanship Center News,* March/April 1982, pp. 38–41. See also

Bruce R. Hopkins, *The Law of Tax-Exempt Organizations,* 3rd ed., (New York: John Wiley, 1979).

43. Andrew H. Malcolm, "Ottawa Runs Into Protests Over Its Huge Advertising Costs," *New York Times,* November 1, 1980, p. 10.

44. Paul Bloom and William D. Novelli, "Problems and Challenges in Social Marketing," *Journal of Marketing,* Spring 1981, p. 80.

45. See the case "U.S. Postal Service," in Lovelock and Weinberg, *Cases in Public and Nonprofit Marketing,* pp. 153–62.

46. The American Marketing Association has published a code of ethics for marketing research. A good discussion of ethical perspectives and problems in marketing research is found in C. Merle Crawford, "Attitudes of Marketing Executives Toward Ethics in Marketing Research," *Journal of Marketing,* April 1970, pp. 46–52.

47. Jack Anderson, "'Blow Your Horn Louder,' Interior Department Told," *Chicago Daily News,* September 28, 1971, p. 13.

48. "Is 'Showbiz' Ruining America's Big Museums?" *U.S. News and World Report,* February 25, 1985, pp. 64–65.

49. Weisbrod, *Statement.*

50. Peter Drucker, "Managing the Public Service Institution," *The Public Interest,* 33 (Fall 1973), pp. 43–60.

51. *Ibid.,* p. 50.

52. See Philip Kotler, "The Major Tasks of Marketing Management," *Journal of Marketing,* October 1973, pp. 42–49.

53. See Philip Kotler and Sidney J. Levy, "Demarketing, Yes, Demarketing," *Harvard Business Review,* November-December 1971, pp. 74–80.

54. Michael L. Rothschild, "Marketing Communications in Nonbusiness Situations or Why It's So Hard to Sell Brotherhood Like Soap," *Journal of Marketing,* Spring 1979, pp. 11–20.

55. Bloom and Novelli, "Problems and Challenges."

56. Rothschild, "Marketing Communications."

CHAPTER 2

The Marketing Philosophy

Initially, hospitals considered marketing to be primarily a matter of influencing doctors. Doctors were seen as the crucial gatekeepers turning on and off the patient flow that was the hospital's lifeblood. Influencing doctors was mainly a problem of equipment and facilities—to attract the most and the best doctors, one had to have available more parking spaces, better and more commodious consulting rooms, the very latest in diagnostic and treatment equipment, and, if at all feasible, nearby subsidized clinic or office space. Attitudes around the hospital were very much dominated by a motto: Thou shalt not rile thy physician staff, for they giveth and they taketh away!

As competition grew and patient censuses declined, hospitals began to become intrigued with what they thought of as the new idea of "marketing." Unfortunately, too many thought of it in terms of image building and promotion. "We're not getting the patients we should," the reasoning went, "because present and potential patients as well as physicians do not fully appreciate what a good institution we are, what good facilities we have, and how caring and competent our employees are." This thinking led to a rash of advertising and promotion campaigns trying to show that Hospital X was more loving, more professional, more crammed with the latest hardware, and more convenient than Hospitals Y and Z down the road. "Somehow, if we could only get the Hospital X story across, all our revenue problems would be solved."

Finally, in the mid-1980s, a wide range of hospitals finally did begin to understand what marketing was really all about. They began to undertake surveys inside and outside their institutions to see what patients (and sometimes physicians) really wanted. Then, rather than trying to convince these target audience members that the hospital *already* was giving them what they wanted, they began to change their present offerings and develop new offereings to meet what their target audiences wanted. This has led to a rash of wellness programs and preventive health care seminars and brochures that have made the hospitals more than curative centers. It was found that patients wanted to be *healthy*, not just to be cured!

Hospitals also began to pay attention to many of the complaints that patients and doctors had been raising for years—and that had often been dismissed by an attitude that said, in effect, "We're giving you the very best health care we can. This is not a hotel or fancy restaurant. If we gave you more amenities, our health care delivery would suffer."

But hospitals have learned that by paying close attention to customer needs, they can bring in clients who would otherwise only have come in dire emergencies. Increased marketing costs have meant more "sales." They have also found that more marketing expenditures can mean higher prices (and, therefore, higher returns).

A case in point is the recent development of luxury hospital suites. A traditional complaint of patients has been the primitiveness of rooms and the poor quality of hospital food. By the end of 1985, twenty-three hospitals had opened luxury wings. At the Good Samaritan Medical Center in Phoenix, a patient can stay in a two-room suite with a portable Jacuzzi, a VCR, and a personal hostess. Meals can include Coquilles St. Jacques and fine wine. Spouses can also stay in the suite. Costs, however, are substantial. Compared to a standard $135 for a semiprivate room, luxury suites at Good Samaritan cost $351 for a single and $445 for a double. Apparently a great many well-heeled patients find this an expenditure well worth making and choose Good Samaritan over its more primitive competitors.

SOURCE: Details on the Good Samaritan suites are found in "Pampered Patients," *Money,* December 1985, p. 13.

A first requirement for effective, successful marketing in *any* organization is that the organization have a clear, deeply ingrained appreciation for what marketing is and what it can do for the organization. We have already seen that a great many of those who look at marketing from the outside are highly critical of it. No wonder. Americans are bombarded with television commercials, "junk mail," newspaper ads, sales calls, and mass retailing. Someone is always trying to sell something. Therefore, it may come as a surprise to most administrators that the most important part of marketing is not selling! Selling is only the tip of the marketing "iceberg." It is only one of several functions that marketers perform, and often not the most important one. In fact, if the appropriate products and services are offered and pricing, distributing, and promoting them are done effectively, these goods and services sell very easily. The amount of promotion and hard selling does not have to be very large. Peter Drucker, a leading management theorist, summarized marketing this way: "The aim of marketing is to make selling superfluous."[1]

Marketing is not a peripheral activity of modern organizations but one that grows out of the essential quest of modern organizations to effectively serve some area of human need. To survive and succeed, organizations must know their markets; attract sufficient resources; convert these resources into appropriate products, services, and ideas; and effectively distribute them to various consuming publics. These tasks are carried on in a framework of voluntary action by all the parties. The organization does not employ force to attract resources, convert them, or distribute them. Nor does it beg for resources or distribute them wantonly. The modern organization relies mainly on offering and exchanging values with different parties to elicit their cooperation. In short, modern organizations rely on *exchange mechanisms,* rather than *threat systems* on the one hand or *love systems* on the other, to achieve their goals.[2]

Misconceptions about what marketing is are fortunately becoming rarer. On the other hand, a true understanding of the marketing philosophy is still relatively rare. A major barrier to greater appreciation is that many of those who *think* they understand marketing really do not. Consider the following examples:[3]

- The director of an urban art museum describes her marketing strategy as "an educational task." "I assemble the best works available and then display them grouped by period and style," she says, "so that the museum-goer can readily see the similarities and differences between, say, a Braque and a Picasso or between a Brancusi and an Arp. Our catalogs and lecture programs are carefully coordinated with this approach to complete our marketing mix."
- The public relations manager of a social service agency claims, "We are very marketing oriented. We research our target markets extensively and hire top-flight creative people with strong marketing backgrounds to prepare brochures. They tell our story with a sense of style and graphic innovation that has won us several awards."
- A marketing vice-president for a charitable foundation ascribes his success to careful, marketing-oriented planning: "Once a year we plan the entire year's series of messages, events, and door-to-door solicitation. We emphasize the fine humanitarian work we do, showing and telling potential donors about the real people who have benefited from donations to us. Hardly a week goes by without some human-interest story appearing in the local press about our work. The donors just love it!"

Each of these executives thinks he or she understands what marketing is all about. *They do not.* Nor are they alone. Permut sampled eighty-eight arts administrators in the late 1970s and concluded that for this population, "marketing was seen as primarily sales promotion, heavily tied to advertising and selling activities (particularly for special programs or unusual events)."[4] In a more recent study, Fine surveyed eighty-nine private non-profits and fifty-nine government agencies engaged in what he has called "idea and social issues marketing" (that is, marketing in which no tangible product or service is involved). The study concluded the following: "If stated objectives are indicative of organizational policy, it appears that public and nonprofit institutions share a pattern of disdain for their clients . . . less than 20% of public and nonprofit institutions and only 33% of the [business] firms consider their principal goal to be satisfying customers."[5] Further, the study found that nonprofit and public sector organizations were less familiar with key marketing concepts and concluded that "institutions sponsoring ideas and social issues certainly do engage in marketing practices, but for the most part, in an ad hoc manner."

Consistent with this view of nonprofit managers as having a narrow or distorted view of marketing is a study of museum directors that showed that, as compared to marketing practitioners, museum directors were

- Less likely to have secured "information from [their] customers regarding what they would like [the museum] to offer."
- More likely to see their product as desirable for everyone rather than as targeted at specific segments.
- Less interested in changing prices to increase revenues.
- Less willing to change their distribution strategy.
- Less willing in the future to "change the nature of the products and services [they] offer [their] customers."[6]

Despite this confusion about marketing, it is not uncommon for these managers to sprinkle their planning documents and casual conversations with terms like "benefit segmentation," "product positioning," "message strategies," "marketing mix," and so forth. But if one were to pay careful attention to the subtle nuances of these managers' attitudes toward their customers and toward what they are offering them, it would become strikingly clear that their approach to marketing resembles what one would have found thirty years ago in the private sector. This approach is very different from that permeating today's modern marketing management.

THE EVOLUTION OF THE MARKETING FUNCTION

To understand modern marketing management, it is useful to trace the evolution of different business orientations in the private sector over the last hundred years. Four orientations can be distinguished.

THE PRODUCT ORIENTATION

When marketing first emerged as a distinct managerial function around the turn of the century, it found itself in an era that venerated industrial innovation in the design of new products. It was a period that saw the development of the radio, the automobile, and the electric light. In this first period, marketing also was decidedly *product oriented.* The belief was that to be an effective marketer, you had simply to "build a better mousetrap," and, in effect, customers would beat a pathway to your door.

Even today, many organizations are in love with their product. They believe strongly in its value even if their publics are having second thoughts. They strongly resist modifying it even if this would increase its appeal to others. Thus, colleges continue to require their students to study a foreign language even though few ever learn the language and most students report the whole experience as a waste of time and money. Museums feature certain works of art year after year even though they attract the attention or interest of virtually no one. And many churches present the same dull Sunday morning sermons year after year as a matter of tradition, ignoring the changing interests of church-goers and the steadily declining attendance. We define a product orientation as follows:

A **product orientation** holds that the major task of an organization is to put out products that it thinks would be good for the public.

THE PRODUCTION ORIENTATION

As the great opportunities for technological and service innovation peaked in the first decade or so of this century, entrepreneurs such as Henry Ford turned their attention to simplifying and making more efficient the production process itself. This was also the case with marketing. New forms of distribution sprang up—first the department store, then the chain store, and later the supermarket. At that point, developing low-cost mass consumption systems became the keystone of many organizations' marketing success. The key was to sell more and more and thereby sell it cheaper and cheaper.

Today one still finds that many organizations focus their attention on running a smooth production process, even if human needs must be bent to meet the requirements of that process. The personnel in many U.S. employment offices, for example, act as though they are processing objects instead of people. Job seekers come in, sit for long stretches, are asked routine questions, and are offered jobs if any are available. One does not have the impression that the personnel in the employment office exist to serve the job-seeking clientele, but rather that the job seekers exist to meet the needs of the "system." As another example, consider the bus driver who speeds past dozens of waiting commuters so that he can make his timetable. We define a production orientation as follows:

> A **production orientation** holds that the major task of an organization is to pursue efficiency in production and distribution.

SALES ORIENTATION

The depression of the 1930s dealt a fatal blow to those profit-centered marketers who defined successful marketing in product or production terms. Building ingenious products, producing them cheaply, and distributing them as widely as possible was a reasonable way to be a successful marketer as long as there were customers out there to buy them. But with the depression, demand shrank dramatically and both factories and distribution systems found themselves with large volumes of excess capacity. In response to this turn of events, marketers reconceived their objectives in competitive terms. The problem was no longer to grind out masses of low-cost, inventive products and distribute them broadly. Now the challenge seemed to be to convince consumers that (1) they should give up their hard-earned money for things other than the bare necessities; and (2) when they did, they should choose the marketer's offering over anyone else's. The key was to persuade consumers that the marketer's offering was *better* than buying nothing or buying competitors' products or services. This new orientation led to significant increases in the role of advertising and personal selling in the marketing mix. "Salesmanship" became the byword of successful marketing. In the 1930s, salesmen and the denizens of Madison Avenue achieved a central role in American folklore. Willy Loman and the "Man in the Grey Flannel Suit" became important symbols of the new business culture.

The selling orientation also continues to be pervasive today. Some organizations believe they can substantially increase the size of their market by increasing their selling effort. Rather than change their products to make them more attractive, these organizations increase the budget for advertising, personal selling, sales promotion, and other demand-stimulating activities. Thus the college president reacts to a decline in enrollment by increasing the budget of the admissions office to permit hiring more recruiters, sending out more direct mail, and improving the looks of the college's brochures. These sales-oriented steps will undoubtedly work to produce more customers in the short run. But their use in no way implies that the college has moved into a marketing orientation that would generate higher sales in the long run. A sales orientation is defined as follows:

> A **sales orientation** holds that the main task of the organization is to stimulate the interest of potential consumers in the organization's existing products and services.

THE CUSTOMER ORIENTATION

The orientations that characterized the three earliest stages in marketing's historical development had one thing in common. They all began marketing planning with the organization and *what it wanted to offer.* In the first two stages, it was expected that grateful customers would come to the organization that had the best or the cheapest offerings. In the "selling" era, the task was somewhat different. The organization was forced to go out and convince customers that they had a really good—perhaps superior—offering. As the economy rebounded after the depression, however, consumers became wealthier and more sophisticated. Consumers became pickier, more responsive to custom-tailored options, less willing to settle for just anything the market tried to persuade them to buy.

At that point, a number of leading marketers came to a very important realization. They realized that they had the marketing equation turned backwards. They had been trying to *change consumers to fit what the organization had to offer.* But truly the customer was sovereign. Whatever he or she chose to buy determined the organization's success. Consumers ultimately decided when transactions were to be made—not the marketer. And if this was so, then *marketing planning must begin with the consumer, not with the organization. Outside-inside marketing must replace inside-outside marketing.*

This simple idea is the essence of the modern approach to marketing. It is, in fact, the philosophy that will guide this volume. We shall see that, for the organization, "customer-centeredness" is attained through hard work. The organization must systematically study customer's needs, wants, perceptions, preferences, and satisfaction—using surveys, focus groups, and other means. The organization must act on this information to improve its products constantly to better meet its customers' needs. The employees must be well selected and trained to feel that they are working for the customer (rather than the boss). A customer orientation will express itself in the friendliness with which the organization's telephone operators answer the phone and the helpfulness of various employees in solving customer problems. The employees in a marketing-oriented organization will work as a team to meet the needs of the specific target markets that are to be served.

It is clear that different organizations within the same industry will vary in the degree to which they truly work for the customer. Consider a service industry such as the airlines. Recently, a British guidebook publisher decided as an aid to air travelers to rate the quality of fourteen different airlines.[7] The staff boarded forty-three transatlantic flights armed with tape recorders and evaluated each trip on such factors as check-in service, baggage delivery, food, cleanliness, friendliness, response to special stress situations such as asking for aspirin, and so on. The scores were combined in a weighted index with a maximum score of 100, and the results showed a great variation, with Delta topping the list at 77 and the worst airline scoring only 36. Airlines and other service institutions can show considerable differences in the degree to which their operations reflect a sensitive and caring attitude toward their customers. We define a customer orientation as follows:

> A **customer orientation** holds that the main task of the organization is to determine the perceptions, needs, and wants of target markets and to satisfy them through the design, communication, pricing, and delivery of appropriate and competitively viable offerings.

This philosophic orientation has a great many implications for the way a nonprofit marketing program ought to be run. As we shall see, adopting a customer orientation does not, as many nonprofit managers fear, mean that the organization must cater to every consumer whim and fancy. It doesn't mean that a symphony conductor or theater manager must give up his or her artistic integrity. Nor does it mean that health care institutions must abandon their professional standards or that college professors must become classroom song-and-dance performers. Those who argue that these consequences will befall the organization if the devil (marketing) is let in the door simply misunderstand what a customer orientation truly means. To restate: It means that marketing planning must *start* with customer perceptions, needs, and wants. It means that, even if an organization can't or ought not change certain aspects of the offering, the highest volume of exchange will always be generated if the way the organization's offering is described, "priced," "packaged," and delivered is fully responsive to what is referred to in the current jargon as "where the customer is coming from."

Consider two small examples. For years, the Buffalo Philharmonic, like many other symphonies, had a serious problem in trying to broaden its audience. It was willing to change its program somewhat, but ultimately it felt that Mozart is Mozart and somehow customers must be made to change *their* attitudes and behavior. Then, in the early 1970s, a modest university research project revealed that many consumers who indicated that they thought they *might* like to attend a concert did not do so because they expected the occasion to be very formal. As these potential target consumers put it, "We can't go because we don't have the proper clothes. We would feel really uncomfortable around all those fancy-dressed people." The orchestra itself was seen as distant, formal, and forbidding. Once the Philharmonic realized that this was where these potential customers were "coming from," they took great pains to humanize the orchestra and the concert-going experience. Orchestra section members began playing shirt-sleeve chamber music programs at neighborhood art fairs and other local outdoor events. Contact was made with local primary and secondary schools. The orchestra itself even performed at halftime at a Buffalo Bills football game!

A new conductor, Michael Tilson Thomas, began appearing on local television and giving brief informal talks to audiences at specific concerts. Concert-going never again had the sense of formality that was clearly keeping many potential patrons away. Attendance figures clearly reflected this new customer-centered orientation.

Another example is national in scope. For years, organizations committed to reducing the incidence of smoking in the United States believed that the major reason individuals did not quit was that they did not realize the consequences of continued smoking, or if they did, they were not frightened enough of these consequences to take action. As a result the marketing programs focused almost exclusively on communicating the very real dangers of smoking to target smokers. In a sense, they were trying to *sell* the stop-smoking idea to what they thought was an ignorant and reluctant audience.

It was only after an extensive review of a large number of consumer studies that organizations like the National Cancer Institute realized that the "product" they were trying to sell—that smoking is bad for you—had already been sold. Seven out of eight smokers reported that they either wanted to quit smoking or had tried to quit several times in the past. Further analysis revealed that these consumers perceived two extremely significant barriers to quitting. First, they felt they did not really know of a technique for quitting that would be effective for them. Second, even in cases where they were vaguely aware of a method that might work, they were reluctant to try to quit because they expected to fail. They had either heard of many who had failed, or had failed themselves many times in the past. For these very reasons, they tended to "turn off" most antismoking commercials, since they saw these commercials as, in effect, asking them to fail again!

Once the cancer organizations finally understood this consumer perspective, the marketing efforts of NCI and its sister nonprofits changed dramatically. Warnings of the dangers of smoking were, of course, continued to deter new, young potential smokers. At the same time, a major new marketing thrust was developed along two fronts. First, efforts were made to develop and get into the field a wide range of quitting techniques. Second, NCI and the American Cancer Society worked to persuade physicians and other health care workers to help smokers implement the newly available techniques and, just as important, to cope with smokers' often desperate fear of failing. The effects on cigarette consumption of this new customer-centered campaign have been considerable.

CUSTOMER-CENTERED ORGANIZATIONS

The Buffalo Philharmonic and NCI examples are dramatic examples of the way individual marketing programs can be developed to respond to consumers' needs, wants, and perceptions, and not just to the organization's own needs. But why, one must ask, did these organizations not develop these solutions sooner? The answer—and it is crucial one—is that the organizations had not (and many still have not) developed a true customer-centered philosophy that had seeped into the consciousness of every member of the organization who had any managerial responsibility or contact of any kind with potential target customers. We define a customer-centered organization as follows:

> A **customer-centered organization** is one that makes every effort to sense, serve, and satisfy the needs and wants of its clients and publics within the constraints of its budget.

One result of a customer-centered orientation is that the people who come in contact with such organizations report high personal satisfaction. They make such comments as, "This is the best church I ever belonged to"; "My college was terrific—the professors really taught well and cared about the students"; "I think this hospital is fine—the nurses are cheerful, the food good, and the room clean." These consumers become the best advertisement for these institutions. Their goodwill and favorable word of mouth reach other ears and make it easy for the organization to attract and serve more people. The organizations are effective because they are customer-centered.

Customer-centered organizations stand out from their competitors in the consumer mind. Recently a major bank interested in improving its service sought to interview persons from companies that had an outstanding reputation for service. The candidates included Delta Airlines, Marriott Hotels, Disney, Inc., and McDonald's. Each of these service organizations managed to imbue their employees with a spirit of service to the customers. Employees at Disney, for example, go out of their way to answer visitors' questions, pick up litter, smile, and be friendly. Disney, Inc., continuously interviews visitors to find out what they thought of their park, food, rides, employee attitudes, and so on. Based on these responses, they constantly try to improve their guests' experiences at the park.

Unfortunately, most organizations are not highly customer-centered. They fall into one of three groups. The first group would like to be more customer-centered but lacks the needed resources or power over employees. The organizations' budget may be insufficient to hire, train, and motivate good employees and to monitor their performance. Or management may lack the power to require employees to give good service, as when the employees are under civil service or are volunteers and cannot be disciplined or fired for being insensitive to customers. One inner-city high school principal complained that his problem was not poor students but poor teachers, many of whom were "burned out" in the classroom and uncooperative but who could not be removed.

A second group of organizations is not customer-centered simply because they prefer to concentrate on other things than customer satisfaction. Thus, many museums are more interested in collecting antiquarian material than in making the material relevant or interesting to museumgoers. The U.S. Employment Service may be more interested in the number of people they process per hour than in how much help each one really receives. When these organizations are mandated to exist or are without competition, they usually behave bureaucratically toward their clients.

Finally, there are always a few organizations that intentionally act unresponsively to the publics they are supposed to serve. A local newpaper exposed that one food stamp office chose to be inaccessible in order to minimize the public's use of its service: "There is no sign on the building indicating that the food stamp office is inside . . . there also was no sign anywhere in the building directing applicants to the basement, no sign on the door leading to the stairs, and no sign on the door to the office itself. The only indication that a food stamp office is located in the building is a small, handwritten sign on the door at the top of the stairs. Adding to the inconvenience, the food stamp office was closed from March 10 to April 8."[8]

A number of studies have demonstrated the extent to which nonprofits lack a customer orientation. Rielly and McCullough, for example, conducted extensive interviews with executives in forty-six nonprofit organizations and performed a detailed analysis of the formal written objectives of thirty-nine of these organizations. They concluded the following:

> Content analysis of these statements of purpose indicated a clear sales orientation for the most part. About 65% of the respondents mentioned sales volume or the number of exchanges occurring during a period as their criterion for success. Only 20% reported the evaluation of consumer feedback as a criterion for defining successful operation.
>
> When asked to define marketing, similar results were obtained. Sales was mentioned by 33% of the respondents while 35% described marketing in terms of advertising or promotion. Ten percent could not define marketing at all and the remainder (22%) define marketing in consumer terms. These results along with the statements of organizational purpose indicate that only a small minority of the firms are actually involved in marketing as represented by defining the organization's purpose in terms of the various constituencies of consumers served. Most were concerned with maximizing output or the stimulation of sales to existing consumers, neither of which is consistent with a marketing orientation.[9]

DETECTING AN ORGANIZATION-CENTERED ORIENTATION[10]

Conversations with nonprofit managers such as those quoted earlier make it abundantly clear that they *wish* to be customer-centered and, in virtually all cases, truly believe they already are. In most cases, they are not. Fortunately, a number of "clues" exist that tend to give away an organization's organization-centered marketing philosophy. These clues, simply stated, are:

1. The organization's offering is seen as inherently desirable.
2. Lack of organizational success is attributed to customer ignorance, absence of motivation, or both.
3. A minor role is afforded customer research.
4. Marketing is defined primarily as promotion.
5. Marketing specialists are chosen for their product knowledge or their communication skills.
6. One "best" marketing strategy is typically employed in approaching the market.
7. Generic competition tends to be ignored.

Each of these clues will be discussed more extensively in the sections to follow, since in some ways it is easier to see what marketing *should* be by seeing what it *should not* be.

CLUE #1: THE OFFER IS SEEN AS INHERENTLY DESIRABLE

The very nature of the offerings promoted in the nonprofit sector often leads their sponsors to have an extremely high opinion of the value of their offering. They simply see their product or service as inherently desirable. They find it hard to believe that anyone would turn them down!

Committed theater managers find it hard to believe that right-thinking people wouldn't wish to attend a well-acted play; charitable organization's cannot accept a consumer's unwillingness to give; and those who head up nonprofit social issues groups often can't see why people won't vote for, say, cleaner air or the ERA. One organization that overcame the notion that its offerings were inherently desirable is the National Cancer Institute. Most women, NCI discovered, agreed that practicing breast self-examination was a good way to ensure early detection of breast cancer, and many knew how to do it. Yet the majority were not practicing breast self-examination, or did so only rarely at best. What was the problem? It turned out that among women who practiced self-examination, the discovery that there was no problem led to a sense of relief the first few times, but eventually the women became bored and stopped the procedure. At the same time, the prospect of finding a problem was so frightening to most other women that they never even tried self-examination. It was only when NCI understood the barriers perceived by the target audience to an obviously beneficial practice that it began to develop more user-oriented marketing programs. NCI's new stance, which is based on assuring women that lumps are often nonmalignant and that progress is being made in the fight against breast cancer, has resulted in significant increases in breast self-examination practices among American women.

CLUE #2: CUSTOMER IGNORANCE AND LACK OF MOTIVATION ARE SEEN AS THE BARRIERS TO SUCCESS

It is, of course, not surprising to find that if a manager believes that wearing seat belts or giving to the United Way is something everyone should do, then if someone does *not* respond to a specific marketing effort, there are really only two explanations. Either potential customers do not *truly* understand the offering (that is, do not share the organization's inherent belief in it), or they are simply not motivated enough to take action. Some managers in nonprofits are willing to accept the "blame" for this deplorable state. They admit that they simply haven't yet found the right way to communicate the benefits of the offering or they just haven't found the right incentives to get target consumers to overcome their "natural" inertia.

These managers have a relatively benign view of consumers. There is, however, a very large number of nonprofit managers who feel—often unconsciously—much hostility towards consumers. Their basic perception is that customers are really *enemies*. The managers feel that it is these recalcitrant customers who are standing in the way of the organization's becoming more successful. Such views manifest themselves in the organization's treatment of consumers at the box office, on the telephone, in the field, or in any other personal encounter. They are evident in the disapproving look of the family planning specialist confronted by an impoverished family unwilling to practice birth control. They are apparent in the resentful faces of fund-raisers turned down by those who are "uninterested" or "too busy" and in the sarcastic voices of box office people trying to explain ticket availability to confused telephone customers.

It is not hard for the consuming public to sense in these encounters the organization's true colors and to perhaps respond in kind. And if they do, of course, they only convince the managers that they were right about consumers in the first place!

A key strategic assumption of managers in organizations with this attitude seems to be that the task of marketing is to get the customer to change to fit the organization rather than the other way around. They do not realize that (1) in a great many nonprofit marketing situations, customers are very hard to change, while the organization is not; (2) the organization is under the manager's control and the consumer is not; (3) changing the organization to accomodate customers, if fully carried out, insures that consumer trends will be carefully monitored and followed.

CLUE #3: A MINOR ROLE IS GIVEN TO CONSUMER RESEARCH

That customer ignorance or lack of motivation is not always the key problem in causing an organization's lack of success was obvious in the National Cancer Institute smoking example discussed earlier. But many organization-centered marketing managers are unlikely to discover this through consumer research. Given their anticonsumerist view of the cause of their lack of success, their opinion about what research is needed is very straight-forward. Since part of the problem is that too many consumers are too ignorant about the organization's offering, they believe one kind of study that is needed is research into the nature and extent of consumer ignorance and into the characteristics of who is ignorant. Further, since motivation is a major problem, research may also be needed to try to map the attitudes of those who are knowledgeable to show why they are so negative and unmotivated. Such research, it is hoped, will yield clues as to how to motivate them to take action.

The low level of consumer research by nonprofit organizations is relatively well documented. Permut, for example, found that of the eighty-eight arts organizations responding to his questionnaire, only one in four said they had done any kind of audience research in the past twelve months.[11] And, given that the respondents in the study were the more responsible and better managed of Permut's sample of three hundred eighty-three organizations, the overall rate of research in the arts must be quite low. Permut found that no research was carried on by fifty-eight organizations, while the most spent for an extensive audience study was $5,800. The latter was estimated to represent only 5.8 percent of the sponsoring organization's available funds.[12]

Despite this low level of research activity, the potential can be dramatic. As most profit sector marketers will attest, research can challenge some managers' most fundamental assumptions about their customers. The example of the antismoking groups' assumptions about consumer ignorance of the dangers of smoking is probably the best case in point.

CLUE #4: MARKETING IS DEFINED AS PROMOTION

If one sees the marketing challenge as one of eliminating ignorance and increasing motivation, then it is inevitable that the tool one will focus on is better communications. Managers will see the need for:

- a better copywriter and better copywriting.
- a better brochure.
- a new image.
- better salespeople with better sales presentations.
- more posters in more places.
- ads placed in prime time rather than in public service announcement (PSA) "media ghettoes".
- more and better press releases.
- better relations with newspapers and TV news departments.
- and, of course, a new advertising agency!

Other elements of the marketing mix like pricing, product redesign, and better distribution are seen as "not really the problem." Again, to resort to Permut's study,

- Promotion was clearly viewed as the preeminent marketing variable, with 72 [arts] administrators (82 percent) rating it "most important."
- Distribution was a concept of apparent irrelevance to respondents.
- Only a handful of administrators mentioned that they viewed the product of their organization in terms of "social/aesthetic experience," "enhanced leisure time pursuits," "cultural development," or other, more broadly defined conceptualizations. This is indeed unfortunate, one might argue, since product intangibles abound in the performing arts.[13]

A good example of the consequences of viewing marketing problems as stemming from consumer ignorance and lack of motivation is found in efforts to secure blood donations. Many blood-collection agency heads believe that the best way to encourage donations is to tell consumers about the good things that donor's blood can do or to stress that giving blood is a civic duty. They believe that people hold back from giving because they don't appreciate the "gift's" virtues or because they are afraid. Thus, agency heads reason, the marketing task is to tell consumers as dramatically and convincingly as possible about the benefits to society of giving blood and to assure them that the costs are trivial, that, indeed, giving is not really such a "big deal."

While these messages work for some people, important segments respond to very different approaches that are not based on impersonal media. Many donation programs, for example, have become more successful by simply changing the distribution strategy and going to major customer groups rather than insisting that they come to the agency, or having the hours of service convenient for potential donors, not just for the medical staff. For example, many men, especially blue-collar workers, can be motivated by challenges to their masculinity. Contrary to the view of the typical donor, the macho man who can brag to his coworkers that he is a 20-gallon donor is really responding to benefits he sees for himself. He may care relatively little about "society." Even more perversely, it may be that the higher the costs of giving, the greater the pain and suffering in the process of giving, the greater the rewards. Thus, campaigns in factories that publicize individuals' giving records (bar charts or 10- and 20-gallon lapel pins) and that (contrary to the usual program) don't downplay the possible psychological and physical costs of giving can be highly effective. In such situations, informal group pressure, rather than persuasion, is the key marketing tool.

On the other hand, social, fraternal, and church group members can be motivated to give blood by the let's-all-participate aspects of a blood-mobile visit. They will respond to messages about camaraderie, about "feeling left out if you don't join in," or about letting the group down if you don't go. Messages of this sort have little to say about the occasion for the get-together or its value to society, recognizing that for these potential donors the key distinction is also selfish: the desire to be wanted and loved by other members of a group. Here again, rather than brochures and advertisements, it is within-group word of mouth stimulated by key opinion leaders that does the job.

Finally, personal selling can be a surprisingly effective marketing tool. One blood bank director even uses sexual attraction as a key element in this marketing strategy. This director found that a small segment of middle-aged men considered the attentions of the pretty nurses well worth any inconvenience involved in giving blood. By hiring the most voluptuous nursing assistants he can, the center director has built a highly loyal following. This innovative marketer has learned that he who listens to potential customers can gain surprising insights about what the target audience wants and what will get it to act. Such persons realize that very often it is not the slick ad or the fancy brochure that gets the job done.

CLUE #5: THE BEST MARKETERS ARE SEEN AS THOSE KNOWLEDGEABLE ABOUT THE OFFERING OR ABOUT COMMUNICATIONS

In most for-profit organizations, marketing managers are typically selected for their skills at *marketing;* the best managers are those who know their consumer markets and competitors well. They make active use of consumer research and they know how to develop and implement systematic marketing plans. They possess insights and skills that in theory could be used to manage *any* functional area within marketing (for example, advertising, the sales force, or public relations) or to market any kind of product or service. Their assumption is that it is always possible to learn the essential mechanics of a particular marketing function or the details of a particular product or service in a few weeks, while it takes years to become a marketing expert. Marketing talent is, in a sense, a generic skill that can be used whenever and wherever it can be most effective.

By contrast, in the nonprofit sector, the situation has often been quite different. In the first stage of the marketing revolution in nonprofits, marketing specialists were typically drawn from within the organization. Those with similar responsibilities, for example the director of advertising or the public relations specialist, were simply encouraged to become "more marketing oriented" (that is, to become instant marketers). In the second stage, this approach persisted with the slight modification that some organizations drafted their marketing people from outside the organization but from similar enterprises. They took this approach because they seemed to believe rather strongly that only if one really knows the product or service can one be a truly successful nonprofit marketer.

Thus, as recently as early 1983 a study of marketing executives in eight hundred nongovernment hospitals showed that despite the fact that hospital marketing is one of the most advanced areas in the nonprofit world, "the data showed that hospitals have tended to make marketers out of planners and others without a marketing background. Three out of every four hospital marketing directors responding had a non-marketing background. . . . Of those who worked elsewhere before taking the hospital marketing post, 28% came from another hospital while another 29% had other healthcare or government-agency background."[14]

This personnel strategy is, of course, perfectly consistent with a product orientation towards marketing. It is also explainable by four other factors. First, since marketing is an unfamiliar subject to many nonprofit heads, they don't know how to evaluate marketing skills (while they *can* evaluate product know-how).

Second, these managers often believe that nonprofit marketing is so different from profit-sector marketing that there can be little transferability of skills.

Third, many top nonprofit administrators accumulate most of their management experience using product-oriented marketing and so are more comfortable working with people who have that orientation. Many business managers of arts organizations, for example, were once active performers or were formally trained in music, theater design, or museum curatorship. Many hospital administrators have either medical or public health backgrounds, and college presidents usually have Ph.D.'s in academic disciplines. Seldom are these administrators selected purely for their management skills.

Finally, the world of nonprofits is a fairly clubby one where key people know others in the same field around the country. Thus, a certain amount of favoritism prevails. A prospective staff member with the proper connections and the right vocabulary stands a much better chance of making it than a total outsider. The profit-sector marketing professional, who probably doesn't know what "needs assessment" or "audience development" means, is at a distinct disadvantage in the nonprofit job market. This means that the customer-oriented marketer who is not part of the "club" and who is brought in to turn an organization around will be seen (whether consciously or not) as a threat.

In the recent third stage of development, a few nonprofits now no longer insist on hiring *product* specialists for their marketing positions. They do tend, however, to choose from the ranks of those with *communications* skills. These potential hirees are typically chosen from advertising agencies or advertising departments of other companies (sponsors, for example). They might come directly from the media (for example, magazine or newspaper writers) or they may be public relations specialists. What these potential "marketers" have in common is that they are good communicators. Of course, the emphasis on communications skills reflects a view of marketing only slightly different from that found in the product-oriented organization.

The problem is still seen as reducing ignorance and providing motivation. But in this group of firms with marketers trained in communications, the emphasis is placed on *persuasion* rather than information. This emphasis on persuasion, it will be obvious by now, is perfectly consonant with a "selling" orientation toward marketing.

CLUE #6: ONE "REALLY GOOD" STRATEGY IS SEEN AS ALL YOU NEED

Since the nonprofit administrator is not often in as close touch with the market as a customer-oriented marketer would be, he or she may view the market as monolithic or at least as having only a few crudely defined market segments. Subtle distinctions are ignored or played down. As a consequence, most nonprofits tend to see the need for only one or two marketing strategies aimed at the most obvious market segments. This climate of managerial certainty precludes experimentation either with alternative strategies or with variations across market subsegments. In this view, the problem is to inform and motivate, and the challenge is about the same for every target consumer.

Also encouraging this approach is the fact that nonprofit managers often come from nonbusiness backgrounds and may fear taking risks. Personal job survival and slow aggrandizement of the budget and staff are often their paramount objectives. And since such administrators are typically responsible only to a volunteer board—which meets irregularly and sometimes prefers to know little about day-to-day operations—they do their best to keep a low profile and avoid causing waves. Simple, consistent strategies that imply well-thought-out analysis are the best choice for career safety. Too much change, too much variation, too much experimentation may seem to imply that one really isn't too sure about what to do. Such a low-profile, risk-averting strategy is, of course, tactically sound if one's organization happens to make up their losses with fundraising or government allocations. In such cases, aggressive marketing strategies are not really necessary.

CLUE #7: THERE IS ASSUMED TO BE NO GENERIC COMPETITION

In the private sector, organizations compete at many different levels, from interbrand competition all the way back to competition at the generic or basic desire levels. In the nonprofit sector, while many organizations do, in fact, compete—the Heart Fund with the American Cancer Society, the Metropolitan Museum of Art with the Whitney or the Museum of Modern Art—many institutions don't have clear competitors because their services or so-called products are intangible or stress unique behavior changes. The competitors faced by those marketing, say, blood donations or forest-fire prevention are not immediately apparent. So it's not surprising that marketers ignore competition at more basic levels. But at the product level, blood banks, for example, undoubtedly compete with other charities (who seek dollars, not blood) for donors. Even institutions with easily identifiable organizational competitors often face product competition from unlikely quarters. Thus, art museums compete with aquariums for family outings, with books and educational TV for art lovers, and with movies and restaurants as places to socialize.

Nonprofit organizations rarely plan strategies to compete at the product level because they lack a customer perspective. And this failure is even more serious at the nonproduct level. Before people will write their congressman in support of ERA, for instance, they must give up their long-held ideas and divert their energies to the new cause. Inertia can be a powerful force, but enthusiastic nonprofit marketers can bring about the necessary rethinking.

CHARACTERISTICS OF CUSTOMER-CENTERED MARKETING MANAGEMENT

The preceding sections have held up a mirror to the product-centered and selling-centered nonprofit organization. We have learned what a true marketing organization is *not*. What, then, are the characteristics that one observes in a nonprofit organization that has fully adopted a modern marketing orientation?

CUSTOMER-CENTEREDNESS

In a sophisticated marketing organization, all marketing analysis and planning begins and ends with the *customer*. A customer-centered organization always asks:

- To whom are we planning to market?
- Where are they and what are they like?
- What are their current perceptions, needs, and wants?
- Will these perceptions, needs, and wants be different in the future when our strategy is to be implemented?
- How satisfied are our customers with our offering?

RELIANCE ON RESEARCH

Since the consumer is central, management realizes that it must constantly track changes in consumer perceptions, needs, and wants so that the organization can respond to subtle shifts as quickly as they occur. Better still, to assure that it is not merely reactive but *proactive* in its strategic planning, an alert market-oriented management will have in place a forecasting capability that can *anticipate* changes in customer needs, wants, and perceptions.

Further, a customer-centered management realizes that any specific strategic or tactical decision will only be effective if it meets two conditions. First, it must be designed with a full appreciation of the consumers it is designed to affect. Second, it must be pretested as much as possible with those target consumers to assure that it truly will have the effect that management intended. Both requirements necessarily put a heavy reliance on integrated market research.

This is not to say that a consistent reliance on research need be expensive. As we shall outline in Chapter 6, there are a great many techniques by which high quality and clearly useful research can be carried out by imaginative managements at relatively modest cost. The critical requirement for achieving these benefits, however, is the proper mind-set. The truly customer-centered manager must continually "think research." The manager should assume that what he or she "believes" is not necessarily what is true. Intuition, casual observation, or "just common sense" do not constitute the ideal bedrock on which to build solid marketing strategies and sound tactical decisions.

Take the case of the Midwestern hospital marketer who believed he had a "foreign doctor" problem. The marketer knew that his hospital had more foreign doctors than major competitors in nearby cities. In part, this situation resulted from the fact that there was a major veteran's hospital nearby and many foreign doctors came there to do their residencies or to carry out a public service obligation. After such service, the doctors, many of whom had begun to develop modest practices in the area, quite naturally decided to stay on in the city permanently.

The marketing manager "knew" that their presence in his hospital constituted a serious problem. After all, he knew the hospital was statistically different in its physician profile. And, besides, he saw these doctors regularly in the building. He had heard patients and staff both complain about having difficulty understanding their "foreign doctors." Finally, the one major malpractice issue the hospital had recently faced had involved a foreign doctor. Thus, the manager *knew* he had a problem.

To cope with this "problem," hospital management began to develop strategies both to change the mix of doctors in the community (and therefore the hospital) and to change patient and staff perceptions about the "foreign doctor problem." Fortunately, at about this time the hospital decided to carry out a field study with about five hundred past and potential patients (costing under $3,000 in out-of-pocket costs). Among the other valuable insights gained from this study was the information that the marketing manager's presumption about consumer perceptions of his foreign doctors was entirely wrong! Consumers were indeed aware that there were many foreign doctors at the hospital, and a few acknowledged that communicating with these doctors was sometimes difficult. But on the whole, they did not see this as a serious problem. In fact, many in the patient sample felt that the foreign doctors were more conscientious and more caring for their patients than were some of their golf-playing, blasé U.S. counterparts! Several respondents said that they thought that cultural and language differences simply made the foreign doctors more conscientious about clearly understanding exactly what the patient really meant and what he or she needed. For many patients, then, the foreign doctors were not a problem but a boon to the hospital.

The lesson, of course, is that for less than $3,000 (much of which was spent for information serving a wide range of other planning needs), the organization saved itself the cost of an extensive communication project that could well have boomeranged.

A Predeliction for Segmentation

Just as the customer-centered manager routinely thinks of the consumer and of the possible need for research before planning programs, so, too, should he or she habitually "think segmentation." That is, in designing any particular marketing program, the nonprofit manager should routinely assume, until shown otherwise, that the market ought best be thought of as a combination of a great many smaller subsegments that may deserve separate marketing programs.

Of course, many nonprofit marketing managers do think of segmentation from time to time, but in our experience, only in the most general terms. Managers of symphony organizations, for example, are well aware that their prospects are better in high- than in low-income households, among women than among men, among the well-educated rather than the less educated, and among the young or old rather than the middle-aged. And this understanding does affect where they concentrate their budgets. But all too often these budgets are spent on a single "best" program, usually aimed at upscale households. (This of course stems from the familiar ignorance-and-motivation definition of the marketing "problem.")

Yet even within this market, many possibilities for more subtle segmentation exist and are all too often passed by. In a recent study for the National Endowment for the Arts, for example, one of the authors and a colleague revealed that, despite wide industry "intuition" to the contrary, the best predictors of likely symphony attendance were not at all the traditional demographic characteristics but lifestyle factors, attitudes toward actual attendance, past experience, and childhood training.[15] Considering only the lifestyle measure, the study clearly showed that there were not just one but *two* major lifestyle groups interested in symphony attendance. One group was the "traditional" cultural lifestyle group. This group made cultural events the center of their leisure pursuits. They tended to patronize the theater, opera, and museums as well as the symphony. They were very much interested in the program content and artists at specific performances and tended to be swayed less by atmospherics and prices. They attended largely for the cultural experience it provided. This group is undoubtedly the one that many theater and symphony marketers have in mind when they design their "one best" strategy.

The research, however, identified a very different lifestyle group that also included excellent prospects for the symphony. This group were very social in their lifestyles. They went out a lot, not only to the symphony but to all sorts of nonclassical events. They liked to give parties and dinners and attend those of their friends. For this group, symphony attendance was largely a social experience. It was an opportunity to meet and talk with their friends. It was an occasion to plan a dinner beforehand and, perhaps, dessert or cocktails afterwards. *Going out* was the thing. What was actually in the program was of less interest than who among their friends were going, what restaurants might be worth trying before the concert, and so forth.

Clearly, the appropriate strategies to reach these two groups are very different. More importantly, a strategy designed to appeal to the one group might very well turn off the other. Suppose, for example, that a symphony manager designed a typical "one best," nonsegmented strategy stressing program elements. Print ads, public relations releases, and interviews by guest artists and the symphony staff would emphasize the works to be performed—perhaps highlighting a first performance locally of a particular composition, the debut of a precocious youngster, the innovativeness or difficulty of a particular program entry, or the conductor's mastery of the "oeuvre" of the composer featured at the concert. All this would be very appealing to those in the Cultural Lifestyle Group. At the same time, it might have just the opposite effect on the Socially Active Group. The latter might see the event as formal and stuffy, a program for the aficionados and definitely not one that they would understand and enjoy. Certainly it would not seem to them to be something that their friends would attend. The group, then, would be very much turned off by this "best" strategy.

On the other hand, a marketing strategy could be chosen that emphasized the informality of the audience and the event, described the possibilities of making "an evening" of the occasion, talked about the ease of parking, and implied that "just about everyone" would be there. The Socially Active potential attendees might well be very attracted by such a prospect. At the same time, the Cultural Group may find this set of appeals vaguely distasteful. The marketing program might signal to them that the concert program would not be very challenging or, perhaps, even particularly well performed. And, even worse, the campaign might suggest to the cultural sophisticates that all those untutored, unsophisticated social types would be in attendance, ill-dressed and applauding in all the wrong places.

Clearly what is needed here are at least two separate and very different strategies. The strategies would say different things and be communicated through different channels. Careful efforts would have to be made to ensure that the strategies rarely overlapped.

The NEA study also showed that these are not the only possible groups to appeal to. The study also identified considerable audience-building potential for relatively uncomplicated strategies emphasizing price reductions (for example, a second ticket at half price) rather than different messages. Price discounting would not greatly affect the attendance of the Cultured Group, which is quite willing to pay for quality arts performances (but would use the cut if it was offered) or the Socially Active Group, which undoubtedly considers the concert ticket price alone to be a relatively minor component of the entire going-out event.

The lesson is obvious. Markets can usually be segmented much further and in much more sophisicated ways than the naive marketer usually imagines. But only if the marketer has a customer- and segmentation-oriented philosophy clearly in mind is he or she likely to look for these potentials. As this extended example shows, ignoring segmentation possibilities can mean not only missing chances for attracting new customers whom one is not now reaching, but driving away important audiences to whom one may have considerable appeal.

Defining Marketing Broadly

In contrast to those who conceive of marketing largely in terms of communications strategies designed to change customers to fit the organization's offering, sophisticated marketers view the marketing function as more diverse and the marketing objective as, above all, meeting customer needs and wants. The true marketer's philosophy considers that it is the organization that must be willing to adapt its offering to the customer, and not vice versa. This necessarily means not just a willingness to talk about the offering in different terms but to actually change it (within the constraints set by artistic and professional standards and the organization's capabilities). The marketer must be willing to change the product, service, or idea *itself* that it wishes the customer to get. For instance, skilled political infighters in any legislature, national or local, are well schooled in the need to adjust proposed bills or regulations to fit the needs and wants of specific senators or members of Congress with whom they are trying to make an exchange. It is not usually effective to take the stance that one knows one's position is *right*. Often one must compromise. Compromising may be seen simply as adaptive marketing.

The marketers must also be willing to change pricing or the place of performance. The marketing director of the Mass Transit District in Champaign-Urbana has found that by offering free or minimal cost bus service on the very coldest, snowiest days, he can induce auto owners who are averse to using buses (but who are perhaps *more* averse to driving and parking their own cars in terrible weather) to try using the bus. The director also cleverly puts extra emphasis on on-time performance at every stop on these nasty days, with the reasonable expectation that customers would believe that punctual performance under such terrible circumstances surely would predict excellent service on normal days. The director also varies the price of his offering through the use of a "generic bus" painted in "plain-wrap," white with black lettering. This bus is randombly assigned to the various city routes as a reward to those who regularly ride the route and as a spur-of-the-moment incentive to those who rarely take the bus. The fares on the generic bus are a bare-bones 25 cents, and "losses" on the routes are subsidized by a local supermarket chain that itself features plain-wrap products. Clearly, this nonprofit marketer has learned well that effective marketing is a lot more than just good advertising. It is the right offerings in the right place at the right time and at the right price.

A Richer Conceptualization of Competition

An organization-centered marketer naturally defines the competition as "other organizations like us." Yet if one begins with customers, the definition of competition can become very different. Competition, in its most basic sense, really becomes whatever the *customer* thinks it is. Thus, if certain customer segments think of treating a particular medical problem *themselves,* then *that* is a hospital or clinic's competition. If a potential donor thinks that money given to the United Way is money that could have gone for a "needed" weekend ski vacation, then that vacation is the competition. If going to the symphony competes with working in the garden or having friends over for pizza in front of the TV, then those activities are the competition.

The Entire Organization Becomes Fully Responsive to Customers[16]

Even if top-management adopts a customer orientation, organizations in both the nonprofit and profit sectors can vary greatly in the extent to which a customer-centered philosophy pervades every corner of the enterprise. This can best be seen in the extent to which the organizational performance is responsive to customer feedback. It can show up dramatically, for example, in how the organization handles consumer queries and complaints. Three levels of customer responsiveness can be identified. The orga-

Table 2-1

THREE LEVELS OF CONSUMER-RESPONSIVE ORGANIZATIONS

	Unresponsive	Casually Responsive	Fully Responsive
Complaint system	No	Yes	Yes
Surveys of satisfaction	No	Yes	Yes
Surveys of needs and preferences	No	No	Yes
Customer-oriented personnel	No	No	Yes
Empowered customers	No	No	Yes

nization can be unresponsive, casually responsive, or fully responsive. The differences are indicated in Table 2-1.

THE UNRESPONSIVE ORGANIZATION

The unresponsive organization is at one extreme. Its main characteristics are:

1. It does not encourage inquiries, complaints, suggestions, or opinions from its customers.
2. It does not measure current customer satisfaction or needs.
3. It does not train its staff to be customer-minded.

The unresponsive organization is typically characterized by a bureaucratic mentality. A bureaucracy exists when an organization tends to routinize its operations, replace personal judgment with impersonal policies, specialize the job of every employee, create a rigid hierarchy of command, and convert the organization into an efficient machine.[17] Bureaucrats are not concerned with innovation, with problems outside their specific authority, with qualifying human factors. They will serve people as long as their problems fall within the limits of their jurisdiction. People's problems are defined in terms of how the bureaucratic organization is set up, rather than setting the organization up to respond to people's problems. Questions of structure dominate questions of substance; means dominate ends.

Many hospitals were bureaucratically operated in the 1960s when they had far more patient demand than beds. Consider the following:

Why is it necessary to awaken a patient a couple of hours before breakfast to wash his face? . . . Why does it sometimes take many minutes for a nurse to answer the patient's light? . . . We've all seen nurses standing in the hallway talking and ignoring call lights. . . . Too many hospitals are drab.[18]

The physician, the house staff member, the nurse, the waiter, the X-ray or emergency room technician, or the admitting clerk who is rude; the maid who bumps the bed while cleaning; the parking lot attendant who is less than helpful when the lot is full; the cafeteria that turns away visitors; the pharmacy that has limited hours for outpatients—all suggest that hospitals operate for their own convenience and not that of the patient and his or her family and friends.[19]

Such an unresponsive organization brings about a host of undesirable consequences. The products and services are usually poor or irrelevant. Citizens or customers become frustrated and dissatisfied. Their dissatisfaction leads to rebellion, withdrawal, or apathy and may ultimately doom the organization.

The Casually Responsive Organization

The casually responsive organization differs from the unresponsive organization in two ways:

1. It encourages customers to submit inquiries, complaints, suggestions, and opinions.
2. It makes periodic studies of consumer satisfaction.

When American universities began to experience a decline in student applications in the early seventies, they began to pay more attention to their students and publics. College administrators who formerly were largely oriented toward problems of hiring faculty, scheduling classes, and running efficient administrative services—the earmarks of the bureaucratic mentality—now began to listen more to the students. They left their door open, made occasional surprise appearances in the student lounge, encouraged suggestions from students, and created faculty-student committees. These steps moved the university into being casually responsive.

The result of such an approach is to create a better feeling among the organization's customers. It is the first step in building a partnership between the served and the serving. Whether or not the increased customer satisfaction continues depends on whether the organization merely makes a show of listening or actually tries to do something about what it hears. It may merely offer a semblance of openness and interest without intending to use the results in any way. It sooner or later becomes apparent to the consumers that this is a public relations ploy. Because of rising consumer expectations, it can lead to greater strain than when the organization was completely unresponsive. If their voices fall on deaf ears, consumers resent the organization and may try to force it into greater responsiveness.

The Fully Responsive Organization

A highly responsive organization takes two additional steps:

1. It not only surveys current customer satisfaction but also researches unmet consumer needs and preferences to discover ways to improve its service.
2. It selects and trains its people to be customer-minded.

Many nonprofit organizations fall short of being highly responsive. Universities rarely take formal surveys of their students' real needs and desires, nor do they offer incentives and train their faculty to be student-minded. Recently, a small liberal arts college recognized this failing, and it developed the following philosophy to guide its professors:

The students are:

- the most important people on the campus; without them there would be no need for the institution.
- not cold enrollment statistics, but flesh-and-blood human beings with feelings and emotions like our own.
- not dependent on us; rather, we are dependent on them.
- not an interruption of our work, but the purpose of it; we are not doing them a favor by serving them—they are doing us a favor by giving us the opportunity to do so.

If this philosophy could be successfully implemented, the college would have moved a long way toward being highly responsive.

There is still a danger that the fully responsive organization will feel free to accept or reject complaints and suggestions from its consumers based on what it thinks is important and what it is willing to do. The public proposes and the organization disposes. A fully responsive organization overcomes the "we-they" distinction by accepting its customers as central to its success. Whenever possible it encourages consumers to participate actively in setting the objectives and strategies of the organization.

Among examples of fully responsive organizations, at least in principle, are "mutual" organizations such as local town democracies, churches, trade unions, and democratic nation-states. In such cases, the organization is seen as existing for and serving the interests of its members. There is no question of the organization going off on its own course to pursue goals that are not in the interest of its members. The organization shows an extreme interest in assessing the will of the members and responding to their wishes and needs.

When these principles are fulfilled, the expectation is that the members will be highly involved, enthusiastic, and satisfied. Recently, a Canadian university was searching for ways to build a more active alumni association.

Just sending out newsletters about the school did not build up alumni pride or interest. The university developed the idea of conferring membership status on its alumni and giving them certain privileges and voting rights on certain issues. Suddenly, the alumni came alive with interest in the school. This gesture proved very meaningful to the alumni, who had hitherto felt that the university was simply using them for their money.

HOW FAR TO GO IN ADOPTING A CUSTOMER ORIENTATION

It would be foolhardy not to recognize the outright fears of marketing that are present in the nonprofit world. We addressed them briefly in Chapter 1. If a manager wishes the organization to be wholly customer-driven, he or she must directly confront the often unspoken fear that this type of marketing orientation will ultimately cause artists, surgeons, librarians, museum directors, and other nonprofit professionals to bend their professional standards and integrity to "please the masses." These professionals rightly fear that going overboard towards a customer orientation can be at variance to many of the most elevated pursuits of society.

First, we too share these concerns. Ultimately, we view marketing's role as one of supporting the organization in achieving its goals. It does this best by devising strategies that start with the customer and not with the organization. But note that marketing is designated as a *means* to achieve the *organization's* goal. It is a tool—really a process and set of tools wrapped in a philosophy—for helping the organization do what *it* wants to do. Using marketing and being customer-oriented should *never* be thought of as goals; they are ways to achieve goals.

Marketing is a subarea of management. It is not necessarily at the top of the organization. Clearly and importantly, top management has a responsibility to decide what role it will allocate to marketing. *Management* must decide which goals marketing can help achieve and how. It is management's prerogative to say that certain decisions will be made with little or no attention to marketing concerns. Thus, the management of a theater company may decide that it will choose the season's program on the basis of the interests of its directors who, in turn, will consider both past programming and the availability of acting and production talent in choosing specific plays and performers. Marketing may then be assigned the task of maximizing audience revenues for that given program. It is important to realize, however, that this does not mean that marketing should fall back upon a selling philosophy. It means that marketing planning must simply start with customers in deciding how to describe, package, price, and distribute a given program. Marketers must merely recognize that the specific program cannot be changed.

At the other extreme, a theater manager may decide to be very customer-driven. He or she may very carefully survey the potential audience, consider past revenues and audience reactions, and consider what artist and plays are available to maximize future attendance. This organization would then establish an offering that limits attention to achieving artistic objectives but that maximizes sales. Note that the two approaches were equally customer-oriented. They simply differ in the management goals they were designed to achieve.

There are, of course, many variations on these two options. The theater management could always choose a middle ground between the two extremes by opting for one of the following approaches to program offering:

1. Mixing artist-driven and customer-driven performances over the season. (As early as 1929, conductor Serge Koussevitzky designed the Boston Symphony Orchestra season himself, except for the last concert, which he let the audience determine.)[20]
2. Alternating seasons of artist-driven and audience-driven programming.
3. Deciding to be audience-driven initially until revenues are great enough to permit the luxury of more artistic offerings later.
4. Letting the content of the season be artist-driven, with talent, costuming, or place of performance audience-driven.

Theater managers, therefore, have a great deal of flexibility in choosing how audience-driven the programming will be for a particular planning period, although how they market the offering in the final analysis should always be purely customer-centered. Other institutions by their very nature may have more or less latitude in the extent to which offerings are customer-driven. At one extreme are organizations that seemingly ought to give marketing a very central role because achieving "sales" is virtually their only objective. This would apply to a great many charitable organizations, alumni associations, and other groups that have as their major objective getting customers to give funds, time, and other resources to the marketer. At the other extreme are organizations that cannot change many elements of their basic offering at all because these elements very much define who they are. Included in this group would be most religious organizations and research institutions.

To repeat, then, the question of "how far marketing should go" is really a variable always under the control of management. Since marketing is merely a means to other ends, those who wish to protect those other ends need not fear marketing. At the same time, it is very important to stress that management should not allow the fears of artists and professionals to compromise marketing's legitimate place. As we shall indicate throughout this volume, marketing can make major contributions to nonprofit success in areas where it is appropriate. It must be controlled by management but not hamstrung by those who are suspicious of it if it is to be truly effective.

INTRODUCING A CUSTOMER-CENTERED PHILOSOPHY

If marketing is to take its rightful place in nonprofit organizations, management must not only understand and accept its function, but also take care to introduce it effectively.[21] Recognizing several considerations can increase the chance that marketing will be able to make a maximum contribution to the organization. When seeking to formally introduce marketing to an organization, remember that:

1. Marketing should not be positioned as a substitute for organizational management (a point we have already made).
2. Other pressures on the organization should be recognized (for example, the need to maintain artistic or professional integrity, to secure major government subsidies, etc.).
3. Limited understanding of marketing by present organization members should be accommodated.
4. The translation of for-profit marketing to the specific nonprofit context should not be done mechanically.
5. It should be granted that the organization is already doing many things that are "marketing." Marketing will be accepted more rapidly if one adopts the existing language, at least initially, rather than trying to change the organization's accustomed language to fit current marketing jargon.
6. Many nonprofit managers have come to their positions from nonbusiness backgrounds and may be defensive about their naivete (although not necessarily hostile to marketing).
7. You should be careful in your selection of early marketing projects. Lovelock and Weinberg suggests that five criteria should be met by such programs:
    • They should be evaluated by explicit performance measures.
    • They should be completed within a short to medium time period.
    • They should use a limited portion of available resources.
    • They should be neither peripheral nor central to the organization.
    • Their results should be obvious to key decision-makers within the organization.[22]
8. In the final analysis, getting marketing accepted in an ongoing organization is much more a *political* activity than a simple attempt to market marketing through persuasion. Allies must be sought—most particularly the chief executive officer. "Enemies" whose view of the organization and of their own turf is threatened by the new approach should be assumed to exist, whether visible or not, and dealt with directly.
9. Setbacks will occur and compromises will have to be made.

The issue of achieving organizational change is a subject beyond the scope of this book. Interested readers may wish to read the works of Argyris and Schon,[23] Quinn,[24] or Weick.[25] How the marketing function should eventually be structured in order to be effective in an ongoing, nonprofit organization will be discussed further in Chapter 9.

SUMMARY

The starting point for an effective marketing strategy is the proper orientation toward the marketing function. Historically, marketing has passed through four stages: a product orientation stage, a production orientation stage, a selling orientation stage, and finally, today's customer orientation stage. The first three stages are characterized by management putting the organization's own needs and desires at the center of the strategic process. It is only when management realizes that it is the customer who truly determines the long-run success of any strategy that the nonprofit firm can join the ranks of the sophisticated marketing strategists typically found in the private sector.

Several clues can be used to identify a nonprofit that is still mired in an organization-centered perspective. They see their offering as inherently desirable. They see the ignorance or lack of motivation of their customers as the major barrier to the organization's success. Research plays a minor role in strategy formulation. Marketing tends to be defined as synonymous with promotion. Marketing specialists tend to be chosen for their product knowledge or for their familiarity with communications techniques. A "one best" strategy is typically used in approaching the market, and generic competition is typically ignored in the process.

By contrast, customer-centered strategists begin with the customer and the customer's needs and wants. They rely heavily on research findings about the customers. They routinely assume—unless shown otherwise—that markets ought to be segmented. They define marketing broadly, not just as communication or promotion. Since they adopt the customer's perspective, they inevitably define competition as coming from widely diverse sources, not just from similar products or services. Finally, they move from being unresponsive or casually responsive to being fully responsive to their customers' needs and wants.

Indoctrinating a nonprofit organization from top to bottom with the proper marketing philosophy is not an easy task. The experience of those who have successfully achieved this objective suggests such strategies as recognizing the limited understanding of others about what marketing really is; allowing for other pressures on the organization that may temporarily mandate non-customer-oriented approaches; picking visible, short-term projects for the first marketing applications; and recognizing that the introduction of a new philosophy is as much a political exercise as a matter of logic and persuasion. Allies must be sought and enemies deflected. Above all, it is essential to secure a top management commitment to the new way of thinking. Without it, a true marketing orientation will not be achieved and customer-centered thrusts in one area will inevitably run afoul of organization-mindedness elsewhere.

QUESTIONS

1. It has been argued that religious organizations "by definition" must adopt a selling orientation. Do you agree? If not, how would you go about helping a particular religious organization become more customer-oriented?

2. It was stated in this chapter that "expert marketing talent is generic." What would you classify as the principal characteristics of "expert marketing talent"?

3. Health educators in nonprofit hospitals state that they are really not marketers in that their basic job is to inform target customers about personal health care practices they ought to adopt. Further, they say they can't be customer-oriented because their customers—even the well-educated ones—simply don't know what they *should* need and want. Is this a selling approach? How could a marketing approach be implemented?

4. The text says that a marketing orientation should pervade the organization from top to bottom. Why should the chief of surgery of a hospital, the artistic director of a ballet company, or the leader of a Girl Scout troop be at all interested in marketing—let alone practice it?

5. Some say that politicans are too customer-centered. How can a marketing orientation, the need to win, and ethics be merged in a political campaign?

NOTES

1. Peter F. Drucker, *Management: Tasks, Responsibilities, Practices* (New York: Harper & Row, 1973), pp. 64–65.

2. Kenneth Boulding, *A Primer on Social Dynamics* (New York: Free Press, 1970).

3. Alan R. Andreasen, "Nonprofits: Check Your Attention to Customers," *Harvard Business Review,* May-June 1982, pp. 105–110.

4. Steven E. Permut, "A Survey of Marketing Perspectives of Performing Arts Administrators," in Michael P. Mokwa, William M. Dawson, and E. Arthur Price, eds., *Marketing the Arts* (New York: Praeger Publishers, 1980), pp. 47–58.

5. Seymour H. Fine, "Concept Sector Within the Economy," in Philip Kotler, O. C. Ferrell, and Charles Lamb, eds., *Cases and Readings for Marketing for Nonprofit Organizations* (Englewood Cliffs, N.J.: Prentice-Hall, 1983), p. 349.

6. Chris T. Allen and Charles D. Schewe, "An Empirical Assessment of the Relative Marketing Orientations of Museum Directors and Marketing Practitioners." Working Paper 81-14, School of Business Administration, University of Massachusetts, Amherst, Massachusetts.

7. "A Guidebook to the Airlines," *Newsweek,* November 26, 1979, p. 88.

8. Bill Grady, "This Food Stamp Office is Hiding," *Chicago Tribune,* May 22, 1980.

9. Mike Reilly and Jim McCullough, "A Survey of Marketing Activity in Nonprofit Organizations," in F. Kelly Shuptrine and Peter Reingen, eds., *Nonprofit Marketing: Conceptual and Empirical Research* (Tempe, Ariz.: Bureau of Business and Economic Research, College of Business Administration, Arizona State University, 1982), pp. 40–43.

10. Much of the material in this section was first presented in Andreasen, "Nonprofits."

11. Permut, "A Survey."

12. *Ibid.,* pp. 52, 53.

13. *Ibid.,* p. 51.

14. John A. Witt and Nelson L. McRoberts, "Lack of Expertise, Funding Shackles Marketing Moves," *Modern Healthcare,* April 1983.

15. Alan R. Andreasen and Russell W. Belk, "Predictors of Attendance at the Performing Arts," *Journal of Consumer Research,* September 1980, pp. 112–120.

16. For approaches to evaluating consumer reactions to offerings, see Chapter 22.

17. See Anthony Downs, *Inside Bureacracy* (Boston: Little, Brown, 1967).

18. Quoted from a speech given by Frank Sinclair at a public relations conference of hospital administrators.

19. Bernard J. Lachner, "Marketing—An Emerging Management Challenge," *Health Care Management Review,* Fall 1977, p. 27.

20. Apparently Koussevitzky was copying an innovation begun sometime earlier by the Philadelphia Orchestra.

21. See Philip Kotler, "Strategies for Introducing Marketing into Nonprofit Organizations," *Journal of Marketing,* Vol. 43 (January 1979), pp. 37–44; William R. George and Fran Compton, "How to Initiate a Marketing Perspective in a Health Care Organization," *Journal of Health Care Marketing,* Vol. 5, No. 1, (Winter 1985), pp. 29–37.

22. Christopher H. Lovelock and Charles B. Weinberg, *Marketing for Public and Nonprofit Managers* (New York: John Wiley, 1984), p. 561.

23. Chris Argyris and Donald A. Schoen, *Organizational Learning: A Theory of Action Perspective* (Reading, Mass.: Addison-Wesley, 1978).

24. James Brian Quinn, *Strategies for Change: Logical Incrementation* (Homewood, Ill.: Richard D. Irwin, 1980).

25. Karl E. Weick, *The Social Psychology of Organizing* (Reading, Mass.: Addison-Wesley, 1969).

Understanding Customer Behavior

For years, marketers in the performing arts have conducted "audience profile" studies. Inevitably these studies have shown that typical consumers of cultural arts activities are decidedly upscale. They have incomes well above average, they have gone to college or beyond, and they have managerial or professional occupations (or are students aspiring to them). Further, those who attend one form of the arts tend to be likely to attend other forms of the arts.

Given this narrow profile, arts marketers have had to rely on relatively obvious strategic options. They have sought out upscale media for their messages, chosen "sophisticated" message themes and classy graphics, advertised in their competitors' programs, and worked over mailing lists from American Express or the fancier department stores in town.

In the mid-1970s, the National Endowment for the Arts began a research program that—among other goals—sought to expand upon this narrow data base. First, they commissioned a study to ascertain what we already knew about cultural audiences. The NEA next funded two University of Illinois researchers to develop richer audience profile data that used some of the latest technology from private-sector consumer research. The researchers reported findings that were original in three ways.

First, they used what is called "expectancy-value" attitude modeling to learn what consumers perceived to be the costs and benefits of attending theater or symphony performances. At the same time they asked them how valuable each of these costs and benefits actually was to them. They isolated specifically which costs were perceived to be high and which benefits were perceived to be low on dimensions ranked as quite important. They were then able to specify areas in which both the reality and the perceptions of the arts event needed to be improved for more of this target audience to attend.

Second, potential and present consumers were segmented on the basis of complex lifestyle profiles derived from an extensive series of questions about their attitudes, interests, and activities with respect to their leisure time. As expected, those exhibiting a culturally oriented lifestyle were prime targets for the symphony and theater. The detailed profile of this group that emerged from the lifestyle analysis yielded a rich set of characteristics that advertisers and others could use to speak intimately and directly to this audience. Interestingly, the lifestyle analysis identified a second leisure lifestyle group that appeared to be an excellent target for the symphony. This group, labeled socially-oriented, indicated that, while the cultural group might attend the symphony because it is a cultural event, there are others who will attend if they see it as a major social event.

Third, the researchers used multivariate regression analysis to identify the set of factors that together best predicted theater and symphony attendance. Separate regression analysis with first a theater group and then a symphony group revealed that likely future attendance at both was best predicted by four factors: (1) lifestyle, (2) attitudes toward attendance, (3) experiences with the specific art form while growing up, and (4) past attendance. What was surprising was that, although the traditional upscale demographic "explainers" were found to correlate well with likely attendance, *not one* of them appeared in either of the regressions. This led the researchers to conclude that past research has really only given us a superficial glimpse of the arts consumer. It appears that the upscale demographic variables have been significant only because they were closely associated with attitudes, lifestyle, and childhood experiences that are the more fundamental determinants of cultural consumption.

SOURCES: The first study mentioned was Paul DiMaggio, Michael Useem, and Paula Brown, *Audience Studies of the Performing Arts and Museums,* Research Report #9, Washington, D.C.: National Endowment for the Arts, 1977. The University of Illinois researchers' study was Alan R. Andreasen and Russell W. Belk, "Predictors of Attendance at the Performing Arts," *Journal of Consumer Behavior,* September 1980, pp. 112–120.

In our view, the bottom line of all marketing strategy and tactics is to influence behavior. Sometimes this necessitates changing ideas and thoughts first, but in the end, it is behavior change we are after. This is an absolutely crucial point. Some nonprofit marketers may think they are in the "business" of changing *ideas,* but it can legitimately be asked why they should bother if such changes do not lead to action. That is, why bother changing whites' attitudes towards blacks unless it leads to fair treatment socially and in the workplace? Is social marketing really successful if the attitudes of a specific white population (for example, teenaged boys in a given neighborhood) are made more positive while their behaviors continue to be prejudicial? If one argues that attitude change alone really does represent success because *eventually* behavior will change, one is simply reinforcing our fundamental position that the bottom line of nonprofit marketing really is—or ought to be—*behavior change.*

If the end product of a particular program is only a change in a mental state, this should more properly be called *educating* or *propagandizing.* It is not really marketing. A great many nonprofit organizations, of course, engage in a great deal of education or propagandization as well as marketing. Besides educational institutions, these include religious organizations and those seeking broad social reforms.

Our definition still leaves a very wide area for the application of marketing principles. Indeed, there are scholars like Bartels and Luck who believe that the arena for marketing is defined too broadly.[1] But all of the following seem to us to be perfectly legitimate opportunities for the application of effective marketing:

- Sales of products and services
- Efforts to get individuals to undertake activities that will be good for their physical and mental health—from brushing their teeth or exercising regularly to undergoing surgery or entering psychoanalysis
- Efforts to get individuals to refrain from certain activities, such as smoking, excessive drinking, and taking harmful drugs
- Efforts of customers to influence *marketers*—for example, to get them to reduce prices, add free accessories, or give free installation

---

THE CENTRAL ROLE OF EXCHANGE

What do all of these contexts have in common? The parties involved all believe they can induce behavior change by offering the other party a *favorable exchange.* People—at least those who are mentally competent—behave in ways that they perceive will leave them better off than if they behaved in some other fashion. Since every action implies perceived costs (if only some anxiety about not taking an alternative action), it follows that people act in certain ways because they perceive *the ratio of the benefits to costs* to be better than for any alternative. Since the costs are in a basic sense the sacrifices the consumer must make to receive the benefits the action will bring, a diverse array of scholars have come to consider the *exchange* to be the most useful way to conceptualize the relationship between marketers and their target consumers. The marketer is offering what the consumer perceives to be benefits but the organization sees as costs, and receives in return what the organization sees as benefits but the consumer sees as costs or sacrifices. The simplest exchange can then be represented as follows:

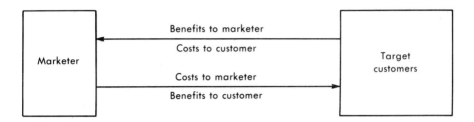

Formally speaking, the exchange perspective assumes that four conditions exist:

1. *There are at least two parties.* In the simplest exchange situation, there are two parties. If one party seeks an exchange more actively than the other, we call the first party a marketer and the second party a prospect. A marketer is someone who is seeking a behavior from someone else and who is willing to offer benefits in exchange. The marketer can be a seller or a buyer.[2]
2. *Each can offer something that the other perceives to be a benefit or benefits.* If one of the parties has nothing that is valued by the other party, the exchange will not take place. Each party should consider what things might be perceived as benefits by the other party. Four categories of things tend to offer such benefits. The first is *physical goods.* A good is any tangible object—food, clothing, furniture, and so on—that is capable of satisfying a human want. The second is *services.* A service is any act that another person or institution might perform that is capable of satisfying a human want. The third category is *money.* Money is a generalized store of value that can be used to obtain goods or services. The final category is *time and effort.* Many marketing exchanges involve marketers seeking to attract any of the previous resources from others. This could include getting others to give blood, serve as volunteers for a charity drive, or provide free advice to the organization's management.
3. *Each is capable of communication and delivery.* For exchange to take place, the two parties must be capable of communicating with each other. They must be able to describe what is being offered and when, where, and how costs and benefits will be exchanged. Each party must state or imply certain warranties about the expected performance in the exchange. In addition to communicating, each party must be capable of finding means to deliver the values to each other.
4. *Each is free to accept or reject the offer.* An exchange assumes that both parties are engaging in voluntary behavior. There is no complete coercion. For this reason, every trade is normally assumed to leave both parties better off. Presumably each ended up with more value than he or she started with, since they both freely entered the exchange.

It is critical to recognize that in attempting to understand consumer behavior, one can distinguish between exchange as a *process* and exchange as an *outcome*. In the present context, exchange as an outcome will be considered a *transaction*. That is, the *process* of "exchanging" results in an outcome called a transaction. If either party is actively trying to create or influence the *nature* of an exchange, that is *marketing*. Merely accepting or rejecting the marketing of another is "exchanging," but by our definition, it is *not* marketing.[3]

TYPES OF EXCHANGES

It is possible to categorize transactions (exchanges) as resulting from two kinds of exchange processes:

1. *Unilateral exchange processes,* where only *one* party seeks to influence the outcome of the exchange process; that is, whether there *is* an outcome and what its terms are (what benefits and costs each party will exchange). Examples of unilateral exchanges would be nonnegotiated sales of goods and services, employment contracts, and requests for blood donations or for fixed charitable contributions.
2. *Bilateral exchange processes,* where *both* sides seek to influence the outcome of an exchange process. Examples include negotiated sales, charitable donations of time and money, or provision of public services in exchange for tax dollars.

Exchanges can also vary in whether they are *two-party* or *multiple-party* and whether they lead to transactions that are *continuing* or of *fixed duration*. Multiple-party exchanges occur in a number of contexts: the "additional" party can be (1) *allied with the customer*—for example, other family members, other members of the neighborhood, or other members of a buying group; (2) *allied with the marketer*—for example, an advertising agency or distribution channel member; (3) *independent* of either prime transactor but necessary to *facilitate* the transaction—for example, a credit card company; or (4) *independent* of either party but *seeking to influence* the existence or content of an exchange—for example, a bystander urging a teenager not to take an offered cigarette or a national politician urging citizens to be sure to vote. These additional parties are unique in the exchange process in that they do not bear any of the direct costs in the transaction but are involved because they expect to reap benefits depending on the nature of the outcome.

"Continuing transactions" are transactions where one or more parties must perform some continuing behavior as their part of the exchange agreement. Thus, a sale is a fixed duration transaction. Renting a car or a motel room for several days or weeks is a transaction taking place over time but of fixed duration. A great many of the transactions sought in the nonprofit sector, however, require the target consumer to *permanently* change some behavior or set of behaviors. Examples include campaigns to induce children to brush their teeth regularly, teenagers to avoid drugs, adults to stop smoking, and couples to practice birth control. Implicit in continuing transactions—and therefore crucial to marketers—is the fact that marketing does not stop and *should not stop* with the parties' agreement to the transaction or when the exchange is first performed under the terms of the transaction.

MARKETERS AND THE EXCHANGE PROCESS

To summarize, we have proposed the following:

1. Marketing is a set of activities designed to influence behavior.
2. Behavior by a target consumer is carried out at the end of an exchange process.
3. An exchange will result in a transaction whenever the target consumer perceives the benefits of the behavior the marketer seeks to exceed the costs or sacrifices the behavior entails *and* this ratio of benefits to costs is better than that achieved by "spending" the costs in any other conceivable way.
4. Behavior by the target consumer yields benefits to the marketer (which was the reason for marketing in the first place), while most of the benefits the consumer receives will involve costs for the marketer.
5. The outcome of an exchange may be of fixed duration or continuing.
6. There may be two or more parties; one or both of whom may be carrying on marketing.

Given the exchange framework, the challenge to the marketer in the case of a single consumer is relatively straightforward. To secure a transaction, the marketer must somehow induce the consumer to perceive the benefit/cost ratio to be more favorable than other alternative actions the consumer is considering—including doing nothing. Assuming that the consumer is not behaving as the marketer wishes, the task is either to increase the perceived benefits and/or reduce the perceived costs of this behavior (or in some cases, reduce the perceived benefits and increase the perceived costs of a competitive alternative). At the aggregate level, the marketer must choose a *set* of strategies to be directed at changing cost/benefit ratios of sets of consumers so that the marketer secures for itself the largest amount of the benefits it desires.

ANALYZING EXCHANGE FLOWS

To give a sense of how this framework can be used in the development of marketing strategy, suppose a hospital in a small town needs to attract a staff physician to replace one who has just retired. The hospital chief of staff makes some inquiries among physicians, medical school professors, and local medical society executives and collects the names of a dozen prospects. Their résumés are screened by a hospital committee, which establishes criteria for what it wants in a prospective physician. These wants can be represented in the following abstract way:

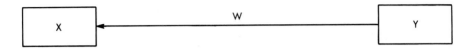

This says that X wants W from Y. In the concrete case, this is expanded to read:

Wants

1. competence
2. high admitting rate
3. cooperativeness
4. cost consciousness

That is, the hospital is looking for a physician who is competent, can bring a lot of patients to the hospital, is cooperative in committee work, and conscious of costs to patients and the hospital. The hospital will usually attach different weights to each of these wants.

Suppose the hospital search committee finds one physician who is highly attractive on these criteria. He has a private practice in a large city and is rumored to be looking for a small-town practice. The chief of staff contacts the physician to gather information on this physician's wants. From informal conversations, he establishes that the physician's wants are as follows:

Wants

1. competent colleagues and staff
2. improved income
3. good facilities and equipment
4. good living area

It would be very helpful to the hospital chief of staff to know the respective weights that the physician puts on these wants.

The hospital has to consider whether it can really make a good "case" to attract this physician (that is, whether it can offer him enough benefits). If the hospital is located in an unattractive area and its facilities are poor, there is little or no *exchange potential.* The hospital would have to offer the physician a substantially higher income to compensate for its deficiencies on this want dimension. On the other hand, the hospital's potential resources may match well the physician's needs and thus create a basis for a transaction.

In the latter case, the hospital would invite the physician for an interview. The staff would show its enthusiasm and the strong points about the hospital. If they liked the visiting physician, the chief of staff would make an offer:

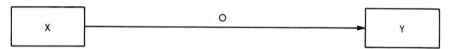

That is, X offers 0 to Y. In more concrete terms, the offer might be:

Offer

1. $80,000 salary
2. Four-week vacation
3. Secretarial service
4. One new piece of equipment worth $40,000

The physician might like the offer but suggest certain additions or modifications (that is, he will engage in marketing also):

Counteroffer

1. $95,000 salary
2. Five-week vacation
3. Secretarial service
4. Two new pieces of equipment worth $80,000

In turn, the chief of staff might make another counteroffer. This process of trying to find mutually agreeable terms is called *bilateral marketing*

or *negotiation*. Negotiation ends in either mutually acceptable terms of exchange or a decision not to transact.

ELABORATING THE EXCHANGE PROCESS

We have examined the exchange process as if it involved only two parties. But additional parties might be involved before an agreement can be struck. The chief of staff needs the board of trustees' approval on the offer terms. The physician needs his wife's approval and willingness to relocate to the small town. Thus, the buyer and seller might not act as two persons but as two organizations, each involving several participants.

We can illustrate a multiparty exchange process by introducing the physician's wife and her wishes into the picture. This is shown in Figure 3-1. The wife wants the hospital to help her find a job in her profession, hopes to find friendly physicians and wives at the hospital, and hopes for a good income and home and a good area for raising chidren. She wants her husband to be happy and to have enough time to give to the family. At the same time, the hospital hopes the wife will support her husband's work and par-

FIGURE 3-1

Three-Party Exchange Map Showing Want Vectors

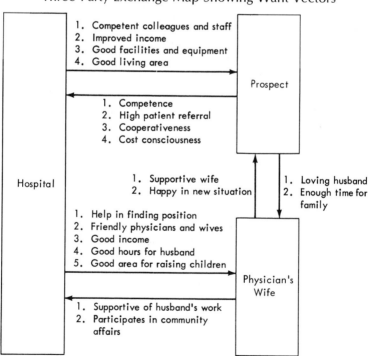

ticipate in community affairs. Finally, the husband wants his wife to be supportive and happy in the new situation. Clearly, the hospital, as marketer, must take these various needs into consideration in formulating an offer to attract the physician.

When marketers are anxious to consummate a transaction, they may be tempted to exaggerate the actual benefits of the product being offered. Thus, the chief of staff might be tempted to overstate the competence of the staff or understate the amount of expected committee work. He may succeed in attracting the physician but the physician will be turned into an unhappy customer. The physician will be dissatisfied because of the difference between his *expectations* and the hospital's *performance.* As an unhappy customer, he can be expected either to complain a lot, talk badly about the hospital to others, or quit, leaving the hospital with the task of finding another physician. In cases like these, the best exchanges are those in which it is realized that it is continuing behavior one is seeking, not a single transaction.

A MODEL OF THE DETERMINANTS OF EXCHANGE

Bagozzi has formulated a comprehensive model of the major determinants affecting exchange. The model is summarized in Figure 3-2. We will apply it to the hospital's problem of attracting the new physician to its staff.

First, we consider the two primary social actors involved in the exchange, namely, the chief of staff (source) and the prospective physician (receiver). The chief of staff and the prospective physician will engage in actions, communicate and exchange information to influence each other. The chief of staff's influence will be a function of several personal qualities, namely, attraction, similarity to the physician, expertise, prestige, trustworthiness, and status. The prospective physician's perception of these qualities will be influenced by his own self-confidence, self-esteem, sex, race, religion, social class, intelligence, and personality. The physician's ultimate decision will additionally be influenced by situational variables such as the availability of alternative sources of satisfaction (other hospitals and career opportunities), the opinion of other parties (wife, children, friends, and other colleagues), physical and psychological variables (time pressure for making a decision, number of issues that have to be considered, pleasantness of the surroundings, type of communication setting), and legal or normative variables (his contract with his present hospital and any normative concerns that might be triggered by the thought of leaving his community).

The physician will also be influenced by his picture of the contrasting outcomes associated with his staying versus leaving his present hospital. Three kinds of outcomes can be envisioned. First, his money income will be influenced by the outcome. Second, he will experience different social rewards in the form of approval, praise, and status. Third, he might also experience some social punishment such as disapproval or blame.

FIGURE 3-2

A Model of the Determinants of Exchange

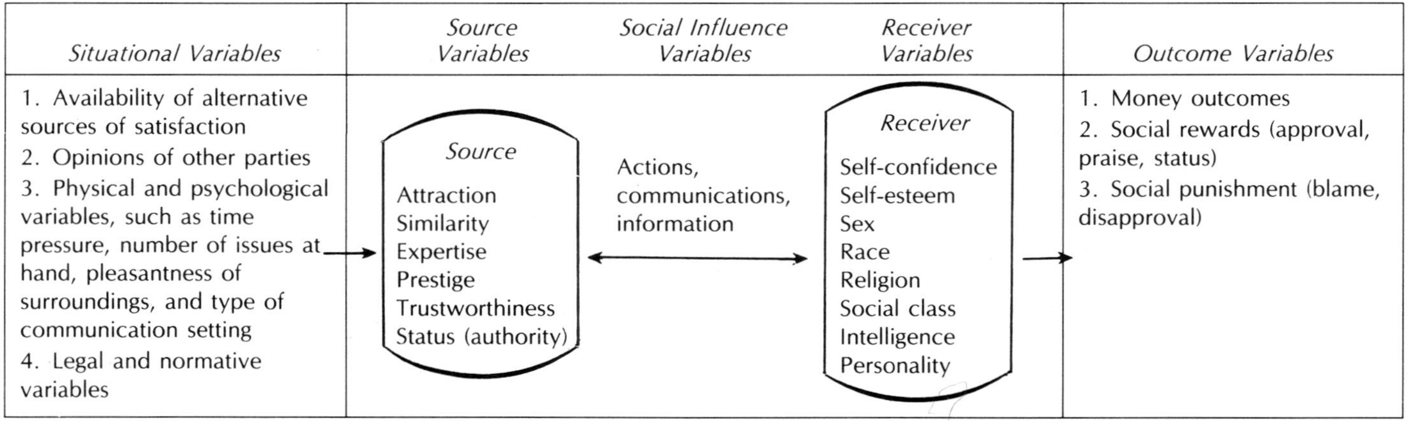

Situational Variables	Source Variables	Social Influence Variables	Receiver Variables	Outcome Variables
1. Availability of alternative sources of satisfaction 2. Opinions of other parties 3. Physical and psychological variables, such as time pressure, number of issues at hand, pleasantness of surroundings, and type of communication setting 4. Legal and normative variables	**Source** Attraction Similarity Expertise Prestige Trustworthiness Status (authority)	Actions, communications, information	**Receiver** Self-confidence Self-esteem Sex Race Religion Social class Intelligence Personality	1. Money outcomes 2. Social rewards (approval, praise, status) 3. Social punishment (blame, disapproval)

SOURCE: Diagram adapted by the authors from prose text in Richard P. Bagozzi, "Marketing as Exchange: A Theory of Transactions in the Market-place," *American Behavioral Scientist*, March–April 1978, pp. 535–56.

Thus, a large number of factors will influence the exchange process involving a hospital and a prospective physician. The direction of influence of most of these factors is pretty clear, although their relative importance varies with each situation. This model is presented not as an elegant predictive theory of how an exchange situation will be resolved, but as a comprehensive view of the factors that the marketer will want to analyze in preparing a marketing plan.

LEVELS OF UNDERSTANDING CONSUMER BEHAVIOR

The marketing manager for a nonprofit organization must understand consumer behavior because the organization's success depends on it. There are four broad classes of management decisions for which an understanding of consumers is especially crucial. The decisions will determine:

1. *How to aggregate consumers into similar groupings for purposes of marketing planning.* This is the issue of *segmentation,* which is taken up in the next chapter.
2. *How to market to each chosen segment, if at all.* These are the *marketing mix* decisions taken up in Part III of this book. The marketer must decide what to offer in costs and benefits (offer and "pricing" decisions), how to communicate these (promotion decisions), and how to make them available (distribution decisions).
3. *How much to market to each segment.* These are strategic allocation decisions, which are considered in Chapter 12. They involve questions about how many dollars in investment and operating budget to put into a particular market, how many personnel to use, and how much to use of one of the scarcest organizational resources—management's own time.
4. *When to apply the marketing efforts to the segment.* These timing decisions are also critical strategic choices. They involve allocations of resources over time as well as sequencing decisions for various tactics within a given strategy.

There are also four levels at which a manager may wish to understand consumer behavior so as to make these decisions better:

1. *Descriptive understanding.* At the simplest level, the manager may wish to profile the characteristics of the market at a given point in time. How many buyers of what age, sex, and occupational status are in market A, creating how many exchanges of type B, in month Y, costing X marketing dollars, and so on. At a more sophisticated level, the manager may wish to categorize consumers in terms of complex indexes such as their social class or family life cycle or their "psychographic profile."
2. *Understanding of associations.* At this level, the manager may desire to know what behaviors or characteristics in the profile are associated with what other behaviors or characteristics at a certain point in time. Thus, the manager may wish to know whether museum attendance is associated with occupation, theater attendance with sex, and attendance at both with age and family composition.

3. *Understanding of causation.* If a curvilinear association between family life cycle and arts attendance is found, a manager may wish to know whether getting older and having children *leads* to less performing arts attendance or whether the two sets of factors just happen to occur together for other reasons. This level of understanding moves beyond association to show determinancy. Such information is particularly valuable if the "cause" at issue is a marketing intervention the manager can control.

4. *Explanation level.* Ideally, a manager would like to move beyond knowing that A causes B to know *why* this is so. That is, the manager may "know" that arts attendance has a curvilinear association with age and that the appearance of children *causes* a decline in attendance. But the manager may only have hypotheses as to why this is so. It is possible, for example, that the explanation is that the appearance of children puts a strain on budgets that precludes former luxuries like arts attendance (an economic explanation). Alternatively, it may be that younger family members put pressure on adult consumers to *not* attend the performing arts (a sociological explanation). Or, the appearance of children may change the consumer's personal priorities. He or she may decide to devote more time to being with the children or more time working to build a firm economic future for the family, which leaves no room for attending the performing arts (a psychological explanation). Quite obviously, what a performing-arts marketer should do to win back families with new children—or whether one should do anything at all—depends on which of these explanations is the most valid.

Developing a sophisticated understanding of various consumer markets is, of course, not easy. It comes with time and experience and the careful use of formal and informal research to accumulate facts, understand relationships, and slowly form patterns from them. But personal observation and formal research are both likely to be much more effective if they are based on an awareness of what we already know about consumers. More importantly, it will be much more useful and effective if this observation, research, and past history are all based on a sound conceptualization or model of consumer behavior. The remainder of this chapter will offer such a conceptualization centered on the fundamental concept of exchange.

INDIVIDUAL DECISIONS

Unilateral Two-Party Marketing

We begin with a situation where a marketer is seeking to influence a consumer to undertake an exchange that is favorable to the marketer. For a *one-time exchange* to take place, a minimum of three steps must occur in the exchange process:

1. The consumer must *need or want* to make an exchange;
2. The consumer must *understand* that the marketer's offering will meet those needs or wants; and

3. The consumer must *behave* as desired (that is, must complete the transaction).

This can be represented schematically as follows:

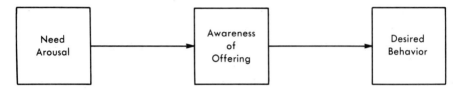

If a *continuing exchange* or repeat behavior is sought, the model would be as follows:

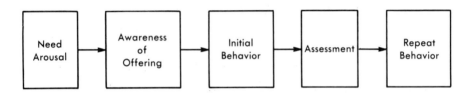

Consumer behavior theorists make a further distinction between *low-involvement* and *high-involvement* exchanges. In effect, this is a distinction that they believe affects the amount of cognition or problem-solving a consumer will undertake during and after the exchange process. As defined by Engle and Blackwell, with respect to products and services,

> **Involvement** is the activation of extended problem-solving behavior when the act of purchase or consumption is seen by the decision-maker as having high personal importance or relevance.[4]

High personal involvement has been found to occur when one or more of the following conditions are operative:

1. The behavior required of the consumer will reflect upon his or her self-image;
2. The economic and personal costs of behaving "incorrectly" are perceived as high;
3. The personal or social risks of a "wrong" decision are perceived as high;
4. Outside (nonmarketer) reference group pressures to act in a particular way are strong and the target consumer's motivation to comply is strong;
5. The decision is being made for the first time.

Thus, exchanges can vary in the extent to which they are personally involving. They can also vary in their *newness* to the decision-maker. There are, of course, exchanges made for the first time and exchanges made after years and years of experience. Thus, we might expect very complex decision-making to occur for exchanges that are highly involving and that are being made for the first time. As the consumer gains experience, however, decisions will be simplified to reflect this experience. At some point, given many repeats of the exchange process, the evaluation process may become relatively routine even though the subject of the exchanges is still highly involving. This distinction is indicated in Table 3-1.

There are also many exchanges, especially in the private sector, where consumers are not personally involved to any great degree. Whether or not they have had any relevant experience, they may make their decisions about what to do with little or no conscious evaluation of alternatives, certainly nothing elaborate. Such exchanges are sufficiently trivial to the individual that they may in fact appear to be behaving *randomly*. In such cases, attempts by marketers to try to develop some complex model of supposedly rational decision-making activity is not at all warranted. Engel and Blackwell warn that complex decision-making may be much rarer than we think: "This [rational problem-solving] occurs, however, with only a minority of product purchases. Most items, quite frankly, are not sufficiently important to justify this kind of activity."[5]

It is likely that a great many of the exchanges nonprofit marketing managers are attempting to influence are high, rather than low involvement. The manager should be extremely careful, however, *not* to assume that the elaborate cognitive model outlined in the next section applies to all consumer decisions about products and services that many nonprofit marketers attempt to sell. It is possible that many other nonprofit exchanges, such as small donations, voting on trivial public issues, signing a simple petition, and so on, are really low-involvement actions. It is our experience that there is the real danger that a myopic company-oriented view of marketing will contaminate the marketer's view of consumer decision-making. Marketers

Table 3-1

A TAXONOMY OF CONSUMER DECISION-MAKING APPROACHES

Experience	Degree of Personal Involvement	
	High	*Low*
None	Extensive Evaluation	Extensive Evaluation
Some	Simplified Evaluation	No Observable Evaluation
Much	Routinized Evaluation	No Observable Evaluation

may assume that the exchange is highly important to consumers since it affects the very success or failure of the organization. The consumer may be assumed to think carefully about the choice, have complex information about the alternatives, engage in at least some information-seeking before deciding, and so on. Substantial resources can be wasted by myopic marketers trying to tease out of consumers data about a complex process that really doesn't exist.

Having raised this important caution, we must repeat our position that a much larger number—perhaps the majority—of exchanges with which marketers in nonprofit organizations are involved are in fact considered high involvement and therefore highly cognitive. Decisions about changing health habits, voting for major candidates, choosing a school or a career, giving a significant donation of time or money, attending the arts, changing religious institutions, supporting tax referenda, obeying the laws, and so forth all may be characterized as:

- Involving very elemental aspects of one's self-image;
- Involving major personal or economic sacrifices;
- Risking major personal or social costs if a wrong choice is made;
- Involving considerable peer pressure for or against.

THE MARKETER'S TASK—AN OVERVIEW

As outlined in Table 3-1, consumer decisions can be of several types and exhibit various levels of evaluation complexity. They can be (1) extensive, (2) simplified, (3) routinized, and (4) unobservable. An understanding of these differences can be very instructive to a marketer. As in the private sector, a given market at any single point in time may contain consumers who differ significantly in the kinds of cognitive behavior they are undertaking. To illustrate the point, let us consider a hypothetical example of a political race for a seat on the city council between the incumbent, David Deacon, and his opponent, Amy Anderson. Exit interviews with a hypothetical family, the Evanses, might turn up the following differences in decision styles among the family members that represent the four levels of evaluation complexity. As will be seen, as one moves to simpler levels of complexity, decisions involve less cognition, less search behavior, simpler decision rules, and less personal involvement in the decision-making process.

Frank Evans, nineteen, is an example of a highly complex decision-maker undergoing extensive evaluations. This election was his first opportunity to exercise his citizen franchise. He was anxious to put to the test his high school civics lessons and to satisfy his commitment to himself that he would be a concerned citizen. Frank carefully read the campaign literature of both candidates and attended most of the debates sponsored by the local

Junior League at Frank's high school. Frank talked about the candidates with his parents; his older sister; his girlfriend, Jean, a senior at State College; and a few politically astute friends. Frank paid careful attention to the endorsements of his favorite local newspaper columnist and the American Civil Liberties Union (to which he planned to belong someday). Frank changed his intentions at least once during the period leading up to the election and admitted he was not entirely certain of his choice until he entered the polling place to cast his ballot for Amy Anderson.

Bert, Frank's father, is an example of someone undergoing simplified evaluation. Bert had only recently become interested in politics. For years, as a foreman in the local dishwasher manufacturing plant, he didn't see how local politics affected him very much. But five years ago, when he moved into an executive position with the company, he realized how much local council actions could affect his firm. He voted for Deacon last time but had not been comfortable with some of his votes on the council. Bert knew what he was looking for in a good councilman and carefully studied the campaign positions of the two candidates before deciding that Deacon's positions were still best for Bert and his company. His decision-making could be characterized as simpler than that of his son due to his experience as a voter, but not as *routine* as was the case for his wife.

Alice Evans, Bert's wife, indicated that the exchange for her vote for the candidate's expected future services and positions on issues was a *routine decision* for her. She had lived in the area for over eighteen years and had voted a number of times. In the last two elections she had voted for David Deacon. She was satisfied with his performance in office and saw no reason to switch to an unknown at this time. She had intended to vote for Deacon from the start and remained true to those intentions to the end of the campaign.

Theresa Evans, twenty-two, was largely an uninvolved decision-maker in this election. She considered the race between Deacon and Anderson just not worth her time and interest. She was off at college and was unsure whether she would ever return to her home community afterward. She felt that the winner could have little effect on her personal well-being. She might have thought more about this election race because the results would affect the rest of her family, but Theresa had become disenchanted with local politics in her hometown. She viewed both candidates as political hacks equally likely to be incompetent in office. Her views of politics were strongly influenced by her peers at college who debated "one-world" issues and tended, in their youthful enthusiasm, to see domestic politics as either irrelevant to what they felt were the broader issues or as downright divisive. Theresa and her friends felt that campaign rhetoric focused people's attention too much on nationalism and patriotic pride that, Theresa thought, got in the way of what she and her friends called "world empathy." For Theresa, casting her vote in the Anderson-Deacon race (which she did) was a very trivial decision. One could not really detect any clear cognitive evaluation in her choice.

Thus, as the Evans family suggests, in any market it is important for the marketer to measure whether target segments are undergoing complex, simple, or routine evaluations or are simply uninvolved. As can be seen in the above example, the marketing manager's approach to each member of the Evans family would be very different simply because of the way they went about making decisions in this contest.

Several points about the makeup of markets according to decision style need to be made.

1. Because a particular target audience member adopts a particular style for a particular exchange does not mean that the marketer should assume that the audience member would use the same process for other decisions, even if they involve similar factors. Thus, Theresa Evans might turn out to be a highly complex decision-maker with regard to a future Senate race because she feels that the candidates are actively debating important world issues. At the same time, Mr. and Mrs. Evans might be uninvolved in the same Senate election because the two of them are very local in their orientation and, in general, feel that who goes to Washington will have no effect on them. Thus, for a marketer to characterize an observed decision style with respect to one decision as a general personality trait applying to many situations would be incorrect. While it is entirely *possible* that a given consumer would treat a number of related decisions similarly (for example, treat all small charitable gifts or all conservation requests as simplified evaluations), a marketer should not automatically assume that this will occur.

2. Because a consumer adopts a decision style on one occasion doesn't necessarily mean that he or she will adopt it next time for the same decision. Three kinds of circumstances could make the next time different from this. First, the consumer could simply acquire more experience, and a highly complex decision could become simplified and then routinized. Next time around, Frank Evans could just repeat his votes from this first time. Second, the consumer could change in his or her perceptions, needs, and wants. Theresa could move back home and, away from the influence of her college friends, see that local issues *can* have important effects on individual lives. This could lead her to decide to become a highly complex decision-maker with respect to local political issues. Third, circumstances surrounding the next decision occasion could change. A charismatic new world-centered candidate could appear who would grab Theresa's attention even though she was still largely under the spell of her college values. Or, David Deacon could die, be involved in a scandal, or choose to run for a different office, leaving Alice with no chance to exercise her routine decision process (unless she chose to repeat what she may define as a "Republican" or "Democratic" choice). An individual's past decision behavior is not necessarily a good predictor of the future.

3. Although the consumers in a market at a given time will undoubtedly represent all four decision styles, the *majority* may be characterizable as one type or another. This may be the case when a crucial subject is at issue and everyone must choose for the first time (for example, choosing two new presidential candidates or voting for or against a new public nonsmoking ordinance or a sales tax referendum). Or it may just be that, although the decision is not new or

unique, the behavior in question is one that is almost always routine (for example, perhaps contributing to the United Way or to a high school spring raffle) or always highly complex (for example, choosing a hospital or a church). 4. Although a certain type of exchange may most frequently involve a particular decision style for most consumers at one point in time, virtually everyone in the market may be predicted to change before the next time they decide. Again, this may be due to the passage of time and the maturing of a market over its life cycle. Thus, when consumers were first asked many years ago to consider relatively narrow antismoking ordinances, the decision for many was highly complex. Today, as society seems to have generally accepted such restrictions on individual freedom, voting on similar ordinances will be more simplified. Alternatively, markets may shift totally as major circumstances change. For years, patients have chosen physicians largely on the basis of word of mouth and have routinely stuck with their doctors despite sometimes less than satisfactory care. Growing sophistication by patients and the availability in some communities of published guides and evaluations of physicians have led many consumers to engage in much more complex doctor-shopping behavior. This doctor-shopping has added one more pressure to an already highly competitive marketplace.

Implications. It is clear that the appropriateness and probable impact of various marketing strategies depends on the depth of cognition undertaken by the market segment to whom the marketing program is directed. To understand these implications, it is necessary to describe our current best understanding of the processes we believe are operative under each of the four decision styles.

We shall begin with highly complex decisions because they are, obviously, the most comprehensive. We turn next to simplified and then routine cognitive decisions since, as we have indicated, they are by definition outgrowths of earlier, more complex processes. Finally, we shall shift our focus to decisions for which it is fruitless to attempt to understand consumers' cognitive activity. "Unobservable evaluations" will be assumed to occur for decisions that are very trivial for the individual. It is possible that such decisions really involve some kind of cognitive activity that is a *very highly* simplified version of the processes in the more elaborate cases. We shall assume, however, that the possiblity of unearthing these cognitions is so remote or so costly that digging them out is simply not worth the marketer's troubles. Further, since the decisions are trivial, even if we could understand the cognitions behind a consumer decision today, the chances are good that they wouldn't apply tomorrow.

HIGHLY COMPLEX DECISIONS

For exchanges in which a consumer has relatively high involvement, a more elaborate representation of the steps from need arousal to behavior (and repeat behavior) suggested at the beginning of the chapter is outlined in Figure 3-3.

FIGURE 3-3

A Model of Complex Evaluations

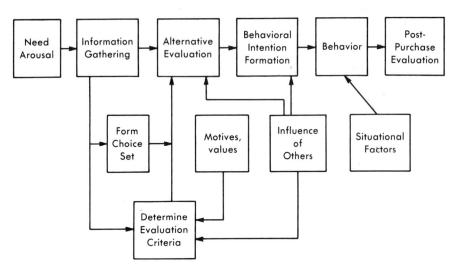

The core of this heavily cognitive model is the evaluation of alternatives. We shall consider this stage first. It involves three components: forming the choice set, determining evaluation criteria, and evaluating alternatives.

Forming the Choice Set. Through the process of gathering information, the consumer arrives at an increasingly clear picture of the major available choices. He or she eliminates certain alternatives and moves toward making a choice among the few remaining alternatives.

This process of *choice narrowing* can be illustrated for Bob Jones as he faced the problem of what he should do after high school. Bob Jones considered a number of alternatives to college, including working, joining the army, traveling, and loafing. He decided that going to college made the most sense. Should it be a community college, a state university, or a private college? Examining his needs and values, he decided to attend a private college.

We can now examine how Bob narrowed his choice to a specific set of colleges. Figure 3-4 shows a succession of sets involved in this consumer's decision process. The *total set* represents all private colleges that exist, whether or not the consumer knows about them; this list runs into the thousands. The total set can be divided into the consumer's *awareness set* (the colleges he has heard of) and the *unawareness set*. Of those he is aware of, he will only want to consider a limited number; these constitute his *consideration set*, and the others are relegated to an *infeasible set*. As he gathers additional information, a few colleges remain strong candidates, and they constitute his *choice set*, the others being relegated to a *nonchoice set*. (Some

FIGURE 3-4

Successive Sets in Consumer Decision-Making

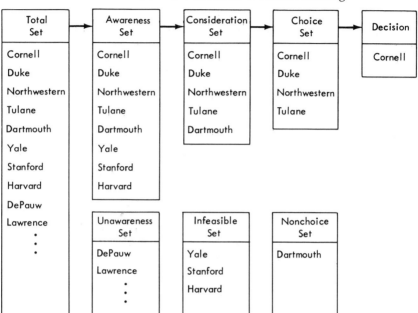

research has suggested that choice sets seldom exceed seven alternatives, plus or minus two.) Let us assume that the student sends applications to the four colleges of his choice set and is accepted by all four. In the final step, he carefully evaluates the colleges in the choice set (we shall examine this process shortly) and then makes a final choice, in this case Cornell University.

The implication of this choice-narrowing process is that a nonprofit marketer potentially competes with a large number of other choices for the consumer's interest. Therefore, before making plans to market to a particular segment, the nonprofit marketer must study consumers to learn (1) whether the organization is in the segment's awareness, consideration, and choice sets and (2) if the organization *is* in the various sets, who the competitors are. If the organization is not in the choice set, for example, then the desired exchange will not be possible. The first marketing task, then, is to get the alternative into the choice set of the target buyers.

Another marketing task is to identify the major competitors. We saw how colleges compete not only with each other but also with alternatives to college, such as going to work or military service. If high school seniors start favoring some of these generic alternatives, then all colleges will suffer. As a result, colleges would have to constantly prove their value to high school students, either in terms of raising their ultimate incomes or their appreciation and enjoyment of life. In addition, each college must watch the trends in the intraform competition. If the high tuitions of private colleges drive more students into community colleges and state universities, private colleges will suffer. Finally, each college must undertake research to determine its closest "brand" competitors (i.e. other colleges) and monitor their strengths and weaknesses. (We shall consider competition further in Chapter 5.)

Forming Criteria.   To make an eventual judgment about which of the alternative behaviors he will select, Bob Jones must develop some basis for forming an overall evaluation of the alternatives in the final choice set. Presumably, developing these criteria is a step he could have taken before or—more likely—during the process of defining his choice set.

Clearly, if a college marketer wants to influence Jones, he ought to understand what is important to Jones. And finding what is important to Jones is really finding out two things: (1) what factors Bob Jones considers in judging the various alternatives, and (2) the relative value he assigns to each factor. We shall refer to the former as *choice criteria* and the latter as *criteria weights*.

One of the key factors determining Bob Jones's criteria in choosing his college is his own needs. While individuals have many basic needs, the marketer must discover which ones apply in this specific case.

FIGURE 3-5
Maslow's Hierarchy of Needs

One of the most useful typologies of basic needs is Maslow's *hierarchy of needs* shown in Figure 3-5.[6] Maslow held that people act to satisfy the lower needs before satisfying their higher needs. A starving man, for example, first devotes his energy to finding food. If this basic need is satisfied, he can spend more time on his safety needs, such as eating the right foods and breathing good air. When he feels safe, he can take the time to deepen his social affiliations and friendships. Still later, he can develop pursuits that will meet his need for self-esteem and the esteem of others. Once this is satisfied, he is free to actualize his potential in other ways. As each lower level need is satisfied, it ceases to be a motivator and a higher need starts defining the person's motivational orientation.

We can ask what basic needs are stimulated by the aroused interest in college. Some high school seniors become concerned about whether they can afford college and meet their basic needs for food and adequate housing. Others wonder about how safe they will be away from home. Still others are concerned with whether they can find people they like and who like them. And others are concerned with self-esteem or self-actualization. A college will not be able to give attention to all of these needs. Thus, we find colleges that primarily cater to the need for belonging (small schools with small classes, a caring faculty, and a good social life), others to the students' need for esteem (many "name" colleges), and still others to the need for self-actualization (many "arty" schools).

Students often want to satisfy several needs, some of which are in conflict, by the same behavior. Thus, a student may have a high need for both achieving and belonging. This can create mental conflict, which can be resolved either by treating one need as more important or by fluctuating between the two needs at different times. Here is where the person's *values* come into play, namely, the principles the person employs to choose among competing ends.

Measurement. Maslow's hierarchy is only one way of looking at the criteria target consumers might apply in a particular decision context. Whatever model or checklist one uses, the nonprofit marketing manager must still discover what specific criteria and weightings apply in a specific complex (or simplified) exchange context. Criteria can be determined by any of four different methods: (1) direct questions; (2) indirect measurements; (3) perceptual mapping; or (4) conjoint analysis. These are outlined in Exhibit 3-1.

Evaluating Alternatives. The bottom line in understanding highly complex decisions is determining how consumers ultimately come to a conclusion about each alternative in the choice set. Although the range of approaches to this very difficult issue would fill several volumes, we prefer to adapt a model developed by a psychologist, Martin Fishbein, at the University of Illinois in the late 1960s and early 1970s.[7] The central features of this approach have received wide acceptance in the private sector and play

EXHIBIT 3-1. Methods for determining decision criteria and weightings

DIRECT QUESTIONING

Most marketing researchers use direct questioning to assess consumer needs and wants. They may conduct an interview with a single individual or lead a focused group discussion. They may use open-end questions, such as "What courses would you like to see added to the college curriculum?" or "What recreational facilities would you like to see added on the campus?" Closed-end questions may also be included, such as "Rank the following activities in terms of your level of interest" or "Rate each of the following services on a scale from one to ten." Closed-end questions are simple to administer and code. They assure uniformity of responses across consumers (they are all responding to the same stimulus). But they have two major disadvantages in comparison to open-ended questions. First, they require that the nonprofit marketer know the "master list" of criteria in advance. The marketer, then, is really asking the consumer *which* of a set of criteria applies (and, perhaps, how heavily weighted each is or will be). Second, direct questions risk influencing how the consumer thinks about the behavior. By telling the interviewee in advance what the *marketer* thinks are the key dimensions, the questioner risks inducing the Heisenberg effect by which the thing being measured is changed by the process of measurement itself.

INDIRECT METHODS

The direct questioning method assumes that consumers are aware of their own needs and wants and are willing to share the information with interviewers. But there are many issues on which they may not know or want to share their true feelings. College students, for example, may mention a desire for more study time when what they really want is less work. Or they may say they want younger teachers when they really believe that younger teachers will be less demanding, and less demanding teachers is what they really want.

Thus, the needs a person verbalizes may mask his or her real needs. Various projective techniques have been proposed to probe more deeply into the real needs of consumers. The four main projective techniques are:

1. *Word association or sentence completion.* Here the person might be asked to name the word that first comes to mind when each of a set of words is mentioned. The interviewer might say "college" and the person might respond with "boring." By mentioning key words, the interviewer hopes to infer a pattern of needs and wants that people connect with a particular object or behavior.

2. *Projection.* Rather than being asked about himself directly, the individual is asked about a vaguely defined "someone else." A

90

EXHIBIT 3-1 (continued)

questioner, for example, might ask an individual what he thinks is the basic reason "most people" go to college. Another approach is to present a picture or drawing of someone and ask the subject what that person is thinking about when considering college. Alternatively, the person might be presented with a set of incomplete sentences and asked to finish them. One sentence might read: "College is for people who_____." The basic assumption of these techniques is that, in the absence of specific information about the other individuals, consumers will project onto them their own true feelings.

3. *Picture completion.* The person is shown a vague picture and asked to make up a story about what he or she sees (called the Thematic Apperception Test or TAT). Or he or she may be shown a cartoon involving two people talking to each other, with one of their remarks deleted. The person is asked to fill in the words, which are thought to reflect the respondent's own attitudes toward the object.

4. *Role playing.* In this technique, one or more respondents are asked to act out a given role in a situation that is described in the briefest terms. One person, for example, may be asked to play the role of a successful business alumnus of a major university and the other the university president asking for a larger contribution. Through role playing, the respondents again project their needs and personalities into the amorphous situation, thereby providing useful clues on fundraising.

PERCEPTUAL MAPPING

The direct and indirect approaches require that the respondents explicitly indicate both the nature and the relative weightings of alternative criteria. A newer approach, called perceptual mapping, permits the researcher or manager to *deduce* either the weightings or both criteria and weightings from consumer judgments about the available alternatives. Two techniques are typically employed in perceptual mapping: direct and indirect. In direct perceptual mapping, consumers are asked to rate the various alternatives on a set of dimensions supplied by the researcher. A mathematical technique called factor analysis is then applied to these responses to yield one or more statistically independent underlying dimensions that best represent the original responses. These factors can then be used to produce a "map" on which the alternatives can be placed.

Factor analysis assumes that the original responses contain a great deal of redundancy and are really just surface outcroppings of more basic underlying criteria (factors). Thus, for example, Bob Jones may constantly give similar ratings to different colleges on scales labeled "student centeredness," "classroom size," and "teacher approachability" because they all reflect an underlying "intimacy" factor that he

EXHIBIT 3-1 (continued)

believes is *really* the important difference between big state colleges and smaller private institutions.

The disadvantages of the direct approach were pointed out earlier: it assumes that the researcher knows all the relevant dimensions in advance, and the questioning process may well influence the consumer's judgments.

The indirect approach does not place these burdens on the research designer. The indirect approach simply asks respondents to rate the alternatives in terms of their similarity to each other, letting the individual apply to these "similarities judgments" whatever criteria he or she wants. Again, a computerized mathematical algorithm is used to reduce the similarities data to one or more underlying dimensions. While this technique does not bias the respondent by presenting dimensions in advance, it does require that the *researcher* label the dimensions after the fact. Such labeling is often as much an art as a science.

CONJOINT ANALYSIS

An even newer technique that can be used in this context is called conjoint analysis. Conjoint analysis was developed, in part, to remedy the problem of more naive direct rating approaches, namely that ratings of alternatives are developed with respect to one benefit or cost dimension at a time. The traditional approach ignores two important features of the real world. First, when target consumers are evaluating courses of action, they implicitly or explicitly realize that the actions will generate *bundles* of benefits and *bundles* of costs. Second, in judging these various bundles, people are often willing to make *trade-offs*. That is, Bob Jones, if asked directly, may say that he prefers small classes to large classes and tuition under $1,000 to tuition over $1,000. Suppose, however, that he were offered the two conjointly. How would he respond if given the choice of (1) classes averaging twelve students and a tuition of $2,500 versus (2) classes averaging forty-five students and a tuition of $800? The answer is that it depends on how he makes trade-offs between the two criteria. This, in turn, depends on the weight he has in mind for the two dimensions. The mathematical algorithm underlying conjoint analysis is specifically designed to reveal these weights, which are known as "part-worths" in the conjoint lexicon.

a central role in basic consumer-behavior texts such as that of Engel and Blackwell.

To understand Fishbein's approach, it is necessary to recall that our principal interest as a marketer is influencing behavior. Further, we proposed earlier that consumers choose whether or not to undertake a particular behavior on the basis of the benefits and costs they expect to result from taking that action. It logically follows that at any point in time, a consumer who has not yet decided whether to take a particular action or which of several actions to take will consider three things:

1. Each consumer will possess a set of perceptions (what we shall call *beliefs*) about the positive and negative consequences of undertaking each act in the choice set (that is, the benefits and costs). These can be stated as the perceived *probabilities* of the consequences that result from particular behaviors. Thus, in a research study, we might ask Bob Jones the following questions about what we will assume are his *only* relevant criteria:

a. How likely is it that classes will be small if you choose to attend each of the following:

	Very unlikely								*Very likely*
1. Cornell	.1	.2	.3	.4	.5	.6	.7	.8	.9
2. Duke	.1	.2	.3	.4	.5	.6	.7	.8	.9
3. Northwestern	.1	.2	.3	.4	.5	.6	.7	.8	.9
4. Tulane	.1	.2	.3	.4	.5	.6	.7	.8	.9

b. How likely is it that you and your family will *not* make a major financial sacrifice if you choose to attend:

	Very unlikely								*Very likely*
1. Cornell	.1	.2	.3	.4	.5	.6	.7	.8	.9
2. Duke	.1	.2	.3	.4	.5	.6	.7	.8	.9
3. Northwestern	.1	.2	.3	.4	.5	.6	.7	.8	.9
4. Tulane	.1	.2	.3	.4	.5	.6	.7	.8	.9

c. How likely is it that you will make many lifelong friends if you choose to attend:

	Very unlikely								*Very likely*
1. Cornell	.1	.2	.3	.4	.5	.6	.7	.8	.9
2. Duke	.1	.2	.3	.4	.5	.6	.7	.8	.9
3. Northwestern	.1	.2	.3	.4	.5	.6	.7	.8	.9
4. Tulane	.1	.2	.3	.4	.5	.6	.7	.8	.9

d. How likely is it that you will have excellent teachers if you choose to attend:

	Very unlikely								*Very likely*
1. Cornell	.1	.2	.3	.4	.5	.6	.7	.8	.9
2. Duke	.1	.2	.3	.4	.5	.6	.7	.8	.9
2. Northwestern	.1	.2	.3	.4	.5	.6	.7	.8	.9
4. Tulane	.1	.2	.3	.4	.5	.6	.7	.8	.9

2. For each of the criteria used to evaluate the alternatives in the choice set, the consumer may be expected to have a sense of the value he or she places on the particular positive or negative consequence. These values we shall refer to as the *criteria weightings*. Thus, Bob Jones might be asked:

e. At the present time, how important to you is it that you obtain the following consequences from your choice of college:

	Very important								*Very unimportant*
Small classes	.1	.2	.3	.4	.5	.6	.7	.8	.9
No major financial sacrifice	.1	.2	.3	.4	.5	.6	.7	.8	.9
Lifelong friends	.1	.2	.3	.4	.5	.6	.7	.8	.9
Excellent teachers	.1	.2	.3	.4	.5	.6	.7	.8	.9

3. For each alternative in the choice set, the consumer's weighting of his or her beliefs on the various dimensions will result in a summary evaluation at that point in time which may be thought of as a "leaning" toward each of the courses of action. These "leanings" are termed *behavioral intentions.* Thus, one could ask Bob Jones the following kind of question:

   f. At the present time, considering all you know about the various alternatives, how likely is it that you will choose to attend the following colleges next fall?

	Very unlikely								Very likely
1. Cornell	.1	.2	.3	.4	.5	.6	.7	.8	.9
2. Duke	.1	.2	.3	.4	.5	.6	.7	.8	.9
3. Northwestern	.1	.2	.3	.4	.5	.6	.7	.8	.9
4. Tulane	.1	.2	.3	.4	.5	.6	.7	.8	.9

Modeling Attitudes.   If this view of highly complex alternative evaluation processes is the correct one, then careful research into our target population should reveal two things:

First, in the absence of significant new information (for example, Bob Jones learns of a rise in tuition at one of the alternative colleges) or some unexpected intervening event (for example, Bob Jones's mother is laid off by her employer), consumers' *behavioral intentions* ought to be very good predictors of their eventual behavior. How good they are as predictors will in turn depend on how involved the given consumer is in the decision and how much cognitive evaluation he or she has completed at the time of the research.

Second, consumers' behavioral intentions should be predicted very well by their beliefs about the various consequences of taking the action *and* the relative importance of these consequences, assuming that these have been measured correctly. To make such a prediction, however, we still need to know how consumers combine (or process) the weightings and belief information.

To understand the possibilities, let us return to Bob Jones and assume that he has revealed his beliefs about the probabilities that his college alter-

Table 3-2

A HIGH SCHOOL STUDENT'S BELIEFS ABOUT FOUR COLLEGES

Alternative	Small Classes	No Large Financial Sacrifice	Many Lifelong Friends	Excellent Teachers
Cornell	.8	.3	.7	.7
Duke	.7	.2	.8	.7
Northwestern	.5	.5	.6	.9
Tulane	.3	.7	.6	.2
Weightings	40	20	30	10

natives will yield the consequences he considers important as indicated in Table 3-2. Table 3-2 also portrays Jones's allocation of an arbitrary one hundred weighting points across the four basic criteria.

Given the belief and importance weightings in Table 3-2, there are several ways in which Jones could process these perceptions. Each has its own, sometimes arcane, label.[8]

CONJUNCTIVE MODEL.   Here the consumer sets minimum acceptable levels for each type of consequence and drops from consideration those behavioral alternatives that fall short on *any* dimension. Thus, Bob Jones might decide that he will only consider colleges where the probability of no large financial sacrifice is at least .3 *and* the probability that he will be in small classes is at least .7. Only Cornell would satisfy him in this case. If more than one of his choices satisfied the minima, however, then some other model, such as the linear additive model described below, would have to be introduced to resolve the decision.

DISJUNCTIVE MODEL.   Here the consumer considers all options that meet at least *one* minimum attribute level. If Jones decides he will consider attending colleges that rate at least .3 on no financial sacrifice *or* .7 on small classes, he would be willing to consider *all* the alternatives. Again, at that point, some other model must be involved to resolve the alternatives.

LEXICOGRAPHIC MODEL.   Here the consumer ranks the consequences in order of importance. He compares all the options on the first ranked consequence and chooses the superior one. If two options are tied, he repeats the process with the second consequence. Jones apparently weights class size as the most important consequence. In that case, he will choose Cornell.

Again, if there is no clear "winner" after the list of consequences is exhausted, a second model must be introduced.

DETERMINANCE MODEL.   In this approach, consumers ignore consequences for which all the alternatives are essentially the same. Bob Jones may decide that the four colleges differ very little in the likelihood that he will make many long-term friends there. Thus, to simplify a complex choice process, he treats all the colleges *as if* they were the same on this dimension. This approach, too, is not strictly a choice model unless all but one alternative are eliminated. Rather, it is a criteria-reduction process yielding a final set of *determinant* consequences that both are important and are dimensions on which the action alternatives vary a great deal. A second stage model is, again, still needed after the salient consequences have been determined.

LINEAR ADDITIVE EXPECTANCY-VALUE MODEL.   Here the consumer combines and then adds the beliefs and weighting data for each alternative. Each *expectation* about a consequence from choosing an alternative is weighted by the *value* of the consequence. All weighted consequences for a given alternative are then added to yield an overall "score" for that alternative. The weighted sum is then considered to be a mathematical representation of an *attitude* toward an act. Algebraically, this is:

$$A_{actj} = \sum_{i=1}^{n} b_{ij}a_i \text{ where:} \qquad (3\text{-}1)$$

A_{actj} = attitude toward act j
b_{ij} = belief about the likelihood of experiencing consequence i from taking act j
a_i = value of consequence i
n = number of salient consequences

In the case of Bob Jones, we would have:

A(Cornell)   = 40 (.8) + 20 (.3) + 30 (.7) + 10 (.7) = 66
A(Duke)   = 40 (.7) + 20 (.2) + 30 (.8) + 10 (.7) = 63
A(Northwestern) = 40 (.5) + 20 (.5) + 30 (.6) + 10 (.9) = 57
A(Tulane)   = 40 (.3) + 20 (.7) + 30 (.6) + 10 (.2) = 46

As a result of these (perhaps subconscious) computations, Bob Jones would be most likely to choose Cornell, followed by Duke, Northwestern, and Tulane, in that order.

Several comments need to be made about this model. First, it is the only model with which a choice is almost always determined. Thus, this processing approach typically comes into play in cases where one of the other models is not determinant. This is one reason that the linear additive model will be the major focus of our remaining discussions of highly complex consumer behavior. The second and more important reason is that the linear additive model has been shown empirically to be *an excellent predictor of behavioral intentions,*[9] and behavioral intentions are good predictors of behavior under certain conditions. All of these conditions make the model potentially very useful for strategic marketing decisions.

There are, however, defects in the linear additive model. First, it does not take into account possible interactions among dimensions. Second, it is a *compensatory* model. That is, low scores with respect to one consequence can be compensated for by high scores with respect to another consequence. Thus, in Bob Jones's case, Cornell and Duke both compensate for their significantly poorer scores on financial sacrifice (that is, they cost more!) by having good scores on the other three dimensions. By contrast, Tulane is perceived to be very good on the financial dimension, but this cannot make up for poor scores in Jones's mind on the other three dimensions.

Key Features of the Fishbein Model.   The first and perhaps most important feature of the linear additive model (sometimes called "the Fishbein

model") is that it reinforces a feature of nonprofit markets that we emphasized in early parts of this chapter. The model emphasizes that what determines Bob Jones's choice in this highly complex, highly cognitive decision
are his *perceptions* of the consequences of taking the action and his *internal
weighting* of these consequences, which, in turn, are a function of his own
personal needs and wants. This simply emphasizes the point that *to be effective marketers in situations where consumers make complex decisions, we
must always start with a clear understanding of the target customers' perceptions, needs, and wants.* Further, since these perceptions, needs, and wants
are interior to the consumer and not directly observable, some kind of formal research must be contemplated by anyone considering developing marketing strategies to influence these complex deliberations.

A second feature of the linear additive model is that it emphasizes
behavior. The predicted consequences of behavior are a central determinant
of action. Unfortunately, many marketers and researchers in both the profit
and nonprofit sectors believe they ought to study individuals' perceptions
of the *attributes of objects* involved in an exchange, rather than the behavioral consequences. In Bob Jones's case, these misguided researchers might
try to study Jones's perceptions of Duke or Cornell itself, not his perception
of going there. This approach can very often yield predictions that are far
off the mark. If one were to ask Bob Jones to evaluate *colleges,* for example,
he might indicate as important *attributes* such features as the reputation of
the faculty for research and scholarship, the attractiveness of the campus,
the innovativeness of curricula, and so forth. All of these may be very
important to Bob Jones's evaluation of these colleges but have little or nothing to do with his evaluation of the opportunity to *attend* them. Questions
about college attributes might never reveal that Jones was very concerned
about whom he might meet there and turn into lifelong friends. It might not
occur to him that this is what an interviewer meant when asking about the
attributes of a college (an object) rather than going there (a behavior).

We are firmly of the opinion that in complex high involvement decisions, it is behavioral intentions that determine behavior, and perceptions
of consequences that determine behavioral intentions (along with other
interpersonal factors to be noted below). Perceptions of objects involved in
the behavior are interesting, but they are not determinant and marketers
should not waste time and resources studying them. This approach will be
central to our consideration of strategic planning throughout the rest of the
book.

Influence of Others.   The evaluation stage leads consumers like Bob
Jones to form A_{Act}. Research has shown, however, that whether or not this
is predictive of *behavioral intention* also depends on *the influence of others.*
As David Reisman pointed out many years ago, many individuals go
through life taking their cues about appropriate behavior largely from what
are called by sociologists "significant others" or "referents." These referent

individuals or groups could be people they know or people they've only seen or read about (for example, movie or rock stars). Further, they can be people they identify with (membership referents), envy and want to be like some-day (aspiration referents), or people they *don't* wish to be like (negative referents). The latter would be exemplified by teenagers who refuse to go to the college where their parents went or to dress or to cut their hair as parents want them to. These referents can provide input into the criteria individuals use to form their personal attitude toward an act. They can also have *direct* influence on behavioral intentions by exerting pressure on the individual to act in certain ways.[10]

Some individuals may be directly influenced by several referents at once. Others may not be affected by referents at all. In the case of Bob Jones, to be able to obtain the best possible estimator of his behavioral inten-tions—and thus to have a true understanding of how his present perceptions affect his behavior—we must "add in" a factor for the possible influence of significant others. In a research context, this would involve three steps.

First, we must identify all of the definable sets of referents to whom Bob Jones might pay attention. These could include parents, high school counselors, brothers and sisters, and friends.

Second, we must ask Jones what he *perceives* each of the significant others as wanting him to do. Fishbein and his disciples refer to this as *Nor-mative Behavior* and define it algebraically as NB_{kj} where k is an index refer-ring to each set of significant others and j refers to the action in question.[11] Normative behavior is measured by asking Jones to what extent he believes each significant other wants him to take a particular action, ranging from, say, "Does not want it at all" to "Wants it very much." It must be empha-sized once again that we must measure here what he *perceives* to be the posi-tion of others. Whether he has an accurate perception of reality does not matter. *"Reality" is what the consumer thinks it is,* a point we shall continue to emphasize.

Third, we must ask Jones how motivated he is, in general, to comply with the wishes of each referent group. This factor, defined as MC_{kj} (moti-vation to conform), is in effect a *weighting factor* for each NB_{kj}. Thus, if one parent is very insistent that Jones choose Cornell but he tends to ignore that parent, that parent should have little effect on his behavioral intention and eventual behavior. On the other hand, if the second parent barely leans toward, say, Duke, and Bob listens to him or her most of the time, this influ-ence on the ultimate choice could prove to be quite significant.[12]

With this consideration of the often important role of significant oth-ers on possible behaviors, we can now expand our model of the predictors of behavioral intention (*BI*) as follows:

$$BI_j = \left(\sum_{i=1}^{n} b_{ij} a_i \right) W_1 + \left(\sum_{k=1}^{m} NB_{kj} \cdot MC_{kj} \right) W_2 \qquad (3\text{-}2)$$

It should be noted that this extended Fishbein model has one additional feature. There are two weighting coefficients, W_1 and W_2, which signify the relative importance of the individual and group influences on behavioral interaction, respectively. In practice, these weighting coefficients are usually derived statistically—that is, they are the product of a statistical technique called multiple regression rather than of a question asked of consumers like Bob Jones. In this procedure, the components of the model set out in (1) above are used to predict behavioral intention (*BI*). If the best fit of the equation to Bob Jones's interview responses yields a value of W_1 greater than W_2, then we would conclude that Jones is what Reisman would call "inner directed," more driven by his own perceptions and needs. On the other hand, if we find that W_2 exceeds W_1, Jones could be characterized as relatively more "other directed," more driven by what he thinks and feels others expect of him.

Behavior.   Behavioral intention may not always directly lead to behavior in complex cases because of unexpected situational inhibitors. Bob Jones, for example, may postpone choosing any college until he acquires more money, his mother is reemployed, he gets a scholarship, or a friend agrees to enroll also. It is possible that all of these situational factors may not clear up and cause Jones eventually to reconsider his intentions. Or, unexpectedly, he may not like the looks of the campus when he visits it. He may be turned off by some of the students or professors he meets. Marketers believe that unanticipated factors in the critical contact situation can have a great influence on the final decision.

Thus, preferences and even behavioral intentions are not completely reliable predictors of actual behavior. They give direction to behavior but fail to include a number of additional factors that may intervene.

For example, the decision of an individual to modify, postpone, or avoid a decision is heavily influenced by perceived risk. Marketers have devoted much effort to understanding exchange behavior as risk-taking. Consumers cannot be certain about the performance and psychosocial consequences of their decisions. This produces anxiety. The amount of perceived risk varies with the amount of economic and social well-being at stake, the amount of consequence uncertainty, and the amount of consumer self-confidence. A consumer develops certain routines for reducing risk, such as avoiding decisions, gathering information from friends, and preferring national brand names and warranties. The nonprofit marketer must understand the factors that provoke a feeling of risk in the consumer and attempt to provide information and support that will help reduce this risk.[13]

Postdecision Assessment.   After going ahead with the behavior, the consumer will experience some level of satisfaction or dissatisfaction. Based on this, the consumer will engage in posttransaction actions that will have implications for the marketer. Here we want to look at the marketing implications of posttransaction satisfaction and subsequent actions.

What determines whether the consumer is highly satisfied, somewhat satisfied, somewhat unsatisfied, or highly unsatisfied with a choice? There are two major theories about this.

One theory, called *expectations-performance theory,* holds that a consumer's satisfaction is a function of the consumer's expectations and the perceived outcome.[14] If the outcome matches expectations, the consumer is satisfied; if it exceeds them, he or she is highly satisfied; if it falls short, he or she is dissatisfied.

Consumers form their expectations on the basis of messages and claims sent out by the seller and other communication sources. If the seller makes exaggerated claims, consumers who go ahead and take the recommendation will experience disconfirmed expectations, which lead to dissatisfaction. Thus, if Cornell fails to perform as Bob Jones was led to expect, Bob will revise downward his attitude toward Cornell and may drop out, transfer, or bad-mouth the college. On the other hand, if the college meets his expectations, he will tend to be a satisfied student.

The consumer's satisfaction or dissatisfaction will be greater the larger the gap between expectations and performance. Here the consumer's coping style also comes in. Some consumers tend to magnify the gap when the outcome is not perfect, and they will be highly dissatisfied. Other consumers tend to minimize the gap and feel less dissatisfied.[15]

This theory suggests that the seller should make claims that faithfully represent the likely outcome so that consumers experience satisfaction. Some sellers might even understate performance levels so that consumers would experience higher-than-expected satisfaction with their choice of behavior.

The other theory of posttransaction satisfaction is called *cognitive dissonance theory.* It holds that almost every choice is likely to lead to some posttransaction discomfort; the issues are how much discomfort and what will the consumer do about it. As stated by Festinger: "When a person chooses between two or more alternatives, discomfort or dissonance will almost inevitably arise because of the person's knowledge that while the decision he has made has certain advantages, it also has some disadvantages. Dissonance arises after almost every decision, and further, the individual will invariably take steps to reduce this dissonance."[16]

Under this theory, we can expect Bob Jones to feel some posttransaction dissonance about his college choice. Problems with professors, other students, housing, or athletics are likely to stir doubts in his mind as to whether he made the right choice. He will undertake certain actions to reduce this dissonance.

The dissonant consumer seeks ways to reduce the dissonance because of a drive in the human organism "to establish internal harmony, consistency, or congruity among his opinions, knowledge, and values."[17] Dissonant consumers will resort to one of two courses of action. They may try to reduce the dissonance by *abandoning* the action, or they may try to reduce the dissonance by seeking information that might *confirm* its high value (or avoiding information that might disconfirm its high value). In the case of Bob Jones, he might withdraw from the college or, alternatively, he might seek information that would lead him to feel better about the college.

Organizations can take positive steps to help buyers feel good about their choices. A college can send a warm congratulatory letter to recently admitted candidates. It can invite their suggestions and complaints after they have spent a few months on the campus. It can develop effective communications describing the college's philosophy and aspirations to reinforce the students' reasons for coming. Postpurchase communications to buyers have been shown to reduce the amount of consumer postpurchase dissatisfaction.[18]

Information Gathering. In the process of making this decision, Bob Jones will seek and be offered information from a range of sources. Of key interest to the marketer are what these major information sources are and the relative influence each will have. Consumer information sources can be classified into four groups: (1) *personal nonmarketer controlled* (family, friends, acquaintances); (2) *personal marketer controlled* (sales representatives); (3) *nonpersonal nonmarketer controlled* (mass media, natural settings); and (4) *nonpersonal marketer controlled* (ads, catalogs). A consumer is normally exposed to all of these sources. The marketer's task is to interview consumers and ask what sources of information they sought or

FIGURE 3-6

Information Sources Influencing the College-Bound Student

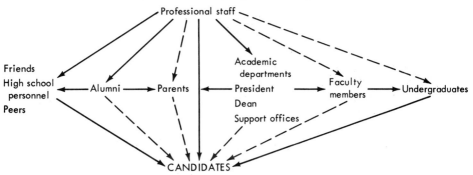

Note: Solid lines imply direct influence in the college-choice process; dashed lines indirect influence

SOURCE: William Ihlanfeldt, *Achieving Optimal Enrollments and Tuition Revenues* (San Francisco: Jossey-Bass, 1980), p. 129.

received in the course of the decision process. On this basis, a picture can be drawn of the most frequent sources. Ihlanfeldt has studied this for the college choice decision and identified the major sources shown in Figure 3-6.

Different sources might appear at different stages of the process as outlined in Figure 3-6. For example, Bob Jones might report that his uncle initiated his interest in college by asking a year ago where Bob planned to go to college. His friends provided considerable information and influence about the types of colleges to consider. His parents acted both as influences and as buyers, since they were paying for his education. Bob Jones, however, made the final decision and was the user of the product.

Bob Jones not only received different information from each source, but he also placed different value on the information from each source. He consciously or unconsciously gave weight to the source's credibility in deciding how to use the information. An information source is more credible when the source is trustworthy, expert, and likeable.[19] Thus, Bob would give more credence to the information provided by an older brother in college than to a college recruiter who is obviously biased.

All this having been said, marketers find it worthwhile to study the consumers' information sources whenever (1) a substantial percentage of consumers engage in active search, and (2) consumers show some stable patterns of using the respective information sources. Identifying the information sources and their respective influences calls for interviewing consumers and asking them how they happened to hear about the alternatives, what sources of information they turned to, what type of information came from each source, what credence they put in each source, and what influence each source of information had on the final decision. Marketers can use the findings to plan effective marketing communications and stimulate favorable word of mouth, issues we shall turn to in Chapter 18.

Two Examples.   The extended model of complex decision-making outlined above has been used by marketing researchers in nonprofit areas with considerable success. Ryan and Bonfield,[20] for example, used the model to predict loan application behavior of ninety-three faculty and staff members at a major southeastern university. The researchers measured beliefs about five outcomes, such as "the loan would be easy to obtain" or "I could get favorable terms," plus normative expectations for four referents: spouse, other family members, credit union employees, and friends and coworkers. Overall, Ryan and Bonfield were able to explain 23 percent of the variance in behavioral intentions using Fishbein's extended model. This is a highly respectable level of explanation in marketing. The contribution of the individual and group components (and their interaction) to the overall explanation of BI was as follows:

	% of Variance Explained
Individual attitude	12
Normative influence	7
Joint effects	4
Total	23

The researchers also found that the two components plus behavioral intention explained 36 percent of the variance in actual loan application behavior.

A more complex test of the extended model using somewhat modified measures and a technique called causal modeling was conducted by Richard Bagozzi to predict blood donation behavior. Bagozzi[21] studied 157 male and female students, faculty, and staff at a medium-sized New England university one week prior to the first of two yearly campus blood drives. Ninety-five respondents who gave their names in the survey were then checked unobtrusively to see whether in fact they did or didn't give blood in the two drives as predicted.

Several interesting findings emerged from Bagozzi's study, including modifications of the basic model:

1. Citing earlier studies by Condie, Warner and Gillman,[22] and Pomazel and Jaccard,[23] and after his own pilot research, Bagozzi decided to include only *negative* consequences in his study (for example, "it would hurt my arm" or "my resistance to colds or infection would be lowered").

2. Attitudes were measured both by the linear additive expectancy-value approach advocated here and by semantic differentials presumably tapping basic underlying feelings (affect) towards donating blood (for example, unpleasant/pleasant or safe/unsafe). The expectancy-value model performed consistently better.

3. "Social normative beliefs" were not found to be significant predictors of either BI or actual behavior. The measure of representative beliefs used, however, was not as detailed as proposed here or as employed by Ryan and Bonfield. Bagozzi lumped together all significant referents as "people whose opinions you value the most."

4. Overall, the level of explanation of behavioral intention (depending on the definition of BI used) varied from 20 to 26 percent using the expectancy-value operationalization. This is very similar to the findings of Ryan and Bonfield and again is quite creditable.

5. On the other hand, Bagozzi had less success than Ryan and Bonfield in explaining behavior in the first blood drive. This is probably attributable to the much greater possibility that other situational factors will intervene between intentions and behavior for a blood drive than for a loan.

6. Finally, Bagozzi found that when measures of *past behavior* were used to predict behavioral intention, levels of explanation increased significantly (to 32 to 40 percent), although past behavior had no effect on the ability to predict actual behavior in the first drive. On the other hand, knowing that a person gave on the first drive permitted excellent prediction of behavior on the second

blood drive (49 percent). This influence of past behavior is a point we shall return to below.

Strategy Implications.   What then does a marketer *do* with research findings such as those hypothesized for Bob Jones? Suppose one is the marketing director for Tulane University—what can one do to improve the university's chances of attracting him (besides hope that the other three colleges turn Bob Jones down!)?

Tulane has five options with respect to Jones's personal attitudes (^{A}Act):

1. *Change beliefs about alternatives.* Tulane could attempt to change Jones's beliefs about Tulane University (his b_{ij}'s) on key dimensions on which Tulane scores poorly. There are two alternatives here, depending on whether Bob Jones's perceptions are accurate or not.
   a. If Jones's perceptions *are* accurate and there are a great many otherwise highly attractive prospective students like him, Tulane might consider reducing its class sizes or improving perceptions of the quality of its teachers (dimensions on which it scores poorly);
   b. If Jones's perceptions are *not* accurate and it is clear he and others have a misunderstanding of what Tulane is really like, then Tulane has a communication problem. By words, pictures, testimonials, informal research reports, and the like, Tulane must tell its story more effectively, being sure that it begins by responding to Bob Jones and his needs and perceptions rather than just telling him what *they* think he should know.
2. *Change beliefs about competitors.* Similarly, Tulane might attempt to change Bob Jones's beliefs about Tulane's competition (which the research has specifically identified as being in his choice set). This would be particularly appropriate if Tulane knew that Jones's perceptions were, in fact, wrong. That is, Tulane could offer comparative data (if such were available) showing that, for example, Tulane had below-average class sizes while major competitors had above-average class sizes.
3. *Change weightings.* A third strategy available to Tulane is to attempt to change the importance weightings assigned to the dimensions. One way to look at Tulane's problem is not that it is perceived badly but that the dimension on which it is rated highly, its lack of financial sacrifice, is not rated highly enough by Bob Jones and his cohorts. Tulane would be the *most favored alternative* if it were to shift its target audience's weights for the four dimensions as follows:

Consequence	Weight
Small classes	10
No large financial sacrifice	50
Many lifelong friends	30
Excellent teachers	10

4. *Call attention to neglected favorable consequences.* Attendance at Tulane may have consequences that Bob Jones didn't realize. These might include better weather or the chance to visit nearby recreational or cultural centers. The college would attempt to have its target audience add these consequences

to their salient criteria, especially if they are features that are not offered by competitors.

5. *Add new favorable consequences.* Just as products add new ingredients or new packaging to revive flagging sales, so too could Tulane offer such new features as the chance to attend a new study-abroad program or participate in a local work-study option that would meet important basic needs of the target audience that they heretofore had not thought relevant to the college decision.

In addition to these actions, Tulane could seek to work through the reference groups found to be important to Bob Jones. Business alumni in Bob's hometown might be contacted to speak to Jones. Letters or phone calls could be directed to his parents. Possibly the applications of Jones and several of his friends could be treated as a "package."

Tulane will need to carefully evaluate these alternative strategies according to their feasibility and cost. The difficulty of implementing each strategy, such as repositioning the college or shifting the importance of weights, should not be minimized. But the marketer can take comfort that, at least for these kinds of first-time complex decisions, there are many points at which the decision can be influenced. As we shall see, however, the marketer's degree of freedom declines as the consumer gains experience.

The reader should note that the beliefs and weightings data can also be used to segment markets, as can the measures discussed in the next section. We shall return to these considerations in Chapter 4.

Simplified Behavior

The complex process undergone by Bob Jones in evaluating his college is typical of many nonprofit decisions because these decisions are highly involving. It was also complex because Jones was making the decision for the first time. If this were a decision that the consumer would be making a second, third, or fourth time, however, we would expect to observe some simplifications of the elaborate process outlined in Figure 3-3 as a result of experience. In such cases, we would still expect considerable information-seeking and information-processing to take place because the decision is an important one. Consumer behavior theory postulates, however, that three kinds of simplification will probably take place:

First, little information-seeking and thinking will be devoted to defining the evaluative criteria. The first time around, say in evaluating charities, a consumer might be expected not only to try to learn about the charities to which he might give but also how he should evaluate his potential behavior. The consumer will take stock of what he or she really wants as benefits from charitable giving and what the costs might be. Friends and co-workers might be asked about how they choose charities. In these circumstances, the marketer has considerable opportunity to influence the criteria since they are still in their formative stage. (This would certainly be the case for the colleges communicating with Bob Jones.) With repeated behavior occasions (additional charity drives), however, it may be expected that after the first time the consumer will have "set" the criteria on which alternatives are assessed. Marketers thus will have very limited opportunity to intervene to change these criteria.

Second, the weights of the criteria may also be largely set, although they will be somewhat more changeable than the criteria themselves. That is, a consumer considering charitable donations from year to year may change the total amount dispensed depending on the *weightings* of a "financial sacrifice" dimension, which in turn might depend on personal economic fortunes or the relative desirability of other types of expenditures.

Third, the choice set may also be relatively well defined in second and third decisions. At least, a core subset of alternatives is likely to be constant from exchange to exchange with marginal alternatives coming and going at the periphery in response to new information or changing criteria or decision rules on the part of the individual consumer.

Thus, in complex cognitive exchanges, the experienced consumer is seen to be primarily evaluating *given* choices on *given* criteria with relatively *constant* weightings. The marketer's first task in such circumstances, therefore, is to learn the contents of the choice set and the set of operative criteria as well as the consumer's beliefs about the consequences of accepting the marketer's alternative or those of competitors. Then, assuming that the marketer is in fact a part of the choice set, the main option available is to devise marketing strategies to modify *beliefs* to secure greater market penetration. In these circumstances, this may be the only area in which the marketer can maneuver. Relatively little can be done at this point to influence criteria or their weighting. In general, it may be expected that the less involving the decision, the faster the consumer will simplify the evaluation process with experience and the less flexibility the marketer will have to improve a flagging market share.

Routine Evaluation

After considerable experience on the consumer's part, one may observe the development of relatively habitual routine behavior. In such cases, relatively little cognitive evaluation will appear to be taking place. Future behavior will be better predicted by past behavior than by attitudes.

This brings us back to Bagozzi's study of prospective blood donors. Bagozzi found that if one only knew expectancy-value attitudes, one could explain from 10 to 22 percent of the variance in behavior at a blood drive one week away. If one knew how often the respondents had given in the past *and* what they did on the first blood drive, however, one could explain *40 percent of the variance* in behavior in the second drive. Since his study participants had given an average 13.08 times in the past five years, they were clearly experienced givers. For many, the behavior may well be described as becoming highly simplified, if not routine. This would explain the greater role of behavioral over attitudinal predictors in Bagozzi's study. In such cases of routinized decisions, it is likely that the best approach to understanding the market is to study past behavior. Studying attitudes may not be particularly useful either because consumers cannot really recall what evaluation they went through many years ago or because their attitudes today have been simplified and aligned to support their behavior! Left with behavior only, the marketer can take several approaches.

First, use past behavior frequencies to segregate the market and concentrate on the "heavy users" (see Chapter 4).

Second, seek to discover behavior modification strategies that "bypass" cognition—for example, use special incentives, free trials, and so on to change behavior (see Chapter 18).

Third, seek to discover persuasion strategies to "shock" habituated consumers into once again undertaking cognitive activity.

Nonobservable Evaluations.   There are many situations in the private sector, and perhaps some in the nonprofit sector, where individual behavior involves virtually *no* active prior cognition. This does not mean that the behavior is not influenced to some extent by the brain and, therefore, that a marketer should always rule out possible influence strategies involving attitude change. But to the extent that they attempt to rely on this kind of research, such strategies are likely to have very limited effect, in part because of the present crudity of most of our attitude measurement technology. On the other hand, it is, of course, always true that marketers could attempt to influence trivial decisions as they do routinized, high-involvement decisions—that is through behavior modification or "shock tactics." But Krugman and others have postulated that a better way to view trivial exchanges is as instances of what is now called *low-involvement* or *incidental learning.*[24] Krugman points out that consumers in developed countries are inundated with hundreds of advertising messages daily. And when these messages are about exchanges about which the consumers are highly involved, they will become perceptually vigilant and process the information vigorously.

The question, then, is what happens to the remaining messages that aren't immediately relevant? Krugman suggests that, precisely because the exchange addressed in the message is one of trivial interest to the consumer, he or she will be neither perceptually vigilant nor perceptually defensive. The message, so the theory goes, bypasses the cognitive evaluation stage and goes directly into long-term memory to be stored in detail or as some vague overall impression. This trace then resides in memory until some cue at the time of purchase reactivates it (perhaps subconsciously). It *then* becomes a factor influencing the immediate choice. Since the more often a given message passes the consumer's sensory field, the more likely it is to become lodged in long-term memory, Krugman's postulation of low-involvement learning has led many marketers in "trivial" categories to emphasize memorable visual images (for example, cartoon characters, Morris the Cat, etc.), jingles or "haunting" melodies (for example, Coke or McDonalds) or outright repetition (for example, the Mr. Whipple Charmin ads) to increase the probability that a subconscious memory trace will be built. Since most non-profits cannot afford the budgets necessary to adopt these tactics, it may be expected that where they (reluctantly) conclude that a particular target segment considers the decision to be trivial, imaginative attempts must be developed to build trace recognitions through visual imagery, clever dialogue, or music that someday can be activated when an exchange is contemplated.

GROUP DECISIONS

This chapter has so far given very extensive consideration to exchanges involving single individuals. But at the outset, we noted that many transactions can be multiparty. This means that the target consumer might not be a single person but a group. One obvious case of a nonprofit group decision would involve *households;* a second would involve *organizations.*

Multiparty decisions vary in the roles played by participants. First, there are occasions on which there will be true joint decisions in which each party shares more or less equally. Households in many cases are likely to function as joint decision-makers when considering such exchanges as donations or legacies or when trying to decide on child-raising, family exercise, or dietary patterns.[25] Similarly, corporations may have committees jointly determining their charitable contributions. Foundations or government agencies may jointly determine budget allocations or decide on program acceptability. In these cases, the actions required in the exchange are actions that *all parties* must undertake.

The second general multiparty situation is the case where different steps involved in the exchange process are specifically allocated to different parties. There are five basic *roles* involved in any exchange:

1. *Initiator.* The initiator is the person who first suggests or thinks of the idea of becoming involved in a particular exchange.
2. *Influencer.* An influencer is a person who offers or is sought out for advice on the decision. This is not simply a *referent* but someone whose advice is heard.
3. *Decider.* The decider is the person who ultimately determines any or all parts of the decision to participate in the exchange: whether to take action, what action to take, how to take action, or when and where.
4. *Transactor.* The transactor is the person who completes the actual transaction.
5. *Exchanger.* The exchanger is the person(s) who then follows through on the transaction.

The decision by a household for a child to have his tonsils removed at a particular hospital, for example, is in many cases a situation where each role would be filled by a different person. The mother might be the *initiator,* noticing an increase in sore throat episodes. The family doctor may then come into play as a key *influencer* suggesting whether or not the problem is serious enough to merit action, making recommendations as to whether delay or urgent action is more appropriate and, finally, offering an opinion about surgeons and hospitals. If the household is strongly patriarchal, the father may be delegated the role of *decider* since "father ultimately pays the bills around here." The *transactor* could then be an older brother or sister who works near the chosen hospital who can sign the necessary admittance papers. And, of course, it is the child who is obviously the *exchanger,* the person whose tonsils are at issue. The implication of this example is, obviously, that if a hospital wishes to increase the amount of elective tonsillectomies performed at its institution, it would do well to know more about the role allocation strategies of target households in its market. The hospital may find that it may need different strategies to "win over" each of the different role types.

1. *Initiators* need to be made aware of opportunities and needs for elective surgery they might not have thought about.
2. *Influencers and deciders* need to have their perceptions, criteria and choice sets subjected to a marketing program that insures that the hospital will be the one chosen.
3. *Transactors* need to find no impediments, clerical *or* psychological, to setting up the transaction.
4. Finally, the *exchanger* needs to be contacted before, during, and especially after the exchange to insure satisfaction, good word of mouth, and behavioral intentions favoring the hospital for future sickness episodes.

The approach that one uses when marketing to multiple party exchangers like organizations should not require very much alteration in the approach one would use if marketing to individuals who would take on all five exchange roles themselves. To see how this is, let us follow the approach the San Francisco Zoo might use to convince a large corporation to make a major grant toward building a new lion house.

NEED AROUSAL

The first step is for the marketer to identify corporate prospects and try to gain their attention and interest in the proposal. Thus, the San Francisco Zoo would approach corporations that have made generous civic gifts in the past. "Qualifying the prospect" can save the marketer a lot of time.

The marketer's next step is to try to understand the basic needs and wants of target organizations. This is fairly straightforward in the case of corporations, whose main objectives are to make money, save money, and be good corporate citizens. The San Francisco Zoo cannot help corporations make or save money, but it can appeal to the corporation's wish to be a good corporate citizen. Most corporations welcome favorable publicity about their "good deeds": in this way, they build a fund of goodwill that they can draw upon when adverse events take place. The zoo can meet this need by offering to name the new lion house after the corporation or arrange for other publicity showing the corporation's generosity.

The marketing organization needs to analyze the mission, goals, plans, and criteria of each prospect organization so that it can develop appropriate appeals. When the San Francisco Zoo seeks a corporate grant, it must respect the fact that money is tight and that the corporation expects the Zoo's needs to be convincingly presented. The Zoo will state its case in a way that meets the issues uppermost in the minds of the corporation.

INFORMATION GATHERING

The buying organization normally needs time to consider the proposition and gather information. The amount of information needed depends on the type of buying situation and on the buying organization's familiarity with the marketer. Robinson et al. distinguished among three types of buying situations, called *buyclasses,* that are not unlike the categories outlined earlier for individual decision makers.[26] They are:

1. *Straight rebuy.* Here the buying organization is buying something similar to what it bought before. Most corporations, for example, set new budgets every year, and in the absence of major new factors, they might approve a budget pretty much like last year's budget, which did or did not include the Zoo. This is analogous to "routinized response behavior" in the individual consumer buying situation. In a straight rebuy, the buyer does not need much information because he knows the proposition and the marketer from previous dealings with him.

2. *Modified rebuy.* The modified rebuy describes a situation in which the buyer is considering modifying something it has purchased in the past. The task calls for "decision-making with experience" and hence requires more information than the case of a straight rebuy. Thus, a corporation might want specific information to evaluate whether the Zoo's lion house needs to be remodeled and what alternatives are available.

3. *New task.* The new task faces an organizational buyer when he is presented with a new offer of an unfamiliar kind from an unfamiliar seller. An example would be a Japanese corporation being asked to build a new lion house at the San Francisco Zoo to improve Japanese-American relations. The Japanese corporation faces a complex problem-solving situation and needs to gather considerable information prior to making any decision.

Another issue deals with the probable sources of information to which the organizational buyer will turn. One source is the marketer, and the marketer can be more effective by supplying relevant and credible information to the buying organization. The marketer should also anticipate other information sources that the organization buyer is likely to tap in developing its marketing plans.

DECISION EVALUATION

Each buying organization has certain well-established ways of evaluating different types of "purchases." Straight rebuy decisions may be in the hands of a single officer who makes the decision in a fairly routine way. Modified rebuys may be in the hands of a small middle-management committee with the members coming from different business functions. New tasks may be in the hands of a high-level management committee, again with members representing different kinds of expertise.

The marketer must attempt to identify the people in the buying organization who are likely to get involved in the buying process. Webster and Wind call the decision-making unit of a buying organization the *buying center,* which they define as "all those individuals and groups who participate in the purchasing decision-making process, who share some common goals and the risks arising from the decisions."[27] The buying center includes all members of the organization who play roles in the buying process.[28]

The marketer's task is to identify the members of the buying center and try to figure out (1) in what decisions they exercise influence, (2) what their relative degree of influence is, and (3) what evaluation criteria each decision participant uses. This knowledge can help the marketer know the key buying influencers who must be reached personally (through multilevel in-depth selling) or through nonpersonal communications.

Organization buyers are subject to many influences when they meet to make their buying decisions. Some of the process is highly rational in that the buyers rate proposals on such attributes as (1) marketer credibility, (2) marketer efficiency, (3) impact of the proposal on profits, costs, and other dimensions, (4) amount of goodwill created, and so on. To the extent that the process is a rational one, the marketer will want to make the strongest case in rational terms.

Marketers also recognize the role of personal motives in the organization buying process, such as buyers who respond to personal favors (self-aggrandizement), to attention (ego enhancement), or to personal risk containment (risk avoiders). A study of buyers in ten large organizations concluded, "Corporate decision-makers remain human after they enter the office. They respond to 'image'; they buy from companies to which they feel 'close'; they favor suppliers who show them respect and personal consideration, and who do extra things 'for them'; they 'over-react' to real or imagined slights, tending to reject companies which fail to respond or delay in submitting requested bids."[29]

This suggests that marketers should also take into account the human and social factors in the buying situations and address more emotional and interpersonal appeals.

DECISION EXECUTION

After the buying organization has decided to favor the offer, it must put the finishing touches on it. The buyer and seller would have to negotiate the exact terms and timing of various steps. Thus, the corporation that agrees to make a gift to the San Francisco Zoo would need to decide on the exact amount, how to pay it, when to pay it, and what compliance conditions to establish. Any of these steps can involve further negotiation. The marketer should anticipate these issues of detail and be prepared to work them through smoothly.

Organization buyers have also been known to cancel or withdraw at the last minute, given new conditions or information. The buyer may have heard something negative about the marketer or might have encountered a cash flow problem. The practical implication is that the marketer's work is not finished after receiving news of a favorable decision. The alert seller wants to keep in touch with the buyer to make sure that the agreement is enacted smoothly and that no snags develop.

POSTDECISION ASSESSMENT

The buying organization usually undertakes a periodic performance audit to make sure that the marketer is performing according to expectations. It is in the marketer's interests to negotiate clear performance goals with the buying organization in the decision execution stage. Then the marketer knows what is expected, and it can periodically supply the buyer with relevant information on performance. The San Francisco Zoo, for example, can keep a large corporate donor informed of the way the money is spent and the results achieved with the grant. By demonstrating responsible performance, the zoo will be able to go back to the same corporate donor some years later and ask for another grant based on the satisfactory results it has produced.

SUMMARY

The ultimate objective of all marketing strategy and tactics is to influence target audience behavior. While the short-term focus may be communicating facts or changing attitudes and values, what distinguishes these activities from education or propaganda is that these aims are not ends but means to other goals. And since the ultimate goal is behavior change and the proper philosophy is customer-centered, it is essential that all strategic planning start with understanding customer behavior.

The targets of nonprofit marketers' influence strategies can be as diverse as legislators, donors, journalists, or consumers. In all cases, the marketer's objective is to bring about exchanges wherein target audience members give up some costs in return for some expected positive consequences. Exchanges may be unilateral or bilateral, involve two or multiple parties, and be of fixed or continuing duration. The starting point for understanding customer behavior thus must be an understanding of the exchange relationship to be effected. Most importantly, that exchange must be seen from the target audience's perspective.

Exchanges in the nonprofit sector are usually high involvement and often concern target audience behaviors where audience members have little or no experience. In such highly complex decision situations, customers begin by gathering information in order to form a choice set of alternative behaviors and to determine the criteria that will eventually be used to choose among them. The criteria, in turn, will be affected by the customer's own needs and wants and by the influences of significant others.

The next step in the typical process is to evaluate the chosen alternative on the relevant criteria and to form attitudes and behavioral intentions toward each. These behavioral intentions will again be influenced by others. In a similar way, the eventual course of behavior will be modified by situational factors such as the availability of funds or time. Finally, behavior will result in experience and subsequent evaluations that will influence both attitudes and behavioral intentions in the future.

Marketers have several options in seeking to influence complex exchanges that are not turning out as the marketer wishes. The marketer can attempt to change the target customer's perceptions of the probable outcomes of choosing the marketer's alternative and/or the alternatives of competitors. Weightings on the criteria can be changed—although this is more difficult—or the customer can be pointed toward new or neglected favorable consequences.

With experience, customers proceed to simplify and then routinize behavioral patterns. In such cases, criteria are relatively fixed and alternatives are narrowed considerably. At the routine stage, behavior may appear to occur with little conscious thought or even appear probabilistic. In cases of low involvement decisions, relatively little cognition may be the norm even when the customer has little experience.

Not all decisions of interest to nonprofit marketers are individual. Where one is dealing with households or organizations, it is first necessary to understand the possible roles various members of the group can play. These roles include initiator, influencer, decider, transactor, and exchanger. But even for such groups, a given decision may be much like that which occurs for individuals in that it may be complex, simplified, or relatively routine.

QUESTIONS

1. Outline the benefits and costs the following target customers might perceive to exist in the exchange relationship: (a) a potential attender at a legitimate theater; (b) an expectant mother choosing a hospital; (c) an undergraduate choosing an MBA program.

2. Which kinds of hospital decisions would you categorize as (a) high involvement and continuous; (b) high involvement and one-time; (c) low involvement and continuous?

3. Assume that research shows that the New York City Opera is not in a major target segment's evoked set but is part of their consideration set. What further information do you need to ascertain what "went wrong?"

4. Who are the significant others who might influence a woman's decision to practice birth control in a developing country? How can a marketer take advantage of these reference groups?

5. Can blood donation behavior be studied as a probabilistic process in which the probability of a future donation is seen to be simply a function only of past behavior? What would be gained or lost by such an approach?

6. What roles might different family members play in getting an alcoholic father into a treatment program? How could a marketer aid them in their goal?

7. Foundations make group decisions on grants and fellowships. Some decisions are complex, some simplified, some routine. How should an arts organization seeking foundation support study them before submitting an application?

NOTES

1. Robert Bartels, "The Identity Crisis in Marketing," *Journal of Marketing,* October 1974, pp. 73–76; David J. Luck, "Broadening the Concept of Marketing—Too Far," *Journal of Marketing,* January 1969, pp. 53–54.

2. See Philip Kotler and Sidney J. Levy, "Buying is Marketing Too," *Journal of Marketing,* January 1973, pp. 54–59.

3. For additional discussion of the concept of exchange in marketing, see Richard P. Bagozzi, "Marketing as an Organized Behavioral System of Exchange," *Journal of Marketing,* October 1974, pp. 77–81; and "Marketing as Exchange," *American Behavioral Scientist,* March-April 1978, pp. 535–56.

4. James F. Engel and Roger D. Blackwell, *Consumer Behavior,* 4th ed. (Chicago: Dryden Press, 1982), p. 24.

5. *Ibid.*

6. Abraham H. Maslow, *Motivation and Personality* (New York: Harper & Row, 1954), pp. 80–106.

7. See Martin Fishbein and Icek Ajzen, *Belief, Attitude, Intention and Behavior* (Reading, Mass.: Addison-Wesley, 1975).

8. See Paul E. Green and Yoram Wind, *Multiattribute Decision in Marketing: A Measurement Approach* (Hinsdale, Ill.: Dryden Press, 1973), Chapter 2.

9. Fishbein and Ajzen, *Belief.*

10. Robert Burnkrant and Alain Cousineau, "International and Normative Social Influence in Buyer Behavior," *Journal of Consumer Research* 1975, pp. 206–15.

11. Michael J. Ryan and Edwin H. Bonfield, "The Extended Fishbein Model and Consumer Behavior," *Journal of Consumer Research* September 1975, pp. 118–136.

12. The reader will note that the relationship among the $NB_{kj}MC_{kj}$ components is compensatory, as is the relationship among the a_i and b_{ij} factors.

13. See Raymond A. Bauer, "Consumer Behavior as Risk Taking," in Donald F. Cox, ed., *Risk Taking and Information Handling in Consumer Behavior* (Boston: Division of Research, Harvard Business School, 1967); and James W. Taylor, "The Role of Risk in Consumer Behavior," *Journal of Marketing,* April 1974, pp. 54–60.

14. See John E. Swan and Linda Jones Combs, "Product Performance and Consumer Satisfaction: A New Concept," *Journal of Marketing Research,* April 1976, pp. 25–33.

15. See Ralph E. Anderson. "Consumer Dissatisfaction: The Effect of Disconfirmed Expectancy on Perceived Product Performance," *Journal of Marketing Research,* February 1973, pp. 38–44.

16. Leon Festinger and Dana Bramel, "The Reactions of Humans to Cognitive Dissonance," in Arthur J. Bachrach, ed., *Experimental Foundations of Clinical Psychology* (New York: Basic Books, 1962), pp. 251–62.

17. Leon Festinger, *A Theory of Cognitive Dissonance* (Stanford, Calif.: Stanford University Press, 1957), p. 260.

18. See James H. Donnelly, Jr. and John M. Ivancevich, "Post-Purchase Reinforcement and Back-Out Behavior," *Journal of Marketing Research,* August 1970, pp. 399–400.

19. Herbert C. Kelman and Carl I. Hovland, "'Reinstatement' of the Communicator in Delayed Measurement of Opinion Change," *Journal of Abnormal and Social Psychology,* Vol. 48 (1953), pp. 327–35.

20. Michael J. Ryan and E. H. Bonfield, "Fishbein's Intentions Model: A Test of External and Pragmatic Validity," *Journal of Marketing,* Spring 1980, pp. 82–95.

21. Richard P. Bagozzi, "Attitudes, Intentions and Behavior: A Test of Some Key Hypotheses," *Journal of Personality and Social Psychology* 1981, pp. 607–627.

22. S. J. Condie, W. K. Warner and D. C. Gillman, "Getting Blood from Collective Turnips: Volunteer Donations in Mass Blood Drives." *Journal of Applied Psychology* 1976, pp. 290–94.

23. R. J. Pomazel and J. J. Jaccard, "An Informal Approach to Altruistic Behavior," *Journal of Personality and Social Psychology* 1976, pp. 317–326.

24. Herbert E. Krugman, "Low Involvement Theory in the Light of New Brain Research," in John C. Maloney and Bernard Silverman, eds., *Attitude Research Plays for High Stakes* (Chicago: American Marketing Association, 1979), pp. 16–22; and "The Impact of Television Advertising: Learning Without Involvement," *Public Opinion Quarterly,* Fall 1965, pp. 349–56.

See also F. Stewart DeBruiker, "An Appraisal of Low-Involvement Consumer Information Processing," in Maloney and Silverman, *Attitude Research,* pp. 112–32.

25. For a review of the family decision-making literature, see Harry L. Davis, "Decision Making Within the Household," *Journal of Consumer Research,* March 1976, pp. 241–60.

26. Patrick J. Robinson, Charles W. Faris and Yoram Wind, *Industrial Buying and Creative Marketing* (Boston: Allyn & Bacon, 1967).

27. Frederick E. Webster, Jr. and Yoram Wind, *Organizational Behavior* (Englewood Cliffs, NJ: Prentice-Hall, 1972), p. 6.

28. *Ibid.,* pp. 78–80.

29. See Murray Harding, "Who Really Makes the Purchasing Decision?" *Industrial Marketing,* September 1966, p. 76. This point of view is further developed in Ernest Dichter, "Industrial Buying is Based on Same 'Only Human' Factors That Motivate Consumer Market's Housewife," *Industrial Marketing,* February 1973, pp. 14–16.

CHAPTER 4

Market Segmentation and Customer Targeting

A major problem for the National High Blood Pressure Education Program (NHBPEP) in developing strategies to get people to control their blood pressure is that different groups have different concerns and respond to different themes. This was dramatically shown in a recent focus group study by Needham Porter Novelli, a Washington social marketing and public relations firm, of male hypertensives who knew they had high blood pressure.

Across the six focus groups, a number of differences were found between the younger and older participants in terms of their attitude toward having high blood pressure and their adherence to treatment.

- Older participants generally tended to take their condition more seriously, whereas younger hypertensives seemed to manifest a "macho" attitude characterized by such statements as "It's not really happening to me" or "I'll take care of it when I get older."

- Although shame or embarrassment about having high blood pressure was not prevalent in any of the groups, younger participants tended to be more adamant than older participants about not wanting other people to know about their condition. As a whole, participants tended to feel that their high blood pressure was their "own private affair and not something to be broadcast."

- Younger participants reacted more negatively than older participants to being told what to do. They also tended to prefer being addressed by one person rather than observing characters address each other in the ad.

- Participants tended to associate believability in a script with realistic situations rather than situations they could not imagine happening. Younger participants appeared to be somewhat more literal-minded than older participants in their interpretations of the commercials.
- While participants as a whole were not reluctant to ask questions of their doctors, younger participants appeared to be less intimidated by doctors than their older counterparts.
- Few of the younger participants were on medication for high blood pressure, as compared to the older participants. The side effects reported most commonly by older participants were sexual dysfunction and fatigue. Younger participants were more concerned about nondrug issues, such as losing weight and salt reduction.

Based on the differences in attitude found between younger and older participants in the groups, it was recommended that a new commercial spot be developed by NHBPEP that specifically addressed the "macho" attitude of younger hypertensives. This new spot would complement several that NHBPEP is currently using.

SOURCE: *Focus Group Study Among Male Aware Hypertensives*, Washington, DC: Needham Porter Novelli, June 1984. Excerpted with permission.

A marketing manager, knowing that marketing strategy should be tailored to customer perceptions, needs, and wants, might see the task as almost overwhelming. There are three reasons for this. First, as Chapter 3 clearly showed, customers involved in a particular exchange can differ from each other in dozens—perhaps hundreds—of ways. Some could be engaged in trivial decisions, some in highly complex, cognitively rich evaluations. Among the latter, some could be inexperienced, some experienced. Customers differ in the size and contents of their evoked sets, in the criteria they use, in where they go for information, in how much they have learned so far, in how malleable their present views are, and on and on. The combinations can seem almost endless, especially when one adds the possibility that target customers also differ in gender, age, geographical location, TV-watching habits, and magazine- or newspaper-reading habits.

Even if the manager could *conceptualize* how to deal with this complexity (and we'll offer some help with this in a moment), the next question is how to apply *numbers* to it? That is, even if a manager could conceive of all of these differences and could speculate on how to capitalize on them, the manager typically has little or no idea of whether any or all of these groups *exist,* and if they do, how big they are. Not all nonprofits have adequate budgets to help them quantify segments. Further, because of the newness of the entire field, few secondary data exist from which a nonprofit marketer might extrapolate to his or her own particular market situation. Finally, neither commercial services nor the government has moved in yet to provide the kind of data bases that are available to traditional marketers of household durables and most consumer convenience items.

Even if the conceptualization and quantification problems could be solved, there remains a series of strategy questions about how to group segments and how to treat them, if at all. That is, just because a marketer can define a separate group, this doesn't necessarily mean that the group should (1) be treated separately and not lumped together with some relatively similar group so that significant scale economies for a particular marketing strategy could be achieved, or (2) be treated at all. One might choose not to treat a group at all, for example, if probable demand within the group was small or had already been effectively captured by a competitor. And, of course, the typical nonprofit marketer not only has few resources for *research* but also few resources—both financial and organizational—to try to treat many diverse sets of segments separately.

Nonprofit organizations have gone through three stages in their thinking about how to operate in these kinds of markets.

- *Mass marketing.* Mass marketing is a style of marketing where the organization mass-produces and mass-distributes one market offer and attempts to attract every eligible person to its use. It is compatible with a selling orientation to marketing. Thus, the Philadelphia Transit Authority could conceivably offer only one form of transportation—buses—and try to attract all commuters to use that form. The argument for mass marketing is that it would result in the lowest costs and prices and therefore create the largest potential market. The mass marketer pays little or no attention to differences in consumer preferences.

- *Product-differentiated marketing.* Product differentiation is a style of marketing compatible with a product orientation to marketing. With this approach, the organization prepares two or more market offers for the market as a whole. The market offers may exhibit different features, styles, quality, and so on. Thus, the Philadelphia Transit Authority could create a bus system and subway system and leave it to commuters to make the choice. The offers are designed, not so much for different groups, but to offer alternatives to everyone in the market.

- *Target marketing.* Target marketing is a style of marketing appropriate to a customer-oriented organization. In it the organization distinguishes between the different segments making up the market, chooses one or more of these segments to focus on, and develops market offers and marketing mixes tailored to meet the needs of each segment. The Philadelphia Transit Authority, for example, could develop a commuter train system designed to meet the needs of affluent commuters for a clean train and comfortable ride, albeit at a high price. At the same time, it could provide inexpensive, small "jitney" buses for those who want frequent, cheap, short rides, say in a downtown area.

FIGURE 4-1

Steps in Market Segmentation and Target Marketing

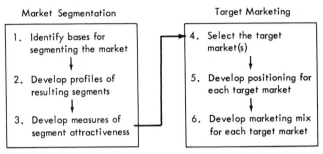

Organizations can be found today practicing each style of marketing. As one might expect, however, there is a strong movement away from mass marketing and product-differentiated marketing toward target marketing. At least three benefits of target marketing can be identified. First, organizations are in a better position to spot market opportunities. They can notice market segments whose needs are not being fully met by current offerings. Second, marketers can make finer adjustments of their offer to match the desire of the market. They can interview members of the target market and get a good picture of their specific needs and desires and track how these change over time. Third, sellers can make finer adjustments of their prices, distribution channels, and promotional mix. Instead of trying to draw in all potential buyers with a "shotgun" approach, sellers can create separate marketing programs aimed at each target market (called a "rifle" approach).

For the marketer wishing to adopt the more sophisticated *target marketing* approach, a process is needed to cope with the sheer enormity of the task. There are really *two* stages to this process. First is a conceptualization and research stage to identify and describe the groups the marketer *may* wish to target. This stage we shall refer to as market segmentation. As can be seen in the left side of Figure 4-1, market segmentation requires (1) identifying the different bases for segmenting the market, (2) developing profiles of the resulting market segments, and (3) developing measures of each segment's attractiveness. The second stage is target marketing, the act of selecting one or more of the market segments and developing a positioning and marketing mix strategy for each. This chapter will describe the major concepts and tools for both stages.

MARKET SEGMENTATION

Markets consist of buyers, and buyers are likely to differ in one or more respects. They may differ in their desires, resources, geographical locations, buying attitudes, buying practices, and so on. Any of these variables can be used to segment a market. We will first illustrate the general approach to segmenting a market.

THE GENERAL APPROACH TO SEGMENTING A MARKET

Figure 4-2A shows a market consisting of six buyers before it is segmented. The maximum number of segments that a market can contain is the total number of buyers making up that market. Each buyer is potentially a separate market, because of his or her unique needs and desires. Ideally, a marketer might study each buyer in order to tailor the best marketing program to that buyer's needs. Where there are only a few buyers, this may be feasible. A therapist, for example, tailors a different treatment to each patient, depending on what each patient needs. This ultimate degree of market segmentation is illustrated in Figure 4-2B.

Most marketers will not find it worthwhile to "customize" their product to satisfy each buyer's specific requirements. Instead, the marketer identifies broad classes of buyers who differ in their product requirements, marketing responses, or both. The marketer may discover, for example, that income groups differ in their product requirements and marketing responses. In Figure 4-2C, a number (1, 2, or 3) is used to identify each buyer's income class. Lines are drawn around buyers in the same income class. Segmentation by income class results in three segments, the most numerous one being income class 1 in the illustration.

FIGURE 4-2

Different Approaches to Segmentation of a Market

A. No market
segmentation

B. Complete market
segmentation

C. Market segmentation
by income classes
1, 2, and 3

D. Market segmentation
by age classes
a and b

E. Market segmentation
by income-age class

On the other hand, the marketer may find pronounced differences in buyer behavior between younger and older buyers. In Figure 4-2D the same individuals are shown, except a letter (a or b) is used to indicate the buyer's age class. Segmentation of the market by age class results in two segments, each having three members.

It may turn out that income and age both count heavily in differentiating the buyer's behavior toward the product. The marketer may find it desirable to partition the market according to those joint characteristics. In terms of the illustration, the market can be broken into the following six segments: 1a, 1b, 2a, 2b, 3a, and 3b. Figure 4-2E shows that segment 1a contains two buyers, segment 2a contains no buyers (a null segment), and each of the other segments contains one buyer. In general, as the market is segmented on the basis of a larger set of joint characteristics, the marketer achieves finer precision, but at the price of multiplying the number of segments and reducing the population in each segment. If the seller segmented the market using all conceivable characteristics, the market would again look like Figure 4-2B, where each buyer would be a separate segment.

As can be seen in Figure 4-3, the problem for management is that as the number of segments treated separately increases, (1) the *impact* of the overall strategy increases but at a decreasing rate, while (2) the *total cost* of the strategy also increases. The manager's task is to estimate at what point the gap between total impact and total costs will be greatest. This would be five segments in the example in Figure 4-3. In practice, of course, estimating these relationships is not an easy task, but its difficulty should not deter the

FIGURE 4-3

Total Costs and Impact as a Function
of Number of Segments

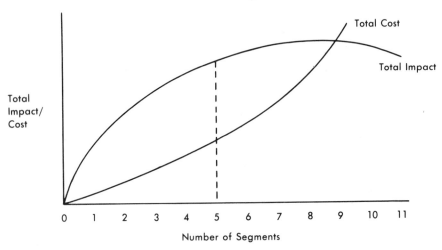

manager from making the attempt. Experience has suggested that, in a large proportion of the markets in which nonprofits must operate, the total impact rises faster than total costs as one begins to segment markets beyond a simple mass-marketing approach. Indeed, it is our position that marketing managers are almost always better off looking for ways to segment, and only if that approach is unfeasible should an undifferentiated strategy be adopted.

CRITERIA FOR SEGMENTATION

There are a great many ways in which a given market can be divided up for purposes of marketing strategy. In determining which way one ought to proceed, the manager should first consider *why* segmentation is to be carried out. Management may wish to consider segmenting a market[1] to help make the following strategic decisions:

1. *Quantity decisions: How much* of the organization's financial, human, and mental resources are to be devoted to each segment (if any)?
2. *Quality decisions: How* should each segment be approached in terms of specific offerings, communications, place of offering, prices, and the like?
3. *Timing decisions: When* should specific marketing efforts be directed at particular segments?

Given the seemingly infinite array of segmentation possibilities, management needs to decide which is best. In theory, the choice is relatively straightforward. A segmentation base is optimal if it yields segments possessing the following characteristics:

1. *Mutual exclusivity.* Each segment should be conceptually separable from all other segments. Breaking donors into present givers and past givers, for example, would be confusing for a respondent who could be both a past and present giver.
2. *Exhaustiveness.* Every potential target member should be included in some segment. Thus, if there is to be segmentation according to household status, one should have categories to cover relationships like unmarried couples and religious communes where the notion of "household head" really does not apply.
3. *Measurability.* This is the degree to which the size, purchasing power, and profile of the resulting segments can be readily measured. Certain segments are hard to measure, such as the segment of white upper-income teenage female drug addicts, since this segment is engaged in secretive behavior.
4. *Accessibility.* This is the degree to which the resulting segments can be effectively reached and served. Thus, it would be hard for a drug treatment center to develop efficient media to locate and communicate with white female drug addicts.
5. *Substantiality.* This is the degree to which the resulting segments are large enough to be worth pursuing. The drug treatment center is likely to decide that white affluent female drug addicts are too few in number to be worth the development of a special marketing program.

6. *Differential responsiveness.* This is perhaps the most crucial criterion. A segmentation scheme may meet all of the above criteria but several or all segments may respond exactly alike to different amounts, types, and timing of strategy. In such cases, although it may be *conceptually* useful to develop separate segments in this way, *managerially* it is not useful.

The last point deserves a brief elaboration. Figures 4-4A and 4-4B show the allocation of a given advertising budget to two geographically separate markets we'll call East and West. Curves marked a-a and b-b depict the responsiveness of each market to different levels of advertising expenditure. The slope of curve a-a as compared to b-b indicates that the West market responds more dramatically than the East market for any given change in ad spending. (That is, the West market is more *advertising-elastic* than the East market.)

The points A_{E1} and A_{W1} represent equal advertising expenditures in the two markets. This allocation strategy yields total response results of $(R_{E1} + R_{W1})$. But it can be seen that if, say, $1,000 is shifted from East to West to yield expenditure levels $(A_{E2}$ and $A_{W2})$, then total response $(R_{E2} + R_{W2})$ rises, even though *total* expenditures are unchanged. This is because the gain in shifting dollars to the West market $(R_{W2} - R_{W1})$ exceeds the loss in the East $(R_{E2} - R_{E1})$. One should continue shifting a given budget into the West market until such point as the incremental gain in the one market just equals the incremental loss in the other. In general, one should shift a given budget among differentially responsive markets until the point is reached where the *total* responses would be unchanged under any further fine-tuning one might do between markets. Technically, this is the point where the marginal responses[2] for the various segments are equal.

FIGURE 4-4

Hypothetical Responses of Two Markets
to Advertising Expenditures

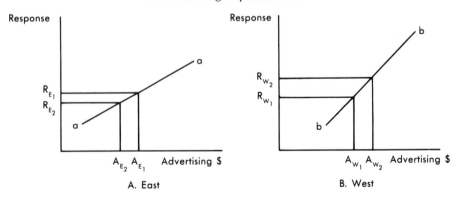

A. East

B. West

As the preceding discussion indicated, it would be ideal if target consumers could be labeled as to how and how much they would respond to specific quantities, qualities, and timing of marketing strategy. Since consumers don't carry such labels, an ideal segmentation approach expressly requires specifications of the responsiveness of different potential segments. However, once specifications are determined either by assumption or through research, the requirement that the segments be differentially *reachable* still means that we must also know something about *where* they might be reached—for example, through what media, what outlets, what personal information sources, etc.—so that we might differentially apply our segmented strategies.

The ideal response-and-reachability-based approach is rarely achieved for two reasons. First, field research to determine responsiveness and information source behavior is costly and time-consuming and not every organization has the funds and the patience to make the necessary investment. Second, the sheer *number* of segmentation decisions a manager must make precludes such care and attention except in rare, very important situations.

As a result, managers typically use *surrogates* for what they *ideally* would like to measure. Segmentation is often based on demographics, for example, because managers assume that such characteristics will be related to likely responses and reachability. Thus, one might choose to segment potential symphony customers on the basis of sex because it is believed (or past research has shown) that women respond more to communications focusing on the performance itself whereas men respond more to communications about the social aspects of attending the symphony *event*. At the same time, it may be found (or assumed) that ads placed in the sports section of a newspaper would reach a predominantly male audience and ads in the metropolitan news section would be an excellent way to reach females. Symphony marketers may initially conclude—with or without past research evidence—that the added costs of placing two such ads in a given paper may be justified by the better *total* responses achieved over a less costly, single ad that tried a middle approach or tried to combine the two approaches in one (possibly confusing) message.

But it should be reemphasized that the demographic approach, responsiveness and reachability are typically estimated rather than known. As we shall note in Chapter 6, however, a strategy of flying blind needn't continue. A careful program of experimentation could directly test which segmentation approach (for example, separate or single ads) generated more mail orders or more box office sales. Once such a research base was begun, further research could experiment with other segmentation bases or use other strategies to attack the chosen segments. Over time, a careful, systematic, low-cost research program could accumulate considerable experience on the responsiveness and reachability of key market segments.

Variables that have been used to segment markets in particular cases vary according to whether they were *primarily* chosen to reflect expected differences in responsiveness or differences in reachability. Frank, Massy, and Wind have developed a useful two-by-two matrix that serves as a useful vehicle for categorizing segmentation approaches that may be used to achieve these ends.[3] These authors note that two important ways in which segmentation variables differ are in the extent to which they are (1) objective or inferred and (2) general or specific. *Objective measures* are those that can be verified by an independent observer—for example, status indicators such as age, income, sex, and the like. *Inferred measures* are mental states peculiar to each respondent; included are such cognitive factors as perceptions, beliefs, importances attached to exchange consequences, and so forth. Inferred variables can only be measured through the candor and cooperation of a target consumer through answers to a questionnaire, a paper-and-pencil test, or similar assessment device.

General variables are those that might apply to any exchange, whereas *specific* variables are those that are unique to one type or class of exchanges, for example, the purchase of a particular brand or patronage of a particular hospital or museum. Thus, the extent to which an individual consumer possesses an "aggressive" or "risk averse" personality would be a general inferred variable, whereas beliefs about the likelihood of getting friendly nursing service or the latest diagnostic procedures at Good Samaritan Hospital would be a specific inferred variable.

Objective General Measures.   In some respects, marketers would prefer to use objective rather than subjective measures as the basis for segmentation. There are several reasons for this. First, there is the *ease* of measuring target consumers. Most objective general measures such as sex and geographic location are instantly observable. Others, such as education level, occupation, household size, and family composition are relatively easily determined and verifiable. Unlike inferred measures, objective indicators do not always require consumer cooperation, nor is there a strong likelihood that an error in measurement would be made either because the wrong wording was used for a question or because respondents did not know the answer or consciously or unconsciously distorted their responses. Second, target consumers can be fairly easily allocated to specific, nonarbitrary categories (that is, the categories are mutually exclusive). Third, the measures can be adapted easily by different researchers to different contexts, permitting extensive comparison of segmentation findings across studies. This is typically not possible with inferred characteristics, where subtle changes in wording can yield major differences in results.

Finally, objective measures are often preferred because they are available in secondary sources. Thus, if one believes that households with young children are the best prospects for a charity drive, then publicly available census data can be used to discover cities or census tracts within cities that have above-average frequencies of households with that characteristic.

Among the most commonly used objective general measures are the following:

GEOGRAPHICAL SEGMENTATION. In geographical segmentation, the market is divided into different geographical entities, such as nations, states, regions, counties, cities, or neighborhoods, based on the notion that consumer needs or responses vary geographically. The organization either decides to operate in one or a few parts of the country as a specialist in meeting their needs or to operate broadly but pay attention to variations in geographical needs and preferences. The State University of New York (SUNY), for example, operates sixty-four college campuses, each with programs adapted partly to the interests of the local inhabitants. This is in contrast to running sixty-four college campuses that are all doing the same thing.

DEMOGRAPHIC SEGMENTATION. In demographic segmentation, the market is divided into different groups on the basis of demographic variables such as age, sex, family size, family life-cycle, income, occupation, education, religion, race, and nationality. Demographic variables have long been the most popular bases for distinguishing consumer groups. One reason is that consumer wants, preferences, and usage rates are often highly associated with demographic variables. Another is that demographic variables are easier to measure than most other types of variables. Even when the target market is described in nondemographic terms (say, a personality type), the link back to demographic characteristics is necessary in order to know the size of the target market and how to reach it efficiently.

Here we will illustrate how certain demographic variables have been applied creatively to market segmentation.

Age. Consumer wants and capacities change with age. Thus churches have developed different programs for children, youths, singles, married adults, and senior citizens. The churches try to "customize" the religious and social experiences to the interests of these different groups. Some churches are even subsegmenting the senior citizens into those between fifty-five and seventy ("the young old") and seventy and up ("the old old"). The young old still feel vigorous and want challenge and variety in their lives, and the old old want to settle into a comfortable and routine existence.

Sex. Sex segmentation appears in many nonprofit sectors, such as male and female colleges, service and social clubs, prisons, and military services. Within a single sex, further segmentation can be applied. The continuing education department of a large university segments the female adult learners into "at homes" and "working outside the homes." The "at homes" are subdivided into homemakers and displaced homemakers. Homemakers are attracted to courses for self-enrichment and improved homemaking skills, while displaced homemakers are more interested in career preparation. The "working outside the home" segment breaks into two subsegments, clerical-technical businesswomen and management businesswomen. Each segment has a different set of motivations for attending college, and different educational programs are appropriate for each. Furthermore, each segment faces certain problems in attending college. By addressing the specific problems of each segment, the college is in a better position to attract more women to its campus.

Income. Income segmentation is another long-standing practice in the nonprofit sector. In the medical field, the standard health insurance policy pays for semiprivate rooms. Most hospitals, however, offer patients the option of a private room at an additional cost in order to cater to the preferences of higher income groups. Some hospitals have designed entire wings and even whole buildings to serve more affluent patients. Hospitals that

FIGURE 4-5

Brochures Designed for Consumer, Physician, and Business Markets

establish outreach ambulatory centers vary the decor and service to match the different income groups.

Role in the distribution system. As shown in Figure 4-5, The Hospital of the Good Samaritan in Los Angeles has developed entirely separate brochures for its ambulatory care center for (a) potential patients, (b) physicians, and (c) businesses.

COMPLEX GENERAL OBJECTIVE MEASURES.   As nonprofit marketers grow more sophisticated in their use of objective segmentation variables, two steps can be taken. First, marketers can be more precise in operationalizing the measures they use. Income, for example, is a frequently used variable in attempts to segment the charity market—for obvious reasons. Miller, however, has found that donation behavior in various zip codes in Oklahoma is often more closely associated with the source of income than the amount of income.[4] He found, for example, that the number of households in a zip code area receiving some form of interest income was a better predictor of total donations than was total adjusted gross income. Predictions of the *percentage* who would donate were better with measures of the percentage of households receiving dividends, or of the percentage receiving interest than with average household income. Clearly, routinely using total income in studies may miss insights that more careful measures might yield.

The second way nonprofit marketers can become more sophisticated is in using objective variables in combination. One approach is the development of relatively complex segmentation matrices like that developed for the "blindness" market in Figure 4-6.

FIGURE 4-6

Segmentation of the Blind Market

		Single Handicapped		Multiple Handicapped	
		Partially sighted	Totally blind	Partially sighted	Totally blind
Congenital	Elderly				
	Working-age adult				
	Child				
Adventitious	Elderly				
	Working-age adult				
	Child				

SOURCE: Adapted from teaching note, *The Richardson Center for the Blind,* prepared by Roberta N. Clarke under the supervision of Benson P. Shapiro.

Another approach is to combine objective measures in a single index. Two such combined measures, social class and family life-cycle, have been used extensively in marketing.

Social class.   Social classes are relatively homogeneous and enduring divisions in a society that is hierarchically ordered and whose members share similar values, interests, and behavior. Social scientists have distinguished six social classes: (1) upper uppers (less than 1 percent); (2) lower uppers (about 2 percent); (3) upper middles (12 percent); (4) lower middles (30 percent); (5) upper lowers (35 percent); and (6) lower lowers (20 percent), using objective variables such as income, occupation, education, and type of residence. Social classes show distinct consumption preferences in the nonprofit area. A recent study of museum-goers attending the King Tut exhibit in New Orleans, for example, showed that attendance came heavily from the upper and middle classes, in spite of the mass marketing of this extraordinary exhibit.[5] Operas, plays, the ballet, symphonies, and lectures also attract the upper classes most heavily. Cultural institutions that wish to overcome their elitist image and attract lower-class audiences to appreciate their art form will have to develop separate marketing programs and strategies.

Family life-cycle.   The family life-cycle concept is based on the notion that over one's lifetime there are critical transition points when major changes in consumer behavior (and other behaviors) take place. These transition points are generally defined in terms of objective variables such as marital status, work force status, and the presence and age of children. Eight stages are typically specified as the modal family life-cycle pattern:

1. Young single (under forty, not married, no children at home)
2. Newly married (young, married, no children)
3. Full nest I (young, married, youngest child less than six)
4. Full nest II (young, married, youngest child six to thirteen)
5. Full nest III (older married, dependent children fourteen or older)
6. Empty nest I (older married, no children at home, head working)
7. Empty nest II (older married, no children at home, head retired)
8. Solitary survivor (older single, working or retired)

Some of the characteristics of the households in each of these stages are indicated in Table 4-1.

It should be noted that while the family life cycle concept can prove a useful segmentation variable, it is not *exhaustive* in that it omits important groups of households. For example, older never-marrieds, and divorced or single parents with spouses absent are not included.[6] For some nonprofit social service marketing programs, such households may be very important.

A third approach to using objective variables in combination is to use

Table 4-1

AN OVERVIEW OF THE FAMILY LIFE CYCLE AND BUYING BEHAVIOR

Stage in Family Life Cycle	*Buying or Behavioral Pattern*
1. Bachelor stage: young, single people not living at home.	Few financial burdens. Fashion opinion leaders. Recreation oriented. Buy: basic kitchen equipment, basic furniture, cars, equipment for the mating game, vacations.
2. Newly married couples: young, no children.	Better off financially than they will be in near future. Highest purchase rate and highest average purchase of durables. Buy: cars, refrigerators, stoves, sensible and durable furniture, vacations.
3. Full nest I: Youngest child under six.	Home purchasing at peak. Liquid assets low. Dissatisfied with financial position and amount of money saved. Interested in new products. Like advertised products. Buy: washers, dryers, TV, baby food, chest rubs and cough medicines, vitamins, dolls, wagons, sleds, skates.
4. Full nest II: Youngest child six or over.	Financial position better. Some wives work. Less influenced by advertising. Buy larger sized packages, multiple-unit deals. Buy: many foods, cleaning materials, bicycles, music lessons, pianos.
5. Full nest III. Older married couples with dependent children.	Financial position still better. More wives work. Some children get jobs. Hard to influence with advertising. High average purchase of durables. Buy: new, more tasteful furniture, auto travel, unnecessary appliances, boats, dental services, magazines.
6. Empty nest I: Older married couples, no children living with them, head in labor force.	Home ownership at peak. Most satisfied with financial position and money saved. Interested in travel, recreation, self-education. Make gifts and contributions. Not interested in new products. Buy: vacations, luxuries, home improvements.
7. Empty nest II: Older married. No children living at home, head retired.	Drastic cut in income. Keep home. Buy: medical appliances, medical-care products that aid health, sleep, and digestion.

Table 4-1 (continued)

Stage in Family Life Cycle	Buying or Behavioral Pattern
8. Solitary survivor, in labor force.	Income still good but likely to sell home.
9. Solitary survivor, retired.	Same medical and product needs as other retired group; drastic cut in income. Special need for attention, affection, and security.

SOURCE: William D. Wells and George Gubar, "Life Cycle Concept in Marketing Research," *Journal of Marketing Research*, November 1966, pp. 355–63, here p. 362. Reproduced with permission. Also see Patrick E. Murphy and William A. Staples, "A Modernized Family Life Cycle," *Journal of Consumer Research*, June 1979, pp. 12–22.

multivariate statistical procedures to determine customized *sets* of predictors that when considered together best segment target markets. These procedures consider *all* possible segmentation variables together and develop (1) a parsimonious subset that jointly does the best job of predicting the behavior in question, and (2) a measure of the relative contribution of each variable to the final predictions. Beik and Smith, for example, collected survey data on 2,261 households in Allegheny County, Pennsylvania, describing their charitable giving of all kinds. They also assembled objective data on the tracts in which the respondents resided.[7] By analyzing these results with a technique called multiple discriminant analysis, the researchers found they could best discriminate between households making donations of $50 or more to medical charities and all other households with the following equation:

$$Y_1 = .58328X_1 + .53414X_3 + .31493X_4 \qquad\qquad (4\text{--}1)$$

where:

Y_1 = Donate $50+ to medical charities (1 = yes, 0 = no)
X_1 = Proportion of households with income $\geq$ \$15,000
X_3 = Proportion of household heads $\geq$ 55 years of age
X_4 = Proportion of household heads in managerial, professional, or entrepreneurial positions.[8]

Note three features of this analysis. First, to discriminate donation behavior, the researchers attempted to use objective variables other than age, income, and occupation such as the proportion of owned homes and the proportion of household heads who were college graduates. These variables, however, turned out in the multivariate analysis framework not to be useful for segmentation. Second, the coefficients in the final equation indicate that income contributed somewhat more as a predictor of medical donations than did age, while both were substantially more important than occupation. Finally, because the predictors are all available in government census data, if one assumed that the Oklahoma results applied elsewhere, one could—in theory—segment every area in the United States as to whether they are likley to be better or poorer prospects for solicitations by medical charities using the three variables and weightings reported in the above equation.

Objective Specific Measures.   For consumer decisions involving little or no cognitive activity, the best predictor of future responsiveness may well be past behavior with respect to the exchange category or closely related exchanges. Among the objective specific variables relating to behavior often used in marketing are the following:

EXCHANGE OCCASION.   Buyers can be distinguished by the occasions when they purchase a product. Commuters using public transportation, for example, include those who are traveling to work, those who are shopping, those who are going to entertainment, and those who are visiting friends. Some public transit companies have launched campaigns to encourage the shopping segment to travel in off-peak hours and have even charged lower fares as an incentive.

USER STATUS.   Many markets can be segmented into nonusers, ex-users, potential users, first-time users, and regular users of a product. This segmentation variable is helpful to antidrug agencies in planning their education programs and campaigns. Much of their effort is directed at identifying potential users of hard drugs and discouraging them through information and persuasion campaigns. They also sponsor rehabilitation programs to help regular users who want to quit their habit. They utilize ex-users in various programs to add credibility to their effort.

In another example, Lovelock has found that one can separate target segments for mass transit in San Francisco as follows:

1. Never used (13.6 percent)
2. Nonuser, used in past (48.5 percent)
3. Occasional user (30.1 percent)
4. Regular user by choice (6.9 percent)

In his study, Lovelock found significant differences across these groups in perceptions of car, bus, and train travel and their knowledge of interurban bus service.[9] He concluded that "the findings presented from the San Francisco area represent a strong link between perceptions . . . and modal choice behavior." However, two features of this research need to be noted. First, the study uses specific rather than general objective measures (of behavior), so the implications about likely responsiveness are more obvious than they would be if general measures like automobile ownership, occupation, or place of residence were used and from which further inferences about transit patronage would have to be made.

Second, the study only showed *links* between the subjective measures and likely behavior. It did not discover the *direction* of the causation. Thus, it could be that favorable perceptions lead to public transit use, but it is also possible that public transit use leads to favorable perceptions. Thus, as Lovelock notes, only a longitudinal design could produce a causal explanation.

USAGE RATE. Many markets can be segmented into light-, medium-, and heavy-user groups for the offer (called volume segmentation). Heavy users may constitute only a small percentage of the numerical size of the market but a major percentage of the unit volume consumed. Marketers make a great effort to determine the demographic characteristics and media habits of the heavy users and aim their marketing programs at them. An antismoking campaign, for example, might be aimed at the heaviest smokers, a safe driving campaign at those having the most accidents, and a family planning campaign at those likely to have the most children. Unfortunately, the heaviest users are the most resistant to change. Fertile families are the most resistant to birth control messages, and unsafe drivers are the most resistant to safe driving messages. The agencies must consider whether to use their limited budget to go after a few heavy users who are highly resistant or many light users who are less resistant.

Semenik and Young segmented the audience attending opera into three attendance level segments—subscribers, frequent attenders, and infrequent attenders—and found significant differences.[10] Subscribers tended to be long-time patrons, attended as husband and wife, and considered themselves to be opera fans. Frequent attenders had similar characteristics but were younger and lower in income, and often attended with a friend rather than a spouse. Infrequent attenders did not consider themselves opera fans but attended because of a featured star or well-known opera. The identification of segment characteristics enables the development of separate market strategies designed to maximize attendance and loyalty.

LOYALTY STATUS. Loyalty status describes the strength of a consumer's preference for a particular entity. The amount of loyalty can range from zero to absolute. We find consumers who are deeply loyal to a brand (Budweiser beer, Crest toothpaste, Cadillac automobiles); an organization (Harvard University, the Republican Party); a place (New England, Southern California), a person (Ralph Nader); and so on. Being loyal means preferring the particular object in spite of increased incentives to switch to something else.

An organization should research its present customers and analyze their degree of loyalty. Four groups can be distinguished: (1) *hard-core loy-*

als, who are exclusively devoted to the organization; (2) *soft-core loyals,* who are devoted to two or three organizations; (3) *shifting loyals,* who are gradually moving from favoring this organization to favoring another organization; and (4) *switchers,* who show no loyalty to any organization. If most of the organization's customers are hard-core loyals or even soft-core loyals, the organization is basically healthy. It might study its loyals to find out the basic satisfactions they derive from affiliation and then attempt to attract others who are seeking the same satisfactions.

Inferred General Variables.   Most of the measures in this category seek to identify consumers in terms of general intrapsychic predispositions that presumably would apply over time and across exchange categories. The most widely used approaches are those that segment consumers by personality, by general needs and wants, and by lifestyle.

PERSONALITY.   It has long been believed consumer variations in personality will be reflected in their marketplace behavior. There have been three approaches to incorporating personality in marketing studies. The first is to define consumers in terms of traditional personality traits such as dominance, narcissism, sociability, and exhibitionism and then see whether these traits predict preferences, behavior, or both. Young, for example, found thirteen personality traits useful in segmenting the cosmetic market,[11] while Ackoff and Emshoff claim that four personality types adequately characterize the beer market.[12]

A second approach is to develop simpler categorizations based on a specific personality theory. Thus, Cohen has used Karen Horney's three orientations toward anxiety—compliant, aggressive, and detached—to predict product and brand usage with some success.[13]

The third approach is to take one particular personality trait and use it to explain a certain behavior. The most frequently used traits in this regard are *dogmatism, self-confidence,* and *risk-taking propensity.* All three have been found to be highly correlated with willingness to accept innovations. In addition, self-confidence has been found to be related to store choice (for example, those with high self-confidence were more likely to use discount stores).

Despite these findings, in the main, general personality measures have not been successful in past studies, in part because they are very difficult to measure (that is, they are highly subjective and unreliable across studies) and therefore very hard to link to specific marketplace actions. On the other hand, these studies have focused on relatively trivial behavior like beer preferences. It may be that in the future, personality measures may finally prove to be helpful in segmenting markets for the more highly involving exchanges that are of interest to nonprofit marketers.

SPECIFIC NEEDS.   It is believed that, just as consumers have distinct personalities, they also have important goals that tend to dominate responses across a wide range of specific situations. Maslow's needs hierarchy (described in Chapter 3) is sometimes used to identify such central needs. Other single needs often studied are consumers' needs for *power, affiliation,* and *achievement.* Many nonprofits clearly attempt (although sometimes haphazardly) to appeal to segments dominated by one or another of these three goals. The Marines seem clearly intersted in individuals with strong power needs. Various social clubs (Boy Scouts, Elks, etc.) appeal to those who have affiliation needs, and the Sierra Club has a natural affinity for those who seek a sense of achievement in their lives.

LIFESTYLES.   Recent dissatisfaction with the overly general personality or dominant-need approaches to inferred segmentation has led to the very rapid growth of lifestyle research in the last ten years. If segmentation by personality is based on the notion that "we do what we do because of the kind of person we are," then lifestyle segmentation is based on the notion that "we do what we do because it fits into the kind of life we are living or want to live." A further distinction is that whereas personality is seen to be a very enduring, perhaps lifelong characteristic, lifestyle is seen as more transient, something that can change even from one year to the next.

There are several different approaches to identifying lifestyle groups in the population. Most, however, are based on measures of consumers' *activities, interests, and opinions* (AIOs). Lifestyle measures developed from these data can be general or more specific as in the case of one's leisure lifestyle. Among the more general approaches, two have received relatively wide publicity; the Needham Harper Worldwide approach and the VALS approach. They are described respectively in Exhibits 4-1 and 4-2.

An example of segmentation based on lifestyles is shown in Figures 4-7 and 4-8. Figure 4-7 shows a point-of-sale placard for oral contraceptives aimed at Cairo women. The very same placard altered to depict more traditional lifestyles outside of Cairo is shown in Figure 4-8.

Inferred Specific Measures.   Segmenting consumers subjectively for specific markets, of course, usually requires original field data. Rarely are such data available from secondary sources. In cases where the exchange at issue is highly involving, a very useful framework for such research is the Extended Fishbein Attitude Model described in detail in Chapter 3. It will be recalled that this model algebraically was as follows:

$$\text{Behavior} = BI = \left(\sum_{i=1}^{n} b_{ij}a_i \right) W_1 + \left(\sum_{k=1}^{m} NB_{kj} \cdot MC_{kj} \right) W_2 \qquad (4\text{--}2)$$

The model contains a wide array of specific subjective measures that can be used to segment markets. Referring to the algebraic notations, these measures include:

1. *j* the exchange alternatives in the evoked set (for example, segmenting those consumers that include your alternative separately from those that do not);

EXHIBIT 4-1. The Needham Harper Worldwide approach

Using a large bank of AIO measures, the advertising agency of Needham Harper Worldwide has identified ten major consumer lifestyles—five for men and five for women. These groups and the percentage of the population in each are as follows:

Ten Lifestyle Groups	
Ben, the self-made businessman (17 percent)	Cathy, the contented housewife (18 percent)
Scott, the successful professional (21 percent)	Candice, the chic suburbanite (20 percent)
Dale, the devoted family man (17 percent)	Eleanor, the elegant socialite (17 percent)
Fred, the frustrated factory worker (19 percent)	Mildred, the militant mother (20 percent)
Herman, the retiring homebody (26 percent)	Thelma, the old-fashioned traditionalist (25 percent)

More detailed descriptions of two of the female groups give a sense of the kind of detail that can be provided in lifestyle profiles:

Mildred, the militant mother. Mildred married young and had children before she was quite ready to raise a family. Now she is unhappy. She is having trouble making ends meet on her blue-collar husband's income. She is frustrated and she vents her frustrations by rebelling against the system. She finds escape from her unhappy world in soap operas and movies. Television provides an ideal medium for her to live out her fantasies. She watches TV all through the day and into the late night. She likes heavy rock and probably soul music, and she doesn't read much except for escapist magazines such as *True Story.*

Cathy, the contented housewife. Cathy epitomizes simplicity. Her life is untangled. She is married to a worker in the middle of the socioeconomic scale, and they, along with their several preteen children, live in a small town. She is devoted to her family and faithfully serves them as mother, housewife, and cook. There is a certain tranquility in her life. She enjoys a relaxed pace and avoids anything that might disturb her equilibrium. She doesn't like news or news-type programs on TV, but she does like wholesome, family TV entertainment.

The data from Needham Harper Worldwide that generated the above profiles have also been used to produce relatively rich descriptions for nonprofit marketing campaigns. Novelli has recently reported the following portrait of Fatalist adult males who agreed with the pessimistic statement "cancer is usually fatal," a very difficult segment to influence for cancer communication strategies.

EXHIBIT 4-1 (continued)

> In their dietary habits, Fatalists show concern for what they eat. They try to eat natural foods most of the time and would be willing to pay more for products containing all natural ingredients. They feel that they eat more than they should, including snack foods. The Male Fatalist tends to be on the compulsive side. He is most comfortable when his house is clean; he doesn't like dirt, and has the urge to empty a full ashtray or waste basket whenever he sees one. He feels as though he's under a great deal of pressure most of the time, and wishes he knew how to relax. While he sees himself as a hard worker, the Male Fatalist despairs of getting ahead, no matter how fast his income rises. Part of this may be that he is not very good at saving money. He sees maximum safety, rather than high interest, as more important in investing, and he feels that the stock market is too risky for most families. When he spends his money, the Fatalist likes to pay cash for what he buys. The Fatalist prefers a quiet, secure, routine life, both at home and on the job. Television is his primary form of entertainment, although he's disturbed by the amount of sex on prime time TV nowadays.
>
> This portrait obviously tells a marketer much more about the person to whom he must market than knowing that Fatalists are also:
>
> 1. Less likely to be college graduates
> 2. More likely to be in the lowest income categories
> 3. Less likely to be a professional worker.

SOURCE: Needham Porter Novelli. Reprinted with permission.

EXHIBIT 4-2. The VALS Approach

> The VALS program represents another widely adopted approach to the problem of developing general lifestyle profiles of the U.S. population that can be used to understand behavior in a wide range of contexts. Unlike the Needham Harper Worldwide approach, VALS (which stands for *Values* and *Life-Styles*) is based on a wide range of inputs, not on just an analysis of scale responses to questions about activities, interests, and opinions. The VALS program, which was developed by *SRI*, Palo Alto, divides the population into four major categories and nine lifestyle groups as follows:

Need-Driven	Survivor lifestyle
	Sustainer lifestyle
Outer-Directed	Belonger lifestyle
	Emulator lifestyle
	Achiever lifestyle

EXHIBIT 4-2 (continued)

Inner-Directed $\left\{\begin{array}{l}\text{I-Am-Me lifestyle}\\ \text{Experiential lifestyle}\\ \text{Societally Conscious lifestyle}\end{array}\right.$

Combined Outer- and Inner-Directed $\left\{\text{Integrated lifestyle}\right.$

The VALS model assumes that while at any point in time a household can be categorized in one lifestyle group, over time the household would be expected to move upward within each major category.

The distribution of the nine lifestyles among the U.S. population aged eighteen and over in 1983 was as follows:

Need-Driven	11 percent
Survivors	4
Sustainers	7
Outer-Directed	67
Belongers	38
Emulators	8
Achievers	21
Inner-Directed	20
I-Am-Me's	3
Experientials	5
Societally Conscious	12
Integrated	2
	100

A description of the nine groups follows.

THE NEED-DRIVEN

The Need-Driven are people so limited in resources (especially financial resources) that their lives are driven more by need than by choice. Much evidence shows that they are the furthest removed from the cultural mainstream, are the least aware of the events of our times, and are most inclined to be depressed and withdrawn. The values of the Need-Driven center on survival, safety, and security. Such people tend to be distrustful, dependent, unplanning. Many live unhappy lives focused on the immediate specifics of today, with little sensitivity to the wants of others and little vision of what could be.

The Need-Driven are divided into two lifestyles: Survivors and Sustainers.

Survivors. Survivors are the most disadvantaged in American society by reason of their extreme poverty, low education, old age, and limited access to the channels of upward mobility. They are people oriented to tradition, but marked by despair and unhappiness. Many, now infirm, once lived lifestyles associated with higher levels of the VALS hierarchy. Others are ensnared in the so-called culture of poverty.

Sustainers. Sustainers are a group struggling at the edge of poverty. They are better off and younger than Survivors, and many have not

EXHIBIT 4-2 (continued)

given up hope. Their values are very different from those of Survivors in that Sustainers have advanced from the depression and hopelessness typical of Survivors to express anger at the system they see as repressing them, and they have developed a street-wise determination to get ahead. Many operate in the underground economy.

THE OUTER-DIRECTED

This large and diverse category is named to reflect the central characteristic of the people within it. The Outer-Directed conduct their lives in response to signals—real or fancied—from others. Consumption, activities, attitudes—all are guided by what the Outer-Directed individual thinks others will think. Psychologically, Outer-Direction is a major step forward from the Need-Driven state in that the perspective on life has broadened to include other people, a host of institutions, shared goals, and an array of personal values and options far more complex and diverse than those available to the Need-Driven. In general, the Outer-Directed are the happiest of Americans, being well attuned to the cultural mainstream—indeed, creating much of it.

The VALS typology defines three principal types of Outer-Directed people: Belongers, Emulators, and Achievers.

Belongers.   Belongers constitute the large, solid, comfortable, middle-class group of Americans who are the main stabilizers of society and the preservers and defenders of the moral status quo. Belongers tend to be conservative, conventional, nostalgic, sentimental, puritanical, and conforming. The key drive is to fit in—to belong—and not to stand out. Their world is well posted and well lit, and the road is straight and narrow. Family, church, and tradition loom large. Belongers are people who know what is right, and they adhere to the rules. They are not much interested in sophistication or intellectual affairs. All the evidence suggests that Belongers lead contented, happy lives and are relatively little vexed by the stresses and mercurial events that swirl around them.

In terms of psychological maturity, Belongers are ahead of the Need-Driven in having a much wider range of associations (both personal and institutional), a longer focus for planning their lives, and a less opportunistic pattern of behavior. These are people well integrated with their surroundings.

Emulators.   Emulators live in a wholly different world from that of Belongers. Emulators are trying to burst into the upper levels of the system—to make it big. The object of their emulation is the Achiever lifestyle. They are ambitious, upwardly mobile, status-conscious, macho, competitive. Many see themselves as coming from the other side of the tracks and hence are intensely distrustful, are angry with the way things are, and have little faith that "the system" will give them a fair shake. Emulators tend not to be open in their feelings for fear of alienating those in authority, on whom they depend to get ahead. The Emulator

EXHIBIT 4-2 (continued)

group contains a higher fraction of minorities (24 percent) than any VALS group other than the Need-Driven.

Psychologically, Emulators are a step ahead of Belongers in that they ask more of themselves and the system and have assumed greater personal responsibility for getting ahead, instead of drifting with events as many Belongers do. On the other hand, Emulators seem often to have unrealistic goals. In truth, many are not on the track to becoming Achievers, but they appear not to know it.

Achievers.   Achievers include many leaders in business, the professions, and government. Competent, self-reliant, efficient, Achievers tend to be materialistic, hard-working, oriented to fame and success, and comfort-loving. These are the affluent people who have created the economic system in response to the American dream. As such, they are defenders of the economic status quo. Achievers are among the best adjusted of Americans, being well satisfied with their place in the system. Only 5 percent of Achievers come from minority backgrounds.

Achievers are psychologically more advanced than Emulators in having a wider spectrum of values, in being more open and trusting, and in clearly having brought their ambitions into better alignment with reality. Achievers are supporters of technology and are open to progress, but they resist radical change. After all, they are on top economically, and too radical a change might shake them off!

THE INNER-DIRECTED

People we call the Inner-Directed* contrast with the Outer-Directed in that they conduct their lives primarily in accord with inner values—the needs and desires private to the individual—rather than in accord with values oriented to externals. What is most important to such people is what is "in here" rather than what is "out there." Concern with inner growth is thus a cardinal characteristic. Inner-directed people tend to be self-expressive, individualistic, person-centered, impassioned, diverse, and complex.

It is important to recognize that, in American society today, one can hardly be profoundly Inner-Directed without having also internalized Outer-Directedness through extensive and deep exposure as a child, adolescent, or adult. One implication is that Inner-Directed people tend not to come from Need-Driven or Inner-Directed families, because some measure of satiation with the pleasures of external things seems to be required before a person can believe in or enjoy the less tangible pleasures of Inner-Directedness. The pleasures of the outer world do not necessarily disappear (for the VALS typology is a nested model), but inner needs become more imperative than outer needs. From the psychological standpoint, then, in today's Western culture, Inner-Direction represents an advance over Outer-Direction in that it adds new values to old, thus increasing the range of potential responses and the number of channels available for self-expression. For children raised in strongly

EXHIBIT 4-2 (continued)

inner-directed families, however, the psychological advance would involve the shift from Inner-Direction to Outer-Direction. This would be true, for example, of people raised according to the tenets of the great Inner-Directed Eastern cultures.

VALS has identified three stages of Inner-Directedness: I-Am-Me, Experiential, and Societally Conscious.

I-Am-Me.   I-Am-Me is a short-lived stage of transition from Outer- to Inner-Direction. Values from both stages are much in evidence. Typically, the I-Am-Me person is young and fiercely individualistic, to the point of being narcissistic and exhibitionistic. People at this stage are full of confusion and of emotions they do not understand; hence, they often define themselves better by their actions than by their statements. They tend to be dramatic and impulsive. Like cats, they have whims of iron. Much of their Inner-Direction shows up in great inventiveness, a willingness to try anything once, and an often secret inner exploration that will later crystallize into lifelong pursuits.

Experiential.   As the I-Am-Me's mature psychologically, they become Experientials. At this stage of Inner-Direction, the intense egocentrism of the I-Am-Me has lessened and the person's focus has widened to include other people and many social and human issues. Experientials are people who most want direct experience and vigorous involvement. Life is a light show at one moment and an intense, often mystical inner experience the next. They are attracted to the exotic (such as Oriental religions), to the strange (such as parapsychology), and to the natural (such as organic gardening and home baking). The most Inner-Directed of any VALS group, these people are also probably the most artistic and most passionately involved with others. This is a thoroughly enjoyable stage of life, full of vigorous activity (although less so than the I-Am-Me stage), and marked by a growing concern with intellectual and spiritual matters.

Societally Conscious.   The Societally-Conscious have extended their Inner-Direction beyond the self and others to the society as a whole—in fact, sometimes to the globe or even, philosphically, to the cosmos. A profound sense of societal responsibility leads these people to support such causes as conservation, environmentalism, and consumerism. They tend to be activist, impassioned, and knowledgeable about the world around them. Many are attacted to simple living and the natural; some have taken up lives of voluntary simplicity. Many do volunteer work. The Societally Conscious seek to live frugal lives that conserve, protect, and heal. Inner growth remains a crucial part of life. Consequently, many Societally Conscious people assume a high degree of self-reliance, which extends to holistic health and a sense that they are guided by inner forces.

THE INTEGRATEDS

At the pinnacle of the VALs typology is a small group we call the Integrateds. These rare people have melded the power of Outer-Direction

EXHIBIT 4-2 (continued)

with the sensitivity of Inner-Direction. They are fully mature in a psychological sense—able to see many sides of an issue, able to lead if necessary, and willing to take a secondary role if appropriate. They usually have a deep sense of the fittingness of things. They tend to be self-assured, self-actualizing, self-expressive, keenly aware of issues and trends, and possessed of a world perspective. These highly unusual people are the Lincolns and Jeffersons and Einsteins and Schweitzers and Huxleys and Hammarskjölds of society.

An Empirical Example of the VALS Approach

In a recent study for the Association of College, University, and Community Arts Administrators, the VALS approach was used to offer insight into attendance patterns, preferences, and motives for a sample of 686 individuals divided into the four key VALS groups. The four groups, Achievers, Societally Conscious, Experientials, and Integrateds, were chosen as likely to be prime prospects for professional arts performances.

Some of the key findings of the study are as follows:

> The Societally Conscious are the best market for professional arts not only per capita (attending some mode of the performing arts 5.5 times yearly on average) but in terms of growth in attendance. Although there are 34 million Achievers and only 20 million Societally Conscious, the former outstrip the Societally Conscious as a total market only on performances of music (accounting for 68 million vs. 59 million of the total annual music audience). The two groups are tied in theater attendance (36 million to 37 million) and dance (14 million each).
>
> Reasons for attending the performing arts are diverse. They vary distinctively by VALS type and by frequency of attendance. ("Frequent" means six or more times in the past year for a given performance mode; "infrequent" means one to five times; "never" means not in the past 12 months.) Across the board, the top reasons for attending are to be entertained and to see a particular show, performer, or group. Achievers are drawn especially by external reasons, such as sociability and business. The Societally Conscious are largely inner-oriented; they attend to be moved, to fulfill themselves, etc. Social/celebration aspects rank high with Experientials. Integrateds and Achievers appear to be "users" of the performing arts, rather then enjoyers. There is a hint that they feel they ought to attend but really don't want to.

* The term "inner-directed" was made famous by Riesman, Glazer, and Denney in *The Lonely Crowd* more than thirty years ago; as used here, the expression has a somewhat different meaning.

SOURCE: For more on the VALS approach, see Arnold Mitchell, *The Nine American Lifestyles* (New York: Macmillan, 1983). The material describing the VALS categories and the empirical example is from *The Professional Performing Arts: Attendance Patterns, Preferences and Motives*. Permission granted by Association of College, University, and Community Arts Administrators, Inc., Madison, WI. 1984.

FIGURE 4-7

Family of the Future Contraceptive Point-of-Sale Placard for Cairo Market

FIGURE 4-8

Family of the Future Contraceptive Point-of-Sale Placard for Non-Cairo Markets

2. i the criteria used to evaluate the alternatives (for example, segmenting those who *consider* consequences you offer from those who don't);

3. a_i the pattern of weightings applied to the criteria (for example, segmenting those who give high weight to the set of consequences at which you excel from those who give them low weight);

4. b_{ij} beliefs about consequences of taking particular action alternatives (for example, segmenting those who accurately see the consequences of choosing your alternative from those who have inaccurate perceptions or segmenting those who have more favorable beliefs about a competitive alternative than about yours from those for whom the reverse is true);

5. k the significant others whose views about the behavior might influence behavioral intentions (for example, segmenting those who consider family only from those who consider peers only);

6. MC_{kj} the pattern of motivations to conform to the views of these significant others (for example, segmenting those who say they are heavily influenced by parents from those who are only "somewhat" influenced);

7. NB_{kj} perceptions of the behavioral expectations of specific significant others (for example, segmenting those whose significant others are generally favorably disposed toward your alternative from those whose significant others are negative);

8. W_1/W_2 the relative weight of the person's own attitude versus the perceived views of significant others in affecting behavioral intentions (for example, segmenting those who are inner-directed from those who are other-directed).

BENEFIT SEGMENTATION.   Use of the a_i and b_{ij} measures means that buyers can be segmented according to the particular benefit(s) that they are seeking through the consumption of the offering. Benefits are reflected in the b_{ij} measures and their weights in the a_{ij} measures. Some consumers look for one dominant benefit from the offering and others seek a particular *benefit bundle*.[14] Many markets are made up of three core benefit segments: *quality buyers, service buyers,* and *economy buyers.* Quality buyers seek out the best reputed offering and are not concerned with the cost. A quality seeker in the college market would consider only the elite universities, and a quality seeker in the hospital market would consider only the best hospitals and surgeons. Service buyers look for the best value for the money and expect the service to match the price. A service-seeker would choose a college that provides a good education and social life for the money, regardless of its reputation. Economy buyers are primarily intersted in minimizing their cost and favor the least expensive market offer. An economy-seeker would go to a community college to keep college costs to a minimum. Benefit segmentation, it should be added, works best when people's preferences for benefits are correlated with demographic and media characteristics, making it easier to reach them efficiently.

In addition to general benefits, each product or service should be evaluated for the specific benefits that different buyers might seek. Goodnow found that adults attending the College of DuPage, a large community college in Illinois, fell into five benefit segments: (1) social improvement learners, (2) career learners, (3) leisure learners, (4) submissive learners, and (5) ambivalent learners. She recommended a separate marketing strategy directed at each benefit segment, based on the segment's characteristics. Thus, the leisure learners could be best attracted to noncredit physical education and creative arts programs that meet informally in small groups for three hours on weekday evenings. This segment could be effectively reached by sending an *Extension Bulletin* appealing to their desire for a "night out." Certain programs might be promoted to this group through women's clubs and the suburban newspaper. A separate marketing strategy can be worked out for each of the other segments, based on the benefit sought and associated characteristics.[15]

In a recent application, Bonaguro and Miaoulis developed eight benefit segments for a multiservice family planning agency. These segments are outlined in Table 4-2.

The eight segments were then combined into more manageable subsets. The Firefighters and Desperates were joined into a group that had in common a sense of urgency about health needs. They only seek information and take action in an emergency, at which point they are likely to be agitated, confused, and perhaps irrational. It was decided to ignore the Worriers and Infertile benefit segments because of the agency's limited budget and to group the four remaining original segments as Rationals. This combined group was likely to seek information on their own as a means of improving their families' health and future prospects. Print media, lectures,

Table 4-2

BENEFIT SEGMENTS FOR A FAMILY PLANNING AGENCY

Benefits Sought	*Segment Name*
Immediate solution to a problem (pregnancy, breast lump, etc.), shoulder to lean on	1. Firefighters
Relief from feeling of desperation, financial stability, marital harmony	2. Desperates
Security about good health, relief from worry	3. Worriers
Conception, birth, children	4. Infertiles
Freedom of choice, control, financial stability, marital harmony	5. Married Rationals
Freedom of choice, financial	6. Married—No Children
Pregnancy prevention, financial stability, avoid social stigma	7. Married—With Children
Pregnancy prevention to avoid social stigma, retain independence, financial stability	8. Singles—Without Children

SOURCE: John A. Bonaguro and George Miaoulis, "Marketing: A Tool for Health Education Planning," *Health Education*, January-February 1983, p.9.

pamphlets and posters all with longer messages were emphasized within the strategy destined for this group under the theme: "A brighter future—plan it now."

Note that in this example, the marketer segmented the market by benefits and then decided to concentrate on only those segments where it could have the best impact for its limited resources.

SACRIFICE SEGMENTATION.   In Chapter 3, we noted that consumers are likely to undertake exchanges if the benefits outweigh the costs. And we further noted that in many cases, there is wide appreciation of the *benefits* of a particular action, while it is the *costs* that are the major inhibitors to action. Thus, the National Cancer Institute found that 80 to 85 percent of smokers were aware of the benefits of giving up their habit but that ignorance about methods of quitting and fear of failure were keeping most of them from taking the desired action.

In Chapter 3, we also noted that Bagozzi, in his study of blood donors, found little difference among consumers in the perceived positive consequences that would follow from their behavior. Bagozzi found considerable variation in perceptions of *negative* consequences and learned that they were good predictors of behavioral intentions. These results give rise to the speculation that some markets could be usefully segmented in terms of the relative weight individuals attach to the various *barriers* to action rather than to the benefits. Thus, in the blood donation case, consumers could be subdivided into those who are highly sensitive to: physiological risks—infections, AIDS, physical pain; social risks—not being "brave" in the eyes of others; and psychological fears—fears of needles, blood, and "hospitals."

STAGES OF BUYER READINESS.   At any point people are in various stages of readiness about buying the product. Some members of the potential market are *unaware* of the product; some are *aware;* some are *informed;* some are *interested;* some are *desirous;* and some *intend to buy.* The distribution of people over stages of readiness makes a big difference in designing the marketing program. Suppose a health agency wants to attract women to take an annual Pap test to detect cervical cancer. At the beginning, most of the potential market is unaware of the concept (see Figure 4-9A). The marketing effort should go into high-reach advertising and publicity using a simple message. If successful, more of the market will be aware of the Pap test but will need more knowledge (see Figure 4-9B). After knowledge is built up, the advertising should be changed to dramatize the benefits of taking an annual examination and the risks of not taking it, so as to move more people into a stage of desire (see Figure 4-9C). Facilities should also be readied for handling the large number of women who may be motivated to take the examination. In general, the marketing program must be adjusted to the changing distribution of buyer readiness.

FIGURE 4-9

Stages of Market Readiness

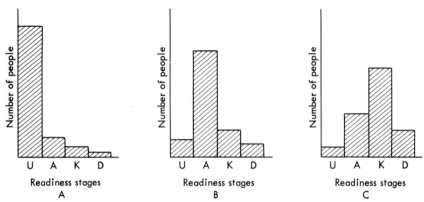

Note: U = unaware; A = aware only; K = knowledgeable; D = desirous.

<small>BASES FOR SEGMENTING ORGANIZATIONAL MARKETS</small>

Public and nonprofit organizations not only market to individual consumers but also have many occasions to market to organizations. A small art museum wants to identify appropriate foundations to solicit for financial support. A state hospital association wants to motivate its local chapters to improve their member services. A local hospital wants to convince adjacent hospitals to use its blood bank services. In all these cases, the organization is seeking to get other organizations to "buy" something. Here we want to examine how a market of organizations can be segmented.

We will use the example of a small art museum trying to identify appropriate foundations for support. Here are some of the major ways to segment organizations as applied to foundations:

1. *Organization size.* Foundations can be divided into large, medium, and small foundations. The small museum could decide that its best chances for a grant lay with small foundations rather than with large or medium-sized ones.
2. *Geographical location.* Foundations can be divided as to whether they are in the same city as the museum, in the same state, or far away. The small museum would decide to focus on the local foundations because they would have stronger contacts with these foundations.
3. *Interest profile.* Foundations have different interest profiles. The museum could identify those foundations that have given the most support to the arts.
4. *Resource level.* Foundations differ in the amount of resources they have and are willing to devote to particular programs. The museum would only want to approach foundations that can give the size grant it seeks.
5. *Buying criteria.* Foundations differ in the qualities they look for in grant

applications. Some foundations emphasize applicants' neediness, others the quality of their management, and still others the amount of social benefit that would be produced. The museum should focus on those foundations whose buying criteria match the museum's strengths.

6. *Buying process.* Foundations differ in how much documentation they require and in the length of their review process. The museum may want to work only with foundations that require little documentation and announce awards early.

TARGET MARKETING

Market segmentation reveals the market segment opportunities facing the organization. At this point, as indicated in the example of the family planning agency, the organization has to decide between three broad market selection strategies. They are shown in Figure 4-10.

1. *Undifferentiated marketing.* The organization can decide to go after the whole market with one offer and marketing mix, trying to attract as many consumers as possible (this is another name for mass marketing).
2. *Differentiated marketing.* The organization can decide to go after several market segments, developing an effective offer and marketing mix for each.
3. *Concentrated marketing.* The organization can decide to go after one market segment and develop the ideal offer and marketing mix.

Here we will describe the logic and merits of each of these strategies.

UNDIFFERENTIATED MARKETING

In undifferentiated marketing,[16] the organization chooses not to recognize the different market segments making up the market. It treats the market as an aggregate, focusing on what is common in the needs of consumers rather than on what is different. It tries to design an offer and a marketing program that appeal to the broadest number of buyers. It would be exemplified by a church that runs only one religious service for everyone, a politician who gives the same speech to everyone, and a family planning organization that tries to promote the same birth control method for everyone.

Undifferentiated marketing is typically defended on the grounds of cost economies. It is "the marketing counterpart to standardization and mass production in manufacturing.[17] Product costs, research costs, media costs, and training costs are all kept low through promoting only one product. The lower cost, however, is accompanied by reduced consumer satisfaction through failure of the organization to meet individually varying needs. Competitors have an incentive to reach and serve the neglected segments, and become strongly entrenched in these segments.

FIGURE 4-10

Three Alternative Market Selection Stategies

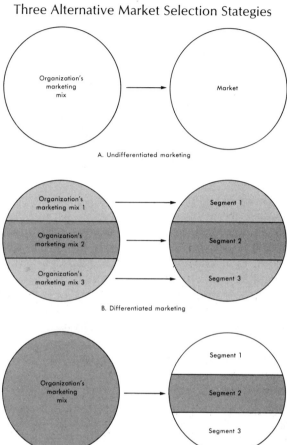

A. Undifferentiated marketing

B. Differentiated marketing

C. Concentrated marketing

DIFFERENTIATED MARKETING

Under differentiated marketing, an organization decides to operate in two or more segments of the market but designs separate offerings and/or marketing programs for each. By offering product and marketing variations, it hopes to attain higher sales and a deeper position within each market segment. It hopes that a deep position in several segments will strengthen the customers' overall identification of the organization with the offer field. Furthermore, it hopes for greater loyalty and repeat purchasing, because the organization's offerings have been bent to the customer's desire rather than the other way around.

The net effect of differentiated marketing is to create more total sales for the organization than undifferentiated marketing. However, it also tends to create higher costs of doing business. The organization has to spend more in offer management, marketing research, communication materials, advertising, and sales training. Since differentiated marketing leads to higher sales and higher costs, nothing can be said in advance about the optimality of this strategy. Some organizations push differentiated marketing too far in that they run more segmented programs than are economically feasible; some should be pruned. The majority of public and nonprofit organizations, however, probably err in not pushing differentiated marketing far enough in the light of the varying needs of their consumers.

CONCENTRATED MARKETING

Concentrated marketing occurs when an organization decides to divide the market into meaningful segments and devote its major marketing effort to one segment. Instead of spreading itself thin in many parts of the market, it concentrates on serving a particular market segment well. Through concentrated marketing the organization usually achieves a strong following and standing in a particular market segment. It enjoys greater knowledge of the market segment's needs and behavior and it also achieves operating economies through specialization in production, distribution, and promotion. This type of marketing is done, for example, by a private museum that decides to concentrate only on African art; or an environmental group that concentrates only on the problem of noise pollution; or a private foundation that awards grants only to transportation researchers.

Concentrated marketing does involve higher than normal risk, in that the market may suddenly decline or disappear. The National Foundation for Infantile Paralysis almost folded when the Salk vaccine was developed. Fortunately, the National Foundation was able to turn its huge fundraising apparatus over to another medical cause.

CHOOSING AMONG MARKET SELECTION STRATEGIES

The actual choice of a marketing strategy depends on specific factors facing the organization. If the organizaiton has *limited resources,* it will probably choose concentrated marketing because it does not have enough resources to relate to the whole market and/or to tailor special services for each segment. If the market is fairly *homogeneous* in its needs and desires, the organization will probably choose undifferentiated marketing because little would be gained by differentiated offerings. If the organization aspires to be a leader in several segments of the market, it will choose differentiated marketing. If *competitors* have already established dominance in all but a few segments of the market, the organization might try to concentrate its marketing in one of the remaining segments. Many organizations start out with a strategy of undifferentiated or concentrated marketing and if they are successful, evolve into a strategy of differentiated marketing.

If the organization elects to use a concentrated or differentiated marketing strategy, it has to evaluate carefully the best segment(s) to serve. The best way to do this is to apply the General Electric strategic business planning grid discussed in Chapter 5. Each segment should be rated on its market attractiveness and the organization's strengths. The organization should focus on market segments that have intrinsic attractiveness and that it has a differential advantage in serving.

SUMMARY

In most markets, target consumers are treated as similar. On the other hand, marketing strategies are more effective and efficient if customers are not treated as all alike. The problems facing the marketing manager, then, are several. First, bases for segmenting the market must be determined. Then, profiles of resulting segments must be identified and their attractiveness assessed. Concern with strategic issues then turns to questions of how to target and develop appropriate marketing mixes for some or all of the identified segments.

Markets are segmented to help management make decisions about the quality, quantity, and timing of marketing efforts. A scheme for segmenting markets for these purposes is ideal if the segments are mutually exclusive, exhaustive, measurable, accessible, substantial, and, finally, if the segments differ from each other in responsiveness to marketing approaches.

Variables that might be used for segmentation can be grouped into those that are objective and those that are inferred. They can also differ to the extent that they are general and apply across many categories or are specific and only apply to one or two. Examples of objective general measures are simple measures of socioeconomic status and more complex measures like social class and stages in the family life cycle. Specific objective measures include the nature of the exchange occasion, user status, usage rate, and purchase loyalty. The most commonly used inferred general measures are personality and lifestyles/psychographics. The Needham Harper Worldwide and VALS lifestyle approaches are now seeing increasing use among nonprofits. The last category, specific inferred measures, includes such indicators as benefits sought and stage of buyer readiness.

Once markets have been segmented, then the marketer must decide whether to pursue them with an undifferentiated, differentiated, or concentrated strategy. Choices among these alternatives depend on market conditions and the organization's own goals and resources. In particular, the organization should seek to focus on the segments where it has a differential advantage.

QUESTIONS

1. Family planning programs in developing countries are frequently mandated to not discriminate against certain types of customers. Does this mean they cannot segment? How would you segment the family planning market, and to which segments would you give priority under a limited budget? Justify your recommendation to a suspicious government minister.

2. How should you segment the market for weight control programs to identify overweight groups that are more ready to change their present behavioral patterns?

3. What behaviors could a museum use to segment its market? Is loyalty to a museum better conceived as a *behavioral* or an *attitudinal* phenomenon?

4. Outline a set of communications themes for a nonprofit hospital oriented to each of the nine VALS types.

5. A major market for the Colorado ski industry is young singles who like difficult skiing and an exciting after-ski lifestyle. Colorado would also like to attract more older skiers and more families, who are often turned off by the prospect of finding too many "swinging singles" where they have chosen to ski. How can Colorado ski marketers cope with this problem when developing their marketing strategy?

NOTES

1. A basic review of the segmentation literature is found in Ronald E. Frank, William F. Massy, and Yoram Wind, *Market Segmentation* (Englewood Cliffs, N.J.: Prentice-Hall, 1972). See also Yoram Wind, "Issues and Advances in Segmentation Research," *Journal of Marketing Research,* August 1978, pp. 317–37.

2. *Marginal response* is the change in response to a unit change in a control variable such as price or advertising expenditure.

3. Frank, Massy, and Wind, *Market Segmentation.*

4. Stephen J. Miller, "Source of Income is a Market Descriptor," *Journal of Marketing Research,* February 1978, pp. 129–31.

5. See John E. Robbins and Stephanie S. Robbins, "Segmentation for 'Fine Arts' Marketing: Is King Tut Classless as well as Ageless?" in Neil Beckwith, Michael Houston, Robert Mittelstaedt, Kent B. Monroe and Scott Ward, eds., *1979 Educator's Conference Proceedings* (Chicago: American Marketing Association, 1979), pp. 479–84.

6. For a more recent approach, see Patrick E. Murphy and William Staples, "A Modernized Family Life Cycle," *Journal of Consumer Research,* June 1979, pp. 12–22.

7. Leland L. Beik and Scott M. Smith, "Practical Segmentation: A Fund Raising Example," Working Paper No. 68, College of Business Administration, Pennsylvania State University, February 1978.

8. Their analysis also included a second function using five variables to separate those who are not large medical givers into those who were large and small donors to all charities.

9. Christopher H. Lovelock, "A Market Segmentation Approach to Transit Planning, Modeling, and Management," *Proceedings, Sixteenth Annual Meeting Transportation Research Forum* (1975).

10. Richard J. Semenik and Clifford E. Young, "Market Segmentation in Arts Organizations," in Beckwith, Houston, Mittelstaedt, Monroe and Ward, eds. *1979 Educators' Conference*, pp. 474–78.

11. Shirley Young, "The Dynamics of Measuring Unchange," in Russell Haley, ed., *Attitude Research in Transition* (Chicago: American Marketing Association, 1972), p. 62.

12. Russell Ackoff and James R. Emshoff, "Advertising Research at Anheuser-Busch (1968–74)," *Sloan Management Review*, Spring 1975, pp. 1–15.

13. Joel B. Cohen, "An Interpersonal Orientation to the Study of Consumer Behavior," *Journal of Marketing Research*, August 1967, pp. 270–78.

14. See Paul E. Green, Yoram Wind, and Arun K. Jain, "Benefit Bundle Analysis," *Journal of Advertising Research*, April 1972, pp. 31–36.

15. See Wilma Elizabeth Goodnow, "Benefit Segmentation: A Technique for Developing Program and Promotional Strategies for Adults in a Community College," unpublished Ph.D. disseration, Northern Illinois University, DeKalb, Illinois, May 1980.

16. See Wendell R. Smith, "Product Differentiation and Market Segmentation," *Business Horizons*, Fall 1961, pp. 65–72.

17. Smith, "Product Differentiation."

CHAPTER 5

The Strategic Marketing Planning Process

The Toledo Hospital is a 1,000-bed hospital competing with nine other major institutions for the 350,000 potential patients in the Toledo Metropolitan area. In 1984, the hospital became aware of a critical need to develop a new strategic plan for its emergency room facilities. As with any hospital, the emergency room (ER) serves as a major source of both revenue and new patients. But in many markets, new competition has forced traditional hospitals to compete harder for ER business. Toledo Hospital, in particular, was seriously concerned that between 1980 and 1984 its emergency room census had fallen from 51,000 to 43,000.

John Horns, marketing director at the hospital, began the strategic planning process by conducting a detailed consumer research study and an in-house assessment of Toledo Hospital's strengths and weaknesses. The consumer research revealed a number of opportunities and threats in the marketplace. First, it was clear that Toledo Hospital was feeling major pressures from newly opened freestanding clinics that provided low-cost routine medical care in attractive, convenient locations. The study also revealed that the Toledo emergency room facility had a very negative image among its target audience and was losing elderly and pediatric patients. Respondents to the study said that it was hard to find the emergency room and then to find a parking place. To be served, patients had to fill out a lot of paperwork and prepay their bill. Waiting times were long and patients often became very anxious. Prices in the ER were seen to be higher than at the freestanding clinics. In addition, elderly patients reported distrust of the ER—they feared that, if they

156

came in, they would risk being admitted to the hospital itself and not being able to go back home. Finally, research within the hospital showed that pediatricians were not actively involved in ER care and, indeed, saw it as potential competition.

On the basis of this extensive situation analysis, Horns put in place a comprehensive strategic plan designed to tackle the overall ER problem and to address specifically the geriatric and pediatric markets. Among the steps aimed at all patients were the following:

- Signs were improved directing patients to the ER.
- A security guard was assigned to meet patients at the curb, escort them into the ER, and park their cars.
- The ER itself was completely renovated.
- Patients coming into the ER were assigned a nurse, who stayed with them throughout their ER treatment. These nurses and other ER employees were given "guest relations" training.
- Patients with serious problems were separated immediately from those who had only minor concerns. The latter were directed to an "Express Care" section of the facility.
- A "Ready Card" was designed for patients, which, when inserted into the ER computer system, yielded detailed data on the patient's medical history and the name of his or her physician.
- Extensive print, radio, billboard, television, and direct mail campaigns were carried out. The last-mentioned targeted a screened list of 100,000 credit-worthy households in selected zip code areas and promoted the Toledo Hospital Ready Card.

For the elderly, Toledo Hospital developed a Ready Line phone service. For a fee, elderly customers could dial one number and be connected with a physician at the ER. The physician could dispense advice, send an ambulance if needed, or trace a call if the patient could not communicate for some reason. Trust among the elderly grew as a result of this service, and elderly patients reported that visits to the emergency room less often caused high anxiety about how they would be treated.

In dealing strategically with the pediatric problem, Toledo Hospital focused more on the physicians. An educational program was developed whereby school classes are invited for a tour of the hospital under the leadership of "Healthy Bear." More importantly, nineteen pediatricians were recruited to become part of the emergency room rotation. Horns found that Toledo pediatricians came to recommend the emergency room to their patients as a place to go for after-hours problems.

The results of Horns's strategic plan were already impressive by early 1985. The ER census had rebounded to 51,000, and the incremental income his program had generated easily exceeded the costs of the various marketing and promotion efforts. Horns, to his credit, did not see the results as the end of the strategic planning process. Toledo Hospital continued to monitor the program's results and expected to fine-tune a number of components in the ensuing months.

SOURCE: Material for this example drawn from "Toledo Hospital Targets ER," *Healthcare Marketing Report,* February 1986, pp. 1, 3, 4, and 12.

Once an organization believes it has understood and internalized a customer-centered orientation up and down its ranks, the next step is to bring the organization up to the frontier of the best in current marketing practice. At this point, we are not talking about the *content* of marketing practice—how to determine a specific marketing position, develop an array of detailed offerings, establish prices, design appropriate distribution channels, or create elaborate promotion programs. These are details that will be reformulated each year within what must be a systematic approach to all marketing strategy problems. The approach we shall advocate to guide these detailed decisions is what we call the *Strategic Marketing Planning Process* (SMPP). Just as "customer-centeredness" is the advocated way of *thinking* about marketing, SMPP is the advocated way of *doing* marketing. It is an approach that can apply equally well to the question of what to do over the next ten years and, in highly simplified form, what to do tomorrow.

The SMPP is a set of steps one must take to decide what to do in any given marketing situation. It is based on the assumption that marketing is a function that must operate within two environments. First, it operates within an organization. Therefore, what marketers do in the future must necessarily fit with what the organization as a whole wishes to do. As we shall see, this does *not* mean that the marketer must take the organization's goals and plans as given and slavishly adapt to them. On the contrary, assuming that the organization is run *openly* and the marketing function is properly located at the very highest level of the organization hierarchy, there should be continual interaction between marketing planning and organization planning. Marketers must tell organizational planners what can and cannot be accomplished in the way of developed or changing consumer markets. At the same time, organizational planners must tell marketers where and how and what they must do to meet the organization's overall needs and plans.

Second, marketers cannot plan willy-nilly to do anything they want (say, meet an observed customer need) without taking very serious account of the organization's *abilities* to take advantage of the opportunity the external world presents. It is essential, then, that any planning process systematically consider organization strengths and weaknesses before it results in suggestions for new ventures, particularly those that take the organization far afield from its present activities.

Marketing also must operate in an external world. We saw in Chapter 2 that marketing plans must adapt to target consumer markets as the organization finds them and as they will evolve in the future. But they must also adapt to expected competitors and to changes in the technological, economic, political, and social environments in which both the organization and its competitors function.

Management has to pay attention to *market evolution* and *strategic fit.* All markets undergo evolutionary development marked by changing customer needs, technologies, competitors, channels, and laws. The organization should be looking out of a *strategic window* watching these changes and assessing the requirements for continued success in each market. The fit between the requirements of a particular market and the organization's competencies is at an optimum for only a limited period. During this period, the strategic window is open, and the organization should be investing in that market. In some subsequent period the organization will find that the evolutionary path of that market is such that the organization can no longer serve it effectively and efficiently. It should then consider disinvesting and shifting its resources to areas of growing opportunity.

The distinction between external and internal environments permits us to define strategic marketing planning as follows:

Strategic planning is the managerial process of developing and maintaining a strategic fit between the organization's goals and resources and its changing market opportunities.

The *strategic marketing planning process* includes the following steps:

1. Determine organization-wide objectives, mission, and specific goals to which marketing strategies must contribute.

2. Assess external environmental threats and opportunities that can be addressed by marketing in the interest of achieving greater organizational success.

3. Evaluate present and potential organization resources and skills to take advantage of the opportunity or repel the threat identified in the external environmental analysis.

4. Determine the marketing mission, objectives, and specific goals for the relevant planning period.

5. Formulate the core marketing strategy to achieve the specified goals.

6. Put in place the necessary organizational structure and systems within the marketing function to ensure proper implementation of the designed strategy.

7. Establish detailed programs and tactics to carry out the core strategy for the planning period, including a timetable of activities and assignment of specific responsibilities.

8. Establish benchmarks to measure interim and final achievements of the program.

9. Implement the planned program.

10. Measure performance and adjust the core strategy, tactical details, or both as needed.

The entire process is illustrated in Figure 5-1.

We shall discuss the first five steps of the strategic marketing planning process in this chapter. The remaining five steps, such as program tactics (pricing, channel design, etc.), marketing research and forecasting, organizational design, and program evaluation and control, will be discussed in detail in later chapters.

DETERMINING ORGANIZATION-LEVEL MISSIONS, OBJECTIVES, AND GOALS

A marketing program is not developed in a vacuum. It must adjust to both internal and external realities. The principal internal reality is where the organization as a whole wishes to go. If the organization is mature and well managed, it should have already completed an organization-wide strategic planning process like that outlined in Figure 5-1. That is, before marketing planning should begin, the organization's top-level managers (including the marketing manager) and its advisory boards should ideally have:

1. Determined the organization-level *long-term* mission, objectives, and goals.

2. Assessed the organization's likely future external environment (of which the *marketing* environment is a subset).

3. Assessed the organization's present and potential strengths and weaknesses (of which marketing strengths and weaknesses are a subset).

In this sense, strategic marketing planning can be seen as a *nested activity,* as suggested in Figure 5-2. That is, marketing strategic planning can—and should—be nested within organization-level strategic planning. Further, if the organization is large enough, the same kind of strategic planning ought to be carried out by subunits *within* the marketing function. In general, the further down the planning hierarchy, the more detailed the planning and the shorter the planning horizons.

Plan formulation involves the organization in determining an appropriate mission, objectives, and goals for the current or expected environment. The three terms are distinguished below:

- *Mission:* the basic purpose of an organization, that is, what it is trying to accomplish.

FIGURE 5-1

Strategic Marketing Planning Process

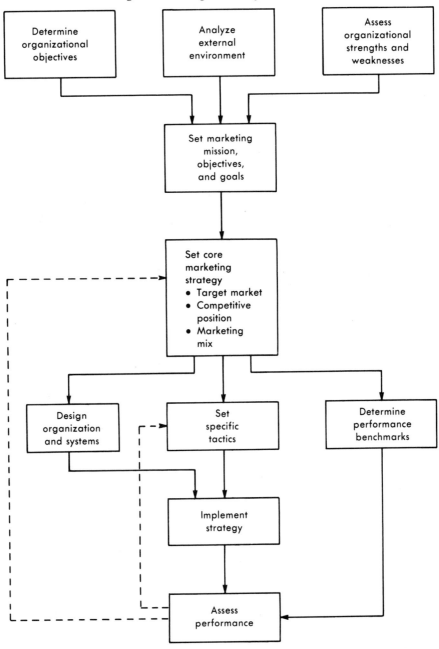

FIGURE 5-2

Nested Strategic Planning

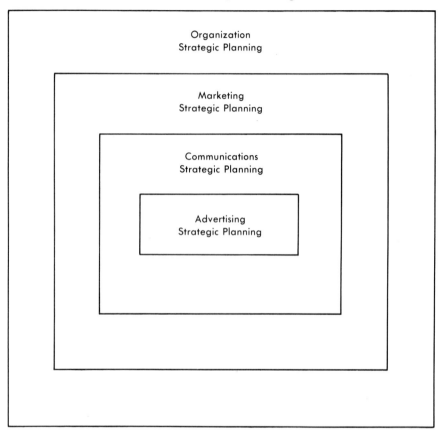

- *Objective:* a major variable that the organization will emphasize, such as market share, profitability, reputation.
- *Goal:* an objective of the organization that is made specific with respect to magnitude, time, and who is responsible.

We examine these concepts in more detail below.

MISSION

Every organization starts with a mission. In fact, an organization can be defined as a *human collectivity that is structured to perform a specific mission through the use of largely rational means.* Its specific mission is usually clear at the beginning. Thus, the original mission of the Northminster Presbyterian Church was to deepen religious faith among believers through offering religious training and worship. Over time, this church added further services to meet other needs of its members, until it is no longer easy to distinguish between the church's core mission and its peripheral missions. Is the church basically a religious center, a social center, or a mental health center? The church's growing responsiveness to other needs is changing its character and its membership composition.

Each organization that wants to be responsive must answer two questions: *responsive to whom and to what?* An organization cannot serve everyone and every need. If it tried to serve everyone, it would serve no one very well. From time to time, each organization must reexamine its mission.

Years ago, Peter Drucker pointed out that organizations need to answer the following questions: *What is our business? Who is the customer? What is value to the customer? What will our business be? What should our business be?*[1] Although the first question "What is our business?" sounds simple, it is really the most profound question an organization can ask. A church should not define its business by listing the particular services it offers. Consistent with a customer-centered philosophy, it should identify the underlying need that it is trying to serve. The church might decide that it is in the "feeling good" business, that is, helping people feel better about themselves and the world. Or it might decide that it is in the "hope" business, that is, helping people feel that they will eventually experience joy and fulfillment, either in this life or in the next. Ultimately, a church has to decide what its mission is so as not to lose sight and confuse it with a lot of intermediate goals and services that it might provide.

Clarifying the organization's mission is a soul-searching and time-consuming process. Different members will have different views of what the organization is about and should be about. One organization held numerous meetings over a two-year period before membership consensus developed on the real mission of the organization.

A helpful approach to defining mission is to establish the organization's scope along three dimensions. The first is *consumer groups,* namely, *who* is to be served and satisfied. The second is *consumer needs,* namely, *what* is to be satisfied. The third is *technologies,* namely, *how* consumer needs are to be satisfied. For example, consider a church that serves mainly senior citizens who only want a simple worship service every Sunday. This church's mission scope is represented by the small cube in Figure 5-3A. Now consider the mission of Northminster Presbyterian Church, which is approximately that shown in Figure 5-3B. This church serves almost all age groups, meets at least four strong needs, and provides services through the chapel, meeting rooms, classes, and outings.

Still other churches will have a different mission scope. A campus church will serve primarily students of a particular religious faith and meet a wide variety of needs (for belief, sociability, counseling, and so on) within the four walls of a religious house. On the other hand, Robert Schuller's

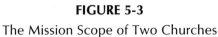

FIGURE 5-3

The Mission Scope of Two Churches

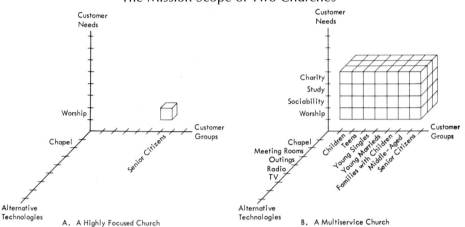

church, Garden Grove Community Church (Garden Grove, Calif.) meets a wide variety of needs of 7,000 members and serves them through such modern technologies as radio, television, and cassettes, in addition to its $16 million "Crystal Cathedral."[2]

An organization should strive for a mission that is *feasible, motivating,* and *distinctive.* In terms of being feasible, the organization should avoid a "mission impossible." Pastor Robert Schuller wants his church to grow from 7,000 members to 25,000 members and may discover this to be infeasible. His followers must believe in the feasibility of this goal if they are to lend their support. An institution should always reach high, but not so high as to produce incredulity in its publics.

The mission should also be motivating. Those working for the organization should feel they are worthwhile members of a worthwhile organization. A church whose mission includes "helping the poor" is likely to inspire more support than one whose mission is "meeting the social, cultural, and athletic needs of its current members." The mission should be something that enriches people's lives.

A mission works better when it is distinctive. If all churches resembled each other, there would be little basis for pride in one's particular church. People take pride in belonging to an institution that "does it differently" or "does it better." By cultivating a distinctive mission and personality, an organization stands out more and attracts a more loyal group of members.

OBJECTIVES

The mission of an institution suggests more about where that institution is coming from than where it is going to. It describes what the institution is about rather than the specific objectives and goals it will pursue in the coming period. Each institution has to develop major objectives and goals for the coming period separate from but consistent with its mission statement.

For every type of institution, there is always a potential set of relevant objectives, and the institution's task is to make a choice among them. For example, the objectives of interest to a college are: increased national reputation, improved classroom teaching, higher enrollment, higher quality students, increased efficiency, larger endowment, improved student social life, improved physical plant, lower operating deficit, and so on. A college cannot successfully pursue all of these objectives simultaneously because of a limited budget and because some of them are incompatible, such as increased cost efficiency and improved classroom teaching. In any given year, therefore, institutions will choose to emphasize certain objectives and either ignore others or treat them as constraints. For example, if Beloit College's enrollment continues to fall, Beloit will make increased enrollment a paramount objective subject to not letting student quality fall below a certain level. Thus, an institution's major objectives can vary from year to year depending on the administration's perception of the major problems that the institution must address at that time.

GOALS

The chosen objectives must be restated in an operational and measurable form called *goals*. The objective "increased enrollment" must be turned into a goal, such as "a 15 percent enrollment increase in next year's fall class." A goal statement permits the institution to think about the planning, programming, and control aspects of pursuing that objective. A number of questions may arise: Is a 15 percent enrollment increase feasible? What strategy would be used? What resources would it take? What activities would have to be carried out? Who would be responsible and accountable? All of these critical questions must be answered when deciding whether to adopt a proposed goal.

Typically, the institution will be evaluating a large set of potential goals at the same time and examining their consistency. The institution may discover that it cannot simultaneously achieve "a 15 percent enrollment increase," "a 10 percent increase in student quality," and a "12 percent tuition increase" at the same time. In this case, the executive committe may make adjustments in the target levels or target dates or drop certain goals altogether in order to arrive at a meaningful and achievable set of goals. Once the set of goals are agreed upon in the goal formulation stage, the organization is ready to move on to the detailed work of strategy formulation.[3]

The issue of determining organizational goals can be broken into two distinct steps: (1) determining what the current goals are, and (2) determining what the goals should be. Sometimes the task of determining present goals is straightforward because they are written down, widely disseminated, and most importantly, understood by everyone as meaning the same thing. But frequently the image of the current goals differs from person to person and group to group in the organization. The president of a college may see the primary goals as upgrading the quality of the student body; the vice-president for admissions may see the primary goal as increasing the size of the student body; and the vice-president for finance may see the primary goal as increasing the number of nonscholarship students in relation to scholarship students. The faculty as a whole may pursue the goal of a reduced teaching load to permit more time for research, whereas the administration may adopt the goal of an increased teaching load to reduce the cost of education. These differences reflect the fact that the organization is really a coalition of several groups, each giving and seeking different things from the organization. On the other hand, in some organizations differences in goals may signal a basic confusion that really ought to be corrected before planning proceeds much further.

Another disconcerting problem occurs when the marketing manager discovers that what the organization *says* its goals are and what they *actually* are constitute two very different things. In the late 1960s a major consumer goods marketer became aware that blacks and Hispanics provided the firm with sales volume well in excess of their share of the total U.S. population. However, members of these minorities felt that the organization was not reciprocating by either giving an adequate share of its advertising and public relations business to minority firms or hiring and promoting more members of the minority within the firm.[4]

After a particularly bitter confrontation, the organization agreed to change its priorities. It made increased employment and upgrading of minority staff a central corporate objective and began to seek more outside minority consultants. After three years of operation, however, the program was found to be languishing well behind its stated objectives. The reasons for the diminished activity were clear. Many local managers had conscientiously tried to meet what they believed were management's clearly expressed social goals. The steps they took, however, were internally costly. As a consequence, their year-end operating profits suffered. And, when they were called by top management to account for this reduced profitability, they quite naturally pointed to the many steps they had taken to seek out, train, and promote minority workers as management had directed them. Management's response was, in effect, "That's admirable. We are pleased that you are taking these important social initiatives. But we do notice that your bottom line has suffered . . . " Very soon these managers learned that the organization's *real* goals were not what management said they were: the real goals were what management *rewarded*.

There are two implications of this kind of experience. First, marketing managers must be aware that many organizations will, in practice, turn out to be schizophrenic in their goal-setting, speaking and acting in different ways. Sometimes this is intentional. It is not so important to the marketing manager to know the true explanation, only that he or she be able to read the proper signals and either respond to what management *really* wants or, if the marketing manager believes management is misguided in what it is doing, try to bring the firm's real goals more in line with stated goals.

The other implication of this company's experience is for the marketing manager's own goal-setting. The manager must be absolutely certain to understand what it is that is *really* being rewarded. What is rewarded will be *de facto* market goals. The manager may choose to *say* something else for public consumption. But it is crucial that the manager *act* in ways that will obtain the performance the department truly wants. The manager should not, for example, speak constantly about bottom-line profitability but reward those whose market share has grown the most if the real goal is profitability, not market share.

ANALYZING EXTERNAL THREATS AND OPPORTUNITIES

The external environment in which an organization operates is complex and constantly changing. The environment consists of four components:

1. The *public environment,* consisting of groups and organizations that take an interest in the activities of the focal organization. The public environment consists of local publics, activist publics, the general public, media publics, and regulatory agencies whose actions can affect the welfare of the focal organization.
2. The *competitive environment,* consisting of groups and organizations that compete for attention and loyalty from the audiences of the focal organization. The competitive environment includes desire competitors, generic competitors, form competitors, and enterprise competitors.
3. The *macroenvironment,* consisting of large-scale fundamental forces that shape opportunities and pose threats to the focal organization. The main macroenvironmental forces that have to be watched are the demographic, economic, technological, political, and social forces. These forces largely represent "uncontrollables" in the organization's situation to which it has to adapt.
4. The *market environment,* consisting of the groups and other organizations that the focal organization directly works with to accomplish its mission. The main groups in the market environment are the clients, marketing intermediaries, suppliers, and supporters. The focal organization must monitor trends and changes in the needs, perceptions, preferences, and dissatisfactions of these key groups.

We shall consider each of these environmental components in turn.

THE PUBLIC ENVIRONMENT

When marketing managers turn to examining the external environment, they realize that it contains several publics, and the organization has

FIGURE 5-4

The University and Its Publics

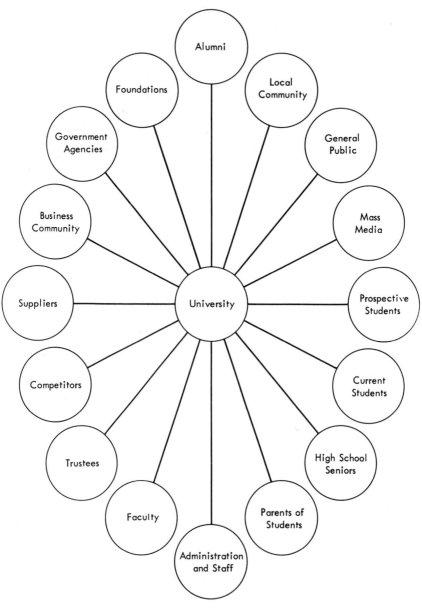

to develop a strategic posture with respect to most or all of them. We define a public in the following way:

A **public** is a distinct group of people, organizations, or both whose actual or potential needs must in some sense by served.

It is fairly easy to identify the key publics that surround a particular organization. Consider a university. Figure 5-4 shows sixteen major publics with which a university deals and whose needs it must consider. This calls for strategic planning.

Not all publics are equally active or important to an organization. Publics come about because the organization's activities and policies can draw support or criticism from outside groups. A *welcome public* is a public that likes the organization and whose support the organization welcomes. A *sought public* is a public whose support the organization wants but which is currently indifferent or negative toward that organization. An *unwelcome public* is a public that is negatively disposed toward the organization and that is trying to impose constraints, pressures, or controls on the organization.

Publics can also be classified by their functional relation to the organization. Figure 5-5 presents such a classification. An organization is viewed as a resource-conversion machine in which certain *input publics* supply resources that are converted by *internal publics* into useful goods and services that are carried by *intermediary publics* to designated *consuming publics*. Here we will look at the various publics more closely.

Input Publics.   Input publics mainly supply original resources and constraints to the organization, and as such consist of donors, suppliers, and regulatory publics.

DONORS.   Donors are those publics who make gifts of money and other assets to the organization. Thus a university's donors consist of alumni, friends of the university, foundations, corporations, and govern-

FIGURE 5-5

The Main Publics of an Organization

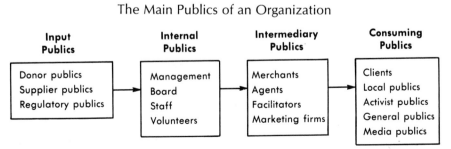

Input Publics	Internal Publics	Intermediary Publics	Consuming Publics
Donor publics Supplier publics Regulatory publics	Management Board Staff Volunteers	Merchants Agents Facilitators Marketing firms	Clients Local publics Activist publics General publics Media publics

ment organizations. Each university runs a development office consisting of a staff of professional fund-raisers. This staff develops a philosophy of fund-raising and specific proposals that might excite possible donors. It tries to match its financial needs with the appropriate donor groups. It tries to build value in the eyes of its donors so that they can feel pride and other satisfactions from their association with the institution.

SUPPLIERS.   Suppliers are those organizations that sell needed goods and services to the focal organization. Nonprofit organizations often try to obtain price concessions or even free donations of goods and services but don't often succeed. In recent times, supply shortages and the rapidly rising cost of supplies have made skillful supply planning and purchasing more important than ever.

REGULATORY ORGANIZATIONS.   The third input public consists of regulatory organizations that impose rules of conduct. The regulatory publics of a university include federal, state, and local government agencies, trade unions, and various academic accreditation associations. The focal organization must keep in close contact with these regulatory organizations and be ready to argue against regulations that will harm their ability to create value for their clients.

Internal Publics.   The various inputs are managed by the organization's internal publics to accomplish the organization's mission. The internal publics consist of up to four groups: management, a board of directors, staff, and volunteers. (Public agencies are an exception and normally lack volunteers, and their "board of directors" may be a congressional committee.) We have already considered the requirement that marketing managers be responsive to those above them in the organization hierarchy, that is, top management and the board of directors. Marketing managers must also be responsive to those below them in the organization.

STAFF.   The staff consists of the various employees who work on a paid basis. This would include middle management, secretaries, workmen, telephone operators, and so on. The staff would also include the skilled practitioners who deliver the organization's services to its consumers, such as the hospital's nurses, the college's professors, the police department's police officers, and the social agency's social workers.

Management faces the normal problems of building an effective staff: defining job positions and responsibilities, recruiting qualified people, training them, motivating them, compensating them, and evaluating them. We discussed earlier all the "marketing" work that one hospital took to recruit one physician, and now this example has to be multiplied by the number of new people an organization hires each year. Employee training is another critical task with significant marketing implications. Those employees who come in contact with consumers must be trained in a "customer service" orientation. A college whose professors are cold or indifferent to the students is much more likely to have falling enrollment than a college with student-oriented professors.

Motivating the staff takes careful planning. The staff wants several things from the organization: adequate salaries, fair treatment, respect and recognition, and the feeling of working for a worthwhile enterprise. Management must create these benefits if it expects to get in return solid work, high morale, and continuous support. Employees are a "market" to which management must creatively communicate and relate.

VOLUNTEERS. Many nonprofit organizations—churches, charities, hospitals—use volunteers as an important part of their operations. The volunteers perform work that usually requires less skill, and this helps to keep down the costs of running the organization. On the other hand, volunteers are less controllable and often less productive. They may not show up for meetings, resist doing certain tasks, and tend to be slow in getting their work done on time. Some organizations claim to be able to accomplish more by increasing the size of the paid staff and reducing the number of volunteers.

At the same time, a better answer might be for the organization to improve its skill in managing and motivating the volunteers. Volunteers are sensitive to small slights like not receiving recognition for a job well done or being pushed hard. They feel that they are giving their time free and want to be appreciated and respected.

The competent volunteer staff manager will be skilled in attracting good and reliable volunteers and in motivating and rewarding them. A marketing approach means understanding the volunteers' needs and meeting them in a way which draws their support and hard work. The volunteer staff manager is likely to sponsor social functions for volunteers, confer awards for many years of service, and arrange a number of other benefits that will recognize their contributions.[5]

Intermediary Publics.   The focal organization enlists other organizations, called marketing intermediaries, to assist in promoting and distributing its goods and services to the final consumers. A college, for example, may decide to offer off-campus educational services to consumers who cannot avail themselves of courses offered on campus. The college may work with four different marketing intermediaries to distribute and promote its educational services and products. They are described below.

MERCHANTS.   Merchants are organizations such as wholesalers and retailers that buy, take title to, and resell merchandise. Suppose the college makes an arrangement with a local bookstore to carry and sell certain textbooks, where the bookstore cannot return the unsold books. The bookstore is performing a merchant role in the distribution system used by the college.

AGENTS.   Agent middlemen are organizations such as manufacturer's representatives, agents, and brokers that are hired by producers to find and/or sell to buyers without ever taking possession of the merchandise. Suppose the college signs a contract with a person who agrees to recruit new students for the college. This person is acting as an agent for the college. The college would have to negotiate the terms on which the agent would be remunerated for services.

FACILITATORS. Facilitators are organizations such as transportation companies, real estate firms, and media firms that assist in the distribution of products, services, and messages, but do not take title to or negotiate purchases. Thus, the college will use the telephone company and the post office to send messages and materials to prospective students. These facilitators are paid a normal rate for their transportation, communications, and storage services.

MARKETING FIRMS. Marketing firms are organizations such as advertising agencies, marketing research firms, and marketing consulting firms that assist in identifying and promoting the focal organization's products and services to the right markets. The college will hire the services of these marketing firms to investigate, develop, and promote new educational services. The focal organization has to select these firms wisely and negotiate terms that are mutually rewarding.

Consuming Publics.   Various groups consume the output of an organization, and in varying senses have needs the marketing manager must meet. They are described below.

CLIENTS.   Customers represent the marketer's primary public, its raison d'etre. Drucker insists that the only valid purpose of a business is to create a customer. He would hold that hospitals exist to serve patients, colleges to serve students, opera companies to serve opera lovers, and social agencies to serve the needy.

Various names are used interchangeably to describe customers, such as consumers, clients, buyers, and constituents. The appropriate term is elusive in some cases. Consider a state penitentiary. The prisoners are clearly the penitentiary's consumers. A psychiatrist in the prison will have certain prisoners as clients. The prisoners are not buyers in the sense of paying money for the service; instead, the citizens are the buyers, and they are buying protection from criminal elements through their taxes. The citizens are also the prison's constituents in that the prison exists to serve their interests. We might conclude that the citizens are the prison's primary customers.

What this illustrates is that a market can have a multiple set of customers, and one of its jobs is to distinguish these customer groups and their relative importance. Consider this issue in relation to a state college. Who is the state college's primary customer? Is it the students, because they consume the product? Is it the students' parents, who expect the college to transmit knowledge and ambition to their sons and daughters? Is it employers, who expect the college to produce people with marketable skills? Is it taxpayers, who expect the college to produce educated individuals? Or is it the college's alumni, who expect their alma mater to do notable things to give them pride?

Clearly, a college must take the interest of all of these "customer" groups into account in formulating its services and policies. At times, the college will aim to increase its service to one group more than to another. If the students complain about poor lectures and unavailable professors, then the administration will have to focus its energy on improving service to the students. This may require putting pressure on the professors to be more responsive to students. At other times, professors may complain that their teaching load is too heavy to get any research done, and the administration may seek additional money from alumni to finance lighter teaching loads. Most of the time the administration is busy balancing and reconciling the interests of diverse customer groups rather than favoring one group all the time at the expense of the other groups.

LOCAL PUBLICS. Every organization is physically located in one or more areas and comes in contact with local publics such as neighborhood residents and community organizations. These groups may take an active or passive interest in the activities of the organization. Thus, the residents surrounding a hospital usually get concerned about ambulance sirens, parking congestion, and other things that go with living near a hospital.

Organizations usually appoint a community relations officer whose job is to keep close to the community, attend meetings, answer questions, and make contributions to worthwhile causes. Responsive organizations do not wait for local issues to erupt. They make investments in their community to help it run well and to acquire a bank of goodwill. This, too, is a marketing activity.

ACTIVIST PUBLICS. Organizations are increasingly being petitioned by consumer groups, environmental groups, minority organizations, and other public interest groups for certain concessions or support. Hospitals, for example, have had to deal with demands by environmental groups to install more pollution control equipment and engage in better waste handling methods.

Organizations would be foolish to attack or ignore demands of activist publics. Responsive organizations can do two things. First, they can train their management to include social criteria in their decision-making to strike a better balance between the needs of the clients, citizens, and the organization itself. Second, they can assign a staff person to stay in touch with these groups and to communicate more effectively the organization's goals, activities, and intentions.

GENERAL PUBLIC. A marketer is also concerned with the attitude of the general public toward the organization's activities and policies. The general public does not act in an organized way toward the organization, as activist groups do. But the members of the general public carry around images of the organization that affect their patronage and legislative support. The marketer needs to monitor how the organization is seen by the public and to take concrete steps to improve its public image where it is weak.

MEDIA PUBLICS.   Media publics include media companies that carry news, features, and editorial opinion: specifically, newspapers, magazines, and radio and television stations. Marketers are acutely sensitive to the role played by the press in affecting their organizations' capacity to achieve their marketing objectives. Organizations normally would like more and better press coverage than they get. Getting more and better coverage calls for understanding what the press is really interested in. The effective press relations manager knows most of the editors in the major media and systematically cultivates a mutually beneficial relation with them. The manager offers interesting news items, informational material, and quick access to top management. In return, the media editors are likely to give the organization more and better coverage.

We will examine the problems of marketing to consumers throughout this volume. We give special attention to the problems of marketing to activist, general, and media publics in Chapter 20. The problems of structuring and managing the marketing department's internal organization are considered in Chapter 9.

THE COMPETITIVE ENVIRONMENT

Today nonprofit marketers are facing increasing competition in their markets. Unfortunately, many nonprofit organizations still deny the existence of such competition, feeling that this is only characteristic of private sector markets. Thus, hospitals until recently did not like to think of other hospitals as competitors, museums tended to ignore other museums, and the Red Cross saw other blood banks as all seeking the same general public goal. They would rather think of their sister organizations as simply helping provide social services and not competing. Yet the reality of competition is driven home when one hospital starts attracting many doctors and patients from another hospital, blood banks compete for donors, or YMCAs start losing members to local racquetball clubs and gymnasiums.

By contrast, there are also nonprofits who recognize the existence of potential competitors but seem to think that competition is "not nice." They feel that since all nonprofits, in some sense, are attempting to achieve the same (obviously desirable) social goals, any attention to competition would divert energies from what each competitor should *really* be doing. Sometimes nonprofit marketers are rudely awakened when a competitor doesn't "play fair."

Consider the case of Population Development Associates (PDA), the dominant nonprofit contraceptive marketer in Thailand. In 1984, PDA found their lowest-priced Mechai brand condom challenged by a new, similar priced brand whose package bore a very strong resemblance to PDA's own brand. This competitive brand—what in Western marketing circles would be considered a me-too brand—was brought to the market not by a private brander or by foreign competition but by a "sister" nonprofit organization, Thailand's affiliate of International Planned Parenthood Foundation (IPPF). PDA's first reaction was one of shock. It complained to the IPPF affiliate that its tactics "weren't fair" and that they should concentrate on the larger issue of getting consumers to practice birth control and not try to beat each other out of sales in the marketplace. However, this reaction was fleeting and PDA, a sophisticated nonprofit marketer, quickly developed a hard-nosed, strictly competitive reaction, drawn straight put of the private sector consumer goods marketing handbook. PDA simply came back with its own new, even lower priced competitive brand targeted specifically at gaining back market share lost to the IPPF products.

What PDA realized is that competition may help rather than hurt the nonprofit marketers' performance in two important ways. First, the existence of two competitors in the marketplace, clamoring for attention, spending two advertising budgets, commanding even more shelf space or media interest, can stimulate increases in *the size of the total market.* Thus, it is entirely possible that PDA might lose market share but discover that, because the entire market grows more than their share loss, PDA's total sales may be higher. And if the higher sales are great enough to cover the increased costs due to the new competition, PDA will clearly be better off after the copycat brand entry than before. More importantly, more total sales of contraceptives would mean that Thailand's population is also better off, which, of course, is PDA's basic mission.

The second virtue of face-to-face competition is that it can sharpen the competitive skills of the embattled marketers. It is a serious danger in the nonprofit domain that marketers will become fat and happy by observing growing sales and pretending there is no competiton. There is nothing like the effect of new competitive activity to give complaisant managers the needed slap to the side of the head. To compete, they have to rethink how their brand is positioned. They have to look to their customers more carefully to see if there are better ways to meet their needs and wants. They have to consider the possibility of changing prices, features, and advertising. This reevaluation and the continuing close attention to marketing details can only help the marketer's overall performance.

This example illustrates competition at only one level. A marketer can face up to four major types of competitors in trying to serve a target market. They are:

1. *Desire competitors*—other immediate desires that the consumer might want to satisfy.
2. *Generic competitors*—other basic ways in which the consumer can satisfy a particular desire.

3. *Service form competitors*—other service forms that can satisfy the consumer's particular desire.

4. *Enterprise competitors*—other enterprises offering the same service form that can satisfy the consumer's particular desire.

We will illustrate these four types of competitors as they were faced by a New York legitimate theatre, the Barrymore, offering the play *Hurlyburly* in the spring of 1985. Consider a young professional woman in New York deciding what to do on a particular evening. Suppose her options are evaluated as shown in Figure 5-6. She realizes that she has several desires she could satisfy—finishing a project at work, getting some exercise, meeting several household responsibilities, or being entertained. Once she determines that the *desire* she will satisfy is to be entertained, she has to consider various *generic* competitors, including TV at home, a movie, or a live performance. Choosing to be entertained by a live performance, she has to consider various *forms* of live entertainment—a symphony, a nightclub performance, a rock concert, or a legitimate play. Finally, after settling on a legitimate play, she has to choose the offerings of various *enterprises*—the Barrymore's *Hurlyburly,* the Winter Garden's *Cats,* or the Promenade Theatre's *Pacific Overtures.*

If the Barrymore Theatre is experiencing poor sales, the causes may be poor marketing strategy at *any or all* of the four levels of competition. The Barrymore may have chosen a poor offering and so loses out to other *enterprise competitors.* Or the play may be terrific, but too many consumers may

FIGURE 5-6

Types of Competitors Facing a Legitimate Theatre

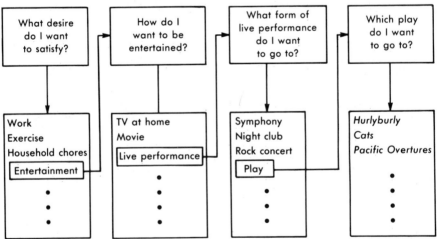

be choosing other *form competitors* such as nightclubs or rock concerts. In the latter case, the marketing manager's challenge would be to focus on those who like live entertainment and convince them that legitimate theatre is a better alternative. This could involve research into why the theatre is losing out to other forms. It may be that competitors in other forms have discovered better ways to meet consumer needs that the theatre might wish to copy (for example, reducing prices, selling popcorn or liquor). Or it might be that more people would choose the theatre except for certain disincentives ("costs") that the marketer could correct. For instance, potential customers could fear for their safety in downtown parking lots (the marketer could build a new structure, put in stronger lights, or hire a bus service to bring fearful people up to the door from a distant, safe lot). Or they could feel their friends might not want to come. In that case, the marketers could offer two-for-one ticket bargains or a "bring-a-friend-free" promotion.

At the next level of competition, if the manager found that too many promising customers were not choosing live entertainment as the preferred generic form of entertainment, the theatre manager might consider joint promotions with its generic comrades (symphony managers, rock concert promoters, nightclub owners) to get people out to "the live world of entertainment tonight." On the other hand, if the problem is at the *desire level* of competition, joint promotion by those in the entertainment industry (live performance promoters, movie house bookers, TV station managers) could compete with other desires by promoting the theme that "in this stressful, work-conscious world, you need more entertainment to relax, to replenish, to grow."

The important points to recognize in this extended example are:

1. Every nonprofit has competition and it is critical to recognize and accept it.
2. If one has competition, good strategic planning requires that the organization evaluate *very carefully* whether it is operating as an effective competitor and, if not, how its strategy should be changed to make it more competitive.
3. Competitive problems can be at any of four levels, *desire, generic, form,* and *enterprise.*
4. Evaluating one's competitive position therefore requires evaluation and potential changes of strategy at one or more of these competitive levels.

For an example of how one hospital analyzed its enterprise competitors, see Table 5-1. This hospital could base a strategy on challenging those hospitals that were not able to deliver comparable customer satisfaction to the same target customers. It could focus, for example, on hospital C attempting to attract their better medical staff and promoting several major services to their potentially vulnerable patients and potential patients.

Table 5-1

HOSPITAL X SUMMARY OF COMPETITOR STRATEGIES

Hospital	Present Position		Plans	Apparent Strategy
	Strengths	*Weaknesses*		
A	• Strong local Image • Good medical-surgical market share; relatively high utilization • Strong psychiatry services (range of services and utilization) • Developing women's program • High visibility media promotion	• Heavy debt load	• Ambulatory care satellite • One-day surgery • Home health • Radiation therapy • Cardiac catheterization • Health Maintenance Organization	• Emphasis on primary/secondary care; outreach and on-site
B	• Teaching affiliation • Increasing medical-surgical utilization • Stable psychiatric utilization • Some specialty programs—neonatal intensive care unit, radiation therapy, open-heart surgery	• Declining obstetrics and pediatrics utilization	• Oncology • Pain center • One-day surgery • Outreach satellites • Physician recruitment • Health Maintenance Organization	• Emphasis on market and program development

C	• Multihospital system • Teaching affiliation • Health Maintenance Organization affiliation (PRUCARE)	• Deteriorating utilization in all major services • Medical staff turnover • Underutilized open-heart surgery	• Wellness services • Elderly day care	• Emphasis on affiliations and development of non-inpatient services
D	• Increasing obstetrics utilization • Stable medical-surgical utilization	• Limited inpatient services—no pediatrics or psychiatry	• Physician office building • Computerized Tomography Scanner replacement	• Emphasis on primary care—attracting patients to site
E	• Increasing medical-surgical utilization • A few strong specialty services • Fourth generation Computerized Tomography Scanner • Alcoholism	• Underutilized, declining obstetrics and pediatrics • Underutilized open-heart surgery	• $32 million expansion on-site approved	• Emphasis on adult inpatient care on site

If strategic planning has its consequences in the future, it is crucial that nonprofit managers understand the broad forces creating the world in which they must operate. These broad forces can be divided into demographic, economic, technological, political-legal, and social-cultural categories. The nature of these forces varies, of course, by the country in which the nonprofit markets, and within a given country, their relative impact varies significantly by region and nonprofit sector. Demographic and political-legal trends are very important for strategic planning in social service agencies. Economic trends are important to charities, technological trends to hospitals and libraries, demographic and economic trends to the armed forces, and social-cultural trends to parks and recreation services and the performing arts.

This volume is not the place to describe in detail the major trends in the macroenvironment that can have major impact on the nonprofit sector. A diverse array of scholarly and popular treatises by futurists have sought to identify these trends. Among the most prominent of the latter are Alvin Toffler[6] and John Naisbitt.[7] Naisbitt described in 1982 what he called ten "megatrends" and he continues to publish *The Trend Report* on a regular basis for corporate and nonprofit subscribers. Besides books and newsletters, nonprofit managers wishing to keep abreast of the latest macroenvironment trends will find academic and trade conferences useful sources of information, along with most trade journals and general business periodicals such as *Advertising Age, Business Week,* and *Fortune.* Many nonprofits also use their own panel of outside experts to help guide them about the probable critical macroenvironmental changes that will affect their future performance.

Nonprofits function within markets with other "players" whom the manager must work with or attempt to influence. One of these, of course, is the set of target consumers the marketer must put at the center of the strategic planning process. We discussed this key group in Chapters 3 and 4. Other key market groups will be discussed below. Chapter 10 considers the role of business and other intermediaries in leveraging the nonprofit's limited assets. Chapter 11 discusses trends in donor groups and Chapter 17 considers the use of channel members to carry out the nonprofit mission.

In all cases, strategically oriented nonprofit managers must recognize that these market players are not static entities, but are themselves changing. In some sectors, change is slow and evolutionary. In others, change can be rapid, even chaotic. Three recent examples of the latter are financial services, communication, and advertising media. Nonprofit mangers who, for example, wish to plan for a future media environment must today carefully consider the challenges and threats posed by the rapid growth in cable television, VCRs and satellite dishes, the shrinkage of network TV audience shares, the consolidation of ownership of local TV stations and newspapers, the fragmentation of radio to serve narrow market segments, the willingness of public TV to carry more corporate messages more closely resembling advertising, the growth of national newspapers, and so on. Keeping up with such rapid change again can be facilitated by close observances of the trade and popular press and the use of outside experts.

SETTING MARKETING MISSION, OBJECTIVES, AND GOALS

Once the marketing manager has completed the first three steps of the strategic marketing planning process, he or she must then integrate what has been learned at these earlier stages into a long-term strategy for marketing. That is, the opportunities and threats in the external environment (step 2) must be compared to the organization's strengths and weaknesses (step 3) to determine what long-term course of marketing action will best achieve what top management has communicated are its real mission and objectives (step 1).

The approach that most sophisticated for-profit marketers have adopted is to use some variation on what is known as *portfolio planning*. The portfolio concept assumes that most modern organizations, including nonprofits, offer *multiple* products or services in *multiple* markets and are constantly facing questions of how to treat simultaneously these sets of existing and potential products or services. They need to decide:

1. Which products or services to pour additional resources into because their future looks bright (building opportunities).
2. Which products or services to essentially maintain in their present posture as doing just fine (holding opportunities).
3. From which products or services to drain resources because they are not promising (harvesting opportunities).
4. Which products or services to drop because their future doesn't look promising or because other product or service prospects look better (divesting opportunities).
5. Which products or services to add to the portfolio over the planning period (new product opportunities).

In essence, the problem is like that of managing an investment portfolio where one must decide which stocks to buy or sell, how much to hold of each, whether to switch from stocks to bonds or real estate, whether to withdraw cash, and so on. The problem for the financial investor as well as for the marketing manager is to constantly evaluate the portfolio against changing market conditions and changing performances of individual units in the portfolio.

There are a number of approaches to the portfolio management problem. The most prominent are those commonly referred to as the Boston Consulting Group (BCG) and McKinsey/General Electric approaches. The two approaches have a number of elements in common. We shall outline these common elements and each approach's distinctive features. Then we shall suggest, first, how the BCG approach might be used by the marketing manager of a diversified family planning program in a developing country, and second, how the McKinsey/GE approach might be used by a college.

The first step in any portfolio analysis is to partition the organization's existing offerings into *strategic business units* (SBUs). These can be individual products and services or groups of similar products or services. Four criteria should be considered when deciding whether individual products and services belong together in a strategic marketing unit:

1. Do they market to essentially the same customers?
2. Are they marketed in essentially the same way? That is, do they use similar media for advertisements or common distributor channels?
3. Do they have essentially the same competitors?
4. Can they be planned for together?

Thus, in a family planning program, the sterilization marketing programs *could* be grouped with programs to market birth control pills and condoms for strategic planning purposes. Further analysis, however, would reveal that they more properly belong with other *medical services* offered by the family planning program. They have in common with the latter two important characteristics: (1) they are offered through the same distribution channel—medical clinics rather than drug stores, and (2) they face the same competitors—other clinics and other private physicians rather than other pharmaceutical manufacturers.

The next step in both BCG and McKinsey/GE approaches is to assess the favorability of the market in which the SBU competes and the SBU's current performance. Here, the two approaches proceed somewhat differently. We shall describe each approach in some detail.

BOSTON CONSULTING GROUP PORTFOLIO APPROACH

BCG's approach calls for rating all of the organization's offerings along two dimensions, namely, market growth and relative market share (see Figure 5-7). Market growth is the annual rate of growth of the relevant market in which the offer is marketed. Relative market share is the organization's performance (for example, sales) relative to that of the leading competitor's, expressed as a ratio.[8] By dividing the market growth axis into high-growth

FIGURE 5-7

Boston Consulting Group Portfolio Approach

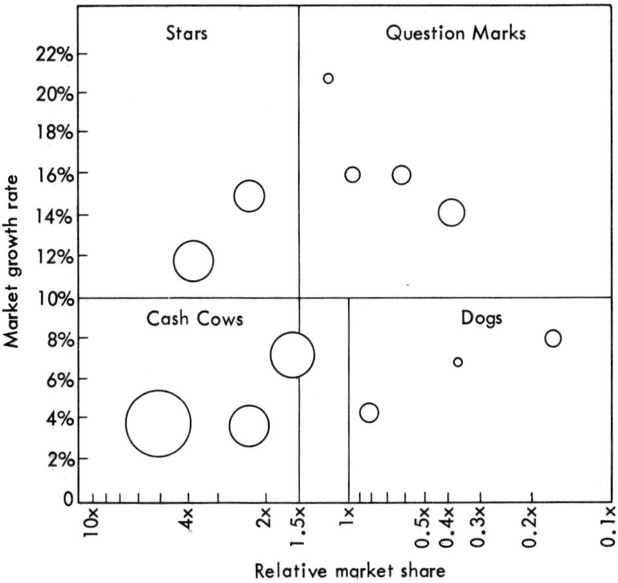

and low-growth and the market share axis into high-share and low-share, four types of SBUs emerge:

1. An organization's *stars* are those SBUs for which the organization enjoys a high relative market share in fast-growing markets. Marketers need to pour increasing resources into its stars to keep up with the market's growth and maintain its share leadership. Because stars have high relative shares, they are usually profitable enough that they can support much of their own growth, although they need some outside resources. This is why they are referred to as "stars."

2. An organization's *cash cows* are those SBUs for which the organization enjoys a high share in slow-growth markets. If they are revenue producers, cash cows, because of their large relative market shares, typically yield strong cash flows to an organization. This excess cash can pay the bills for other offerings that cannot support themselves. Unfortunately, many nonprofits have no cash cows and thus need continuous outside subsidies.

3. An organization's *question marks* are those SBUs for which the organization has only a small relative share in a fast-growth market. The marketers here continually face the decision of whether to increase investments in these question marks hoping to make them stars, or to reduce or terminate the investment on the grounds that the funds could find better use elsewhere in the business. Obviously, the major sources of funding for question marks are the cash cows, although external bank or capital market funding can be solicited for particularly promising ventures.

4. An organization's *dogs* are those SBUs that have a small market share in slow-growth or declining markets. Dogs usually bring little into the organization. Organizations often consider shrinking or dropping dogs unless they are necessary for other reasons.

Applying this scheme to the situation of a contraceptive marketer in a developing country, the marketer might find that its low-cost condoms are *stars* in that it has a high market share in a high-growth market. Its highly profitable clinics may be *cash cows* spinning off funds for the rest of the organization. Attempts to offer noncontraceptive items such as oral rehydration salts through its social marketing channels would be *question marks.* Its attempts to market certain non-health-related product lines may turn out to be *dogs.*

The BCG evaluation is particularly useful for organizations interested in tracing the cash implications of their product portfolios. High sales generate cash and high growth consumes cash. To the extent that nonprofit organizations do not seek rapid growth or high market share, they could be less interested in these criteria for evaluating current products and seek a different set of criteria.

McKinsey/General Electric Approach

General Electric (GE) has formulated another approach to portfolio evaluation that has more applicability to nonprofit organization. They call it the *strategic business planning grid* (see Figure 5-8); it uses two basic dimensions, market attractiveness and organizational strength. The best programs to offer are those that serve attractive markets and for which the organization has high organizational strength.

Market attractiveness is a composite index made up of such factors as:

- *Market size.* Large markets are more attractive than small markets.
- *Market growth rate.* High-growth markets are more attractive than low-growth markets.
- *Profit margin.* High-profit-margin programs are more attractive than low-profit-margin programs.
- *Competitive intensity.* Markets with many strong competitors are less attractive than markets with a few weak competitors.
- *Cyclicality.* Highly cyclical markets are less attractive than cyclically stable markets.
- *Seasonality.* Highly seasonal markets are less attractive than nonseasonal markets.
- *Scale economies.* Programs where unit costs fall with large volume production and marketing are more attractive than constant cost programs.
- *Learning curve.* Programs where unit costs fall as management accumulates experience in production and distribution are more attractive than programs where management has reached the limit of its learning.

FIGURE 5-8

General Electric Portfolio Approach
(Called the Strategic Business Planning Grid)

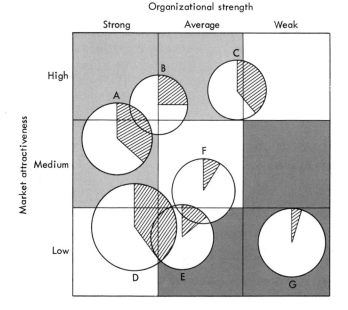

Marketing strength is a composite index made up of such factors as:

- *Program quality.* The higher the program quality relative to competitors, the greater its organizational strength.
- *Efficiency level.* The more efficient the organization is at producing the program relative to competitors, the greater its organizational strength.
- *Market knowledge.* The deeper the organization's knowledge of customers in that market and their needs and wants, the greater its organizational strength.
- *Marketing effectiveness.* The greater the organization's marketing effectiveness, the greater its organizational strength.

The factors making up each dimension are scaled and weighted so that each current SBU achieves a number indicating its market attractiveness and marketing strength and therefore can be plotted in the grid.

The grid is divided into three zones—green, yellow, and red. The green zone consists of the three cells at the upper left, indicating those SBUs that are located in attractive markets and for which there is marketing strength. The implication is that the organization should "invest and grow" these SBUs. The yellow zone consists of the diagonal cells stretching from the lower left to the upper right, indicating SBUs that are medium in overall attractiveness. Here the organization gives serious consideration to harvesting or divesting. Finally, the red zone in the three cells at the lower right represent definitely unattractive situations where divestment is in order.

For an example, consider program G shown in Figure 5-8. The graph indicates that program G is in an unattractive market and that the marketing group does not have strong strengths to bring to it. It is a fairly large volume product (indicated by the size of the circle) and the organization has only a small market share (indicated by the shaded wedge). The organization will want to consider phasing this product down or out.

Other portfolio approaches have been developed. As an example, consider a college administration trying to determine how much support to give to each academic department. One college developed the following criteria:

- *Centrality.* The degree to which an academic program is central to the mission of the college.
- *Quality.* The quality and reputation of the academic department relative to those in other colleges.
- *Market viability.* The degree to which the market for the academic program is sufficient in size and growth.

The three criteria can be combined in the grid shown in Figure 5-9. Each criterion is divided into high, medium, and low. (Market viability is represented by MV and its level is represented by H, M, or L, for high, medium, or low, respectively.) According to Figure 5-9, the administration rates the psychology department high in centrality, quality, and market viability.

FIGURE 5-9
Academic Portfolio Model

Centrality

		High	Medium	Low
Quality	High	Psychology (MV–H) Decision: ·Build size ·Build quality		Home Economics (MV–H) Decision: ·Build size ·Build quality
	Medium		Geography (MV–M) Decision: ·Hold size ·Hold quality	
	Low	Philosophy (MV–L) Decision: ·Reduce size ·Build quality		Classical Languages (MV–L) Decision: ·Reduce size or terminate

Because the psychology department is one of the stars, the administration may want to increase its budget further. On the other hand, classical languages' rating fell in the lower right. The administration feels that classical languages are not central to its purpose, that the faculty is poor, and that the market viability is low insofar as few students enroll in the course. The administration will give serious thought to reducing or dropping classical languages.[9]

Ideally, under any portfolio, the marketing manager should take one *further* step before taking action. This step is to *forecast the future locations* of the offerings on the grid under the assumption that there are no changes in the organization's own strategy.

Once the marketing manager completes the present portfolio and makes a nonchange forecast analysis, it is necessary to step back and evaluate the portfolio determining what needs to be done. Two features of the portfolio approach must be kept in mind at this point. First, portfolios require balance. To take the BCG model, for example, an organization cannot exist with too many question marks and too few cash cows, since the latter are necessary to feed the former. Nor can it keep too many dogs, because these can drain time and resources from stars. Thus, if there are too few cash cows the manager must make one of three plans. Over the planning horizon, some of the question marks could be sacrificed. Alternatively, a project that is categorized as a star may have to be temporarily, but *purposely,* allowed to become a cash cow by reducing the amount of resources put into it. Finally, if neither of these strategies is deemed appropriate, the manager can seek to support the question marks with outside grants or increased donations. Sound marketing management, however, suggests that seeking outside funding should serve as a last resort and not as a crutch to justify neglectful planning of the rest of the portfolio.

The second feature of portfolios that the no-change projection should make abundantly clear is that they evolve over time. Again, to take the BCG approach, a normal progression for SBUs over their life cycle is that they begin as question marks. This is because one usually looks for new ventures in *growth markets,* where they will initially have low market shares. With careful environmental analysis, thoughtful strategic planning, and imaginative implementation and follow-up, the question marks should increase their relative market share and become stars. After a time, most markets "top out" and cease to grow dramatically. Under such conditions stars become excellent candidates to be treated as cash cows. Then, either as their overall market begins to decline or as the organization's maintenance strategy causes the SBU to lose market share, it eventually becomes a dog. The critical decisions implied by this schema involve deciding when to do the following:

1. Add new question marks to be groomed to replace present stars that are soon to fall into the cash cow quadrant.

2. Give up on question marks that really seem unlikely to move into the star category and that will continue to drain resources from better uses.
3. Begin harvesting (milking) a star whose upward momentum has pretty well sputtered out.
4. Eliminate dogs, though this seems to be especially difficult for nonprofit managers to confront.

The ultimate decision as to whether to change the portfolio may well depend on the marketing manager's or the organization's attitude toward risk. Some managers might on some occasion be quite averse to risk. A marketing manager hoping for a renewal grant from a funding agency, for example, would pursue a cautious, no-change strategy that would guarantee that the program would appear reasonably successful at the end of the period. The manager would prefer this to a riskier strategy that could look sensational but could also fail sensationally.

OPPORTUNITY IDENTIFICATION

Portfolio planning is very useful as far as it goes. Its implications for the coming planning period are clear: managers can (1) delete or develop question marks, (2) delete dogs, or (3) harvest cash cows. But these planning models *don't* help the manager with two of the most difficult problems the manager faces—determining (1) how to find and nurture new offers, and (2) how to *grow* new offers into stars.

Needed is a systematic approach to opportunity identification. A useful device for doing this is known as the product/market opportunity matrix (see Figure 5-10).[10] Originally a two-by-two matrix proposed by Ansoff, it is here expanded into a three-by-three matrix. Markets are listed at the left and offerings along the top.

Each cell in Figure 5-10 has a name. Potential opportunities—in this case, for a college—are listed in small letters. The administration should first consider cell 1, called *market penetration.* This cell raises the question of whether the college can maintain or expand its enrollment by deepening its penetration into its existing markets with its existing products. If further market penetration does not look likely, then it will have to look for ideas in another cell.

Cell 2, *geographical expansion,* raises the question of whether the college should consider expanding into new geographical markets with its existing products. The college could open a branch in another part of the city, or in a new city, or start a new campus in another country. Southern Methodist of Dallas is offering courses in its M.B.A. program in Houston. Similarly, Notre Dame now grants an M.B.A. in London, and Antioch operates campuses in several countries.

The administration then moves to cell 3, *new markets,* and considers

FIGURE 5-10

Product/Market Opportunity Matrix

Offerings

		Existing	Modified	New
Markets	Existing	1. Market Penetration	4. Product Modification • short courses • evening program • weekend program • new delivery system	7. Product Innovation • new courses • new departments • new schools
	Geographical	2. Geographical Expansion • new areas of city • new cities • foreign	5. Modification for Dispersed Markets • programs offered on military bases or at U.S.-based firms abroad	8. Geographical Innovation
	New	3. New Markets A. Individual • senior citizens • homemakers • ethnic minorities B. Institutional • business firms • social agencies	6. Modification for New Markets A. Individual • senior citizens • homemakers • ethnic minorities B. Institutional • business • government	9. Total Innovation • new courses • new departments • new schools

possibly offering its existing products to new individual and institutional markets. Colleges are increasingly recruiting nontraditional student groups such as senior citizens, homemakers, and ethnic minorities. Iowa State University, for instance, has instituted "Eldercollege," a program for retired and older adults, which meets once a week for two months. In additon, colleges are trying to interest business firms, social agencies, and other organizations in buying educational and training programs to be delivered in-house by the faculty.

Next the marketing manager can consider whether the organization should engage in *product modification* to attract more of the existing market (cell 4). Standard courses can be shortened in the evening or on weekends. For example, Alverno College, a private women's school in Milwaukee, instituted a weekend college and drew large numbers of housewives and employed women. Some colleges are beginning to offer courses in the very late evening or very early morning, having discovered a number of working people for whom these hours would be more convenient.

Cell 5 is named *modification for dispersed markets.* The University of

Maryland, for example, offers modified programs for members of the armed forces both domestically and abroad.

Modification for new markets (cell 6) may be a more realistic growth approach for colleges and universities. To penetrate the senior citizen market, for example, may require a modification of standard courses. Specifically, the time period might need to be shorter and less reading might be required, with more comfortable seats and probably books with larger print.

Product innovation (cell 7) involves developing new courses, departments, or schools for existing markets. A business school, for example, might develop a new program in managing nonprofit organizations to offer to its students.

Geographical innovation (cell 8) involves finding new ways to serve new geographical areas. Illinois Bell, for instance, has developed an electronic blackboard that allows a professor to write on a blackboard in one location and have it transmitted over telephone lines to a distant city. With the advent of home computers, interactive television, and other new media technologies, it will be possible to offer courses to a national audience.

The final category, *total innovation,* refers to offering new products for new markets. The "university without walls" college where learning takes place away from a campus is an example.

The product/market opportunity matrix helps the administration imagine new opportunities in a systematic way. These opportunities are evaluated and the better ones pursued. The results of the product/market analysis and the previous portfolio analysis allow the organization to formulate its strategic plans.

DEVELOPING THE CORE MARKETING STRATEGY

Once the decision is made broadly as to how the organization wishes to treat each SMU, the next step in the strategic planning process outlined in Figure 5-1 is to develop a set of core marketing strategies to achieve the desired positions.

> **Core Marketing strategy** is the selection of a target market(s), the choice of a competitive position, and the development of an effective marketing mix to reach and serve the chosen customers.

We shall examine the three basic components of a core marketing strategy in terms of the following example:

> Desert University [name disguised], located in the Southwest, operates a liberal arts college and several professional schools. One of these, the journalism school, enjoys a good local reputation. Although it has attracted a large number of students in the past, the number of applicants has fallen in recent

years because of the growing difficulty of finding journalism jobs for graduates and the low pay. The dean of the journalism school allowed enrollment to decline rather than lower the school's admission standards. The university president, however, is upset with the enrollment decline. The president wants the journalism school to remain at its present size and quality and wants the dean to develop a marketing strategy for the late 1980s that will adapt the school to its best opportunities.

Target Market Strategy.   The first step in preparing a marketing strategy is to understand the market thoroughly. We define a market as follows:

> A **market** is the set of all people who have an actual or potential interest in an exchange and the ability to complete it.

Thus, the journalism student market is the set of all people who have an actual or potential interest in studying journalism and the ability and qualifications to buy this education. At the outset, it becomes clear that the national market must be quite large and that Desert University would only need a small share of it to fill its classes. But the administration realizes that not every person in this market would know about Desert University, find it attractive, or be able to attend. Nor would Desert University find every person attractive. When looked at closely, every market is heterogeneous, that is, it is made up of quite different types of consumers, or market segments. Therefore, the administration would benefit from constructing some market segmentation scheme that would reveal the major groups making up the market. Then it could decide whether to try to serve all of these segments (mass marketing) or concentrate on a few of the more promising ones (target marketing).

There are many ways to segment a market.[11] A market could be segmented by age, sex, income, geography, lifestyle, and many other variables. The market analyst tries different approaches until a useful one is found. Suppose the administration settles on the product/market segmentation scheme shown in Figure 5-11. Three customer markets for journalism are shown: college-age learners, adult learners, and practicing journalists. And three product types are shown: broadcast journalism (radio and TV), print journalism (newspapers and magazines), and public relations (a program found in most schools of journalism). Suppose the journalism school at Desert University at present caters to all nine market segments but is not doing a distinguished job in any. At the same time, competitors are beginning to concentrate on certain market segments and doing a first-class job: the University of Texas in training college-age students for broadcast journalism, Northwestern University in training college-age students for print journalism, and so on. The dean is wondering whether to pursue target marketing, and if so, what pattern of target marketing to choose.

FIGURE 5-11

Segmentation of the Journalism Product Market

Markets

	College-age Learner	Adult Learner	Practicing Journalist
Broadcast Journalism			
Print Journalism			
Public Relations			

Products

The dean will recognize that there are five basic patterns of market coverage possible with a product/market segmentation scheme. They are shown in Figure 5-12 and described below:

FIGURE 5-12

Five Patterns of Market Coverage

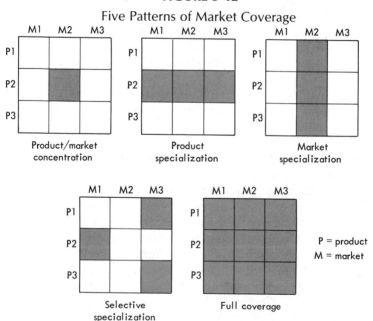

SOURCE: Adapted from Derek F. Abell, *Defining the Business: The Starting Point of Strategic Planning* (Englewood Cliffs, N.J.: Prentice-Hall, 1980), Chapter 8.

1. *Product/market concentration* consists of an organization concentrating on only one market segment, here teaching print journalism to adult learners.
2. *Product specialization* consists of the organization deciding to produce only one product (here print journalism) for all three markets.
3. *Market specialization* consists of the organization deciding to serve only one market segment (adult learners) with all the journalism products.
4. *Selective specialization* consists of the organization working in several product markets that have no relation to each other except that each constitutes an individually attractive opportunity.
5. *Full coverage* consists of an organization making the full range of products to serve all the market segments.

After researching these alternatives, the dean decides that the most attractive one for the school is product specialization, here print journalism. The journalism school does not have the funds to buy expensive television and radio equipment and sound rooms for student training and would only be doing a second-rate job compared to the neighboring University of Texas with its $12 million facility for teaching broadcast journalism. And the school's program in public relations is quite weak and cannot be the basis for building a distinguished journalism school. The region lacks a good print journalism school, which happens to be Desert University's strong suit. And it would be best to develop print journalism programs for all three markets, because the number of college-age students is shrinking.

Having decided on product specialization, the administration should now proceed to developing a finer segmentation of the market for print journalism education. Figure 5-13 shows one possible *subsegmentation* of the print journalism market. The columns show different geographical areas from which the journalism school can try to actively recruit students. The school can concentrate on attracting journalism majors from the local area, using easy admission standards since the market is quite small. Or it can try

FIGURE 5-13

Subsegmentation of the Print Journalism Market

Career Objectives	Geography: Local	Geography: Regional	Geography: National
News Writing			
Feature Writing			
Advertising			
Media Management			

to compete for students in the Southwest region, which will require a larger recruiting budget and contacts with a larger number of newspapers and magazines for placing students. Or it can try to develop national eminence and attract journalism students from all over the nation. The rows show that journalism majors have different career objectives—some seeking training in news writing, others in feature writing, still others in advertising, and finally some in managing media organizations. Looking at the subsegmentation, the dean may decide to cultivate the regional market and emphasize careers in news-writing and feature-writing. Although the school will also teach advertising and media management, it will seek to build its reputation as a writer's training school.

Competitive Positioning Strategy.   Having selected its target market, the journalism school will now have to develop its competitive position strategy vis-à-vis other journalism schools serving the same target market. Suppose there are three other journalism schools in the Southwest that do a good job of training students in print journalism. If the four schools are similar, then high school students going into journalism would not have much basis for choice among the four. Their respective market shares would be left to chance. The antidote for this is competitive positioning, defined as follows:

> **Competitive positioning** is the art of developing and communicating meaningful differences between one's offer and those of competitors serving the same target market.

The key to competitive positioning is to understand how members of the target market evaluate and choose among competitive institutions. Suppose the target market judges journalism schools by the extent to which they offer high- or low-quality teaching or whether their curriculum is oriented to vocational or liberal arts. Figure 5-14 shows the perceived competitive positions of the other three journalism schools (A, B, C) and Desert University's journalism school (D). Schools A and B are perceived as liberal-arts-oriented journalism schools of low quality, B being somewhat larger and slightly better in quality than A. They are locked in competition for the same students, since their differentiation is negligible. School C is seen as a high-quality vocationally oriented journalism school and draws well students who are seeking this type of program. Desert University's journalism school is shown as D, because it comes closest to being perceived as having a high-quality, liberal-arts-oriented program. Fortunately, it has no competition in this preference segment. The only question is whether there are enough students seeking a high-quality liberal-arts-oriented journalism program. If not, then D is not a viable competitive position and D's administration has to think about repositioning the program toward a part of the market in which the demand is larger.

FIGURE 5-14

Competitive Positioning of Four Colleges

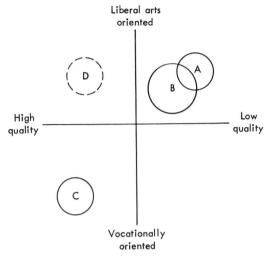

The next step in marketing strategy is to develop a *marketing mix* and a *marketing expenditure level* that supports the school's ability to compete in the target market.

Marketing mix is the particular blend of controllable marketing variables that the firm uses to achieve its objective in the target market.

Although many variables make up the marketing mix, they can be classified into a few major groups. McCarthy formulated a popular classification called the "four Ps": *product, price, place,* and *promotion.*[12] The particular marketing variables under each P are shown in Figure 5-15. The figure emphasizes that the marketing mix must be adapted to the target market.

The organization chooses a marketing mix that will support and reinforce its chosen competitive position. Since the journalism school wants to maintain and project a reputation as having a high-quality liberal-arts-oriented journalism program, it will hire high-quality faculty, require students to take many liberal arts courses, develop high-quality school catalogs and brochures, send them to potential students seeking this type of school, and so on. In other words, the chosen competitive position dictates the elements of the marketing mix that will be emphasized.

As for the marketing expenditure level, this depends on estimating how much money is needed to accomplish the school's enrollment objectives. If past experience shows that the school has spent about $400 per stu-

FIGURE 5-15

The Four Ps of the Marketing Mix

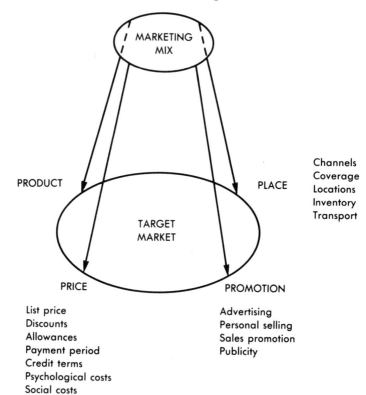

dent recruited, and the school wants to recruit one hundred students, it will need a marketing budget of $40,000. If the market shrinks or if competitive schools increase their marketing budgets, it may cost, say, $500 per student recruited and the budget would have to be raised to $50,000 to do the job. We shall say more about establishing the marketing budget in Chapter 12.

This illustration shows that strategic planning must be supported by marketing strategy in order for the organization to adapt optimally to its market opportunities.

REMAINING STEPS IN THE SMPP PROCESS

DEVELOPING STRUCTURE, TACTICS, AND BENCHMARKS

The next level of the strategic marketing management process outlined in Figure 5-1 is to take three steps more or less simultaneously to set the stage for implementing the core marketing strategy defined in the preceding stage. These steps are the following:

1. Developing an *organizational structure* and a set of *management systems* within the marketing group to carry out the marketing strategy. In any particular strategic planning cycle, this may involve adjusting an existing structure or set of systems or may require the development of entirely new ones. We take up these issues in Chapter 9. It may also involve creating bases of support from others in terms of goods, services, and/or skills (discussed in Chapter 10) or implementing specific fundraising activities (discussed in Chapter 11).

2. At the same time, detailed *tactics* must be specified for carrying out each aspect of the core strategy. This will involve decisions about what offerings to make (Chapters 13, 14, and 15), what channels to use and how to use them (Chapter 16), how to manage consumer costs (Chapter 17), and what communications tactics to use through advertising and sales promotion (Chapter 19), personal selling (Chapter 20), and public relations (Chapter 21).

3. *Benchmarks* must be developed reflecting the core strategy's goals and objectives so that, after implementation, marketing management can learn whether its strategy, structure, and tactics are achieving what is expected of them.

Implementing and Assessing Marketing Strategy.   If the strategic planning process has worked well, the task of implementation should be straightforward. The process is not complete, however, until management consciously and systematically assesses how well it is performing. While we discuss these issues in more detail in Chapter 22, management must realize that this assessment step is crucial both to permit short-run and on-the-run fine-tuning of core strategy, marketing organization structure, and marketing tactics and to feed into subsequent cycles of this critical strategic marketing planning process.

SUMMARY

Once the organization has developed the appropriate customer orientation and has carefully assessed its customer markets and given preliminary thought to how it might segment them, the next critical task is to to develop a strategic marketing plan. Out of this plan will emerge day-to-day marketing tactics. To insure careful, consistent marketing planning, the organization should follow a Strategic Marketing Planning Process (SMPP).

The first step in the strategic planning process is to identify the organization's mission, objectives, and specific goals. The next step is to determine threats and opportunities in the external environment. This requires, first, an evaluation of the many publics the organization must consider. Organizations carry on exchanges with several publics. A public is a distinct group of people and organizations that have an actual or potential interest in or impact on an organization. Publics can be classified as input publics (donors, suppliers, and regulatory publics), internal publics (management, board, staff, and volunteers), intermediary publics (merchants, agents, facilitators, and marketing firms), and consuming publics (clients, local publics, activist publics, general publics, media publics, and competitive publics). A public from which an organization seeks some response is called a market. A market is a distinct group of people, organizations, or both that have resources that they want to exchange, or might conceivably be willing to exchange, for distinct benefits.

The next step is to analyze the competitive environment. Here the organization must recognize that it has competitors at several levels: desire, generic, service form, and enterprise. Finally, the strategic planner must analyze the relevant macroenvironment and the specific market environment the organization faces.

The next step in the strategic planning process is to compare the opportunities and threats in the external environment to the organization's strengths and weaknesses to develop specific marketing goals, missions, and objectives that will achieve what top management has determined are real long-term objectives. One useful approach to this task is portfolio planning, in which the strategic planner assesses current and potential organizational offerings to determine which he or she should build, maintain, harvest, or terminate.

Following this analysis, the organization must develop core marketing strategies for each offer. This means selecting a target market segment or segments, choosing a competitive position, and developing an effective marketing mix to reach and serve the chosen customers. The marketing mix consists of the particular blend of offer, price, place, and promotion that the organization uses to obtain its objectives in the target market.

Once the core marketing strategy is set, the strategist must assure that the proper organizational structure and management systems are put in place, specific performance benchmarks are chosen, and detailed marketing tactics determined. The final steps then merely involve implementing the strategy and tactics and carefully assessing performance against the predetermined benchmarks. This final assessment then feeds back either immediately into on-the-run changes in core marketing strategy or more slowly into subsequent cycles of the strategic planning process itself.

QUESTIONS

1. The proliferation of cable television systems and the growing impact of videocassette recorders create a new environment for public television stations. What are the major threats and opportunities these changes present to local public television? Do these stations have a "strategic window" here?

2. How should the following organizations define their mission: (a) New York Museum of Modern Art, (b) Boy Scouts of America, (c) The American Automobile Association, (d) Planned Parenthood, and (e) Cedars-Sinai Hospital.

3. What are the desire, generic, service form, and enterprise competitors of (a) KCET, the Los Angeles public television station, (b) the YMCA, and (c) United Way of America.

4. Conduct a BCG portfolio analysis for a religious organization, club, or fraternity with which you are familiar.

5. Outline a set of quantitative benchmarks the Chicago Museum of Science and Industry could use to assess whether it is meeting its strategic objectives each year.

NOTES

1. See Peter F. Drucker, *Management: Tasks, Responsibilities, Practices* (New York: Harper & Row, 1973), Chapter 7.

2. See C. Peter Wagner, *Your Church Can Grow* (Glendale, Calif.: G/L Publications, 1976.)

3. For an advanced example of goal-setting in a university environment, see David P. Hopkins, Jean-Claude Larreche and William F. Massy, "Constrained Optimization of a University Administrator's Preference Function," *Management Science,* December 1977, pp. 365–77.

4. For a broader discussion of these issues, see S. Prakash Sethi, ed., *The Unstable Ground: Corporate Social Policy in a Dynamic Society* (New York: John Wiley, 1974).

5. See David L. Sills, *The Volunteers—Means and Ends in a National Organization* (Glencoe, Ill.: Free Press, 1957). Also note that the National Center for Voluntary Action, 1785 Massachusetts Avenue, N.W., Washington, D.C., 20036, researches, runs seminars on, and disseminates up-to-date techniques on managing volunteers.

6. See Alvin Toffler, *Future Shock* (New York: Bantam Books, 1970) and *The Third Wave* (New York: Bantam Books, 1980).

7. John Naisbitt, *Megatrends: Ten New Directions Transforming our Lives* (New York: Warner Books, 1982).

8. This definition of market share is called "relative market share." Thus, a relative market share of 10 means that the organization sells ten times as much as the next largest organization. It should not be confused with absolute market share, which measures the organization's sales as a percentage of the total market size.

9. For additional readings on portfolio analysis applied to universities, see Peter Doyle and James E. Lynch, "A Strategic Model for University Planning," *Journal of the Operations Research Society,* July 1979, pp. 603–609; and Gerald D. Newbould, "Product Portfolio Diagnosis for U.S. Universities," *Akron Business and Economic Review,* Spring 1980, pp. 39–45.

10. H. Igor Ansoff, "Strategies for Diversification," *Harvard Business Review,* September–October 1957, pp. 1123–24.

11. See Chapter 4.

12. E. Jerome McCarthy and William D. Perreault, *Basic Marketing: A Managerial Approach,* 9th ed. (Homewood, Ill.: Richard D. Irwin, 1984).

CHAPTER 6

Marketing Research

The United Way of America, through its various local and national programs, collects almost $3 billion per year, making it the equivalent of a Fortune 100 company. In recent years, the United Way of America has sought to bring its expenditures for marketing research up to a level appropriate for an operation of its size. One major effort in this regard is the series of over 11,000 workplace interviews conducted at cooperating firms between 1982 and 1984.

In a recent analysis of 5,000 of these surveys, the United Way of America's marketing research unit sought to assess the effectiveness of various marketing strategies in the workplace. Respondents were asked about which campaign tools they were exposed to. Eighty percent said they were exposed to a pledge card, 70 percent to campaign literature, 66 percent to a letter or memo, 57 percent to a personal conversation, 51 percent to a meeting or rally, 47 percent to a film, and 27 percent to a telephone conversation. Although most workers had multiple exposures, United Way's researchers found that these broke down into eight basic campaign patterns. Analysis showed that two of these patterns were most effective: (1) using all techniques *except* a telephone call, and (2) using all techniques except a telephone call *and* a personal conversation. The analysis concluded, "While one-on-one solicitation undoubtedly works, these results suggest that a personal conversation is perhaps not always as crucial to giving as we believed."

The research analysis also examined the issue of excessive pressure. Overall, two-thirds of the givers did not feel any pressure. While some attitudes and beliefs influence perception of pressure, certain types of personal contact are strongly related to perception of pressure. Looking only at those personal contacts which the respondents felt had a "great deal" of influence on them, pressure was much more likely to be perceived when this "influencing contact" was made by a manager or supervisor. If the "influencing contact" was made by a co-worker, someone who had been helped by a United Way agency or by a United Way representative, perception of pressure was much lower.

One conclusion was, "It appears that the perception of pressure can be minimized by downplaying the role management and supervisors play in directly contacting employees about United Way."

The study also found that those who did perceive pressure have less favorable attitudes toward United Way. And, at higher levels of income, perception of excessive pressure apparently decreased the size of the gift.

SOURCE: Adapted from Robert J. O'Connor, "Can We Campaign Smarter?" *Community*, Volume 4, Number 4, pp. 4–10, with permission.

We saw in the preceding chapters the critical role marketing research must play in understanding customer behavior and planning marketing strategy. We define marketing research as follows:

Marketing research is the planned acquisition and analysis of data measuring some aspect or aspects of the marketing system for the purpose of improving an organization's marketing decisions.

Marketing research can be very diverse. It can involve conducting one-time field research studies. It can comprise the analysis of data provided by internal record systems or by secondary sources of information. It can involve experiments or panel studies. What distinguishes it from simple observation and "straight thinking" is that it is (1) planned, and (2) tied to specific decision-making situations.

MARKETING RESEARCH IN NONPROFIT ORGANIZATIONS[1]

Nonprofit organizations carry out much less marketing research than they can *or ought to*. This is a consequence of their limited budgets, their relative newness in the marketing field, and their limited research expertise. Increasing the amount of marketing research, therefore, calls for both education and motivation, showing nonprofit executives what marketing research can do and how to do it properly as well as encouraging them to do it more often.

Five myths keep nonprofit managers from engaging in more marketing research.

- The "big decision" myth
- The "survey myopia" myth
- The "big bucks" myth
- The "sophisticated researcher" myth
- The "most-research-is-not-read" myth

If nonprofit managers are to even consider doing more research, these five myths must be directly challenged.

THE "BIG DECISION" MYTH

Too often marketing research is considered necessary only for decisions involving large financial stakes, and in such cases it should always be carried out. But research should be viewed from a cost/benefit perspective. Its costs are usually of two types—the expenses for research itself and the amount of sales and competitive advantage lost by delaying a decision until the results are in. The benefits are measured in improvements in the decision under consideration. The value of the improvement, in turn, is a function of the stakes involved and how certain the manager is about the rightness of the contemplated decision.

The cost/benefit ratio may often come out against research even when the stakes are high. Take the case of the hospital manager who was thinking of adding an outpatient plastic surgery clinic and investing in a series of advertisements to promote this new service. He called in a research professional to design a study of consumer interest in plastic surgery that would show how likely acceptance of such a service would be. Although such a study could cost several thousand dollars, the researcher determined in extended discussions with the manager that unless the survey found virtually no interest in outpatient plastic surgery, the manager should go ahead with the decision to add the clinic.

The manager was highly uncertain about the market, but he was certain that his decision to add the clinic was best. The researcher convinced the manager that the research expenditure was unnecessary and that the money could more productively be used to ensure that the new clinic got the advertising send-off needed to have the best chances of succeeding.

On the other hand, research can often be justified even when the amount at stake is not very great. This is the case whenever the research can be done inexpensively, will not take very long to complete, and will help clarify which actions to take.

These conditions often accompany advertising copy decisions. While total expenditures are small, managers usually have two or three candidate ads, each of which seems to have potential worth. Showing the ads to a small but representative set of prospective target customers—very modest research—usually reveals one superior candidate, or at least, by pointing out serious defects in one or two candidate ads, allows the choice to be narrowed. This process has the fringe benefit that once in a while it produces extremely good suggestions for entirely different ads.

Research may also be justifiable when the stakes initially appear modest but later turn out to be high. In this regard, it is generally useful to think through the monetary consequences of making a poor decision. When one considers the possible side effects of a bad decision on such things as the organization's reputation, its ability to attract funding and staff, and its sales of related products, the costs may be very high indeed. Such is often the case when nonprofits venture beyond their national borders and assume that what works in their home countries will work overseas. The international community is replete with horror stories of marketing gaffes with long-term consequences that could have been avoided with a little research.

One may grant these arguments but then assert that there is no low-cost research to meet these challenges, that the research suggestions made previously involve the proverbial quick-and-dirty study that may well be worse than no research at all. The only good research, one might argue, is a survey carefully done. This contention leads to the second major misconception about the use of research.

THE "SURVEY MYOPIA" MYTH

Any reliable information that improves marketing decisions can be considered marketing research. If one takes this view, many alternatives to formal survey research come to mind. Consider a contraceptive social marketing manager thinking of introducing a new intrauterine device who has no idea whether the target market will accept the product or, once it is accepted, how quickly it can be expected to break even. If successful, the new product would produce profits of only a few thousand dollars in the first few years. The manager could conduct a survey to reduce this uncertainty. However, to make the research 95 percent certain of being within two percentage points of the break-even market share figure of 10 percent, the manager must use a sample of nine hundred people.

An experienced survey researcher would estimate that, assuming the questionnaire and sampling plan are already designed and ignoring analysis and report preparation costs, simply completing the interviews would cost between $3,000 and $7,000. (The amount would depend on the duration and type of interviews done.)[2]

Clearly, such research would eat up the manager's initial years' contribution profits. More important is the question of whether the research would yield valid data in any case. One should ask whether it is reasonable to expect respondents to be candid about or even to know their likely behavior with respect to this new IUD, especially if many do not want to disappoint the interviewer or the research sponsor by showing little enthusiasm for the product.

How else, then, might the survey research objectives be achieved at lower cost? The company could try test marketing in representative markets. This approach has the virtue of not only lowering costs but yielding useful data (that is, it shows what people will actually do, not what they say they will do). Testing in a number of markets also allows alternative marketing strategies to be systematically evaluated.

Another low-cost approach would be to commission focus group interviews of eight to twelve members of the target audience at a time.[3] Although the results are not strictly projectable to the larger market because the groups are not randomly selected, these results can cut the cost of interviewing by a quarter or a half. Interviewers can sometimes develop richer data in the relaxed, chatty format of the focus group. Also, the groups can alert management to problems with the new product. When a company commissions several focus group sessions covering the range of people likely to be target market members for the new IUD, officials can spot serious problems mentioned by a modest number of participants and, if necessary, abort the product launch. Elaborate probability sampling designs are simply not necessary to satisfy this objective.

THE "BIG BUCKS" MYTH

We have already seen that there are often low-cost alternatives to the kinds of field surveys most nonprofit managers normally consider. To be knowledgeable users of marketing research, managers must know how and when to do traditional survey research and how and when to use a wide range of alternative low-cost research techniques. We shall consider these low-cost research techniques in later sections since nonprofits typically have seriously restricted budgets.

THE "SOPHISTICATED RESEARCHER" MYTH

Just as marketing research need not involve complex sampling and elaborate designs, a high level of sophistication in sampling techniques, statistics, and computer analysis is not essential. Of course, executives of nonprofits planning to undertake research programs should acquaint themselves with at least the rudimentary principles of random sampling, questionnaire design, and graphic presentation of results.

Even when managers need high levels of sophistication—for example, if elaborate experiments or careful field study projects are being planned—they can get low-cost assistance on an ad hoc basis. Professors at local colleges are one resource. An alternative particularly appropriate to nonprofit organizations is the voluntary help of local professional researchers. Nonprofits contemplating extended research programs may want to ask marketing research professionals to sit on their boards of directors.

THE "MOST-RESEARCH-IS-NOT-READ" MYTH

Executives who would rather not bother with research or who subconsciously fear the results use this last rationale for their inaction. Poor research certainly is undertaken, but when it is, it is usually a testimonial to poor planning. In our experience, few pieces of well-planned research are rejected as unhelpful, although they may be ignored on other, often political, grounds.

How can one ensure that research will not be wasted effort? The responsibility rests with both the manager requesting the research and the researcher doing it. Research will be most valuable when:

1. It is undertaken after the manager has made clear to the researcher what the decision alternatives are and what it is about those decisions that necessitates additional information.
2. The relationship between the results and the decision is clearly understood.
3. The results are communicated well.

MARKETING RESEARCH STRATEGY

Once a nonprofit manager has overcome the myths just outlined, it is necessary to develop a strategy for carrying out a planned program of market research. As with any other aspects of marketing strategy, the manager must develop (1) a mission, (2) a broad strategy, (3) a budget, (4) detailed steps for implementing the strategy, (5) an organization to carry it out, and (6) a system of evaluation and control. We shall comment on (1) through (4) here and on (5) and (6) briefly at the end of the chapter.

THE MARKETING RESEARCH MISSION

An important first step in planning marketing research is for the manager to determine whether the purpose of the research is description, explanation, or prediction.

Description. Marketing research can be designed to tell a nonprofit manager what his or her marketing environment is like. It can, for example, tell a hospital manager how many patients were served in each hospital facility each hour of each day of each year and indicate the sex and home address of the patient, his or her attending doctor, any previous admissions to the hospital, and the diagnosis.

While internal records can often provide these data to hospital management, additional descriptive information could be acquired from a telephone survey to ascertain the patient's family status, occupation, education, media habits, satisfaction with various hospital services, and intentions as to word of mouth and future patronage. At the same time, the manager could acquire from published sources descriptive data on competitors' pricing and advertising expenditures as well as information on national trends in payment methods, wages of specific hospital departments, cost of equipment, and so on. All of these data have in common the fact that they are descriptions of one point in time or descriptions of trends or pattern changes over time. Descriptive data usually serve management decisions in three ways: (1) monitoring performance to indicate whether strategy changes are needed; (2) describing consumers for segmentation decisions; and (3) serving as the basis for more sophisticated analysis.

Explanation.   Usually a manager is not satisfied with merely seeing what the market environment looks like. He or she would typically like to know what makes it "tick." In principle, there are really three possible levels of explanatory sophistication that a manager could attempt to build into the nonprofit organization's marketing research system. Each succeeding level has higher costs and greater resource requirements than the one preceding it, but it also has higher potential payoff.

ASSOCIATION.   The simplest level of explanation is to discover what seems to be associated with what. Thus, the hospital manager might like to know which socioeconomic and demographic characteristics of patients characterize those who are repeat users of the hospital, or those who are satisfied or dissatisfied with past services, or those who are not favorably disposed toward competitors' offerings. Such data would be very useful in helping management decide which segment to address through what channels with which general strategy.

CAUSATION.   A nasty feature of associations data that is learned by every freshman statistics student is that association is not the same as causation. Thus, the hospital manager may find that OB/GYN patients are more satisfied with their hospital care than those who were admitted for treatment of, say, urological problems. The manager may be tempted to think that the former service is doing a better job than the latter in terms of the technical quality and warmth of service offered. But suppose the manager had data like that displayed in Figure 6-1 showing patients' perception of the hospital before and after admission. The manager would quickly see that at admission, urology patients thought worse of the hospital than OB/GYN patients, but that the attitudes of OB/GYN patients *worsened* over the course of their treatment in the hospital, while the attitudes of urology patients improved. An "association" level of explanation would have given misleading indications about causation. For a manager to be sure of taking appropriate action,

FIGURE 6-1

Hypothetical Attitudes Towards Hospital Service Before and After Admission

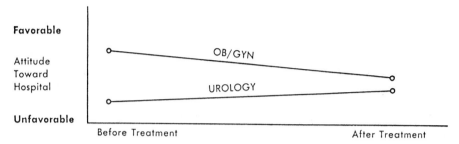

he or she must know what causes what. If the hospital manager took action to improve OB/GYN satisfaction scores, it would be critical to know whether these actions in fact led to the necessary changes. Only when the research strategy is specifically designed to trace antecedents and consequents, to measure effects under very controlled conditions, or to be subject to rather rigorous statistical procedures, does the strategy yield causative explanations.

REASONS WHY. The ultimate level of explanation for marketing researchers is to know not only that A caused B, but *why* A caused B. Thus, the hospital manager looking at the data in Figure 6-1 may be willing to conclude that treatment by the urology service leaves patients satisfied, while treatment by the OB/GYN service does not. Before rushing to reward one service and castigate the other, the manager should have a better understanding of the nature of the causation, that is, of the "reasons why." To consider just one possibility, it may be that a significant number of patients in urology at the time of the study were there for treatment of kidney stones and were simply relieved to have them removed. Any set of nurses or doctors who treated them in *any* way, from very competently and warmly to very incompetently and coldly, would have found them happier after treatment than before. If treatment per se, not staff, is the reason for the pattern of causation in Figure 6-1, then clearly, rewards are not due to the urology staff. Indeed, there could even be serious problems on the urology floor that the warm afterglow of treatment is hiding. Management must often dig beneath simple causation if research is to lead to the right decision and action.

Prediction.   Of course, descriptions or explanations of what exists or existed in the past are only useful to the manager if they tell about the future. Suppose the hospital manager in our hypothetical example finds that the reason for the posttreatment decline in OB/GYN patients' perceptions of the hospital is real and is due to the professional style of the staff, who emphasize doing the job right and efficiently rather than investing a lot of time in being solicitous and talkative with patients. But suppose it is also true that there are many patients who prefer this style—for example, those who have more education, those who are not having their first child, and those who are having birth complications. For the hospital manager to make a judgment about whether to try to change the style of the OB/GYN service to emphasize "warmth," it is essential to know what the future pool of potential patients will be and which strategic competitors will attack them. This clearly requires a different set of information than is available from a typical descriptive or explanatory study.

The mission statement for the marketing research department obviously requires that the marketing manager think through the major decisions that will be made over the planning horizon. These include *routine decisions* to be made over and over, such as where to place advertising, which products or services to promote, what to do with prices and channels of distribution, and so forth. The planning period typically also includes *one-time decisions* such as whether to add a specific new product or service, reposition the enterprise, focus on a new target group, seek new funding sources, drop certain products, services, or customers, and so on. Some of these one-time decision needs can be anticipated and built into the mission statement, but some cannot. The manager must build excess capacity into the research system, the amount of which can be more precisely estimated with experience.

The implication of the foregoing is that the only marketing research worth undertaking is that which will be applied. One could argue that *no* market research should be undertaken unless it leads directly into a decision. For nonprofit organizations with very limited budgets, we would argue forcefully that this ought to be the *only* rule when planning a marketing research program.

Where one has a more generous budget, however, a nonprofit marketer might want to undertake one or both of two other kinds of research. One is *basic research*. Basic research has no immediate application to specific management decisions but is generally expected to lay the groundwork for better decisions somewhere down the road. Thus, the Association of College, University, and Community Arts Administrators has used part of its members' dues in recent years to explore the potential of life-style research—specifically, the VALS approach—to understand consumers' reactions to the performing arts.[4]

The other type of research a nonprofit might undertake alone or jointly is *methodological research,* that is, research designed to improve the organization's ability to do more effective research in the future. Organizations involved in contraceptive marketing programs in developing countries, for example, have invested in two kinds of methodological research in recent years. One research stream has focused on figuring out how to measure the impacts of contraceptive marketing programs on a country's marketing system. The organizations need to know whether contraceptive program sales come at the expense of existing private sector firms or whether subsidized contraceptive marketing programs expand the entire market. In this connection, SOMARC, one of the key groups involved in international contraceptive social marketing, is currently looking into the possibility of using panels of pharmacies or even consumer panels to generate needed sales data in target countries. What is unknown is how and whether such data can be collected in developing countries where education is limited, record-keeping systems are poor, and local retailers are unsophisticated.

Another more difficult methodological problem in family planning programs is how to get valid information on consumer attitudes and behavior concerning family planning. In this highly sensitive subject area, respondents very often distort the truth, withhold information, and make claims of use (or nonuse) that simply do not reconcile with, say, known sales data. In some cultures, research has discovered significant differences even within given households with respect to relatively simple matters such as whether the family has ever actually used a particular method. Tackling this crucial methodological dilemma must be part of the marketing research mission of one or more of the key players in the social marketing arena over the next several years. Explanatory or predictive studies of what does or will work will simply not be possible if the dependent variables in such studies (that is, attitudes or behavior) are invalid or unreliable.

RESEARCH STRATEGY

Assuming that a nonprofit organization wishes to carry out a program of applied research, the next question is what specific kinds of research should be conducted this year and who should do it?

The range of specific studies open to a researcher is indicated in a 1983 American Marketing Association study of 599 private sector companies in consumer and industrial goods, advertising, and financial services.[5] Table 6-1 shows the proportions carrying out each of thirty-three kinds of research.

The *kinds* of studies most heavily used in Table 6-1 are the ones that also should be used most heavily by mature nonprofits. These include:

- Short- and long-range forecasting
- Business trends studies
- Competitive offerings studies
- Measurements of market potentials
- Market share analyses
- Determination of market characteristics
- Sales analyses

Table 6-1

RESEARCH ACTIVITIES OF 599 RESPONDENT COMPANIES

	% Doing
Advertising Research	
A. Motivation research	47
B. Copy research	61
C. Media research	68
D. Studies of ad effectiveness	76
E. Studies of competitive advertising	67
Business Economics and Corporate Research	
A. Short-range forecasting (up to 1 year)	89
B. Long-range forecasting (over 1 year)	87
C. Studies of business trends	91
D. Pricing studies	83
E. Plant and warehouse location studies	68
F. Acquisition studies	73
G. Export and international studies	49
H. MIS (Management Information System)	80
I. Operations research	65
J. Internal company employees	76
Corporate Responsibility Research	
A. Consumers "right to know" studies	18
B. Ecological impact studies	23
C. Studies of legal constraints on advertising and promotion	46
D. Social values and policies studies	39
Product Research	
A. New product acceptance and potential	76
B. Competitive product studies	87
C. Testing of existing products	80
D. Packaging research: design or physical characteristics	65
Sales and Market Research	
A. Measurement of market potentials	97
B. Market share analysis	97
C. Determination of market characteristics	97
D. Sales analysis	92
E. Establishment of sales quotas, territories	78
F. Distribution channel studies	71
G. Test markets, store audits	59
H. Consumer panel operations	63
I. Sales compensation studies	60
J. Promotional studies of premiums, coupons, sampling, deals, etc.	58

SOURCE: Dik Warren Twedt, *1983 Survey of Marketing Research* (Chicago: American Marketing Association, 1984), p. 41. Reprinted with permission.

The development of a specific research plan for a particular organization should not be difficult. An example of a master plan for a hospital marketing research strategy is outlined in Figure 6-2.

BUDGETING

The next research planning problem is setting the overall research budget. While not all nonprofits have a marketing research department, specific funds for research purposes must be set aside annually. Four basic methods are used in both the nonprofit and for-profit sectors. Despite their popularity, they are decidedly inferior to the cost/benefit approach outlined in the next section.

- *Historical increment.* The manager simply looks at the research budgets of the last several years and adjusts the figures upward or downward by some percentage based on the expected activity level of the organization in the current year.
- *Percent of revenues.* The manager applies a standard percentage to the amount of expected revenues. If private sector experience is any guide, this percentage could range anywhere from .10 percent to .80 percent of revenues.
- *Competitive matching.* An estimate is made of either the dollar amount or percentage of revenues spent on market research by major competitors or similar organizations last year. The manager then sets the nonprofit's own budget to equal, stay proportionate with, or exceed these comparison organizations.
- *Affordable.* Budgets are first set for other "necessary" activities. Then the amount that is left over from projected revenue levels is divided between advertising and marketing research.

Collectively, there are a number of defects with these four approaches:

1. They imply that market research is a discretionary expenditure rather than an essential tool for effective management.
2. They ignore the fact that one should expect applied marketing research to produce better revenues. Rather than setting a research budget that would help increase revenues, these four approaches use revenues to determine marketing research budgets.
3. They are cyclical by definition. When revenues are up, more will be allocated to marketing research, and when revenues are down, less will be allocated. Yet a good case can be made for making marketing research budgets contracyclical. That is, in strong, buoyant markets where revenues are up, a wide range of decisions may prove successful. In such cases, marketing research can improve management decisions only marginally. By contrast, when the market is difficult, management will be much more uncertain about which way to go, and wrong decisions can be devastating. In such cases, marketing research will be more helpful. Obviously, when research can be more helpful, more should be spent on it.
4. Rule-of-thumb approaches to budgeting marketing research ignore enterprise life cycles. When many new activities are being proposed or just getting

FIGURE 6-2

Proposed Marketing Research Strategy for a Hospital

Questions To Be Answered	Hospital Records Analysis	Patient Survey[1]	Hospital Records Analysis	Physicians' Survey[2]	Secondary Source Data Analysis	Market Area Survey[1] (Population)	Market Area Survey (Physicians)[2]	Market Area Survey (Hospitals)
Recent Patients								
Who are the Hospital's recent patients and how is the mix of patients changing?	X	X						
What Hospital services have patients experienced and what are their attitudes toward the Hospital?		X						
To what extent are patients aware of the Hospital's services which they have not experienced?		X						
What needs do patients have which might be served by the Hospital but currently are not being met?		X						
Affiliated Physicians								
Who are the Hospital's affiliated physicians?	X							
What experiences have these physicians had and what are their attitudes toward the Hospital?				X				
To what extent are these physicians aware of the Hospital's total services?				X				
What needs do these physicians have which might be served by the Hospital but currently are not being met?				X				
General Population/Service Area								
Who lives in the Hospital's geographic market (services) area and how is the population mix changing?					X	X		
What experiences has this population had with health care organizations and what are their attitudes toward those organizations?						X		
To what extent is the population aware of the Hospital's services and what are their general attitudes toward the Hospital?						X		
What health care needs does the population have which might be served by the Hospital and might not be available through health care institutions serving the Hospital's geographic market area?						X		
Nonaffiliated Physicians								
Who are the nonaffiliated physicians serving the Hospital's geographic market area?					X		X	
To what extent are these physicians aware of the Hospital's services and what are their general attitudes toward the Hospital?							X	
What needs do these nonaffiliated physicians have which might be served by the Hospital and are not now available at other health care institutions in the area?							X	
Competitors								
What organizations compete with the Hospital in providing health care services to residents in the Hospital's market area and how do they compete?		X			X	X	X	X

[1] Patient and market area general population survey may use a combined survey instrument.
[2] Physician and market area general population survey may use a combined survey instrument.

SOURCE: Dennis J. Cunningham and William C. Jackson, "Marketing Research in a Competitive Health Care Environment," *Health Care Focus*, Vol. 6, No. 3, June/July 1980, p. 3. Arthur Young & Co., Publisher. Reproduced with permission.

off the ground, much more research ought to be carried out, yet this is often a period when relatively little revenue is available to "pay" for such research.

The Cost/Benefit Approach.   The cost/benefit approach calls for the manager to follow the procedure suggested above for specifying research *needs* for the planning period and then costing out the research and comparing these costs to the expected benefits. Specifically, the steps are

1. List all possible projects that might be undertaken for the planning period. Develop this list by asking marketing managers to ascertain their upcoming information needs.
2. Estimate the costs for meeting each set of information needs, noting whether they can be met by secondary analysis of existing data, purchase of outside services, or whether they require original research.
3. Estimate the likely improvement in organizational performance as a result of each proposed study, that is, the study's "benefits." This involves considering several factors. First, the marketing research manager should ascertain the stakes involved in the various decision alternatives that the line manager is considering. An attempt should be made to estimate the economic *opportunity loss* of choosing the *wrong* course of action in each instance and the probability that such a loss might occur. This "expected" opportunity loss would then constitute the research's maximum possible benefit. This figure would constitute an upper limit on the amount that could be spent on aiding the manager's decision-making through research.[6]
4. Adjust the calculated benefit from the research by the probability that the research at the proposed budget level will, indeed, provide right answers as to which decision to make.
5. Compare costs to expected benefits and include *all* projects where the latter exceed the former. The total of these project costs will comprise the year's research budget.

This cost/benefit approach is illustrated in Exhibit 6-1.

IMPLEMENTATION

Once the marketing research strategy is worked out, the researcher is ready to design and carry out the specific studies. The research manager will be concerned about two criteria: *effectiveness* and *efficiency*. Effectiveness in the research context can be measured in terms of the study's *usefulness* for making management decisions. Efficiency is achieving usefulness at the lowest possible cost. We shall discuss low-cost research techniques later in the chapter. We consider here the more difficult problem of making research projects effective.

Being effective in research is the result of three major factors. First, the researcher needs a *research design process* that gives the greatest likelihood that the research will meet management's needs. Second, the researcher needs to know the *full array of methodologies* that might be used to solve

EXHIBIT 6-1. Using the cost/benefit approach to researching a library decision

Assume that a library marketer is considering adding a line of rental videocassettes to her library's offerings for a two-year test period. She decides she would have to invest about $8,000 to have an adequate beginning stock. She would charge $1.75 for each overnight rental (compared to $3.00 elsewhere in the city). Costs of rental (bookkeeping, staff time, etc.) would be largely variable at about $0.95 per unit. Since the project is to be given two years to break even, a second set of more up-to-date videocassettes would have to be acquired at the start of the second year at an estimated cost of $4,000. She assumes that salvage costs for all used videocassettes would be about 15 percent of original value if the project is aborted after year two. An article she found in the October, 1984, issue of *MART*, a monthly trade journal on consumer electronics products, reported that families that rented videotapes in 1984 rented about fifty tapes per year. Secondary sources also indicate that 20 percent of all households have videocassette recorders and 87 percent of these rent tapes. The librarian knows that her library has about 2,300 active members based on a recent study of library card usage; of these, then, about four hundred would have VCRs and rent tapes. Finally, given that she would have a narrower collection than competing commercial outlets, the librarian estimates that each renter who used the library's collection would only meet half of his or her needs there, or about 25 tapes.

The critical unknown for the librarian is, of course, what demand will be. How many of the library's active patrons with videocassette recorders who rent movies would use the service? Her best guess without research is that one-half of the 400 households would do so. Rentals of twenty-five videocassettes per year for two years for these 200 households would be 10,000. To this would be added another 2,000 rentals to new patrons attracted to the library for the first time by this new offering.

Profits from these rentals would be 12,000 × ($1.75 − .95) = $9,600, from which would be subtracted the write-off of the cassettes over two years of $10,200, leaving her a *loss* of $600 on the venture. She realizes that she could be wrong in her estimate, either pleasantly or unpleasantly. That is, demand could be weaker or stronger than she projected.

She must decide whether to do any research to help her with the decision to go ahead with the videocassettes, and, if so, how much to spend. If she used a percent-of-revenues approach, she would figure about .10 to .80 percent of $12,000, or anywhere from $12 to $96, could be spent for research! If one looks specifically at the *go-no-go* decision she faces, however, a different result appears. To see this we need to first summarize the available information in a useful way. The framework that we shall use is formal decision theory. This approach says that decisions can be specified in terms of the following properties:

1. The decision alternatives

EXHIBIT 6-1. (continued)

2. The factors likely to affect the success or failure of each alternative
3. The outcome (for example, profit) associated with the combination of each choice alternative and each factor
4. The estimated probabilities that each factor will occur (either independently of the choice or contingent upon the choice).

Suppose our librarian visualizes three possible levels of demand for her videocassettes: rentals of 12,000 (her best guess), a level 20 percent higher, and a level 25 percent lower. Further, she estimates the following probabilities:

Expected sales of 12,000 (moderate demand)—60 percent chance
20 percent higher sales (strong demand)—30 percent chance
25 percent lower sales (weak demand)—10 percent chance

Finally, she realizes that buying an inventory of videocassettes will tie up capital that could have been invested in the bank at 6 percent. Thus, if she did nothing, she could earn 6 percent on the original $8,000 for two years and on the $4,000 for one year. Assuming she would reinvest the first interest when it was paid at year's end, she would forego interest of $1,020 by going into the videocassette business.

The calculations below indicate the hypothetical payoff matrix for two years.

	Critical Future Factors			
Action	Weak Demand	Moderate Demand	Strong Demand	Weighted Average
Add Videocassettes	−3,000	−600	+3,240	+312
Do nothing	+1,020	+1,020	+1,020	+1,020
Probability	.10	.60	.30	

Thus, the weighted average payoff of each alternative is:

Add Videocassettes	$ 312
Do nothing	$1,020

EXHIBIT 6-1. (continued)

Clearly without research, decision theory says she should do nothing as she would be $708 ahead by leaving her capital in the bank. But should she conduct research to determine more accurately what the demand is likely to be?

The first point to realize is that research information is only valuable to the extent that it helps our librarian decide what to do. The formal decision theory approach indicates how a rational decision-maker would decide without further information. It can also indicate whether to spend for further information, as we shall see in a moment. But, the librarian may not be a "rational decision-maker." She may believe that *unless* research can show her that the prospects were very bleak, she will go ahead. We have all encountered decision-makers who say, in effect, "Don't bother me with the facts, I've already made up my mind." In the librarian's case, she may wish to add videocassettes for any number of noneconomic reasons: to impress potential donors with the library's vitality; to enliven the day-to-day jobs of her employees and build group spirit; to add a "development" item on her résumé; and so on. It is crucial to remember that research is *only* valuable if it has a chance of affecting decisions. As Sudman has perceptively noted, the value of information is a very personal concept, which depends on an individual's knowledge and beliefs. The same information may have great value for some people or some organizations, and no value for others. It depends on what the person already knows. . . . Thus, whenever we talk about the value of information, we must specify for whom."

If the librarian wants to act rationally, she must estimate the value of further information. The value of further information is equal to the *loss due to uncertainty*. One way of measuring this value is to calculate the difference between *perfect* knowledge about what to do and *present* knowledge about what to do. Perfect knowledge could be acquired only if one could conduct a perfect study.

If the librarian could buy a perfect study, she would learn whether demand was actually weak, moderate, or strong. At present, her best guesses about their likelihoods are .10, .60, and .30, respectively. *After* the perfect study comes in, the best decision is clear. If the study says that demand will either be weak or moderate, the librarian should do nothing and earn the $1,020 in interest. If the study says demand will be strong, she should rent videocassettes and reap the $3,240 estimated reward. By weighting these possible outcomes after the perfect study by their respective probabilities, she can get a measure of the "expected outcome with perfect information":

$$EOPI = .1(\$1,020) + .6(\$1,020) + .3(\$3,240) = \$1,686$$

Recall that the librarian's expected outcome in her present state of uncertainty from her best strategy (do nothing) is $1,020. The difference

EXHIBIT 6-1. (continued)

between these two values ($666) is, in reality, an economic measure of her *loss due to uncertainty*. We define this as follows:

> **Loss due to uncertainty** is the difference between the expected value of the best course of action *with perfect information* and the expected value of the best course of action *given present knowledge.*

The librarian must now consider two additional factors. First, what is the cost of one or more possible research designs? The most, theoretically, that she should pay for a *perfect* study is, of course, one dollar less than $666. But the other factor to consider is that the study won't be perfect! Given the expenditure range she will have to work with—say, $100 to $665—the chances are that the quality will not be very great. On the other hand, a lot can be done for very little money. She has a list of her active library users (presumably on computer file). Labels could be produced cheaply, as could a sensible one-page questionnaire. Printing and labeling costs plus first-class postage for, say, one questionnaire mailer could be on the order of 25 cents. Assuming a 40 percent response rate and adding an average return postage of 6 cents, this would yield a total cost of, say, 31 cents per mailed questionnaire. If a budget of $310 was spent, 1,000 questionnaires could be mailed. Statistical theory would show that, with a 40 percent response that (1) was a random sample of all active users, not just those interested in the tapes, and (2) did not involve bias due to respondent exaggerations or attempts to please the librarian, she could estimate the proportion within 1.4 percentage points of all active users likely to rent videocassettes with 95 percent confidence. If the sample size were doubled and $620 spent, she would still only come within 1 percentage point of the true figure at the 95 percent confidence level!

The final research issue is *bias.* Would the sample be random and would the respondents tell the truth? We have no reason to believe the latter would be a problem, especially if the cover letter for the questionnaire conveyed the right tone. The randomness issue is more serious: it is likely that those who respond will be more interested in the videotapes than those who do not. There are several ways of handling the problem:

1. The librarian could simply estimate the extent of systematic bias due to nonrandomness; she could, for example, determine in advance to subtract, say, 20 percentage points from the percentage derived from the study.
2. A question could be asked about videocassette recorder *ownership,* and, assuming the library cardholders are representative of the

EXHIBIT 6-1. (continued)

community, reweight the answers of those with videocassettes and those without, as follows:

Videocassette Owners	% of Respondents	% likely to Rent	% in Population	Weight
Yes	70	60	20	.2
No	30	0	80	.8

The resulting estimate would not be $(.7 \times .6) + (.3 \times 0) = 42$ percent as *achieved* in the actual sample, but $(.2 \times .6) + (.8 \times 0) = 12$ percent after reweighting.

3. She could conduct a small telephone study of nonrespondents and adjust the achieved percentage by the percentage likely to rent among nonrespondents as follows:

	% of Population	% Likely to Rent
Respondents	40	60
Nonrespondents	60	5

The resulting estimate would be $(.4 \times .6) + (.6 \times .05) = 27$ percent. (Note that in both examples, the confidence intervals would have to be recalculated to take account of the weighting.)

SOURCE: The Sudman quote is from Seymour Sudman, *Applied Sampling* (New York: Academic Press, 1976), p. 91. For an excellent discussion of the potential for bias in field research, see Gilbert A. Churchill, Jr., *Marketing Research: Methodological Foundations*, 3rd ed. (New York: Dryden Press, 1983, pp. 411–421.)

the particular problem. Third, the researcher needs to know how to minimize the *research bias*.

In the following sections, we will first consider the problem of developing an effective *process* for researching. Next, we will outline several more advanced research techniques, and finally, we will point out some major pitfalls that the unwary researcher might expect in carrying out a specific research design.

THE RESEARCH PROCESS[7]

The standard approach to the research process is to start by defining the problem. The problem is then translated into a research methodology. This leads to the development of research instruments, a sampling plan, coding and interviewing instructions, and other details. The researcher takes to the field, examines the resulting data, and writes a report. The executive then steps in to translate the researcher's findings into action. The executive has, of course, already devoted some thought to the application of the results.

In the more typical case, however, managers leave the problem vague and general. They say, in effect, "Here are some things I don't know. When the results come in, I'll know more. And when I know more, then I can figure out what to do." This approach makes it highly likely that the findings will be off target.

We advocate instead a procedure that turns the traditional approach to research design on its head. The procedure stresses close collaboration between researcher and decision-makers. It markedly raises the odds that the organization will come up with findings that are not only "interesting" but also actionable.

The "backward" approach advocated here rests on the premise that the best way to design usable research is to start where the process usually *ends* and then work backward. Each stage in the design is developed on the basis of what comes after it, not before. The procedure is as follows:

1. Determine how the research results will be implemented (which helps to define the problem).
2. Determine what the final report should contain and how it should look in order to be implemented.
3. Specify the analysis necessary to "fill in the blanks" in the research report.
4. Determine the kind of data that must be assembled to carry out these analyses.
5. Scan the available secondary sources and syndicated services to see whether the specified data already exist or can be obtained quickly and cheaply from others.
6. If no such easy way out presents itself, design instruments and a sampling plan that will yield the needed data.
7. Carry out the field work, continually checking to see whether the data will meet your needs.
8. Do the analysis, write the report, and watch it have its intended effect.

As one might expect, the first step is the most important.

Step 1

To most managers, the research "problem" is seen as a lack of important facts about their marketing environment. A manager may say, "The problem is that I don't know if source A is preferred over source B." Or, "The problem is that I don't know if my distributors are more satisfied with my organization than my competitor's distributors are with theirs, and if they aren't, what they're unhappy about."

If the problem is defined in this way, the "solution" is simply a reduction in the level of ignorance. The data elicited may be very "interesting" and may give managers a great deal of satisfaction in revealing things they didn't know. But satisfaction can quickly turn to frustration and disappointment when the executive tries to use the results.

Take, for example, a life-style study done not long ago on over-the-counter drugs. Some respondents who claimed they were always getting colds and the flu frequently went to doctors, but the doctors were never of much help. They thought that the over-the-counter drugs were often very beneficial, but they weren't sure why. This information, together with other details, caused the researchers to label this group "the hypochondriacs."

What can be done with these results? As is usually the case with segmentation strategies, there are quantity and quality decisions to make. The company has to decide whether to pump more marketing resources into the hypochondriac group than its proportion of the population would justify. The marketing vice-president might first say yes because the hypochondriacs are heavy drug users.

But the picture is more complicated than that. Perhaps hypochondriacs are sophisticated buyers, set in their purchase patterns, and very loyal to favorite brands. If so, money aimed at them would have little impact on the market shares. Light users, on the other hand, may have fragile loyalties, and throwing money at them could entice them to switch brands. Of course, just the opposite might be true: the hypochondriacs, being heavy users, might prove to be very impressionable and responsive to compelling ads.

On the qualitative side, life-style research could be much more helpful. Since it generates a rich profile describing each group's jobs, families, values, and preferences, this research could tell the company what to say. But the frustrated manager is not likely to know where to say these things. There is no *Hypochondriac's Journal* in which to advertise, and there may be no viewing and reading patterns that apply to heavy users specifically—hypochondriacs or not.

A self-selection strategy could be tried in which the organization develops an ad speaking to hypochondriacs' fears and worries in the hope that they will see the message and say to themselves, "Ah, they're talking about me!" But nonhypochondriac heavy users who read the ad might say, "Well, if this product is really for those wimpy worrywarts, it certainly is not for sensible, rational me! I'll take my patronage elsewhere." In this case, the research will be very interesting (fine fodder for cocktail party banter) but not actionable.

But suppose that the company had first laid out all the action alternatives it might take after the study. If the marketing vice-president had made it clear that his problems were (1) whether to allocate marketing dollars differently and (2) whether to develop marketing campaigns aimed at particular, newly discovered segments, he would have launched the project in a more appropriate direction.

In the first case, discussions with the researcher would help the vice-president determine the criteria that would justify a different allocation. The manager needs research on the likely responses of different segments to advertising and promotional money. In the second case, the manager needs to know whether there are effective channels for reaching these segments. Only by first thinking through the decisions to be made with the research results will the project have a high likelihood of actionability.

STEP 2

After Step 1, management should ask, "What should the final report look like so that we'll know exactly what moves to make when the findings are in?" Now the collaboration between the researcher and the manager should intensify and prove dynamic and exceedingly creative.

Scenarios are a good technique for developing ideas for the contents of the report. The initiative here lies with the researcher, who generates elements of a hypothetical report and then confronts management with tough questions, like "If I came up with this cross-tabulation with these numbers in it, what would you do?"

The first payoff from this exercise arises from improvements in the research itself. These results can move the project forward by sharpening the decision alternatives and backward by indicating the best design for the questionnaire or how the analysis of the findings should be carried out.

Suppose the manager is considering canceling a multiple-purchase discount offer because most of the people taking advantage of it may be loyal customers who are already heavy users, are upscale, and are largely price inelastic. The manager speculates that the discount mainly represents lost revenue. To decide whether to eliminate the discounts, one must of course predict the responses of old and new customers to this step. The researcher hypothesizes tables showing various results.

Suppose the first iteration shows long-time customers to be price inelastic and new customers to be price elastic. This result suggests to the manager to offer no discount except to new customers. In considering this alternative, the manager will need to know whether potential new customers can be reached with the special offer in a way that will minimize or eliminate purchases at a discount by long-time customers.

This new formulation of the decision leads to a discussion of results set out in another set of dummy tables showing responsiveness to the one-time discount by past patronage behavior. Other tables would then reveal what television shows various consumer segments watch and what they read or listen to, which will indicate whether they are differentially reachable. And so goes the process of recycling between the decision context and the research design.

The recycling will reveal what research is needed. Sometimes, the researcher will present contrasting tables of regression results only to discover that management would take the same course of action no matter what the results. This is actually a *prima facie* case for doing away with that part of the research design altogether.

Management participation in the design decision has other advantages. It serves to win managers' support of marketing research and deepens their understanding of research details. That understanding permits the researcher to simplify the report immeasurably. Working with contrasting, hypothetical tables can make the manager eager for the findings and unlikely to be startled by surprising results. Participation will also sensitize management to the study's limitations. Managers are often tempted to go far beyond research "truth" when implementing the results, especially if the reported truth supports the course of action they prefer to take anyway.

STEP 3

The form of the report will clearly dictate the nature of the analysis. If management is leery of multivariate analysis, the researchers should design a series of step-by-step cross-tabulations. If management is comfortable with the higher reaches of statistics, the researcher can draw on more advanced analytic procedures. In general, the analysis phase should be straightforward. If the exercise of scenario-writing has gone well, the analysis should amount to little more than filling in the blanks.

STEP 4

The backward approach is very helpful in data-gathering. In one study, management wanted to gauge young consumers' knowledge of and preferences for the organization's offering. Not until the researcher had prepared mock tables showing preference data by age and sex did the manager's wishes become clear. By "young," the manager meant children as young as ten. The manager believed that preteens, being a very volatile group, undergo radical changes from year to year, especially as they approach puberty. Design plans to set a low age-cutoff for the sample at thirteen and to group respondents by age category—such as thirteen to sixteen and seventeen to twenty—went out the window. If the researcher had been following the usual design approach, the manager's expectations may not have surfaced until the study was well under way.

Backward design can also help determine the appropriateness of using strict probability techniques. If, for example, management wants to project certain findings into some universe, the research must employ precise probability methods. On the other hand, if the manager is chiefly interested in frequency counts (say, of words used by consumers to describe the organization's offerings or of complaints voiced about its staff), sampling restrictions need not be so tight. Researchers often build either too much or too little sampling quality for the uses the organization has in mind. Similarly, scenario-writing will usually also reveal that management wants more breakdowns of the results, requiring larger sample sizes or more precise stratification procedures than initially planned. Through simulating the application of the findings, the final research design is much more likely to meet management's needs with substantially lower field costs.

Steps 5–8

The first four steps encompass the major advantages of the backward technique. Steps 5 through 8 revert to a traditional forward approach that applies the research decisions and judgments made earlier. If all parties have collaborated well in the early stages, the last four steps will carry through what has already been largely determined.

RESEARCH ALTERNATIVES

The second requirement for effective implementation is to choose the right research methodology. When the nonprofit researcher thinks of carrying out primary research, the technique that usually comes to mind first is the one-time field survey, usually a mail or telephone study using conventionally designed questionnaires. However, this technique can be very expensive. Later in the chapter we shall describe some techniques for reducing its costs. Here we wish to suggest some approaches that can either materially upgrade the value of the traditional one-time survey or can substitute for it.

In upgrading the traditional survey, the mature researcher should consider the following possibilities:

Sophisticated Attitude Measures

Consumers typically undertake complex decision processes in deciding whether to take a particular action in which nonprofit marketers are interested. Tapping into that process with the types of measures and models described in Chapter 3 can be very useful. Andreasen and Belk, for example, found that a complex attitude model best predicted likely future attendance at a symphony and theatre in the South. The attitude measures proved not only good predictors but also offered a number of diagnostic insights for strategy.[8]

Using Conjoint Research Techniques

Conjoint analysis provides measures of the importance of various criteria affecting the nonprofit consumer's decision process. Currim, Weinberg, and Wittinck reported a study for the Lively Arts Program (LAP) at Stanford using this technique.[9] A mail survey of current LAP subscribers asked respondents to rank order three paired comparisons of attributes of a subscription series drawn from the following set of factors.

Attribute	Levels
Driving time	$\leq$30 min; >30 min.
Number of series events	5; 8
Seating priority	Yes; no
Single ticket price	$5; $8; $12
Subscription discount	30%; 15%; none
Performer renown	World; national; regional

Only three comparisons were needed since the researchers could reasonably assume a preference ordering for the levels of each attribute (that is, everyone would prefer less driving to more, seating priority over no priority, a ticket for $5 over one at $8, and so forth). By looking at the trade-offs consumers made among these factors, the researchers concluded that driving time was most important, followed by performer renown, price, seating priority, number of events, and percentage discount.

The power of the conjoint techniques is found in the interactions it can detect.

PANEL STUDIES

Researchers who wish to monitor the performance of a target market over time can choose among four change measures. For example, they can study changes in consumer behavior

1. *Retrospectively,* by asking a single sample of consumers what they are doing now and what they did at some past point in time;
2. *Cross-sectionally,* by comparing behaviors of a single sample of consumers presumed to be earlier or later in a process (for example, comparing seat-belt usage of twenty-one- to thirty-year-olds with that of thirty-one- to forty-year-olds, or those never exposed to a particular campaign with those exposed for two, four, and six months).
3. *Cross-sectionally over time,* by asking about behaviors of different samples at two points in time (for example, as in traditional polling).
4. *Longitudinally over time,* by taking behavioral measures of the same panel of consumers at different points over time.

The value of the last approach, panel studies, as compared to cross-sectional polls, is suggested in the following hypothetical but realistic example. Suppose a political candidate, Frank Allison, makes a major statement on a key issue, say, in favor of paying women equal to men for jobs of comparable worth. Further, suppose that polls before and after the speech using *different* samples showed that the proportion of female voters planning to vote for him rose from 40 to 50 percent. Understandably, the candidate would be pleased with such results. But this pleasure is based on a belief that if one studied the same consumers before and after the speech, the shifting of consumer preferences over time would look like that shown in Table 6-2a. The true result in a worst-case scenario, however, could be like Table 6-2b.

In Table 6-2a, Allison's speech added nicely to his present core of supporters. In Table 6-2b, his speech alienated *all* his core supporters and attracted a few of his opponents' supporters and *all* those previously undecided. Under the 6-2b scenario, Allison would realize he had to move fast to win back "his people" while at the same time trying to hold on to the possibly fickle "undecideds" who have just switched over to him. Learning this crucial information is *only* possible with panel data. Only panel data can show *who* changed. Such data may be absolutely crucial to an organization that wishes to move quickly and correctly in a volatile marketplace.[10]

EXPERIMENTATION[11]

A major problem with survey research is that it relies upon information volunteered by consumers. The quality of the measurements can well be compromised by interviewee or interviewer bias. Many private organizations have sought to develop more objective behavioral measures through experimentation. Experimental opportunities abound. Too many nonprofit organizations ignore excellent opportunities to learn about their market-

Table 6-2

HYPOTHETICAL PANEL STUDY RESULTS

	a		*b*		
	After Speech		*After Speech*		
Before Speech	*Prefer Allison*	*Prefer Opponent*	*Prefer Allison*	*Prefer Opponent*	*Total*
Prefer Allison	40%	0%	10%	30%	40%
Prefer Opponent	10%	20%	10%	20%	30%
No Preference	0%	30%	30%	0%	30%
Total	50%	50%	50%	50%	100%

place by applying different marketing strategies to different subsamples of the target population. For example, the librarian described earlier in Exhibit 6-1 could

> 1. Send out solicitations of interest in her videocassette proposal to library cardholders suggesting one price to one sample and offering this price plus an introductory discount to another. She would learn not only who would be interested in rentals, but which strategy would prove most profitable. If the discount "worked," she could then offer it to the entire membership. If it didn't "work," she would not have lost much.
>
> 2. Place the rental videocassettes (or notices about them) in different parts of the library for randomized periods of time to see which generated the most "impulse" rentals or inquiries.
>
> 3. Advertise the service in area newspapers on different days with different size ads and with different copy to see which generated the most rentals or inquiries.
>
> 4. Send out coupons of differing value to subsets of the library's mailing list to assess impact.
>
> 5. Send out different solicitations to potential nonmember renters in high probability, upscale zipcode areas or on special mailing lists to see whether and to what extent the extra effort is justified.

These experimental manipulations require very little effort on the librarian's part. Careful attention, of course, must be paid to randomness and to the problems of ensuring that the control group really is a control group (see Exhibit 6-2). But as a great many organizations have discovered, the informational payoff can be high.

OTHER LOW-COST TECHNIQUES

There are a number of other useful techniques for carrying out marketing research at lower cost.

Focus Group Interviewing.[12]   This technique calls for interviewing consumers in groups. Groups of eight to twelve target consumers, usually (but not always) a relatively homogeneous group, are brought together to discuss a specific set of issues under the guidance of a leader trained to stimulate and focus the discussion. Although the results of focus groups are not projectable to the universe, they can often provide rich insights into consumer perceptions and preferences regarding a product, service, or organization. They are useful as a means of testing product concepts and proposed advertisements, package designs, posters, instructions, and so forth. Finally, they are useful in generating lists of factors to consider in more elaborate field studies and so are often part of the development phase of major research programs.

EXHIBIT 6-2. Problems of experimental control in the MRFIT study

Conducting major experimental social research projects in the health care field presents significant methodological and ethical problems of control. This was most apparent in a massive seven-year, multimillion project to attack coronary heart disease. Twenty-eight institutions and 250 investigators participated in the project, which was called MRFIT (Multiple Risk Factor Intervention Trial). The methodological problems are outlined in the following editorial comment from the *Journal of the American Medical Association.*

The MRFIT study was a randomized primary prevention trial designed to test the effect of a program of intervention with hypertension, cigarette smoking, and blood cholesterol in high-risk men in the United States on mortality from coronary heart disease. The results were that risk factor levels did decline, and there may have been a reduction in coronary heart disease mortality.

Unfortunately, the fundamental question facing the investigators at the beginning of the experiment remains unanswered. It is, What will happen if one takes a large group of men at high risk of dying of coronary heart disease because of the presence of multiple risk factors, intervenes in their lives by successfully reducing three such factors, and then follows the group over several years? To answer that question definitively will require a comparable control group on whom *no* intervention is practiced. For reasons explained as methodological and ethical, no such group was identified and followed in this study.

The experiment reported herein is one of a division of subjects into special intervention (SI) and usual care (UC) groups for test and control. This approach was intentional and well thought out. It was theorized that the expected mortality in the UC group would eventuate and that the UC group would thus constitute an appropriate control. That is not what happened. Both groups experienced substantially lower mortality than anticipated, reducing the statistical power of the comparison. Therefore, the experiment that is reported was one of testing the SI *vs.* the UC approach. Unfortunately for the study, the UC group was really not a "usual care" group. Both the UC members, and the physicians who cared for them, knew that they were part of a high-risk study and that they were not selected for the SI group, returned annually for follow-up (which served both as a reminder of their high-risk category as well as a time for data gathering), and had the results of such follow-up sent to their physicians.

It would seem that the investigators underestimated the effects of the following:

1. Identifying patients as high risk and informing them of it.
2. Notifying physicians that their patients were in a high-risk control group.
3. Providing original and annual data to the physicians.

227

SOURCE: George D. Lundberg, M.D., "MRFIT and the Goals of *The Journal*," *Journal of the American Medical Association*, Vol. 248, No. 12, September 24, 1982, p. 1501, Copyright 1982, American Medical Association, Reproduced with permission.

Convenience Sampling. A nonprofit organization with a very limited budget often can get useful data (although again not projectable) from respondents close at hand. Hospitals, for example, could study patients, visitors, and service delivery people coming into the hospital. These groups would obviously know more about the hospital and may be more biased. Still, the hospital might argue that these people are their target market and knowing more about them (and the differences among them) could be very useful.

Snowball Sampling. Participants in the above study could be asked to suggest the names of others "like them" who could be contacted. This would add a group that (1) did not have the familiarity biases of the first group; (2) would be likely to cooperate in the study (especially if the initial respondents allowed their names to be used as references); and (3) would closely *match* the first sample in all other socioeconomic characteristics but that which characterized the initial sample (for example, people already coming to the hospital). Snowball sampling is a particularly good technique for finding rare populations. A hospital trying to broaden its appeal to hemophiliacs, for example, might ask those hemophiliacs already attending the hospital to identify others. Conducting a full-scale random sample to find rare populations like paraplegics or handicapped bus riders or the deaf would be prohibitively expensive. Yet such rare groups may well be known by many others like themselves.

Piggybacking. Nonprofit organizations may be able to add questions onto studies undertaken by others. Several national research organizations regularly conduct omnibus surveys that combine questions from a number of sponsors. Nonprofits could add questions for close to the incremental cost of the question or questions. These or other private firms with a public service inclination may be willing to add such questions at no charge or at reduced rates.

Volunteer Field Workers. Nonprofits such as hospitals or charities may enlist volunteers to conduct telephone, mail, or "convenience" interviews, or to tabulate questionnaires.

Student Projects. Students in business schools and sometimes in psychology and sociology departments are frequently looking for outside, real-world term projects. They can be an excellent source of thought and legwork for nonprofit organizations. However, certain caveats should be observed. First, student interviewers are not the same as trained professional interviewers. The nonprofit manager must give them guidance or be sure that a professor is overseeing the research process. Second, plenty of lead time is necessary. Student projects must fit within semester or quarter academic systems. Third, the nonprofit manager should set time aside to consult with the students—they are doing this to learn. Finally, the nonprofit manager should be sensitive to the university's research norms. The students cannot be ordered to do the research in a particular way, the professor cannot be treated as a paid consultant or a field supervisor, and the professor may request that the results be made public (although possibly in disguised form).

Secondary Sources. Various published sources can provide comparative data or suggestions for question-wording, sample design, and data analysis. Trade articles, marketing journals, and government reports can all prove very valuable, especially at the beginning stages of a project.

Board of Directors. Most nonprofit organizations select board members who will serve the nonprofit in some beneficial way. A typical board has lawyers, bankers, accountants, and individuals who have access to influential financial and political figures. There is every reason to add a marketing research professional (and advertising, public relations, and other marketing professionals) to the board. Such experts can provide useful advice, and possibly offer the services of their agency gratis or at reduced rates.

RESEARCH BIASES[13]

Research can only be effective if it avoids major sources of error. Detailing all of the things that can go wrong with field research is beyond the scope of this book. The nonprofit manager should be aware, however, of the major pitfalls. First, it should be made clear that there are two major kinds of error: sampling error and systematic bias.

Sampling error is the error brought about because only a sample was taken from the universe. This type of error can be reduced by simply increasing the sample size or by adopting sophisticated stratification techniques.

Systematic bias is more difficult to handle. It refers to all those "glitches" that cause the expected value of the sample to be different from the true value. The "expected value" is the value the research would yield if the design were repeated a very large number of times. As shown in Figure 6-3, in an unbiased sample, the expected value for the mean $(E(\overline{X}_1))$ is the same as the true value for the mean (μ). The standard error $(\sigma_{\overline{x}})$ would be a measure of the sampling error around this expected value. Its size would depend on (1) the true variability of the value being studied in the overall universe, which the researcher cannot influence, and (2) the sample size, which the researcher can influence. As shown in Figure 6-3, *bias* is the difference between the expected value from the particular research procedure and the true value (that is, $\mu - E(\overline{x}_2)$) when they are *not* the same.

Consider once again the example of the librarian's videocassette study described in Exhibit 6-1. Because those replying to her mail questionnaire were more likely to be interested in videocassettes than the true universe would be, the librarian could do the study repeatedly and even with larger sample sizes, but the average proportion likely to rent videocassettes across *all* these replications would be much higher than the true value. This is what we mean by systematic bias.

Systematic bias in a survey usually comes about in the following ways:

1. *Frame bias.* This is caused by drawing a probability sample from a poor representation of the universe. For example, estimating the proportion of households who moved in the last twelve months by sampling from the telephone directory would systematically underestimate the true value since recent movers are much less likely to be listed in a given directory.

2. *Selection bias.* This is caused when the procedure for drawing actual sample members *always* excludes or underrepresents certain types of universe (frame) members. This would occur if telephone interviewers only telephoned during the day, thus underrepresenting men and households where everyone works.

FIGURE 6-3

Sampling Error and Systematic Bias in Field Research

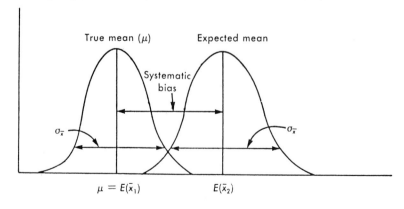

It would also occur in field surveys where interviewers were allowed to pick and choose whom to interview. If interviewers were told to stand at a street corner or at a shopping mall and interview people "selected at random," they would probably ignore "unsavory characters" as well as people hurrying and people who had pestering children. "Nice" people or people with characteristics similar to the interviewers would have a much better chance to be interviewed.

3. *Nonresponse.* This results when a particular group of those contacted declines to participate out of lack of interest, antagonism or busyness.

4. *Interviewer bias.* In this situation, an untrained interviewer deliberately or inadvertently leads the respondent to deviate from the truth. This can occur, for example, when interviewers read or "clarify" a question in a way that suggests that a particular answer is preferred.

5. *Questionnaire bias.* Systematic error can arise due to poor or confusing wording, leading questions, identification of the research sponsor, or omission of important possible responses.

6. *Respondent bias.* In this instance, the respondent misremembers something, lies, or unwittingly distorts an answer. Often this source of bias results not from malice, but from a misplaced attempt to "help out," as when an interviewee tries to please the interviewer by "yea-saying" everything.

7. *Processing bias.* This would occur if the interviewer (or respondent in a written study) wrote down the wrong answers, the office entered the answers into the computer incorrectly, or—heaven forbid—the computer analysis was programmed incorrectly.

Catching all of these glitches is not easy. It takes careful attention to the design process, to interviewer training, to checking on data-processing, and so on. It should be said that research funds are often better spent on catching glitches than on increasing the sample size. As one can see in Figure 6-2, the band of sampling error around the expected mean could be reduced somewhat by increasing N, but the potential for reduction of systematic bias is *much greater.* Dollars spent reducing the latter will undoubtedly have much greater impact than just dragging in more (biased) sample members.

ORGANIZATION[14]

We noted earlier many ways in which the research function can be organized. Among the key questions to be decided are

1. Is the marketing research function to stand alone, or is it to fit within a broader marketing or management information system? The answer depends on management's perception of the research mission (whether it is largely to provide descriptive, explanatory, or predictive information) and also on the overall budget.[15]

2. Which of the marketing research functions are to be farmed out to outside suppliers and which kept in-house? New nonprofit research departments will farm more out and with maturity gather them back in.

3. Where should the research function be placed in the organization? We

believe it should be high in the organization, since we believe that effective marketing is informed marketing. It should not be placed in a position (for example, in accounting) where its value may be compromised and its use limited.

EVALUATION AND CONTROL

The nonprofit's marketing research strategy should be routinely and formally evaluated. Questions should be raised about methodologies and personnel. Managers should be queried about the value of the information they received and asked for possible improvements. From time to time, an independent outside consultant should be brought in to ascertain the quality of the research given the available budget.

SUMMARY

Most nonprofit organizations carry out much less marketing research than they should. This is because they have accepted certain myths. They assume that marketing research should only be used for major decisions, that it involves big surveys, that it takes a long time, that it is always expensive, that it requires sophisticated researchers, and, when it is finished, that it is usually not read or used. But research using a diversity of techniques, many at low cost, can be extremely valuable to a wide range of decisions.

Research can help managers by describing, explaining, or predicting market characteristics. Most nonprofit research is applied, although some could be basic or methodological research. The applied nature of the research provides a good framework for decisions about budgets and for designing specific research projects.

There are several approaches to budgeting research, including historical increment, percent-of-revenues, competitive matching, and affordable budgeting. A cost-benefit approach is preferable, however, because it explicitly takes account of the uses to which the study's results are to be put. Formal decision theory allows the manager to estimate the economic loss due to present uncertainty about the best action to take. This clearly indicates the upper limit of a research budget. The actual amount to spend would then depend on the likely quality that the expenditure could achieve.

An applied orientation also recommends a "backward" research design process. Here the research manager first looks to the decisions to be made using the research results and then works backwards to design a study that would best inform such decisions. A second step would be determining what report format would provide the most managerially useful information. The report form would then suggest the type of analysis needed, which, in turn, would specify how the data are to be collected and processed.

Management of individual projects must involve careful attention in advance to potential biases and then to a careful evaluation of accomplishments or failures after the project has been completed. Such evaluation and control is especially essential as the organization develops a continuous program of strategic research over several years.

QUESTIONS

1. The Los Angeles Actors Theater facility has four theaters of varying sizes for varying types of performances. It opened in 1985 and management wishes to forecast future sales and determine sales responsiveness to future pricing strategies. Describe a procedure for determining the budget for such a study.

2. The Executive Management Program at the University of Illinois needs information on its attendees' backgrounds, perceptions, satisfactions, and probable future reenrollment behavior. What criteria should Illinois use to decide whether to do the necessary research itself or hire an independent consultant?

3. List the biases that could occur if a museum decided to have volunteers interview every tenth person entering the museum next Thursday morning between 9:00 A.M. and 1:30 P.M. In each case, suggest how you would reduce or eliminate the bias.

4. Design an experiment that would "prove" that a specific mail solicitation for a charity was more effective than some alternative and was more effective with some target consumers than with others.

5. Prepare a set of hypothetical tables to report the results in question 4. Show what data collection procedures are needed to fill in the tables.

6. Under what circumstances would the director of a local chapter of the American Red Cross be justified in spending $500 on a specific research study?

NOTES

1. This section draws upon Alan R. Andreasen, "Cost-Conscious Marketing Research," *Harvard Business Review,* July–August 1983, pp. 74–77.

2. For further information on research costs, see Seymour Sudman, *Reducing the Costs of Surveys,* (Chicago: Aldine, 1967).

3. See, for example, James B. Higgenbotham and Keith K. Cox, eds., *Focus Group Interviews: A Reader* (Chicago: American Marketing Association, 1979).

4. *The Professional Performing Arts: Attendance, Preferences and Motives* (Madison, Wis.: Association of College, University, and Community Arts Administrators, 1977).

5. Dik Warren Twedt, *1983 Survey of Marketing Research* (Chicago: American Marketing Association, 1984).

6. This approach makes use of Bayesian analytic techniques. For an introduction to this approach, see Robert Schlaifer, *Probability and Statistics for Business Decisions* (New York: McGraw-Hill, 1979). For other cost/benefit treatments of this problem, see Frank M. Bass, "Marketing Research Expenditures: A Decision Model," *Journal of Business,* January 1963, pp. 77–90, and Ralph L. Day, "Optimizing Marketing Research Through Cost Benefit Analysis," *Business Horizons,* Fall 1966, pp. 45–54.

7. This section is drawn from Alan R. Andreasen, "'Backward' Marketing Research," *Harvard Business Review,* May–June 1985, pp. 176–182.

8. Alan R. Andreasen and Russell W. Belk, "Predictors of Attendance at the Performing Arts," *Journal of Consumer Research,* September 1980, pp. 112–120.

9. Imran Currim, Charles B. Weinberg, and Dick R. Wittinck, "Design of Subscription Programs for a Performing Arts Series," *Journal of Consumer Research,* June 1981, pp. 67–75. For other examples, see Yoram Wind and Lawrence K. Spitz, "Analytical Approach to Marketing Decisions in Health-Care Organizations," *Operations Research,* September–October 1976, pp. 973–990, and Linda J. Golden, Mark I. Alpert, and John F. Betak, "A Programmatic Research Approach to Transit Marketing," *Traffic Quarterly,* Vol. 34, No. 4, October 1980, pp. 627–647.

10. For further discussion, see Seymour Sudman and Robert Ferber, *Consumer Panels* (Chicago: American Marketing Association, 1979).

11. A good introduction to alternative field experimental designs is found in Donald T. Campbell and Julian C. Stanley, *Experimental and Quasi-Experimental Designs for Research* (Chicago: Rand McNally, 1966). For a good example of a nonprofit experiment, see Richard A. Winett, Ingrid N. Lecklite, Donna E. Chinn, and Brian Stahl, "Reducing Energy Consumption: The Long-Term Effects of a Single TV Program," *Journal of Communications,* Summer 1984, pp. 37–51.

12. See Higginbotham and Cox, *Focus Group Interviews.*

13. See Gilbert A. Churchill, Jr., *Marketing Research: Methodological Foundations,* 3rd ed. (Chicago: Dryden, 1983), pp. 412–420. See also Leslie Kish, *Survey Sampling* (New York: John Wiley, 1965), especially Chapter 13.

14. See, for example, Lee Adler and Charles S. Mayer, eds., *Readings in Managing the Marketing Research Function* (Chicago: American Marketing Association, 1980).

15. For a description of the development of a marketing information system for UCLA's Department of Fine Arts, see Lee G. Cooper and Daniel Jacobs, "Marketing Information Systems for the Profession and Science of Arts Management," *The Journal of Arts Management and the Law,* Vol. 14, No. 1, Spring 1984, pp. 77–89.

Market Measurement and Forecasting

Since 1973, the National Research Center for the Arts has conducted surveys tracking changes in the attitudes and behaviors of Americans toward the performing and participative arts. The study of 1,504 adult Americans in March of 1984 identified a major change in the arts market. The National Center researchers found a significant decline in the amount of discretionary time households have available for leisure pursuits. In more families, both husbands and wives work, while the median number of hours people spend working has risen from 40.6 hours in 1973 to 47.3 hours in 1984.

In the face of this, the Center finds it not at all surprising that the rapid growth in arts attendance and participation that marked the 1970s has slowed. The slowdown, however, has not been uniform across arts categories. A number of arts are still growing rapidly. Attendance at live popular performances rose from 53 percent of responding households in 1980, to 60 percent in 1984. Attendance at the opera and musical theater rose from 25 to 34 percent of the households surveyed, and classical music and ballet rose from 25 percent to 34 percent each. On the other hand, attendance at museums has not increased at all.

The attitudes held by respondents in the latest study continue to be very positive. The vast majority of American adults consider the arts to be essential to their own and their community's welfare. They believe that the arts contribute significantly to the quality of life and to the economic vitality of their local community. They would like to see more arts education available in their public schools and believe that such programs should be supported out of the regular school budget.

The public feels that both the government and the private sector should contribute more to support the arts financially. The respondents contribute significantly themselves and indicate that they would be willing to pay more taxes if their money went to the arts. The Center found that fifty-three percent of the sample would pay an extra $25 in taxes if it went to fund the arts. The comparable figure in 1975 was only forty-one percent.

SOURCE: Adapted from National Research Center for the Arts, Inc., *Americans and the Arts* (Washington, D.C.: Louis Harris and Associates, Inc., October 1984).

A great many marketing decisions require a full understanding of the current and probable future market for a good or a service. Whether a nonprofit should venture into a new market or whether it is getting a reasonable share of the existing market are questions that can be answered only after present and future market potential have been carefully determined. This in turn requires that the manager be able to answer the following questions:

1. Who is the market? (market definition)
2. How large is the current market? (current market size measurement)
3. What is the probable future size of the market? (market forecasting)

These questions will be examined in the following sections.

DEFINING THE MARKET

Every organization faces the task of defining who is in its market. It knows that not everyone is a potential customer of its market offer. Not everyone is in the market for a college education, or day-care center services, or cancer treatment, or a job with the police department. Organizations must distinguish between their customers and noncustomers.

To define the market, the organization must carefully define its market offer. Take the case of a small private college. We can talk about the market for the college's bachelor's degree, or for its sociology program, or for its specific course on the sociology of religion. The market definition and size would vary in each case. Even the market for the course on the sociology of religion would be affected by the cost of the course and the place and time it is offered. The more specifically we can define the product, the more carefully we can determine the market's boundaries and size.

We define a market as follows:

A **market** is the set of actual and potential consumers of a market offer.

Two comments are in order. The term "consumers" is shorthand for a number of other possible terms, such as buyers, clients, adopters, users, and responders. Furthermore, the consumers can be individuals, families, groups, or organizations. The term "market offer" is also shorthand for a tangible good, service, program, idea, or anything that might be put out to a group of responders.

Those in the market for something have three characteristics: *interest, ability to transact,* and *access.* To illustrate this, consider the following situation:

> The chairman of a French department at a small college is concerned with the declining number of students signing up for French. One faculty member has already been dismissed, and another will be dismissed if the market for studying French continues to shrink. The French department chairman is thinking of offering an evening noncredit course on French culture to adults in the community. He is interested in estimating whether enough adults in the community would be in the "market" for this course.

The first thing to estimate is the number of adults in the community with a potential interest in a course on French culture. There are a number of ways to do this. The chairman could contact other colleges offering this course and find out their enrollment levels as a proportion of their area's adult population. A more direct approach would be to phone a random sample of adults in the more affluent and educated sectors of the community and ask about their level of interest in a French culture course. The following question could be asked: "If a noncredit French culture course is offered in the evening at our college, would you definitely take it, probably take it, or not be interested in taking it?" Suppose 4 out of 100 say they would definitely take the course, 6 say they might take it, and 90 say they would not take it. At the most, it appears that 10 percent have an interest in this course.[1] This percentage can be multiplied by the adult population in the community to estimate the potential market for this course. We define the potential market as follows:

The **potential market** is the set of consumers who profess some level of interest in a defined market offer.

Now consumer interest is not enough to define a market. If a price is attached to the offer, potential consumers must have adequate income to afford the purchase. They must be able to buy besides being willing to buy. Furthermore, the higher the price, the lower the number of people who will stay in the market. The size of a market is a function not only of the interest level but also of the ability to transact.[2] In certain circumstances, this "ability" would include goods or time to donate, blood with adequate hemoglobin to give, and so on.

Market size is further cut down by personal *access* barriers that might prevent response to the offer. Interested consumers may not be able to take the French course at the place and time it is offered. Access factors make the market smaller. The market that remains is called the available market. We define the available market as follows:

> The **available market** is the set of consumers who have interest, ability to transact, and access to a particular market offer.

In some market offers, the organization will establish some restrictions regarding with whom they will transact. Although a college sells football tickets to everyone in the community wishing to attend a game, it may not be willing to accept everyone who wants to take a course in French culture. The college may choose to accept only adults who (1) are twenty-four years old or older, and (2) have a high school diploma. These adults constitute the qualified available market:

> The **qualified available market** is the set of consumers who have interest, ability to transact, access, and qualifications for the particular market offer.

Now the college has the choice of going after the whole qualified available market or concentrating its efforts on certain segments. In the latter case, we need the concept of the served market. We define the served market as follows:

> The **served market** is the part of the qualified available market that the organization attempts to attract and serve.

Suppose the college prefers to attract primarily middle- and upper-class adults to its evening classes and, as a result, promotes the French culture course primarily in certain sections of the city. In that case, the served market would be somewhat smaller than the qualified available market.

Once the course is advertised, it will attract an actual number of adult learners that will represent some fraction of the served market. The number who enroll is called the penetrated market. We define the penetrated market as follows:

The **penetrated market** is the set of qualified available consumers who are actually consuming the product.

Figure 7-1 brings all the preceding concepts together. The bar on the left illustrates the ratio of the potential market—all interested persons—to the total population, here 10 percent. The figure on the right illustrates several breakdowns of the potential market. The available market—those who have interest, ability to transact, and access—is 40 percent of the potential consumers. The qualified available market—those who would meet the college's admissions requirements—is 20 percent of the potential market, or 50 percent of the available market. The college is actively trying to attract half of these, or 10 percent of the potential market. Finally, the college is shown as actually enrolling 5 percent of the potential market in the course.

These definitions of a market are a useful tool for marketing planning. If the organization is not satisfied with the size of its penetrated market, it can consider a number of actions. First, it could try to attract a larger percentage of people from its served market. If it finds, however, that the nonenrolling part of the served market has chosen to study French culture at a competing college, this college might try to widen its served market by

FIGURE 7-1

Levels of Market Definition

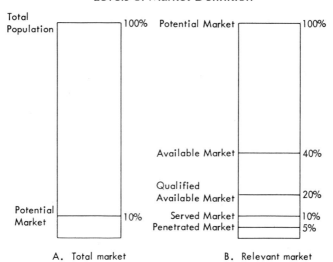

A. Total market   B. Relevant market

promoting the course in other parts of the city. Beyond this, the college could relax the qualifications for admission, thus expanding the qualified available market. The next step would be to consider expanding the available market by lowering the tuition, improving the location and time of the course offering, and doing other things to reduce cost and access. Ultimately, the college could try to expand the potential market by launching a campaign to convert noninterested consumers into interested consumers.

✤ MEASURING CURRENT MARKET DEMAND

We are now ready to examine practical methods of estimating current market demand for a market offer. There are four types of estimates that an organization will want to make: *total market demand, segment market demand, total industry demand,* and *organization market share.*

ESTIMATING TOTAL MARKET DEMAND

Total market demand is defined as follows:

Total market demand for a product is the total volume of exchanges that would be made by a defined consumer group in a defined geographical area in a defined time period in a defined marketing environment under a defined marketing program.

The most important thing to realize about total market demand is that it is not a fixed number but a function of the specified conditions. One of these conditions, for example, is the marketing program (psychological and economic cost, product features, promotional expenditure level, etc.), and another is the state of the economy. The dependence of total market demand on these conditions is illustrated in the response curve in Figure 7-2. The horizontal axis shows different possible levels of marketing expenditure by the organization in a given time period. On the vertical axis is shown the resulting demand level. The curve represents the estimated level of market demand associated with different marketing expenditure levels by the organization. We see that some base volume (called the *market minimum*) would take place without any demand-stimulating expenditures by the organization. Positive marketing expenditures would yield higher levels of demand, first at an increasing rate, then at a decreasing rate. Marketing expenditures higher than a certain level would not stimulate much further demand, thus suggesting an upper limit to market demand called the *market potential.*

The distance between the market minimum and the market potential shows the overall *marketing sensitivity of demand.* We can think of two extreme types of markets, the *expansible* and the *nonexpansible.* An expan-

FIGURE 7-2

Market Demand

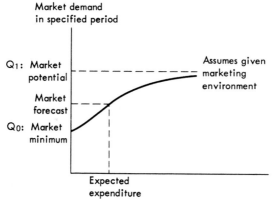

A. Market demand as function of marketing expenditure
(assumes particular marketing environment)

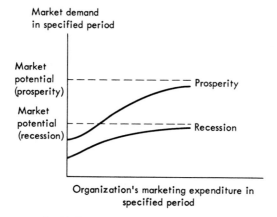

B. Market demand as function of marketing expenditure
(two different environments assumed)

sible market, such as a market for a new sport such as racquetball, is quite affected in its total size by the level of marketing expenditures. In terms of Figure 7-2A the distance between Q_0 and Q_1 is relatively large. A nonexpansible market, such as the market for opera, is not much affected by the level of marketing expenditures; the distance between Q_0 and Q_1 is relatively small. The organization operating in a nonexpansible market can take the market's size (the level of *primary demand*) for granted and concentrate its marketing resources on getting a desired market share (the level of *selective demand*).

Only one of the many possible levels of marketing expenditure will actually be chosen by the organization. The market demand corresponding to this expenditure level is called the *market forecast*. The market forecast shows the expected level of market demand for the expected level of organizational marketing expenditure in the given environment.

If a different environment is assumed, the market demand function would have to be freshly estimated. The market for theatregoing, for example, is higher during prosperity than recession because market demand is income-elastic. The dependence of market demand on the environment is illustrated in Figure 7-2B.

The main point is that the marketer should carefully define the situation for which market demand is being estimated. The marketer can use a method known as the *chain ratio method* to form the estimate. The chain ratio method involves multiplying a base number by a succession of percentages that lead to an estimation of the defined consumer demand. Here is an example:

> The U.S. Navy seeks to attract 112,000 new male recruits each year from American high schools. The question is whether this is a high or low target in relation to the market potential. The market potential has been estimated by the chain ratio method as follows:

Total number of male high school graduating students	10,000,000
Percentage who are militarily qualified (no physical, emotional, or mental handicaps)	× .50
Percentage of those qualified who are potentially interested in military service	× .15
Percentage of those qualified and interested in military service who consider the Navy the preferred service	× .30

This chain of numbers shows the market potential to be 225,000 recruits. Since this exceeds the target number of recruits sought, the U.S. Navy should not have much trouble meeting its target, if it does a reasonable job of marketing the Navy. But many of the potential recruits are lost somehow. They are not contacted; their parents talk them out of military service; they hear negative things from friends; they form a bad impression at the recruiting office. The result is that the Navy barely manages to recruit the targeted number. Knowing the market potential therefore provides the Navy with a basis for knowing whether it is doing well or poorly in comparison to what it *could* do.

Often, when purchases of goods and services are involved, the marketer has to estimate the total revenue that might be realized through a market offer. This is accomplished by multiplying the number of consumers by the price of the product. Suppose, however, that consumers can buy more than one unit, as is the case of adult learners who can take from one to four courses during a semester. The total potential revenue would be estimated using the following formula:

$$R = NQP \qquad (7\text{-}1)$$

where:

R = total potential revenue
N = number of buyers in the specific product market who might buy under the given assumptions
Q = quantity purchased by an average buyer
P = price of an average unit

Thus, if there are 1,000 potential adult learners in a community who might sign up for courses, and the average adult enrolls in two courses a semester, and the average tuition is $30 a course, the total potential revenue would be $60,000 (= 1,000 × 2 × $30).

ESTIMATING SEGMENT MARKET DEMAND

The market demand for a product or service varies by segment. Given this fact, the organization has to decide on the specific segments deserving the most attention. These will normally be the segments having the highest market demand, although some segments may have to be served for reasons other than maximizing demand.

There are a number of ways to estimate the relative attractiveness of different segments. We illustrate these ways in connection with the following situation involving geographic segmentation.

The Organic Theatre of Chicago attracts most of its season ticket subscribers from Chicago and nearby suburbs. The management feels that additional theatregoers can be attracted from more distant suburbs such as Oak Park, Hinsdale, Arlington Heights, and Highland Park. However, the theatre cannot mount a campaign to promote subscriptions in all of these suburbs and wants to identify the suburbs with the highest potential.

Four methods of estimating area market potential will be described in the following paragraphs.

Area Analysis of Current Sales.   A common approach is to study the areas that current subscribers are coming from. One can prepare a dot map showing the number of consumers in different areas. Suppose the management finds that 6 percent of its audience comes from Oak Park and 2 percent from Hinsdale. The management will conclude that Oak Park is a better "market" than Hinsdale, in that it might have more people who like theatre. The further implication is that Oak Park might deserve three times the marketing effort as Hinsdale.

Although this is a common way to estimate area market potential, it can be misleading. Current area sales reflect not only differences in market potential but also differences in market cultivation. Maybe the Organic Theatre mailed more promotional literature to Oak Park residents than to Hinsdale residents. In the extreme, suppose the Organic Theatre had run a direct mail campaign in Oak Park and no campaign in Hinsdale. One might then conclude that Hinsdale might have substantially more potential since 2 percent of the audience came from Hinsdale without the benefit of any promotion. Furthermore, even if we believe that Oak Park had three times as much market potential as Hinsdale, it does not follow that Oak Park deserves three times the effort. It may deserve four times the effort, two times the effort, or the same effort. We would have to estimate the marginal response to additional promotional effort that would occur in each community.

Single-Factor Index.   Here management tries to discover a single measurable factor that would reflect the market potential of different communities. Suppose management believes the best single indicator of the propensity to attend theatre is the "number of college-educated people in the community." Using this criterion, if Oak Park has 6,000 college-educated residents and Hinsdale has 4,000, we could argue that Oak Park deserves more marketing effort—indeed, something like 50 percent more than Hinsdale.

Multiple-Factor Index.   Often, management feels that it cannot put its whole confidence in a single factor. Instead, two or more factors may seem to indicate the level of market potential in a community. The problem is to form an index that combines these factors. Suppose the Organic Theatre management believes that two factors are highly associated with demand: (1) "the number of college-educated people," and (2) "the number of people earning over $20,000." Suppose statistics are not available on the combined variable. Figure 7-3 shows how a multiple factor index can be formed.

The rows list the communities in greater Chicago that are accessible to the theatre. The first two columns list the two factors. The third and fourth columns convert these two factors into percentages expressing each community's share of the total of each column. Thus, Oak Park has 6 percent of the total college-educated people in the greater Chicago area and 4 percent of the high earners. We can take a simple average of the two percentage figures for each community and call this the multiple factor index number.

FIGURE 7-3

Multiple Factor Index

	(1)	(2)	(3)	(4)	(5)
	Number of College Educated	Number Earning More Than $20,000	Percent of Total College Educated	Percent Earning More Than $20,000	Multiple Factor Index
Oak Park	6,000	8,000	6	4	5
Hinsdale	4,000	4,000	4	2	3
•	•	•	•	•	•
•	•	•	•	•	•
•	•	•	•	•	•
	100,000	100,000			

Thus, Oak Park can be said to have about 5 percent of the total market potential, whereas Hinsdale has 3 percent. These numbers can be used to guide the percentage of the promotional budget to spend in each community.

The multiple factor index can be refined in a number of ways. First, management may want to use more than two factors, and this would require additional columns. Second, management may want to assign unequal weights to the factors instead of taking a simple average. Third, some of the factors may not be expressible in percentage terms, and it may be necessary to convert all the row numbers into standard scales (say, 1- to 10-point scales), which are then weighted. The general approach outlined here is the one used to develop the "index of consumer buying power" that is used by business to determine the market potential of different geographical areas for basic products.[3]

Distance-Adjusted Index.   One more factor should be taken into account in developing the market potentials of different communities. Studies show that market potential drops with distance from the site of the offer, because people view travel as a cost and would prefer to patronize outlets nearer their residence. In fact, some early studies indicated that market attractiveness falls off with the square of the distance of the buyer from the seller. Market potential is considered positively correlated with the size of the target population and inversely correlated with the squared distance of the target population from the seller.[4] Thus, each of the indexes in column 5 of Figure 7-3 could be divided by the square of the distance from the center of the community to the Organic Theatre to produce a new distance-adjusted index.

There is a simpler way to make an adjustment for distance. Management could decide, arbitrarily, to reduce the multiple factor index by 1 percentage point for every 8 miles of distance between the community and the theatre. Oak Park happens to be 8 miles from the theatre and Hinsdale is 16 miles away. Instead of Oak Park's multiple factor index standing at 5, it would be reduced to 4; Hinsdale's index, instead of standing at 3, would stand at 1. Thus, Oak Park is seen to have five times the potential for the sale of theatre tickets over Hinsdale, and not just 1⅔ the potential as in Figure 7-3.

Estimating Total Industry Demand

Besides measuring potential demand, an organization will want to know the current number of exchanges taking place in its market. This requires identifying the other organizations serving the same market. This is not as simple as it sounds because of the many definitions of a market. Grant Hospital, for example, would have to identify other alcoholic treatment centers in the greater Chicago area where some of its potential consumers might have gone. Should this include Highland Park Hospital, which is a long distance away but might have some alcoholism patients? The organization must carefully define its real competition as the first step in developing an estimate of total sales and its share of sales.

Then the organization has to estimate the volume for each competitor. How can this information be obtained? The easiest way is to contact each competitor and offer to exchange information. In this way, each organization can measure its performance against every other organization and against the total volume for the industry. However, this solution is not always available. Trading competitive information is illegal in some industries. In other cases, particular competitors are not willing to divulge this information. In the latter case, the organization can still compare its performance to that of the cooperating organizations.

Another solution calls for the trade association to collect the data and publish the results of each organization, the industry total, or both. In this way, each organization can evaluate its performance against specific competitors or the industry as a whole. If such a trade association does not exist, nonprofit competitors may see the need for comparative data as the very reason to create a trade association.

If this solution is not available, the organization must estimate the volume of one or more competitors through indirect methods. Grant Hospital, for example, might infer the number of inpatient alcoholism treatments at a particular competitive hospital by knowing the number of beds, the size of the staff, or other clues. In the industrial world, a company may estimate the sales of another company by finding out how many shifts the factory is operating or how much raw material it is ordering from suppliers. In the retail sector, this is often accomplished by multiplying square footage of competitors' outlets by estimated sales per square foot (based, for example, on one's own sales per square foot).

ESTIMATING ORGANIZATION MARKET SHARE

The organization's own volume does not tell the whole story of how well it is doing. Suppose the organization's volume is increasing at 5 percent a year and its competitor's volume is increasing at 10 percent. This organization is actually losing its relative standing in the industry. Organizations will therefore want to compare their volume with that of competitors.

Organizations can estimate at least three market share figures. Ideally, the organization should know its (1) share of the total market, (2) share of the served market, and (3) share relative to the leading competitor or leading three competitors. Each of these measures yields useful information about the organization's market performance and potential.

FORECASTING FUTURE MARKET DEMAND

Having looked at ways to estimate current demand, we can now examine the problem of estimating future demand. Very few industries lend themselves to easy forecasting. The few cases generally involve a product or service whose absolute level or trend is fairly constant and whose competition is nonexistent or stable. In the vast majority of markets, total market demand and specific organization demand are not stable from year to year and good forecasting becomes a key factor in effective performance. This is particularly true for nonprofits in which these problems are compounded by a lack of good historical data. In such cases, poor forecasting can lead to excess or insufficient personnel and supplies. The more unstable the demand, the more critical is forecast accuracy, and the more elaborate is forecasting procedure.

In approaching forecasting, one should list all the factors that might affect future demand and predict each factor's likely future level and effect on demand. The factors affecting demand might be classified into three categories: (1) *noncontrollable macroenvironmental factors* such as the state of the economy, new technologies, and legal developments; (2) *competitive factors* such as competitors' prices, new products, and promotional expenditures; and (3) *controllable organizational factors* such as the organization's prices, new products, and promotional expenditures.

In view of the many factors that might be involved, organizations have turned to various approximation methods to forecast future demand. Five major methods are discussed below. They arise out of three information bases for building a forecast. A forecast can be based on *what people say, what people do,* or *what people have done.* The first basis—what people say—involves systematic determination of the opinions of buyers or of those close to them, such as salespersons or outside experts. It encompasses three methods: (1) buyer intentions surveys, (2) middleman estimates, and (3) expert judgments. Building a forecast on what people do involves another method: (4) market testing. The final basis—what people have done—involves using statistical tools to analyze records of past buying behavior, using either (5) time-series analysis, or (6) statistical demand analysis. Each of these methods is described and illustrated below.

Buyer Intentions Surveys

Forecasting is particularly difficult when one is dealing with new offerings or markets that have dramatically changed. One way to form an estimate of future demand is to ask a sample of target buyers to state their buying intentions for the forthcoming period. Suppose a college is trying to estimate the number of majors to expect next year in each of its disciplines. The objective is to schedule enough courses and faculty to service the level of demand for the various majors. A small number of sophomores can be asked to indicate their intended major next year. If 20 percent say that they intend to make economics their major, the college can multiply this against the size of the sophomore class and infer the number of actual students who plan to major in economics.

The reliability of buyer intentions forecasts depends on (1) buyers having clear intentions, (2) buyers being likely to carry out their intentions, (3) buyers being willing to describe their intentions to interviewers, and (4) little time elapsing between the forecast and the behavior. To the extent that these assumptions are weak, the results must be used with caution. Suppose a theatre at midseason asked its subscribers about their intentions to renew their subscription for the following year. The problem is that the current subscribers may not have thought about renewal and they may want to finish the series before forming their intentions. Buyer intentions data in this case would be weak.

They would also be weak in the case of new products, services, or ideas with which consumers are unfamiliar. Thus, asking voters in 1985 about their intention to support a "flat" income tax may yield highly unreliable estimates. Consumers are also notoriously poor predictors whenever much time elapses before the predicted behavior itself. Certainly, Jimmy Carter would have dropped out of the presidential race of 1976 if he had believed that a poll indicating that less than 10 percent of the population intended to vote for him was a good predictor of the eventual outcome.

Buyer intentions could be assessed in a number of ways. A yes-or-no form of the question would be: "Do you intend to buy a season ticket next year?" This requires the respondent to make a definite choice. Some researchers prefer the following form of the question: "Will you (a) definitely buy, (b) probably buy, (c) probably not buy, or (d) definitely not buy a season ticket next year?" These researchers feel that the "definitely buys" would be fairly dependable as a minimum estimate and some fraction of the "probably buys" could be added to arrive at a forecast. More recently, some researchers have recommended using a *full purchase probability scale:*

Do you intend to buy a season theatre ticket for next year?

.00	.10	.20	.30	.40	.50	.60	.70	.80	.90	1.00
No chance	Very slight possibility	Slight possibility	Some possibility	Fair possibility	Fairly good possibility	Good possibility	Probably	Very probably	Almost	Certain

The researcher uses various fractions of the positive responders to form an estimate. The researcher can improve the system over time by checking the forecasts against the actuals and seeing what weights would have improved the forecast.

Finally, it may be noted that even when the *absolute* levels of demand derived from buyer intentions are unreliable, the relative levels are often reliable. Thus, if a nonprofit organization measures buyer intentions over several years, it may know that *each* estimate is fallible but that if the buyer intention index is up 20 percent between periods, demand may be expected to rise. Even where past indexes are unavailable, forecasts of *relative* demand for different kinds of market offerings can be derived by asking target audience members a series of "what if" questions (see Exhibit 7-1).

MIDDLEMAN ESTIMATES

If reaching ultimate buyers is difficult or too expensive, another way of developing a forecast is to ask people who are close to the buyers what those buyers are likely to do. The college that is trying to anticipate enrollments to different majors, for example, might ask each department chairperson to estimate these enrollments. The chairpersons will examine past data and what they have recently heard and prepare a forecast. Some chairpersons will overestimate (the optimists) and some will underestimate (the pessimists). If individual chairpersons are fairly consistent overestimators or underestimators, their forecasts can be adjusted by the administration for their known bias before using the forecasts for planning purposes.

When business firms use this method, they ask for estimates from their sales force, distributors, and dealers, since all of these are presumably closer to the customers and can render an opinion about likely demand. Nonprofit organizations can also find similar "experts." Thus a national fundraising organization can ask its regional chairpersons to make estimates, and they in turn can ask their individual fund-raisers for estimates. Asking people

EXHIBIT 7-1. Expanding the audience for symphony and theater

Traditional approaches to forecasting demand for the arts have relied on trend extrapolation or econometric models describing the relationship between selected socioeconomic characteristics and past attendance behavior. These approaches are of limited value for arts marketers interested in *changing* past relationships to broaden the base of arts attendance. To remedy this, Andreasen and Belk collected data forecasting the probable responses of theater and symphony audiences in four southern cities to a series of "what if" questions.

The approach adopted was designed, not to forecast absolute levels, but to provide indexes of the relative effectiveness of specific concrete strategies known to be available to most arts marketers. Thus, past attenders and nonattenders of theater and symphony were asked to indicate whether they would increase or decrease (if possible) their attendance *if* certain changes were made. Among the changes suggested were:

1. *Product changes*
   a. Changes in types of performance
   b. Changes in the quality of performances
   c. Increases in the amount of explanation
      about performances
2. *Place changes*
   a. Performances nearer to home
   b. More informal dress at performances
3. *Price Changes*
   a. Increases or decreases in individual ticket prices
   b. Changes in series ticket discounts
   c. Offering half-price tickets the day of the performance
   d. Offering second tickets at half price
   e. Offering telephone credit purchases

These strategic changes were attempts to reflect plausible offerings and trade-offs. An indication of the kinds of responses in the case of symphony offerings is reported in Table 7-1. Figures are reported as numbers showing greater or lesser effects compared to an "average impact" score of 100. Results are reported for both past attenders and nonattenders and in total.

The final columns of Table 7-1 indicate clearly that the two most potent means of increasing symphony patronage among this set of alternatives is offering second tickets at half price or scheduling more famous conductors or performers. Least effective would be more choral music or more modern compositions. These options had the same effect on both past attenders and nonattenders. Thus, unfortunately, a powerful means of attracting past nonattenders, offering a second ticket at half price, is just as attractive to past attenders, implying that new revenues from such a strategem will be offset by losses from regular attenders who take advantage of the offer but who would have paid full price. Two cases showing major differences between attenders and nonattenders

EXHIBIT 7-1. (continued)

are having a more convenient site and making the occasion seem less formal. Nonattenders find these options significantly more appealing. However, the potential user of these results is confronted by the dilemma in Table 7-1 where regular attenders appear potentially turned off by such a move.

These results cannot be taken to indicate *absolute* levels of response to the various offerings. The results of asking consumers about future behavior in hypothetical situations must be interpreted cautiously. *If* one is willing to assume that such biases are constant across offerings, however, then the data can be interpreted to indicate the *relative* effectiveness of each offering.

---

who come in contact with the buyers for their estimates is called "grassroots forecasting." In using the method, the grassroots forecasters should be given a set of basic assumptions about the coming year, such as the state of the economy, the organization's tentative marketing plans, and so on. This is preferable to allowing each expert to make personal assumptions about major demand influences that will operate next year.

Grassroots forecasting has two major advantages. Since people involved in the marketing process submit them, these people will have more confidence in the derived sales quotas they get back and they will have more incentive to achieve them. Also, grassroots forecasting results in estimates broken down by product, territory, customer, and estimator, which makes the setting of individual quotas easier.

EXPERT FORECASTS

Buyer intentions or middlemen predictions may be helpful for near-term forecasting, especially for new offerings. When carrying out long-term forecasting, however, these groups may not have sufficient perspective, experience, or wisdom to be able to see the forest for the trees. Take, for example, the problem of the marketing manager of UCLA's executive education program in trying to estimate the long-run demand for MBA degree programs for senior executives. Several techniques may be used for such longer range forecasts. The most casual approach is to subscribe to one or another social trend forecasting services such as those offered by SRI International or Public Policy Forecasting, and attempt to extrapolate their insights to the executive MBA problem.

SRI International in Palo Alto has a Business Intelligence Program (BIP) with SCAN options. This system involves 150 SRI consultants in California, Washington, Tokyo, and London looking routinely for signals of change. They then use electronic mail to "discuss" their findings with other

Table 7-1

INDEXES OF EFFECTIVENESS OF SYMPHONY OFFERINGS AMONG PRIOR
ATTENDERS AND NONATTENDERS

Offerings	Past Year Symphony Attenders		
	Attenders	Nonattenders	Average
Product Variations			
Type of Performance:			
More classical music	102	107	105
More romantic music	107	90	97
More modern music	53	54	54
More concertos	56	57	57
More choral music	31	49	43
Quality of Performance:			
More famous performers/conductors	150	166	161
Extent of Learning Opportunities:			
Short talk	101	121	114
Context Variations			
Location/Convenience:			
Nearer, less attractive, 20% discount	76	112	100
Formality of Atmosphere:			
Dressing more informally	61	100	87
Price Variations			
Couples Discount:			
Second ticket one-half off	199	180	186
Clearance Discount:			
One-half off day of performance	106	121	116
Effort to Secure tickets:			
Telephone/credit purchasing.	77	81	80
Base ticket price decrease	112	124	120
Base ticket price increase	99	84	89
Series discount	96	112	107
Favorite program with ticket price increase	93	87	89
Average	100	102	100

SOURCE: Alan R. Andreasen and Russell W. Belk, *Audience Development: An Examination of Selected Analyses and Prediction Techniques Applied to Symphony and Theatre Attendance in Four Southern Cities* (Washington, D.C.: National Endowment for the Arts, 1981).

experts. Once a month, twenty experts assemble in Menlo Park, California, and see if the "weak signals" from the field constitute a trend.

Public Policy Forecasting is the brainchild of Graham T. T. Molitar. Molitar assumes that shifts in public policy in European countries toward social, environmental, and health care issues are good predictors of what will happen later in the United States, usually eight to twenty-two years later. He feels Sweden and Norway are particularly relevant and spends several weeks each year sniffing out trends for his corporate (AT&T, Citibank, Coca-Cola, Standard Oil), university (Stanford, MIT, Harvard) and government (Federal Trade Commission, General Accounting Office, Federal Food and Drug Administration) clients.

These techniques, however, are not usually very specific to an organization or industry. Another possibility is what might be called "scenario analysis." This technique, championed by the Hudson Institute, takes past and present developments and offers several pathways into the future. Thus, in UCLA's case, they may propose these possibilities:

Scenario 1: General demand for executive MBA programs will rise through 1992 as managers promoted to senior ranks continue to have formal undergraduate training in areas other than business (for example, engineering) and need MBAs. At the same time, competitors for this executive market will accelerate even faster, resulting in a decline in UCLA's market share toward the end of this period. After 1992, industry demand will drop sharply, competitors will be slow to leave the market, and UCLA's enrollment will drop sharply.

Scenario 2: Industry demand will increase through 1992, but competitors will not increase as fast as the industry, particularly competitors at UCLA's "quality level." After 1992, declining demand will encourage other high quality competitors to leave the market rapidly, leaving UCLA with a growing market share in a declining market.

Scenario 3: Industry demand will increase to 1992 and then drop as far as senior executives are concerned. The fact that more senior executives enter the top ranks after 1992 with business training, however, will put even greater pressure on those remaining managers who lack MBAs and this will sustain the upward trend in the industry through 2000.

Managers and the scenario writers may then apply probability estimates to each scenario (and others that could emerge) to serve as their forecast. A major virtue of this technique is that it forces the nonprofit manager to think about contingency plans should the most likely scenario not take place.

A competing technique called the Delphi Method permits interaction among diverse experts, who can be widely separated geographically.[5] The Delphi approach is based on a forecast-feedback-reforecast process as follows:

1. In the first round, experts are asked to (a) extrapolate past trends to some distant future point, and (b) write down the major environmental factors they considered in making their extrapolations.

2. The results of the expert forecasts are then pooled, the key environmental factors summarized, and the findings reported back to the original survey group.
3. The experts are then asked to revise their forecasts if they wish and to indicate any new considerations they have introduced.

This pattern may be repeated over additional cycles until a consensus is reached and the variance around the group's estimates is reduced considerably. The technique is costly but the Stanford Research Institute (SRI) found it extremely useful in attempting to estimate how the American populace will budget their time and expenditures for leisure activities fifteen to thirty years in the future.

MARKET TESTS

In the case where buyers do not plan their future behavior carefully or are very erratic in carrying out their intentions or where experts are not likely to be very good guessers, a more direct market test of probable behavior is desirable. A direct market test is especially desirable in forecasting the sales of a new product or the probable sales of an established product in a new channel of distribution or territory. Where a short-run forecast of likely buyer response is desired, a small-scale market test is usually a highly accurate and reliable method.

TIME-SERIES ANALYSIS

As an alternative to costly surveys or market tests, many organizations prepare their forecasts on the basis of a statistical analysis of past data. The underlying logic is that past time series reflect causal relations that can be uncovered through statistical analysis. The findings can be used to predict future demand.

A time series of past performance can be analyzed into four major components.

The first component, *trend (T)*, reflects the basic level and rate of change in the size of the market. It is found by fitting a straight or curved line through the time-series data. The past trend can be extrapolated to estimate next year's trend level.

A second component, *cycle (C)*, might also be observed in a time series. Many behaviors are affected by periodic swings in general economic activity. If the stage of the business cycle can be predicted for the next period, this would be used to adjust the trend value up or down.

A third component, *season (S)*, would capture any consistent pattern of movements within the year. The term "season" is used to describe any recurrent hourly, daily, weekly, monthly, or quarterly pattern. The seasonal component may be related to weather factors, holidays, and so on. The researcher would adjust the estimate for, say, a particular month by the known seasonal level for that month.

The fourth component, *erratic events (E),* includes strikes, blizzards, fads, riots, fires, war scares, price wars, and other disturbances. This erratic component has the effect of obscuring the more systematic components. It represents everything that remains unanalyzed in the time series and cannot be predicted in the future. It shows the average size of the error that is likely to characterize time-series forecasting.

Here is an example of how time-series forecasting works:

> A county historical museum had 12,000 visitors this year. It wants to predict next year's December attendance in order to schedule enough guards. The long-term trend shows a 5 percent attendance growth rate per year. This implies attendance next year of 12,600 (= 12,000 × 1.05). A business recession is expected next year, however, and this generally depresses attendance to 90 percent of the expected trend level. This means attendance next year will more likely be 11,340 (= 12,600 × .90). If attendance is the same each month, this would mean monthly attendance of 945 (= 11,340 ÷ 12). December is an above-average month, however, with a seasonal index standing at 1.30. Therefore, December attendance may be as high as 1,229 (= 945 × 1.3). No erratic events, such as public transportation strikes or new competitive exhibits, are expected (but they may occur). Experience has shown that such events could leave a forecast off plus or minus 3 percent. Therefore, the best estimate of next December's attendance is 1,229 with a possibility it could be as high as 1,276 or as low as 1,201.

STATISTICAL DEMAND ANALYSIS

Numerous real factors affect the demand for anything. *Statistical demand analysis* is a set of statistical procedures designed to discover the most important real factors affecting behaviors and their relative influence. The factors most commonly analyzed in the case of products and services are prices, income, population, and promotion.

Statistical demand analysis consists of expressing sales (Q) as a dependent variable and trying to explain sales variation as a result of variation in a number of independent demand variables $X_1, X_2, \ldots, X_n$; that is,

$$Q = f(X_1, X_2, \ldots, X_n) \tag{7-2}$$

This says that the level of sales, Q, is a function of the levels of the independent factors $X_1, X_2, \ldots, X_n$. Using a technique called multiple regression analysis, various equation forms can be statistically fitted to the data in the search for the best predicting factors and equations.[6]

Here is an example:

A central library wanted to forecast book circulation next year at each of its ten branch libraries. The following equation was fitted to past data:

$$Q = 5000 - 300X_1 + 1000X_2 \qquad (7\text{-}3)$$

where

X_1 = average education level in the branch's neighborhood
X_2 = age of the branch library

For example, the Lincoln branch library would be ten years old next year and was located in a neighborhood whose residents averaged twelve years of formal education. Using (7-3), we would predict that book circulation would be:

$$Q = 5000 - 300(10) + 1000(12) = 14,000 \qquad (7\text{-}4)$$

If this equation predicts book circulation satisfactorily for the various branches, then the central library can assume that it has identified two key factors influencing book circulation. It may want to explore the exact influence of these factors, as well as other factors that might be added to improve the equation's forecasting accuracy.

Note, however, that this technique requires an independent estimate of the predictor variables. Thus, if the library wanted to forecast circulation ten years hence, somebody would have to first make a forecast of education levels. Sometimes good estimates are available from other sources. Sometimes the managers must make their own "guesstimates." If the issue is important enough, management may wish to develop a second, prior equation predicting a value that is then "plugged into" the forecasting equation.[7]

A structural model was recently used by Hanssens and Levien to study the effects of environmental and marketer-controlled factors on U.S. Navy recruitment.[8] Using measures for thirty variables collected at forty-three Navy recruiting districts between January, 1976, and December, 1978, the researchers constructed and estimated a multiplicative (log-linear) model to explain the number of advertising leads secured and delayed-entry and direct-shipment recruitment contracts achieved. They concluded the following:

> Overall, changes in the environment have a more dramatic impact on recruiting performance than changes in marketing efforts. . . . [I]ncreased marketing spending does not fully compensate for a much more difficult recruiting environment (e.g., a declining unemployment rate). At the district level, differences in youth attitudes toward the Navy, degree of urbanization, proportion of high school seniors and blacks in the target market are primarily

responsible for the variability in recruiting performance across [Navy Recruiting Districts], in spite of the fact that poorly performing NRDs have received more recruiters, local advertising and recruiter aid support on a per capita basis.*

SUMMARY

In order to carry out their responsibilities for marketing planning, execution, and control, marketing managers need measures of current and future market size. We defined a market as the set of actual and potential consumers of a market offer. Being in the market means having interest, ability to transact, and access to the market offer. The marketer's task is to distinguish various levels of the market that is being investigated, such as the potential market, available market, qualified available market, served market, and penetrated market.

The next step is to estimate the size of current demand. Total current demand can be estimated through the chain ratio method, which involves multiplying a base number by a succession of appropriate percentages to arrive at the defined market. Area market demand can be estimated in four ways: area analysis of current sales, single factor index, multiple factor indices, or distance-adjusted indices. Estimating actual industry demand requires identifying the relevant competitors and using some method of estimating the sales of each. Finally, the organization should compare its sales to industry sales to find whether its market share is improving or declining.

For estimating future demand, the organization can use one or any combination of five forecasting methods: buyer intentions surveys, middleman estimates, market tests, time-series analysis, or statistical demand analysis. These methods vary in their appropriateness with the purpose of the forecast, the type of product, and the availability and reliability of data.

QUESTIONS

1. Define the potential market, available market, qualified available market, served market, and penetrated market for the Los Angeles Museum of Contemporary Art. Should strategies be developed for each level of market definition?

2. A psychiatric hospital in a city of 200,000 is considering developing and promoting an outpatient alcoholism and drug abuse program. None of its five competitor hospitals has such a program. How can the hospital develop an estimate of likely revenues for the first five years? How accurate does such an estimate really need to be?

3. The U.S. Coast Guard wishes to use market share as one measure of the success of its recruiting programs. What are the alternative ways it could

---

*Reprinted by permission of Dominique M. Hanssens and Henry A. Levien, "An Econometric Study of Recruitment Marketing in the U.S. Navy," *Management Science*, Volume 29, Number 10, October, 1983, © 1983 The Institute of Management Sciences.

measure share? Under which measure is it likely that the Coast Guard would look best and under which would it look worst?

4. How could you go about developing a statistical forecast of the number of visitors coming to the United States from Canada for vacation purposes in 1988? What would be *two* best predictor variables?

5. A performing arts center is afraid to market test price cuts for seatings at individual performances for fear of alienating some customers. Management feels it sufficient to just ask present patrons about their probable behavior under various pricing plans. Evaluate both their fears and their alternative plans.

NOTES

1. Some analysts use all the "definites" and some arbitrary fraction of the "probablys" to estimate the demand level. Thus, they may say that the demand is made up four "definites" and half of the six "probablys," namely seven people, or 7 percent of the population.

2. It must be added that for many nonprofit organization markets, income is not a defining variable, because the consumer is not expected to pay for the service. Thus, in such cases as the Girl Scouts, U.S. Army cigarette smokers, and so on, the target consumer's income is not a factor in the size of the market.

3. See "Putting the Four to Work," *Sales Management,* October 28, 1974, pp. 13 ff.

4. See George Schwartz, *Development of Marketing Theory* (Cincinnati: Southwestern, 1963), pp. 9–36.

5. See Philip Kotler, "A Guide to Gathering Expert Estimates," *Business Horizons,* October 1970, pp. 79–87.

6. See William F. Massy, "Statistical Analysis of Relations Between Variables," in David A. Aaker, ed., *Multivariate Analysis in Marketing: Theory and Applications* (Belmont, Calif., Wadsworth, 1971), pp. 5–35.

7. For other statistical approaches, see Gary L. Lilien and Philip Kotler, *Marketing Decision Making: A Model Building Approach* 2d ed. (New York: Harper & Row, 1983).

8. Dominique M. Hanssens and Henry A. Levien, "An Econometric Study of Recruitment Marketing in the U.S. Navy," *Management Science,* Vol. 29, No. 10 (October 1983), pp. 1167–1184.

C H A P T E R   8

Marketing Planning

In the late 1970s, WILL-TV, the public television station of the University of Illinois at Urbana-Champaign, faced a major decision about its capital expenditures for the coming year. To resolve the problem, station management set aside a weekend for all of its management personnel to repair to a nearby resort area for some serious away-from-the-telephone thinking about the station's future. A faculty consultant was recruited as a key facilitator.

The immediate issue at hand seemed simple enough. WILL -TV had to decide whether to purchase several state-of-the-art video recording and playback machines. But, like all budgetary decisions of this magnitude, the decision was complex because it meant taking funds from other areas. The area that was resisting most vigorously was local production. Subtle and not-so-subtle infighting between factions at the station was the major factor precipitating the planning weekend. Top management felt that, if nothing else, getting away to thoroughly discuss the issues would help clear the air and improve internal morale.

The weekend's initial discussions made it immediately clear to the consultant that WILL -TV was at a major crossroads. The issue of the video recorders revealed that the station really had no long-range plan. Specifically, it had not decided whether its long-range mission was to focus on local programming—interviews, news features, cultural programming, and so on—or on effectively using the higher quality programming available from the Public Broadcasting System and a wide range of independent sources, especially several in England. The latter strategy choice would require the acquisition of a significant number of VCRs, since this plan would require the station to record substantial amounts of material from several satellite sources while juggling regular PBS and station programming.

Discussion quickly turned to the needs and wants of the station's target audience (and *potential audience*) and the nature of present and probable future competition (both from other TV stations and from other sources of the kind of news and cultural programming WILL -TV could provide). Also considered were the station's present strengths and weaknesses and the hopes and desires of the management personnel present at the weekend planning meeting. It was clear that the choice of long-range strategy would very much determine the kind of station WILL -TV was to be and what rewards would be available to those who worked there. The choice would not only affect what equipment was purchased but what kind of staff would be needed, what future research would have to be undertaken, how success would be measured, and how managers would be judged and rewarded.

Once the planning issues were crystallized, the staff could come to grips with the truly fundamental problems facing them all. The weekend experience led not only to a resolution of the immediate dilemma but to a year-long series of additional planning meetings within and across departments to work out the short- and medium-range planning implications of the weekend's decisions.

But perhaps the most important outcome of the weekend—at least as far as most of those who attended were concerned—was that *they became part of the planning process.* The occasion was not (as many expected) a griping session, but an opportunity for mutually grappling with their joint futures. Not everyone was happy with the basic choices (satellite-based programming won out). Some left the station because they realized that it was not going to be the kind of public television station they wanted to be a part of. But because the key issues had been aired, they resigned, not in anger, but in relief, respecting the organization for its straightforwardness about where it was going. The resignations were also good from the organization's standpoint since potential malcontents were removed yet left as goodwill ambassadors for the station. Among those who stayed, those whose preferences had prevailed were, of course, content. Those who would have liked a different long-run mission at least felt that their position had received a fair hearing and that they had chosen to stay aboard under no false pretenses.

The work carried out in marketing research, marketing measurement, and forecasting makes its maximum contribution when it is incorporated in a systematic and formal marketing planning process. Yet many nonprofit managers have resisted instituting a formal planning system. A university president gave the authors five reasons why he did not believe in formal planning systems:

1. The department heads (deans and chairpersons) do not have the time to write formal plans, nor does the top administration have the time to read them.
2. Most department heads would not be able to plan even if they were asked. They head their departments because they are scholars or leaders in their field, not because they are managers. They might refuse to plan, or plan poorly, and this would be tolerated as long as they were performing well in other respects.
3. The department heads would not use their plans. The plans would be window dressing and filed away. The plans might even be obsolete the day they were written, with so much change occurring in the academic world.
4. The administration has plans which are best kept secret from the department heads, because some department heads would feel threatened by them. The department heads should not be encouraged to come up with unrealistic ideas of what they want that the president would have to reject.
5. Installing a formal planning system and making it work would cost too much in money and time.

Without denying some validity to these arguments, this chapter will argue that formal planning and control systems are beneficial on the whole and needed for the improvement of organizational performance. The fact that many business firms use modern planning and control systems and that an increasing number of nonprofit organizations are introducing these systems indicates some apparent satisfaction with the results of these systems. Melville C. Branch has perceptively summarized the main benefits of a formal planning system:

1. Encourages systematic thinking ahead by management
2. Leads to a better coordination of company efforts
3. Leads to the development of performance standards for control
4. Causes the company to sharpen its guiding objectives and policies
5. Results in better preparedness for sudden developments
6. Brings about a more vivid sense in the participating executives of their interacting responsibilities.[1]

In Chapter 5, we outlined the essential features of a formal strategic planning process. In very general terms, this system is divisible into three parts: planning, implementation, and control (see Figure 8-1).

The first step calls upon the organization to plan its marketing effort, specifically to identify attractive target markets, develop effective marketing strategies, and develop detailed action programs. The second step involves executing the action programs in the marketing plan, both geographically and over time. The third step calls for marketing control activity to make sure that the objectives are being achieved. Marketing control requires measuring results, analyzing the causes of poor results, and taking corrective actions. The corrective actions consist of adjustments in the plan, its execution, or both.

We will deal with marketing planning in this chapter and then with marketing evaluation and control in Chapter 22. Matters dealing with execution will be left to later chapters.

FIGURE 8-1

The Marketing Planning and Control System

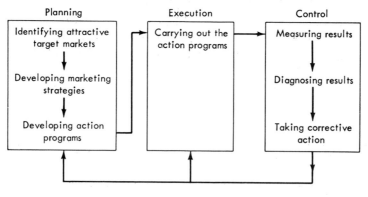

MARKETING PLANNING

When an organization *establishes* a marketing planning system it faces three questions: (1) How sophisticated should the planning system be? (2) What procedures should be used to carry on the planning process? (3) What should the contents of a marketing plan be?

DEGREES OF SOPHISTICATION IN MARKETING PLANNING

Most organizations start with little or no formal planning and over the years upgrade their planning systems. In fact, planning systems tend to evolve through the following stages:

Unplanned Stage.   When organizations are first established, their organizers are so busy soliciting funds, attracting clients, and seeking facilities that they have little time for formal planning. Management is totally engrossed in making the day-to-day decisions required for survival. There is no planning staff and hardly any time to plan.

Budgeting System Stage.   Management eventually recognizes the desirability of installing a budgeting system to improve the management of the organization's cash flow. Management estimates the expected income and costs for the coming year. Each department manager prepares a department budget. These budgets are financially oriented, not strategically oriented. Budgets are not the same as plans.

Project Planning Stage.   Many organizations find that they need to develop plans for specific projects. Thus, a university needs to plan new buildings and usually establishes a planning office to carry out this work. Yet the university's planning department is not concerned with strategic or annual planning.

Annual Planning Stage.   Management eventually recognizes the need to develop an annual planning system based on *management by objectives.*[2] It has three options.

The first is *top-down planning,* so called because top management sets *goals* and *plans* for all the lower levels of management. This model is taken from military organizations where the generals prepare the plans and the troops carry them out. In nonprofit organizations this goes along with a ory X view of employees, that they dislike work and responsibility prefer to be directed.[3] Top-down planning is most prevalent in government agencies where each level establishes the plans for the next lower level.

The second system is *bottom-up planning,* so called because the various units of the organization prepare their own goals and plans based on the best they think they can do, and they send them to upper management for approval. This style is based on Theory Y thinking about human nature, that employees like work and responsibility and are more creative and committed if they participate in the planning and running of the organization. Bottom-up planning is most often found in collegial organizations and smaller organizations.

Most companies use a third system known as *goals down—plans up planning.* Here top management takes a broad look at the organization's opportunities and requirements and sets organizational goals for the year. The various units of the organization are responsible for developing plans designed to help the organization reach these goals. These plans, when approved by top management, become the official annual plan.

Long-Range Planning Stage.   In this stage, the organization refines the planning system in a number of directions to improve its overall effectiveness. The major change is the addition of *long-range planning.* Management realizes that annual plans make sense only in the context of a long-range plan. In fact, the long-range plan should come first, and the annual plan should be a detailed version of the first year of the long-range plan. The long-range plan, however, is reworked each year (called *rolling planning*) because the environment changes rapidly and requires an annual review of the long-run planning assumptions.

As the company gains experience with planning, an effort is made to *standardize the plan formats* so that higher management can make more meaningful comparisons among similar units. It is important that the plans written for comparable units, such as divisions, departments, and programs, follow the same or similar formats to permit intelligent comparisons by higher management.

Strategic Planning Stage.   A further development is that the various plans begin to take on a more *strategic character.* When an organization first turns to long-range planning, it usually assumes that the future will largely be an extension of the present and that past strategies, organizational forms, and procedures will remain appropriate. Eventually, management begins to recognize that the environment is full of probabilities, not certainties, and broader strategic thinking is required. The planning format is redesigned to stimulate managers to contemplate and evaluate alternative strategies that will leave the organization as well off as possible.

As the strategic planning orientation takes hold in the organization, further improvements are introduced. Managers receive more training in the use of *financial analysis* and are required to justify their recommendations not only in terms of enrollment, attendance, contributions, and so on, but also in terms of financial measures such as cost/benefit ratios or cost effectiveness of an activity. Personal computers or computer terminals become a common tool to help managers examine the impact of alternative marketing plans and environments on "sales" and "profit." The managers might also be asked to develop *contingency plans* showing how they would respond to specific major threats and opportunities that might arise. These and other developments mark the emergence of a true strategic planning culture in the organization.

DESIGNING THE MARKETING PLANNING PROCESS

A planning system doesn't just happen. An appropriate system must be designed that will be acceptable to the managers and compatible with the level of information and skill at their disposal. Often the initial system will be designed simplistically so that managers can get accustomed to writing plans. As they gain experience, changes and improvements will be made in the planning system to increase its effectiveness. Eventually, the managers accept planning, not as a chore to meet their boss's needs but as a tool to increase their own effectiveness.

Someone has to be responsible for developing the initial planning system. The following three-step procedure is recommended. First, top management appoints a committee to study whether a formal planning system is needed, and if so, what kind of system, and when and how it should be established. The second step is to hire an outside consultant who has broad experience in designing management planning systems for other organizations. The outside consultant can provide valuable perspectives on planning as well as specific procedures and forms. The third step involves hiring a director of planning. The planning director would take responsibility for designing the final system.

The planning director's job is not to write the plans but to educate and assist the managers in writing their plans. A maxim of planning is that planning should be done by those who must carry out the plans. By involving the line managers in planning their operations, they are (1) stimulated to think out their business objectives and strategies, and (2) motivated to achieve their goals.

One major task of the planning director is to develop a calendar for the planning process. The normal calendar steps are:

1. Develop a set of relevant environmental facts and trends to distribute to the managers in preparation for their planning.
2. Work with top management to develop a set of overall corporate objectives for the coming year to pass on to the managers in preparation for their planning.
3. Work with individual managers to complete their marketing plans by a certain date.
4. Work with top management to review, approve, or modify the various plans.
5. Develop a consolidated official plan for the organization for the coming period.

This calendar sequence underscores the critical role of marketing planning in the overall management planning process. Individual managers start the process by setting marketing goals (for attendance, enrollment, contributions, etc.) for their programs for the coming period, along with proposed strategies and marketing budgets. Once top management approves these marketing goals and strategies, decisions can be made on how many personnel to hire, how much supplies to order, and how much money to borrow. Thus, a commitment to a set of marketing goals precedes decisions on personnel, production, and financial requirements.

THE FORMAT OF A MARKETING PLAN

Another major task of the planning director is to design the appropriate standard format that managers should follow in preparing their marketing plans. The topics and their sequence can make a difference in the quality of planning results. A marketing plan should contain the following major sections: *executive summary, situation analysis, objectives and goals, marketing strategy, action programs, budgets, and controls.* These sections will be discussed in the context of the following situation:

The concert manager of the Pick-Staiger Concert Hall at Northwestern University asks each manager to develop a plan for his or her area of responsibility. One of them is Janet Smith, who is responsible for building up general audience attendance at the Performing Arts Series.

Executive Summary.   The planning document should open with a summary of the main goals and recommendations presented in the plan. Here is an abbreviated example:

> The 1986 marketing plan for community audience development seeks to attract 2,000 new first-time "nonuniversity" attenders to the Performing Arts Series at Pick-Staiger. Assuming an average attendance of one performance per new attender, and an average ticket price of $7, this step, if successful, will add $14,000 to concert hall revenue. To accomplish this, the plan calls for a marketing expenditure of $10,000. Of this, $2,000 will be spent on marketing research to measure present levels of community awareness and interest in the Performing Arts Series, and $5,000 will be spent in buying appropriate mailing lists and producing a new "hard-selling" brochure about the series. Finally, $3,000 will be spent on radio and newspaper ads to stimulate interest in the series.

The purpose of the executive summary is to permit higher management to preview the major thrust of each plan and read further in search of the information that is critical in evaluating the plan. To facilitate this, a table of contents should follow the executive summary.

Situation Analysis.   The first major in-depth section of the plan is the *situation analysis,* in which the manager describes the major features of the situation facing his or her operation. The situation analysis consists of four subsections—background, normal forecast, opportunities and threats, and strengths and weaknesses.

BACKGROUND.   This section starts with a summary of key performance indices for the last few years. An example (hypothetical) is shown in Table 8-1 for the Pick-Staiger Concert Hall.

Row 1 shows that the concert hall has increased the number of performances in the Performing Arts Series from twenty to forty a year over a three-year period. Row 2 shows the annual capacity, that is, the maximum number of tickets that could have been sold. Row 3 shows that a growing audience has been attracted, and Row 4 shows that audience as a percent of capacity has been growing. Row 5 shows that the average ticket price has been rising from $5 to $7 over the three-year period. Row 6 shows that total revenue has risen substantially over the three-year period. Rows 7, 8, 9, and 10 show how performers' cost, marketing cost, and administrative cost have risen over the same period. Finally, Row 11 indicates that the concert hall's loss has increased over the period in spite of higher attendance and ticket prices.

Clearly, the concert hall is making progress in a sales sense, but not in a financial sense. These data should be followed by a description of major

Table 8-1

BACKGROUND DATA

	1983	1984	1985
1. Number of performances	20	30	40
2. Annual capacity[1]	20,000	30,000	40,000
3. Audience	5,000	9,000	10,000
4. Audience as % of capacity	25%	30%	40%
5. Average ticket price[2]	$5	$6	$7
6. Total revenue	$25,000	$54,000	$70,000
7. Performers' cost	$35,000	$60,000	$83,000
8. Marketing cost	$6,000	$8,000	$12,000
9. Administrative cost	$20,000	$24,000	$30,000
10. Total cost	$61,000	$92,000	$125,000
11. Net operating loss	$36,000	$38,000	$55,000

[1]One thousand seats are available for each performance, and this is multiplied by the number of performances to find annual capacity.
[2]Average ticket price is found by dividing total ticket revenue by the number of tickets distributed, whether they were sold at full price, discounted price, or free.

developments occurring in the marketplace, such as changes in audience size and interests, trends in ticket prices, new competition, and other factors that would throw light on the marketplace and provide guidance in the development of an effective strategy.

NORMAL FORECAST.   The background information should be followed by a forecast of future output or "sales" under "normal conditions," that is, assuming no major changes in the *marketing environment* or *marketing strategies.* This forecast could be obtained in a number of ways. The assumption could be made that output would stay constant, or grow at the most recent rate of growth, or even decline. The basis of the forecast could be statistical curve fitting, surveying a sample of target audience members, or similar procedures.

The forecast would have to be revised if quite different environmental conditions are expected or strategies are planned. If the forecast does not satisfy higher management, the planner would have to consider new strategies, hopefully finding one that promises a higher level of growth.

OPPORTUNITIES AND THREATS.   The normal forecast should be followed by a section in which the manager identifies the main opportunities and threats facing the organizational unit. Usually, the manager is aware of a number of these but should be required to put them down on paper. Higher management can review this list and raise questions about threats and opportunities that are listed or missing. In the following year, management can see how many opportunities were acted on and what threats really occurred.

Table 8-2A shows the opportunities and threats listed by a manager at the concert hall. The opportunities and threats describe *outside* factors facing the organization. They are written so as to suggest some actions that might be warranted. The manager may be asked to rate the opportunities and threats for their potential impact and probability as an indicator of which deserve the most planning attention.

Table 8-2

AN EXAMPLE OF OPPORTUNITIES, THREATS, STRENGTHS, AND WEAKNESSES

***A.** Opportunities and Threats Facing the Concert Hall*

OPPORTUNITIES

1. There is a large potential audience in the nearby suburb of Winnetka that is unaware of Pick-Staiger Concert Hall who could be attracted to the Performing Arts Series.
2. Many of Chicago's large corporations would buy blocks of tickets if they could be effectively reached.
3. If Ticketron would handle Pick-Staiger tickets, citywide distribution would be guaranteed.

THREATS

1 The expected downswing in the economy may reduce the subscription renewal rate.
2. The increasing parking problem is producing a lot of unhappy patrons.
3. Top performing groups are planning to raise their fees by an average of 20 percent, resulting in higher costs to the concert hall.

***B.** Strengths and Weaknesses of the Concert Hall*

STRENGTHS

1. The audience has been highly satisfied with most of the past performers.
2. The acoustics of the concert hall are among the best in the Midwest.
3. The concert hall has an air of warmth and excitement.

WEAKNESSES

1. The staff, though enthusiastic, is not well trained in handling the various tasks that have to be done.
2. The access roads to the university are slow and discourage people from coming at greater distances.
3. The ticket office is open only from 1:00 to 5:00 P.M. and some sales are lost as a result.

STRENGTHS AND WEAKNESSES.   The manager should next list the main internal strengths and weaknesses of the organization (see Table 8-2B). The list of strengths has implications for strategy formulation, while the list of weaknesses has implications for investments to correct weaknesses. Higher management can raise critical questions about the strengths and weaknesses identified by each manager.

Objectives and Goals.   The situation analysis describes where the organization stands and where it might go. Now management must propose where that organization should go. Specific objectives and goals have to be set. Top management typically promulgates overall goals for the coming period for the organization as a whole. The top management of the Pick-Staiger Concert Hall might state that they want to achieve (1) a 15 percent growth in audience size, and (2) an operating loss not to exceed $40,000.

Each manager develops goals for his or her department within the context of these overall goals. Thus the general audience manager, reviewing top management's goals, decided on the following specific goals: (1) to attract 2,000 new first-time attenders at an average ticket price of $7, and (2) to spend $10,000 to accomplish this. Other goals would also be listed here.

Marketing Strategy.   The manager next outlines a marketing strategy for attaining the objectives. The marketing strategy describes the "game plan" by which the manager hopes to "win." We define marketing strategy as follows:

> **Marketing strategy** is the fundamental marketing logic by which an organizational unit intends to achieve its marketing objectives. Marketing strategy consists of a coordinated set of decisions on (1) target markets, (2) marketing mix, and (3) marketing expenditure level.

TARGET MARKETS.   Management should introduce criteria to identify the most attractive markets, defined in terms of age, education, income, and geographic and other variables. Various markets should be rated on these criteria and the markets selected with the greatest probable response to a unit of marketing effort. Thus management might conclude that the suburbs of Skokie, Wilmette, and Winnetka are likely to deliver a larger audience increase than Highland Park, Glenview, and Deerfield.

MARKETING MIX.   The organization should develop a *strategic marketing mix* which answers such basic questions as whether to emphasize subscriptions or single-performance tickets, or whether to rely on word-of-mouth or mass media. It should then develop a *tactical marketing mix.* For the Winnetka market, the manager may decide on local newspaper advertising and a telephone campaign. For the Skokie market, the manager may decide to mail free tickets for one performance to every resident of Skokie.

MARKETING EXPENDITURE LEVEL. Marketing strategy also calls for deciding on the marketing expenditure level. Organizations typically establish their marketing budget at some percentage of the sales revenue. For example, the concert manager might be willing to spend 20 percent of sales revenue on marketing. Clearly the more spent on marketing, the larger the audience will be. What an organization needs to know is the point where increased sales no longer bring increased profits and, in fact, cut into profits. Most nonprofit organizations do not allocate nearly enough to marketing. While for-profit organizations may spend 15 to 25 percent of sales on all forms of marketing, many nonprofit organizations allocate less than 1 percent to it.

Action Program.   The marketing strategy needs to be turned into a specific set of actions for accomplishing the marketing goals. Each strategy element should be elaborated into appropriate actions. The strategy element, "decrease the personal cost of attending performance to off-campus people," for example, could lead to the following actions: "increase the parking space available to off-campus attenders," "improve traffic management for incoming and outgoing traffic," and "arrange for a bus to bring people to the campus." The actions which appear most cost-effective should then be assigned to specific individuals with specified completion times.

The overall action plan can take the form of a table, with the twelve months (or fifty-two weeks) of the year serving as columns and various marketing activities serving as rows. Dates can be entered when various activities or expenditures will be started, reviewed, and completed. This action plan can be changed during the year as new problems and opportunities arise.

Budgets.   The goals, strategies, and planned actions allow the manager to build a budget, which is essentially a projected profit-and-loss statement. On the revenue side, it shows the forecasted unit sales and the expected net realized price. On the expense side, it shows the costs of production, marketing, and administration. The difference is the projected profit or loss. Management reviews the budget and either approves or modifies it. Once approved, the budget is the basis for marketing operations, financial planning, and personnel recruitment.

Controls.   The last section of the plan describes the controls that will be applied to monitor the plan's progress. Normally, the goals and budgets are spelled out for each month or quarter. This means that higher management can review the results each period and spot those managers who are not attaining their goals. These managers will be asked to indicate what actions they will take to improve the results.

SUMMARY

Systematized processes for making, carrying out, and reviewing marketing strategies are essential to the effective management of mature nonprofit organizations. Such a system is typically divided into three parts: planning, implementation, and control. Marketing planning has evolved through six stages from an unplanned stage through to an annual planning stage and, in the most sophisticated systems, to a strategic planning stage.

A long-range planning orientation is appropriate to an organization that thinks strategically. Annual planning and budgeting are still carried out, but the organization is more concerned with evaluating each undertaking in terms of its consequences for the nonprofit's long-term market position and cash and investment status.

Establishing any planning system is not easy. Managers may initially resist the process but will eventually see its value in organizing and managing their own efforts. Most formal plans are comprised of the following sections: summary, situation analysis, objectives and goals, marketing strategy, action programs, budgets, and controls. The most critical section of this process is the situation analysis, in which the manager must assess the threats and opportunities in the environment and the organization's strengths and weaknesses in potentially taking advantage of the predicted environment.

QUESTIONS

1. What indicators would suggest that a nonprofit organization was ready to move from the project planning stage to the annual planning stage?

2. The director of a local charity states that the needs of the organization she represents change greatly from year to year and that the economy is unpredictable in its effects on individuals' propensity to donate. Thus she contends that long-range planning would be pointless. Make an argument as to why this position is shortsighted.

3. Develop a set of questions that a manager might submit to his or her subordinates to initiate a bottom-up planning process.

4. Assume that the charity director in question 2 has almost completed her annual plan for the coming year. What major contingencies should she plan for and what should such contingency plans look like?

5. Develop a situational analysis for yourself as a nonprofit entity to be marketed for your first job or for a promotion or raise on your present job. Be sure to indicate threats and opportunities in the environment you face and your own strengths and weaknesses in facing them.

NOTES

1. Melville C. Branch, *The Corporate Planning Process* (New York: American Management Association, 1962), pp. 48–49.

2. See D. D. McConkey, *MBO for Nonprofit Organizations* (New York: AMACOM, 1975).

3. See Douglas McGregor, *The Human Side of Enterprise* (New York: McGraw-Hill, 1960).

Organizing for Implementation

UCLA is a large, complex, and often unwieldy institution. In 1985, the University's Administrators and Supervisors Association invited a panel of representatives from different departments on campus to discuss current principles in the corporate world that might be applicable to UCLA's particular situation.

The discussion focused extensively on the concept of "corporate culture" recently brought to prominence in the book *In Search of Excellence* by Thomas J. Peters and Robert H. Waterman, Jr. In their book, Peters and Waterman point out that their excellent companies tend to have such characteristics as a "bias toward action," a "stick-to-your knitting philosophy," "loose-tight control," and an approach to leadership called "managing by walking around."

Most participants agreed that UCLA's culture, while sometimes ineffective, is of prime importance to its continued success. "To understand the University's culture, managers and supervisors have to understand the value of their work, and communicate those values constantly to department employees," said William Kastenberg, chair of UCLA's Department of Mechanical, Aerospace and Nuclear Engineering. "By expressing their values to employees, [the supervisors' values] become the staff's values as well, and the supervisor will wind up with the kind of department he or she wants."

Participants said that a nontraditional style of mangement at the department level should also prove important and applicable at UCLA. They maintained that in successful companies much of the red tape, memo writing, and paper shuffling is discarded in favor of simplified procedures and actions, which are aided by good working relationships with employees.

A company's "bias toward action" leads to productivity, and communication at all levels within an organization will foster and motivate workers toward that goal, said Newton Margulies, Dean of the UC Irvine Graduate School of Management and Director of the UC Management Institute.

"Innovation can be encouraged among employees in a variety of ways," he said, adding that a company or group must first be willing to tolerate some faltering steps.

An environment reflecting "loose-tight control" can be found in the best run companies. By being loose on the rules, and tight on the values, managers can give employees enough autonomy to perform their jobs without cramping their styles, said Margulies.

Brad Volkmer, management services officer in the Department of Medicine, cautioned the audience that all too often communication problems within departments will lead to an "Ivory Tower" brand of arrogance which will divide department employees and create adversarial "we-they" relationships.

"The MBWA approach to managing, or 'managing by walking around,' is a good way of encouraging communications," Volkmer said. "From that, a certain amount of two-way trust will develop between staff and managers, and since managers have to trust their employees, that mutual trust will mean your department's decisions are sound."

SOURCE: Adapted from Diane Ainsworth, "Measuring the University Structure: A Corporate Comparison, *UCLA Today*, (January 9–19, 1986), p. 7. Reproduced with permission.

As we noted in Chapter 1, the concept of marketing has progressed through three stages of acceptance in the nonprofit sector: introduction, growth, and its present entry into the maturity phase. This has also been the typical pattern within individual nonprofit organizations.

The introductory phase within an organization is the period when marketing is first proposed as a philosophy and set of techniques for improving the organization's performance. This introduction typically comes about in one of two ways. One pattern is for marketing to be *pushed* into the organization by one or more key individuals who have been exposed to its potential in outside seminars or in formal academic training. This is a pattern that is common in the performing arts, and, in earlier days, in education. These potential change agents shuttle about the organization trying to convince others, most importantly the CEO, of the wisdom of their newfound views. They frequently encounter considerable intraorganization resistance, which is often reflected in disparagement of the marketing function and frequent allusions to its nastier manifestations. Unless the change agents are very highly placed in the organization or are extremely convincing in their promotion campaigns, the introduction period is likely to be quite prolonged under a "push" scenario.

The other common pattern for the introductory period is for marketing to be *pulled* into the organization by environmental forces. This condition occurred in health care as market conditions increased the pressures on nonprofit hospitals to improve performance. Marketing comes to be viewed as a potentially highly useful approach to such improvement. Pressures to introduce marketing are further heightened if one or more direct competitors begins to use marketing or is rumored to be beginning soon. Marketing is likely to be introduced much faster under a "pull" scenario than if it is "pushed" into a sometimes reluctant institution.

In the growth phase following marketing's introduction, attempts are made to expand marketing's role and formalize its position in the organization. Typically, marketing is first formalized as a staff function *coordinating* programs and providing advice to others. Only later, as marketing proves its value and/or environmental pressures become more intense, is it often changed into a specific line function with its own staff and reponsibilites for programs and specific volume results.

Even when marketing becomes a formal department during the growth phase, its role may be inconsequential. The mature phase can therefore be identified by the transition of marketing from being just another division or function to being a top-level management concern. In this phase, marketing philosophy has permeated much of the organization's planning. Marketing has relatively few detractors and virtually no effort is needed to market marketing itself. Concern has shifted to the issue: how to market *well.*

We will now consider some organizational issues that marketing must face during each development phase.

THE INTRODUCTION STAGE

In the beginning, there will be much resistance to setting up a formal marketing function. Among the arguments against formally accepting marketing are the following:

- Some organizations think that formal marketing is inappropriate. Thus, the faculty of a college might be contemptuous of the notion that education has to be marketed.
- Some organizations think that marketing is everyone's job. They fear that appointing a marketing director will lead employees to think that marketing is something done by a marketing director rather than everyone in the organization, and they will sit around expecting the marketing director to miraculously solve their problems.

- Some organizations feel that they are getting all the marketing they need from their directors of public relations, planning, and development. They identify marketing with these functions.
- Some organizations feel that they would be better off hiring marketing expertise as needed—from marketing consultants, advertising agencies, and marketing research firms—instead of hiring a full-time marketing director.

  Some organizations feel that a director of marketing would not contribute enough to pay for his or her salary. They believe that they can buy more important things with the same money.
- Some organizations are too small or too poor to afford a marketing director.

Some of these arguments undoubtedly reflect personal biases against what the individual believes marketing to be. The majority reflect an absence of a formal assessment of whether the organization really needs a marketing person, department, or program. At the outset, it should be realized that whether an organization should install a formal marketing function is not the issue of whether it should do marketing. All organizations do marketing whether or not they organize it in a formal way. Colleges, for example, search for prospects (students), develop products (courses), price them (tuition and fees), distribute them (announce time and place), and promote them (college catalogs). Similarly, hospitals, social agencies, museums, and other nonprofit organizations also carry on marketing. When this dawns on a nonprofit organization, the response is much like that of Molière's character in *Le Bourgeois Gentilhomme* who utters, "Good heavens! For more than forty years I have been speaking prose without knowing it."

Some organizations feel that they are not only doing marketing but that they already have formal staff positions responsible for marketing. Therefore, they don't need to add another staff position called "marketing." A college president may feel that the admissions director, the public relations director, the planning vice-president, and the development vice-president are the institution's professional marketers. This may or may not be correct, however. Many admissions directors are sales oriented rather than marketing oriented. They are good at "pounding the pavement" for prospective students but not skilled in marketing research and marketing strategy that would make this selling job easier. Most public relations directors are skilled in journalism and communication but are not trained in analyzing, researching, and planning for markets. Planning vice-presidents may concentrate on developing the physical plant and on financial problems without having much marketing knowledge or aptitude. Development vice-presidents are often sales oriented and fail to put their fund-raising efforts on a modern marketing management basis. Though these officers should be professional marketers handling their respective markets, they typically are not.

The president may acknowledge this but feel that there are several ways to get marketing resources without going through the expense of establishing a formal marketing position. In fact, the nonprofit organization that cannot afford or chooses not to install formal marketing can get some marketing resources in the following ways:

1. Appoint a marketing executive to the board of directors, hoping to get help or advice from this marketing executive as needed. Also, invite voluntary help from other marketing executives in the community.
2. Invite help from the marketing faculty of a business school, such as using a marketing research class to research a problem facing the organization.
3. Hire a marketing consulting firm, marketing research firm, or advertising agency to do specific projects when needed.
4. Send key staff to marketing seminars and workshops to learn marketing.

Although these makeshift ways of acquiring marketing services do not do the full job of creating a market-oriented organization, they normally produce good value in the short term. But certain cautions must be exercised. In drawing on the voluntary services of marketing executives in the community, it should be realized that they will be offering advice without the benefit of research data or much time to analyze the problem. Furthermore, they will be heavily influenced by their own industry background. A P&G soap marketing executive will put heavy emphasis on advertising spending because this is what works in the soap industry; an IBM marketing executive will put heavy emphasis on personal selling because this is what works in the computer industry. Every marketing executive has biases as to what works best and the nonprofit organization must maintain a critical attitude. If extensive use of such part-time advisors is contemplated, however, briefly introducing them to some of the differences between profit and nonprofit marketing as outlined in Chapter 1 would be helpful.

If the nonprofit organization decides to get marketing help by hiring marketing firms as needed, it must be able to discriminate between good, average, and poor firms. A poor advertising agency, for example, will try to solve a membership decline by creating an instant advertising campaign. An average ad agency will ask management questions to help clarify the nature of the membership decline and then create an advertising campaign. A good ad agency will ask about the organization's overall mission, goals, and plans and do some research with members and ex-members before developing an advertising campaign. Naturally, the nonprofit organization will get the most value from a market-oriented advertising agency.

If the foregoing alternatives are deemed unsatisfactory or if the organization has outgrown them, the organization may consider installing a formal marketing function. As a first step, the organization should appoint a marketing committee charged with three objectives:

1. Identifying marketing problems and opportunities facing the organization
2. Assessing the felt need of different department heads for professional marketing assistance

3. Recommending whether the organization should establish a formal marketing position

The marketing committee should include representatives from a cross-section of the organization's departments that might have a stake in marketing. Thus, a university's marketing committee should include the vice-president of faculty, some deans and department chairpersons, the admissions director, the public relations director, the development vice-president, the planning vice-president, a board member, and possibly a student representative. The marketing committee might also include an outside marketing executive or paid marketing consultant to provide professional guidance. This committee should gather information from various groups (deans, chairpersons, students) as to how they see the environment (its opportunities and threats), the organization's strengths and weaknesses, the organization's strategy, the organization's marketing problems and possible solutions, and so on. Many surprising, if not shocking, things will be discovered in this process.

The committee should digest the information and prepare a report for the president. This report of marketing findings and recommendations is called a *marketing audit*. Although it is an inside audit done by a committee of nonprofessionals, it is likely to be highly useful. The organization always has the option of hiring a marketing consulting firm to do a full-scale marketing audit, which will cost more and be likely to yield even greater value because of the marketing auditor's independence, objectivity, and experience in doing marketing auditing in a large number of industries.

THE GROWTH PHASE

At some point, the nonprofit organization will become committed to installing a formal marketing function. The organization may find the makeshift use of outside marketing resources to be too costly or unreliable, or it may find that its marketing needs are extensive enough to hire a full-time person. The organization should recognize that establishing a marketing function is undertaken at some risk if the rest of the organization is still resistant or the new appointee is not given sufficient authority to carry out his or her responsibilities. If the organization decides to move forward, however, it must decide on (1) the level at which to hire, (2) the job description, and (3) the recruiting strategy.

The major issue concerning level is whether marketing will initially be a staff or a line function. The decision operationally is whether to hire a *director of marketing services* who would advise but not have direct responsibility over programs and people or *a vice-president of marketing* who would have line responsibility. The former person is hired at a middle-management level and basically acts as a resource person or internal marketing consultant to various other managers in the organization who need marketing services. In effect, a marketing directorship is a staff position, not a line position. This director can help define marketing problems, arrange for marketing research, and hire advertising agency services as needed. He or she may be located in the planning department under the vice-president of planning or in public relations or development, though these functions might overspecialize the use to which marketing is put. Some hospitals and colleges have preferred to call the person an "assistant to the president" who reports directly to the president.

Alternatively, the organization might establish a vice-president of marketing. This is an upper-level management position that gives more scope, authority, and influence to marketing. A vice-president of marketing not only coordinates and supplies services to others in the organization but also participates in the setting of policy and direction for the institution. This person has a better chance to help create a marketing orientation in the organization. The position is much closer to being a true line position. The vice-president of marketing would be responsible for planning and managing relations with several publics of the institutions. In fact, if full delegation of line authority were given, this person would manage client relations, donor relations, public relations, and government relations. The person's title might be "vice-president of institutional relations" or "vice-president of external affairs" to avoid unnecessary semantic opposition to the term "marketing." A vice-president of marketing would cost the institution more but might ultimately contribute more to the institution.

Which position should it be initially? Some organizations prefer to make marketing a staff position on the assumption that the position costs less, its value can be tested, and, if the director proves effective and intraorganizational opposition is diffused, he or she can be promoted to a line position. Other organizations feel that a staff marketer can only accomplish minor things because he or she would not have the ear of the president, would not participate in strategy formulation, and would not have the necessary line authority. The authors favor establishing a vice-president of marketing with line responsibility initially because marketing's job is to transform the thinking of top management into a marketing mode.

Suppose, however, that the organization decides initially to hire a staff director of marketing services. A job description that outlines the functions, responsibilities, and major liaison relations associated with the job is needed. A sample job description for a university director of marketing services is shown in Table 9-1.

Before searching for a qualified person to fill the job, the organization will want to further define the desirable age of the person, years and type of marketing experience, salary range, and planned budget for the job. The organization may decide that it wants a person with substantial marketing training and experience in industry rather than a person who has worked in

Table 9-1

JOB DESCRIPTION: A UNIVERSITY DIRECTOR OF MARKETING SERVICES

Position title: Director of Marketing Services

Reports to: Vice-President, University Relations

Scope: University-wide

Position concept: The Director of Marketing Services is responsible for providing marketing guidance and services to university officers, school deans, department chairpersons, and other agents of the university.

Functions: The Director of Marketing Services will:

1. contribute a marketing perspective to the deliberations of the top administration in its planning of the university's future

2. prepare data that might be needed by an officer of the university on a particular market's size, segments, trends, and behavioral dynamics

3. conduct studies of the needs, perceptions, preferences, and satisfactions of particular markets

4. assist in the planning, promotion, and launching of new programs

5. assist in the development of communication and promotion campaigns and materials

6. analyze and advise on pricing questions

7. appraise the workability of new academic proposals from a marketing point of view

8. advise on new student recruitment

9. advise on current student satisfaction

10. advise on university fundraising

Responsibilities: The Director of Marketing Services will:

1. contact individual officers and small groups at the university to explain services and to solicit problems

2. prioritize the various requests for services according to their long-run impact, cost-saving potential, time requirements, ease of accomplishment, cost, and urgency

3. select projects of high priority and set accomplishment goals for the year

4. prepare a budget request to support the anticipated work

5. prepare an annual report on the main accomplishments of the office

Major liaisons: The Director of Marketing Services will:

1. relate most closely with the President's Office, Admissions Office, Development Office, Planning Office, and Public Relations Department

2. relate secondarily with the deans of various schools and chairpersons of various departments.

---

its field—whether education, health, the arts—but who has only weak training in marketing. The organization normally finds it easier to educate a person about the field than to train a person from the field as a marketer.

The search will use the normal recruitment channels—job ads in the

Wall Street Journal or *Marketing News* (published by the American Marketing Association), phone calls to business school professors for leads, use of an executive search firm, and so on. This should produce a large number of leads, leaving the organization to prune the list and interview a few of the most promising candidates.

The kinds of individuals recruited into nonprofit marketing have been changing dramatically as the field matures. This was demonstrated in a 1984 "National Hospital Marketer's Survey" by Allied Research Associates.[1] The study showed clearly that those who had been in a hospital marketing position for six or more years were more likely to have degrees no higher than a B.A. or B.S. and to come from a communications background. This lack of formal marketing training is a serious problem. The report stated that "the older hospital marketers who come from a nonmarketing background are frustrated because they don't know how to cope with the new demands of hospital marketing." By contrast, the growing maturity of the field was reflected in the fact that those who reported that they had come into hospital marketing in the previous year were more likely to have a master's degree, to be trained in marketing, and to be paid a higher salary. That marketing was not yet in a maturity phase in many hospitals, however, was indicated by the fact that almost half the marketers in these hospitals had formal titles involving public relations or community relations.

A broader based survey of 800 hospitals in 1983 by Witt Associates, Inc., confirmed these patterns. This study showed that hospital marketers typically came from nonmarketing backgrounds and needed further training to be effective marketers. Three out of four came from nonmarketing backgrounds. In larger hospitals and chains, they tended more often to come into marketing from a planning role while in smaller hospitals they came from public or community relations. When hospitals hired from outside their own organizations they tended to hire those with experience in health care but "who lack[ed] functional marketing skills or understanding."[2]

Marketing was not a full-time responsibility for many of the participants in the study. Administrators or CEOs held marketing responsibilities in 29 percent of the hospitals studied. Marketing people in another 47 percent of the reporting hospitals had other responsibilities besides marketing. The researchers concluded that "hospital marketing hasn't yet come of age in terms of acceptance, understanding and use. Rather many institutions seem to favor the make-do or do-it-yourself approach. The many job titles that hospital marketing directors hold underscore the tentativeness and fragmentation of health care marketing."

DEVELOPING INITIAL MARKETING PROJECTS

If marketing is to achieve a steep upward trajectory during the intra-organization growth phase, the new marketing director will want to demonstrate that marketing thinking can contribute to the organization. Many members of the organization will be critical of marketing, arguing that it is inappropriate or a waste of money, or that the money could be spent better elsewhere. Others will be puzzled about what marketing is or does. Only a few will see it as a strong opportunity for the organization.

In the face of this skepticism, the new director must carefully choose initial projects which, if successfully executed, demonstrate the value of marketing. The marketing director can devise these projects, but it would be better if he or she meets key groups and conducts a needs assessment to get ideas on important marketing needs. For example, a new marketing director at a hospital should meet with department heads, individually or in groups, describe the work that can be done (marketing analyses, new program assessment, communication planning, and so on), and ask about any projects they might be interested in seeing done. This approach will build goodwill and understanding with various people in the organization and lead to many project ideas, often more than can be handled by a single marketing director operating with a small budget. The director should not promise to do work on any project until he or she reviews the possible projects and chooses the best ones. The best early projects to undertake would have four characteristics:

1. A high impact on making money or saving money for the institution
2. A relatively small cost to carry out
3. A short period of time for completion
4. A high visibility potential if successful

Presumably, some projects will stand up better than others under these criteria. The main thing is to avoid major projects that will take a long time, cost a lot of money, and not yield definitive results. The organization will not have the patience to support costly, drawn-out marketing projects, at least not until the marketing function is well established and respected.

Expanding the Market Function

If the marketing director does a good job that is recognized by others in the organization, more resources will be made available and more responsibility will be accorded.[3] The marketing executive may want to hire one or more assistants to specialize in marketing research, advertising, new services evaluation, and other marketing functions. It pays to hire a full-time expert in any specialized marketing function that the organization needs to cover on a continuous basis.

THE MATURE STAGE

As the organization matures, marketing people become well accepted and marketing planning is better integrated into the corporate planning cycle. The number of people in the marketing department can grow substantially. This can come about as organizational designers recognize that heretofore separate functions like fundraising, public relations, and customer education need to be coordinated in one place. Such coordination would be consistent with the view proposed here that nonprofit organizations are already doing marketing in many parts of their enterprise—they are trying to influence behaviors of different target audiences whether they be potential donors, politicians, customers, the general public, or employees. At the mature stage, then, the marketing department will be given (1) the responsibility for maximizing the number of exchanges between the organization and its various clienteles, and (2) line authority over most, if not all, of the tools within the organization needed to get the job done.

This can lead to the establishment of a separate marketing department with its own budget and a substantial staff. An example of such a mature department is that created at the U.S. Postal Service.[4]

> Marketing activities within the USPS are centered in the Customer Department, which is headed by a former Procter and Gamble executive. The department is divided into eight divisions: special events division, planning and management division; office of stamps; office of international postal affairs; office of advertising; office of product management; office of customer marketing; and office of consumer advocate. Each division, in turn, has subdivisions. For example, the office of product management has six subdivisions: letter mail, parcel mail, retail products, special services, electronic mail, and market research. Many of the division heads are ex-marketing executives from private industry.

ORGANIZATIONAL DESIGN

As the marketing department grows in physical size, how to organize it internally becomes a critical question. This will affect not only how the department is run but what kinds of people can be employed. The options typically found in the private sector as design alternatives can be adapted to nonprofit marketing with limited rethinking. These alternatives are (1) functional organization, (2) product/service-centered organization, (3) customer-centered organization, and (4) mixed organization.

Functional Organization. Most growing nonprofit marketing units first take on the appearance of a functional organizational structure as shown in Figure 9-1a.

As the marketing group absorbs once-separate functions such as public relations, advertising, and marketing research, it is natural to keep them as separate functional units within marketing. Each function may initially be the responsibility of a single employee. As the marketing group grows, the functional units inevitably grow, and each function may well have its own manager. The kinds of functions a large mature organization such as the

FIGURE 9-1

Alternative Organizational Designs

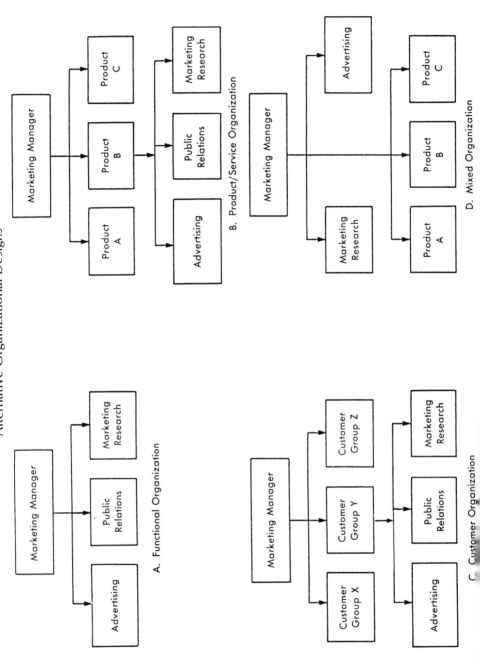

A. Functional Organization

B. Product/Service Organization

C. Customer Organization

D. Mixed Organization

post office, YMCA, or Red Cross, could eventually *possibly* have (although few will have all of them) are outlined in Table 9-2.

The organization may choose to retain a functional structure for a long time. One obvious reason for this would be if the subunits never become larger than one or two persons. But even if they did, many in the private sector believe that keeping marketing people aligned with their functional specialty has many advantages:

1. *Economies of scale.* A single public relations or advertising group can produce mass communications programs at much less cost or can develop more "clout" with significant outside agencies than can individual advertising or public relations people scattered throughout a complex nonprofit organization.
2. *Functional skill synergies.* Several advertising or public relations people working together in physical proximity will stimulate each other to produce much higher quality work.
3. *Professional affinities.* A functional organization is consistent with the natural affiliation of those it hires. That is, other things being equal, advertising people will feel more comfortable with other advertising people, public relations people with other public relations people. Even if they are initially located apart, they will gravitate toward each other. Therefore, why not put them together in the first place?

In mature organizations, functional structures are desirable under two conditions. First, the product and customer mix should be relatively homogeneous. Second, the industry to be served should not be particularly dynamic. If the former is not the case, there is serious danger that functionally oriented specialists will ignore product or service groups that don't interest them. In rapidly changing markets, focus on individual specialties and not on products or customers may lead functionally oriented departments to miss major changes in consumer behavior, competitve strategies, or both.

The functional approach also has other disadvantages.

1. Informal criteria of performance may become centered on what the *function* values and not on what is good for the nonprofit enterprise. Thus, advertising people working with each other may tend to feel rewarded for "impressive" advertisments. Public relations people may pride themselves on industry awards for their brochures or public education campaigns. Peer accolades will take the place of market performance.
2. Coordination is more cumbersome. If the organization has several products or services, the general marketing manager will have to spend a lot of time running between functional specialists to ensure that campaigns complement each other, that work is done on time and in proper sequence, and so on.
3. Bottom-line responsibility is diffused. If a product or service is unsuccessful or if a major customer group is stolen away by a competitor, functional specialists will blame "the other guy." If, for example, a new adult extension program in a hospital is a flop, the advertising people may blame the public relations people for not getting enough free TV time or news releases in local

Table 9-2

GENERIC MARKETING POSITIONS

MARKETING MANAGER

1. Other names: vice-president of marketing, marketing director, chief marketing officer, marketing administrator.

2. The marketing manager heads the organization's marketing activities. Tasks include providing a marketing point of view to the top administration, helping to formulate marketing plans of the organization; staffing, directing, and coordinating marketing activities; and proposing new products and services to meet emerging market needs.

PRODUCT MANAGER

1. Other names: program manager, brand manager.

2. A product manager is responsible for managing a particular product or program of the organization. Tasks include proposing product objectives and goals, creating product strategies and plans, seeing that they are implemented, monitoring the results, and taking corrective actions.

MARKETING RESEARCH MANAGER

1. Other names: marketing research director.

2. The marketing research manager has responsibility for developing and supervising research on the organization's markets and publics, and on the effectiveness of various marketing tools.

COMMUNICATIONS MANAGER

1. Other names: advertising manager, advertising and sales promotion director.

2. The communications manager provides expertise in the area of mass and selective communication and promotion. Person is knowledgeable about the development of messages, media, and publicity.

SALES MANAGER

1. Other names: vice-president of sales.

2. The sales manager has responsibilitiy for recruiting, training, assigning, directing, motivating, compensating, and evaluating sales personnel and agents of the organization and coordinating the work of sales personnel with the other marketing functions.

NEW-PRODUCTS MANAGER

1. Other names: new-products director.

2. The new-products manager has responsibility for conceiving new products and services; screening and evaluating new product ideas; developing prototypes and testing them; and advising and helping to carry out the innovation's introduction in the marketplace.

DISTRIBUTION MANAGER

1. Other names: channel manager; physical distribution manager; logistics manager.

Table 9-2 (continued)

2. The distribution manager has responsibility for planning and managing the distribution systems that make the organization's products and services available and accessible to the potential users.

PRICING MANAGER

1. Other names: pricing executive.

2. The pricing manager is responsible for offering advice about or actually setting prices on the organization's services and programs.

CUSTOMER RELATIONS MANAGER

1. Other names: customer service manager, account manager.

2. The customer relations manager has responsibility for managing customer services and handling customer complaints.

GOVERNMENT RELATIONS MANAGER

1. Other names: legislative representative, lobbyist.

2. The government relations manager provides the organization with intelligence on relevant developments in government and manages the organization's program of representation and presentation to government.

PUBLIC RELATIONS MANAGER

1. Other names: public affairs officer.

2. The public relations manager has responsibility for communicating and improving the organization's image with various publics.

TERRITORY MANAGER

1. Other names: regional manager, district manager.

2. The territory manager has responsibility for managing the organization's products, services, and programs in a specific territory.

papers describing the program. For their part, the public relations people may blame the adult education staff for not being customer-oriented enough in actually running the classes. No one person takes final responsibility for the disappointing performance.

Product/Service-Centered Organization.   Many of the leading private sector marketers have turned their functional departments into product/service-centered organizations as shown in Figure 9-1b. One person is put in charge of a specific product or service (or a set of relatively similar products and services) and charged with making them a success. Responsibility is inescapable. If the organization is large enough, each product/service manager would manage his or her own advertising, public relations, and marketing research specialists. In smaller organizations such as one often encounters in the nonprofit sector, it may be necessary to adopt a mixed form of organization like that in Figure 9-1d, which attempts to capture at least the major features of the product/service design. In the mixed format, functional *staff* departments are established along with product/service departments. Each product/service manager then "buys" their services, coordinating their use and ensuring that the "purchased" service provider pays strict attention to market performance.

The product/service-centered organization has a number of advantages:

1. Responsibility is clear. If the product or service fails, there is only one person to blame. If it succeeds, one person probably deserves most of the credit (and the rewards that go with it).
2. This single responsibility forces close attention to market dynamics, shifts in customer tastes and preferences, and competitors' current and planned strategies and tactics. The product/service structure typically is much "faster on its feet" than the functional system.
3. General management skills are developed. Marketing proves to be a good training ground for future top managers. Since all product/service managers have their own little "businesses" to manage, they should become very good at overall strategic planning, budgeting, coordination, and personnel management, all skills that should quickly qualify them for higher level management positions.
4. Small products or services are not neglected.
5. Intraorganizational competition is fostered. Hospital OB-GYN marketing programs could be set in competition with its programs for emergency or outpatient care or for adult education. This internal competitiveness in the private sector seems to keep marketers even more alert and aggressive than other structural designs.

Despite these important advantages, the product/service manager system can have serious limitations. Some are inherent. Broad general management skills are necessary in this kind of system, but often the product/service managers filling the ranks are young and not yet experienced enough to handle the complex managing job effectively. Further, a product/service emphasis can mean relatively weak skill development in functional areas. Thus, the product/service manager may not be particularly strong in advertising or marketing research or public relations and will need to defer too much operational responsibility to functional specialists. Finally, the product/service structure may encourage top management to assign product/service roles to persons with deep product/service knowledge rather than marketing skills and customer sensitivity. Thus, an older nurse with a large family may be seen as the best person to head up the OB-GYN program. The adult fitness program may be assigned to the hospital "fitness freak," while the outpatient program is assigned to the young man who dropped out of medical school for a management career.

Clearly, the major disadvantage of the product/service manager approach is that the manager is not given direct line authority over his or her functional specialists. Thus, product/service managers need great persuasive skill to get staff functional specialists to do what is needed *when* it is needed. With other product/service managers competing for the same staff specialists, there is a great chance that programs will be poorly coordinated. Further, where authority does not equal responsibility, product/service managers will feel considerable frustration at being held accountable for things they cannot totally control.

If there is the danger of this frustration occurring, three steps must be taken. First, top management must back up the product/service manager by according them an important role in the overall organization and by stressing to functional staff people that their job is to serve the product/service managers and not to decide what should or should not get done. Second, product managers should be chosen partly for their interpersonal and persuasive skills. Third, reward systems should explicitly make allowances for situtional factors the product/service manager cannot control.

Customer-Centered Organization.   If, as we have argued, successful marketing organizations should be customer-centered, then it might reasonably be asked why this shouldn't apply to their marketing systems as well. Take the case of the YMCA, for example. The Y has many "products"—physical fitness programs, arts and crafts programs, educational programs, and so on. A product management system would call for appointing a person to head each major program. Thus, a physical fitness director would study people's needs and interests in physical fitness and would develop plans for expanding the offerings and attracting more users, as well as for pricing the programs. This person would advise various local Y units on how to make their physical fitness programs stronger.

The Y also serves a variety of markets divided by sex (male, female) and age (teens, young adults, adults, senior citizens). In a marketing system organized by customer group, a person would be appointed to head each major market. Thus, the market manager for teens would study their needs and develop programs that satisfy their needs. This person would consult local Ys that are having trouble attracting teens and propose new programs that might be offered.

The potential for such a shift to a customer-centered orientation is captured in the experience of the Office of Cancer Communications at the National Cancer Institute, as shown in Exhibit 9-1.

IMPLEMENTING A CUSTOMER ORIENTATION

Establishing the marketing structure appropriate to a particular organization does not necessarily make the organization market-oriented. Indeed, it is crucial that the departments and key managers and staff elsewhere in the institution have the proper philosophy. Inculcating this philosophy may be the marketing manager's most important task. The marketing

EXHIBIT 9-1. A proposal for a customer-centered organization at the National Cancer Institute

The Office of Cancer Communications at the National Cancer Institute (OCC/NCI) is responsible for a number of communications programs dealing with detecting, treating, and helping families cope with various kinds of cancer. Among the programs they actively promoted in the early 1980s were those dealing with breast cancer, smoking, and industrial workplace cancers (for example, those contracted by some workers handling asbestos). These programs were initially organized by type of cancer (that is, by program). Over time, the first two programs evolved two separate and distinct marketing thrusts.

One thrust aimed at the general public. The other thrust was directed at potential cooperating organizations. Thus, the smoking program managers developed an effective liaison with physcians who became key educators about the consequences of smoking and communicators of how-to-quit information. Simultaneously, the breast cancer program recruited major corporations with large female work forces such as AT&T to help develop communications materials for their workers and to organize training sessions in breast self-examination.

A 1983 audit of these two programs recommended switching to a customer-centered program development system:

> It is recommended that reorganziation along *customer* lines be explored. Under such a reorganization, staff would be specialists for specific target customer groups, rather than being "smoking" or "breast" specialists. Thus, someone would be responsible for *all* cancer communications programs directed at physicians and nurses, another for those directed at blue collar worksites or schools, still another for those directed at unions or the elderly or Hispanic or rural "customers." This market-centered organizational innovation is gaining increased use in the private sector.* It is used by Xerox, Mead, and Heinz. The latter, for example, has specialists for groceries, commercial restaurants, and institutions, with the latter further divided into schools, colleges, hospitals, and prisons.

> For OCC, this organizational design would have several advantages:

> 1. It would reinforce efforts to make staff more customer-oriented. They would have clear motivation to understand better the needs, wants, and perceptions of their particular clients since staff, in effect, would be rewarded in terms of their success in creating behavior changes in these groups. (As it is now, each program deals with so many clients that it is just not possible to learn a great deal about any one.)

> 2. It will permit separation of those working with intermediaries from those working with "final consumers." The skills, insights, and approaches needed for the one are very different from those needed for the other. It is not unlike the split in sales forces and

EXHIBIT 9-1 (continued)

other marketing specialists between industrial or retail/wholesale buyers and final consumers in private sector companies.

3. Successful programs with specific target audiences can be followed up quite naturally with other programs. For example, if the breast cancer education program with AT&T or the smoking program with the Navy is successful and a good working relationship has developed, the customer specialist can be thinking ahead to introducing the next program (e.g., breast cancer education in the Navy, or antismoking at AT&T).

4. The synergism possible by applying research findings from one area to another can be enhanced.

5. OCC's image and capabilities can become sharper in target customer eyes since OCC will be personified by only one or two specific staff members. As it is now, a given customer group could conceivably be contacted by different OCC staff people not altogether clear on what each other is doing. Customers will prefer dealing with *one* OCC contact.

6. There would be incentive for OCC to promote the visibility and credibility of the staff person in the eyes of the target audience. Thus, staff might well be selected or assigned in terms of whether they will impress the target audience (e.g., having the "right" educational background, the "right" experience). They can be encouraged to participate in conferences attended by target audiences (especially intermediaries) and from time to time give papers or present workshops.

7. There would be incentive for the staffer to develop extensive contacts among target audience members. Thus, they would learn who the key media gatekeepers are and who opinion leaders/early adopters are in the target population. They could develop and then continually refine a computerized mailing list for all of the target audiences or at least its key members.

8. Duplication of effort would be reduced. For example, if under the present system, a breast program was to be developed for the Navy, much already known about the Navy to the OCC smoking staff person would have to be acquired and contacts already made would have to be made by a second person.

9. Since there may be a certain diminished enthusiasm on the part of some staffers who have been involved a long time in one or the other programs, such a reorganization would revitalize them. In particular, the necessity of trying to apply what was learned in one program to other existing and new programs could prove particularly stretching.

10. Specific, important target customer groups (e.g., rurals, minorities, the elderly) are less likely to be ignored.

11. Advisory committees could be formed from each target group as a means of providing program inputs and of heightening OCC's profile. Such a grouping may be more "natural" than the present grouping by program.

12. Recruiting business financial support for publishing and/or promotional activities may well be easier since businesses more

EXHIBIT 9-1 (continued)

> often identify with audiences than with programs. Thus, for example, a given business marketing to the Navy might be approached to help produce a booklet on smoking and, if that didn't spark an interest, a series of posters on breast cancer or colon-rectal cancer or on toxic chemicals could be proposed until something is found that is mutually rewarding.
>
> *See Mack Hanan, "Reorganize Your Company Around Its Markets," *Harvard Business Review*, November-December, 1979, pp. 63–74.

SOURCE: Alan R. Andreasen, *Second Marketing Audit of Smoking and Breast Cancer Program* (Washington, D.C.: Office of Cancer Communications, National Cancer Institute, 1981).

manager has a limited influence on how others in the organization think and behave toward customers and other publics. The marketing officer in a college, for example, cannot order professors to show a stronger interest in their students. A marketing vice-president in a hospital cannot require nurses to smile and act promptly to meet patient needs. The marketing manager, instead, must work patiently to build up a market-oriented organization. It is not possible for a non-market-oriented organization to be transformed into a fully responsive market-oriented organization overnight. Installing the marketing concept calls for major commitments and changes in the organization. As noted by Edward S. McKay, a longtime marketing consultant:

> It may require drastic and upsetting changes in organization. It usually demands new approaches to planning. It may set in motion a series of appraisals that will disclose surprising weaknesses in performance, distressing needs for modification of operating practices, and unexpected gaps, conflicts, or obsolescence in basic policies. Without doubt, it will call for reorientation of business philosophy and for the reversal of some long-established attitudes. These changes will not be easy to implement. Objectives, obstacles, resistance, and deep-rooted habits will have to be overcome. Frequently, even difficult and painful restaffing programs are necessary before any real progress can be made in implementing the concept.[5]

Any attempt to reorient an organization requires a plan. The plan must be based on sound principles for producing organizational change. Achieving a customer orientation calls for several measures, the sum of which will hopefully produce a market-oriented organization within three to five years. These measures are described below.

Top Management Support

An organization is not likely to develop a strong marketing orientation until its chief executive officer (CEO) believes in it, understands it, wants it,

292

and wins the support of other high-level executives for building this function. The CEO is the organization's highest "marketing executive," and has to create the climate for marketing by talking about it and agitating for it. The CEO of a university, for example, must remind the faculty, bursar, housing director, and others of the importance of serving the students. By setting the tone that the organization must be service-minded and responsive, the CEO prepares the groundwork for introducing further changes later (see Exhibit 9-2).

EFFECTIVE ORGANIZATION DESIGN

The CEO cannot do the whole marketing job. Eventually, a marketing manager must be added to the organization, in either a staff or a line position.

As we saw earlier, a staff marketing director essentially operates as a *resource manager* who takes responsibility for building and coordinating marketing resources and activities. A marketing director operates as a high-level *strategy and policy manager,* capable of influencing other top managers to take a market-oriented view of the organization's customers and publics. The cost of failing to establish an adequate marketing function is described below:

> An illustration of the failure to position the marketing function properly within the organization is that of a large city hospital which made the mistake of assigning the organization's marketing to a mid-level supervisor already overloaded with administrative tasks. Not only was the supervisor unable to spend adequate time analyzing the hospital's major markets and competitive stance, but also the supervisor found that he was unable to obtain support for the few (quite reasonable) marketing actions he recommended. Because no one in top management had initiated the analysis from which the recommendation came and no top level manager was responsible for the marketing function, no one with the power to implement the recommended marketing actions would support them. The result was a frustrated supervisor who spent a good deal of his overallocated time on a nonproductive task and a hospital which missed out on two substantial market opportunities.[6]

IN-COMPANY MARKETING TRAINING

An early task of the new marketing executive should be to develop a series of workshops to introduce marketing to various groups in the organization. These groups are likely to have incorrect ideas about marketing and little understanding of its potential benefits.

The first workshop should be presented to top corporate and divisional management. Their understanding and support is absolutely essential if marketing is to work in the organization. The workshop may take place at the organization's headquarters or at a retreat; it may consist of a highly

EXHIBIT 9-2. Memo from a college president on the need for a customer orientation

As surely as there are "Fifty Ways to Leave Your Lover," as the popular song says, there are fifty ways and fifty reasons for a student to end his love affair with his college. Short-term campaigns to accommodate students meet the urgency of the moment, but do not build long-term goodwill. Some research indicates that students leave colleges not for big reasons, but for accumulations of little reasons that erode their justifications of college choice.

The problem is how to inculcate responsiveness, or "marketing consciousness," within the entire collegiate community, making everyone connected with the institution aware that (1) no one *has* to attend your college; (2) no one has to *remain* at your college; and (3) everyone wants to be treated with respect, and to be appreciated. In modern society, no service- or people-oriented establishment can prosper without a sense of responsiveness, a may-I-help-you approach on the part of all.

An educational institution has a responsibility to set a high example in valuing humankind. A surly clerk in the registrar's office, a defensive custodian, an irritable residence director, an abrasive secretary can easily undo in moments the goodwill created by the warm friendship of a professor or the congeniality of a dean. How may we heighten the marketing consciousness of the whole institution? How do we assure the student consumer that he is entitled to as much courtesy and kindness at his or her school as at the bank, airlines, clothing shop, grocery, and so on?

At the heart of a consumerist approach in any *service* industry is an adaptation of an old rule: Perform your service as if you were on the *receiving* point rather than the delivery point of the transaction. If teachers would teach as they would like to be taught, custodians cleaned as they would like their houses cleaned, questions were answered as we would want our own questions answered, the world would be happier, and the college would be a better place. In truth, marketing consciousness will have to be promoted (perhaps "marketed") within the college community.

1. The president, as chief executive, will have to strike the official posture with an initial memo or position paper in which he makes it clear that: (a) students and all publics are due the utmost courtesy, consideration, and thoughtfulness; (b) temper tantrums, "telling people off," deviousness have no part in the academic setting; (c) this is not just a passive policy, but everyone should be constantly asking, How can I be of help? The clientele is the key to institutional good fortune, personal prosperity, and a clear conscience toward consumers and the society.

2. Since most institutions now use some sort of evaluative process, included among performance standards for personnel judgments could be the matter of marketing consciousness. How does the individual reflect the institution's commitment to a consumer-

EXHIBIT 9-2 (continued)

istic approach? That standard then feeds into salary decisions just as do job skill, productivity, professional growth, and so on.

3. Short seminars and workshops for different classes of employ-ess can point up the priority the college gives to marketing con-sciousness. The airlines and the telephone companies have been very good at instilling this approach—I have never been treated with anything but the utmost courtesy and kindness by telephone operators and airline personnel. It would be worthwhile to assem-ble the custodians to say: Be responsive to student needs and requests; be looking for helpful things you can accomplish that may not be in your job description; see to it that leaky faucets get fixed, light bulbs replaced, trash bins emptied, spills cleaned. Offer short courses to secretaries and clerks in telephone manners and good reception techniques. Chances are there are resource persons on every campus who could provide such instruction.

4. Put a statement in the catalog declaring the college's intent. You may want to note that constraints of purpose, law, finances, propriety will not permit the institution to say "yes" to everything. But it is institutional intent to be responsive, consumeristic, cour-teous, and conscientious in all matters.

5. Place statements in the faculty handbook and in personnel policy manuals concerning the college's commitment to a high level of marketing consciousness.

6. Place squawk boxes in a few prominent places so that anyone who feels he's been dealt less than the minimum of human kind-ness may report the incident. A follow-up by the worker's super-visor will impress the point that the institution is serious about its commitment.

7. Encourage supervisory personnel to make a special effort to reward and compliment those who consistently go the extra mile, and who exhibit a heightened concern for the welfare of the clien-tele. Let the president write thank yous for exceptional courtesy and responsiveness. Word will spread.

8. If the institution publishes an internal newsletter, each issue could highlight a particular example of consumer concern: a fac-ulty member's visit to the hospital bedside of a student recovering from an accident; a student providing a spontaneous campus tour in response to the request of a "walk-on" visiting alumnus; a sec-retary's detailed explanation of a complicated Bureau of Immigra-tion form for the benefit of a befuddled international student.

Human kindness ought to be in generous supply among the humane personnel of the learning community. Such will also prove to reduce attrition and to be good for the institution.

SOURCE: Written by Thomas E. Corts, president, Wingate College of Wingate, North Carolina, and included with his permission.

professional presentation of concepts, cases, and marketing planning exercises. From there, further presentations can be made to the operations people, financial people, and others to enlist their understanding. These presentations should cover such topics as market opportunity identification, market segmentation, market targeting and positioning, marketing planning and control, pricing, selling, and marketing communication.

BETTER EMPLOYEE HIRING PRACTICES

Training can only go so far in inculcating the right attitudes in employees. If a college faculty has grown accustomed to concentrating on research instead of good teaching, it will be hard to change their attitudes. The college can gradually rectify the imbalance by hiring faculty who are more teaching- and student-oriented. The first principle in developing a caring faculty is to hire caring people. Some people are more naturally service-minded than others, and this can be a criterion for hiring. Delta Airlines does most of its flight attendant recruiting from the deep South where there is a tradition of hospitality; it avoids hiring in large northern cities because people from these cities tend to be less hospitable. Delta operates on the principle that it is easier to hire friendly people than to train unfriendly people to be friendly.

New employess should go through a training program that emphasizes the importance of creating customer satisfaction. They can be taught how to handle complaining and even abusive customers without getting riled up. Skills in listening and customer problem solving would be part of the training (see Exhibit 9-3).

REWARDING MARKET-ORIENTED EMPLOYEES

One way for top management to convince everyone in the organization of the importance of customer-oriented attitudes is to reward those who demonstrate these attitudes. The organization can make a point of citing employees who have done an outstanding job of serving customers. Many colleges have "best teacher" awards based on student voting. Some hospitals carry a picture in their employees' magazine showing the "nurse-of-the-month" and describing how this person handled a difficult situation. By calling attention to examples of commendable customer-oriented performance, it is hoped that other employees will be motivated to emulate this behavior.

PLANNING SYSTEM IMPROVEMENT

One of the most effective ways to build a demand for stronger marketing is to improve the organization's planning system. Suppose the nonprofit organization has neither strong marketing nor strong planning. The organization might first design and install a business planning system. To

EXHIBIT 9-3. Walt Disney Enterprises—a highly responsive organization

Service organizations—colleges, hospitals, social agencies, and others—are increasingly recognizing that their marketing mix consists not of four Ps but five: product, price, place, promotion, and people. And people may be the most important P. The organization's employees come in continuous contact with consumers and create good or bad impressions about the organization, as the case may be. Service organizations are eager to figure out how to produce a genuine customer orientation and service-mindedness in their employees.

Not many organizations have really figured out how to motivate their inside people (employees) to serve their outside people (customers). Consider the following things that the Disney organization does to market "positive customer attitudes" to its employees:

1. The personnel staff at Disney makes a special effort to welcome new job applicants and make a good impression on them. The initial impression is very important. Those who are hired are given clearly written instructions on what to expect—where to report, what to wear, and how long each training phase will take.

2. On the first day, new employees report to Disney University for an all-day orientation session. They sit four to a table, receive name tags, and enjoy coffee, juice, and pastry. The four new employees at each table are asked to get acquainted and then introduce each other. As a result, each new employee immediately knows three other people and feels part of a group.

3. During the next eight hours, the employees are introduced to the Disney philosophy and operations through the most modern audiovisual presentations. The new employees learn that they are in the entertainment business. They are "cast members" whose job it is to be enthusiastic, knowledgeable, and professional in serving Disney's "guests." Each division in the organization is described, and how these divisions relate to each other to produce the "show." They are then treated to a free lunch, and in the afternoon, the new employees are given a tour of the park and also shown the private recreational area set aside for the employees' exclusive use, consisting of a lake, recreation hall, picnic areas, boating and fishing, and a large library.

4. The next day, the new employees report to their assigned jobs, such as security hosts (policemen), transportation hosts (drivers), custodial hosts (street cleaners), or food and beverage hosts (restaurant workers). They will receive a few days of additional training before they go "on stage." When they really know their function, they receive their "theme costume" for that function and are ready to go on stage.

5. The new employees receive additional training on how to answer the scores of questions guests frequently ask about the park. When they don't have the answer, they can dial a special number where a cadre of switchboard operators armed with thick factbooks stands ready to answer any question.

6. The employees regularly receive an eight-page 8½ × 11 news-

EXHIBIT 9-3 (continued)

paper called *Eyes and Ears* that features all sorts of activities, employment opportunities, special benefits, educational offerings, and so on. Each issue contains a generous number of employee pictures, all of them smiling.

7. Each Disney manager spends a week each year in "cross-utilization," namely, giving up the desk and heading for the front line, such as taking tickets, selling popcorn, or loading or unloading rides. In this way, management stays in touch with the daily challenges of running the park and problems of maintaining quality service to satisfy the millions of people who visit the theme park yearly. All the managers and employees wear name badges and address each other on a first-name basis, regardless of rank.

8. All exiting employees receive a questionnaire to indicate how they felt about working for Disney, particularly any dissatisfactions they might have had. In this way, Disney's management can measure how good a job they are doing in producing employee satisfaction and ultimately customer satisfaction.

No wonder the Disney people have had such huge success in satisfying their "guests." Their exchange with employees makes the latter feel important and personally responsible for the "show." The employees' sense of "owning this organization," of being worthwhile members of a worthwhile organization, results in their satisfaction spilling over to the millions of visitors with whom they come in contact.

SOURCE: This is a summary of the major points found in N. W. Pope, "Mickey Mouse Marketing," *American Banker,* July 25, 1979; and "More Mickey Mouse Marketing," *American Banker,* September 12, 1979.

make this system work, strong marketing data and analysis are necessary. The planners will see that business plans must begin with an analysis of the market. This will require strengthening the organization's marketing function. Top management will see that business planning is largely an empty gesture without good marketing data and analysis.

SUMMARY

The role of marketing in a nonprofit organization typically evolves through three stages. In the introductory stage, there is resistance because organization members are opposed to marketing in principle or because they feel they are already doing it. If the organization wishes to proceed without a formal department, it can make use of outside resources. Should a formal marketing function be contemplated, a marketing committee should carefully consider what form it should take and how it should be introduced.

Marketing will clearly be a separate function during the growth phase. At this point, a major issue is whether marketing should be established as a line or a staff function. There may also be a question of what kind of background is appropriate for marketing positions. While it may be expedient to use someone with an advertising or journalism background initially, most organizations eventually turn to individuals with formal marketing training.

Initial projects for the marketing group should have a high economic impact yet be relatively inexpensive to implement. They should be completed in a short period of time and have high visibility if successful.

Once the mature phase is reached, marketing is well established. The organizational question at this stage is what form is best. The major alternatives are a functional orientation, a product/service orientation, a customer orientation, or some mixture. While the specific form chosen should depend on the experience, market conditions, and mission of the organization, the customer-centered firm must explicitly incorporate the philosophy emphasized in this book. And even when the customer-centered form is not chosen, it is essential that the organization adopt such a perspective. This can be accomplished by careful hiring and training, explicit top management support, and a reward structure that reinforces customer-centered behavior.

QUESTIONS

1. The family planning program in Egypt has several products, including IUDs, condoms, and oral pills. It serves urban and rural areas and frequently must work through physicians and hospitals. It also has to market itself to government agencies and to the media. What type of marketing organization would you recommend for this program?

2. A university alumni organization is thinking of adding a marketing specialist, and the alumni director favors an advertising copywriter for the position. What arguments would you make for hiring someone with a B.A. or M.B.A. in marketing?

3. A museum of natural history has hired a marketing person for the first time. What projects do you suggest this person undertake first to assure that marketing is fully accepted?

4. The public relations director for a nonprofit hospital believes that the hospital may be ready to institute a formal marketing department. What factors would suggest that the organization is, indeed, ready for such a step?

5. What questions would you ask of a potential marketing director to assure yourself that he or she truly has a customer orientation?

NOTES

1. "A New Breed of Marketer Evolves as Hospitals Get Serious about Marketing," *Marketing News,* January 18, 1985, p. 8.

2. John A. Witt and Nelson L. McRoberts, "Lack of Expertise, Funding Shackles Marketing Moves," *Modern Health Care,* April 1983.

3. Sometimes, unfortunately, the reverse happens. At one college, the director of marketing helped improve recruitment effectiveness substantially. At this point, the president terminated the position, feeling that all the value had been obtained. Needless to say, other marketing problems emerged down the road, and the president realized that he had been hasty. Marketing is not a "fair weather" function, but one that has a continuous job to perform in an organization.

4. See "United States Postal Service," in Christopher H. Lovelock and Charles B. Weinberg, eds., *Cases in Public and Nonprofit Marketing,* (Palo Alto, Calif.: Scientific Press, 1977), pp. 153–62.

5. Edward S. McKay, *The Marketing Mystique* (New York: American Management Association, 1972), p. 22.

6. Roberta N. Clarke, "Marketing Health Care: Problems in Implementation," *HCM Review,* Winter 1978, p. 24.

CHAPTER 10

Leveraging Limited Resources

A public service campaign launched in March 1985 to aid parents of missing children has mushroomed into the most extensive effort to date on behalf of this worthy cause, according to Rochelle Dishon, director of public relations at Supermarket Communications Systems, Inc. (SCS), in Norwalk, Connecticut.

The project—a joint effort between SCS, Nestle Foods Corporation, the National Center for Missing and Exploited Children, and national and regional supermarket chains—involves the placing of children's photographs on "Good Neighbor" message center displays in 5,500 supermarkets coast to coast.

Each week, as many as 90 million people view the displays, which feature a toll-free national hotline as well as six to eight photos of children who are victims of stranger or parental kidnappings, she said.

SCS owns and maintains the message centers, distributes the photos, and replaces them monthly, while the National Center for Missing and Exploited Children staffs the hotline in Washington, D.C. Nestle has thus far committed more than $250,000 to the project.

Participating supermarkets include Pathmark, A&P, Stop & Shop, and Acme in the Northeast; Kroger, Jewel, Dominicks in the Midwest; Alpha Beta, Lucky, and Ralphs on the West Coast; and Pantry Pride in the South. And SCS expects even more chains to sign on as the campaign progresses.

"This project is an example of how a direct marketing/literature distribution company can use its resources to affect an important and vital community effort," Dishon said.

Giving the campaign an additional boost are TV and radio public service announcements featuring Brian Patrick Clark of "General Hospital," Daniel J. Travanti of "Hill Street Blues," and New Jersey Democratic Senator William Bradley. These announcements, which have been run by stations across the country since August of 1985, urge the public to visit the displays.

SOURCE: Adapted from "Supermarket Chains Join in Quest for Missing Children," *Marketing News,* October 11, 1985, p. 22.

For one who wishes to manage a nonprofit or public service marketing organization, it is essential to understand the special place society accords these organizations and the implications that special place has for managerial effectiveness. As is evident from both its actions and its attitudes, society considers nonprofit and public service organizations and those who work for them to be motivated not just by different goals but by *higher* goals. Elsewhere in this volume, we have suggested several of the disadvantages this status has for nonprofit organizations. We have noted that a major problem facing most nonprofit organizations is that they lack adequate time, manpower, skills, and financial resources to achieve the mission they or society has established for them. To be successful, they have to augment these resources by securing the assistance of others. This assistance comes in three forms, manpower, skills and volunteered or reduced-cost goods and services. Some of this assistance is provided routinely either as required by law (for example, tax concessions) or by common (often written) agreement (for example, the provision of free television air time for public service announcements). For the most part, however, securing assistance is itself a *marketing* task. Those who could assist must be brought to the point where they agree to exchange their goods and services (or their "normal" markup or profit) in return for certain benefits.

It is our position that while the special elevated status of nonprofit and public service organizations offers a highly positive platform for seeking help, the organization must also explicitly or implicitly have other benefits to offer as well. Doctors who could help with an antismoking campaign or contribute to a charitable activity may agree that what you're doing is admirable and ought to be supported. But they have many demands on their time by other organizations and, indeed, make their social contribution by providing free services to impoverished patients. To get their help, the nonprofit marketer must make them see that the benefits exceed the cost of the

help *and* that the benefit/cost ratio for this contribution is better than anyone else's.

In the next chapter we shall consider steps nonprofits can take to augment their financial resources by seeking out foundation and other support.
In this chapter, we will be concerned with the opportunities and challenges
nonprofits have for leveraging their special status by securing other needed
resources. Specifically, we will be concerned with three resources: manpower, skills, and specific goods and services. It should be pointed out, however, that we consider the special status of nonprofits that affords them these
leveraging possibilities to be a *mixed* blessing. Put most simply, when goods
and services are acquired at more or less full price on the open market, the
acquirer has almost total discretion over how they are to be used. As the
expression goes, he who pays the piper calls the tune. When the provider of
the acquired goods and services offers a special dispensation, all too often
they want a say in what the "tune" will be. The transaction has strings, and
these strings may seriously impair the performance capability of the nonprofit. In the sections to follow, we shall alert the manager to these possibilities and suggest methods for coping with them.

RECRUITING AND MANAGING VOLUNTEERS

One common feature of many nonprofit organizations is their use of
volunteers, both to keep down expenses and to provide a channel for high-
minded people to contribute time to a cause they believe in. Among the
organizations that make heavy use of volunteers are hospitals, political parties, trade associations, arts organizations, charitable institutions, churches,
and social reform organizations. Also, smaller volunteer units are found in
schools and social service organizations.

The core concept of voluntarism is that individuals participate in
spontaneous, private, and freely chosen activities that promote or advance
some aspect of the common good, as it is perceived by the persons participating in it. These activities are not coerced by any institution in society
and the behavior is engaged in not primarily for financial gain. Over 92 million Americans act as regular or periodic volunteers each year. In 1985, the
economic value of volunteer time exceeded $65 billion.[1] In recent years,
however, the number of volunteers has been declining due to the rise in the
proportion of working women. Organizations have to give increased attention now to the problem of volunteer attraction and satisfaction and
management.

This problem has been made more difficult because of several important trends in volunteerism. Eva Schindler-Rainman and Ronald Lippitt
have recently highlighted several of these trends:[2]

1. While people are still volunteering because they feel it's a good thing to do

or because they have been taught to do so, new motivations are emerging, such as:

    a. The desire to change society.

    b. The desire to obtain experiences that can eventually be useful on a "regular" paid job.

    c. The desire to help a specific cause, such as improving the environment, electing a specific candidate, helping the elderly, removing discrimination, and so on.

    d. The desire to improve one's life through meeting others and attempting to make a difference.

    e. The desire to prepare for a volunteer career upon retirement.

    f. The desire to get inside important institutions (for example, government or a social movement) to see what it is doing and to make sure it is doing what it says it is doing.

2. A wider spectrum of people are volunteering. Rather than just the healthy, vigorous middle classes, we now find the "served" (for example, the elderly or the handicapped) and professionals also offering their services.

3. Volunteers are more demanding. They want more "input" into what they are doing and are no longer willing to only be a drone in a larger enterprise.

4. Some groups are challenging the ultimate social desirability of volunteerism. While unions have traditionally worried that volunteerism was taking employment from those who could have been paid, the women's movement has recently challenged volunteerism as perpetuating the notion that what women do (that is, housework, volunteering) is not really valuable because it is unpaid.

The major consequence of these trends is that securing volunteers in the future may not be as easy as it was in the past.[3] The pool of those who come forward with little or no encouragement is shrinking. Those who might come forward are more hard-headed about their choices and are likely to be approached by many more competitors crying for their volunteer commitment. The need for effective strategic marketing aimed at this crucial resource is becoming even more apparent. We shall consider the problems of recruiting and managing volunteers in turn.

RECRUITING VOLUNTEERS

As with any other marketing task, a crucial starting point for recruiting is understanding the target audience. Volunteer motivations are as diverse as consumer motivations. One classification of motivations is based on Maslow's higher order needs:

- *Belonging:* Help others; meet friends; feel part of something bigger than oneself
- *Status:* Get recognition; impress others; add to résumé; make contacts
- *Self-Actualization:* Feel altruistic; learn a skill; feel one is having an impact on something important

Schindler-Rainman and Lippitt suggest that one might look upon the decision to volunteer as a response to forces pulling towards and away from volunteering. They suggest that such forces be separated into (1) individual internal forces, (2) external interpersonal forces, and (3) situational forces.[4] These forces are outlined in Exhibit 10-1.

To identify the critical motivations in their own volunteer situation, the more sophisticated nonprofits have turned to marketing research as the

EXHIBIT 10-1. Forces affecting the decision to volunteer or not volunteer

Forces supporting "yes" decisions	Forces inhibiting "yes" decisions and supporting "no" decisions
———————————————→	←———————————————
Forces from Inside Self ("Own Forces")	
It sounds like fun ————————————→	It sounds like routine "scut" work ←———————————————
	Their work isn't as important as it used to be—it's not where the
I want to be where the action is ————————————→	action is ←———————————————
I want to get out of my "box," away from daily routine boredom ————————————→	I owe my time and energy to my family ←———————————————
	I don't feel I have any skill that's
What they are doing is very important ————————————→	needed ←———————————————
They really need and want me ————————————→	I'm scared of what I might get into ←———————————————
	I worked hard to develop my
It's a chance to learn new skills ————————————→	skills—I should be paid ←———————————————
It's a chance to learn things that would help me get ahead ————————————→	I think I am too old for that ←———————————————
	It's not clear what kind of help and
The visibility could help me on my job ————————————→	support I'd get ←———————————————
	The last time I said yes it was a
It could help me with my personal life ————————————→	waste of my time ←———————————————
I've gotten a lot of help. Now it's my turn to repay ————————————→	It might tie me down at times—I'd want to be free to do other things ←———————————————
It's a critical need; I've got to do my part	I need to earn extra money in my spare time

EXHIBIT 10-1. (continued)

	It's unpopular; I'll be involved in conflict
I need something to do ——→	←——
I'll have a chance to really influence what happens ——→	
I'll waste my time if I don't commit it to something ——→	

Forces from Relations with Others ("Interpersonal and Group Member Forces")

Service is a tradition in our family—it's expected ——→	They don't trust volunteers to do the important things ←——
It's one of the things our group members do, part of our program ——→	My colleagues would raise their eyebrows at my getting into that ←——
My best friend is asking me ——→	I might lose my job ←——
He's an important person. I don't feel I can say no ——→	My family would object ←——
She wouldn't ask me if it wasn't important ——→	They are paying others for the same thing ←——

"Situational Forces"

	I'd have to go too far from where I live: transportation is not clear ←——
It would be a new world, an adventure ——→	
We'd have our own office and telephone ——→	There's no place for the volunteers to meet and have a space of their own ←——
They'll fit it to the hours I have free to give ——→	They are too rigid in the time schedule they want ←——
There'll be several of us working at the same place ——→	That area is dangerous ←——
The national leadership has declared it a national priority ——→	
I'd make new friends ——→	

SOURCE: Reprinted from Eva Schindler-Rainman and Ronald Lippitt, *The Volunteer Community: Creative Use of Human Resources,* 2d ed. (La Jolla, Calif.: University Associates Inc., 1977), pp. 48–50. Used with permission.

next step in their strategic planning. Such research falls into one or more of four categories:

1. *Segmentation Studies.* Here the interest is in isolating the demographic, motivational, and lifestyle characteristics that separate *current* volunteers from nonvolunteers. The studies assume that the best prospects for future volunteers will resemble those who have volunteered in the past.

2. *Prospect Studies.* Here the interest lies in recruiting volunteers from new segments. The focus is on learning more about clusters of candidates who might have values or lifestyles to which the organization can appeal. Particular attention is given to reaching new groups through understanding either their media habits or their likely accessibility to interpersonal influence.

3. *Motivational Studies.* Nonprofits have recognized the relatively superficial nature of responses obtained through surveys. Thus, recent interest has developed in qualitative methodologies such as focus groups, projective techniques, and in-depth personal interviews as efficient, effective ways to reveal more fundamental reasons for volunteering and—just as importantly—for not volunteering.

4. *Positioning Studies.* Organizations that may feel they understand motivations typically progress to image studies as a basis for potentially changing organizational marketing strategies. They recognize that their success or failure as recruiters of particular segments of potential volunteers is tied closely to those segments' perceptions of the organization and their perceptions of other organizations that are in their set of evoked alternatives.

With information derived from such studies, the volunteer recruiter is then in a position to decide whom to focus on, what to say to get them to volunteer, how to say it (for example, with what appeals, with what spokesperson), and where to say it.

There are many sources of volunteers. Over the last two decades, universities have been a major source of volunteer help. In recent years, student volunteerism has been growing. Harvard found that 51 percent of graduating seniors had devoted some time to community service in 1985, up from 35 percent in 1982. At the University of California at Berkeley in 1985, nine sororities and seven fraternities enrolled 1,000 students willing to give at least one week to supervising after-hours activities at Berkeley public schools.[5]

Once recruited, volunteers must be retained. Retention has become a very important problem in recent years as the demand on people's time and energy increase. Two techniques have proven particularly valuable. First, *former* volunteers should be studied to determine who they are and how they differ from volunteers who stayed on, why they left the organization, and what steps could be taken to get them to revolunteer.

Second, the organization should carry out routine formal assessments of *present* volunteers' satisfactions and dissatisfactions. Among the factors that frequently surface in these kinds of studies are the following:

1. Unreal expectations when volunteering. This is sometimes the recruit's own fault in that he or she has unrealistic fantasies about how exciting it would be to join the Peace Corps, participate in a political campaign, or become part of the "United Way team," or about how much time would be involved. But just as often the culprit is the nonprofit organization, which, in its zeal to get recruits, paints an excessively optimistic picture of the volunteer's time commitment, type of work, and probable influence.
2. Lack of appreciative feedback from clients and co-workers.
3. Lack of appropriate training and supervision.
4. Feelings of second-class status vis-à-vis full-time staff.
5. Excessive demands on time.
6. Lack of a sense of personal accomplishment.

Managing Volunteers

The use of volunteers is not an unmixed blessing for a nonprofit organization. The mix of volunteers and full-time staff can be a volatile one. There can be problems on both sides. On the side of the volunteer, many have the attitude that because they are donating their services to the nonprofit and are not paid by them (1) they don't really *work* for the organization and so shouldn't be *told* what to do, rather, they should be *asked* if they would be willing to do something; (2) they should have a great deal to say about the content and timetable for their assignments; and (3) they deserve continual appreciation for their generosity and commitment. Further, some individuals volunteer, not because they really want to work, but because they have been coerced into volunteering by an employer or peers or because they wish to add an item to their résumé. One manager of a large volunteer force has developed what he calls his "rule of thirds." One-third of his volunteer force works avidly with very little direction and encouragement. One-third will work only with considerable motivation and are only effective with careful supervision. And one-third will not work at all under any circumstances and are best ignored.

On the organization side, there is considerable opportunity for friction to develop if the professional full-time staff looks on the volunteers as second-class workers. Among the opinions professionals have been known to offer are

1. Volunteers are dilettantes. They are not there for the long haul and so don't have to live with the consequences of their impulsive or lethargic performance.
2. Volunteers never really pay attention to their training and instruction because they are only part-time and so commit tactical and ethical missteps that hurt the organization.

3. Volunteers often come from occupations in which they boss others and so cannot or will not take direction.
4. Volunteers are often well-to-do members of the leisure classes who (a) consider themselves better than the professional staff (the "Junior Leaguers"), and (b) are unwilling to perform grubby tasks like licking envelopes or cleaning bedpans.

The potential for conflict between volunteers and professional full-time employees is therefore considerable. The situation can be exacerbated if management does not take firm control of the situation. Again, it is a matter of *attitude*. If management's attitude is dominated by feelings of gratitude that individuals have so kindly volunteered, all is virtually lost. Management will be unwilling to ruffle the feathers of volunteers. This will only encourage the volunteers' tendencies toward undisciplined performance. At the same time, management will be likely to squelch grumblings of the paid staff for fear that they will upset these needed volunteers. This will only cause unrest and surreptitious insubordination among the staff. The result will be that management loses control of *both* full-time and volunteer staff.

The solution that the more experienced programs have developed is simply to treat volunteers as much as possible as professional, full-time workers indistinguishable from paid staff. Among other things, this means using the following standards and managerial practices:

1. Assessing the volunteer's skills and as nearly as possible matching these skills to the tasks to be performed in the organization.
2. Setting out job responsibilities clearly and in detail in advance.
3. Setting specific performance goals and benchmarks.
4. Clearly informing the volunteers of these goals and of the fact that they are expected to achieve them.
5. Informing the volunteers that if they do not perform satisfactorily in their job, they will be let go or assigned elsewhere (the most difficult task).
6. Following through on the standards of accountability, knocking heads and dismissing volunteers until the word gets around that management is serious in its commitments (the most crucial task).

This straightforward, professional style of volunteer management may seem risky to the inexperienced manager. But both volunteer and professional staff respond very favorably to it. Most volunteers like to be taken seriously and challenged. They appreciate the opportunity to be well trained and well supervised. Those who don't are the one-third you don't want anyway. Full-time staff appreciate management's firmness and the fact that they, too, can treat the volunteer seriously, giving orders as necessary and reprimands as required. Performance standards for both groups improve enormously and the nonprofit's effectiveness, efficiency, and morale rise noticeably. Indeed, the organization's volunteer positions can be highly coveted.[6]

ATTRACTING SKILLS, GOODS, AND SERVICES

Nonprofit marketers are not only understaffed and underfinanced. Their relative newness and frequent lack of commercial marketing training often means that they lack marketing capability. Two areas in which assistance is often needed are advertising and marketing research. Some of the steps a nonprofit can take to leverage its goodwill to get skilled help in these areas from various sources are described in the following sections.

COMMERCIAL AGENCIES

Probably the best-known source of leverage for nonprofits is professional advertising agencies that are willing to donate their skills and services in the public interest. Almost every major community has agencies that are willing to make such contributions. An example of what can result from the support of just one advertising agency is given in Figure 10-1.

There are a number of reasons for such generosity:

- They may believe that the nonprofit organization will have important community executives among its other volunteers and so a volunteer campaign will be a major opportunity to make business contacts.
- Goodwill can be obtained by such public-spiritedness.
- Agency executives and staff can achieve personal psychic benefits from working on important social issues rather than just "selling soap."
- Opportunities in the campaign for individual creativity, agency creativity, or both may be considerably greater than when a paying client is "calling the tune." The agency may see a chance to make a major public impression with a highly innovative campaign.
- The campaign presents an opportunity to give experience to junior staff people where a major client isn't at risk.

Like volunteers, volunteer-leveraged advertising services can be a mixed blessing. First, if the donated campaign is costly, the agency may skimp on production values. If it assigns junior people, the execution may not be of the highest quality. On the other hand, if the agency focuses too narrowly on the campaign as merely a chance to make a major creative impact, it may lose sight of the nonprofit organization's basic advertising goals. If nonprofit managers are alert to these potential dangers, however, they can typically be avoided with timely interventions. Again, as with volunteers, it is up to the nonprofit to treat the donated relationship *as if* it were a professional, fully-paid-for relationship rather than a "charity case" for which the nonprofit organization should be grateful (and thus noninterfering).

Probably the best-known example of donated advertising agency services is the operation of the Advertising Council. The Council was founded

FIGURE 10-1
Promotion Seeking Media Cooperation

Please.

Make Smokey's Birthday Wish Come True.

A-1

Run these ads.

SOURCE: Needham Porter Novelli. Reprinted with permission.

in 1942. In 1984, it serviced over twenty-five public service advertising campaigns using contributed services of advertising agencies and volunteer industry coordinators. These campaigns were able to obtain space and time contributed by the media valued at over $700 million annually.[7] Among the campaigns for which the Ad Council's work has been particularly memorable over the years are:

- The U.S. Forest Service (Smokey the Bear—see Exhibit 10-2 and Figure 10-1)
- The United Negro College Fund ("A mind is a terrible thing to waste")
- The American Red Cross
- The Statue of Liberty renovation project
- The National Highway Traffic Safety Administration (see Figure 10-2)
- The U.S. Justice Department ("Take a Bite Out of Crime" campaign—see Exhibit 10-3)

EXHIBIT 10-2. Smokey Bear Program for the U.S. Forest Service, U.S. Department of Agriculture, and the Advertising Council

The Forest Service account has been a public service client of Foote, Cone & Belding's Los Angeles office since 1942. The Smokey Bear Program is the longest-running public service campaign on record, and it has been handled by FCB since its inception. Further, an awareness study done by the U.S. Advertising Council in 1976 showed that Smokey Bear is the second most widely recognized advertising symbol in America, second only to the Coca-Cola bottle.

The Ad Council's study also showed that 98 percent of the respondents not only recognize Smokey Bear but also know that he stands for forest fire prevention. In addition, more than half the respondents can complete the Smokey Bear slogan, "Only you . . ." can prevent forest fires.

The Smokey campaign, for which new material is created by FCB every year, includes public service advertising materials as well as posters and handouts for use by foresters and teachers to help teach children to be careful with fire in the forest.

HISTORY OF SMOKEY BEAR

Smokey celebrated his fortieth birthday in 1984 and is the subject of a television documentary.

Smokey the Bear has a long history.

During the Second World War, a Japanese submarine shelled the Southern California coast, and forestry officials were afraid that future attacks might start widespread forest fires. The government was alerted to the danger to its national forests. Because of this, the Cooperative Forest Fire Prevention campaign was organized by the USDA Forest Service.

The campaign needed to take its message directly to the American people, so the newly formed Wartime Advertising Council was asked for their advice. The Council agreed to help, and Foote, Cone & Belding of Los Angeles became the volunteer advertising agency.

At first, during 1942 and 1943, wartime slogans were used on forest fire prevention posters. Then Walt Disney's Bambi was used on a 1944 poster. After Bambi's success, the Forest Service and the Wartime Advertising Council decided to choose their own animal to represent forest fire prevention. The agreed-on animal: a bear. This bear was described as follows: "nose short (panda type), color black or brown; expression appealing, knowledgeable, quizzical; perhaps wearing campaign (or Boy Scout) hat that typifies the outdoors and the woods."

The first poster (1944–1945) showed the bear, named "Smokey," pouring water on a campfire.

When the war was over, the Wartime Advertising Council was renamed the Advertising Council. But they continued to sponsor public service campaigns, including Smokey Bear's message. The famous mes-

EXHIBIT 10-2. (continued)

sage, "Only *you* can prevent forest fires," was created in 1947. It is still in use today.

By 1952, Smokey Bear had become so well known that his image needed protection by law. So Congress passed the Smokey Bear Act. The Act did several things: 1) it prohibited the use of Smokey Bear without permission of the Forest Service; 2) it permitted the Forest Service to license the use of Smokey Bear and collect royalties; and 3) it allowed the Forest Service to keep the royalties and put them into a fund to be used only for forest fire prevention. The Act also prohibited the wearing of a Smokey Bear costume without permission.

The first Smokey Bear stuffed toy was made in 1952 by Ideal Toys. With permission from the Forest Service, a card was inserted with each toy to be mailed to the Forest Service as an application to become a "Junior Forest Ranger." Children readily responded. By 1955 there were 500,000 Junior Forest Rangers.

Elementary school children were taken with the message of Smokey Bear. State forestry people and Forest Service rangers visited classrooms, telling the students about forest fire prevention. Children were encouraged to write Smokey for their very own Junior Forest Ranger Kit. By 1965, Smokey Bear was given his own zip code number. Requests for Junior Forest Ranger Kits from children are still being sent to Smokey today.

Has all this effort to prevent forest fires had a result? In 1942 over 10 million acres of wildlands were burned. In 1981, only 3 million acres were burned—representing a savings of over $20 billion for the American taxpayers.

SOURCE: Foote, Cone & Belding, Chicago.

Marketing research agencies can also be helpful. Research organizations can provide advice on specific design strategies, research instruments, and analysis plans. They can carry out the research on a voluntary or at-cost basis. Finally, they can append research questions of interest to the nonprofit organization to questionnaires designed for other purposes.

An example of a campaign done by an individual agency is described in Exhibit 10-4.

BUSINESS FIRMS

Sometimes business firms will contribute staff time for particular nonprofit projects. Computer firms will assist with data processing. Major accounting firms will keep the books, conduct audits, and prepare annual reports for nonprofit organizations routinely as part of their "pro bono"

DRUNK DRIVING CAMPAIGN

for National Highway Traffic Safety Administration

"Empty City"   30 SECONDS

Use expires Nov. 21, 1984.   CNTD-3130

(SFX: WIND, PAPER BLOWING, ETC.)   More than the population of Salt   (SFX: SCREECHING OF CAR)
ANNCR: (VO) In the last 10   Lake City.   The drunk driver.
years, he's killed over 250,000
people.

Tougher laws are being passed.   But nothing can protect you   It doubles your chances of
                                        from him like your seat belt.   surviving.

                                        Don't let drunk drivers do a   (SFX: WIND BLOWING)
                                        number on you.   Wear your seat belt.

CTND-3230 (:30) May be run before and
during National Drunk and Drugged Driving
Awareness Week Dec. 11-18

A Public Service Campaign of the Advertising Council

VOLUNTEER COORDINATOR: VOLUNTEER ADVERTISING AGENCY:
Michael Fink, Block Drug, Inc.   Foote, Cone & Belding

SOURCE: Reproduced with Permission. Foote, Cone & Belding, Chicago, IL.

professional responsibilities. Similarly, law firms and some management consultants will devote some of their staff time, albeit junior staff time, to pro bono work. They often provide this help collectively, as in the case of Business Volunteers for the Arts—Chicago. Under this umbrella organization, sixty-four executives from thirty-six corporations offered time and skills to metropolitan Chicago's nonprofit arts organizations in 1985.

EXHIBIT 10-3. A research evaluation of "taking a bite out of crime"

The public service campaign, "taking a bite out of crime," was begun in October, 1979, under the sponsorship of the U.S. Department of Justice and the Coalition Against Crime. The campaign features an animated dog, "McGruff," who is dressed in a trenchcoat and describes a real example of someone personally combating a crime and asking the audience to follow this example. The PSA campaign focused heavily on television but also included radio, magazines, and newspapers. In the first phase, the campaign offered individuals suggestions on protecting houses and property. The second phase encouraged individuals to observe and report suspected criminal behavior. The third phase promoted the organization of neighborhood and local groups to support various community crime prevention activities.

In an attempt to assess the effects of this campaign over its first two years, the National Institute for Justice carried out an evaluation study through the University of Denver. This study relied upon data from two sources (1) a national probability sample of 1,200 households conducted in November, 1981, and (2) reinterviews in November, 1981, of 426 panel respondents in three cities who were previously interviewed three months before the beginning of the campaign (September, 1979).

Both the national survey and the panel data showed that a very broad range of the population was exposed to and influenced by the campaign. In particular, the studies found that those exposed to the campaign reported (1) they now knew much more about crime prevention, (2) they felt more positively about the likely effectiveness of private citizens taking actions against crime, and (3) they felt more personally competent in protecting themselves against crime. On the other hand, the campaign didn't make them feel more threatened by crime and, in fact, the panel felt less likely to be burglarized.

Effects on actual behavior were also apparent. The PSAs appeared to influence the panel to (1) leave outdoor lights on, (2) have neighbors watch the house, (3) use timer lights, (4) watch the neighborhood themselves, (5) report suspicious behavior to the police, and (6) join with others to prevent crime. All were advocated by the PSAs. Curiously, the study also found an increase in the proportion of the households "acquiring a dog for security purposes." Clearly McGruff had other influences besides the specific measures he advocated.

SOURCE: Adapted from Garret J. O'Keefe, "'Taking a Bite Out of Crime': The Impact of a Public Information Campaign," *Communication Research*, Vol. 12, No. 2 (April 1985), pp. 147–178.

EXHIBIT 10-4. Foote, Cone & Belding and the Boy Scouts of America

The Boy Scouts of America has been handled as a public service by Foote, Cone & Belding's New York office since the late 1970s. During that time a number of different campaigns have appeared, the most popular being the "Celebrity" campaign featuring outstanding male

EXHIBIT 10-3. (continued)

Americans who had been Scouts. (See Figure 18-6, p. 531). These celebrities included former president Gerald Ford, Hank Aaron, James Stewart, Henry Fonda, Howard K. Smith, Mark Spitz, Arthur Godfrey, Bruce Jenner, Rich Little, and many more.

The campaign, including print ads and TV spots, began in 1978 and ran for several years.

The campaign background is as follows:

The Boy Scouts of America is a seventy-five-year-old private organization serving just under four million boys between the ages of seven and twenty.

Local organizations in every community in the United States support the Scouting program through more than 132,000 charters. These Charter Partners provide a source of volunteer leadership, access to the youth of their community, and stable, convenient meeting places.

The relationship between the National BSA Organization and the Charter Partners faced an array of problems.

Fewer major local organizations were willing to give more than nominal support.

Organizations like PTAs experience substantial turnover, which compromised the needed continuity among volunteer leaders.

Traditionally supportive groups like religious organizations had suffered a decline in community influence.

The BSA "Celebrity" campaign, prepared as a public service by Foote, Cone & Belding's New York office, was conceived to address these problems. The message speaks to both current and potential Charter Partners and underscores the contribution that Scouting plays in offering youth the challenge necessary to develop character and personal values that foster the pursuit of excellence.

SOURCE: Reproduced with permission. Foote, Cone, & Belding, Chicago, IL.

Business organizations often offer their own premises for nonprofit activities. This can involve relatively simple contributions such as allowing charity gum machines to be placed in a retail store or permitting the use of a conference center or meeting rooms for nonprofit board meetings. Recently, a major firm allowed the United Way to conduct a major attitudinal and motivation study on the organization's own employees using the firm's reproduction facilities, mail system, and computer.

Charities have also benefited for years from free goods and services provided by the soft drink, beer, and food service industries. Firms will announce charity campaigns in their employee publications, permit blood donations to be taken on their premises, and loan executives to give lectures or demonstrations at schools and civic meetings. Two of the most elaborate series of contributions from the private sector involved the 1984 Summer Olympic Games in Los Angeles and the annual Muscular Dystrophy drive.

UNIVERSITIES AND COLLEGES

Universities and colleges can be an important source of advice and manpower. University faculty can provide advice on technical matters like research design and analysis. They can develop seminars for nonprofit staffers on marketing principles. They can also serve as consultants on specific nonprofit marketing problems.

Students can also be helpful. We have already noted their value as volunteers. Many marketing and management courses and even entire degree programs may require some kind of field study experience. Nonprofit organizations usually qualify for such projects as much as for-profit enterprises. Similarly, marketing research and advertising students are often looking for places to complete a term project or otherwise apply their newly developed skills. In some institutions, students' involvement with the nonprofit may be under close faculty supervision. In other cases it may not, and one should obviously be cautious in accepting advice and analysis from students who have limited experience and training. On the other hand, with the proper supervision, students may often provide manpower to carry out research studies, experiments, forecasts, or other marketing projects that would otherwise not be completed for the lack of manpower, skills, or both.

ASSOCIATIONS

As the nonprofit field has matured, organizations have sought to develop an infrastructure for self-support. Perhaps the most ambitious of these is the Washington-based Independent Sector. Formed in March of 1980 under the chairmanship of John W. Gardner, Independent Sector now has over 540 members split almost evenly between donors (foundations and corporations) and national voluntary organizations. Independent Sector programs include

- *Public education* about the contributions and problems of the independent sector
- *Government relations* at the national, state, and local levels to influence critical legislation and regulatory activity
- *Research* to build the knowledge base of the independent sector
- *Communication* among members about community problems and opportunities through periodicals, research reports, monographs, and conferences

A major concern of the Independent Sector is improving management skills in the nonprofit area.

SECURING LEVERAGED ASSISTANCE

Leveraged assistance for nonprofits is of two types, one-time and continuing. Securing one-time assistance for a particular charity drive or a research project involves three steps. First, the nonprofit must define its project and frankly recognize where it should not attempt some parts or all of an activity and should seek outside help. Second, the universe of possible sources of assistance from universities, firms, service agencies, individuals, and the like should be arrayed and ranked according to (1) degree of potential contribution, and (2) likelihood of offering help. In the latter regard, the nonprofit agency should put heavy weight on the possible benefits that each potential contributor will recognize—or can be made to recognize—as following from their cooperation. In the former regard, it must be recognized that, like a lot of other volunteer help, free goods and services may well come with strings, which should be carefully assessed. Experienced but opinionated professionals may insist on doing things their way or not at all. Inexperienced amateurs may want to do things their own way and may botch an otherwise potentially useful contribution.

The final step is, of course, to market directly to the top-ranked potential contributor. This means playing up the benefits they might derive and playing down any costs or inconveniences. Certainly, this is much easier if the match between project needs and the contributor's needs is high. When it is not, marketing creativity must be brought into play. The reputation of the organization is certainly a major factor. Well-known community nonprofits have relatively more success in getting outside help. Indeed, they have more offers of help than they need. More obscure agencies (for example, minor charities, neighborhood service agencies, and the like) have a much more difficult time. The nonprofit should *not* simply assume, however, that because the "sell" is difficult it should not be attempted. Going it alone may have even greater costs.

One way of securing continuing help from for-profit organizations and individuals is to create a blue-ribbon Marketing Advisory Board to bring key marketing professionals onto the nonprofit's board of directors, or both. Nonprofits are usually farsighted enough to see the need to put partners from major accounting firms and law firms in their communities onto their boards. Yet very useful continuing advice can be obtained by adding to the board a senior vice-president of marketing from a for-profit organization (preferably from a consumer goods or service company), the head of a local major advertising agency, or the director of one of the area's largest marketing research agencies. Not only will these executives provide useful ongoing advice, but they will often volunteer their organizations' facilities or services (or they can be *asked* to volunteer them) for specific one-time marketing needs.

SUMMARY

Nonprofits have limited resources. As a consequence, they must become experts at securing additional manpower, skills, and financial resources. This, too, is a marketing task. Others must be convinced that the benefits of helping exceed the costs.

Nonprofits are unique in needing volunteers to help them accomplish their basic goals. Strategies for recruiting and managing volunteers must take into account changes in the environment. Today's volunteers cover a wider spectrum of people. They are more demanding and have different motivations than they had in the past. More importantly, some groups are challenging the basic value of volunteer service.

Recruiting volunteers involves knowing the target audiences through segmentation, prospect, invitational, or positioning studies. The nonprofit should also know how to retain volunteers. Studies of former volunteers and the satisfaction and dissatisfaction of present volunteers can be helpful in this regard. The problems that may emerge may involve volunteers' expectations, training, supervision, and feedback.

Managing volunteers can also be a problem if the organization is not truly professional in its approach. Many volunteers work hard and effectively with little incentive or guidance. Some hardly work at all under any circumstances. Most, however, respond best to being treated as professionals. This means matching responsibilities to skills, setting clear, achievable goals, and then holding volunteers to achieving them.

Nonprofits must also secure important outside help in critical skill areas like advertising and marketing research. Commercial agencies may be quite willing to help out for both altruistic and self-interested reasons. The Advertising Council is a prime example of such help. Business firms can also help by loaning space, staff, or equipment and by providing specific advice. Faculty and students at local colleges and universities are another major source of assistance. An effective vehicle for coordinating all of these efforts is through a Marketing Advisory Council.

QUESTIONS

1. Outline the principal benefits that can be offered to someone who would volunteer for (1) a hospital, (2) a library, or (3) a charity drive. Are the benefits different, and would this suggest what kind of target audience each should seek out?

2. What are the *costs* a target audience might perceive in volunteering in each of the cases in question 1? How can these costs be lowered?

3. Develop a research instrument to assess the satisfaction and dissatisfaction of United Way volunteers.

4. List the kinds of material, financial, and skill assistance a public television station would need for an on-the-air raffle.

5. Role-play a conflict between an upper-class volunteer and a middle-

class professional staffer at a museum over the volunteer's lack of punc-
tuality and tendency not to show up when scheduled.

NOTES

1. Statistics are taken from a discussion draft of the *Report of the Task
Force on Measureable Growth in Giving and Volunteering,* (Washington,
D.C.: The Independent Sector), August, 1985.
2. Eva Schindler-Rainman and Ronald Lippitt, *The Volunteer Community:
Creative Use of Human Resources,* 2d ed. (La Jolla, Calif.: University Associates, 1977), pp. 21–45.
3. See also Gordon Mauser and Rosemary H. Cass, *Volunteer at the Crossroads* (New York: Family Service Association of America, 1976), and Jon
Vantil, "In Search of Voluntarism," *Volunteer Administration,* Vol. 12, No.
2, Summer 1979.
4. Schindler-Rainman and Lippitt, *Volunteer Community,* pp. 48–50.
5. Fox Butterfield, "Universities Take Lead in New Volunteer Efforts,"
New York Times, October 17, 1985, p. 12.
6. For other information on voluntarism, the reader should contact the
National Center for Voluntary Action, 1214 16th Street N.W., Washington,
D.C. 20036.
7. The Advertising Council, *Report to the American People, 1983–84.*
Washington, D.C.: The Advertising Council, 1984.

CHAPTER 11

Fundraising

Executives don't do good works quite the same way everybody else does. Their motives are complex. Consider, for example, how a big-league charity dinner is put together. Robert Williams, director of public relations for the Boy Scouts of New York, describes his organization's method, which is fairly standard: "There is always someone to be honored with the Good Scout Award—the honoree and the chairman are selected a year in advance. We explain to the honoree that we want to present him the award and we ask him to help us to raise money. Then there'll be a discussion of how to do that. Usually, the honorees give us a list of their vendors." Companies that sell goods and services to the honoree's company will be asked to buy tables at $2,500 apiece. Williams goes on: "Sometimes the man will say, 'Okay, I'll accept the award and ask my friend to be chairman.' Sometimes we get someone who will be the chairman and then he asks a friend to get the award." The charity gets lists of vendors from both of them.

In selecting an honoree, prestige is important. The executive director of another big New York City charity notes, "One hard thing is picking the guy who is going to be the hot man in town next year—we're looking hard at John Reed of Citicorp now." And what's the worst thing that can happen? Having the honoree get fired or die a month before the event, the experts say.

Diverse motives impel executives into good works. This holds true whether the good work consists of serving on the board of a nonprofit organization or showing up for the twentieth banquet of the season—

"Not filet mignon, new potatoes, and green beans *again*." The mix of motives also governs an executive's choice of causes to tie up with; typically, a myriad present themselves for his consideration. In a speech last May to the National Conference of Boys' Clubs, the uncommonly forthright Minot K. Milliken, vice-president and treasurer of the big textile company that bears the family name and president of the Boys' Club of New York for nineteen years, listed several of these motives.

Predictably, the desire to do some good heads Milliken's list. But executives also get involved, he says, because they want to show what they can do beyond their workaday endeavors. Some "seek a different kind of social acceptability or social mobility." Some want to meet "prospective customers or clients" or even competitors from whom they might learn something. Another reason for serving on a nonprofit board, he says, "is the desire to control—other people, or ideas, or programs." In short, to exercise power. And for some, he concludes, "It makes them feel less guilty about having more when they are helping people who have much less."

The awful truth in all this: good works not only benefit the charity on whose behalf they've performed, but also the worker. Roderick Gilkey, a psychologist and professor at the business school of Emory University in Atlanta, notes that studies of male development—there aren't yet comparable studies of women—show that particularly for men in their forties and older, some form of public service helps fulfill the developmental task of achieving "generativity." A generative individual passes on to others some of what he has learned and been given, thereby achieving a smidgen of immortality for his accomplishments. This link to development may help explain why baby-boom executives sometimes don't seem as interested in charity work as their elders.

SOURCE: Condensed from: Walter Kiechell, III, "On the Charity Circuit," *Fortune*, October 14, 1985, pp. 223–225. Reprinted with permission. © Time Inc. All rights reserved.

The major resource attraction problem of nonprofit organizations is attracting money to carry on their activities. For-profit organizations get their funds primarily through issuing equities and debentures. They cover the costs of these "borrowed" funds by charging prices for their goods and services that exceed their costs. Nonprofit organizations, in the absence of owners and profit-oriented price-setting, must rely on other sources of funds to support their activities. Public organizations receive their funds primarily from the public treasury through the mechanism of taxation. Private nonprofit organizations rely mainly on gifts from generous donors.

Fundraising strategy is, therefore, an essential component of all nonprofit organizations.

The total amount of charitable money raised by all organizations in 1984 was $74.23 billion. Eighty-three percent of all contributions came from *individuals* ($61.55 billion), with the remainder coming from *bequests* ($4.89 billion), *foundations* ($4.36 billion), and *corporations* ($3.45 billion). Almost 50 percent of the money was raised by religious organizations ($35.56 billion); the rest was raised by health and hospital groups ($10.44 billion), educational institutions ($10.08 billion), social welfare groups ($8.01 billion), arts and humanities groups ($4.64 billion), civic and public organizations ($4.08 billion), and other groups ($3.44 billion).[1] About one out of every three dollars was raised by mail or mail-assisted campaigns and the rest by personal contact campaigns.

The art of fundraising has passed through various stages of evolution. Its earliest form was *begging,* in which needy people and groups would implore more fortunate people for money and goods. Beggars perfected many techniques to gain the attention and sympathy of their target audience, such as simulating pain or blindness or showing their children with bloated stomachs. The next stage consisted of *collection,* in which churches, clubs, and other organizations would regularly collect contributions from a willing and defined group of supporters. In recent times, *campaigning* emerged; in the form of fundraising, organizations appoint a specific person or group to be responsible for soliciting money from every possible source in a systematic fundraising campaign. Most recently, fundraising has been reinterpreted as *development,* in which the organization systematically builds up different classes of loyal donors who give consistently and receive benefits in the process of giving. Today's organizations vary considerably in their concept of raising money, some seeing it as begging, others as collection, others as campaigning, and still others as development.

STAGES OF MARKETING ORIENTATION

Organizations that raise money typically pass through three stages of marketing orientation in their thinking about how to carry on fundraising effectively.

- *Product orientation stage.* Here the prevailing attitude is "We have a good cause; people ought to support us." Many churches and colleges operate on this concept. Money is raised primarily by the top officers through an "old boy network." The organization relies on volunteers to help raise additional funds. A few loyal donors supply most of the funds.
- *Sales orientation stage.* Here the prevailing attitude is "There are a lot of people out there who might give money, and we must go out and find them and convince them to give." The institution appoints a development director who eventually hires a staff. This staff raises money from all possible sources, typ-

ically using a "hard sell" approach. The fundraisers have little influence on the institution's policies or personality since their job is to raise money, not improve the organization. A majority of large nonprofit organizations are in this stage.

- *Strategic marketing stage.* Here the prevailing attitude is "We must analyze our position in the marketplace, concentrate on those donor sources whose interests are best matched to ours, and design our solicitation programs to supply needed satisfactions to each donor group." This approach involves carefully segmenting the donor markets; measuring the giving potential of each donor market; assigning executive responsibility for developing each market; and developing a plan and budget for each market based on its potential. More and more large nonprofit organizations have moved into this stage as fundraisers become aware of the differences between a sales approach and a marketing approach.

This chapter will analyze fundraising from a marketing perspective. The first section will examine four major donor markets: individual givers, foundations, corporations, and government. Section two will examine how organizations organize their fundraising effort internally. Section three will consider the important task of setting fundraising objectives and strategies, while section four will take a look at the multiplicity of fundraising tactics. The fifth section will consider how organizations can evaluate and improve their fundraising effectiveness.

ANALYZING DONOR MARKETS

An organization can tap into a variety of sources for financial support. The four major donor markets are: *individuals, foundations, corporations,* and *government.* Small nonprofit organizations frequently solicit funds primarily from one source—often wealthy individuals—to meet their financial needs. Larger organizations tend to solicit all sources and, in fact, make specific executives responsible for each market. Ultimately, they seek to allocate the fundraising budget in proportion to the giving potential of each donor market. Here we will examine the institutional and behavioral characteristics of each donor market.

INDIVIDUAL GIVERS

Individuals are the major source of all charitable giving, accounting for some 83 percent of the total. Almost everyone in the nation contributes money to one or more organizations each year, the total amount varying with such factors as the giver's income, age, education, sex, ethnic background, and other characteristics. Thus relatively more money is contributed by high-income people, people in their middle years, and people of high education. At the same time, giving levels vary substantially within each group. Some wealthy individuals give little and some lower income individuals give a lot. Among wealthy people, for example, physicians tend to give less than lawyers.

Charitable causes vary in their appeal to individuals. In a study sponsored by Save the Children Foundation, the public was asked: "Which of the five (categories of charity) would rate as the most worthwhile?" The ranking turned out to be: (1) needy children, (2) disaster victims, (3) medical research, (4) aid to the handicapped, and (5) religious organizations.[2] That is, Americans would be most ready to give to a cause involving needy children, followed by disaster victims, and so on. Paradoxically, they give relatively small amounts to these causes in relation to the amounts they give to their churches.

Within each category of charity, the appeal levels also vary greatly. For example, within medical charities people give readily to the American Cancer Society ($220.5 million), American Heart Association ($128 million), March of Dimes ($92 million), Muscular Dystrophy Association ($81.9 million), and National Mental Health Association ($24 million) (figures as of 1985).

Some of the difference in the amount raised is due to the fact that these organizations have different life spans and different degrees of effectiveness at fundraising. A larger part of the difference in giving levels is due to the opinions people hold about specific diseases, particularly about the disease's *severity, prevalence,* and *remediability.* Thus, heart disease and cancer are severe diseases—they kill—whereas arthritis and birth defects are considered less serious since they do not kill. Cancer has a higher prevalence than muscular dystrophy and therefore attracts more support. Finally, people believe that cures or preventions are possible for heart disease and less so for birth defects and this leads to more giving. Figure 11-1 shows the hypothetical positions of three diseases on the three variables. If the March of Dimes wants to attract more funds for its cause—birth defects—it must try to increase the perceived severity, prevalence, and remediability of birth defects.

Why do individuals give to charity? Nonprofit organizations need a good understanding of the motives for giving to be effective at fundraising. The answer called "altruism" tends to mask the complex motives that underlie giving or helping behavior. The position of this book is that the individuals give in order to get something back. In other words, donations should not be viewed as a *transfer* but as a *transaction.* The question is, what does the donor *get?* Table 11-1 lists several motives underlying giving behavior. People give to get response or recognition, reduce fear, reduce social pressure, or feel "altruistic."

Is there such a thing as giving without "getting"? Some people give and say that they expect nothing back. But, actually, they have "expectations." They expect the organization to use the money efficiently, they expect the fundraiser to show gratitude, and so on. Even the anonymous giver who

FIGURE 11-1

Public's Perception of Different Medical Causes (Hypothetical)

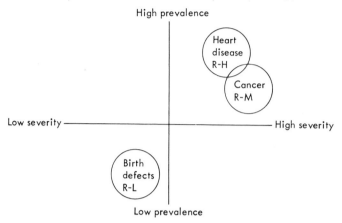

Note: The third variable, remediability (R), is shown for each disease with an indication of level: low (L), medium (M), and high (H).

wants no acknowledgment may privately enjoy the self-esteem of being "big enough" to give money without requiring recognition.

The various motives for giving provide clues to marketing strategy for fundraisers. Harold Seymour has suggested that in many mass donor markets, one-third of the people are *responsible* (they donate without being solicited), one-third are *responsive* (they donate when they are asked), and one-third react to *compulsion* (they donate because of pressure).[3] Each market can be investigated further to discover the specific motive segments that exist. One group of givers to a university might respond to "pride," another to "let's catch up to the competition."

Too many organizations ask people to give to them as a needy organization rather than to support promising programs. The former approach is close to begging. The latter is more effective. People respond to what they sense as the relevance, importance, and urgency of a giving opportunity. Seymour suggests that the case for giving must be bigger than the institution. And it must be presented in a way that catches the eye, warms the heart, and stirs the mind.

Another important principle for segmentation is the donor's "giving potential." Fundraisers distinguish between small, medium, and large donors. Many fundraisers prefer to concentrate all or most of their energy on large potential donors, feeling that attracting a few large gifts would produce more funds than attracting many small gifts. It is not uncommon to hear fundraisers claim that 10 to 20 percent of the givers generate 50 to 80 percent of gifts. If a college fundraiser spends thirty hours with a wealthy alumnus who ends up giving $1 million, the fund raiser's productivity is much greater than trying to raise $100 each from 10,000 alumni. For this reason, many college fundraisers in the past neglected building up the number of alumni donors and concentrated instead on increasing the size of the average gift received. This is now changing as more colleges are thinking strategically, seeking to involve all alumni in school support and giving and to build a solid long-term base of donors.

Table 11-1

INDIVIDUAL GIVING MOTIVES

1. *Need for self-esteem.* These people attempt to build their self-esteem and self-image by playing "God," or feeling good from giving. The opposite of this would be shame or guilt.

2. *Need for recognition from others.* These people attempt to build their social status or enhance their prestige in the eyes of others. They have a strong need to belong.

3. *Fear of contracting the problem.* This need centers on people's fear that they or members of their families will contract a particular disease or fall into poverty or neglect in their old age. They hope in some sense to buy "protection."

4. *The habit giver.* These people give out of habit for no real reason other than a desire not to be embarrassed by not contributing to the cause. They are indifferent to contributions, but feel that they must give to someone because everyone else does. A benefit may be not having to agonize over choosing charities (for example, *not* giving to a needy cause).

5. *Nuisance giver.* These people only give to get rid of the caller. They feel that contributing to a cause is of no real significance, but would rather donate a few dollars than be troubled by others.

6. *Required to give.* These people are required to give at work; they feel they are under pressure from superiors to donate part of their checks to a fund. They therefore demand efficiency and credibility from the organization that they contribute to.

7. *Captive givers.* These people feel real sorrow for someone they know who has a particular problem. They are other-centered in that they earnestly would like to aid the victim in some way. Givers in this category may contribute at the death of a friend rather than sending flowers, etc.

8. *People-to-people givers.* These people have a real feeling of the "commonness of man," a solidarity with other people. This group of people has internalized the idea of helping others because they want to.

9. *Concern for humanity.* This segment of givers is concerned about others for religious reasons and because they are "God's children." They feel a moral obligation to contribute to a charity. They have accepted the love-for-humanity idea because it is a requirement of their faith.

Seeking the "large gift" is still the most important part of fund raising for many organizations. Fundraisers use a five-step approach: *identification, tion, introduction, cultivation, solicitation,* and *appreciation.* They first identify wealthy individuals who could conceivably have a strong interest in the organization. They identify others who might supply information and arrange an introduction. They cultivate the person's interest without asking for any money. By asking too early, they may get less than is possible. Eventually, they do ask for money and, upon receiving it, they express their appreciation.

Large individual gift fundraising is most effective when the organization has developed a "wish list" of exciting projects to show the prospective donor. Large hospitals classify their wished-for gifts in several financial sizes, ranging from the small pieces of medical equipment for under $10,000 to the building of an entire wing for over $3 million. One of the most powerful appeals is to allow donors to have their names (or the names of loved ones) attached to physical facilities, research funds, distinguished chairs, and the like. Here, the exchange is very clear and dramatic. In addition, fundraisers can offer these individuals all kinds of ways to make their gifts, including direct cash payments, gifts of stock and other property, and bequests in which they will assign part or all of their estate to the organization upon their death. Organizations have worked up a variety of gift plans that can be tailored to the needs of individual wealthy donors.

FOUNDATIONS

Currently there are over 23,700 foundations in the United States, all set up to give money to worthwhile causes. They fall into the following groups:

1. *Family foundations,* set up by wealthy individuals to support a limited number of activities of interest to the founders. Family foundations typically do not have permanent offices or full-time staff members. Decisions tend to be made by family members, counsel, or both.
2. *General foundations,* set up to support a wide range of activities and usually run by a professional staff. General foundations range from extremely large organizations such as the Ford Foundation and the Rockefeller Foundation, which support a wide range of causes and give most of their money to large, well-established organizations, to more specialized general foundations that give money to a particular cause, such as health (Johnson Foundation) or education (Carnegie Foundation).
3. *Corporate foundations,* set up by corporations and allowed to give away up to 5 percent of the corporation's adjusted gross income.
4. *Community trusts,* set up in cities or regions and made up of smaller foundations whose funds are pooled for greater impact.

With 23,700 foundations, it is important for the fundraiser to know how to locate the few that would be the most likely to support a given project or cause. Fortunately, there are many resources available for researching foundations. The best single resource is known as the Foundation Center, a nonprofit organization with research centers in New York, Washington, and Chicago which collects and distributes information on foundations. In addition, many libraries around the country carry important materials describing foundations and how to approach them. The most important materials are:

1. *The Foundation Grants Index,* which lists the grants that have been given in the past year by foundation, subject, state, and other groupings. The fundraiser, for example, could look up visual arts and find out all the grants made to support the visual arts and identify the most active foundations in this area of giving.
2. *The Foundation Directory,* which lists over 2,500 foundations that either have assets of over $1 million or award grants of more than $500,000 annually. The directory describes the general characteristics of each foundation, such as type of foundation, types of grants, annual giving level, officers and directors, location, particular fields of interest, contact person, and so on. The directory also contains an index of fields of interest, listing the foundations that have a stated interest in each field and whether or not they gave money to this field last year.
3. *The Foundation News,* which is published six times a year by the Council on Foundations and describes new foundations, new funding programs, and changes in existing foundations.
4. *Fund Raising Management,* which is a periodical publishing articles on fundraising management.

The key concept in identifying foundations is that of *matching.* The nonprofit organization should search for foundations matched to its *interests* and *scale of operation.* Too often a small nonprofit organization will send a proposal to the Ford Foundation because it would like to get the support of this well-known foundation. But the Ford Foundation accepts about one out of every 100 proposals and may be less disposed toward helping small nonprofit organizations than more regional or specialized foundations would be.

After identifying a few foundations that might have strong interest in its project, the organization should try to estimate more accurately their level of interest before investing a lot of time in grant preparation. Most foundations are willing to respond to a letter of inquiry, telephone call, or personal visit and indicate how interested they would be in the project. The foundation officer may be very encouraging or discouraging. If the former, the fund-seeking organization can then make an investment in preparing an elaborate proposal for this foundation.

Writing successful grant proposals is becoming a fine art, with many guides currently available to help the grant-seeker.[4] Each proposal should contain at least the following elements:

1. *A cover letter* describing the history of the proposal, and who has been contacted, if anyone, in the foundation
2. *The proposal,* describing the project, its uniqueness, and its importance
3. *The budget* for the project
4. *The personnel* working on the project with their résumés

The proposal itself should be compact, individualized, organized, and readable. In writing the proposal, the organization should be guided by knowledge of the "buying criteria" that the particular foundation uses to choose among the many proposals that it receives. Like any other marketing communication, it must be customer-centered. Many foundations describe their criteria in their annual reports or other memos, or their criteria can be inferred by looking at the characteristics of the recent proposals they have supported or talking to knowledgeable individuals. Among the most common guiding criteria used by foundations are:

1. The importance and quality of the project
2. The neediness and worthwhileness of the organization
3. The organization's ability to use the funds effectively and efficiently
4. The importance of satisfying the persons who are doing the proposing
5. The degree of benefit that the foundation will derive in supporting the proposal

If the proposing organization knows the relative importance of the respective criteria, it can do a better job of selecting the features of the proposal to emphasize. If the particular foundation is likely to be influenced by who presents the proposal, for example, the organization should send its highest ranking officials to the foundation. On the other hand, if the foundation attaches the most importance to the quality of the proposal, the organization should put a lot of effort into fine-tuning the writing of the proposal.

Nonprofit organizations should not contact foundations only on the occasion of a specific proposal. Each organization should cultivate a handful of appropriate foundations in advance of specific proposals. This is called "building bridges" or "relationship marketing." One major university sees the Ford Foundation as a "key customer account." The development officer arranges for various people within the university to get to know people at corresponding levels within the foundation. One or more members of the university's board arrange to see corresponding board members of the foundation each year. The university president visits the foundation's president each year for a luncheon or dinner. One or more members of the university's development staff cultivate relations with foundation staff members at their levels. When the university has a proposal, it knows exactly who should present it to the foundation and whom to see in the foundation. Furthermore, the foundation is more favorably disposed toward the organization because of the long relationship and special understanding they enjoy. Finally, the organization is able to do a better job of tracking the proposal as it is being reviewed by the foundation.

CORPORATIONS

Business organizations represent another distinct source of funds for nonprofit organizations. Corporations have been especially supportive of such causes as higher education, the United Way, and health, civic, cultural, and social services. In 1984, American business contributed $3.45 billion of the $74.25 billion received in total charity. This amounts to slightly less than 1 percent of business's pretax income. Since business organizations are allowed by law to give up to 5 percent of their pretax income to charity, considerable potential for more corporate giving exists.

Corporate giving differs from foundation giving in a number of important ways. First, corporations regard gift-giving as a minor activity, in contrast to foundations where it is the major activity. Corporations vary their giving level with the level of current and expected income. They have to be sensitive to the feelings of their stockholders, to whom they have the first obligation both in terms of how much to give to charity and what particular charities to support. Corporations are more likely to avoid supporting controversial causes than are foundations. Corporations typically handle the many requests for support they receive by setting up a foundation so that corporate officers are not personally drawn into gift decision-making.

Second, corporations pay more attention than foundations to the personal benefit that any grant might return to them. If they can show that a particular grant will increase community goodwill (as a grant by a cigarette company to a cancer research foundation) or train more manpower that they need (as a grant by an engineering company to an engineering school), these grants will be more acceptable to their board of directors and stockholders.

Third, corporations can make more types of gifts than foundations can. The nonprofit organization can approach the business firm for *money, securities, goods* (asking a furniture company for some furniture or a computer firm for PCs or software), *services* (asking a printing company for some free printing or printing at cost), and *space* (asking a company for the use of its auditorium for a program). In the extreme, the nonprofit organization should be able to get office equipment, marketing research, advertising, and so on, free or at cost if it can identify the right corporate prospects to approach.

Effective corporate fundraising requires that the nonprofit organization know how to identify good corporate prospects efficiently. Of the millions of business enterprises that might be approached, relatively few are appropriate to any specific nonprofit organization. Furthermore, the nonprofit organization ordinarily does not have the resources to cultivate more than a handful of corporate givers. The best prospects for corporate fundraising have the following characteristics:

1. *Local corporations.* Corporations located in the same area as the nonprofit organization are excellent prospects. A hospital, for example, can base its appeal on the health care it offers to the corporation's employees, and a performing arts group can base its appeal on its cultural offerings. Both improve the local climate and thus help corporations attract and keep top-flight talent. Corporations find it hard to refuse to support worthwhile organizations in their area.

2. *Kindred activities.* Corporations located in a field kindred to the nonprofit organization's are excellent prospects. Hospitals can effectively solicit funds from pharmaceutical companies, and colleges can attract funds from companies that hire many of their graduates.

3. *Declared areas of support.* Nonprofit organizations should target corporations that have a declared interest in supporting that type of nonprofit organization. Thus, a "support-the-arts" organization might approach the Borg-Warner Corporation because of the latter's active purchase of contemporary art.

4. *Large givers.* Large corporations and those with generous giving levels are excellent prospects. Yet fundraisers must realize that these corporations receive numerous requests and favor those nonprofit organizations in the local area or a kindred field. Regional offices of major corporations are often not in a position to make a donation without the approval of the home office.

5. *Personal relationships or contacts.* Nonprofit organizations should review their personal contacts to obtain clues to which corporations they might solicit. A university's board of trustees consists of influential individuals who can open many doors for corporate solicitations. Corporations tend to respond to peer influence in their giving.

6. *Specific capability.* The fundraiser may identify a corporation as a prospect because it has a unique resource needed by the nonprofit organization. Thus, a charity hospital might solicit a paint manufacturer for a donation of paint to repaint the rooms in an old wing of a hospital.

The preceding criteria will help the nonprofit organization identify a number of corporations that are worth approaching for contributions. Corporations in the organization's geographical area or field are worth cultivating on a continuous basis ("relationship marketing") aside from specific grant requests. When the organization is seeking to fund a specific project, however, it needs to identify the best prospects and develop a marketing plan from scratch. We will illustrate the planning procedure in connection with the following example:

> A well-known private university was seeking to raise $5 million to build a new engineering library. Its existing library was wholly inadequate and a handicap to attracting better students to the engineering school. The university was willing to name the new library after a major corporate donor who would supply at least 60 percent ($3 million) of the money being sought. This donor would be the "bell cow" that would attract additional corporate donors to supply the rest.

The first step called for the university to *identify one or more major corporations* to approach. The fundraisers recognized that major prospects would have two characteristics: they would be wealthy corporations and they would have a high interest in this project. The fundraisers developed the matrix shown in Figure 11-2 and proceeded to classify corporations by their giving potential and their interest potential. In classifying corporations, they realized that oil companies fell in the upper left cell. Oil companies have high profits ("giving potential") and a high interest in engineering schools ("interest potential"). They also want to give money to good causes to win public goodwill. The university decided that approaching an oil company would make good sense.

Which oil company? Here the university applied additional criteria. An oil company located in the same geographical area had already given a major donation to this university for another project; it was ruled out. The university considered whether it had any good contacts with other oil companies. The university identified one oil corporation in the East in which several of its graduates held important management positions. In addition, a member of the university's board of trustees—a major bank president—

FIGURE 11-2

Classifying Prospective Corporate Donors by Level of Interest and Giving Potential

		Giving Potential		
		High	Medium	Low
Interest Potential	High			
	Medium			
	Low			

knew the president of the oil company. It was decided on the basis of these and other factors to approach this oil company for support.

The next step called for preparing a *prospect solicitation plan*. As a start, the university fundraisers researched the oil company's sales, profits, major officers, recent giving record, and other characteristics. This information was useful in deciding whom to approach at the corporation, how much to ask for, what benefits to offer, and so on. A decision was made to approach the corporation's president, ask for $3 million for the new engineering library, and offer to name the library after the corporation.

The final step called for *plan implementation*. The bank president arranged an appointment to visit the oil corporation's chairman, who was an old friend. He was accompanied by the university's president and also the vice-president of development. When they arrived, they met the chairman and the oil company's foundation director. They made their presentation, and the chairman said the proposal would be given careful consideration. A subsequent meeting was held on the university's campus, and ultimately the oil corporation granted the money to the university.

The oil company responded positively to this solicitation because the proposal stood high on its major criteria. The oil company foundation rated each proposal on four criteria:

1. The proposal had to be worthwhile from a societal point of view. In this case, an engineering library would contribute toward better trained engineers in the United States.
2. The corporation had to feel that the soliciting institution was worthwhile and would handle the grant well. Here, the oil company had full confidence in the particular university.
3. The proposal should create some direct benefit, if possible, for the oil company. In this case, the oil company recognized a number of benefits: it would have an "in" with the best new graduates, it would memorialize its name on the campus, and it would get good publicity for supporting this private university.
4. The oil company foundation placed value on the personal relationships involved. The fact that an important bank president had taken the time to personally present the proposal to the oil company chairman was an important factor in having the proposal carefully considered.

In general, corporations pay attention to these criteria in considering whether to "buy" a particular proposal, and therefore the seller ("fundraiser") should weave them into its planning and presentation.

GOVERNMENT

Another major source of funds is government agencies at the federal, state, and local levels that are able to make grants to worthwhile causes. As an example, the federal government set up the National Endowment for the

Arts (NEA) to make grants to support museums, ballet companies, art groups, and other arts organizations, large and small. The NEA had a budget of $163 million in 1985. $148 million went to programs, the remainder to administrative costs. Arts organizations, as well as individual artists, regularly subscribe to NEA's *Guide to Programs* and *The Cultural Post* to review the types of grants recently made by NEA as a basis for preparing their own proposals.

Other government agencies make grants to support health care, university teaching and research, social services, and other worthwhile causes. Large nonprofit organizations appoint a staff member as director of government grants to concentrate on cultivating opportunities in this sector. The director monitors announcements of government grant opportunities that might have potential for his or her organization, as well as spends time in Washington and elsewhere getting to know officers at these various agencies.

Government agencies normally require the most detailed paperwork in preparing proposals. On the other hand, the agencies are very willing to review proposals, placing the main weight on the proposal's probable contribution to the public interest. Certain topics become "hot," such as cancer research, environmental health, and so on, and the granting agencies look for the best proposals they can find on these topics. They pay less attention to agency benefit or to personal relations with the requesting organizations.

ORGANIZING FOR FUNDRAISING

Nonprofit organizations must develop a strategic approach to fundraising. They cannot simply rely on money coming over the transom; this would make funding too erratic. Small organizations normally rely on one person who is chiefly responsible for fundraising. This person may be the organization's head or a director of development. He or she will be responsible for identifying fundraising opportunities and activating others—officers, employees, and volunteers—to assist when possible.

Large nonprofit organizations such as the American Red Cross and American Heart Association have entire departments of development consisting of dozens of staff members plus volunteers numbering in the thousands. In these large organizations, development staff members take responsibility for specific *donor markets, services, marketing tools,* or *geographical areas.* We shall illustrate this by showing how a large private college typically organizes its fundraising.

A model organization for university fundraising is shown in Figure 11-3. The board of directors has the ultimate responsibility for overseeing the financial health of the university and does this by making personal and company contributions, arranging donor contacts, and suggesting new fundraising ideas. The college president is the chief fundraiser when it comes to meeting important people and asking for money. The vice-president of

FIGURE 11-3

A Large University Fundraising Organization

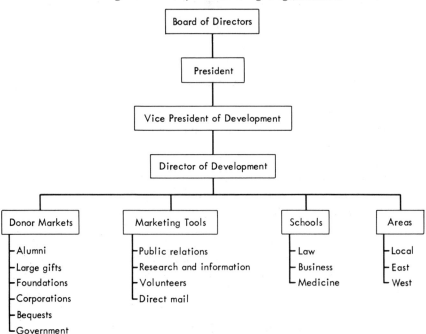

development is the chief planner of the fundraising strategy for the institution and also personally asks for money from potential donors. Day-to-day administration is often handled by a director of development to free the vice-president of development for strategic planning and outside travel. The remaining development staff carry out specialized activities. Some staff specialize in donor markets—thus, there are directors of alumni affairs, foundations, corporate giving, and so on. Other staff members manage marketing functions such as public relations, research, and volunteers.

Others handle various schools, where they get to know the faculty and fundraising needs and opportunities. Finally, some staff members may manage regions of the country. Cornell, for example, runs offices in eight cities that handle fundraising, alumni relations, and public relations.

The staff's effectiveness is amplified by a large number of volunteers such as alumni, wealthy friends of the institution, deans, faculty, students, and so on. Stanford, for example, runs a special program called the Inner Quad program for those who give (or may give) over $1,000 annually to Stanford. This program is run by eight professional staff members working through 250 volunteers operating in sixteen regions of the country.[5] In this case, the staff really functions to activate the volunteers, who are the main fundraising arm of the university. It achieves considerable gains in efficiency *and* effectiveness in this manner (see Exhibit 11-1).

The university's effectiveness in fundraising is also influenced by the quality of its information system. The development office needs to maintain up-to-date and easily accessible files on donors and prospects (individuals, foundations, corporations, etc.) so that past and potential givers can be identified and previous solicitations can be reviewed. To the extent that these files are computerized and data can be retrieved by year, school, giving level, and other key variables, the fundraiser is in a much better position to allocate his or her time effectively.

Universities can help each other out in the organization of charities by coordinating the vast resources represented by their student bodies. In October of 1985, seventy-five university presidents under the leadership of the presidents of Brown, Georgetown, and Stanford Universities announced a program "to match students seeking volunteer work with agencies that need help."[6]

FUNDRAISING GOALS AND STRATEGY

Organizations must set annual and long-range goals for fundraising. As an example, the March of Dimes set the following goals:

- To become the leading charitable organization in the area of birth defects
- To increase annual contributions received each year by an average of 10 percent
- To keep the expenses-to-contributions ratio below 20 percent
- To increase the median size of contributions by 10 percent
- To increase grants from the government by 15 percent

Presumably, these goals would have to be checked for consistency and prioritized in terms of importance.

Every organization tends to set an annual goal for contributions because this allows the organization to (1) know how much to budget for fundraising, (2) motivate the staff and volunteers to high exertion, and (3) measure fundraising effectiveness. Organizations use several different approaches to arrive at their fundraising goal.

1. *Incremental approach.* Here, the organization takes last year's revenue, increases it to cover inflation, and then modifies it up or down depending on the expected economic climate. Thus, the American Heart Association may decide to raise about 15 percent more than it did in the preceding year.

2. *Need approach.* Here, the organization forecasts its financial needs and sets a goal based on its needs. Thus, a hospital's administration will estimate future building needs and costs, staff salaries, energy costs, and so on, subtract other funds sources, and set the portion that has to be covered by fundraising as its target.

EXHIBIT 11-1. Stanford tailors its fundraising tactics to each alumni segment

To raise money from its alumni, Stanford University's development office distinguishes different categories of alumni—according to the school they attended while at Stanford and also the year of their graduation. The development office then applies the most cost-effective method of fundraising to each category. For this purpose, Stanford further divides its alumni into groups according to their estimated giving potential: those who are believed able to give $1,000 or more; $100–$999; and less than $100. Personal solicitation has proven most effective with the two groups that give over $100. Phonathons have proved especially effective for getting nondonors to start giving and small donors to increase their gifts. A phone call from a classmate asking the alumnus to give a little more is often successful. On the other hand, mail appeals are more cost-effective in reaching alumni who have given under $50 in the past and who are not located in a geographical area where there is a large concentration of Stanford alumni (which is necessary to achieve economies of scale in a phonathon). Even here, the development office divides the under-$50 group into several segments: (1) gave last year, first time, over $25; (2) gave last year, first time, under $25; (3) gave last year, regular donors, over $25; (4) gave last year, regular donors, under $25; (5) gave only in the previous year; (6) gave only two or more years ago; and (7) never gave. Each of these groups receives a different pattern of mail. Those who gave last year, first time, over $25, receive up to five solicitation letters before the school gives up. The first mail appeal, for example, comes from the school that the alumnus attended and describes its recent activities and accomplishments as a way of building pride. If this doesn't work, a second letter comes from a former classmate. If this doesn't work, a third letter comes from a school faculty member reporting on recent research. This is followed, if necessary, by the school's dean sending a letter. The final effort might be a letter from the university president or the chairman of the fund drive. Such an extensive mailing plan would be too expensive to use on those alumni who give small amounts less frequently, so this latter group would only receive up to four solicitation letters; those who have never given only receive up to two letters. Although these different mailing treatments seem arbitrary, they are based on experimenting with different approaches to each group and determining the most cost-effective approach by comparing response rates and average gifts to mailing costs.

SOURCE: Adapted from "Stanford University: The Annual Fund," in Christopher H. Lovelock and Charles B. Weinberg, eds., *Cases in Public and Nonprofit Marketing* (Palo Alto, Calif.: Scientific Press, 1977), pp. 73–88.

3. *Opportunity approach.* Here, the organization makes a fresh estimate of how much money it could raise from each donor group with different levels of fundraising expenditure. It sets the goal of maximizing the net surplus. This approach can be illustrated with Figure 12-2 (p. 366). The sales response function shows the gross revenue that would be raised with different levels of fund-

raising expenditure. Nonmarketing expenditures can be subtracted to reveal the gross surplus before marketing expenditures. The 45° line shows marketing expenditures on fundraising. The vertical distance between the sales response and expense curves shows the net surplus associated with various fundraising expenditures. The highest point on the surplus curve shows the marketing expenditure level that will maximize net surplus.

The opportunity approach is the most sound. The vice-president of development would be responsible for preparing this analysis by analyzing the potential of each donor group. If this goal is accepted, the vice-president of development knows how much staff effort to allocate to each donor group.

After setting its fundraising goal, the organization has to develop an overall strategy. It must decide on how to present its case to the donors. The American Heart Association, for example, has to decide whether to base its case on "hope," "fear," or some other major motive for giving. It has to decide how to allocate scarce staff time to different donor groups and geographical areas.

The role of the vice-president of development in influencing the organization's objectives and strategies varies greatly among organizations. Most organizations treat the development officer as a technician rather than a policy-maker. The president, board, or both decide how much money is needed, select the broad fundraising strategy, and then assign its implementation to the development officer. This unfortunately robs the organization of a valuable contribution that the development officer can make. Some organizations grant more scope to the development officer. This officer participates with the other officers in developing the organization's institutional positioning and personality. By helping the organization develop a better position in the market, the development officer can raise money more easily.

FUNDRAISING TACTICS

Fundraising strategy sets the overall parameters for the fundraising effort, which the development officer must fill in with specific actions. The organization's job is to send messages to the potential donors through the most effective message channels and allow the donors to return money through the most efficient collection channels. This view of the channel options is shown in Figure 11-4.

The various channel opportunities give rise to a whole set of specific, well-known fundraising tactics. Table 11-2 lists the major tactics that are effective in four markets: the mass anonymous small gift market, the members and their friends market, the affluent citizens market, and the wealthy donors market.

The *mass anonymous small gift market* consists of all citizens who

FIGURE 11-4

Communication and Collection Channels for Fundraising

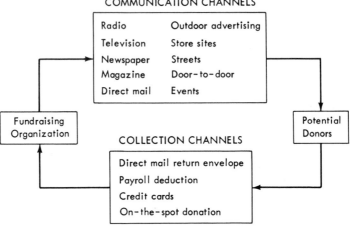

COMMUNICATION CHANNELS

Radio	Outdoor advertising
Television	Store sites
Newspaper	Streets
Magazine	Door-to-door
Direct mail	Events

Fundraising Organization

Potential Donors

COLLECTION CHANNELS

Direct mail return envelope
Payroll deduction
Credit cards
On-the-spot donation

might be induced to contribute a small sum (say, under $50) to a cause. The key idea is to use low-cost methods of fundraising, since the contributions from noninvolved individuals are expected to be low. One of the oldest forms of mass fundraising is the use of volunteers for street and sidewalk solicitation. The volunteers stand in high traffic areas holding out a can (Crippled Children), offering tags (Veterans' Day), ringing bells (Salvation Army), or distributing religious materials (Hare Krishna). Somewhat more costly is door-to-door solicitation because more time is involved and many people won't be home. Yet door-to-door canvassing is the preferred method of the American Heart Association (AHA), which has a massive army of volunteers organized by city, neighborhood, and block, who ring doorbells once a year for the AHA. Block volunteers are typically homemakers who solicit their neighbors for money and make a substantial contribution themselves. Some charities enlist retailers to keep donation cans in their establishments near the cash register where people might deposit their spare change.

In recent years, direct mail has become an extremely important marketing tool to reach the mass anonymous small gift market. There are three reasons for this. First, the cost of personal solicitation has increased dramatically. Second, the growing availability of *highly* specialized mailing lists permits careful targeting of the market. And, third, the emergence of the small business and personal computer has permitted charitable organizations to use and refine mailing lists at very low costs. Direct mail is relatively easy to get started. The first year's returns largely pay back the cost of the mailing lists and the system. This investment then pays off in subsequent

340

years. With computers, charities can personalize correspondence and keep track and code into their data files who responds to what. With special mailing lists, they can tailor appeals to segments with known interests and lifestyles. Each mailing allows the charity to build in more experience and fine-tune its approach. While small organizations can start up for $300 to $400, one national charity invested $200,000 at the beginning and in 1981 was taking in $30 million annually from direct mail.[7] Mailings to acquire new donors vary in their results. The Zoological Society of San Diego found that by investing $80,000 in a high-quality, computer-personalized letter, modest premiums (free passes to the children's zoo and a zoo decal), and high-quality graphics, it generated $130,000 in membership revenues. Lists are carefully tested and analyzed and mailings are coordinated with television,

Table 11-2

FUNDRAISING METHODS

Mass Anonymous Small Gift Market

Charity cans in stores	Raffles
Direct mail	Rummage sales
Door-to-door solicitation	Sporting events
Street and sidewalk solicitation	Tours
TV and radio marathons	Walkathons, readathons, bikeathons,
Thrift shops	danceathons, jogathons,
Plate passing	swimathons
	Yearbooks

Members and Their Friends Market

Anniversary celebrations	Dances
Art shows	Dinners, suppers, lunches,
Auctions	breakfasts
Benefits (theatre, movies, sports events)	Fairs
Bingo games	Fashion shows
Book sales	Parties in unusual places
Cake sales	Phonathons (also called telethons)

Affluent Citizens Market

Convocations	Parlor meetings
Dinners (invitational and/or testimonial)	Telephone calls from high-status
Letters from high-status individuals	individuals

Wealthy Donors Market

Bequests	Testimonial dinner for wealthy
Celebrity grooming	individuals
Committee visit to person's home, office	Wealthy person invited to another's
Memorials	home or club

radio, newspaper, and outdoor ads. These ads create an "awareness umbrella" that has helped triple the Zoological Society's membership from 45,000 to over 118,000 in the past seven years.[8]

The *members and their friends market* consists of the people who belong to the organization and their friends, who have a personal interest in supporting the organization. This market can be tapped for donations in a number of ways. Art museums, for example, favor raising money through selling memberships and running theatre benefits, dinners, and tours. Churches, on the other hand, typically raise money by sponsoring bingo games, rummage sales, cake sales, plate passing, and raffles. Each of these fundraising methods requires careful planning in order to maximize its potential revenue. Fashion shows, for example, have to be planned and promoted far in advance of the day of their occurrence; the same can be said of dances and fairs. Fundraising consultants can be found who specialize in each method and know how to stage it for maximal effectiveness. These consultants can recommend the most effective and appropriate fundraising methods to an organization. Furthermore, they continue to invent new approaches each year.[9] No sooner had walkathons become popular than other organizations created "readathons," "bikeathons," and "jogathons." Each organization seeks to give a special or distinctive twist to its events. The Boys Clubs of Chicago, for example, looked for an unusual place to hold a dinner for its members and decided on a black-tie dinner dance to be held in the Lion House of Lincoln Park Zoo, with the lions stalking around as the dinner guests dined and danced.

The *affluent citizens market* consists of persons whose income and interest in the organization or cause could lead them to give anywhere from $50 to several hundred dollars as a donation. The affluent citizens market is worth pursuing with more than direct mail. A highly effective technique is to issue invitations for special dinners or events. Political parties, for example, run $100- or $500-a-plate dinners to raise money for aspiring political candidates. Or the dinner might be free, with donations solicited after a round of enthusiastic speech-making and drinking, both calculated to loosen the purse strings. Another popular method is letters and phone calls from supporters of the organization to their affluent friends asking for donations.

The *wealthy donors market* consists of persons whose wealth and potential interest is such that they might be induced to contribute anywhere from $1,000 to several million dollars to a cause or organization. These wealthy donors are usually well known in their community, and they are solicited by many organizations for financial support. Many of them set up foundations to handle these solicitations so that they do not have to be personally bothered. Yet some fundraisers spend inordinate amounts of time with these individuals in the hope of attracting a major grant to their institutions. One fundraiser from a major private Eastern university has already spent seven years cultivating the friendship of a wealthy Chicago widow without yet receiving a major grant, yet he is not giving up. Some universities are skillful in putting on weekend retreats for wealthy donors in order to attract substantial money. One well-known private university invited fifty of its wealthiest alumni to an all-expense-paid weekend on the campus, flying them in on private planes from their homes in various parts of the country. These alumni were put up in the best hotel, treated to some fine lectures, led in a religious service by the university president, and treated to a football game won brilliantly by the school's team. Their spirits were so high that the typical alumnus attending that weekend gave a check to the university for over $100,000.

All of these fundraising tactics can be organized under the umbrella concept of a campaign. We define a campaign as follows:

> A **campaign** is an organized and time-sequenced set of activities and events for raising a given sum of money within a particular time period.

Fundraisers distinguish between an *annual campaign* and a *capital campaign*. Colleges, hospitals, churches, and charitable organizations such as the United Way plan an annual campaign to raise a target amount of money each year. The campaign plan spells out the "case," goals, events, and so on. A well-known person may be invited to be the campaign chairperson to energize and symbolize that year's campaign.

Organizations also run capital campaigns from time to time to raise a large amount of money for major undertakings or expansions. In 1972, Stanford launched a five-year, $300 million capital campaign, and in 1974 Yale launched a three-and-a-half-year, $370 million capital campaign. These campaigns require the most careful planning. Here are some of the major considerations:

1. An organization cannot run a capital campaign too often. After Stanford ended its five-year capital campaign, it would not launch another capital campaign for at least three to five years. This "spacing" is necessary if the capital campaigns are to retain their specialness in the minds of the donors.
2. The organization has to make decisions about the capital campaign's goal and duration. The goal should be achievable, for there is nothing more embarrassing than failing to reach the goal. And the campaign should not last too long because it will eventually lose its momentum.
3. The organization should try to add a matching gift feature to the campaign, where some wealthy donors or organizations promise to match, say, $1 for $1 of the money raised. Early in the planning, the organization has to find and cultivate challenge grants.
4. The organization should prepare an attractive booklet showing the main items that the money will buy (called a *wish list*). Thus, MIT prepared a book-

let showing what different amounts of money would buy, including buildings, endowed chairs, and so on.

5. A capital campaign should not be begun until much of its goal *has already been reached.* That is, larger donors must be solicited for major grants before announcing the campaign kickoff. This will give the campaign significant momentum right at the start, creating a bandwagon effect and erasing doubts that the project is not needed or that it will not soon achieve its goal.

An issue in designing a campaign is to decide whether potential donors should be "coached" in how much to give or whether this should be left to their judgment. In fact, there are three possibilities:

1. Don't specify any amount.
2. Suggest a specific dollar amount on the low side.
3. Suggest a specific dollar amount on the high side.

The first approach is the most common. People differ in what they can give, and it is felt that this is best left to their individual judgments.

Suggesting a specific amount on the low side is seen as accomplishing two things. It helps prospects know what is considered a minimum proper amount to give. And the "low-amount feature" allows people to get into the habit of giving (the "foot-in-the-door theory").[10] While there is the problem that many people might have given more, research suggests that the technique can be quite effective. Brockner et al. found that in a campaign for a relatively obscure charity, the National Reye's Syndrome Foundation, concluding the sales presentation with the phrase "even a dollar will help" resulted in *twenty times* as much money being raised as when this suggestion was not made.[11] Further, this was more effective than saying "even five dollars will help." The researchers found that the latter yielded more total dollars than the control condition (no request), but *less* than the "even a dollar" condition. This was due to increased frequency of donating under the "dollar" condition, rather than larger amounts being donated. Finally, the research found that the technique applies to both telephone and face-to-face solicitation. Citing earlier research, they also claim that the technique has been shown to work for at least three *different* charities, Reye's Syndrome, the American Cancer Society, and the Heart Association.[12]

Suggesting a high amount to give works on the theory of the "door-in-the-face." It stretches people's idea of what they should give, and it is hoped that they will give this much or something close to it. Thus, the United Fund might suggest that citizens give 1 percent of their income, or a church might suggest that members give 5 percent of their income. Most people regard these amounts as too high, but end up giving more than they normally would (see also Exhibit 11-2).

EXHIBIT 11-2. How not to ask for money in a face-to-face situation

A successful young lawyer had a recent experience that graphically illustrates several subtle points about personal solicitation. He received a phone call from a person who said that he was from the lawyer's alma mater and would like to make an appointment to talk to the lawyer. At the appointed time the visitor appeared, a tall good-looking man with gray hair who looked like a college president. The visitor started to talk about the university's plan for the eighties and showed pictures of new buildings that the university needed. The lawyer now knew that the visitor was a development officer seeking a donation. After describing the university in glowing terms for fifteen minutes, the development officer came to the point: "In view of our needs and your affection for the university, I would like you to consider making a donation of $10,000 to your university." The lawyer at this point felt stunned by this request ("door-in-the-face"). He had never been asked for such a large contribution by any organization. He felt flattered that someone could think he could make such a large contribution; this meant that he had "arrived." On the other hand, he felt somewhat miffed to be asked without warning for such a large amount of money by a relative stranger. He told the development officer that he appreciated learning about his university's needs and would think it over, and hopefully would give, if not that amount, something substantial in any event. The officer looked a little disappointed, but thanked him for his time and left. At the time of this writing, the lawyer still had not made any donation to his university.

This episode illustrates several mistakes in the development officer's approach to the particular prospect. (Try to imagine these mistakes before reading on.) The development officer should have said over the phone who he was and his purpose for visiting. He should have sent an advance mailing describing the university's campaign, needs, and accomplishments. He should have considered bringing along an eminent lawyer who had also graduated from the same university. He should have done less talking and more listening, asking the lawyer how he felt about the university and what memories he had. The development officer should have asked for a more reasonable gift—say, $5,000. When the lawyer balked, the officer should have continued to try to "close the sale." He might have said that the lawyer could make a contribution of $5,000 over a five-year period in $1,000 annual amounts; this would ease the financial burden. Or he could have suggested a tangible benefit that would flow from this gift, such as a scholarship named after the lawyer to support a worthwhile student. Or he could have said that this would be a leadership gift, and the lawyer's name would be listed along with those of other leading contributors. Or he could have said that he would phone in two weeks to see how much the lawyer might be able to give. The development officer did not do any of these things, and his approach showed poor planning of this sales call.

EVALUATING FUNDRAISING EFFECTIVENESS

Each fundraising organization must make a continuous effort to improve the effectiveness of its strategies through evaluating its most recent results, especially in the face of increasingly sophisticated competition and scarce funds. The organization can evaluate its results on the macro and micro levels.

MACROEVALUATION

Organizations use several methods to evaluate their overall fundraising effectiveness. They are described below.

Percentage of Goal Reached.   For organizations that set an annual goal, the first thing to look at is how close they came to achieving the goal. Every organization wants to achieve at least its goal or better. This creates a temptation to set the goal low enough to be achieved. Often, the development officer favors a low goal so that he or she will look good. The organization's president, however, is tempted to set a high goal to induce the development office to work hard.

Composition of Gifts.   The organization should examine the composition of the money raised, looking at trends in the two major components:

Gifts = number of donors $\times$ average gift size

NUMBER OF DONORS.   Each organization hopes to increase the number of donors each year. The organization should pay attention to the number of donors in relation to the potential number of donors. Many organizations have a disappointing "reach" or "penetration." For example, 29 percent of Stanford's alumni have given each year. The question is not why Stanford has 29 percent penetration but why 71 percent of its alumni do not give. The development officer should interview a sample of alumni nongivers and identify the importance of such reasons as: "did not enjoy Stanford as a student, " "do not like the way Stanford is evolving," "disagree with policies of the school in which I graduated," "couldn't care less," "was never asked," and so on. Each of these reasons suggests a possible plan of action.

AVERAGE GIFT SIZE.   A major objective of the fundraising organization is to increase the size of the average gift in given donor segments. The development office should review the size distribution of gifts. It should estimate the potential number of gifts that might be obtained in each size class and compare it to the current number to determine the size classes of gifts that deserve targeted effort in the next period.

Market Share.   For some organizations, share or rank in fundraising among comparable organizations can be a revealing statistic about whether the institution is doing a competent job. A private midwestern university, for example, compared its results to the results of five comparable universities and found it was trailing in the number of alumni givers and in the amount raised through government grants. This led to more effort being directed to these two donor directions. As another example, the Chicago Lung Association found that while it managed to raise more dollars each year, its rank among charitable causes had slipped from third place to eighth place. It was losing its "share of heart" in the giving community and needed to find ways to reverse this relative decline.

Expense/Contribution Ratio.   The fundraising organization is ultimately interested in its net revenue, not gross revenue. At one time the American Kidney Fund spent $740,000 to raise $779,434 and created a scandal. It is more normal for the expense-to-contributions ratio to run between 10 and 20 percent, and the public generally accepts this. The American Red Cross runs its expenses at 5 percent of its contributions. Many large donors, including corporations, look at this key ratio before they decide whether to support an organization.

MICROEVALUATION

The organization should also rate its individual staff members on their fundraising effectiveness. This is not always done. One university vice-president of development said he had a general idea of the funds brought in by each staff member but not specific numbers. Many gifts were the result of several staff people working together: one identifying the prospect, another grooming him or her, and still another getting the check. Still, it would be worthwhile evaluating each individual to help train them better or dismiss them if they are not tapping the existing potential. As an example, one university rates the staff that works with foundations by using the following indicators (the numbers are illustrative):

Number of leads developed	30
Number of proposals written	20
Average value of proposal	$40,000
Number of proposals closed	10
Percentage of proposals closed	50%
Average value closed	$39,000
Average cost per proposal closed	$6,000
Cost per dollar raised	.20

SUMMARY

One of the major problems of nonprofit organizations is fundraising. Organizations are gradually shifting from a product orientation to a sales orientation and then to a marketing orientation. A marketing orientation calls for carefully segmenting donor markets, measuring their giving potential, and assigning executive responsibility and resources to cultivate each market. Marketers assume that the act of giving is really an exchange process in which the giver also gets something that the organization can offer.

The first step in the fundraising process is to study the characteristics of each of the four major donor markets: individuals, foundations, corporations, and government. Each donor market has its own giving motives and giving criteria.

The second step is to organize the fundraising operation in a way that covers the different donor markets, organization services, marketing tools, and geographical areas.

The third step is to develop sound goals and strategies to guide the fund-raising effort. Goals are set on either an incremental basis, need basis, or opportunity basis.

The fourth step is to develop a mix of fundraising tactics for the various donor groups. Different tactics are effective with the mass anonymous small gift market, the members-and-their-friends market, the affluent citizens market, and the wealthy donors market.

The fifth step is to conduct regular evaluations of fundraising results. A macroevaluation consists of analyzing the percentage of the goal reached, the composition of the gifts, the average gift size, the market share, and the expense/contributions ratio. Microevaluation consists of evaluating the performance of each individual fund-raiser.

QUESTIONS

1. What motives are likely to stimulate large donations to a state university like UCLA? How would these motives differ from those of donors of smaller amounts? How would they differ from the motives of those giving large donations to a *private* university like the University of Southern California?

2. What might a potential donor of a large amount to UCLA perceive to be the major costs of such a donation? In each case, how could a UCLA fundraiser seek to diminish that "cost"?

3. Many corporations are headquartered in Columbus, Ohio. What criteria should a local social service agency specializing in drug and alcohol abuse programs use in prioritizing corporations for fundraising solicitations? Would the criteria be the same for a local art gallery?

4. If you were asked to develop a data bank on past, present, and potential individual donors for the zoo in a major metropolitan area, what information would you *ideally* like to record about each individual on his or her computer record? Draw up a sample entry and, for each item, indicate how the needed information would be obtained.

5. Suppose that you were asked to set the goals for fundraisers responsible for particular target groups under your general jurisdiction and that you had made realistic estimates of what you thought each target group would probably contribute on the basis of past experience. How would you translate these "expected receipts" into specific goals for each of your subordinate fundraisers? Would the goals be equal to or above your estimates? If above, how much above, and why this amount? Would the relationship between your expectations and assigned goals differ across your fundraisers, and if so, on what basis?

NOTES

1. For additional information, see *Giving USA—1985 Annual Report: A Compilation of Facts and Trends on American Philanthropy for the Year 1985* (New York: American Association of Fundraising Council, 1980).

2. "How Do We Choose the Charities We Support?", *Chicago Tribune,* July 30, 1972, Section 5, p. 9.

3. Harold J. Seymour, *Designs for Fund-Raising* (New York: McGraw-Hill, 1966).

4. Here are some useful books and articles on grantsmanship. Virginia P. White, *Grants: How to Find Out About Them and What to Do Next* (New York and London: Plenum Press, 1975); Lois DeBakey and Selma DeBakey, "The Art of Persuasion: Logic and Language in Proposal Writing," *Grants Magazine,* Vol. 1, No. 1 (March 1978), pp. 43–60; F. Lee Jacquette and Barbara J. Jacquette, *What Makes a Good Proposal* (New York: Foundation Center, 1973); and Robert A. Mayer, *What Will a Foundation Look For When You Submit a Grant Proposal?* (New York: Foundation Center, 1972).

5. See "Stanford University: The Annual Fund," in Christopher Lovelock and Charles B. Weinberg, eds., *Cases in Public and Nonprofit Marketing* (Palo Alto, Calif.: Scientific Press, 1977), pp. 73–88.

6. Fox Butterfield, "Universities Take Lead in New Volunteer Efforts," *New York Times,* October 17, 1985, p. 12.

7. Belinda Hulin-Salkin, "Strategies of Charities," *Advertising Age,* January 19, 1981, p. 5–22 ff.

8. Cliff Underwood, "Building Donor Relationships Strengthens Zoo's Membership," *Fundraising Management,* January 1984, pp. 37–43.

9. For several examples, see Suzanne Seixas, "Getting More from Givers," *Money,* September 1976, pp. 79–82.

10. In a study by Freedman and Fraser, the experimenters asked subjects to comply with a small initial request. Two weeks later, they were contacted and asked to comply with a large request. It was found that 76 percent of the experimental participants *agreed* to comply with the large request, compared to a 17 percent compliance rate by those subjects approached with *only* the large request. See J. L. Freedman and S. Fraser, "Compliance Without Pressure: The Foot-in-the-Door Technique," *Journal of Personality and Social Psychology,* Vol. 4 1966, pp. 195–202. See also Chapter 18.

11. Joel Brockner, Beth Guzzi, Julie Kane, Ellen Levine, and Kate Shaplen, "Organizational Fundraising: Further Evidence of the Effect of Legitimizing Small Donations," *Journal of Consumer Research,* June 1984, pp. 611–613.

12. Peter H. Reingen, "On Inducing Compliance With Requests," *Journal of Consumer Research,* September 1978, pp. 96–102; Robert B. Cialdini and David A. Schroeder, "Increasing Compliance by Legitimizing Paltry Contributions: When Even a Penny Helps," *Journal of Personality and Social Psychology,* October 1976, pp. 599–604.

CHAPTER 12
===

Designing and Analyzing Marketing Programs

In an intriguing social experiment, enterprising heart researchers are seeking to ascertain the influence of different marketing mixes on heart health behaviors such as eating, smoking, and exercise.

The experiment is being funded by the National Heart, Lung, and Blood Institute in an effort to knock out the nations's number one killer: heart disease. The project involves sending professional health educators into seven American cities—Monterey and Salinas, California; Mankato, Bloomington, and Moorhead, Minnesota; Fargo, North Dakota; and Pawtucket, Rhode Island—to convince residents that their unhealthy habits have been learned and can be unlearned and to recruit citizens to help spread the word.

The idea behind the long-term study is that if the people in these communities are bombarded with enough heart health messages and peer pressure, they can change their harmful life-styles and cut the risk of heart disease. The heart disease rates of people in the seven cities can then be compared with those of residents in comparable communities that have no such programs.

It was the success of an earlier Stanford University program that spurred the current seven-city study, says Dr. Elaine Stone of the Heart, Lung, and Blood Institute. When the university conducted community-wide health education programs in Gilroy and Watsonville, California, from 1972 to 1975, heart disease risk factors among the population aged twenty-five to seventy-four dropped by more than 20 percent.

In Mankato, Mary O'Sullivan, the community coordinator, indicated

"Our goal was to get between 60 percent and 70 percent of the target-age population to come through the center and have their risk factors measured. We figured it would take two years to do that, and we hit it right on the head. We got about 65 percent of the people by December, 1983."

To recruit people for the assessment, program staff and volunteers sent letters to everyone in town and then followed up with phone calls and, in some cases, door-to-door visits.

Mankato, Minnesota, for example, began with a Dining à la Heart Program, in which local restaurants featured heart-healthy foods. Also, most grocery stores marked low-fat, low-sodium items on their shelves, and billboards reminded residents to look for them. After several taste testings in markets of foods such as bean chili, and low-fat, low-sodium pumpkin bars, sales of ingredients for the products soared. Mankato community leaders began getting into the act, too. One Sunday, Rev. Walter Flesner of the United Methodist Church jogged down the aisle in a sweat suit to preach the benefits of fitness. In May of 1984, about seventy employees of Hubbard Milling Company took a fifteen-minute walk together at lunchtime to launch their participation in the Shape-Up challenge, a month-long contest in which fifty-six local organizations competed to log the most exercise hours among workers.

On the other hand, the heart program in Monterey and Salinas relied heavily on mass communications. That's because the media have been so effective in promoting good health in this country, says Stanford Professor Nathan Maccoby. Slick, attractive publications such as *The Exercise Book For People Who Don't Exercise* and *Staying Healthy: The Stanford Guide to a Good Life* were distributed in libraries and other public places. "We also coproduce segments for local television news," Maccoby said. Each five-part series described a different heart risk, and each weekday a different aspect of the risk was discussed.

There are no official reports yet on the overall effectiveness of the campaigns, each of which is scheduled to run for nine years, "but we can certainly say that awareness of heart disease risk factors is greatly increased," Maccoby said. Some preliminary indications of the effectiveness of the various marketing mixes are slowly emerging. There are, for example, encouraging results from stop-smoking programs in schools. "After three years the smoking rate among students in Saratoga [California] schools, where we introduced the program, was 5 percent. In a control school in Mountain View, California, the smoking rate was 16 percent." The results in Mankato are equally dramatic: a 40 percent lower smoking rate last year among the city's seventh-graders than among seventh-graders elsewhere, according to Dr. Russell Luepker of the University of Minnesota, which directs the Minnesota programs.

SOURCE: Adapted from Norma Peterson, "Heartfelt Efforts," *American Way,* Inflight Magazine of American Airlines, September 1984, pp. 117–120, copyright ©1984 by American Airlines. Reprinted with permission.

Once the core marketing strategy has been developed in light of the manager's analysis of target customers, probable future environmental changes, potential competition, and the organization's strengths and weaknesses, and once the appropriate organization structure and resources have been put in place, the next critical strategic planning task is choosing and developing cost-effective marketing programs. This chapter examines the planning and budgeting tools available to marketing managers in the nonprofit sector to make such determinations. Later chapters examine specific marketing elements—product, price, place, and promotion.

To be cost-effective in its marketing programming an organization must face the following four issues:

1. How can the organization choose among competing marketing programs? (Benefit/cost analysis)
2. What marketing/financial objectives should be pursued? (Detailed goal specification)
3. How much should the organization spend on marketing? (Optimal marketing expenditure level)
4. How can the organization determine the best mix of marketing tactics? (Optimal marketing mix)

CHOOSING AMONG COMPETING PROGRAMS THROUGH BENEFIT/COST ANALYSIS

A common problem facing nonprofit organizations is choosing between alternative programs that all fall within the scope of the organization's objectives. Consider the following situations:

- The American Cancer Society is trying to decide between sponsoring a national cervical cancer detection program or a national breast cancer detection program.
- A public school system is trying to decide between establishing a gifted children program or a retarded children program.
- A police department is trying to decide between a campaign to educate people against pickpockets or adding a few more permanent policemen to the force.
- An art museum is trying to decide between establishing an arts library within the museum or adding a few more major paintings to its collection.
- A university is trying to decide between building some badly needed dormitories and building a badly needed student union.
- A public library is trying to decide between adding a bookmobile to bring books into neighborhoods or using the same funds to permit opening the library on Sundays.

These examples involve organizations facing a choice between two programs. They can choose one of the programs or allocate funds to both programs and operate them on a smaller scale than planned. In principle, the nonprofit organization can make a calculation similar to that of a profit organization. It should attempt to measure the benefits and the costs expected from each program. The benefits are all the contributions that the particular program will make to the organization's objectives. The costs are all the deductions that the particular program will require from alternative organization objectives. A particular program is considered worthwhile when its benefits exceed its costs.

THEORY OF BENEFIT/COST ANALYSIS

Suppose a nonprofit organization is considering a choice between three programs, X, Y, and Z. All programs are estimated to cost about the same— say, 10 (in thousands of dollars). The programs, however, are estimated to yield different levels of benefits. The data on the three programs are shown in Table 12-1A.

All three programs show a positive net benefit $(B - C)$ as well as a benefit/cost ratio (B/C) greater than one. On both criteria, the best program is X, the next Y, and the last Z. If the organization has funds of only 10, it should invest in program X. If the organization has funds of 20, it should invest in programs X and Y. If the organization has funds of 30, it should invest in all three programs, because in all programs the benefits exceed the costs.

Now consider the data in Table 12-1B, where the three programs differ in costs as well as benefits. In this case, the net benefits and the benefit-cost ratios do not show the same rank order. Program X stands highest in net benefit but lowest in benefit-cost ratio. Which criterion should dominate?

Table 12-1

EXAMPLES OF BENEFIT-COST COMPARISONS

Program	B Benefits	C Costs	B − C Net Benefit	B/C Benefit-Cost Ratio
A. Equal Costs				
X	60	10	50	6
Y	30	10	20	3
Z	20	10	10	2
B. Unequal Costs				
Program	B Benefits	C Costs	B − C Net Benefit	B/C Benefit-Cost Ratio
X	60	30	30	2
Y	30	10	20	3
Z	20	5	15	4

Generally, the benefit-cost ratio is the more rational criterion because it shows the productivity of the funds. If funds of 5 are available, they should be spent on Z because they will yield four times the benefit per dollar of cost. If funds of 15 are available, they should be spent on Y and Z to yield total benefits of 50, which is an average benefit-cost ratio of 3⅓ per dollar of cost. Notice that program X, although yielding net benefits of 30, only shows a benefit-cost ratio of 2. The only time program X would be preferred would be if the three programs were mutually exclusive, funds of 30 were available, and the objective was to maximize the net benefit.

We will now ask how these benefits and costs can be quantified in the first place.

The organization is usually in a position to quantify the dollar costs of a program. If the program leads to some social costs, these are harder to estimate. A city government, for example, typically looks at the cost of building a crosstown expressway in financial terms. But an expressway destroys certain neighborhoods and increases local pollution and noise. These social costs should be included in the total evaluation of costs.

Evaluating benefits poses many tough problems. Identified benefits tend to fall into three groups: They are

1. Monetarily quantifiable benefits—benefits whose total value can be expressed in dollars
2. Nonmonetary quantifiable benefits—benefits whose total value can be expressed in some specific nonmonetary but numerical measure, such as "lives saved"
3. Nonquantifiable benefits—benefits whose total value cannot be expressed quantitatively, such as amount of happiness created or beauty produced.

Suppose a certain program is estimated to have several benefits, all of which can be measured in dollars. This is the easiest case to handle.

A second possibility occurs when all the benefits can be measured in terms of a common nonmonetary value, such as "lives saved." In this case, we sum up the lives saved as a result of each benefit of the program. (If one assigned a dollar value to each of those lives, then the problem could be considered under the first category.)

A third possibility occurs when the various benefits do not all share a common value. Some analysts prefer to make a two-stage analysis, the first stage including only the quantifiable benefits and costs. If the benefit-cost ratio exceeds one, the program is considered good unless there is a conviction that the nonquantifiable costs substantially exceed the nonquantifiable benefits. If the benefit-cost ratio is less than one, the program may nevertheless be good if the nonquantifiable benefits substantially exceed the nonquantifiable costs.

The value of trying to quantify the benefits in dollars or some other common denominator is readily apparent. This has led to a number of ingenious ways to try to determine the dollar value of a benefit. The first approach is to try to find an existing market price for this benefit. If a school dropout prevention program persuades a certain number of students to stay in school, the present value of their increased lifetime earnings can be used as a measure of the value of the program. If a farmer fertilizer-education program increases farm output, the expected market value of the additional crops attributable to the educational program could be used as the monetary value of this benefit.

The second approach is used when there is no existing market price for the type of benefit being created by the program. Here people can be asked how much they would be willing to pay for that benefit. If a tennis court is being considered for a local park, local residents could be asked how much they would pay per hour to use it or how much additional taxes they would accept. If the National Aeronautics and Space Administration is contemplating a ten-year program to send a manned flight to Mars, it might ask people how much they would be willing to pay over a ten-year period to achieve a successful mission.

PROBLEMS IN BENEFIT-COST ANALYSIS

Some of the problems in putting benefit-cost analysis to practical use should now be apparent. Even if one manages to devise dollar values for the various benefits and costs, the technique makes certain assumptions that should be stated clearly.

First, the technique assumes that the program, if adopted, would not yield outputs sufficient to change the market prices that were used to estimate the benefits of the program. If school dropout prevention programs are introduced throughout the country, for example, they will increase the skill level of the population and probably result in a fall in the market price of skilled workers. Therefore, the life earnings calculation based on today's earnings of skilled workers overstates the market value of the benefit.

Second, the technique makes no allowance for redistributional benefits caused by the program. A vocational education program and a gifted children program, for example, may both improve lifetime incomes to the same extent. But the vocational education program may improve the incomes of the poor and a gifted children program may improve the incomes of the well-off. Some analysts believe the technique should give weight to desirable redistribution effects.

Third, the technique assumes that economic value should be given the main weight in deciding between programs. Critics resent the notion that everything worthwhile can be measured in dollars or that the growth of the GNP is the major goal. They see the value of a school dropout prevention program not so much in increased dollars of earnings but in terms of increased self-esteem and improved social attitudes.

Finally, the technique assumes that the rank ordering of projects is insensitive to the particular measure of benefit used. In a study of the net benefit of investing in different disease control programs, the ailment of arthritis did not seem important when the criterion "lives saved" was used because arthritis does not kill people. On the other hand, arthritis rates as a high-priority research problem when the criterion "dollars saved through avoiding medical treatment" is used.[1] Thus, various programs may rank differently depending on the benefit measure used.

These difficulties are not created by the technique but exist because the world is complex. The technique was never intended to replace judgment, but to systematize and quantify it where possible. Benefit-cost analysis suggests which important factors should be considered and what information is needed. It introduces relevant data into what otherwise would be a wholly subjective act of decision-making. It rests on the premise that organized ignorance is preferable to disorganized ignorance in making decisions.

ESTABLISHING THE MARKETING/FINANCIAL OBJECTIVES

A major requirement in the marketing programming process is to clarify the organization's overall objective in the marketplace. This can be facilitated by developing a marketing/financial equation and viewing various objectives in terms of this equation. The purpose of the equation is to show the factors that influence the size of the surplus or deficit incurred by the organization in carrying out alternative marketing activities.

We start with the definition of a *surplus ($)* as being the difference between *total revenue (R)* and *total cost (C);* that is,

$$\$ = R - C \qquad\qquad (12\text{-}1)$$

The total revenue *(R)* can have from one to four components, the *average price (P)* charged by the organization times the *quantity sold (Q)*, *donations (D)*, and/or *grants (G)*:

$$R = PQ + D + G \qquad\qquad (12\text{-}2)$$

Some nonprofit organizations may operate only with grants and donations. Some may have extensive internally generated sales revenues.

The total cost *(C)* is made up of *total variable production cost (V)*, *total fixed cost (F)*, and *total marketing cost (M)*. Variable cost *(V)* is the *unit cost (c)* times the *quantity sold (Q);* that is, $V = cQ$. Then total cost is:

$$C = cQ + F + M \qquad\qquad (12\text{-}3)$$

Substituting (12-2) and (12-3) into (12-1), the equation for surplus is:

$$\$ = PQ + D + G - cQ - F - M$$

or

$$\$ = (P - c)Q + D + G - F - M \tag{12-4}$$

The term $(P - c)$ is called the gross surplus per unit, since it represents the markup of price over cost.

In order to use equation (12-4), we have to ask what influences Q, the number of units sold. Clearly, Q is influenced by the price (P) and the marketing expenditures (M); that is:

$$Q = f(P,M) \tag{12-5}$$

This expression says that Q is a function of price and marketing expenditure, and is called *the sales response function* (or *demand function*). The vector (P,M) is called the *marketing mix*. To the extent that D and G are also a function of P and M (and possibly of Q itself), we can also speak of a *donation response function* and a *grant response function*.

ALTERNATIVE OBJECTIVES OF NONPROFIT ORGANIZATIONS

We are now ready to contrast eight alternative marketing/financial objectives that might be pursued by nonprofit organizations. Some are more desirable from a social standpoint than others.

Surplus Maximization.   Some nonprofit organizations pursue the objective of maximizing their surplus. A performing arts group, for example, might want to accumulate as much cash surplus as possible in order to build a new theatre. This does not mean that it will charge the highest possible ticket price, because this would reduce attendance. It would need to know how the quantity of tickets sold is affected by price, as well as how the donations are affected.[2] Nor will the group spend the least on marketing to keep costs low; it knows that more marketing will pull in larger audiences. It wants to know how attendance and donations are affected by the marketing expenditure level. This enables it to find the price and marketing expenditure level that will maximize the organization's surplus.

Revenue Maximization.   An alternative objective is to maximize the total revenue $(PQ + D + G)$, even though high costs might be incurred. A public transportation company, for example, might feel that a high total revenue tells the market that the organization is important and doing a good job. Management might feel that increased revenue would lead to greater confidence in the organization.

Usage Maximization.   Many nonprofit organizations are primarily interested in maximizing the number of users of their services. Thus, art museums and zoological parks are eager to maximize the annual number of visitors, because this is taken as a sign that they are providing worthwhile educational and recreational services to the community. The city council will look at each institution's attendance growth to determine how much budget to grant it *(G)* for next year.

Usage Targeting.   Organizations with fixed service capacities typically set their price and marketing expenditures to produce a capacity audience, Q^*. For example, a symphony orchestra experiencing low attendance might lower its price in order to fill more of the seats in the auditorium. If the potential ticket-seekers exceed capacity, the orchestra would raise prices to improve its revenue while filling the auditorium.

Full Cost Recovery.   Many nonprofit organizations are primarily interested in breaking even each year. They would like to provide as much service as they can as long as their sales revenue plus donations and grants just cover their costs. Many universities want to be in this position of spending just short of the amount at which they would have to report a deficit. Many public agencies also have this objective, making sure to spend any remaining funds toward the end of the year to avoid showing a surplus that might lead to receiving a lower budget during the next year.

Partial Cost Recovery.   Other organizations operate with a chronic deficit each year. Examples in the past have included most performing arts organizations and many local public transportation companies. There is no reasonable price and marketing expenditure level that would bring these organizations close to breaking even. Instead, their aim is to keep the annual deficit from exceeding a certain amount. Public authorities or private foundations or individual donors are solicited to cover the annual deficit.

Budget Maximization.   Many nonprofits, particularly those in social services, act as if they are attempting to maximize the size of their staffs, the number of programs they offer, and their operating expenditures. They seem to seek program grants and donations without fully considering their ability to use the contributed funds effectively. They are also reluctant to trim programs or staff even in the face of evidence that these are nonproductive. Trimming operations would, of course, make the organization seem less "successful" in the staff's own eyes and—they believe—in the eyes of their peers.

Producer Satisfaction Maximization. Many nonprofit organizations are as eager to satisfy the wants of their own staffs as those of the publics they serve. One often hears the criticism that hospitals place the needs of doctors ahead of those of patients and colleges place the needs of faculty ahead of those of students. One can imagine the members of a symphony orchestra playing primarily music that pleases them, whether or not it attracts a large audience. This introduces a new variable not shown in the equation, maximization of producer satisfaction. According to Etgar and Ratchford: "the product is created mainly for the satisfaction of producers themselves. . . . The organization will modify its product away from the one which gives its own members the most satisfaction only insofar as is necessary to obtain enough revenue from these customer groups to survive financially."[3] McKnight goes further and argues that most nonprofit organizations and professionals are basically self-serving and oriented toward maximizing their own interests.[4]

Examples of Revenue Functions

The preceding analysis used the simple sales revenue function, PQ. This function, when elaborated, reveals a large number of marketing actions that an organizaton can take to increase its revenue. Three examples are shown in the sections that follow.

Hospital Revenue Function. A hospital gets its revenue from operating a number of "businesses," including inpatient services, outpatient services, a gift shop, and so on. Each of these requires pricing and marketing expenditure planning. Consider the case of inpatient services. Here the hospital is interested in filling its beds to capacity; that is, it seeks a high occupancy rate. Its revenue function, PQ, can be divided into the following elements:

$$\begin{matrix} \text{Inpatient} \\ \text{revenue} \end{matrix} = \begin{bmatrix} \begin{matrix} \text{Average revenue per} \\ \text{patient per day} \end{matrix} & \times & \begin{matrix} \text{Annual number} \\ \text{of admissions} \end{matrix} & \times & \begin{matrix} \text{Average length of} \\ \text{patient stay in days} \end{matrix} \end{bmatrix}$$

Hospitals have recently been experiencing declining inpatient revenue because one or more of the three factors has declined. First, as hospitals take on a larger proportion of Medicaid and Medicare patients, their average revenue falls because government reimbursement covers less of the cost. Second, the annual number of admissions has declined in many hospitals because of changing neighborhoods and new forms of competition. Third, the average length of stay has been declining because the government is putting pressure on hospitals to get patients out as fast as possible.

Hospitals can attempt to offset each of these factors by taking positive marketing actions. The average revenue per patient can be increased by raising prices where allowed and seeking a more profitable mix of patients. The annual number of admitted patients can be boosted by attracting more active physicians, improving patient care, and adding high-growth specialties. The average length of stay can be boosted by the hospital emphasizing those specialties that produce longer patient stays.

Trade Association Revenue Function.   A trade association gets its revenue from three major sources: membership dues, publications, and conferences. The revenue function can be modeled as follows:

$$
\begin{aligned}
\text{Revenue} = &\begin{bmatrix} \text{Annual} \\ \text{dues} \end{bmatrix} \left[\left(\begin{matrix} \text{Number of last} \\ \text{year's members} \end{matrix} \right) \left(\begin{matrix} \text{Percentage} \\ \text{who renew} \end{matrix} \right) + \begin{matrix} \text{Number of} \\ \text{new members} \end{matrix} \right] \\
&+ \begin{bmatrix} \text{Price per} \\ \text{issue} \end{bmatrix} \begin{bmatrix} \text{Average number of} \\ \text{copies sold per issue} \end{bmatrix} \begin{bmatrix} \text{Number of} \\ \text{issues/yr.} \end{bmatrix} \\
&+ \begin{bmatrix} \text{Registration} \\ \text{fee} \end{bmatrix} \begin{bmatrix} \text{Average number of} \\ \text{attendees per conference} \end{bmatrix} \begin{bmatrix} \text{Annual number} \\ \text{of conferences} \end{bmatrix}
\end{aligned}
$$

This elaboration of the revenue function helps pinpoint positive marketing actions that can be taken. First, the trade association can consider raising the annual dues, although it must take into account the impact of a dues increase on the membership renewal rate and number of new members attracted. The trade association can also improve the job it is doing to encourage membership renewal and attract new members. Second, the trade association can increase its publication revenue by raising the price per issue, increasing the average number of copies sold per issue, increasing the number of issues per year, or instituting some combination of these possibilities. Third, the trade association can increase its conference revenue by raising the registration fee, attracting a larger average number of attendees per conference, and increasing the annual number of conferences. Each of these variables can be influenced by specific marketing actions. The organization, in fact, can build up its marketing plans by examining each revenue component and determining what can be accomplished.

Church Revenue Function.   A church gets revenue from three major sources: donations, facility rental, and sale of complementary services. Specifically, the revenue function looks like this:

$$
\begin{aligned}
\text{Revenue} = &\begin{bmatrix} \text{Average} \\ \text{contribution} \\ \text{per visit} \end{bmatrix} \begin{bmatrix} \text{Average number} \\ \text{of visits per} \\ \text{member per year} \end{bmatrix} \begin{bmatrix} \text{Number of} \\ \text{church} \\ \text{members} \end{bmatrix} \\
&+ \begin{bmatrix} \text{Average} \\ \text{rental fee} \end{bmatrix} \begin{bmatrix} \text{Average number of rentals} \\ \text{per facility per year} \end{bmatrix} \begin{bmatrix} \text{Number of} \\ \text{facilities for rent} \end{bmatrix} \\
&+ \begin{bmatrix} \text{Net revenue from} \\ \text{complementary services} \end{bmatrix} + \begin{bmatrix} \text{Donations due to} \\ \text{impact of services} \end{bmatrix}
\end{aligned}
$$

In its marketing planning, the church will want to consider how to attract more contributions at its weekly worship services. The number of attendees, frequency of attendance, and average contribution are a function of religious service times, the inspirational quality of the religious service, parking, child care services, and a number of other factors. Churches are increasingly seeking to improve the quality of their worship services through hiring dynamic ministers, easing the dress code, and having a social hour after the services. Facility revenue is dependent on attracting weddings, receptions, baptisms, socials, and funerals. The number of functions attracted is dependent upon the public awareness of the facility's availability, rental fee, use restrictions, and so on. Complementary services such as bingo, bake sales, and bazaars will yield some revenue after cost and also tend to increase the cash and time donations to the church.

Thus, we see that marketing planning can be aided by elaborating the relevant revenue and cost elements and seeing what each suggests in the way of appropriate marketing actions.

DECIDING ON THE OPTIMAL LEVEL OF MARKETING EXPENDITURES

Many nonprofit organizations that turn to formal marketing raise the question, "What is the proper amount to spend on marketing?" One college president specifically asked: "How many marketing dollars should we budget to increase our enrollment by 10 percent?" Unfortunately, the answer is not simple. We will describe the five major approaches available to organizations to establish their marketing budgets.

Affordable Method.   Many organizations set the marketing budget on the basis of what they think they can afford. Thus, a college president will assess all the competing claims for funds and arrive at an arbitrary residual amount that can be spent on recruitment, publicity, and fundraising efforts. Setting budgets in this way is tantamount to saying that the relationship between marketing expenditures and sales is unknown and unknowable. As long as the organization can spare some funds for marketing, this will be done as a form of insurance. The basic weakness is that this approach leads to a changing level of marketing expenditure each year, making it difficult to attain consistent long-run results.

Percentage-of-Sales Method.   Many organizations prefer to set their marketing budget as a specified percentage of sales (either current or anticipated). Thus, a private college might decide to spend 5 percent of the average annual tuition per recruited student to cover admissions office salaries, advertising, and brochure preparation. If the college aims to recruit 2,000 freshmen and 5 percent of the average tuition is $100, then the admissions office would receive a budget of $200,000.

The main advantage of the percentage-of-sales method is that it leads to a predictable budget each year, once the sales goal is set. It also keeps marketing costs within reasonable control. Nevertheless, the method has little else to recommend it. The method does not provide a logical basis for the choice of a specific percentage, except what has been done in the past or what competitors are doing. It discourages experimentation with counter-cyclical advertising, since if sales are down, by this method, marketing expenditures should decline also. It does not encourage the development of budgets on an opportunity basis.

Competitive-Based Method.   Some organizations set their marketing budgets specifically in relation to competitors' outlays. Thus, a college may decide on its marketing budget by investigating what its main competitor is spending on marketing. The college may decide to spend more, less, or the same. Assuming that the colleges are roughly the same size, it would spend more if it wants to overtake or surpass the other college. It would spend less if it believes that it can use its funds more efficiently or influentially. It would spend the same if it believes that the competitor has figured out the proper amount to spend or if it believes that maintaining competitive parity would avoid an aggressive reaction by the competitor.

Knowing what the competition is spending on marketing is undoubtedly useful information. Basing one's spending on this information alone is not warranted, however. Marketing objectives, resources, and opportunities are likely to differ so much among organizations that the budget of one organization is hardly a guide for others to follow.

Objective-and-Task Method.   The objective-and-task method calls upon marketers to develop their budget by (1) defining their marketing objectives as specifically as possible, (2) determining the tasks that must be performed to achieve these objectives, and (3) estimating the costs of performing these tasks. The sum of these costs is the proposed marketing budget.

As an example, consider the private college that seeks to recruit 2,000 freshmen. The admissions office might estimate, on the basis of past experience, that the college would have to mail 20,000 letters to select high school seniors, which would result in approximately 8,000 inquiries, which would produce 4,000 applications, 3,000 admissions, and finally 2,000 acceptances. Each step requires a specific set of activities, the cost of each of which can be estimated. Table 12-2 shows a hypothetical estimate of costs involved in recruiting 2,000 freshmen. The admissions director builds the marketing budget by defining the objectives, identifying the required tasks, and costing them.

This method of setting the marketing budget is superior to the preceding methods. It requires that management think through its objectives and marketing activities. Its major limitation is its failure to consider alternative marketing objectives and marketing budgets in the search for the optimal

Table 12-2

HYPOTHETICAL BUDGET FOR COLLEGE RECRUITING

20,000 leads	Purchase of names	$ 4,000
	Mailing cost	20,000
	Office processing	6,000
	Staff costs, including travel	50,000
	Advertising	33,000
8,000 inquiries	Staff cost	16,000
	Mailing cost	24,000
4,000 applications	Staff cost	40,000
	Mailing cost	2,000
2,000 acceptances	Staff cost	4,000
	Mailing cost	1,000
		$200,000

NOTE: Cost per recruited student = $200,000/2,000 = $100.

course of action. We now turn to what is theoretically the soundest method for setting the marketing budget.

Sales Response Optimization Method.   Sales response optimization requires that the manager estimate the relation between sales response and alternative levels of the marketing budget. The estimate is captured in the sales response function, which is defined as follows:

> A **sales response function** forecasts the likely sales volume during a specified time period associated with different possible levels of a marketing element.

The best-known sales response function is the demand function, illustrated in Figure 12-1A. This function shows that the lower the price, the higher sales are in any given period. In the illustration, a price of $24 leads to sales of 8,000 units in that period, but a price of $16 would have led to sales of 14,000 units in that period. The illustrated demand curve is curvilinear, although other shapes are possible.

Suppose that the marketing variable is not price but total marketing dollars spent on sales force, advertising, and other marketing activities. In this case, the sales response function is likely to resemble Figure 12-1B. This function states that the more the organization spends in a given period on marketing effort, the higher the sales are likely to be. The particular function is S-shaped, although other shapes are possible. The S-shaped function says that low levels of marketing expenditure are not likely to produce many sales. The reason is that in most competitive markets a minimal level of marketing effort is necessary merely to attract notice. Higher levels of marketing expenditure per period produce much higher levels of sales. Very high expenditures per period, however, may not add much more sales and would represent "marketing overkill." Thus, at the high end of the curve, sales response would again flatten out.

The occurrence of eventually diminishing returns in response to increases in marketing expenditures is plausible for a number of reasons. First, there is an upper limit to the total potential demand for any particular product. The easier sales prospects are sold first; the more recalcitrant sales prospects remain. As the upper limit is approached, it becomes increasingly expensive to stimulate further sales. Second, as an organization steps up its marketing effort, its competitors are likely to do the same, with the net result that each organization experiences increasing sales resistance. Third, if sales were to increase at an increasing rate throughout, natural monopolies would result. A single organization would tend to take over in each industry because of the greater level of its marketing effort. Yet this is contrary to what we observe in industry.

How can a marketing manager estimate the sales response function? Essentially, three methods are available. The first is the *statistical method,* in which the manager gathers data on past sales and levels of marketing mix variables and estimates the sales response functions using statistical estimation procedures.[5] Despite its apparent attractiveness, there are a number of problems with this method. First, a relatively large amount of data is required for the estimation to be reliable. Second, it requires enough variation in the marketing mix variables that a significant range of the response

FIGURE 12-1

Sales Response Functions

 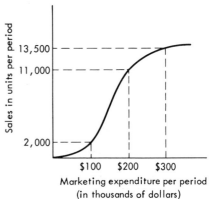

A. Price function   B. Marketing expenditure function

function is covered. Third, it requires that each historical data point represent a glimpse of the same response function and not the results of, say, two or three significantly different functions. The latter situation, however, may not be a serious problem if industry and competitve conditions have remained relatively stable over the analysis period.

The second method is the *experimental method,* which calls for deliberately varying the marketing expenditure levels in matched samples of geographical or other units and noting the resulting sales volume.[6] The third is the *judgmental method,* in which experts are asked to estimate the probable sales response.[7]

Once the sales response function is estimated, how is it used to set an optimal marketing budget? We would have to define the organization's objective. Suppose the organization wants to maximize its surplus. Graphically, we must introduce some further curves to find the point of optimal marketing expenditure. The analysis is shown in Figure 12-2. The key function that we start with is the sales response function. It resembles the S-shaped sales response function in the earlier Figure 12-1B except for two differences. First, sales response is expressed in terms of sales dollars instead of sales units, so that we can find the surplus-maximizing marketing expenditure. Second, the sales response function is shown as starting above zero sales on the argument that some sales might be made even in the absence of marketing expenditures.

To find the optimal marketing expenditure, the marketing manager subtracts all nonmarketing costs from the *sales response function* to derive

FIGURE 12-2

Relationship between Sales Volume, Marketing Expenditures, and Surplus

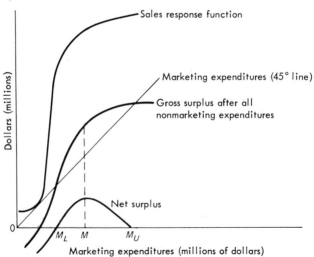

the *gross surplus curve*. Next, marketing expenditures are drawn in such a way that a dollar on one axis is projected as a dollar on the other axis. This amounts to a 45° line when the axes are scaled in identical dollar intervals. The *marketing expenditures curve* is then subtracted from the *gross surplus curve* to derive the *net surplus curve*. The net surplus curve shows positive net surplus with marketing expenditures between M_L and M_U, which could be defined as the rational range of marketing expenditure. The net surplus curve reaches a maximum at M. Therefore, the marketing expenditure that would maximize net surplus is $\$M$.

DEVELOPING A COST-EFFECTIVE MARKETING MIX

The impact of a given marketing budget on demand depends not only on the size of the budget, but also on how the budget is allocated to the various marketing acitivities. An organization has many options concerning how to spend a given budget. A college recruitment office, for example, can spend the marketing budget on recruiting staff, direct mail, media advertising, marketing research, publicity, and so on. The key task is to decide, for any given marketing objective, on the most cost-effective marketing mix.

Before looking at how the marketing mix *should be* established, let us consider how it *is* established in practice. Most organizations develop rules of thumb to guide the budget's allocation to marketing activities. One college may find that sending out recruiters to select high schools produces the greatest number of applications and thus decide to commit over 50 percent of its budget to supporting a recruiting staff. Another college may find that direct mail works well in producing inquiries and make this the largest part of its budget. After a certain division of the funds gets established, management tends to adhere to it year after year. Management only gives thought to a drastic redeployment of its budget if major changes occur in the known effectiveness or cost of different marketing tools. The cost of travel, for example, has recently increased so much that college recruiters are reducing the number of high school campuses they visit and increasing the use of mail and telephone recruiting. In principle, each marketing element can substitute for another to some extent. A college can seek more students by lowering tuition, or increasing the number of recruiters, or using more direct mail. The organization must constantly try to assess the relative sales productivity of these different tools. This is another reason why marketing departments should be created—mainly to achieve administrative coordination over all of the interrelated tools of marketing.

THEORY OF THE OPTIMAL MARKETING MIX

We want to explore how the optimal marketing mix would be determined in principle. Assume that a college recruiting office uses advertising and sales forces as the two major elements of the marketing mix. Clearly, there are an infinite number of combinations of spending on these two items. This is shown in Figure 12-3A. If there are no constraints on advertising and sales force expenditure, then every point in the A–S plane shown in Figure 12-3A is a possible marketing mix. An arbitrary line drawn from the origin, called a *constant-mix line,* shows the set of all marketing mixes where the two tools are in a fixed ratio but where the budget varies. Another arbitrary line, called a *constant-budget line,* shows a set of varying mixes that would be affordable with a fixed marketing budget.

Associated with every possible marketing mix is a resulting sales level. Three sales levels are shown in Figure 12-3A. The marketing mix (A_1S_2)— calling for a small budget and a rough equality between advertising and sales force—is expected to produce sales of Q_1. The marketing mix (A_2S_1) involves the same budget with more expenditure on advertising than on sales force; this is expected to produce slightly higher sales, Q_2. The mix (A_3S_3) calls for a larger budget but a relatively equal split between advertising and sales force, and a sales estimate of Q_3. Given these and many other possible marketing mixes, the marketer's job is to find the sales equation that predicts the Qs.

For a given marketing budget, the money should be divided among the various marketing tools in a way that gives the same marginal profit on the marginal dollar spent on each tool. A geometrical version of the solution is shown in Figure 12-3B. Here we are looking down at the A–S plane shown in Figure 12-3A. A constant-budget line is shown, indicating all the alternative marketing mixes that could be achieved with this budget. The curved lines are called *iso-sales curves.* An iso-sales curve shows the different mixes of advertising and sales force that would produce a given level of sales. It is

FIGURE 12-3

The Sales Function Associated with Two Marketing Mix Elements

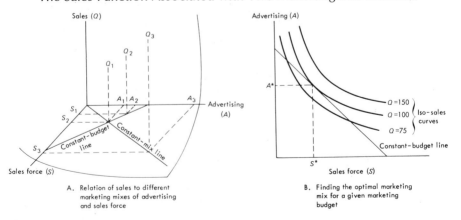

A. Relation of sales to different marketing mixes of advertising and sales force

B. Finding the optimal marketing mix for a given marketing budget

Table 12-3

MARKETING MIXES AND ESTIMATED NUMBER OF INQUIRIES

Marketing Mix No.	Price (P)	Advertising (A)	Sales Force (S)	Inquiries (Q)	Surplus ($)
1.	$16	$10,000	$10,000	12,400	$16,400
2.	16	10,000	50,000	18,500	13,000
3.	16	50,000	10,000	15,100	−7,400
4.	16	50,000	50,000	22,600	−2,400
5.	24	10,000	10,000	5,500	19,000
6.	24	10,000	50,000	8,200	16,800
7.	24	50,000	10,000	6,700	−4,200
8.	24	50,000	50,000	10,000	2,000

a projection into the A–S plane of the set of points resulting from horizontal slicing of the sales function shown in Figure 12-3A at a given level of sales. Figure 12-3B shows iso-sales curves for three different sales levels: 75, 100, and 150 units. Given the budget line, it is not possible to attain sales of more than 100 units. The optimum marketing mix is shown at the point of tangency between the budget line and the last-touching iso-sales curve above it. Consequently, the marketing mix (A^*S^*), which calls for somewhat more advertising than sales force, is the sales-maximizing (and in this case profit-maximizing) marketing mix.[8]

PRACTICAL METHOD FOR DETERMINING THE OPTIMAL MARKETING MIX

The preceding theory can be turned into a practical method for evaluating different marketing mixes. Suppose a college admissions director, Ms. Barbara Smith, has to make three decisions regarding the recruitment program: the application fee *(P)*, the amount to spend on advertising *(A)*, and the amount to spend on the sales force *(S)*. Last year, the office charged $16 for an application fee and spent $10,000 on advertising and another $10,000 on sales force. The office now wants to consider possibly departing from this low price, low sales force strategy, which has drawn around 12,400 inquiries. Barbara Smith is considering raising the application fee to $24, and possibly spending as much as $50,000 on either advertising or sales force or both. She develops a set of alternative marketing mix strategies from among which to make a choice. Suppose Ms. Smith generates the eight strategies shown in the first three columns of Table 12-3 (the first listed strategy is the one used last year). These strategies were formed by assuming a high and low level for each of the three marketing variables.

Her next step is to estimate the likely number of inquiries (Q) that would be attained with each alternative mix. These estimates cannot come out of statistical analysis of past data because her office never charged an application fee of $24 or spent more than approximately $20,000 on marketing. She and her associates have to make educated guesses based on their "feel" for the market. The resulting estimates are shown in the next-to-last column of Table 12-3. The whole table represents Barbara Smith's picture of the sales response function $Q = f(P,A,S)$, where the number of inquiries is a function of price, advertising, and sales force.

The optimal marketing mix strategy will depend on the organization's objective. If the college wants to maximize the number of inquiries, the best strategy is marketing mix number 4, consisting of a low application fee of $16 and a high expenditure of $50,000 each on advertising and sales force. But the college should be aware of the cost of this marketing mix strategy. Suppose the admissions office's fixed costs are $38,000 and unit variable costs are $10 for each inquiry handled. Using the earlier surplus equation (12-4), we find:

$$S = (P - c)Q + D + G - F - M$$
$$S = (16 - 10)22,600 + 0 + 0 - 38,000 - \$100,000 = -\$2,400$$

That is, the admissions office will contract a deficit of $2,400 by using this strategy. The surpluses (deficits) yielded by the other strategies are shown in the last column of Table 12-3.

Suppose the admissions office wanted to avoid a deficit and in fact wanted to maximize its surplus at the inquiry stage of the recruiting process to help pay for the costs of evaluating applications later. Then the optimal marketing mix strategy would be number 5, a fee of $24 and a low budget of $10,000 each spent on advertising and sales force. Unfortunately, although it will yield a high surplus of $19,000, this mix will produce only 5,500 inquiries, far fewer than the number needed to result in the target level of enrollment. The main point is that Ms. Smith should prepare these sales response estimates in order to determine the strategy that would produce the best balance among the competing objectives of inquiries and cost. Marketing mix strategy number 2 would produce substantially more inquiries than last year (18,500 instead of 12,400) at a slightly lower surplus ($13,000 instead of $16,400), and thus seems to be more attractive than last year's strategy.

USING COST-EFFECTIVENESS ANALYSIS FOR MARKETING MIX DETERMINATION

Once a global marketing mix strategy is chosen, there are further marketing mix decisions of a more tactical nature to make. Suppose the admissions office decided to use global marketing mix number 4 because it is anxious to produce the largest possible number of inquiries, even though this will cause a deficit at this stage of the admissions process. In deciding to spend $50,000 on advertising, it must allocate this to competing advertising media, such as direct mail, newspaper ads, and radio ads. As an aid to determining the optimal media mix, the admissions office can use *cost-effectiveness analysis.* Cost-effectiveness analysis is the general name given to researching the effect of variations in cost on results. Figure 12-4 shows Barbara Smith's estimates of how many inquiries would be produced by using different advertising media at different levels. She sees direct mail producing a linear growth in inquiries. Newspaper advertising is seen to produce a low level of response if used at a low level, increasing returns if used at a medium level, and diminishing returns if used at a high level. Radio is seen to produce a high number of inquiries if used at a low level and rapidly diminishing incremental returns thereafter.

Given the cost-effectiveness functions shown in Figure 12-4, which method is the most cost-effective to produce inquiries? The answer depends on how many inquiries the college is seeking. If the college would be satisfied to attract fewer than n_1 inquiries, then radio is the most cost-effective medium. If the college is trying to attract between n_1 and n_2 inquiries, then direct mail is the most cost-effective medium. If the college is trying to attract between n_2 and n_3 inquiries, then newspaper advertising is the most cost-effective single method. If the college is trying to attract more than n_3 inquiries, then direct mail is once again the most cost-effective single medium.

If these media reach entirely different segments of the market, it would

FIGURE 12-4

Cost-Effectiveness Functions

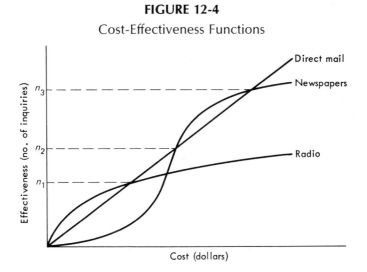

be better to use a combination of media to attract a given number of inquiries. Each medium would be used to a level at which the marginal productivities of all media are equal.

ADDITIONAL FACTORS INFLUENCING THE CHOICE OF THE MARKETING MIX

We have examined the appropriate marketing mix in terms of sales response functions. We will now go behind those sales response functions to see what real factors influence the appropriate mix. The appropriate marketing mix is influenced by the following four factors: (1) the type of consumer—individual versus organizational, (2) the communications task to be accomplished, (3) the stage of the offer life cycle, and (4) the economic outlook.

The Type of Consumer—Individual versus Organization.   Historically, there has been a considerable difference in the marketing mixes used by organizations selling services to households and those selling to other organizations. The mix differences are illustrated in Figure 12-5. Advertising is believed to be the most important tool in marketing to households and personal selling the most important tool in marketing to organizations. Sales promotion is considered to have a smaller influence, but one that is equally important in both markets. And publicity is considered to be even less important, but again its influence is equal in both markets. These proportions, however, are not to be taken as authoritative, and many cases exist where marketers adopted different proportions with good success.

FIGURE 12-5

Communications Mix as a Function of Type of Market
and Buyer Readiness Stage

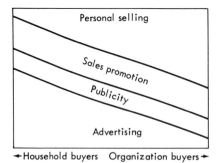

A. Normal marketing mix for
household buyers versus
organization buyers

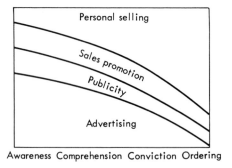

B. Marketing mix cost
effectiveness at different
buyer readiness stages

The Communications Task.   The optimal marketing mix also depends on the stage of buyer readiness at which the market is presumed to be. Figure 12-5B shows the general findings of a number of studies.[9] Advertising, sales promotion, and publicity are the most cost-effective tools at the initial stage in building buyer awareness; they are better than "cold calls" from sales representatives. Advertising is highly cost-effective in producing comprehension at the next stage, with personal selling coming in second. Buyer conviction is influenced most by personal selling, followed by advertising. Finally, placing an order is predominantly a function of the sales call, with an assist from sales promotion.[10]

These findings have important practical implications. First, the organization could effect promotional economies by cutting back on the involvement of salespeople in the early stages of the selling job so that they can concentrate on the vital phase of closing the sale. Second, when advertising is relied on to do more of the job, it should take different forms, some addressed to building product awareness and some to producing comprehension.

The Stage of the Offer Life Cycle.   The effectiveness of marketing expenditures varies at different stages of the offer life cycle, as will be discussed in greater detail in Chapter 14. The typical offer life cycle has four stages: introduction, growth, maturity and decline.

Advertising and promotion are important in the introduction stage because the market is not aware of the offer, and the cost per exposure is low. Sales promotion in particular stimulates interest in and trials of the new offer.

In the growth stage, word-of-mouth processes begin to work for the new offer and partially replace or supplement the organization's promotion efforts. If the organization wants to build its market share, it should continue to promote vigorously during the growth stage.

The maturity stage is marked by intensified promotional expenditures to meet competition and to advertise new uses and features. There is generally an increase in *sales promotion* effort relative to *advertising* effort.

In the decline stage, many organizations reduce their promotion expenditures to improve their profit margins and turn their products into "cash cows." Publicity is cut down, the sales force gives the product only minimal attention, and advertising is cut down to a reminder level. Sales promotion is probably the most exercised promotion tool at this stage.

The Economic Outlook.   Organizations would do well to revise their marketing mixes with shifts in the economic outlook. During inflation, for example, buyers become highly price-conscious. They look for value. The organization can do at least three things to respond: (1) it can increase its sales promotion relative to advertising, since people are looking for deals;

(2) it can emphasize value and price in its communications; and (3) it can develop messages that help customers know how and where to buy intelligently.

SUMMARY

This chapter deals with four tasks in developing and choosing cost-effective marketing programs.

The first task is to choose between alternative products or programs. Here cost/benefit analysis is helpful. The programs with the highest benefit-cost ratio are preferred. To calculate benefits and costs, monetary and quantitative measures are preferred, although ultimately nonquantifiable benefits should be taken into account.

The second task is to choose between alternative marketing objectives. Expressing the situation in terms of a "profit" equation allows the evaluation of different objectives. The most common objectives of nonprofit organizations are surplus maximization, revenue maximization, usage maximization, usage targeting, full cost recovery, partial cost recovery, budget maximization, and producer satisfaction maximization.

The third task is to decide on the marketing expenditure level. Organizations decide on their expenditure level using one of five methods: affordable method, percentage-of-sales method, competitive-based method, objective-and-task method, and sales response optimization method.

The fourth task is to develop an optimal marketing mix of product, price, place, and promotion. The optimal marketing mix can be set if the sales response function for each separate marketing mix element is known. The appropriate marketing mix varies with the type of buyer (individuals or organizations), the communication task, the stage of the offer life cycle, and the economic outlook.

QUESTIONS

1. A public librarian is considering two alternative capital expenditures. One would add a "story area" for future programs of films and story-telling for younger children. The area could also be used to keep young children amused while older family members look for materials elsewhere in the library. The other project would add an inventory of original art for low-cost rental. The projects require the same investments. How would the librarian quantify the benefits and costs of each program to help choose between them?

2. The Federal Trade Commission receives complaints about products, services, and marketing practices from many consumers. Some staff members feel that more weighting should be given to the problems of disadvantaged consumers than those of middle-class and higher income consumers. How could the FTC develop a differential weighting scheme?

3. The text mentions eight alternative marketing/financial objectives for nonprofits. Give examples of how each might apply to the U.S. Army's recruiting program.

4. The S-shaped response function in Figure 12-1 is often used in the private sector. Is there any reason to believe it would *not* be appropriate in a nonprofit environment? Two alternative forms would, of course, be more-or-less linear functions or convex functions reflecting diminishing returns for increased expenditures at *all* levels.

5. A symphony orchestra manager has calculated separate response functions for radio, television, and direct mail expenditures. She thinks, however, that they may interact; for example, a direct mail campaign would be *more* effective if it follows a television campaign than if it doesn't. How can she incorporate possible interactions into her marketing mix decision-making?

NOTES

1. "Benefit/Cost Analyses for Health Care Systems," *Annals of the American Academy of Political and Social Science,* January 1972, pp. 90–99, esp. p. 94.

2. Weinberg has argued in favor of theatres charging a low rather than a high price. His argument is that a low price will lead to a larger audience, and a larger audience will lead to more people who know about the theatre and who will contribute money to its support. See Charles B. Weinberg, "Marketing Mix Decision Rules for Nonprofit Organizations," in Jagdish Sheth, ed., *Research in Marketing,* Vol. 3 (Chicago: JAI Press, 1980), pp. 191–234.

3. Michael Etgar and Brian T. Ratchford, "Marketing Management and Marketing Concept: Their Conflict in Non-Profit Organizations," *1974 Proceedings* (Chicago: American Marketing Association, 1974).

4. John McKnight, "Professional Service Business," *Social Policy,* November-December 1977, pp. 110–16.

5. As an example of this method, see David B. Montgomery and Alvin J. Silk, "Estimating Dynamic Effects of Market Communications Expenditures," *Management Science,* June 1972, pp. 485–501.

6. As an example, see Russell Ackoff and James R. Emshoff, "Advertising Research at Anheuser-Busch," *Sloan Management Review,* Winter 1975, pp. 1–15.

7. See Philip Kotler, "A Guide to Gathering Expert Estimates," *Business Horizons,* October 1970, pp. 79–87.

8. For additional theory, see Robert Dorfman and Peter O. Steiner, "Optimal Advertising and Optimal Quality," *American Economic Review,* December 1954, pp. 826–36; and Robert Ferber and P. J. Verdoorn, *Research Methods in Economics and Business* (New York: Macmillan, 1962), p. 535.

9. "What IBM Found About Ways to Influence Selling," *Business Week,*

December 5, 1959, pp. 69–70; and Harold C. Cash and William J. Crissy, "Comparison of Advertising and Selling," in *The Psychology of Selling,* Vol. 12 (Flushing, N.Y.: Personnel Development Associates, 1965).

10. Swinyard and Ray have challenged the finding that advertising is more effective when it precedes the sales call. They found that female household residents who were contacted by a Red Cross volunteer followed by some mailings expressed a higher intention to donate blood than a similar group who first received the mailings and then received the sales call. See William R. Swinyard and Michael L. Ray, "Advertising-Selling Interactions: An Attribution Theory Experiment," *Journal of Marketing Research,* November 1977, pp. 509–16.

CHAPTER 13

Developing New Offerings

Performing arts centers traditionally operate at a deficit and so constantly search for ways to broaden their offerings. In the early 1980s the associate director of Krannert Center for the Performing Arts at the University of Illinois realized that many potential patrons who were obviously in the socially active lifestyle group considered going out to dinner with friends as the major alternative to attending the arts. But having to rush dinner before an 8:00 p.m. performance was not very graceful, let alone relaxing. So they often avoided the arts altogether. The Krannert Center executive, however, decided to open a Bavarian pastry shop in one unused corner of the performing center's lobby. Sales in the pastry shop were intended both for those interested in lunch rather than art, as well as for theater and symphony patrons interested in an evening of arts entertainment combined with dinner or dessert.

The Intermezzo pastry shop has been a great success. An estimated one in five attendees of performances at Krannert Center purchases something at the pastry shop before or after the concert. The original investment of $75,000 was paid off in twenty months, well in advance of the projected four years. Sales currently run at $180,000, up twenty-two percent over two years earlier. The shop is now venturing into the business of catering meetings and a separate gift shop was opened in 1982. Management now believes strongly that the pastry shop is not only an important source of additional revenue for KCPA but also has brought about changes in attendees' and the community's feelings about the approachability of the center itself.

A prime characteristic of the nonprofit environment in the late 1980s is the extent to which competition has run rampant. Nonprofits once assumed that the future was rosy, that "friendly rivals" would *never* try seriously to take away their market share, and that the coffers of generous donors were bottomless. No longer. To survive, nonprofits have been forced to innovate. Indeed, the successful nonprofits in such diverse areas as education, social services, hospital care, and the arts have had to develop new products and services and innovative ways to market them and their traditional offerings just to stay even with their enterprising competitors. In this chapter, we will consider the problem of developing strategies for new offerings. In the next chapter, we shall consider the problems of launching and managing such offerings into the competitive marketplace.

OFFER MANAGEMENT—A PROBLEM OF STRATEGIC PLANNING

Offer management should be treated as a problem of strategy. The first task is to determine the basic mission of the organization with respect to its offerings. The nonprofit organization can adopt nine basic strategies (see Table 13-1). First, it can decide to focus on its existing offerings and existing markets (cell 1). For this strategy, it can choose among three substrategies. It can seek to grow by more actively penetrating its existing market either through market expansion or through inducing patronage-switching by those already in the market. It can decide not to grow significantly, but become more efficient at marketing to its present clients. Or it can choose to maintain the status quo. While it may seem that neither of the last two

Table 13-1

OFFER STRATEGY OPTIONS FOR NONPROFIT ORGANIZATIONS

	Existing Offerings	New Offerings: Similar	New Offerings: Dissimilar
Existing Markets	1. a. Market penetration b. Cost reduction c. Share maintenance	4. Offer extension	7. Offer development
New Markets: Similar	2. Market Extension	5. Continuous Diversification	8. Offer Diversification
New Markets: Dissimilar	3. Market Development	6. Market Diversification	9. Radical Diversification

strategic postures would appeal to many organizations, there are two situations in which they make sense:

> a. *Declining markets.* If the market demand is declining, as in the need for funding for polio research and treatment, the marketer might want to treat the program as a "cash cow," pull out resources, or become more efficient, thus producing a surplus to be used elsewhere.
> b. *New competition.* A market leader always faces a rearguard action when new competitors enter. Thus, a major hospital may be perfectly content to maintain its present level of emergency room volume after a new emergency care center enters the market.

The second posture the organization can take is to seek out new markets for its existing offerings (cells 2 and 3). Firms can add market segments that are similar to their present markets, as when contraceptive social marketers seek to take programs that worked in Bangladesh and introduce them in nearby countries like India or Nepal (cell 2, market extension). More daring and therefore more challenging would be an attempt to adapt the programs to more dissimilar markets such as West or East Africa, Tibet, or aboriginal tribes in New Guinea (cell 3, market development).

Carrying out these strategies does not require major changes in the organization's offerings. Rather, it requires more attention to other marketing mix variables like advertising, distribution channels, personal selling, and price and cost management. It can also involve minor aspects of offer management such as packaging, redesign of features, and so on.

In this chapter, our attention turns to the six strategies suggested in Table 13-1 involving new offerings. The nonprofit organization can add new offerings that are relatively similar or relatively dissimilar to their present offerings. In either case, they can focus on existing markets (cells 4 and 7), similar new markets (cells 5 and 8), or dissimilar new markets (cells 6 and 9). Clearly, the riskiest stance of all is cell 9, where entirely new offerings (especially offerings new to the world) are brought to radically different markets. Getting very young children to learn to read by speaking into a voice-reading computer would be an example of such a venture. A system of this type is currently being explored by Educational Development Associates of Newton, Massachusetts.

Consider an organization that has explored offerings in all six of the new offering cells in Table 13-1, Population Development Associates (PDA), Thailand's major contraceptive social marketing organization:

> 1. *Offer Extension (cell 4).* PDA has added new *types* of contraceptives (that is, new oral pill formulations) to serve its existing customer markets.
> 2. *Offer Development (cell 7).* It has made syringes, aspirin, and other noncontraceptive products available to villagers in the homes of its village contraceptive distributors and change agents.

3. *Continuous Diversification (cell 5).* PDA has added noncontraceptive health care services in its family planning clinics, to which any person can come.

4. *Offer Diversification (cell 8).* PDA has begun helping households in the villages it serves with procedures and funding for building much-needed water tanks for storing rain water.

5. *Market Diversification (cell 6).* PDA has developed a program for providing health tests in schools and hospitals, using excess capacity among its full-time medical staff.

6. *Radical Diversification (cell 9).* PDA has taken advantage of serendipitous circumstances and is developing programs to market Czechoslovakian tractors through its rural field offices and to manage a small tourist resort in a remote province of Thailand.

As for these radical diversification ventures, a recent evaluation concluded that PDA management lacked a systematic approach to developing and introducing new offerings. Most ventures came about serendipitously—for example, through personal contacts with possible suppliers or chance conversations or visits to programs in other countries.

These new ventures are the result of the natural enthusiasm of young organizations still in their growth phase. The remainder of this chapter will concern itself with the question of how a *mature* nonprofit organization ought to carry out an offer strategy involving *new offerings.*

It should be noted at the outset that nonprofit organizations have greater hurdles to overcome than for-profit firms with regard to successfully launching new offerings:

1. Nonprofit organizations have typically not faced or recognized competition and therefore lack a spur to do better.

2. Nonprofits usually lack the budgets to experiment with new products or methods. Furthermore, legislators, their boards, or both often refuse to support innovation.

3. Nonprofit managers are typically not entrepreneurial. Their training consists of a specialty (for example, social work, art history, etc.) or administration with an emphasis on running existing organizations rather than creating new ones.

4. Nonprofit organizations see their services as necessary and not requiring justification or marketing.

Nevertheless, every nonprofit sector contains a few organizations that can be called "innovators." However, a will to innovate is not enough. Many organizations launch new services that fail.

A 300-bed hospital in southern Illinois got the bright idea of establishing an Adult Day Care Program as a solution to its underutilized space. It designed a whole floor to serve senior citizens who required personal care and services in an ambulatory setting during the day, but who would return home each evening. The cost was $16 a day to the patient's family, and transportation was to be provided or paid for by the patient's family. About the only research that was done on this concept was to note that a lot of elderly people lived within a three-mile radius. The Adult Day Care Center was opened with a capacity to handle thirty patients. Only two signed up!

There are many reasons why this and similar new programs fail:

1. A top administrator pushes the idea through in spite of the lack of supporting evidence.
2. There are poor organizational systems for handling ideas for new offerings (poor criteria, poor procedures, poor coordination of departments).
3. There is poor market size measurement, forecasting, and market research.
4. There is poor marketing planning, such as poor positioning, poor segmentation, underbudgeting, and overpricing.
5. The distinctiveness of the offer or of consumer benefits is not sufficiently clear.
6. The offer is poorly designed.
7. Development costs are unexpectedly high.
8. The competitive response is unexpectedly intense.
9. Promotion is inadequate.

In the sections to follow, we shall describe processes and tools to overcome these problems.

THE NEW PRODUCT DEVELOPMENT PROCESS

An organization that wishes to be entrepreneurial must set up systems that will lead to successful new product launches. There is an effective methodology for introducing new products, which, while it does not guarantee success, usually raises the probability of success. Figure 13-1 shows the overall steps involved in new product development. These steps are described in the following sections.

IDEA GENERATION

Organizations differ in their need for new product ideas. Some organizations are quite busy carrying out their current activities and do not need new things to do. A social security office, for example, is mandated to carry out certain procedures and is not interested, or even legally able, to consider undertaking new ventures not related to its main business. Other organizations need one or two big new ideas because their main business is taking a turn for the worse. In the early 1970s, the March of Dimes had to come up with an entirely new focus when polio was effectively controlled. Still other organizations need several new ideas simply to keep up with the changing environment. Colleges, for example, need to consider new courses and pro-

FIGURE 13-1

Major Stages in New-Product Development

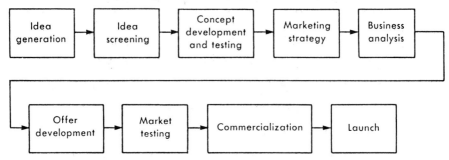

grams to meet the changing interests of the public. Similarly, the YMCA needs to develop new programs as interest in some of its existing programs fades.

The idea generation stage is most relevant to organizations that need one or more ideas to maintain or expand their services. Indeed, it may be argued that, given the high failure rate of many new ideas, the more ideas an organization generates—and the more diverse they are—the more chance there will be of finding *successful* ideas. Ideas can occur spontaneously from the following "natural" sources:

- Personal inspiration of one or more members of the organization.
- Serendipitous stimuli from the environment—for example, learning of a new idea from a competitor or in discussion with nonprofit managers from other parts of the country or the world.
- Client requests for new offerings or modification of existing offerings.

Such sources have two major shortcomings. First, they obviously rely on a chance combination of an idea appearing *and* management's alertness in recognizing it. Reliance on these approaches may be acceptable for a fledgling nonprofit with a limited budget. However, they are definitely not the type of approaches a mature nonprofit organization ought to adopt. These casual approaches have a second problem. As noted by Crompton: "There is a great deal of evidence which suggests that many efforts to produce new programs which meet client needs are incestuous. That is, there is a tendency to reach for prior experiences, prior approaches, or moderate distortions of old answers, as opposed to really searching for new ideas. We become victimized by habit."[1]

If an organization is to be both systematic and creative in its idea generation, four steps must be taken.

1. A *commitment* must be made to routinely and formally seek new ideas.
2. *Responsibility* for this task must be specifically assigned to someone or some group.
3. A *procedure* must be put in place for *systematically* seeking new ideas.
4. The procedure must contain a *creative* component if truly new ideas are sought.

Procedures for Gathering New Ideas.   Establishing the idea generation *procedure* involves the organization in outlining all possible sources for new ideas and then a strategy for generating or collecting ideas routinely from each source. Major sources and procedures for mining them are listed here:

1. *Similar organizations*
   (a) A jointly funded *clearing house* could be established to share new ideas.
   (b) Routine visits or telephone conversations with similar organizations on *specific dates* (for example, the first week of every February and every July) should be scheduled.
2. *Competitors*
   (a) If the competitor has publicly traded stock, a few shares should be purchased to acquire regular reports.
   (b) If board meetings are open to the public, someone should be assigned to attend them.
3. *Journals, newspapers, magazines*
   (a) Probable written sources of ideas should be identified, subscriptions acquired, and someone (or several people) assigned to peruse these sources routinely.
   (b) A clipping service might be subscribed to.
   (c) A librarian might be hired and assigned these tasks.
   (d) A computer-based information retrieval system could be subscribed to.
4. *Conferences, trade shows, lectures*
   (a) People should be routinely assigned to attend important gatherings to collect ideas and useful literature.
5. *Customers and middlemen*
   (a) The organization should *solicit* customers for their ideas rather than wait until they spontaneously offer them. Many organizations obtain most of their best new ideas by soliciting or actively listening to customers.[2]
6. *Employees and staff*
   (a) The organization should *solicit* employees for suggestions and reward them monetarily or in some other way.

In this idea generation system, three features should be applied to each component. First, where relevant, specific dates should be set for carrying out each information-gathering technique. Second, a formal reporting and assessment mechanism should be developed to assure that each idea can come before the appropriate group for consideration. Finally, the system should be *unblocked*. Lower-level managers should not be able to kill ideas as "too outrageous" or "not really appropriate for us right now." Such judgments must be top management's.

One technique for improving the likelihood that new ideas will emerge is to assign responsibilities to someone who might be called an *idea manager*. Kotler has recently suggested that an idea manager would perform six major functions, which can together be roughly classified as *idea generation and advocacy.*

> 1. *Idea finding.* The idea manager would conduct an organized and continuous search for new ideas by reading journals and newsletters, attending conferences, and talking to consultants.
> 2. *Idea stimulating.* The idea manager would use creativity-generating techniques to stimulate others to create new and useful ideas.
> 3. *Idea collecting.* The idea manager would serve as a receiving station for the good ideas spotted by others. Everyone would know that they should send their good ideas to this person.
> 4. *Idea evaluating.* The idea manager would do a preliminary analysis and evaluation of the ideas that flow in and make an effort to identify the really good ones, those that help the target customers and the organization.
> 5. *Idea disseminating.* The idea manager would know to whom to send each worthwhile idea.
> 6. *Idea advocating.* The idea manager would act as an idea champion of the better ideas.[3]

Now the idea manger need not necessarily be a full-time person hired to do only this. On the contrary, this important responsibility *should be assigned to someone who has some power and stature in the organization.* Two good candidates are the managers of strategic planning and marketing. Both managers must produce new ideas that will ensure a future for their institution. It is essential, however, that the nonprofit organization's president "buy" the idea of assigning idea managment to one of these people.

Procedures for Stimulating Creativity.   The above techniques involve either routinely scanning or prodding various systems for ideas. This will yield a high proportion of at least modest ideas or extensions of existing approaches. If an organization seeks "breakthrough-quality" ideas, it can apply a number of proven techniques. Some techniques can be used by individuals; most are best done in groups where members can spark ideas off each other.[4]

Attribute Listing.   Here, the major attributes of the product, service or idea are listed and then each attribute is scrutinized to see if it can be adapted, minified, magnified, substituted, rearranged, reversed, or combined. The traditional approach to borrowing a book from a library, for example, involves (1) going to the library; (2) looking up the book in the card catalogue; (3) going to the shelf to obtain the book; (4) taking it to a central counter; (5) having the book stamped and the borrowing details recorded; (6) taking the book home; and (7) bringing it back to the library when the borrower is finished. The idea-generating process would involve trying to think of new ways to accomplish each of the seven steps to produce

greater "sales." Step 1, for example, could be done by using a telephone or
the mail; by using a computer terminal; by bringing the "library" to the borrower's home or neighborhood in a mobile van; by hiring a courier to bring
the book for a fee; or by asking the librarian to copy the necessary pages and
mail them to the borrower. Then one would proceed to steps 2 and 3, imag-
ining innovative ways to look up and retrieve the book, including voice-
activated computer systems and the use of automatic conveyor belts, or
even robots.[5]

Forced Relationships.   Here, several objects or elements are listed and
each is considered in relation to the other. Thus, a library list might include
children's storytelling hours, card catalogues, and reference books. An analysis of possible relationships might suggest stories to be told to children to
indirectly teach them what reference books are and how the library's catalogue can help find them.

Problem Analysis.   Here consumers are asked about problems they
encounter in making a particular exchange. Each problem can be the source
of new ideas. Library patrons, for example, could express frustration at
sometimes having to wait a long time to check out a book. The librarian
might think of installing some form of amusement—for example, a computer game, an interesting exhibit, or closed-circuit television—to distract
patrons while waiting.

Brainstorming.   Probably the best-known technique for forcing creativity, brainstorming involves putting six to eight people, preferably of diverse
backgrounds, together in a room and giving them a very broad problem
mandate. They are then told (1) to come up with as many solutions as possible; (2) that the wilder the solutions, the better; and (3) that nobody is to
evaluate—most particularly, criticize—*any idea at this stage.* The objective
is to place the participants in a nonthreatening environment where they can
let their imaginations soar as they use each other's input to suggest new and
(one hopes) increasingly creative solutions. William J. J. Gordon suggests
that it is sometimes useful to make the topic as broad as possible, such as,
"How can the library match people and ideas?" and only later in the session
narrow it to specific issues, such as, "How can a library use its limited budget to have the most reference material available for the most users?"[6]

IDEA SCREENING

Once the idea-generating system has accumulated a significant array of
ideas, some of them patently outlandish, some attempt must be made to
winnow the set to the most promising ideas. The purpose of idea screening
is to take a preliminary look at the new ideas and eliminate those that do
not warrant further attention. There is some chance that screening might

result in an excellent idea being prematurely dropped (a drop-error). What might be worse, however, is accepting a bad idea for further development (a go-error) as a result of not screening. Each idea that is developed takes substantial management time and money. The purpose of screening is, therefore, to eliminate all but the most promising ideas.

As an example, in the early seventies De Paul University was looking for ideas for new programs to expand its educational services in the greater Chicago area. Among the new program ideas were (1) a new program of women studies, (2) a new program of black studies, (3) a school of dentistry, (4) a new adult degree program, and (5) a weekend executive master's degree program in business. De Paul did not have the resources to launch more than one of these new programs, and so it needed a way to identify the most attractive program.

Several steps are necessary to ensure effective idea screening for an organization like De Paul:

1. A formal screening committee should be established to evaluate new ideas. The committee should include representatives of each key functional department that has expertise that bears on one or more of the proposed undertakings.
2. Regular meetings should be scheduled to evaluate new ideas.
3. Criteria should be developed against which the ideas are to be evaluated. The criteria would be consistently applied over many evaluation sessions. Examples of such criteria include the following:
   a. Size of potential target audience
   b. Size of financial investment necessary
   c. Probable demand on management's time and energy
   d. Newness of the idea to the target audience and organization
   e. Consequences for the organization's desired public image
   f. Extent of probable competition
   g. Likelihood of outside funding assistance
   h. "Downside" consequences if venture fails.
4. Weights for the criteria should be developed prior to *each* evaluation session. These weights should be set by top management since they will directly affect where the organization wishes to go in the future. Giving a heavy weight to "newness of idea to the organization" (a negative trait), for example, inevitably means that the organization will accept more ideas nearer to its present offerings. Alternatively, giving a low weight to this factor implies that the organization is more likely to undertake relatively bold innovations.
5. Prior to the committee evaluation meeting, one or more staff members should prepare briefs on each idea as a basis for group discussion. Each brief should present data that is relevant to each of the major criteria.
6. The group should meet and discuss each idea. Afterwards, they should rate each idea either individually or collectively on each criterion. (A form should be devised for this purpose.) Each evaluator (or the group as a whole) should also indicate how confident he or she is of the rating on each criterion.
7. A weighted value rating for each new idea should be computed along with a weighted certainty rating.
8. Candidate ideas should then be arranged by value and certainty ratings, as illustrated in Figure 13-2.

FIGURE 13-2

Hypothetical Array of New Programs for De Paul University

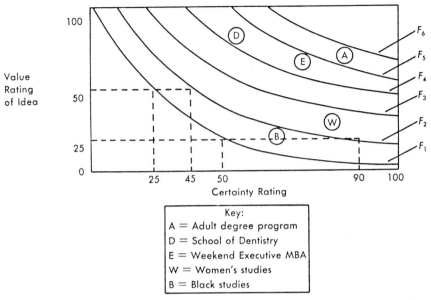

Key:
A = Adult degree program
D = School of Dentistry
E = Weekend Executive MBA
W = Women's studies
B = Black studies

9. The best ideas should be moved on to the next stage. These choices will involve management trade-offs between value and certainty ratings. These trade-offs are shown by the F equivalence curves in Figure 13-2. Thus F_1 shows that management feels that a new venture with a value rating of 50 and a certainty rating of 25 is just as acceptable as an idea with a value rating of 25 and a certainty rating of 50. Management would then decide how many projects to consider by using F_1, F_2, and so on, as the feasible frontier. If it chose F_5, for example, management would only consider the adult degree program; if it chose the more generous frontier F_3, it would also consider the executive MBA and the school of dentistry.[7]

CONCEPT DEVELOPMENT AND TESTING

Those ideas that survive screening must undergo further development into full concepts. It is important to distinguish between an idea, a concept, and an image. An *idea* is something the organization can see itself offering to the market. A *concept* is an elaborated version of the idea expressed in meaningful consumer terms. An *image* is the particular picture that consumers acquire of an actual or potential innovation.

Concept Development.   As a result of screening the various new program ideas, De Paul University decided the best one was a new adult degree program.[8] This is an offer *idea*. De Paul's task was to turn this idea into an appealing concept. Every idea can be turned into several concepts, not all of them equally attractive. Among the concepts that might be created around this idea are

- Concept 1. An evening program with a liberal arts orientation, mostly required courses, and no credit for past experience.
- Concept 2. An evening program with a career development orientation, much latitude in the courses that could be taken, and credit for past experience.
- Concept 3. An evening program with a general education orientation for people over fifty years of age who want a bachelor's degree.

Clearly, one idea can give rise to a number of alternative concepts.

Concept Testing. Concept testing calls for gathering the reactions of target consumers to each concept. Each concept should be presented in written form in enough detail to allow the respondent to understand it and express his or her level of interest. Here is an example of concept 2 in more elaborate form:

> An evening program, called the School for New Learning, with a career development orientation and much latitude in the courses that can be taken. The program would be open to persons over twenty-four years of age; lead to a bachelor's degree; give course credit for past experiences and skills that the individual has acquired; give only pass-fail grades; and involve a "learning contract" between the student and the school.

Target consumers are identified and interviewed about their reaction to this concept. One approach is to use questions like those in Table 13-2. The last question in Table 13-2, for example, assesses the consumer's *intention to act* and usually reads: "Would you definitely, probably, probably not, definitely not enroll in this program?" Suppose that 10 percent of the target consumers said "definitely will enroll" and another 5 percent said "probably will enroll." De Paul would apply this percentage (or a slightly lower one) to the corresponding size of the target market to estimate whether the estimated number of enrollees would be sufficient. Even then, the estimate is at best tentative because people often do not carry out their stated intentions. Nevertheless, by ranking the alternative concepts with target consumers in this way, De Paul would learn which product concept has the best market potential.

An alternative approach would involve the technique of conjoint analysis described in Chapter 3 (p. 67). Suppose DePaul identified key dimensions of the program offer and levels of each as follows:

1. Orientation: (a) liberal arts; (b) general education; (c) career development
2. Credit for past experience: (a) yes; (b) no
3. Student body: (a) mostly under 35; (b) mostly 35 to 50; (c) mostly over 50

Table 13-2

MAJOR QUESTIONS IN A CONCEPT TEST FOR A NEW EDUCATIONAL
PROGRAM

1. Is the concept of this adult degree evening program with its various features clear to you?
2. What do you see as reasons why you might enroll in this program?
3. What expectation would you have about the program's quality?
4. Does this program meet a real need of yours?
5. What improvements can you suggest in various features of this program?
6. Who would be involved in your decision about whether to enroll in this program?
7. How do you feel about the tuition cost of this program?
8. What competitive programs come to mind and which appeal to you the most?
9. Would you enroll in this program?

4. Cost per semester: (a) $800; (b) $950; (c) $1,200
5. Nightly attendance per week: (a) 4–5 times; (b) 2–3 times; (c) once.

The target audience could then be offered combinations of these dimensions described in some detail as potential program offerings (that is, concepts) and asked to rank them. This technique would then not only suggest which alternative is rated highest overall, but would indicate the implicit weights the target audience was assigning to each dimension.

MARKETING STRATEGY FORMULATION

At this point, the organization should develop a preliminary concept of the marketing strategy it would use to introduce the new program to the target audience. This is necessary so that the full revenue and cost implications of the new program can be evaluated in the next stage of business analysis.

The marketing strategy should be spelled out in a statement consisting of three parts. The first part describes the size, structure, and behavior of the target market, the intended positioning of the new offering in this market, and the volume and impact goals for the first few years. For De Paul, this might be as follows:

> The target market is adults over twenty-four living in the greater Chicago area who have never obtained a bachelor's degree but have the skills and motivation to seek one. This program will be differentiated from other programs by offering course credit for relevant past experience, as well as in its career

development emphasis. The school will seek a first-year enrollment of 60 students with a net loss not to exceed $100,000. The second year will aim for an enrollment of 100 persons and a net income of at least $20,000.

The second part of the marketing strategy statement outlines the offerings' intended price (if any), distribution strategy, and marketing budget for the first year.

> The new program will be offered at the downtown location of De Paul University. All courses will take place once a week in the evening from 6:00 to 9:00 P.M. Tuition will be $500 per course. The first year's promotion budget will be $80,000, $50,000 of which will be spent on advertising materials and media and the remainder on personal contact activities. Another $10,000 will be spent on marketing research to analyze and monitor the market.

The third part of the marketing strategy statement describes the intended long-run goals and marketing mix strategy over time:

> The university ultimately hopes to achieve a steady enrollment of 400 students in this degree program. When it is built up to this level, a permanent administration will be appointed. Tuition will be raised each year in line with the rate of inflation. The promotion budget will stay at a steady level of $50,000. Marketing research will be budgeted at $10,000 annually. The target income level for this program is $100,000 a year, and the money will be used to support other programs that are not self-paying.

BUSINESS ANALYSIS

As soon as a satisfactory offer concept and marketing strategy have been developed, the organization is in a position to do a hardheaded business analysis of the attractiveness of the proposal. De Paul, for example, must estimate the possible revenues and costs of the program for different possible enrollment levels. *Break-even analysis* is the most frequently used tool in this connection. Suppose De Paul learns that it needs an enrollment of 260 students to break even. If De Paul manages to attract more than 260 students, this program will produce a net income that could be used to support other programs; if there is a student shortfall, De Paul will lose money on this new program.

OFFER DEVELOPMENT

If the organization is satisfied that the concept is financially viable, it can begin giving the concept concrete form. The person in charge of the concept can begin to develop brochures, schedules, ads, sales plans, and other materials to implement the program. Each of the developed materials should be *consumer tested* before being printed and issued. A sample of prospects in the target audience, for example, might be asked to respond to a mock-up of the brochure describing the new program. This usually results in very valuable suggestions leading to an improved brochure.

MARKET TESTING

When the organization is satisfied with the initial materials and schedules, it can set up a market test to see if the concept is really going to be successful. Market testing is the stage at which the offer and marketing program are introduced into an authentic consumer setting to learn how many consumers are really interested in the program. Thus, De Paul University might decide to mail 10,000 brochures to strong prospects in the Chicago area during the month of April to see whether at least thirty students can be attracted. If more than thirty students sign up, the market test will be regarded as successful and full-scale promotion can be launched.

Test markets are the ultimate form of testing the target market's reaction to a new product. The organization can use two or more sites to measure the new program's viability without installing it wholesale throughout the system. The market test can serve an important second function—determining which of several alternative marketing strategies is best. Suppose that the State University of New York (SUNY) was considering the same new program as De Paul. SUNY consists of sixty-four campuses, not just one campus. SUNY could develop the concept and test it at one of the campuses to see how well it works, or it could test it at several campuses. One campus could emphasize direct mail to alumni, a second could purchase a mailing list of non-alumni who might be interested, a third could use primarily local newspaper ads, and a fourth could advertise in regional editions of national magazines like *Time* or *Newsweek*. As a result, SUNY could develop valuable insights into the cost-effectiveness of different promotional approaches. If the new program proved successful in one or all of the test markets, it could then be launched at other campuses where appropriate.

COMMERCIALIZATION

Commercialization is the set of activities undertaken following the test market's "go" recommendation to actually bring the new offering to market. The first step is to make four crucial decisions about the launch (although not all four will apply in every case).

1. *When* to launch. Factors to consider are (a) whether there is a need to first phase out an old program (for example, use up existing supplies of a product); (b) whether there is a seasonal peak time for introducing the item (for example, a new museum for children at the start of summer or a drunk-driving program just before the Christmas holidays); (c) whether further work on the offer could profitably be carried out; and (d) whether there is any risk that important rivals will reach the market first (or otherwise compromise favorable launch circumstances).

2. *Where* to launch. If the offer is potentially to be marketed in a wide geographic area, the organization must decide whether to tackle the whole market at once or to start slowly, rolling out the offer on a market-by-market basis. A social service program, for example, could be aimed at the entire city or state or tried out neighborhood by neighborhood. The "whole market" approach has the advantages of scale economies, of preempting competitors, and of achieving significant advertising and public relations impact. It does, however, assume that the program has pretty well been finalized and that its chances of ultimate success are excellent. The advantages of the roll-out introduction, which can well compensate for its slower speed and greater total cost, are that (a) one can learn as one goes, and (b) if optimistic projections are not realized, the project can be aborted or "sent back to the drawing boards" at lower economic cost and with less embarrassment to the organization.

3. *To whom* to aim the launch. Even in a local roll-out, the program manager must decide whether to aim at all eventual consumers or to focus at first on (a) those most likely to respond to the offer, (b) those most likely to have an important leadership role for others, or (c) both of these groups. We shall treat this issue in the next chapter in our consideration of postlaunch strategies.

4. *How* to launch. Tactical decisions must be made about how to achieve the maximum impact at launch date and thereafter. Included are decisions about teaser ads, degree of secrecy, amount and type of media coverage, and so on.

A second step in the commercialization process is to assign responsibility for the launch and introductory period to some individual or group. Here, management must decide whether to have a separate venture management group (or individual) for the new offer, a separate new venture *department* to launch *all* new ventures, or to fold the new venture in with the responsibilities of an existing individual or sales department.

The last step is to set up a formal scheduling procedure to ensure that all the needed tasks are (1) done in the right order; (2) done on schedule; and (3) done at the least possible cost. There are a number of valuable scheduling tools, such as PERT, CPM, etc., for this scheduling task.[9] Most of them provide (1) directions for individuals who must accomplish each step; (2) a forecast of probable launch dates; (3) a critical series of steps (called *the critical path*) whose delay will mean postponing the launch date; (4) a monitoring tool with checkpoints to ensure that the process is on schedule; and (5) a decision-making capability that would permit the launch manager to decide which activities along the critical path to speed up if the project falls behind schedule. An example of a simple planning system for the introduction of two new contraceptive products in Jamaica is given in Figure 13-3.

SUMMARY

To be successful in today's nonprofit environment, organizations must learn to effectively and efficiently develop new offerings. These may involve new or existing offerings in combination with new or existing markets. Extensions into new offerings or markets may involve undertakings that are similiar or dissimilar to present marketing programs.

FIGURE 13-3

Flow Chart for Introduction of Low-Dose Oral and Ultra-Thin Condom Jamaica Family Planning Project, September 26, 1983

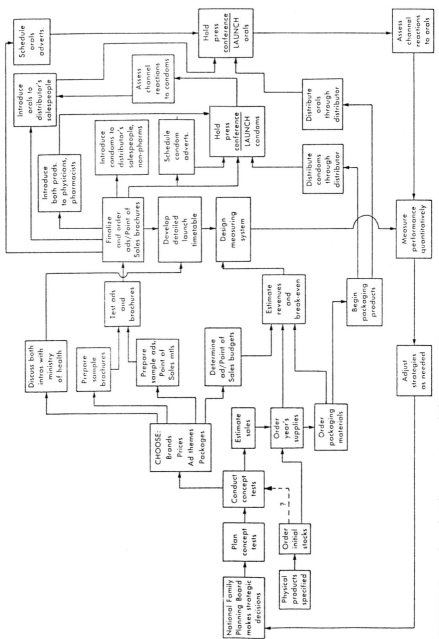

SOURCE: Reproduced with permission of The Futures Group.

393

To be successful in developing new offerings, the organization must be both creative and systematic. The first stage of the process is to generate ideas for new offerings. This can involve careful searching of available information or attempts to create new ideas through a variety of artificial idea-generation techniques. Once the ideas have been produced, it becomes necessary to screen them to eliminate those that do not meet established organization goals.

The next stage involves elaborating the idea into a concrete concept that can be subjected to formal testing. The concept, if successful, must then generate a specific marketing strategy which, in turn, must survive a rigorous business analysis. The final stages of the development process then involve specific offer development and market testing, followed by a carefully orchestrated and timed commercialized process. Critical path techniques may be used to assure that the project meets any crucial timing and cost objectives.

QUESTIONS

1. The Girl Scouts are facing a new competitive environment and a changing youth market. Suggest new offerings they might add in each of the nine cells of Table 13-1.

2. List the attributes of a blood donation experience. Suggest ways in which each attribute could be adapted, minified, magnified, substituted, rearranged, reversed, or combined.

3. List the criteria you feel that a nonprofit hospital should use in screening ideas for new services it should offer or new markets it should seek to penetrate.

4. Develop three alternative conceptualizations for a weight reduction program the YMCA might offer. Draw up a set of criteria for determining which to eventually use and test each concept with a few friends.

5. A hospital in a major metropolitan area has developed and launched six new offerings in the last five years. Two were very successful, one was moderately successful, and the rest were clearly flops. Develop a checklist of questions that those involved in the development and launch of these innovations should ask themselves to learn how the new offering development process could be improved for the future.

NOTES

1. John Crompton, "Developing New Recreation and Park Programs," *Recreation Canada*, July 1983, p. 29.
2. Eric A. von Hippel, "Users as Innovators," *Technology Review*, January 1978, pp. 3–11.
3. Philip Kotler, "Idea Management: A Way to Increase Health Services' Marketing Effectiveness," presentation to Academy of Health Services Marketing, Las Vegas, Nevada, March 11, 1985.

4. For a useful discussion of creativity techniques, see Sidney J. Parnes and Harold F. Harding, eds., *Source Book for Creative Thinking* (New York: Scribner's, 1962).

5. See Alex F. Osborn, *Applied Imagination,* 3d ed. (New York: Scribner's, 1963) pp. 286–87.

6. *Ibid.,* p. 156.

7. See also Barry M. Richman, "A Rating Scale for Product Innovation," *Business Horizons,* Summer 1962, pp. 37–44; and John T. O'Meara, Jr., "Selecting Profitable Products," *Harvard Business Review,* January-February 1961, pp. 83–89.

8. "De Paul's New Study Plan," *Chicago Tribune,* January 6, 1974.

9. For example, see Yoram J. Wind, *Product Policy: Concepts, Methods and Strategy,* (Reading, Mass.: Addison-Wesley, 1982), pp. 237–239; also, Glenn L. Urban and John Hauser, *Design and Marketing of New Products* (Englewood Cliffs, N.J.: Prentice-Hall, 1980), p. 469.

CHAPTER 14

Managing Offerings Over the Life Cycle

After decades in which the United States seemed to be an irresistable lure to all foreign tourists, international travel to the United States has fallen on hard times. In 1984, 6.9 percent of all visits to foreign countries were made to the United States. This represented a significant decline from 7.4 percent in 1983 and 7.6 percent a year earlier. The decline represents a substantial loss of income to the United States. Foreign tourists annually spend over $100 billion worldwide, but the U.S. share of that pie, while very large, has been dropping. The U.S. share was 11.4 per cent in 1984, down from 11.9 percent in 1983. The losses are particularly troublesome for some states. In 1983, foreign tourists spent an estimated $2.65 billion in Florida and $1.57 billion in New York State.

Many factors have contributed to this decline phase of American tourism marketing. First among these was the growing strength of the U.S. dollar up until late 1985, which, along with a very high standard of living, has made the country too expensive for more and more tourists. A second factor is undoubtedly the growth of commercial centers outside the United States. Business people now more often travel to Milan, Hong Kong, Tokyo, and Frankfurt to do their business—and, often, to begin vacations of varying lengths.

Foreign governments are also providing stiffer competition. The U.S. government lags far behind other countries in spending per capita on tourism. The total U.S. budget to promote foreign tourism is exceeded by those of Belgium, Hong Kong, Korea, Jamaica, and Bermuda. The budgets of Canada, Spain, the U.K., and Bermuda are all three times that of the United States in total dollars.

The Reagan administration was the first in recent years to recognize the potential economic benefits of foreign tourism. A revitalization of America's tourism promotion was clearly needed. Despite an increase in budget for the United States Tourism and Travel Agency (USTTA), however, major changes did not come about until Donna F. Tuttle, a personal friend of the Reagans, was put in charge of the agency. As Jack Honomichl put it in *Advertising Age,* despite having no experience in managing an enterprise the size of USTTA and none in the travel industry, "Tuttle hit the ground running." In a very few weeks, she established important links to Congress, revitalized USTTA's industry advisory board, improved USTTA staff, hired a public relations specialist, and began funding significant amounts of marketing research for the first time. Most significantly, she issued a solicitation for an advertising agency to prepare a major new promotional campaign to be tested in West Germany in the fall of 1985.

The solicitation was won by N. W. Ayer, which already had other major travel accounts. Ayer immediately began informally soliciting ideas for the travel-America campaign from its foreign offices and affiliates. It also conducted an intensive five-week background study in nine countries at a cost to USTTA of $100,000. Based on this research and Ayer's own creative thinking, a theme was developed: "America: Catch the Spirit." Undoubtedly taking a cue from the Los Angeles Summer Olympic Games in 1984, the new campaign was designed to emphasize what is exciting, stimulating, vast, and yet accessible about the United States. Advertisements featuring this theme were created and placed in consumer magazines and magazines aimed at the travel industry in West Germany in December of 1985, and further magazine supplements were planned for the spring of 1986. At the same time, an elaborate measurement system was put in place to assess the effects of the campaign via in-flight interviews with returning German travelers, pre- and postadvertising awareness and attitude studies in West Germany, and counts of returned coupons and other requests for information about travel to the United States.

While fluctuations in currency rates will undoubtedly have an important effect on the outcome of the campaign, USTTA is targeting a 10-percent growth in German tourism to the United States. If the market test is successful and Congress appropriates the funding, one can expect a major reinvigoration of America's efforts to entice tourists—and their pocketbooks—to its shores.

SOURCE: Developed from information in Jack L. Honomichl, *Honomichl on Marketing Research* (Lincolnwood, Ill.: NTC Business Books, 1986).

The performance of a new offering launched into the marketplace typically follows an S-shaped pattern over a period known as the *offer life cycle* (OLC) (Figure 14-1). The S-shaped curve is marked by the following four stages:

1. *Introduction* is a period of slow growth as the offering is introduced in the market.
2. *Growth* is a period of rapid market acceptance.
3. *Maturity* is a period of slowdown in growth because the offering has achieved acceptance by most of the potential buyers.
4. *Decline* is the period when performance shows a strong downward drift.

The offer life cycle concept can be defined further according to whether it describes an offer *class* (mental health service), an offer *form* (psychoanalysis), or a *brand* (Menninger Clinic). The OLC concept has a different degree of applicability in each case. Offer classes have the longest life cycles. The performance of many offer classes can be expected to continue in the mature stage for an indefinite duration. Thus, "mental health service" began centuries ago with organized religion and can be expected to continue in the mature state for an indefinite duration. Offer forms, on the other hand, tend to exhibit more standard OLC histories than offer classes. Thus, mental health services are dispensed in such forms as psychoanalysis, bioenergetics, group therapy, and so on, some of which are beginning to show signs of maturity, while others, such as "rolfing," may well be in their decline stage.

FIGURE 14-1

Typical S-Shaped Offer Life Cycle

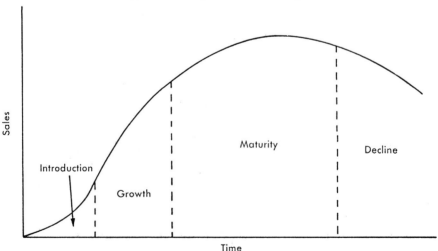

Offer forms still have very long life cycles in which they retain small coteries of adherents, often for decades. As for brands, they are the most likely to have finite histories. Thus, the Menninger Clinic is a well-known psycho-analytically oriented clinic that had a period of rapid growth and is now mature. It will pass out of existence eventually, like most brands and institutions.

Not all products exhibit an S-shaped life cycle. Three other common patterns are

1. *Scalloped pattern.* (Figure 14-2A.) In this case, the offer during the mature stage suddenly breaks into a new life cycle. The new life is triggered by modi-fications, new uses, new users, changing tastes, or other factors. The market for psychotherapy, for example, reached maturity at one point, and then the emer-gence of group therapy gave it a whole new market. At the brand level, interest in the March of Dimes was waning until the organization shifted its focus to birth defects.

2. *Cyclical pattern.* (Figure 14-2B.) The performance of some offerings shows a cyclical pattern. Engineering schools, for example, go through alternating periods of high enrollment and low enrollment, reflecting changes in demand and supply in the marketplace. Preferences for political parties also seem to follow this pattern. The decline stage is not a time to eliminate the offer, but to maintain as much of it as possible, waiting for the next up cycle.

3. *Fad pattern.* (Figure 14-2C.) Here, a new offer comes on the market, attracts quick attention, is adopted with great zeal, peaks early, and declines rapidly. The acceptance cycle is short and the offer tends to attract only a limited fol-lowing of people who are looking for excitement or diversion. Some art and therapy forms exhibit the pattern of a fad.

While the fact that offers have life cycles may at first seem like just common sense, it turns out to be a very useful strategic planning device because it alerts management to the fact that they need to adjust the focus of their marketing thinking depending on the OLC stage they currently are

FIGURE 14-2

Three Anomalous Product Life Cycle Patterns

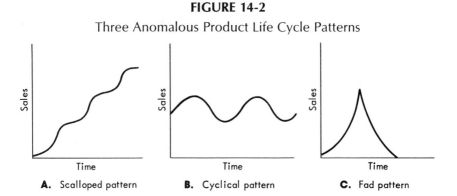

| **A.** Scalloped pattern | **B.** Cyclical pattern | **C.** Fad pattern |

in. The first part of this chapter describes marketing strategies for the introduction and growth stages. Then the chapter moves on to discuss marketing
strategies for the maturing and decline stages.

INTRODUCTION AND GROWTH STAGES

One way to characterize the changes sought by all marketers it to distinguish between first-time and repeat acceptance of the marketer's offering.
Obviously, the strategic problems of getting people to take an action initially
are very different from those of getting them to repeat or continue a given
behavior. Thus, getting someone to give blood the first time, begin contraception, or even vote Democratic for the first time can be very difficult.
Once over this hurdle, the marketing task is infinitely easier, especially if the
initial experience is satisfying.

Following this line of reasoning, the offer life cycle can be divided into
the two parts shown in Figure 14-3. For some nonprofit offerings, the OLC
may *only* involve first-time use. Thus, a male only needs to have one vasectomy; there is no need to repeat the operation. This however, is relatively
rare. Most strategies involve trial and repeat exchanges. Repeat exchanges
may differ, however, as to whether we mean *repeating* an action like giving
blood or attending an opera or whether we mean *continuing* a newly
adopted behavior pattern like not smoking.

SECURING TRIAL

Many social science disciplines have been interested in the issue of
how to get target audiences to begin something new. Cultural anthropolo-
gists have researched how ancient cultures adopted new metals, new pot-
glazing techniques, and new crops. Rural sociologists have studied how

FIGURE 14-3

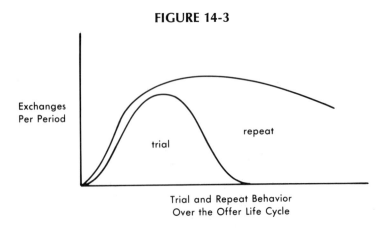

Trial and Repeat Behavior
Over the Offer Life Cycle

farmers have adopted new fertilizing and farm management practices and new types of seeds. Economists have investigated how firms adopt new manufacturing technologies like oxygen lancing in steel-making, while educators have studied the dynamics of adopting teaching innovations, such as the "new math" or "new English." Social psychologists have studied the processes by which individuals acquire smoking, drug, and drinking addictions. And marketers, of course, have long studied new product adoptions.

The findings from these studies can help nonprofit managers reflect on how to induce first-time behaviors. First, they provide insight into the characteristics of those who adopt an innovation at different points during its introduction, growth, and even maturity phases and into the interactions among these characteristics. Second, they model the stages that individuals go through to adopt a given innovation. Finally, they differentiate the characteristics of offerings that will be relatively easy to introduce from those that will not.

FINDING POTENTIAL INNOVATORS

The earliest approach used by new offer marketers for launching a new offering was a *mass market approach.* A hospital, for example, might start a first aid course and try to attract everyone to take it. A mass market approach, however, has two drawbacks: (1) it requires heavy marketing expenditures, and (2) it involves a substantial number of wasted exposures to nonpotential and low-potential buyers. These drawbacks led to a second approach, *target marketing,* in which the offer is directed to the groups that are likely to be most interested. This makes sense, provided that strong prospects are identifiable. But even within strong prospect groups, persons differ in how much interest they show in new ideas and in how fast they can be drawn into trying them. Certain persons are early adopters, and the marketer of an innovation ought to direct marketing efforts to them. *Early-adopter theory* holds that

1. Persons within a target market differ in the amount of time that passes between their exposure to a new offering and their trial of it.
2. Early adopters are likely to share some traits that differentiate them from late adopters.
3. There exist efficient media for reaching early-adopter types.
4. Early-adopter types are likely to be high on opinion leadership and therefore helpful in "advertising" the new offer to potential buyers.

The differences among individuals in their response to new ideas is called their *innovativeness.* Specifically, innovativeness is the degree to which an individual is relatively earlier in adopting new ideas than the other members of his or her social system. On the basis of their innovativeness, individuals can be classified into different *adopter categories.* In each product area, there are apt to be "consumption pioneers" and early adopters. Some women are the first to adopt new clothing fashions or new appliances, such as the microwave oven, some doctors are the first to prescribe new medicines,[1] and some farmers are the first to adopt new farming methods.[2]

Other individuals, however, tend to adopt innovations much later. This has led to a classification of people into the adopter categories shown in Figure 14-4.

FIGURE 14-4

Adopter Categorization on the Basis of Relative Time of Adoption of Innovations

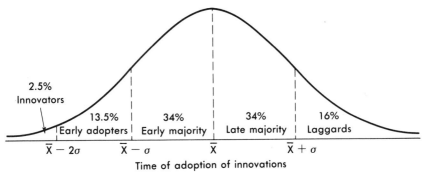

The adoption process is represented as following a normal (or near normal) distribution when plotted over time. After a slow start, an increasing number of people adopt the innovation, the number reaches a peak, and then it diminishes as fewer persons remain in the nonadopter category.

Convenient breaks in the distribution are used to establish adopter categories. Thus innovators are defined as the first 2½ percent of the individuals to adopt a new idea; the early adopters are the next 13½ percent who adopt the new idea, and so forth.

Rogers has characterized the five adopter groups in terms of their central values.[3] The dominant value of innovators is *venturesomeness;* they like to try new ideas, even at some risk, and are cosmopolitan in orientation. The dominant value of early adopters is *respect;* they enjoy a position in the community as opinion leaders and adopt new ideas early with an eye to whether the adoption will enhance their status as trendsetters. The dominant value of the early majority is *deliberateness;* these people like to adopt new ideas before the average member of the social system, although they are rarely leaders. Indeed, this group more often comprises the followers who pay attention to the advice given or the example set by the opinion leaders who preceded them. The dominant value of the late majority is *skepticism;* they do not adopt an innovation until the weight of majority opinion seems to legitimize its utility. They typically pay little attention to the opinion leaders, relying more on market cues of general acceptance. Finally, the dominant value of the laggards is *tradition;* they are suspicious of any changes, and adopt the innovation only because it has now taken on a measure of tradition itself.

Rogers has characterized the earlier adopters as follows:

> The relatively earlier adopters in a social system tend to be younger in age, have higher social status, a more favorable financial position, more specialized operations, and a different type of mental ability from later adopters. Earlier adopters utilize information sources that are more impersonal and cosmopolite than later adopters and that are in closer contact with the origin of new ideas. Earlier adopters utilize a greater number of different information sources than do later adopters. The social relationships of earlier adopters are more cosmopolite than for later adopters, and earlier adopters have more opinion leadership.[4]

These findings have obvious implications for the kind of strategy one should adopt as one moves through the introductory and growth phases.

Innovators. This group enters the market during the introductory phase of the OLC. The marketer can largely ignore the group, however, for three reasons. First, they are a relatively small group. Second, because of their venturesomeness, they are likely to discover the innovation even without the marketer's help. Finally, they have little or no influence on those who follow later. Since the early adopters and early majority tend to look upon the innovators as "try-anything-once" oddballs, the marketer runs a severe risk of cutting off further adoption by identifying too closely with this group.

Early adopters. Early adopters are the key to the success of most innovations. If one does not win them over, the introductory period will be prolonged, or the innovation may totally fail. Thus, an important first step in any marketing program involving an innovation is to identify the opinion leaders. Unfortunately, opinion leadership is not a generalized trait. Particular consumers or households may be innovators in one area but not in another. The fraternity or sorority fashion leader may not be the first to give blood or attend the latest movies. Furthermore, past research has shown that opinion leaders are not necessarily the elite of a society; they can be found in all social strata. On the other hand, there is some evidence that the same opinion leaders may be found for similar innovations. Thus, the early adopters of protective car seats for their babies might be good prospects as opinion leaders supporting airbag legislation. Yet, they should be tested. Three approaches to identifying leaders are possible:[5]

- *Self-reporting.* Individuals can be directly asked whether they would classify themselves as opinion leaders either in general or in ways related to the innovation in question.
- *Reputational.* Individuals may be asked to identify others to whom they might go for information or advice in this particular category. They can be asked to

describe the most salient characteristic of these significant others.

- *Sociometric.* The researcher could directly map the interaction among members of a population and use this to determine the most influential members. Thus, Coleman, Katz, and Menzel found that by asking physicians in a particular community whom they would contact (a) to refer a patient, (b) to secure advice on a medical problem, and (c) to socialize with, they could rather accurately predict who would be the early adopters of a new drug and who was likely to follow them when they did.[6]

Early majority. Some time will elapse before the marketer's strategy of attracting opinion leaders has its effect. The marketer should then make it clear to the early majority that the opinion leaders have already adopted—and, therefore, legitimized—the innovation. This can be accomplished by testimonials, editorials, and news and feature items. A good example of the use of opinion leadership has been the role of former First Lady Betty Ford in trying to get others to follow her lead in detection of breast cancer and in the treatment of drug abuse.

The late majority and laggards. Once the early majority has been heavily penetrated, tactics should shift from securing trial to emphasizing repeat behavior. This is desirable on two grounds. First, if a good trial rate has been achieved, competitors will enter the market and attention will shift to providing superior offers. Second, the emergence of more suppliers and offers will send a clear signal to the late majority that the innovation is accepted. By changing a campaign that says "try this" to one that says "try ours, not theirs," the marketer can make the late majority realize that the innovation is no longer risky. Whether such tactics will have an effect on the laggards is unclear.

The Innovation Adoption Process

Rogers and Shoemaker[7] have identified four steps that individuals typically go through in adopting some new pattern of behavior.

1. *Knowledge.* First, the target consumer must (a) become aware of the innovation, and (b) learn enough about it to deduce that it has some relevance to his or her needs, wants, and life-style.
2. *Persuasion.* Next, the target consumer must move from simple awareness and vague interest to being motivated to take action. This is primarily a matter of attitude change, although it is also possible that a behavioral response could be achieved through *incentivization* or *coercion* with relatively little attitude change.
3. *Decision.* At some point, the target consumer thinks through the probable consequences of the proposed behavior change and makes a decision to adopt or reject it. This stage might well involve a vicarious or personal trial. Thus, a person suffering from hypertension might reduce salt intake for a few days or quiz others who have tried this approach.

Managing Offerings Over the Life Cycle

4. *Confirmation.* After the initial decision, it is hoped that the target consumer will continue the behavior. This can be a major problem for social change agents. For example, over seventy percent of smoking quitters resume the habit within a year. In the case of seat belts, Lovelock and Weinberg showed that seat belt usage rose and then fell after mandatory seat belt usage legislation was enacted in British Columbia, Canada:[8]

	Percentage Using Seat Belts	
	Drivers	*Passengers*
Before announcement of legislation	29	24
Immediately after legislation	72	66
Sixteen months after legislation	54	43

The value of the Rogers-Shoemaker adoption model is threefold. First, it points to the *sequence* of tasks necessary to move a given target segment to adopt. Thus, early messages must create awareness and interest, subsequent messages persuade, and later messages secure and reinforce decisions.

Second, it provides a monitoring device to identify reasons for a slow rate of acceptance. Thus, research on quitting smoking shows that many smokers are blocked at the decision stage. Persuasion attempts are no longer necessary, and effort should focus on inducing a decision.

Finally, the model can lead to a segmentation strategy. Suppose that research has identified three target segments for a new health program: males working in blue-collar jobs, pregnant women, and senior citizens. Suppose that target audience members have reached the stages of the process listed in Table 14-1.

Table 14-1

DISTRIBUTION OF TARGET AUDIENCE MEMBERS ACROSS ADOPTION CATEGORIES

Stages of Adoption Process	*Blue-Collar Male*	*Pregnant Women*	*Senior Citizens*
No awareness	4%	12%	53%
Knowledge	26	51	35
Persuasion	61	14	6
Decision	2	23	4
Confirmation	7	0	2
	100%	100%	100%

Obviously, strategies aimed at a blue-collar male sample should seek to produce action. As for pregnant women, some messages should create interest in the health program; other messages should reinforce the behavior of those who have already acted. (Research differentiating these two subpopulations could lead to finer tuning of strategy.) Finally, senior citizens are not being reached by current messages. New messages, better execution, or better media are warranted.

INNOVATION CHARACTERISTICS

The innovations's characteristics will affect the rate of adoption. Five characteristics have an especially important influence on the adoption rate. The first is the innovation's *relative advantage,* the degree to which it appears superior to previous ideas. The greater the perceived relative advantage (higher quality, lower cost, and so on), the more quickly the innovation will be adopted. Thus, a five-day smoking cessation program that has a 35 percent intitial success rate will be adopted faster than a three-month program that has 20 percent initial success rate—even though both programs may have the same *long-term* effectiveness.

The second characteristic is the innovation's *compatibility,* the degree to which it is consistent with the values and experiences of the individuals in the social system. Thus, persuading Moslem women to practice birth control when they believe that their number of children is "in God's hands" will take more time than persuading them to boil water before drinking it, because the latter has no religious significance.

The third characteristic is the innovation's *complexity,* the degree to which it is relatively difficult to understand or use. More complex innovations take a longer time to diffuse, other things being equal. Condoms, for example, are easier to introduce in a given country than intrauterine devices (IUDs).

The fourth characteristic is the innovation's *divisibility,* the degree to which it may be tried on a limited basis. The evidence of many studies indicates that divisibility helps increase adoption. Thus, a severe hypertensive will be more ready to adopt a salt-restricted diet than corrective heart surgery, since the latter is an all-or-nothing proposition.

The fifth characteristic is the innovation's *communicability,* the degree to which the results are observable or describable to others. Innovations whose advantages are more observable will diffuse faster in the social system. Thus, obese people will adopt new eating and exercise habits faster than hypertensives because the former will observe their weight loss, whereas hypertensives will not observe any change unless they use a blood pressure gauge.

The marketing strategist should research how any proposed innovation is perceived by the target market in terms of these five characteristics before developing the marketing plan. Preliminary studies of the potential for injectible, longer-term contraceptives in developing countries, for example, have brought to light the following characteristics:

1. *Relative advantage.* Three advantages are clear. First, the technique puts less of a burden on the woman in terms of memory and possible interference with sex (real or perceived). Second, it is a technique that can be adopted easily and in private. Thus, it permits women to secure protection without their parents, friends, and sometimes their husbands or boyfriends knowing about it. Third, depending on the formulation, protection from one injection lasts one to three months.

2. *Compatibility.* Women are used to taking injections for other purposes so that the concept is not as "strange" as the IUD.

3. *Complexity.* There is an understandable problem for women in that the side effects are diverse and sometimes quite pronounced in early months. The problem is also complex for physicians because the U.S. Food and Drug Administration has banned the drug because of a small risk that it might produce breast cancer. Doctors face a tough ethical choice between endangering the mother due to the drug and endangering her health from too frequent pregnancies.

4. *Divisibility.* Divisibility exists because the drug can be stopped and another technique substituted. Several months have to elapse, however, before the woman can become pregnant again.

5. *Communicability.* The drug's effectiveness in preventing pregnancies can be easily communicated. There are problems at the confirmation stage in convincing women that the strong side effects are not serious and will disappear soon.

After learning how the innovation is perceived by the target audience, the marketer can then proceed to make the innovation relatively more advantageous, more compatible, more divisible, less complex, and more communicable.

THE MATURITY STAGE

When market growth for the new offering begins to level off, three important shifts in the external and internal marketing environments take place. First, word-of-mouth dynamics between opinion leaders and followers tend to die out. When a new product or service is "old hat," there is no payoff for opinion leaders to promote it and no need for the followers to worry about "checking it out" before going ahead. This puts renewed pressure on the marketer. A second source of pressure is competition. For years, the general public was attracted by the local YMCA's low prices to learn such skills as camping, snorkeling, calisthenics, and racquetball. Just at the point when broad interest began to develop in these programs, the private sector began to offer deluxe snorkeling vacations, luxury campgrounds and campfests, fancy health centers, and exercise videotapes, all tending to attract away the market that the "Y" had built to its maturity stage. By the late 1970s, the YMCA had become the bargain basement of the physical fitness industry with many of the negative connotations this implies. It did not plan ahead for the mature stage of the offer life cycle. It now faces an uphill battle to regain its old patrons, although innovations are being tried in Washington, D.C. and Los Angeles.[9]

The third problem is an internal one. As competition increases, the organization's staff experiences a sense of frustration and helplessness. First, there is the feeling that the present situation is unfair: after all, "we built the market." Second, the staff recognizes that they have become "fat and happy" and lack the competitive skills or drive to fight back. Many observers believe that these attitudes characterized the U.S. Postal Service when it faced the new private rapid mail delivery services in the early 1980s. Considerable managerial energy and often staff reassignments are necessary to recover lost momentum.

Faced with a maturing market, management must decide on the position it wants to occupy relative to its competitors. The choice will depend on management's assessment of future competitive conditions and the organization's strengths and weaknesses. The organization might strive for any of four long-term positions:[10]

- *Market leader.* If the organization has an excellent offering, is well regarded, has superior distribution, has broad resources for future battles, and competition is expected to be relatively weak, the organization can choose to maintain or enhance its leadership position. The U.S. Post Office has recently adopted this posture with considerable success.
- *Market challenger.* If the market leader is formidable and has clear long-term advantages, an organization has three options. The first of these is not to cede but to challenge the market leader. Contraceptive social marketers in several countries, while cooperating with government programs, have often acted as market challengers to prove that their way of marketing is superior in the long run.
- *Market follower.* Another option is to play follow the leader. There are many excellent reasons for adopting this strategy. First, it is a good choice if the market leader is tough or has substantial resources that would make a challenger strategy too costly. Second, imitating but not challenging a smart and innovative leader can lead to effective results. The market follower can save countless dollars and a great deal of managerial time and mental energy by not having to continually develop effective challenging strategies. Finally, a follower strategy often makes good sense as part of an overall portfolio strategy. A "follower" offering can often serve as a "cash cow," providing resources to other sectors of the enterprise. Thus, a me-too strategy is appropriate for book and gift shop operations in many museums and hospitals. These shops can watch what the Hallmark, Rizzols, or Waldenbooks of the area are currently doing and follow their lead.
- *Market nicher.* This final strategy is one that is adopted by a number of nonprofits. The organization finds a set (or sets) of target customers whose needs are not well met by other marketers and devotes itself to that segment. Thus,

a theatre group in a large city might decide to specialize in producing only the plays of Shakespeare and therefore serve only the interests of theatregoers who love Shakespeare.

These four strategic options for the mature stage have further ramifications in terms of both choice requirements and tactical suboptions. Each will be discussed in turn.

MARKET LEADER STRATEGIES

In mature markets, there is usually a market leader who signals pricing changes, develops innovations, leads on legislative tactics, and so on. The leader may or may not be admired or respected. In the private sector, market leaders include General Motors, Kodak, and IBM. The nonprofit sector also has its leaders, including the Metropolitan Museum of Art in New York (art galleries), Harvard Business School (executive education programs), the United Way (charities), the Metropolitan Opera (opera companies), the Sierra Club (environmental protection agencies), Ralph Nader (consumer spokespeople), and the American Red Cross (blood donation agencies).

Unless the dominant firm enjoys a legal monopoly, it must maintain constant vigilance. Other firms will challenge its strengths or take advantage of its weaknesses. The dominant firm might look old-fashioned compared to newer and more aggressive rivals, as is the case for many old-line hospitals facing competition from high-tech, high-efficiency walk-in medical centers.

Dominant firms want to remain number one. This calls for action on three fronts. First, the firm must find ways to expand total demand. Second, the firm must protect its current market share through good defensive and offensive actions. Third, the firm can try to expand its market share further, even if market size remains constant.

Expanding the Total Market.   The dominant firm normally gains the most when the total market expands for one reason or another. If Americans are persuaded to allocate more to private charities, the United Way stands to gain the most. The United Way benefits if it convinces more people to give or persuades current givers to give more frequently or to give larger amounts. In general, the leader should look for *new users, new uses,* and *more usage* of its products.

NEW USERS.   Every offering has the potential for attracting buyers who are unaware of the offer or who are resisting it because of its perceived cost or lack of certain features. An organization can search for new users among three groups. A university survey research center, for example, can try to convince academic departments that do not use research to do so *(market penetration strategy).* It can convince private firms to start using the university's research capability *(new market strategy)*. Or it could sell its services in other cities or states *(geographical-expansion strategy)*. The University of Michigan's Survey Research Center has now developed a national and even an international clientele, to whom it sells special and continuing studies as well as reports, monographs, and books. Its survey of consumer buying intentions is eagerly awaited each quarter by business people, politicians, and the general media.

NEW USES.   Markets can be expanded by discovering and promoting new uses for a product or new ways of making exchanges. Thus, museums hold concerts, free admission days, or special tours or lectures as ways of promoting increased usage.

MORE USAGE.   The market leader can attempt to convince people to use more of the product or service per use occasion. Thus, universities and hospitals have devised a number of innovative estate planning arrangements to get wealthier individuals to transfer more of their wealth to the institution. Performing arts centers provide restaurants or bar facilities and operate gift shops as a means of getting higher expenditures from each visitor.

Protecting Market Share.   While trying to expand total market size, the dominant firm must continuously protect its current business against competitive attacks. The leader is like a large elephant constantly being stung by bees. What can the leader do to protect itself? The most constructive response is *continuous innovation,* in which the leader refuses to be content with the way things are and leads the industry in new-product ideas, customer services, distribution improvement, and cost-cutting. It keeps increasing real and perceived value to customers. The leader applies the military principle of the offensive by exercising initiative, setting the pace, and exploiting competitors' weaknesses. The best defense is a good offense.

The leader, even when it does not launch offensives, must guard its fronts and not leave any flanks exposed. It must keep its costs down, and its prices must be consonant with the value the customers perceive in the offering. The leader must "plug holes" so that the challengers don't jump in. Thus, a major art museum may add a collection of contemporary art to forestall the formation of a new contemporary art museum.

Expanding Market Share.   Market leaders can also try to grow by increasing their market share, even if the total market has stabilized. A series of studies in the private sector has led some management experts to conclude that firms with higher market shares enjoy higher returns. Thus, the well-publicized *Profit Impact of Management Strategies* (PIMS) studies indicate that *profitability* (measured by pretax return on investment) rises linearly with *market share.*[11] The rationale offered for these findings is lowered costs. First, as an organization grows, it achieves scale economies not available to its smaller rivals. Thus, it can produce its products or services cheaper, buy its television or magazine advertising at less cost, and borrow its capital at lower rates. Second, as it grows, it learns how to produce and market in better ways. Thus, if one is producing five television ads or direct mail pieces per quarter, one gets a lot better at it (especially if one continually experiments and conducts evaluation studies) than a rival who prepares only one ad or mailer per quarter.

Other studies have suggested that a V-shaped relationship between market share and profitability in many industries is "more correct."[12] Such industries have one or a few highly profitable leaders, several profitable small and more highly focused firms, and a large number of medium-sized firms with poorer profit performances. As an example, many medium-sized management consulting firms don't do as well as small specialized firms or the large leaders who share stronger reputations and resources. The message is that medium-sized organizations need to figure out how to break into the big league or else settle in specialized niches where they can do outstanding work.

Medium-sized organizations must not think, however, that gaining increased market share will automatically improve their performance. Much depends on their strategy for gaining increased market share, whether it is through offering higher quality, lower cost, or some other procedure. There are many high-market-share companies with low profitability and many low-market-share companies with high profitability. The cost of buying higher market share may far exceed its revenue value.

MARKET-CHALLENGER STRATEGIES

The organizations that occupy second, third, and lower ranks in an industry can still be quite large in their own right, such as the Columbia Graduate School of Business and the New York City Opera Company. These runner-up firms can adopt one of two postures. They can attack the leader and other competitors in an aggressive bid for further market share (market challengers). Or they can simply watch the leader and mimic what seems to work for them (market followers).

A nonprofit organization that decides to be a market challenger must first define its strategic objective. Basically, the challenger can choose to attack one of three types of firms:

- It can attack the market leader. This is a high-risk but potentially high-payoff strategy and makes good sense if the leader is not a "true leader" and is not serving the market well. The "terrain" to examine closely is consumer need or dissatisfaction. If a substantial consumer group is unserved or poorly served by the leader, it offers a great strategic target. Alternatively, the challenger might attempt to out-innovate the leader across the whole segment.

- The challenger could attack organizations of its own size that are doing a poor job or that are underfinanced. Both consumer satisfaction and innovation potential should be examined for opportunities.
- The challenger could attack smaller organizations that are not doing the job and are underfinanced. Many major hospitals are growing not by taking away each other's customers so much as by gobbling up the "small fry" competitors.

Critical to choosing opponents and objectives is the need for systematic competitive analysis. The nonprofit organization must collect current and comprehensive information on competitors. The organization should be able to answer the following questions:

- Who are our competitors?
- What are each competitor's sales, market share, and financial standing?
- What are each competitor's goals and assumptions?
- What is each competitor's strategy?
- What are each competitor's strengths and weaknesses?
- What changes is each competitor likely to make in its future strategy in response to environmental, competitive, and internal developments?

Several strategic alternatives are available to the market challenger.

1. *Price discount strategy.* Challengers can try to attract patrons with an offering comparable to the leader's at a lower price. Thus, a college can charge a lower tuition but offer comparable quality. For a price discount strategy to work, three assumptions must be fulfilled. First, the challenger must convince buyers that its product and service are comparable to the leader's. Second, the buyers must be price-aware and price-sensitive. Third, the market leader must fail to respond to the competitor's price discount.

2. *Cheaper goods strategy.* Another strategy is to offer the market a lower-quality product than the competitor's at a lower price. This works when there are enough buyers who are primarily interested in the price. Organizations that get established through this strategy, however, may be attacked by firms whose prices are even lower. In defense, they might try to upgrade their quality over time. Some mail-order nonprofit educational institutions appear to be following this strategy.

3. *Prestige goods strategy.* A market challenger can launch a higher-quality product and charge a higher price than the leader. Stanford, Wharton, and Northwestern all argue that they offer higher quality (for example, more analytical) executive programs than the leader, Harvard. Some prestige goods organizations later roll out lower-price products to take advantage of their prestige.

4. *Product proliferation strategy.* The challenger can attack the leader by launching a larger number of offerings. UCLA's Performing Arts Center offers its potential subscribers over a dozen different packages of events to compete with the nearby Ambassador Auditorium and the Los Angeles Music Center.

5. *Product innovation strategy.* The challenger may try to be more innovative than the leader. Thus, the New York City Opera offers less commonly performed quality operas, compared to the traditional fare of the Met. The public

often gains the most from challenger strategies oriented toward offer innovation.

6. *Improved services strategy.* The challenger might find ways to offer new or better services to customers. A performing arts center that builds better parking facilities would be following this strategy.

7. *Distribution innovation strategy.* A challenger might discover or develop a new channel of distribution. Goodwill Industries in Los Angeles now places semitrailers in shopping mall parking lots to make it easier for shoppers and nearby residents to donate used goods.

8. *Operating-cost reduction strategy.* The challenger might seek to achieve lower operating costs than its competitors through more efficient purchasing, lower labor costs, and more modern production equipment. The organization can use its lower cost to price more aggressively in order to gain more market share.

9. *Intensive advertising and promotion.* Some challengers attack the leader by increasing their expenditures on advertising and promotion. Substantial promotional spending, however, is usually not a sensible strategy unless the challenger's product or advertising is distinctive or superior to the competitor's.

A challenger rarely improves its market share by relying on only one strategy element. Its success depends on designing a strategy made up of several elements that will improve its position over time.

MARKET FOLLOWER STRATEGIES

Many organizations do not attempt to wrest more shares from the leader or others. They may be content to play a follower role.

A market follower needs to know how to hold current customers. The market follower must keep its costs low and its quality high. It must also enter new markets as they open up. Followership is not the same as being passive or a carbon copy of the leader. The follower has to define a growth path, but one that does not create competitive retaliation. Three broad followership strategies can be distinguished:

- *Following closely.* Here, the follower emulates the leader in as many market segments and marketing-mix elements as possible. Some followers even appear to be parasitic in that they put very little into stimulating the market, hoping to live off the market leader's investments.

- *Following at a distance.* Here, the follower maintains some differentiation but follows the leader in terms of major market innovations, general price levels, and distribution. This follower is quite acceptable to the market leader, who may see little interference with its market plans and may be pleased that the follower's market share helps the leader avoid charges of monopolization. The distant follower may achieve its growth through acquiring smaller organizations in the industry.

- *Following selectively.* This organization follows the leader quite closely in some ways and sometimes goes its own way. The organization may be quite innovative, yet it avoids direct competition and follows many of the strategies of the leaders.

Market followers, although they have lower market shares, may be as profitable or even more profitable than the leader. A recent study reported that many companies with less than half the market share of the leader had a five-year average return on equity that surpassed the industry median.[13] The keys to their success were conscious market segmentation and concentration, effective research and development, profit emphasis rather than market-share emphasis, and strong top management.

Almost every industry includes organizations that specialize in parts of the market where they avoid clashes with the majors. These organizations occupy market niches that they serve effectively through specialization and that the majors are likely to overlook or ignore. These firms try to find one or more market niches that are safe and profitable. The niche should have the following characteristics:

- The niche is of sufficient size and purchasing power to be profitable, or at least self-paying.
- The niche has growth potential.
- The niche is of negligible interest to major competitors.
- The organization has the required skills and resources to serve the niche effectively.
- The organization can defend itself against an attacking major competitor through the customer goodwill it has built up.

The key idea in nichemanship is specialization. The firm has to specialize along market, customer, product, or marketing-mix lines. Here are several specialist roles open to a market nicher:

- *End-use specialist.* The organization specializes in serving one type of end-use customer. A welfare agency, for example, can specialize in serving only poor unmarried mothers.
- *Vertical-level specialist.* The organization specializes at some vertical level of the production-distribution cycle. A university research center, for example, could specialize in research design, field work, or data analysis.
- *Customer-size specialist.* The organization sells to small-, medium-, or large-size customers. Many nichers specialize in serving small customers who are neglected by the majors.
- *Specific-customer specialist.* The organization limits its selling to one or a few major customers. Some nonprofit consulting firms have the government as their only client.
- *Geographic specialist.* The organization sells only in a certain locality, region, or area of the world. Thus, the Chicago Trust limits itself to supporting good causes in the Chicago area.
- *Product or product line specialist.* The organization produces only one product line or product. Museums can specialize in one type of art, pianists in one type

of music, and some small colleges in one type of curriculum (for example, liberal arts).

- *Product-feature specialist.* The organization specializes in producing a certain type of offering or offer feature. The University of Western Ontario specializes in the case method of teaching, while Carnegie Tech emphasizes quantitative analysis.
- *Job-shop specialist.* The organization produces customized products as ordered by the customer. Some colleges will design educational or training programs for particular firms.
- *Quality or price specialist.* The organization operates at the low or high end of the market. The University of Southern California specializes in the high-quality, high-price end of the executive education market in Los Angeles.
- *Service specialist.* The organization offers one or more services not available from other firms. An example would be a hospital that permits new fathers to sleep in the hospital room with the new mother and child.

Niching carries a major risk in that the market niche may shrink or be attacked. That is why *multiple niching* is preferable to *single niching.* By developing leadership in two or more niches, the organization increases its chances for survival. Even some large organizations prefer a multiple-niche strategy instead of serving the total market. Thus, Northwestern University has developed an excellent reputation in several professional education areas, including business, engineering, law, and medicine.

DECLINE STAGE

Most offer forms and brands eventually enter a stage where total volume declines. The decline may be slow, as in the case of barbershop quartet singing, or rapid, as in the case of politicians who fall out of public favor. Volume may plunge to zero and the offer may be withdrawn from the market. Or volume may petrify at a low level and continue for many years at that level. Many universities have witnessed a long-term decline in their schools of education and social work and have wrestled with decisions about what to do with these weakening offerings.

Volume declines for a number of reasons. Technical advances may give birth to new forms and brands, which become effective substitutes. Changes in fashion or tastes may lead to customer erosion. These developments intensify overcapacity and competition.

As volume declines, some organizations withdraw from the industry in order to invest their resources in more attractive markets. Those remaining in the industry tend to reduce their number of offerings. They withdraw from smaller market segments and weaker distribution channels. The promotion budget is reduced. The price may also be reduced to halt the decline in demand.

Unless strong reasons for retention exist, carrying a weak offering is very costly to the organization. The cost of maintaining a weak offering is not just the amount of uncovered cost. No financial accounting can adequately convey all the hidden costs. The weak offering tends to consume a disproportionate amount of management's time; it often requires frequent price adjustments; it requires both advertising and sales force attention that might better be diverted to making the "healthy" offerings more profitable; its very unfitness can cause customer misgivings and cast a shadow on the organization's image. The biggest cost imposed by carrying weak offerings may lie in the future. By not being eliminated at the proper time, these offerings delay the aggressive search for replacements; they create a lopsided offer mix, long on yesterday's breadwinners and short on tomorrow's breadwinners; they reduce current cash flow and weaken the organization's foothold on the future.

An organization faces a number of tasks and decisions in handling its aging offerings.

Identifying the Weak Offerings

The first task is to establish a system that will identify offerings that are in a declining stage. Six steps are involved:[14]

1. An offer review committee is appointed with the responsibility for developing a system for periodically reviewing weak offerings in the organization's mix.
2. This committee meets and develops a set of objectives and procedures for reviewing weak offerings.
3. The controller's office fills out data for each offering showing trends in market size, market share, prices, and costs.
4. This information is run against a computer program that identifies the most dubious offerings. The criteria include the number of years of sales decline, market share trends, and cost trends.
5. Offerings put on the dubious list are then reported to the managers responsible for them. The managers fill out forms showing where they think sales and costs on dubious offerings will go with no change in the current marketing program and with their recommended changes in the current program.
6. The offer review committee examines the offer rating form for each dubious offer and makes a recommendation to leave it alone, to modify its marketing strategy, or to drop it.

Determining Marketing Strategies in Declining Markets

In the face of declining sales, some organizations abandon the market earlier than others. The organizations that remain enjoy a temporary increase in sales as they pick up the customers of the withdrawing organizations. Thus, any organization faces the issue of whether it should be the one to stay in the market until the end.

If it decides to stay in the market, the organization faces further strategic choices. The organization could adopt a *continuation strategy* in which it continues its past marketing strategy: same market segments, channels, pricing, and promotion. Or, it could follow a *concentration strategy* in which case it concentrates its resources in the strongest markets while phasing out its efforts elsewhere. Finally, it could follow a *harvesting strategy,* in which it sharply reduces its expenses to increase its positive cash flow, knowing that this will accelerate the rate of sales decline and the ultimate demise of the offering.

THE DROP DECISION

When an offering has been singled out for elimination, the organization faces some further decisions. First, it has the option of selling or transferring the offering to someone else or dropping it completely. Second, it has to decide whether the offering should be dropped quickly or slowly. Third, it has to decide on the level of service to maintain to cover existing customers.

Recently, various government units have adopted "sunset" proposals for the review and termination of government programs on a regular cycle. Each federal program would receive a review on a five- or six-year cycle. The reviewing government committee would determine whether the current program had met its objectives and whether it should be continued at the same budget level or with higher or lower funding.

SUMMARY

New offerings follow an S-shaped pattern over their life cycle. They move through introductory, growth, maturity, and decline stages. The strategic issues facing the nonprofit marketing manager differ across these stages.

In the introductory stage, the manager must first be concerned with securing trials of the new offering. Five groups may be identified on the basis of when they are likely to enter the innovation adoption process. First are the innovators, who will try almost anything that is new and who are considered odd by the rest of the population. They can usually be ignored by the new offer manager. The second group, the early adopters, cannot be ignored because they are the opinion leaders who influence the next large group, the early majority. The late majority, which enters next, pays less attention to others in making their decisions to adopt and must be convinced that the new offering is not a fad. The last group, the laggards, can typically also be ignored because they are very tradition-oriented and very slow to try anything new.

There is a clear set of stages through which anyone goes in adopting an innovation, from knowledge to persuasion to decision and confirmation. Innovations that have significant relative advantages over old approaches, that are compatible with the culture, and that can be communicated easily and tried out before full adoption will diffuse faster than other innovations.

In the maturity phase, the organization must decide whether to pursue a market leader, market challenger, market follower, or market nicher strategy. Market leaders have to decide further whether they will emphasize expanding the total market, protecting market share, or expanding market share. Challengers must decide whom to challenge—the market leaders, other firms their own size, or firms smaller than themselves. Market followers must decide whether to follow closely, at a distance, or selectively. The market nicher must decide on the basis of their niching strategy. For many, a multiple-niching strategy is the most effective and safest.

In the decline stage of the offer life cycle, management must be careful not to retain weak offerings long after they have ceased to contribute to the organization. While there may be valid reasons for keeping some losing offerings, this decision should be made rationally in full recognition of the hidden costs that weak offerings often incur.

QUESTIONS

1. Who are the market leaders, market followers, market challengers, and market nichers among social and health-related charitable organizations?

2. How would one find early adopters for family planning programs in developing countries? What kind of marketing strategy would you devise to try to win them over to such a program?

3. Which of the following is likely to be more rapidly adopted in a South American country—an intrauterine contraceptive device or oral rehydration salt solutions (a treatment for severe infant diarrhea)? Support your reasoning.

4. Suggest a strategy for a new local charity seeking support for a food relief program in a major city. In particular, show how existing competition will be dealt with in such a strategy.

5. Many hospitals have programs, facilities, and services that are no longer profitable. Yet each has its particular supporters within the institution. Devise a checklist you would use to assess which of these weak offerings were least desirable and most likely to be given up by the institution.

NOTES

1. See James Coleman, Elihu Katz, and Herbert Menzel, "The Diffusion of an Innovation Among Physicians," *Sociometry,* December 1957, pp. 253–270.

2. See J. Bohlen and G. Beal, *How Farm People Accept New Ideas,* Special Report No. 15 (Ames, Iowa: Iowa State College Agricultural Extension Service, November 1955).

3. Everett M. Rogers, *Diffusion of Innovations* (New York: Free Press, 1962).

4. Ibid., p. 192.

5. Everett M. Rogers and David G. Cartano, "Methods of Measuring Opinion Leadership," *Public Opinion Quarterly,* Fall 1962, pp. 43–45; and George Booker and Michael J. Houston, "An Evaluation of Measures of Opinion Leadership," in Kenneth L. Bernhardt, ed., *Marketing 1776–1976 and Beyond* (Chicago: American Marketing Association, 1976), pp. 562–564.

6. Coleman, Katz, and Menzel, "Diffusion of Innovation."

7. Everett M. Rogers with F. Floyd Shoemaker, *Communication of Innovations* (New York: Free Press, 1971).

8. Christopher H. Lovelock and Charles B. Weinberg, *Marketing for Public and Nonprofit Managers* (New York: John Wiley, 1984), p. 77.

9. "Putting On the Ritz at the Y" *Time,* July 21, 1986, p. 65.

10. This material is adapted from Philip Kotler, *Marketing Management: Analysis Planning and Control,* 5th ed. (Englewood Cliffs, N.J.: Prentice-Hall, 1984), Chapter 12. For another approach, see Michael E. Porter, *Competitive Strategy: Techniques for Analyzing Industries and Competitors* (New York: Free Press, 1980).

11. Robert D. Buzzell, Bradley T. Gale, and Ralph G. M. Sultan, "Market Share—a Key to Profitability," *Harvard Business Review,* January-February 1975, pp. 97–106.

12. John D. C. Roach, "From Strategic Planning to Strategic Performance: Closing the Achievement Gap," *Outlook,* Spring 1981, p. 22

13. R. G. Hamermesh, M. J. Anderson, Jr., and J. E. Harris, "Strategies for Low Market Share Businesses," *Harvard Business Review,* May-June 1978, pp. 95–102.

14. For further details, see Philip Kotler, "Phasing Out Weak Products," *Harvard Business Review,* March-April 1965, pp. 107–118.

Strategies for Products, Services, and Social Behaviors

"I've bitten my nails down to the quick; I chew gum like crazy; and I've gained ten pounds," said a university student who recently quit smoking cigarettes. "But it's worth it," she said. "My hair, clothes, and breath smell fresher since I quit. I don't have nicotine stains on my fingers and my teeth, and I save 80 cents a day," said the ex-smoker. "Besides that, I save myself all the aggravation of dying for a cigarette in the no-smoking section of a restaurant, running out of cigarettes late at night, and bugging my nonsmoking friends when I light up. So I quit cold turkey."

That's just how the American Cancer Society's five-day Stop Smoking Clinic at the University of Illinois's McKinley Health Center suggests that people quit. "You're supposed to make a commitment and quit the first day," said Bonnie Berger, student intern at the center and coordinator of the program. "The next four days you 'buddy-up' with another member of the program to help keep you from smoking again," she said.

The clinic includes movies, a panel of ex-smokers, and a series of speakers such as psychologists and medical doctors to help teach the group how to quit smoking permanently.

Another five-day clinic was undertaken at the Seventh-Day Adventist Church. According to Kenneth Harding, pastor of the church and director of the program, "The five-day stop-smoking clinic of the Seventh-Day Adventist Church is the granddaddy" of all the stop-smoking clinics. The Seventh-Day Adventist Church started its program before the American Cancer Society agreed with a 1965 study that found that smoking was dangerous. The clinic also included films and guest speakers and cost $10.

Other stop-smoking plans also exist. "If you don't quit one way, you're not a failure," said Rosann Sherrill, a nurse at the Carle Foundation Hospital and director of the hospital's Chicago Lung Association stop-smoking clinic. The Chicago Lung Association and Dr. Charles Gruder of the University of Illinois psychology department, Circle campus, developed a "smoking by the clock" stop-smoking program that allows the smoker a certain number of cigarettes to be smoked at scheduled time intervals, Sherrill said.

The idea is to break the chain of smoking by letting the smoker have a cigarette only on the hour or the half hour, depending on the person, Sherrill said. They even use a chart, she said. "[Smoking is] not quite as enjoyable that way," Sherrill said. "A lot of people who have been smoking for a long time are afraid of quitting, and they seem to like the interval approach."

"What we're trying to do is break the cue from the behavior," co-director Connie Poor said. "You're trying to disassociate the reward from the act of smoking." You might not want to smoke on a schedule, so you do one of two things: you either smoke without enjoying it as much as usual, or you don't have a cigarette, Poor said. The intervals between cigarettes are increased until the smoker becomes an ex-smoker.

"We encourage people to break their negative habit (smoking) with positive habits, such as exercise," said Polly Bowers, a health consultant at the Chicago Lung Association smoking and health department. The interval reduction program also uses a reward system, such as taking money saved from not buying cigarettes to go to the movies, or sleeping in or taking a bubble bath, she said. "They set their own goals and the clinic guides them."

SOURCE: Condensed from; Kathy Mehler, "Smokers Inhale Final Cigarettes with Group Help," *Daily Illini,* April 8, 1982, pp. 15–18, reprinted with permission.

The marketing activities of any nonprofit organization have in common the goal of ultimately affecting behavior. This new behavior is brought about as the result of an exchange in which the marketer offers benefits and imposes (minimal) costs in return for the target customer's acquiescence or active behavioral cooperation. The exchange may be one of three basic types:

1. *Product sales:* sales of physical goods for money, such as sales of museum gifts or Sierra Club calendars.

2. *Service sales:* Leasing of persons, places, or facilities to meet a personal need, such as occurs at museums and libraries.

3. *Social behavior changes:* Changes of personal behavior in response to non-economic incentives, such as wearing seat belts, voting Republican, or practicing contraception.

Nonprofits may simultaneously engage in marketing in all three categories, as the following examples show:

- Population Development Associates in Thailand sells condoms, T-shirts, and aspirins, rents hotel rooms, provides day-care services, and lobbies to get legislators to pass a law creating a new form of nonprofit (and nontaxed) private organization.
- The Krannert Center for the Performing Arts at the University of Illinois sells cream cakes and espresso, rents seats to concert attendees, and sponsors arts awareness programs for school children.
- The U.S. Postal Service sells commemorative stamps to collectors, "rents" its mail service to corporate and private subscribers, and from time to time tries to induce oversight committees to allow them to raise prices.
- The American Marketing Association sells publications, sends members on tours, offers them conferences, and tries to improve the public's perception of the field of marketing

Thus, nonprofit organizations must manage an *offer mix.* As nonprofit organizations mature and become more entrepreneurial, their offer mix often shifts. As noted in Chapter 1, museums are now doing much more product marketing to complement their traditional collection renting. Many performing arts organizations have shifted into more competitive service marketing since their attempts to affect granting agency behavior have become less successful. Many health organizations have swung their attention increasingly to selling wellness programs in such areas as better nutrition, smoking cessation, and stress management. As these shifts take place, marketers need to realize what kinds of problems they will face.

In this chapter, we shall examine the offer management challenges that an organization faces when it is engaged in product, service, or social behavior marketing. We begin with products but give this subject somewhat less attention, since it is the marketing topic about which the most has been written and for which many of the principles outlined in this volume have been developed.

PRODUCT MARKETING

Most nonprofit organizations offering products have multiple items in their portfolio. They have products, product lines, and product mixes. For clarity, we will use the following definitions:

A **product** is anything that can be offered to a market to satisfy a need. The category can include physical objects, services, persons, places, organizations, and ideas. Other names for a product would be an offering, value package, or benefit bundle.

A **product mix** is the set of all product lines and items that a particular organization makes available to consumers.

A **product line** is a group of products within a product mix that are closely related, either because they function in a similar manner, are made available to the same consumers, or are marketed through the same types of outlets.

A **product item** is a distinct unit within a product line that is distinguishable by size, appearance, price, or some other attribute.

PRODUCT ITEM DECISIONS

In developing a product to offer to a market, the product planner has to distinguish three levels of the concept of a product: the core, tangible, and augmented levels.

Core Product.   At the most fundamental level stands the core product, which answers the questions; What is the consumer really seeking? What need is the product really satisfying? UCLA markets educational programs, but students seek friendships and future earning power. The Sierra Club sells calendars, but purchasers are buying an organizing tool, aesthetic pleasure, and feelings of helping a "good cause." The marketer's job is to uncover the essential needs hiding under every product so that product benefits, not just product features, can be described. The core product stands at the center of the total product, as illustrated in Figure 15-1.

Tangible Product.   The core product is always made available to the buyer in some tangible form. That is, potential mothers seek family planning because it gives the core benefits of more free time and better economic circumstances. Birth control, however, comes in the form of tangible items like pills, intrauterine devices, spermicidal tablets, and condoms. A tangible product can be described as having up to five characteristics. First, it has certain *features;* for example, the birth control pill has high or low hormone levels or does or does not contain iron. Second, it has certain *styling;* some birth control pills are brightly colored and monogrammed, others are drab and featureless. The tangible product also has a certain *quality level;* it is made well or badly. Fourth, it has a certain *packaging.* Birth control pills come in various kinds of blister packs and purse-sized compacts designed

FIGURE 15-1

Three Levels of Product

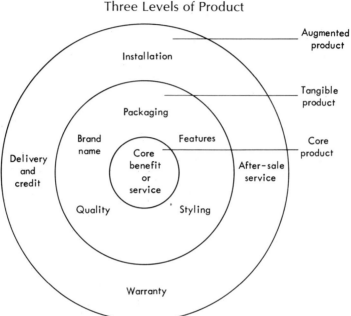

to make the product appealing and method of use straightforward. An attractive compact case for a birth control pill may increase its appeal; by contrast, an inconspicuous but high quality package may be just right for a condom. Fifth, the tangible product can have a *brand name.* Thus, the birth control pills used in Egypt are known to their users as Noridette, Norminest, Triovular, Microgynon, and so on. We will examine these five controllable characteristics of a tangible product in more detail.

FEATURES. Features represent individual components of the tangible product that could be added or subtracted without changing the product's style or quality. Consider a calendar marketer seeking to expand sales to international travelers. It might offer the following feature improvements:

1. Reference materials on the back of the calendar (U.S. and International time zones, foreign currency values)
2. Days and months in several languages
3. Dates of major foreign holidays.

The use of features has many advantages. The organization can go after specific market segments by selecting features that would appeal to these segments. Features are a tool for achieving product differentiation vis-à-vis competitors. They have the advantage of being easy to add or drop, or they can be made optional at little expense. They are often newsworthy and can attract free media publicity.[1]

STYLING.   Styling means giving a product or service a distinctive look or "feel." Much of the competition in durable goods—such as automobiles, watches, and electronic products—is style competition. The style of a product can be established before or after the target market is identified. An American condom manufacturer can try to sell his style of condom without modification in, say, Egypt. Or the manufacturer could adopt a market-oriented view and design the style for the intended audience by redesigning a package cameo figure to represent a more "Egyptian" countenance.

QUALITY.   Quality is the perceived level of performance in a product. Products that have a service feature in particular are tremendously variable in quality, depending upon who is providing the service and how much control the organization exercises over its service providers. A basic issue is how sales response varies with the level of quality in a particular market. Figure 15-2A shows a plausible relationship between sales and quality level. The curve shows that higher perceived quality leads to higher sales. It also says that very high quality may not add much additional sales, either because consumers cannot perceive very high quality or do not value it that much.

An organization must not only set an initial standard for quality but must also manage its quality level over time. Assume that the publications of a nonprofit organization are of average quality. It has three options (see Figure 15-2B). It can attempt to improve its quality level over time through better writing, photographs, reproduction, or packaging. This quality improvement should lead to improved market interest and response. The second option is to maintain its present level of quality and put its emphasis

FIGURE 15-2

Quality Level Strategies

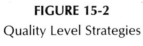

A. Relationship between service quality level and sales

B. Three strategies for service quality management through time

on other dimensions of the operation. The third option is to allow its quality to decline over time. This may be done deliberately when the institution wants to gradually withdraw from the product market. Otherwise, it indicates poor management, makes little strategic sense, and leads the organization down the road to extinction.

PACKAGING.   Packaging is the container or wrapper surrounding the specific product or service. We know that good packaging can add value beyond that perceived in the product itself; consider the contribution of the fancy perfume bottle to the "feeling" of the perfume. In the case of a service, packaging is a contribution of the larger context in which the product is found. Thus, a college campus's environment serves as the packaging of the academic product. Sturner recognizes the importance of the campus environment in contributing to the goals of a college: "The architecture, topography, and landscaping of a campus should support the educational function of the university. . . . The campus should evoke the feeling of a tone poem, a festival, a composition that washes over the inhabitants. It should combine all the senses—sight, sound, touch, taste, and scent—becoming a street scene, a block party, a family gathering, a tactile encounter, a tribute to the intermeshing of the sights and sounds of human beings."[2]

BRANDING.   Most products are branded, that is, given a name, term, sign, symbol, design, or some combination of these, which identifies them as the marketer's and differentiates them from competitors' offerings. Branding can also benefit the user, helping the user recognize a product, know its quality in advance, and so on. The seller might also gain. The Family of the Future (FOF) repackaged its basic condom in a new gold-and-white wrapper and branded the new offering as "Golden Tops." Although the tangible product was unchanged, the image of quality permitted FOF to reap a one-third higher price per unit with no loss in sales. (Indeed, the higher price itself probably added to the "quality" image.)

The brand name can also help define the product. We are offered Girl Scout Cookies and "Instant Lottery" tickets. The brand name or trademark can tie together a line of items and indicate a general standard of quality, as when all Family of the Future birth control products are marked with the organization's official symbol.

The creation of a brand name to symbolize the organization's product can contribute a number of values to the organization itself. An organization feels a proprietary interest in its brand name and normally works hard to ensure the quality and consistency of its service. It wants its brand name to create buyer confidence in its service and lead to consumer brand preference and repeat purchases.

Augmented Product.   The marketer can offer to the target market additional services and benefits that go beyond the tangible product, thereby producing an augmented product. Thus, a physician offering a Family of the

Future IUD can offer to insert it (utilizing training given him or her by FOF) and provide a booklet about IUDs that FOF has prepared. Organizations augment their tangible products to meet additional consumer wants, to differentiate their products from the competition, or both. Final outcomes depend as much or more on the augmented benefits as on the tangible product. As stated by Levitt, "The *new competition* is not between what companies produce in their factories, but between *what they add to their factory output in the form of packaging, services, advertising, customer advice, financing, delivery arrangements, warehousing, and other things that people value.*"[3]

Thus we see that a product is not a simple thing; rather, it is a complex blend consisting of a core need-satisfying offering, a set of tangible characteristics, and a set of augmented benefits. The organization should examine each of its products and design them in a way that will distinguish them from competitors' offers and carry the intended qualities to the intended target market. The more the product can be taken out of the commodity class and moved toward the branded class, the more control the organization will have over the level, timing, and composition of demand for its product.

PRODUCT MIX DECISIONS

An organization's product mix can be described in terms of its length, width, and depth. These concepts can be illustrated in a hypothetical example. Figure 15-3 shows a simplified product mix of a museum cafeteria. We see that the product mix, in terms of its length, consists of three product lines: main courses, desserts, and beverages. Each product line has a certain width. Thus, the dessert line includes ice creams and pastries. Finally, each product item has a certain depth: there are eighteen ice cream flavors and ten pastries.

Suppose the museum's cafeteria operated at a profit and the museum wanted to attract more sales. It could choose any of three alternatives. It

FIGURE 15-3

Length, Width, and Depth of a Museum Cafe's Product Mix

◄──────────────── Product Mix Length ────────────────►

Product Line Width	Main Courses	Desserts	Beverages
	Egg Dishes (4)	Ice Cream (18)	Soft Drinks (4)
	Mexican Dishes (3)	Pastries (10)	Coffee/Tea (2)
	Sandwiches (5)		Beer (3)
	Salads (6)		Wine (3)

could broaden its product mix by adding a line of appetizers or breakfast combinations. Or, it could expand one or more of its product lines, perhaps adding Italian or French entrees to its main course line, fruit or cheese offerings to the dessert line, or mineral water or fruit juices to its beverages. Finally, it could deepen any of its present ten product items, for example, by adding ten foreign beer brands, three imported wines, another sandwich variety, or six new ice cream flavors. The museum would have to assess which of these product mix choices would increase volume, patronage, or profit the most, depending on its objective.

On the other hand, the museum may want or need to prune the product mix in order to save money, free management time and energy, or focus its image better. Again it has three alternatives. It could make some product items "shallower." A more serious move would be to cut out an item altogether. Most radical, of course, would be to eliminate an entire line.

In reviewing the product mix, we should recognize that the products differ in their roles and contributions to the enterprise. Some are the enterprise's core products and others are its ancillary products. Furthermore, certain products play a major role in attracting patrons. They are called *product leaders* or *flagship products.* Often, an organization seeks to add a star product to its mix. The restaurant may offer a well-publicized torte from a famous Vienna restaurant for which customers save up their calories for weeks. An organization can showcase its flagship product as a symbol in its literature and promotion. The high cost of acquiring one crown jewel is often well repaid by the public relations value it produces.

A nonprofit organization should periodically reassess its product mix. Its product mix establishes its position vis-à-vis competitors in the minds of consumers, and it is also the source of its costs. The organization must be constantly alert to products whose costs have begun to exceed their benefits, the elimination of which would release funds for bringing new, more worthwhile products into its product mix.

SERVICE MARKETING

One of the major developments in post-World War II America has been the phenomenal growth of service industries. From constituting about 35 percent of the GNP in the mid-1940s, services now account for almost half of the GNP. Furthermore, two-thirds of the nongovernment labor force is engaged in service industries, and this percentage is expected to increase as the United States becomes a more postindustrial society. As a result of rising affluence, increasing leisure, and the growing complexity of products that require increased servicing, the United States has become the world's first service economy.

Service industries are quite numerous and varied. The whole government sector, with its courts, employment services, hospitals, lending agencies, military services, police and fire departments, post office, regulatory agencies, and schools, is in the service business. The private nonprofit sector, with its museums, charities, churches, colleges, foundations, and hospitals, is in the service business. And, of course, a good part of the business sector, with its airlines, banks, computer service bureaus, hotels, insurance companies, law firms, management consulting firms, medical practices, motion picture companies, plumbing repair companies, and real estate firms, is in the service business.

NATURE AND CHARACTERISTICS OF A SERVICE

A service can be defined as follows:

> A **service** is any activity or benefit that one party can offer to another that is essentially intangible and does not result in the ownership of anything. Its production may or may not be tied to a physical product.

Thus, attending a play, calling the police for assistance, traveling on public transportation, seeing a mental health counselor, and attending church are all exchanges involving a service.

Services have five distinctive characteristics that must be given special consideration when designing service marketing programs.

Intangibility.   Services are intangible, that is, they cannot be seen, tasted, felt, heard, or smelled before they are bought. Thus, a patient getting plastic surgery cannot see the result before the purchase; a patient walking into a psychiatrist's office cannot know the content or value of the service in advance since there is no tangible product involved. Under the circumstances, one makes a purchase on the basis of one's confidence in the service provider.

Service providers can do certain things to improve the client's confidence. First, they can increase the service's tangibility by a number of devices. A plastic surgeon can make a drawing or clay model showing the patient's expected appearance after the surgery. Second, they can manipulate the "atmospherics" surrounding the service encounter by having high quality furniture, medical school diplomas on the wall, attractive staff people, expensive books or magazines (and some professional journals) to read, and so on. Third, service providers can emphasize the benefits of using the service rather than just describing its features. Thus, a college admissions officer can talk to prospective students about the great jobs its alumni have found instead of just describing the job placement procedure. Fourth, service providers can put brand names on their service to increase buyers' confidence; this has been done by the American Red Cross, Salvation Army, and Friends of the Earth, among others. Fifth, service providers can use highly regarded personalities to add tangibility to the service, as muscular dystrophy has done with its Jerry Lewis telethons.

Inseparability.   A service is inseparable from the source that provides it. The very act of creating the service requires that the source, whether a person or a machine, be present. Thus, production and consumption occur simultaneously with services. This is in contrast to products, which continue to exist whether or not their source is present. Consider going to a Billy Graham religious happening. The spiritual impact is inseparable from the performer. It is not the same service if an announcer tells the audience that Billy Graham is indisposed and that they will play his record instead, or that John Smith will substitute. What this means is that the number of people who can experience a Billy Graham religious meeting is limited by the amount of time Billy Graham is willing to give to performances.

Several strategies exist for getting around this limitation. The service provider can learn to work with larger groups. We have seen Billy Graham's organization rent baseball or football stadiums to accommodate more people. Or the service provider can learn to provide the same service in less time, so that more groups can be accommodated. Or the service organization can train additional service providers and build up client confidence in them; for example, the Billy Graham organization can train other evangelists to run local meetings.

Variability.   Since a service is so closely linked to its source, it can be highly variable, depending on who is providing it and when it is being provided. A heart operation by Milton DeBakey is likely to be of higher quality than the same operation performed by a recently graduated M.D. And Doctor DeBakey's quality can vary depending on his energy and mental state at the time of the operation. Purchasers of services are aware of this high variability, and when there is a good deal at stake, will engage in extensive risk-reducing behavior such as talking to others and trying to learn who is the best provider.

Service firms should make an effort to deliver consistent quality. The major step is to develop a good personnel selection and training program. Airlines, banks, and hotels, for example, spend substantial sums of money to train their personnel to provide uniform and friendly service. Far too many nonprofit museums and hospitals rely on untrained volunteers and do very little to train their paid staffs to provide consistent high quality. They apparently do not appreciate how a few bad experiences can permanently damage a services provider's position. A second step is to routinize or even automate many parts of the services. A third step for controlling variability is to develop adequate customer satisfaction monitoring systems. The main tools are suggestions and complaint systems, customer surveys, and comparison shopping.[4]

Art museums could take a number of steps to make the experience that they and the customer *jointly produce* more meaningful:

- Study the types of visitors coming to the museum and what they are looking for. According to Andreasen, the types include *aesthetes,* those interested in the artistic merits of specific works; *historians,* those interested in where the work fits in the stream of art history; and *romantics,* those who want to know about the artist behind the work.[5] Visitors also differ in other respects. There are those who are willing to read the needed information and those who want to be talked to; those who will visit for a brief period and those who stay longer; and those who are visiting for the first time and those who are familiar with the museum.
- Provide separate suggested itineraries through the museum for each type of visitor.
- Provide guidebooks, wall posters, tape-recorded guides, and docent tours for the different types of visitors.

Perishability.   Services cannot be stored. A car can be kept in inventory until it is sold, but the revenue on an unoccupied theatre seat is lost forever. The reason many doctors charge patients for missed appointments is that the service value only existed at that point when the patient did not show up. The perishability of services is not a problem when demand is steady, because it is easy to staff the services in advance. When demand fluctuates heavily, however, service firms have difficult problems. Public transportation companies, for example, have to use much more equipment because of peak demand during rush hours than they would if public transportation needs were steady during the day.

Service organizations have several means available to try to produce a better match between demand and service capacity. Sasser has described several strategies for managing demand and supply.[6] On the demand side, the strategies include the following:

1. *Differential pricing* can be used to shift some demand from peak to off-peak periods. An example would be lower fares for riding buses in off-peak hours.
2. *Nonpeak demand can be developed* through marketing campaigns. The Miami Beach Chamber of Commerce has attempted to convince people to vacation in Miami Beach during the summer months.
3. *Complementary services* can be developed during peak time to provide diversions or alternatives to waiting customers. Physician's offices provide magazines for patients to read while waiting.
4. *Reservation systems* are a way to presell service, know how much service is needed, and reduce consumer waiting. Some hospitals, for example, assign patient beds by requiring physicians to make reservations.

On the supply side, these strategies may be used:

1. *Part-time employees* can be used to serve peak demand. Colleges add part-time teachers when enrollment goes up.

2. *Peak-time efficiency routines* can be introduced. Some computer centers do not permit large data sets to be loaded during peak periods.

3. *Consumer participation* in the tasks can be increased. New patients may be asked to fill out their own medical histories before seeing a physician during busy periods.

4. *Shared servcies* can be developed. Several hospitals can agree to shift patients among themselves, depending on load.

5. *Expandable facilities can be planned.* A nursing home can make arrangements with a nearby motel for extra beds during periods of excess demand.

Customer Involvement.   Many service exchanges involve the customer as an integral part in the production of the service itself. The customer therefore plays a crucial role in the ultimate nature and quality of the experience. At one extreme is client-centered psychological counseling, in which much of the value of the experience depends on the patient. Another example is the patient in the foreign hospital who cannot understand the staff, cannot figure out the telephone system, and cannot make his or her food preferences known and so considers foreign hospitals inferior and unpleasant, a judgment that can easily be projected onto the quality of care.

There are two approaches to incorporating consumer-as-producers into the marketing strategy. First, the marketer can study customers, observing the kinds of skills, biases, and perceptions the customer brings to the encounter. The marketer can then adopt a next-worst-case design strategy for the service. That is, a library designing an on-line information retrieval system may not wish to prepare an idiot-proof system that would satisfy the most inept user. This would be prohibitively costly. Rather, they should consider a degree of idiot-proofing that accommodates the first significant cluster of problem customers. The library could, for example, prepare many simple "help" commands that would solve the problems of 95 percent of the library patrons.

CLASSIFICATION OF SERVICES

There are many types of services, so it is difficult to generalize about them. First, we can ask to what extent the service is *people-based* or *equipment-based*. Thus, a psychoanalyst can serve patients with little equipment—a couch, perhaps—whereas a researcher needs an expensive piece of equipment called a computer. Among people-based services, we can distinguish between those involving professionals (professors, physicians, curators), skilled labor (typists, keypunch operators), and unskilled labor (museum guards, janitors). In equipment-based services, we can distinguish among services involving automated equipment (blood analyzers, vending machines), equipment operated by relatively unskilled labor (buses, motion picture projectors), and equipment operated by skilled labor (airplanes, computers).[7] Even within a specific service industry, different service providers vary in the amount of equipment they use; contrast James Taylor with his one guitar and the Jacksons with their tons of audio and visual equipment. Sometimes the accompanying equipment adds value to the service (stereo amplification) and sometimes it exists to reduce the amount of labor needed (automatic elevators).

Second, we can ask the degree to which the *client's presence* is necessary to the service. Thus, brain surgery involves the client's presence but church organ repair does not. To the extent that the client must be present, the service provider has to be considerate of his or her needs. Thus, modern hospital rooms need to be nicely decorated and comfortable because they are part of the service.

Third, we can ask about the client's *purchase motive,* whether the service meets a personal need (personal services) or a business need (business services). Hospital physicians, for example, price physical examinations differently depending upon whether they are serving personal patients or providing a prepaid service to the employees of a particular organization. Service providers can develop different service offers and marketing programs for personal service versus business service target markets.[8]

SOCIAL BEHAVIOR MARKETING

A large proportion of the nonprofit world is engaged in marketing strategies designed to get individuals, groups, or entire nations to change their behavior in ways that the marketer believes are good for the target market or for society as a whole.[9] This can include

- Encouraging people to adopt behaviors like exercising, wearing seat belts, or taking certain medicines that will make their lives better.
- Encouraging people to take actions that will benefit "everyone," like driving 55 miles per hour, not littering, or conserving water and energy.
- Encouraging individuals, corporate heads, and national and world leaders to support causes like nuclear disarmament, equal rights for minorities, or smaller U.S. defense budgets.

These efforts to alter the behavior of target publics go under different names. They are called *propaganda efforts* by their critics and *educational efforts* by their supporters. They are normal activities that occur in all societies. Every group has its cause and actively attempts to market its viewpoint to others. In a totalitarian society, only one group is allowed to propagandize *openly* for official causes, although others may be found agitating for change surreptitiously. In a free society, all groups propagate their viewpoints in "the marketplace of ideas."

Marketers seeking social behavior change are known by many names—propagandists, agitators, charismatic leaders, publicists, lobbyists, change agents, and so on. Many of them see their task in narrow terms, as that of developing and disseminating persuasive messages. We shall argue, however, that effective communication is only one part of the task required to successfully market social behavior change. The adoption of a social behavior, like the adoption of any product, requires a deep understanding of the needs, perceptions, preferences, reference groups, and behavioral patterns of the target audience, and the tailoring of messages, media, costs, and facilities to make changing easy. We use the term *social behavior marketing* to cover these tasks. We believe that social behavior marketing provides an effective conceptual system for thinking through the problems of bringing about changes in the ideas or practices of a target public.

Before proceeding, however, it is desirable to answer the objection that social behavior marketing provides Machiavellian guidance on how to get people to do what they do not want to do, or not do what they want to do— that is, it provides a means of social manipulation and control. In the first place, it is very difficult to change people's behavior with respect to issues that are important to them. Those who work face to face with individual clients and have their trust, such as psychiatrists, social workers, physicians, or relatives, know how difficult it is to change another person. It is even more difficult to change a whole group of people when the means are mass media ads that appear infrequently and are seen as coming from a biased source. Although social behavior marketing attempts to harness the insights of behavioral science and exchange theory to the task of social change, its power to bring about actual change, or bring it about in a reasonable amount of time, is very limited. The greater the target group's investment in a value or behavioral pattern, the more resistant it is to change. Social behavior marketing works best where the type of change is one people don't care about very much.

We define social behavior marketing as follows:

Social behavior marketing is the design, implementation, and control of programs designed to ultimately influence individual behavior in ways that the marketer believes are in the individual's or society's interests.[10]

The critical features that distinguish social behavior marketing from product and service marketing are that in the latter two types (1) money is paid by the consumer for something he or she can personally consume, and (2) the marketing entity has a major interest in maximizing its *own* returns. Social behavior marketing, by definition, implies that the social marketer is largely motivated by a desire to benefit *others*. While we recognize that not all social behavior marketers operate selflessly, we offer it as the ideal and the distinguishing feature of this type of exchange. It is the area of marketing that in principle is the *most customer-centered*. Paradoxically, it is also the area that many recipients feel is the least customer-centered. They resent "fanatics" who believe *they* know what's best for everyone. Enthusiasts for a cause are sometimes remarkably insensitive to the *customers'* reluctances and their needs and wants. They don't hide their disappointment in prospects who do *not* immediately donate money, stop smoking, or join the movement.

Finally, in stating that social behavior marketing involves customer behavior that the marketer thinks is socially desirable, we make no judgments about whether in any given circumstances they are right. Sound marketing approaches and techniques can be used as easily by a Hitler or a Charles Manson as by a Mother Theresa or a Pope John. Our purpose is to show social behavior marketers how to do strategic marketing, not to debate whether they should use it in certain cases and not in others. Our hope is that by making social marketing technology available to everyone, no one side of an issue will have a greater advantage than any other side.[11]

THE EMERGENCE AND EVOLUTION OF SOCIAL BEHAVIOR MARKETING

The roots of social behavior marketing lie in the informational approach, in the form known as *social advertising.* Many cause groups, struck by the apparent effectiveness of commercial advertising, began to consider its potential for changing public attitudes and behavior. Family planning organizations in India, Sri Lanka, Mexico, and several other countries have sponsored major advertising campaigns attempting to persuade people to have fewer children. Messages on billboards and over radio tell the public that they can be happier (Sri Lanka) or have a higher standard of living with fewer children (India). Nutrition groups have also used advertising extensively to encourage people to adopt better eating habits.

Properly designed, these campaigns can influence attitudes and behavior. The problem is that all too often these campaigns are the only step taken to motivate new behavior, and by themselves they are usually inadequate. First, the message may be inadequately researched. Media campaigns to encourage people in developing countries to improve their diets, for example, miss the point that many people lack knowledge of which foods are more healthful; they may lack the money to buy these goods; and in remote areas, they may not find certain foods available. Second, many people screen out the message through selective perception, distortion, and forgetting. Mass communications have much less direct influence on behavior than has been thought, and much of their influence is mediated through the opinion leadership of other people. Third, many people do not know what to do after their exposure to the message. The message "Stop smoking—it might kill you" does not help the smoker know how to handle the urge to smoke or where to go for help.

As these limitations were recognized, social advertising evolved into a broader approach known as *social communications.* Social communicators make greater use of personal selling and editorial support in addition to mass advertising. Thus, the family planning campaign in India utilizes a network of people—physicians, nurses, barbers—who "sell" the cause. Later, the campaign uses various sales promotion tools such as lotteries, editorials, buttons and signs, speeches, and press conferences to dramatize the message.

Only recently has *social behavior marketing* begun to replace social communication as a larger paradigm for effecting social change. Social behavior marketing adds at least four elements that are missing from a pure social communication approach.

One element is sophisticated *marketing research* to learn about the market and the probable effectiveness of alternative marketing approaches. Social advertising amounts to a shot in the dark unless it is preceded by careful marketing research. Thus social marketers concerned with smoking would examine the size of the smoking market, the major market segments, and the benefit-cost perceptions of different segments, and then they would design appropriate campaigns for each.

The second element added by social marketing is *offer development.* Faced with the problem of getting people to lower their thermostat settings in winter, a social advertiser or communicator would see the problem largely as one of exhorting people to lower the thermostat settings, using patriotic appeals, fuel-cost-saving appeals, or whatever seems appropriate. The social behavior marketer, in addition, would consider existing or potential products that would make it easier for people to adopt the desired behavior. Thus, thermostats may be equipped with an optional voice synthesizer that warned when settings are too high or too low and that when reset will rewind. Alternatively, adjustable governors may be added to the thermostat to prevent children from wasting energy. Whenever possible the social behavior marketer does not stick with the existing offer and try to sell it (a sales approach) but searches for the best offer to meet the need (a marketing approach).

The third element added by social behavior marketing is *the use of incentives.* Social communicators concentrate on composing messages dramatizing the benefits or minimizing the costs of different kinds of behaviors. Social behavior marketers go further and design specific incentives to increase the level of motivation. Social marketers, for example, have advised public health officials who are running immunization campaigns in remote villages to offer small gifts to people who show up for vaccinations. Some hospitals in South America run "price specials" on certain days during which people who come in for health checkups pay less than the normal charge. The sales promotion area is rich with tools that the marketer can use to promote socially desirable behaviors.

The fourth element added by social behavior marketing is concern for *response channels.* The marketer realizes that people wishing to change their behavior must invest time and effort, so the marketer considers ways to make it easier for them. Smoking cessation classes, for example, must be conveniently located and professionally conducted. Marketers are keenly aware of the need to develop convenient and attractive response channels to complement the communication channels. They are concerned not only with getting people to adopt a new behavior, but also with finding ways to facilitate maintenance of the behavior.

Thus, social behavior marketing goes beyond social advertising and social communication in that it involves all four "Ps," not just one. Social communicators usually come into the planning process after the objectives, policies, and products have been determined. They have little or no influence on product design, pricing, or distribution. Their job is to promote the organization's objectives and products using communication media. Social marketers, on the other hand, participate actively in the organizations's planning. They advise what products will be acceptable to the target publics, what incentives will work best, what distribution systems will be optimal, and what communication program will be effective. They think in exchange terms rather than solely in persuasion terms. They have as much interest in improving the organization's offer as in modifying the target market's attitude toward the offer. Whereas propagandists take the product, price, and channels as given, social marketers treat them as variables.

FACTORS AFFECTING THE SUCCESS OF SOCIAL BEHAVIOR MARKETING

Success in marketing social behavior change depends on the society's readiness for that change, which varies at different times. Ralph Nader could not have made much headway with consumerism if he campaigned for it in the late 1950s. Consumerism was successfully launched in the mid-1960s because all of the conditions were ripe. These conditions, according to Smelser, are structural conduciveness, structural strain, growth of a generalized belief, precipitating factors, mobilization for action, and social control.[12] These six conditions have been applied by Kotler to explain why consumerism could be successfully launched in the mid-1960s (see Figure 15-4).[13]

Structural conduciveness refers to basic developments in the society that eventually create potent reactions. Three developments were particularly noteworthy in the 1960s:

1. U.S. incomes and educational levels were advancing continuously. This portended that many citizens would eventually become concerned with the quality of their lives, not just with their material well-being.
2. U.S. technology and marketing were becoming increasingly complex, and this would inevitably create consumer problems.
3. The environment was progressively exploited in the interests of abundance. Observers began to see that an abundance of cars and conveniences would produce a shortage of clean air and water. The Malthusian specter of mankind running out of sufficient resources became a growing concern.

FIGURE 15-4

Factors Contributing to the Rise of Consumerism in the 1960s

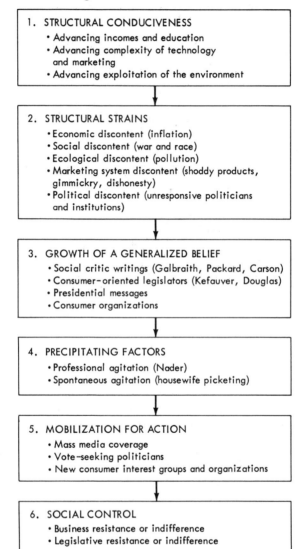

1. STRUCTURAL CONDUCIVENESS
   - Advancing incomes and education
   - Advancing complexity of technology and marketing
   - Advancing exploitation of the environment

2. STRUCTURAL STRAINS
   - Economic discontent (inflation)
   - Social discontent (war and race)
   - Ecological discontent (pollution)
   - Marketing system discontent (shoddy products, gimmickry, dishonesty)
   - Political discontent (unresponsive politicians and institutions)

3. GROWTH OF A GENERALIZED BELIEF
   - Social critic writings (Galbraith, Packard, Carson)
   - Consumer-oriented legislators (Kefauver, Douglas)
   - Presidential messages
   - Consumer organizations

4. PRECIPITATING FACTORS
   - Professional agitation (Nader)
   - Spontaneous agitation (housewife picketing)

5. MOBILIZATION FOR ACTION
   - Mass media coverage
   - Vote-seeking politicians
   - New consumer interest groups and organizations

6. SOCIAL CONTROL
   - Business resistance or indifference
   - Legislative resistance or indifference

These developments produced major *structural strains* in the society. The 1960s were a time of great public discontent and frustration. Economic discontent was created by steady inflation that left consumers feeling that their real incomes were deteriorating. Social discontent centered on the sorrowful conditions of the poor, the race issue, and the tremendous costs of the Vietnam war. Ecological discontent arose out of new awarenesses of the world population explosion and the pollution fallout associated with technological progress. Marketing system discontent centered on safety hazards, product breakdowns, commercial noise, and gimmickry. Political discontent reflected the widespread feelings that politicians and government institutions were not serving the people.

Discontent is not enough to drive change. There must grow a *generalized belief* about both the main causes of the social malaise and the potential effectiveness of collective social action. Here again, certain factors contributed importantly to the growth of a generalized belief.

1. The writings of social critics such as John Kenneth Galbraith, Vance Packard, and Rachel Carson provided a popular interpretation of the problem and of actionable solutions.
2. The hearings and proposals of a handful of congressmen such as Senator Estes Kefauver held out some hope of legislative remedy.
3. The presidential "consumer" messages of President Kennedy in 1962 and President Johnson in 1966 helped to legitimate belief and interest in this area of social action.
4. Old-line consumer testing and educational organizations continued to call public attention to the consumers' interests.

Given the growing collective belief, consumerism only awaited some *precipitating factors* to ignite the highly combustible social material. Two sparks specifically exploded the consumer movement. The one was General Motors' unwitting creation of a hero in Ralph Nader through its attempt to investigate him; Nader's successful attack against General Motors encouraged other organizers to undertake bold acts against the business system. The other was the occurrence of widespread and spontaneous store boycotts by housewives in search of a better deal from supermarkets.

These chance combustions would have vanished without a lasting effect if additional resources were not *mobilized for action.* As it turned out, three factors fueled the consumer movement.

1. The mass media gave front-page coverage and editorial support to the activities of consumer advocates. They found the issues safe, dramatic, and newsworthy. The media's attention was further amplified through word-of-mouth processes into grassroots expressions and feelings.
2. A large number of politicians at the federal, state, and local levels picked up consumerism as a safe, high-potential vote-getting social issue.
3. A number of existing and new organizations arose in defense of the consumer, including labor unions, consumer cooperatives, credit unions, product testing organizations, consumer education organizations, senior citizen groups, public interest law firms, and government agencies.

Of course, the progress and course of an incipient social movement depends on the reception it receives by those in *social control,* in this case, the industrial-political complex. A proper response by the agents of social control can drain the early movement of its force. But this did not happen. Many members of the business community attacked, resisted, or ignored the consumer advocates in a way that only strengthened the consumerist cause. Most legislative bodies were slow to respond with positive programs, thus feeding charges that the political system was unresponsive to consumer needs and that more direct action was required.

Thus, all the requisite conditions were met in the 1960s. Even without some of the structural strains, the cause of consumerism would have eventually emerged because of the increasing complexity of technology and the environmental issue.

As we indicated in Chapter 14, after a social behavior successfully takes hold, it goes through a life cycle. Cameron does not believe there is any one pattern:

> There is no characteristic life cycle of social movements. . . . If we quantify the development of a movement by counting members, amounts of income and expenditures, number of outside persons needed, number of pieces of literature and so on, we find great variations. . . . Some movements grow very slowly . . . others seem blessed with the vitality and reproductiveness of a mushroom and accumulate personnel and property with great rapidity . . . some skyrocket into prominence and then almost as quickly decline.[14]

Although there is great variation in the rates of growth and decline of social movements, many of them pass through certain well-defined stages. Each stage is characterized by a particular set of problems, strategic options, and leadership styles. One of the more typical patterns consists of four stages— the crusading stage, the popular cause stage, the managerial stage, and the bureaucratic stage.[15]

A great number of social behavior campaigns start out as crusades led by a few zealous individuals who have a knack for dramatizing a social ill. To the extent that their message is effective, new supporters are attracted and the cause may reach the stage of a popular movement. As a popular movement, it is still led by the original leaders, whose primary qualities are total absorption in the issues and personal charisma. But as the ranks of the movement swell, new problems must be coped with, such as developing clear definitions of roles and responsibilities and attracting adequate resources to keep the organization going. New types of leaders start being favored—those who have organizational skills—and the campaign passes into the managerial stage. The reins are tightened and more specific goal-setting, planning, and coordination take place. Nevertheless, with luck, the new leaders retain some of the original zeal. Finally, the movement passes into a bureaucratic phase in which the original zeal is lost, and the social behavior campaign is in the hands of functionaries whose main concern is organizational survival. The campaign is run like any other business with a product to sell; it has a rigid hierarchy, established policies, much functional specialization, and so on. Even the job of maintaining a following and support is handled as a specialist function.

These four stages are not inevitable or irreversible. A new leader may appear who gives a flabby movement a new vitality. The political right was in a slump for years until people like Milton Friedman and Ronald Reagan gave it a new respectability. On the other hand, other cause organizations that once commanded power and public attention, such as the Women's Christian Temperance Union, limp along well into the decline stage hoping, but not being able, to regain their former glory.

DISTINCTIONS AMONG TYPES OF SOCIAL BEHAVIOR CHANGE PROGRAMS

Social marketing aims to produce an optimal plan for bringing about a desired social change. The fact that the plan is optimal, however, does not guarantee that the target change will be achieved. It depends on how easy or difficult the targeted social change is. Without social marketing thinking, it may be that the desired social change has only a 10 percent chance of being achieved; the best social marketing plan may only increase this probability to 15 percent. In other words, some social changes are relatively easy to bring about, even without social marketing; others are supremely difficult to bring about, even with social marketing.

Three major dimensions determine the difficulty of successfully changing social behavior. In Chapter 3, we made the distinction between exchanges that were (1) low involvement or high involvement; (2) one-time or continuing; and (3) by individuals or groups. Examples of social behavior change programs in each of the six categories produced by these dimensions are indicated in Table 15-1.

Other things being equal, it is more difficult to change behaviors that are (1) high involvement, (2) group decisions, (3) continuing, or some combination of these. We shall discusss some of the problems of marketing one-time and continuous behavior changes.

One-Time Behavior Changes.   One-time behavior changes require that the target market comprehend something and take a specific action based on this comprehension. Action involves a cost to the actors. Even if their attitude toward the action is favorable, their carrying it out may be impeded by such factors as distance, time, expense, or plain inertia. For this reason, the marketer has to arrange factors that make it easy for target persons to carry out the one-time action.

Consider mass immunization campaigns. Medical teams in Africa visit villages in the hope of inoculating everyone. Over the years, medical teams have evolved a procedure to increase the number of villagers they attract. A marketing team is sent to each village a few weeks before the

Table 15-1

A TAXONOMY OF SOCIAL BEHAVIOR CHANGE PROGRAMS

One-Time Behavior	Low Involvement	High Involvement
Individual	Donating money to a charity Registering to vote Signing up for Medicaid	Donating blood
Group	Voting for a change in a state constitution	Voting out restrictive membership rules in a club
Continuing Behavior		
Individual	Not smoking in elevators	Stopping smoking or drug intake Practicing family planning
Group	Driving 55 M.P.H. Driving on the right side of the road	Supporting the concept of an all-volunteer army

appearance of the medical team. The marketers meet the village leaders to describe the importance and benefits of the program so that the leaders in turn will ask their people to cooperate. The marketers offer monetary or other incentives to the village leaders. They drive a sound truck around the village announcing the date and occasion. They promise rewards to those who show up. Posters are placed in various locations. The medical team arrives when scheduled and uses inoculation equipment that is relatively fast and painless. The whole effect is an orchestration of product, price, place, and promotion factors calculated to achieve the maximum possible turnout.

Another example in the mid-1960s involved Medicare sign-ups. Medicare was enacted into law to provide medical benefits for the *elderly.* The following year, Medicaid was enacted into law to provide medical benefits for the *indigent and handicapped.* In the state of New York, persons and families earning under $6,000 were eligible for Medicaid. One year after Medicaid was enacted, only one million of the three million eligible persons in New York City were enrolled. A survey revealed three factors behind the low enrollment rate:

1. A widespread lack of knowledge of Medicaid and its benefits.
2. Confusion of Medicaid with Medicare by elderly indigents who failed to realize the additional benefits available from Medicaid.
3. A mistaken belief that one had to be literally on the welfare rolls to be eligible.

The city of New York decided to launch a one-month campaign in June, 1967, to increase the number of eligible persons who signed up for Medicaid. The plan for social marketing Medicaid included the following elements:

1. The mayor declared the month of June as Medicaid Month.
2. Health educators in thirty health districts went into the community to organize public support. They enlisted the support of professional leaders, active lay leaders, informal leaders, volunteers from the police auxiliary, and persons from antipoverty programs.
3. Personnel and sound trucks appeared at busy locations on different days to answer questions.
4. Information tables were placed in three department stores in Brooklyn to reach shoppers who might be eligible for Medicaid.
5. Literature was distributed in the streets and through department stores, banks, post offices, supermarkets, and schools.
6. Publicity was placed in newspapers, radio, and television.
7. Car cards were placed in the city subway system.
8. Posters were distributed at hospital outpatient clinics, health centers, and antipoverty offices.

This campaign was so successful that it was extended into the month of July and in the two months, a total of 450,000 additional persons were enrolled in Medicaid.[16]

Continuing Behavior Change.   Getting individuals or groups to permanently change their behavior is harder than getting them to make one-shot action changes. People must unlearn old habits, learn new habits, and freeze the new pattern of behavior. In the area of birth control, for example, couples have to learn how to use new devices such as condoms or diaphragms and get into the habit of using them regularly without anyone being around to help them or to reinforce the behavior. In the area of safer driving, drivers who have a tendency to drink heavily at social gatherings must learn either to drink less or to know when they are not fit to drive their own car. Various campaigns have been directed at problem drivers to condition them to be aware of the problem and the penalties.

LOW INVOLVEMENT, CONTINUING BEHAVIOR CHANGE.   A good example of securing continuing group behavior change in a low involvement area was the effort to get the Swedish motoring public to change their driving habits. This project is outlined in Exhibit 15-1.

EXHIBIT 15-1. Sweden turns to the right

At five o'clock in the morning of September 3, 1967, Sweden changed her rule of the road from driving on the left to driving on the right. For the people of Sweden—almost 8,000,000 of them—this meant that an old and extremely well learned pattern of behavior would have to be changed. From that time, 2,000,000 motor vehicles and 1,000,000 other vehicles would have to be driven on the right instead of on the left, and people would have to pass each other on the left instead of on the right. In addition they would have to learn how to find their way about in the large towns, where traffic engineers were taking the opportunity to make a thorough reorganization of traffic and to introduce, for example, many new one-way streets.

The reorganization meant that the whole population—and of course those who happened to be visiting Sweden at the time—would have to be supplied with information telling them that traffic was to be reorganized, when and how the reorganization was to be effected, what traffic rules would be in force afterwards, and what local changes had been made for the regulation of traffic. For two weeks before September 3, therefore, and after that date until the end of the year, an information campaign of seldom-experienced dimensions was put into action. All conceivable media were used in the campaign—between three and four TV programs a day; an average of two daily radio programs and more than ten trailers; a thirty-two-page brochure of which 7,900,000 copies were printed and which was distributed to every household in Sweden. The brochure was translated into nine languages and was directly distributed to aliens resident in Sweden. It was also issued in editions for the deaf, the blind, and other special groups.

Every pupil in Sweden's schools received study materials adapted to the various stages of education from kindergartens to higher secondary schools and other advanced types of schools. Special printed matter was also produced for other public institutions such as pensioners' homes, hospitals, and prisons. For weeks after the changeover, practically every poster site in the country was used, and along the highways reminder signs were set up every three to five kilometers.

An advertising campaign was carried on in all the 130 daily newspapers and in weeklies and trade papers, from the last weeks in August until November. Even comics of the "Donald Duck" type carried advertising with traffic information adapted to their readers. In addition radio, TV, and newspapers gave information about the changeover in their news. On September 4, facts about right-hand traffic took up one-third of column space in the dailies.

Advertising films were shown before the main feature in movie houses and a sound track reminded audiences of right-hand traffic before they left at the end of the show. Spectators were given similar reminders at sports contests and other events. Traffic information and notices of various kinds were also given on, for example, milk cartons, soft drinks, plastic cups, coffee cans, and department stores' carrier-bags. Private enterprise produced right-hand traffic games, men's under-

EXHIBIT 15-1. (continued)

pants suitably marked with admonitions, and warning devices of the most diversified kinds for car drivers.

During the autumn of 1967, detailed analyses of the accident statistics showed that bicycle and moped accidents were at a relatively high figure during the first two weeks after the changeover, and also that head-on collisions were two to three times more than "normal" during the period from September to November. In both these cases, preventive measures were taken.

The conclusion that can be drawn from the course of developments after the changeover must reasonably be that it is possible to change the public's attitudes in traffic matters, that it is possible considerably to increase road users' traffic knowledge, and that it is possible to make a radical change in people's behavior in traffic.

SOURCE: "Getting all Swedish Drivers to prepare for a switch to the right-hand side of the road," condensed and reprinted from *Progress*, Vol. 53, No. 279 (Quarter, 1968), pp. 26–32. Reproduced with permission.

Change agents rely primarily on mass communication to influence permanent changes in behavior. In some cases, mass communication can be counterproductive. In the late sixties, when many young people were experimenting with hard drugs, advertising agencies, social agencies, and legislators felt that advertising could be a powerful weapon for discouraging hard drug usage. Much money was funded privately and by the government, with donations of time by advertising agencies and media organizations. Fear appeals were first tried, followed by more informational advertising. Soon some people began to voice doubts about the good that this was doing. UN Secretary-General Kurt Waldheim, presenting a drug evaluation study to the UN, cautioned in 1972: "Special care must be exercised in this connection not to arouse undue curiosity and unwittingly encourage experimentation."[17] Antidrug messages, especially on television, reach a lot of young persons who may never have thought about drugs. These young persons do not necessarily perceive the message negatively and might in fact develop a strong curiosity about the subject. This is accompanied by the feeling that if the older generation is spending that much money to talk them out of something, there must be something good in it. They start discussing drugs with their friends and soon learn where to obtain illegal drugs, how to use them, and that their peers think they are not that dangerous if used carefully. Thus, mass advertising might provoke initial curiosity more than fear and lead the person into exploration and experimentation.[18] The main point is that nonprofit organizations often resort to advertising with insufficient knowledge of the audience or testing of the probable effects of their message upon the audience.[19] And they fail to create mechanisms that enable people to translate their motivation into appropriate actions.

HIGH INVOLVEMENT CONTINUING BEHAVIOR CHANGE.   The most difficult kind of behavior to change is that which first requires a major change in values. When values are highly resistant to change, many social behavior marketers prefer to use the law to coerce new behaviors even if the laws are not accompanied by efforts to change attitudes. The theory is that as people comply with the new law, forces will be set into motion that will produce the desired attitude change. Consider the hundred years of persuasive effort to get southern schools in the United States to voluntarily desegregate. All attempts to change racially prejudiced attitudes failed. These attitudes were not only ideological but practical in supporting the system of white supremacy in the South. Unable to wait any longer for an attitude change, the Supreme Court in 1954 declared that all schools had to be desegregated. In the years that followed, school districts and citizens were forced to comply with a law that they did not like. Some resisted the court orders so that their behavior would be congruent with their attitudes. Others who complied gradually found their attitudes softening somewhat to come more into line with their behavior. The passage of a widely disliked law sets several forces in motion that may accelerate the adoption of the targeted attitude change.

1. The new law helps the law's supporters gain new strength. They coalesce their forces and work harder for its implementation.
2. The new law stimulates more radical proposals, leading citizens to accept the original change in order to ward off the more radical proposals.
3. The new law creates sustained media attention and word-of-mouth discussion, which leads people to examine their ideas and values more carefully.
4. The new law elicits conformity on the part of citizens who believe laws are to be obeyed. Conformity eventually leads from mere compliance to acceptance through processes of dissonance reduction.

Thus, when it comes to changing basic attitudes, the most effective means may be to pass laws requiring behavioral conformity, which set forces into motion that might accelerate the acceptance of new values. In this case, the social marketer's role is to build a climate favorable to the passage and acceptance of the new law.

SUMMARY

Most nonprofit organizations are multiproduct firms. They make decisions on product mix, product lines, and product items. An organization's product mix can be described in terms of its length, width, and depth. Some of the organization's products constitute its core products; others are its ancillary products. Organizations like to develop a flagship product or crown jewel product to advertise the organization.

A product itself can be defined as anything that can be offered to a market to satisfy a need. The category includes physical objects, services, persons, places, organizations, and ideas. Three levels of the concept of a product can be distinguished. The core product answers the question, What need is the product really meeting? The tangible product is the form in which the product exists. It is comprised of the product's features, styling, quality, packaging, and brand name. The augmented product consists of the tangible product and the additional services and benefits such as installation, after-sale service, delivery, credit, and warranty. As competition increases, organizations augment their product offers to compete.

Most nonprofit organizations, public and private, are primarily in the service business. Services can be defined as activities or benefits that one party can offer to another. Such services are essentially intangible, inseparable, variable, perishable, and often call for customer involvement. Services can be classified according to whether they are people- or equipment-based, whether the client's presence is necessary for the service to be performed, and whether the client is a consumer or a business. Service industries have lagged behind manufacturing firms in adopting and using marketing concepts. Yet rising costs and increased competition have forced service industries to search for new ways to increase their productivity and responsiveness.

Finally, many nonprofit organizations are involved in marketing ideas and causes in order to change the behavior of certain groups or individuals. Behavior can be changed using legal, technological, economic, and informational approaches. The informational approach became refined into social advertising and later social communication. Social marketing is a more sophisticated approach that combines informational, economic, and technological approaches. Social marketing is the design, implementation, and control of programs designed to ultimately influence individual behavior in ways the marketer believes are in the individuals' or society's interests.

QUESTIONS

1. Outline the criteria a library should use in determining the length, width, and breadth of its line of products and services.

2. How should a hospital choose a "crown jewel" service to promote? Should this jewel change over time, and if so, what should determine the best time to change?

3. An army recruit helps determine the nature of the army experience he or she achieves. How should this fact influence army recruiting strategy?

4. Develop a checklist of questions to help determine which of several states or localities are most ready for a social behavior change program such as one reducing cholesterol in the diet or getting passengers in automobiles to wear seat belts.

5. Why is it more difficult to change social behaviors that are high-involvement, continuing, and that involve group decisions?

NOTES

1. See John B. Stewart, "Functional Features, Product Strategy," *Harvard Business Review*, March-April 1959, pp. 65–78.

2. See William F. Sturner, "Environmental Code: Creating a Sense of

Place on the College Campus," *Journal of Higher Education,* February 1972, pp. 97–109.

3. Theodore Levitt, *The Marketing Mode* (New York: McGraw-Hill, 1969), p. 2.

4. See for example G. M. Hostage, "Quality Control in a Service Business," *Harvard Business Review,* July–August 1975, pp. 98–106.

5. Alan R. Andreasen, "Non-Profits: Check Your Attention to Customers," *Harvard Business Review,* May-June 1982, pp. 105–110.

6. See W. Earl Sasser, "Match Supply and Demand in Service Industries," *Harvard Business Review,* November–December 1976, pp. 133–40.

7. See Dan R. E. Thomas, "Strategy Is Different in Service Businesses," *Harvard Business Review,* July-August 1978, p. 161.

8. For additional classifications of services as well as an excellent general reference, see Christopher H. Lovelock, *Services Marketing* (Englewood Cliffs, N.J.: Prentice-Hall, 1984).

9. Philip Kotler and Gerald Zaltman, "Social Marketing: An Approach to Planned Social Change," *Journal of Marketing,* July 1971, pp. 3–12. This section is based partly on this article and a more recent one by Karen F. A. Fox and Philip Kotler, "The Marketing of Social Causes: The First Ten Years," *Journal of Marketing,* Fall 1980, pp. 24–33. The interested reader should also see Seymour Fine, *The Marketing of Ideas and Social Issues* (Columbus, Ohio: Grid, 1981), and Richard Manoff, *Social Marketing* (New York: Praeger, 1985).

10. The narrower term "social marketing" unfortunately has taken on other usages since then. Some authors use it to describe the whole of "nonprofit organization marketing," which is better called "societal marketing."

11. For a discussion of ethical issues posed by social marketing, see Gene R. Laczniak, Robert F. Lusch, and Patrick E. Murphy, "Social Marketing: Its Ethical Dimensions," *Journal of Marketing,* Spring 1979, pp. 29–36.

12. See Neil J. Smelser, *Theory of Collective Behavior* (New York: Free Press, 1963).

13. See Philip Kotler, "What Consumerism Means for Marketing," *Harvard Business Review,* May-June 1972, pp. 48–57.

14. W. B. Cameron, *Modern Social Movements* (New York: Random House, 1966).

15. See Philip Kotler, "The Elements of Social Action," *American Behavioral Scientist,* May-June 1971, pp. 691–717.

16. Raymond S. Alexander and Simon Podair, "Educating New York City Residents to Benefits of Medicaid," *Public Health Reports,* September 1969, pp. 767–72.

17. "Wrong Publicity May Push Drug Use: UN Chief," *Chicago Sun-Times,* May 8, 1972, p. 30.

18. See "Drug Ed a Bummer," *Behavior Today,* November 13, 1972, p. 2.

19. See Michael L. Ray, Scott Ward, and Gerald Lesser, *Experimentation to Improve Pretesting of Drug Abuse Education and Information Campaigns: A Summary* (Cambridge, Mass.: Marketing Science Institute, September 1973.)

CHAPTER 16

Managing Perceived Costs

It is no great revelation to parents of teenagers today that sending their sons and daughters to college is an expensive proposition. Costs for prestigious schools like Princeton are now $15,000 per year, while at smaller state schools they are still on the order of $6,000 to $9,000. Many parents despair at the prospect of trying to give their children the kind of advanced education they know is now virtually required for most white-collar careers and for many of the so-called trades and crafts.

To help parents cope with the prospect of these major expenditures, a few creative college marketers have developed imaginative tuition prepayment plans designed to cover the tuition costs of a given child at some fixed future date. The prototype for such plans was created by Duquesne University in Pittsburgh in the spring of 1985. Under the program, parents pay a one-time fixed amount which, given Duquesne's ability to reinvest such funds, would be sufficient to cover the tuition costs of a four-year college career at a specific future date. The amount to be put down, of course, depends on the age of the child and therefore the number of years until he or she would be enrolled. Thus, in 1986, a student planning to enroll at Duquesne in 1991 would have to deposit $16,785, while parents investing for a one-year-old's college education beginning in 2004 would only have to put down $5,802.

Money magazine calculates that this is a very good investment for parents. Not only will it force the necessary setting aside of college education funds, it represents a return likely to be better than most parents can achieve on their own. Duquesne's current tuition is $5,850 per year and is growing at an annual rate of 7 percent. By the year 2004, this could mean a four-year tuition bite of $93,942. If the parents of the one-year-old invested their $5,802 prepayment themselves in 9½ percent treasury bonds maturing between 2004 and 2008, they would only secure $40,000.*

Thus, the tuition prepayment plan is a creative way of reducing parents' costs while at the same time giving the institutions that use it a competitive edge in the student marketplace. It should be noted, however, that the prepayment plan is not risk-free for the parents. The colleges do not guarantee admission to a student who prepays. Thus, if the student proves ineligible—or on his or her own decides not to attend—the college will merely refund the fixed prepayment and will not pay interest on the amount.

*SOURCE: "Pay Now, Study Later?" Money, March 1986, p. 16.

Our view of the marketing task is that it starts with consumers and their perceptions of the costs and benefits to be derived from undertaking the behavior the marketer wants. In the preceding two chapters, we have considered some of the tactics a manager might use to increase the real and perceived benefits that flow from a product, service, or social behavior. In the present chapter, we look at the other side of the exchange equation, its prices. The reader will note that we said "prices," not "price." This distinction is crucial to the manager's understanding of this component of the marketing task.

THE NATURE AND ROLE OF PRICES

Consumers balance the expected benefits from an action against the expected costs. Money payment might be only one of these costs or sacrifices—a price in the traditional economic sense. Consider the case of a woman who is deciding whether to go to a doctor's office to have a breast examination because she has a history of breast cancer in her family. She has been exposed to social behavior marketing urging her to have regular examinations and to learn self-examination techniques. The visit to the doctor will cost her money. She will have to pay the doctor (or make a co-payment along with her insurance company). If she is an hourly worker and has no automobile, she will have to pay money for transportation and lose perhaps three hours of wages. If she is at home with a young child and drives, she may have to pay for a baby-sitter, an expressway toll, gasoline, and a parking fee.

Getting to and from the doctor involves nonmonetary costs in terms of physical energy or effort. For many, this may not be an important cost.

For an elderly person, however, such a cost can be very dramatic. Then there are a number of psychic costs, including

- Awkwardness at having to ask for time off from work.
- Embarrassment at having to explain to coworkers where you are going (or lying to them).
- Aggravation at having to find a taxi and find one quickly so as not to wait long (or, if she drives, aggravation at traffic delays and wasting time looking for a parking space).
- Worry that the doctor will be late in seeing her.
- Embarrassment at having her breasts examined.
- Fear that the examination might hurt (for example, if a biopsy has to be done).
- Fear that something will be found.
- Worries that, if something is found, treatment will be costly, consume even more time, and be painful.
- Worries that treatment might involve breast removal, which can cause "disfigurement," problems for her marriage, and embarrassment with her husband, children, and friends.

All of these "perceived costs" will run through her mind. A marketer who focuses primarily on promoting the *benefits* of having a periodic breast examination will probably fail to motivate many women. Many women know the benefits. It is the vast array of perceived costs that keep them from completing the action the marketer wants. In a great many of the exchanges a nonprofit marketer seeks, managing the perceived costs is often much more important than managing the benefits. Furthermore, the nominal *money* price tag on the exchange may be the least important of the perceived costs the consumer is concerned about; in social behavior exchanges, there usually is no price tag at all. We define perceived costs as follows:

> A **perceived cost** is any negative outcome of a proposed exchange perceived by a target consumer.

THE DUALITY OF PRICES

In an exchange, what is a benefit for one side is typically a cost for the other. Thus, a marketer who provides benefits to the consumer in the form of high quality service, nice surroundings, and a satisfaction guarantee does so at a cost to the marketer's own organization. These are the economic costs *the marketer* has to pay. On the other hand, a consumer paying money in exchange for these benefits provides a benefit for the marketer. Therefore, where an exchange involves a money price tag, the marketer is faced with an odd dilemma. There are many nonmoney costs the marketer will work hard to *minimize* so as to secure more exchanges. At the same time, there is at least one cost the marketer would like to *maximize* so the organization can stay in business and grow. To complicate matters even further, there may be occasions when the marketer may not want to minimize nonmoney costs and, indeed, may want to *increase* them. Often a marketer wishes to increase a nonmoney cost because the marketer will enjoy economic savings, which, in turn, will mean more profits from the exchange that could be used to reduce costs elsewhere or permit lower prices overall. Thus, a transit authority may reduce the frequency of its service in a high-income area (thus increasing waiting time and frustration for this market) so as to provide more service in a low-income area, invest in a subway system, or reduce the subsidy required from city or county revenues. Or, a hospital may require a patient to walk in for simple outpatient surgery and bear some of the physical, economic, and psychic costs of managing his or her own convalescence in order to keep the patient's out-of-pocket costs as low as possible.

COSTS MANAGEMENT

This dual nature of cost management presents a delicate problem for the nonprofit marketer. An optimal cost management strategy from the marketer's standpoint is one that maximizes the number of exchanges (or revenue) for a given cost to the marketers. How can such a strategy be developed? The marketer must begin by researching consumer perceptions of the costs they must pay. Otherwise, marketers may miss crucial but subtle barriers affecting particular consumer segments. Consider the following examples:

- The National Cancer Institute only realized within the last ten years that a perceived cost keeping many people from trying to quit smoking was the fear of failure.
- In rural villages in many countries, women who personally want to practice contraception do not do so because all the methods they know require that someone (or many people) become aware of their behavior.
- Some potential attenders of symphony concerts won't go because they believe they have to "dress up."
- Many elderly people do not attend theatre in downtown areas because they believe they will be mugged or robbed.
- Many elderly people will not accept nursing home care because this involves admitting that they are old.
- Many alcoholics avoid treatment because they don't want to admit to themselves that they are alcoholics.
- Some males do not take medication for high blood pressure because they believe it will make them sterile.
- Many uneducated women do not use IUDs because they believe that (1) an unexpected baby could be born with the IUD embedded in its body, or (2) the IUD will work its way through the women's body, causing all sorts of unimaginable problems.
- Some organizations won't hire consultants because to do so would be an admission that they lack some competence.

- Sanitary water systems are resisted in some villages because they disrupt established social intercourse systems (for example, the twice-daily congregation at the village well).
- Many potential theatre, ballet, opera, and symphony attenders avoid going because they don't want to feel ignorant about what's being presented.

Once these costs are understood, the marketer can consider the following questions:

1. Are there strategies that can be used to reduce the perceived costs?
2. What is the cost to the marketer of reducing a perceived cost to the customer?
3. What is the probable responsiveness of the consumer to given levels of perceived cost reduction expenditure by the marketer?

We shall consider how marketers can answer these questions from a theoretical and then a practical perspective.

A THEORETICAL APPROACH

The traditional microeconomic pricing model presents a useful theoretical framework for thinking about these cost issues. Consider the hypothetical case presented in Figure 16-1a. The horizontal axis represents the number of exchanges (or sales). The vertical axis represents both revenue and cost per unit of exchange to the marketer. In the typical for-profit case, the vertical axis would represent price and cost per unit. Each step moving *down* the vertical axis represents something given up by the marketer (that is, the difference between the current price and the amount the marketer could have obtained at the next highest price). On the other hand, reducing prices lowers the cost to consumers, and this should generate more exchanges (sales). Conversely, a step *up* the vertical axis means more retained revenue per unit to the marketer. This revenue, in a sense, is taken away from the customer (that is, the cost to the consumer is increased, as is the benefit to the marketer), thus lowering sales.

The problem for the marketer, then, is to choose the optimal balance between what the marketer receives and what burdens are put on customers (for example, the economic, social, or psychological "costs" he or she must pay). Two of the curves presented in Figure 16-1a suggest a solution. The four curves may be defined from the marketer's perspective as follows:

Average revenue is the average return to the marketer for each unit of exchange (where this exchange involves the sale of goods or services, average revenue equals price; it is equivalent to the total revenue divided by the number of units exchanged).

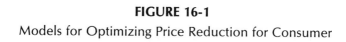

FIGURE 16-1

Models for Optimizing Price Reduction for Consumer

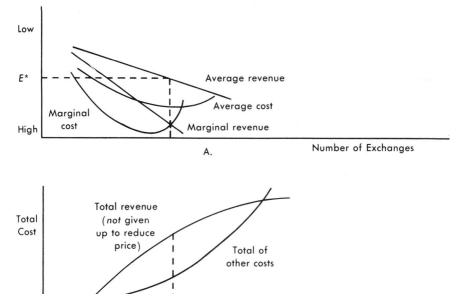

Average cost is the average amount the marketer spends to create a unit of exchange (for goods or services, this would be the average dollar cost per unit; it is equivalent to the total cost divided by the number of units exchanged).

Marginal revenue is, at each volume level, the amount of revenue the marketer gained by creating the last unit of exchange (it is equivalent to total revenue at the given level of volume minus total revenue at one unit less volume).

Marginal cost is, at each level of volume, the amount of cost the marketer would incur in creating the last unit of exchange (it is equivalent to total cost at the given level of volume minus total cost at one unit less volume).

Note that at low volume levels, marginal revenue exceeds marginal cost. As long as this is the case, the marketer is correct in encouraging increased units of exchange (presumably by lowering the perceived costs to the consumer and, of course, increasing the marketer's own expenditures). That is, each unit added brings in more revenue than it costs to create it. On the other hand, at high levels of exchange (to the right of Figure 16-1a), the opposite is true—creating additional units is a mistake if marginal cost exceeds marginal revenue.

Clearly, then, the optimal price to impose on one's customers is the one that will generate the volume level where marginal cost just equals marginal revenue. This point, marked E^*, is also where total revenue exceeds total costs by the widest amount, as shown in Figure 16-1b.

At the same time, this theoretical approach is difficult to implement in practice because it is hard to estimate the response function (AR). (It is easier to estimate the cost functions.) There are four possible estimation approaches:

1. *Historical analysis.* The marketer observes the amount of exchanges that did take place at different levels of the particular price. This approach requires that there be enough variation in the price variable (across time or across markets to permit analysis and that all other factors are constant or that their differentiated effects can be "removed" from the analysis.

2. *Experimental analysis.* The marketer systematically manipulates the price and watches what happens to the number of exchanges.

3. *Intentions research.* The marketer asks potential consumers how likely they are to undertake the exchange at various price levels.

4. *Subjective estimation.* The manager or other experts make their best guess as to the shape of the response curve.

PRACTICAL MANAGEMENT OF THE COST BUNDLE

The difficulty of precisely estimating the revenue response function should not discourage the marketer. If there is a single clearly important cost that drives consumer demand (for example, money price), then a formal analysis of the single response curve may well be justified. Consumer responses to offers, however, are usually a reaction to a *bundle* of costs (and, of course, a bundle of benefits). The problem in managing *costs* rather than *a cost* (singular) is to figure out *which* of many costs to reduce and *how much* to reduce them. For these decisions, the marketing manager needs to know *relative responses.* That is, for a given amount of the marketer's expenditure, which cost or costs could it be applied to to yield the largest net gain in the number of exchanges.

Suppose a clinic is considering reducing one of several customer costs. Suppose further that preliminary research indicates that four nonmoney costs keep potential patients from coming in more often (for example, for checkups) or drives them to other clinics or doctors. These costs are

- Parking costs and the accompanying frustrations.
- Waiting time in the office.

- Inconvenience in filling out forms (for example, for insurance).
- The general unpleasant experience of waiting in unattractive facilities.

The marketer should first determine ways to reduce each cost. Assume that the marketer can spend increments of $5,000 to bring about improvements in each area. For $5,000 to improve appearances, for example, the waiting and other rooms could be painted and new curtains installed. For $10,000, the clinic could acquire new waiting room furniture. Fifteen thousand dollars would also allow recarpeting. And so on. What the marketer now needs is a set of estimated response functions, as in Figure 16-2.

As we can see, the best place to put the first $5,000 is toward improving parking. This yields the largest gain in exchanges. The next $5,000 should also go for parking. At that point, a further $5,000 should be spent on appearance. Given that the marketer can estimate the economic value of the extra exchanges generated by each expenditure increment, he or she can expend $5,000 amounts until the gain in value from the added number of patients is no greater than the last expenditure.

The level of precision the marketer needs for this task is not great. It may be adequate simply to secure intentions data from a representative sample of current and past clinic customers.

FIGURE 16-2

Hypothetical Response Curves
for Alternative Cost Reduction Strategies

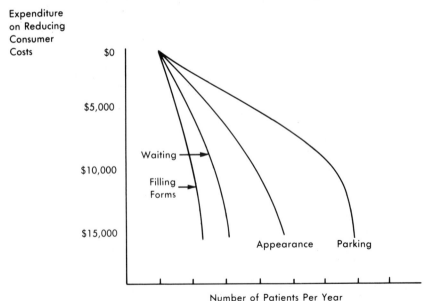

Number of Patients Per Year

Since a major determinant of the demand for many of the offerings of nonprofit organizations is money price, we shall devote more attention to this part of the bundle. Money prices are placed on a great range of goods and services and go by various names:

Money price is all around us. You pay RENT for your apartment, TUITION for your education, and a FEE to your physician or dentist. The airline, railway, taxi and bus companies charge you a FARE. The local utilities call their price a RATE, and the local bank charges you INTEREST for the money you borrow. The price for driving your car on Florida's Sunshine Parkway is a TOLL, and the company that insures your car charges you a PREMIUM. The guest lecturer charges an HONORARIUM to tell you about a government official who took a BRIBE to help a shady character steal DUES collected by a trade association. Clubs or societies to which you belong may make a special ASSESSMENT to pay unusual expenses. Your regular lawyer may ask for a RETAINER to cover her services. The "price" of an executive is a SALARY; the price of a salesperson may be a COMMISSION; and the price of a worker is a WAGE. Finally, although economists would disagree, many of us feel that INCOME TAXES are the price we pay for the privilege of making money!

In addition, price includes subsidiary decision elements. *List price* refers to the stated price of the product or service. *Actual price* may be greater or smaller, depending upon the presence of a *premium* or *discount*. Discounts can be extended to special groups such as seniors and students. If the buyers finance the purchase, they will be interested in the *credit* terms, that is, the monthly cost and time period of payments. Finally, the actual price might include additional charges representing *delivery, taxes,* and so on. All these elements can be varied as part of a pricing strategy.[1]

In handling the complex issues in money pricing, an organization should proceed through three stages. First, it should determine the *pricing objective,* whether it is to maximize profit, usage, fairness, or some other objective. Second, it should determine the *pricing strategy,* whether it should be cost-based, demand-based, or competition-based. Third, it should determine when and whether a *price change* is warranted and how to implement it.

SETTING THE PRICING OBJECTIVES

The first thing an organization must decide in developing a price or pricing policy is the objectives that it wants to achieve. Often the objectives are in conflict, and a choice must be made. Consider the following statement made by a camp director: "I want to keep my camp tuition fees as low as possible to enable more people to enjoy a summer camping experience, but I also must keep the price high enough to ensure that the camp will not lose money in the long run."[2] In this case, the camp director is in conflict over the two opposing goals of *audience size maximization* and *cost recovery maximization.*

However, these are only two of several possibilities. Five different pricing objectives can be distinguished: surplus maximization, cost recovery, market size maximization, social equity, and market disincentivization. Returning to the camp illustration, the camp may aim for surplus maximization on conferences, full cost recovery on weekend retreats, market size maximization for its summer camp program, and lower prices for all events for low-income families.

SURPLUS MAXIMIZATION

One would think that nonprofit organizations never use the principle of profit or surplus maximization. This is not so. There are many situations in which a nonprofit organization will want to set its price to yield the largest possible surplus. Thus, a charity organization will set the price for attending a major benefit dinner with the objective of maximizing its receipts over its costs. A university whose faculty has developed patented inventions will price these inventions to maximize its profits.

As indicated in Chapter 12, surplus-maximizing pricing requires the organization to estimate two functions, the response (demand) function and the cost function. These two functions are sufficient for deriving the theoretical best price. The demand function describes the expected quantity demanded per period (Q) at various prices (P) that might be charged. Suppose the firm is able to determine through demand analysis that its demand equation is

$$Q = 1,000 - 4P \qquad (16\text{-}1)$$

This says that demand is forecasted to be at most 1,000 units, and for every $1 increase in price, there will be four fewer units sold. Thus, the number of units pruchased at a price of say, $150, would be 400 units [$Q = 1,000 - 4(150)$].

The cost function describes the expected total cost (C) for various quantities per period (Q) that might be produced. Suppose the company derived the following cost equation for its product:

$$C = 6,000 + 50Q \qquad (16\text{-}2)$$

With the preceding demand and cost equation, the organization is in a position to determine the surplus maximization price. Two more equations are needed, both definitional in nature. First, total revenue (R) is equal to price times quantity sold:

$$R = PQ \qquad (16\text{-}3)$$

Second, total surplus ($) is the difference between total revenue and total cost:

$$\$ = R - C \tag{16-4}$$

With these four equations, the organization is in a position to find the surplus maximizing price. The surplus equation (16-4) can be turned into a pure function of the price charged:

$$\$ = R - C$$
$$\$ = PQ - C$$
$$\$ = PQ - (6{,}000 + 50Q)$$
$$\$ = P(1{,}000 - 4P) - 6{,}000 - 50(1{,}000 - 4P)$$
$$\$ = 1{,}000P - 4P^2 - 6{,}000 - 50{,}000 + 200P$$
$$\$ = -56{,}000 + 1{,}200P - 4P^2 \tag{16-5}$$

Equation 16-5 shows total surplus expressed as a function of the price that will be charged. The surplus maximizing price can be found in one of two ways. The researcher could use trial and error, trying out different prices to determine the shape of the profit function and the location of the maximum price. The surplus function turns out to be a parabola or hatlike figure and surplus reaches its highest point ($34,000) at a price of $150. At this price, the organization sells 400 units that produce a total revenue of $60,000.

This model for finding the surplus maximizing price, in spite of its theoretical elegance, is subject to four practical limitations:

1. The model shows how to find the price that maximizes short-run surplus rather than long-run surplus. There may be a trade-off between short-run and long-run surplus maximization, as when clients get angry at high prices and eventually switch to other sellers.
2. There are other parties to consider in setting a price. The model only considers the ultimate consumer's response to alternative prices. Other groups that may respond are competitors, suppliers, middlemen, government, and the general public. A high price might lead competitors to raise their price, in which case the demand would be different than that suggested by the demand function if it assumed no competitive reaction. Various suppliers, employees, banks, and raw material producers may take the price to reflect the organization's ability to pay and may raise their prices accordingly, in which case the cost function would be different than that assumed with no supplier reaction. Middlemen who handle the product may have some strong feelings about the proper price. The government, acting in the interests of the public, might establish a price ceiling, and this may exclude the surplus maximizing price. Finally, the general public might complain about the organization if its price appears to be too high.
3. This pricing model assumes that price can be set independently of the other elements in the marketing mix. But the other elements of the marketing mix affect demand and must be part of the demand function in searching for the optimal price. Thus, a ballet company can charge a higher price if it advertises extensively and builds up consumer interest.

4. This pricing model assumes that the demand and cost function can be accurately estimated. In the case of a new service, there is no experience upon which to base these estimates. Unless data are available on a similar service, estimates are likely to be highly subjective. Because the demand and cost equations are estimated with an unknown degree of error, the criterion of maximizing surplus may have to be replaced with the criterion of maximizing *expected* surplus. In any situation of risk and uncertainty, the pricing decision-maker will want to see how sensitive the theoretically calculated price is to alternative estimates of the demand and cost functions.

COST RECOVERY

Many nonprofit organizations seek a price that would help them recover a "reasonable" part of their costs. This is the idea behind the pricing of toll roads, postal services, and public mass transit services. Although the organizations could conceivably charge higher prices and increase their revenue (because of their monopolistic position), they do not want to incite an adverse reaction from the public or legislature.

How much cost should the organization try to recover through its pricing? Some organizations—such as universities and public mass transit organizations—aim at recovery of their operating costs. This would not provide money for expansion; they would rely on gifts or bond issues to raise the needed capital. Other organizations aim for *full cost recovery,* because they cannot rely on raising sufficient funds from other sources.

MARKET SIZE MAXIMIZATION

Some nonprofit organizations—public libraries and museums, for example—want to maximize the total number of users of their service. These organizations feel that the users and society profit from their services. In this case, a zero price will attract the greatest number of users. Even here there can be exceptions. Consider the following situation.[3]

> Family planners in India initially believed the distribution of free contraceptives would lead to the greatest level of usage. However, they discovered two flaws in the reasoning. Some potential consumers interpreted the zero price to signify low quality and avoided the free brand. In addition, many retailers would not carry it or display it prominently because it did not yield them profit, with the result that fewer units were ultimately available to consumers.

In most situations, a low price normally stimulates higher usage *and* may produce more revenue in the long run. Weinberg advocates that theatres should set low ticket prices because this attracts a larger audience, many of whom would eventually make donations to the theatres that would more than make up for the lower ticket prices.[4]

SOCIAL EQUITY

Organizations may wish to price their services in a way that contributes to social equity. In a study of who pays for library services, Weaver and Weaver concluded that "public libraries actually distribute income from the poorest to the more affluent strata of the community."[5]

One of the principal arguments leading to this conclusion is that because the poor rarely use the public library and because public libraries are often supported out of general tax revenues, the poor are paying for the nonpoor's libraries. Admittedly, there are other situations, such as city parks and welfare services, where the reverse is true. Our concepts of social equity hold that, wherever possible, public (and by extension, nonprofit) services should not operate to transfer wealth from the poor to the rich. In the public library case, the goal of social equity might be achieved by charging users for library services, perhaps charging even more for services (such as video-cassette rentals) that the upper classes use relatively more often.

MARKET DISINCENTIVIZATION

Pricing might be undertaken for the objective of discouraging as many people as possible from purchasing a particular product or service. There are many reasons an organization might want to do this. It might consider the product to be bad for people; it might want to discourage people from overtaxing a facility; it might be trying to ration demand to solve a temporary shortage; or it might want to discourage certain classes of buyers.

The purpose of the high government tax on cigarettes and liquor is to discourage the use of these products. But the price is never raised high enough because the government has come to rely on the substantial revenue produced by these taxes. A tax that is truly disincentivizing would yield the government no revenue and possibly create a large black market.

The Golden Gate Authority of San Francisco resorted to disincentive pricing when it learned that the famous bridge structure was overtaxed with traffic. A motorist was charged according to how many passengers were in the car, with the highest fee charged to cars with only the driver. This led to the formation of more driving car pools, although not as many as the authority had hoped.

Public mass transit companies have considered using disincentive pricing to discourage commuting during rush hours. These companies are in a weak financial situation because they have to finance the purchase of enough equipment to cover needs during the rush hours while the equipment sits idle the rest of the time. The pricing possibilities include raising the fare during rush hours or offering a lower fare at off-hours.

The emergence of shortages of gasoline, natural gas, and electrical energy from time to time increases the interest of organizations in disincentive pricing. The theoretical pricing model described earlier can be used to find the price that would achieve a specified reduction in usage.

CHOOSING A PRICING STRATEGY

After the organization has defined its pricing objective, it can consider the appropriate strategy for setting a specific price. Pricing strategies tend to be cost-oriented, demand-oriented, or competition-oriented.

COST-ORIENTED PRICING

Cost-oriented pricing refers to setting prices largely on the basis of costs, either marginal costs or total costs including overhead. Two examples are markup pricing and cost-plus pricing. They are similar in that the price is determined by adding some fixed percentage to the unit cost. *Markup pricing* is commonly found in the retail trades where the retailer adds predetermined but different markups to various goods. Museum gift shops use markup pricing in pricing their various items. *Cost-plus pricing* is used to describe the pricing of jobs that are nonroutine and difficult to "cost" in advance, such as some kinds of marketing research.

Nonprofit organizations vary in where they peg their price in relation to their costs. The American Red Cross charges a price for its blood that covers the "irreducible cost of recruiting, processing, collecting, and distributing the blood to the hospitals." On the other hand, several nonprofit organizations have historically charged less than their costs (called cost-minus pricing). Tuitions at private colleges and ticket prices for symphony orchestras often cover less than 50 percent of the total cost of these services; the remaining costs are covered by donations and interest on endowment funds.

The most popular form of cost-oriented pricing is known as *breakeven analysis.* The purpose of breakeven analysis is to determine, for any proposed price, how many units of an item would have to be sold to cover fully the costs; this is known as the *breakeven volume.* To illustrate, the director of a summer camp wants to set a tuition for an eight-week summer session that would cover the total costs of operating the camp. Suppose the fixed costs of the camp—real estate taxes, interest charges, physical property, insurance, building maintenance, vehicle expense, and so on—are $200,000. This is shown on the breakeven chart in Figure 16-4 as a horizontal line at the level of $200,000. The variable cost for serving each camper—food, handicraft supplies, camper insurance, and so on—is $500 per camper. This is shown as the variable cost line, starting at $200,000 and rising $500 for each camper. Finally, the camp director initially considers charging $1,000 tuition per camper. This is shown as the total revenue line, which begins at $0 and rises $1,000 per camper. The number of campers needed to break even is determined by the intersection of the total revenue and the total cost curves, here 400 campers. If the camp fails to attract at least 400 campers at $1,000 each, it will suffer a loss varying with the number of campers attracted. If the camp attracts more than 400 campers at $1,000 each, it will generate profits. The camp director's task is to estimate whether it will be easy or difficult to attract 400 campers at a tuition of $1,000.

The breakeven volume can be readily calculated for any proposed price by using the following formula:

$$\text{Breakeven volume} = \frac{\text{Fixed cost}}{\text{Price} - \text{Variable cost}} \tag{16-6}$$

Using the numbers in the previous example, we get:

$$\text{Breakeven volume} = \frac{\$200,000}{\$1,000 - \$500} = 400$$

On the other hand, if the camp director thought of charging $700 tuition, equation (16-6) indicates that he would have to attract 1,000 campers to break even.

Suppose the camp has a capacity to handle 1,000 campers and the camp director would like to attract that number. He can try to estimate a demand curve showing how many campers would be attracted at each price. Figure 16-3 shows the estimated demand curve. Accordingly, the $1,000 tuition would succeed in attracting 400 campers and allow the camp to break even. But the $700 tuition would attract only 800 campers, not 1,000 campers, and result in a loss. The camp director may decide to bear the loss, making it up through fundraising, in order to attract 800 campers. If he wants to attract 1,000 campers, a $550 tuition would be required according to Figure 16-3, thus creating an even larger loss.

Figure 16-3

Estimated Demand Curve for a Summer Camp

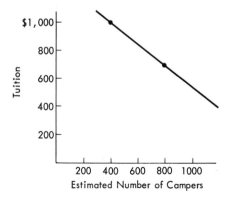

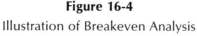

Figure 16-4

Illustration of Breakeven Analysis

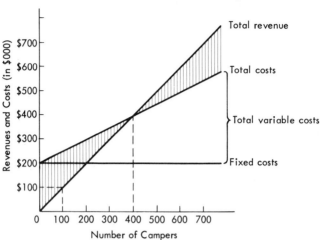

Cost-oriented pricing is popular for a number of reasons. First, there is generally less uncertainty about costs than about demand. By basing the price on cost, the seller simplifies the pricing task considerably; there is no need to make frequent adjustments as demand conditions change. Cost-plus pricing is also easier to implement for organizations that have a great many items to price, such as museum bookstores or Boy Scout equipment centers. Second, when all organizations in the industry use this pricing approach, their prices are similar if their costs and markups are similar. Price competition is therefore minimized, which would not be the case if competitors paid attention to demand variations. Third, there is the feeling that cost-markup pricing is socially fairer to buyers and sellers. Sellers do not take advantage of buyers when the demand becomes acute, yet sellers earn a fair return on their investment. It is also seen as socially fair when different prices must be charged to different users. Thus the popularity of cost-oriented pricing rests on its administrative simplicity, competitive harmony, and social fairness.

DEMAND-ORIENTED PRICING

Demand-oriented pricing looks at the condition of demand rather than the level of costs to set the price. Demand-oriented sellers estimate how much value buyers see in the market offer, and they price accordingly. Thus, a fine arts organization might set a ticket price of $40 for an Isaac Stern concert and $15 for a violin concert by a less well-known performer. The premise is that price should reflect the *perceived value* in the consumer's head. A corollary is that an organization should invest in building up the perceived value of the offer if it wants to charge a higher price. Thus, a private college that builds a reputation for excellence in teaching and research can charge a higher tuition than can an average private college.

A common form of demand-oriented pricing is price discrimination, in which a particular product is sold at two or more prices. Price discrimination takes various forms. Pricing that discriminates on a customer basis occurs when a museum charges a lower price to students than to the general public. Pricing that discriminates on a product-version basis occurs when the U.S. Postal Service charges more for registered mail than for unregistered mail. Pricing that discriminates on a place basis occurs when a symphony charges more for front-row seats than back-row seats. Pricing that discriminates on a time basis occurs when a public golf course charges higher greens fees on weekends than on weekdays. Another example is when high prices are charged for a new product or service when it is first introduced. This is called *skimming pricing* and is practiced when performing arts organizations charge higher prices on opening night.

For price discrimination to work, certain conditions must exist.[6] First, the market must be segmentable, and the segments must show different intensities of demand. Second, there should be no chance that the members of the segment paying the lower price could turn around and resell the product to the segment paying the higher price. Third, there should be little chance that competitors will undersell the firm in the segment being charged the higher price. Finally, the cost of segmenting and policing the market should not exceed the extra revenue derived from price discrimination.

COMPETITION-ORIENTED PRICING

When an organization sets its prices chiefly on the basis of what its competitors are charging, its pricing policy can be described as competition-oriented. It may choose to charge the same as competition, a higher price, or a lower price. The distinguishing characteristic is that the organization does *not* seek to maintain a rigid relation between its price and its own costs or demand. Its own costs or demand may change, but the organization maintains its price because competitors maintain their prices. Conversely, the same organization will change its prices when competitors change theirs, even if its own costs or demand have not altered.

The most popular type of competition-oriented pricing occurs when an organization tries to keep its price at the average level charged by the industry. Called *going-rate* or *imitative pricing,* it is popular for several reasons. Where costs are difficult to measure, it is felt that the going price represents the collective wisdom of the industry concerning the price that would yield a fair return. It is also felt that conforming to a going price would be least disruptive of industry harmony. The difficulty of knowing how buyers and competitors would react to price differentials is still another reason for this pricing.

Going-rate pricing primarily characterizes pricing practice in homogeneous product or service markets. The organization selling a homogeneous product has little choice about the setting of its price. Daring to charge more than the going rate would attract virtually no customers. Deciding to charge less is unnecessary either because the organization can sell its current output at the going price or because it fears that competitors will cut their prices too.

In markets characterized by *product differentiation,* organizations have more latitude in their price decision. Product differences serve to desensitize the buyer to existing price differentials. Organizations such as private universities try to establish themselves in a pricing zone with respect to their competitors, assuming the role of a high-tuition university, a medium-tuition university, or a low-tuition university. Their product and marketing programs are made compatible with this chosen pricing zone or vice versa. They respond to competitive changes in price to maintain their pricing zone.

CHANGING THE PRICE

Pricing is challenging when the organization is thinking about initiating a price change. The organization may be considering a *price reduction* in order to stimulate demand, to take advantage of lower costs, or to gain on weaker competitors. Or it may be considering a *price increase* in order to take advantage of strong demand or to pass on higher costs. Whether the price is to be moved up or down, the action will affect buyers, competitors, distributors, and suppliers, and can attract the interest of government as well. The success of the move depends on how the parties respond. Yet their responses are among the most difficult things to predict. Thus, a contemplated price change carries great risks. Here we will examine methods of estimating probable customer reactions to price changes.

PRICE ELASTICITY OF DEMAND

The traditional analysis of buyers' reactions to price change is based on the assumption that all buyers learn of the price change and take it at face value. The magnitude of their response to the price change is described by the concept of *price elasticity of demand.* This term refers to the ratio of the percentage change in demand (quantity sold per period) to the percentage change in price.[7] A price elasticity of −1 means that sales rise (fall) by the same percentage as price falls (rises). In this case, total revenue is left unaffected. A price elasticity greater than −1 means that sales rise (fall) by more than price falls (rises) in percentage terms; in this case, total revenue rises. A price elasticity lower than -1 means that sales rise (fall) by less than price falls (rises) in percentage terms; in this case, total revenue falls.

Price elasticity of demand allows more precise answers to the question of whether the organization's price is too high or too low. For example, suppose the price elasticity for the Massachusetts Turnpike is $-\frac{1}{2}$. This means that the Massachusetts Turnpike could raise the present toll and increase its total revenue. A 1 percent increase in the toll will lead to only a $\frac{1}{2}$ percent decline in usage. If, on the other hand, the price elasticity of the Massachusetts Turnpike is -2, it could increase its total revenue by lowering the toll. This is why it is critical to measure price elasticity.

In practice, price elasticity is extremely difficult to measure. There are definitional as well as statistical hurdles. Definitionally, price elasticity is not an absolute characteristic of the demand facing a seller, but a conditional one. Price elasticity depends on the magnitude of the contemplated price change. It may be negligible with a small price change and substantial with a large price change. Price elasticity also varies with the original price level. A 5 percent increase over a current price of $1 may exhibit quite a different elasticity than a 5 percent increase over a current price of $2. Finally, long-run price elasticity is apt to be different from short-run elasticity. Buyers may have to stick with the seller immediately after a price increase because choosing a new seller takes time, but they eventually stop purchasing from him or her. In this case, demand is more elastic in the long run than in the short run. Or the reverse might happen; buyers drop a seller in anger after he or she increased prices but then return later. The significance of this distinction between short-run and long-run elasticity is that sellers might not know how wise their price change is for a while.

Promotional Pricing

Often a nonprofit organization will maintain its list price but introduce "price specials" in order to stimulate increased buying. Promotional pricing can take many forms. Consider a theatre performing group that wants to attract a larger audience to its performances. Here are some promotional pricing options:

1. The theatre group can promote a series subscription that represents a savings over buying individual tickets to all of the performances. A popular way to express the savings is "See five plays for the price of four." Newman strongly favors discounts for subscription series on the grounds that the savings are a prime motivator for buying a subscription.[8] But Ryans and Weinberg, in a survey of subscription buyers for the American Conservatory Theater (ACT) in San Francisco, found that subscribers reported that the main reason for buying subscription series was not the savings but to make sure they went to the theatre more often and were assured of a good seat. ACT abandoned the discount in the next season with no palpable impact on subscription sales.[9]

2. The theatre group can offer an "early bird" discount on the series subscription to those subscribing up to two months in advance of the first performance.

3. The theatre group can offer second tickets at half price. Andreasen and Belk found potential theatregoers reacting extremely favorably to this proposal. It tapped into the notion of bringing a date or a friend to the theatre.[10]

4. The theatre group can offer unsold tickets at half price on the day of the performance. This method is used successfully by the ticket kiosks in New York City, Washington, D.C., Boston, and San Francisco. The theatre gets not only the extra seat revenue it would have lost, but also the revenue from the sale of drinks and candy during intermission.[11]

SUMMARY

Nonprofit marketers seek to influence exchanges. From the target consumer's perspective, these exchanges involve trading bundles of benefits for bundles of costs. Costs are the prices the customers perceive they must pay to participate. They can be monetary, nonmonetary, or mixed. Nonmonetary costs include psychic pain, the need to change old habits or ideas, expenditures of time and energy, and dislocations of social arrangements.

The nonprofit manager has a dual task in managing these costs. Some costs must be kept reasonably high to assure continuing revenues to the organization. Other costs must be reduced as much as possible to lower barriers to customer action. Since it will cost the organization to reduce each of these costs, it needs to know the relative responsiveness of target customers to each of these reductions.

In developing a strategy for monetary prices, the organization must first establish objectives. It could seek surplus maximization, cost recovery, market size maximization, social equity, or market disincentivization. Its specific strategy to meet these objectives may be primarily cost-oriented, demand-oriented, or competition-oriented. Organizations that are planning to change an existing price should take into account the price elasticity of demand and perceptual factors in the target audience's response.

QUESTIONS

1. The Muscular Dystrophy Association is seeking large donations. What are some of the "costs" a potential major donor would worry about when considering giving to the Association? In each case, how could the Association reduce the costs to make the donation more likely?

2. How should the U.S. Postal Service determine how much to spend on manpower to reduce customer waiting time at its post offices? Should it have faster lines for some customers (for example, businesses) than for others?

3. Many potential customers for programs treating socially unacceptable problems like alcoholism, drug abuse, or excessive fears (of heights, animals, etc.) can advertise to reduce the perceived costs of enrollment. What research approaches would you propose for learning both the nature and seriousness of such costs? How could the research results be used to segment the market?

4. Should social equity be a goal in the pricing strategy of the Southern California Rapid Transit District? If so, how should such a goal be achieved?

5. Most hospital-based programs for the treatment of eating disorders are full-time inpatient programs. These compete primarily with individual psychiatric office consultations. The neuropsychological center at a major West Coast university is thinking of introducing an evening eating disorders program directed at working young people. It would meet five days a week from 5:30 to 8:30 P.M. and would feature supervised eating, group and individual counseling, exercise classes, and lectures. How should the center go about determining a price (or set of prices) for this new program?

NOTES

1. David J. Schwartz, *Marketing Today: A Basic Approach,* 3d ed. (New York: Harcourt Brace Jovanovich, 1981), p. 271.

2. Quoted from an article by Ben F. Doddridge, "Toward the Development of a Practical Approach for a Solution of the Pricing Dilemma," *Christian Camping International,* January-February 1978, pp. 19–22.

3. See T. R. L. Black and John Farley, "Retailers in Social Program Strategy: The Case of Family Planning," *Columbia Journal of World Business,* Winter 1977, pp. 33–43.

4. Charles Weinberg, "Marketing Mix Decision Rules for Nonprofit Organizations," in Jagdish Sheth, ed., *Research in Marketing,* Vol. 3 (Greenwich, Conn.: JAI Press, 1980), pp. 191–234.

5. Frederick S. Weaver and Serena A. Weaver, "For Public Libraries the Poor Pay More," *Library Journal,* February 1, 1979, pp. 325–355.

6. See George Stigler, *The Theory of Price,* rev. ed. (New York: Macmillan, 1952), p. 215 ff.

7. In symbols,

$$Eqp = \frac{(Q_1 - Q_0)/^{1/2}(Q_0 + Q_1)}{(P_1 - P_0)/^{1/2}(P_0 + P_1)}$$

where:

    Eqp = elasticity of quantity sold with respect to a change in price
    Q_0, Q_1 = quantity sold per period before and after price change
    P_0, P_1 = old and new price

8. Danny Newman, *Subscribe Now!* (New York: Publishing Center for Cultural Resources, 1977).

9. Adrian B. Ryans and Charles B. Weinberg, "Consumer Dynamics in Nonprofit Organizations," *Journal of Consumer Research,* September 1978, pp. 89–95.

10. Alan R. Andreasen and Russell W. Belk, "Consumer Response to Arts Offerings: A Study of Theater and Symphony in Four Southern Cities," in Edward McCracken, ed., *Research in the Arts* (Baltimore: Walters Art Gallery, 1979), pp. 13–19.

11. "New York City Opera Rolls Back Prices," *The Cultural Post,* VII, March-April 1982, p. 9.

Managing the Marketing Channel

The Mayo Clinic has long been synonymous with excellence in medicine. Since the late nineteenth century, people have traveled there from all over the world in the search to discover what ails them.

Now the Mayo is ready to spread beyond Rochester, a town of 60,000 in southeastern Minnesota, and will soon attempt to spread its brand of medicine to other parts of the nation. Branches of the clinic are to open in Jacksonville, Florida, in 1986 and in Phoenix, Arizona, in 1987. Each will employ up to thirty physicians.

"The sky is the limit," said Dr. W. Eugene Mayberry, Chairman of the Board of Governors, in an interview. "It seemed to us that the best opportunity for physician-directed, national group practice resided with the Mayo Clinic. If we thought that that was the case and we had a unique model, did we not have an obligation to society to try to perpetuate that model to a greater degree than we have in the past?"

The Mayo is more than a prestigious medical facility. It describes itself as "a private trust for public purposes." Its fees are below the national average, but it generates about $600 million annually from 275,000 patients from the United States and abroad. It employs 820 physicians and scientists, 1,500 residents and other trainees, 5,600 paramedical workers, and 6,000 others in its two affiliated hospitals.

The Mayo grew out of the medical partnership of two brothers, Charles and William Mayo, who expanded the small clinic set up by their father in 1889 into the nation's first group practice. It began to grow in the early 1900s, attracting many young physicians as well as prominent scientists for training and research.

This year [1987] it has allocated about $53 million for research. Some 6 percent of that amount comes from patient fees, which is in keeping with the founders' notion that the patients of today should help cure the patients of tomorrow. Federal grants contribute $35 million.

Its school, which began granting degrees last spring after severing a seventy-year tie to the University of Minnesota, has 160 students.

The Mayo Clinic is known as a place that treats many of the world's most prominent people. But, Dr. Mayberry said, "If we had to pay our bills with those visits, we'd sure be a lot smaller than we are."

"The backbone of the Mayo Clinic," he continued, "has always been the midwestern farmer and his family. That's still true to this day." About 85 percent of the patients come from within a 500-mile radius of Rochester.

The Mayo has three main components: the clinic, the medical school, which receives 1,000 applications a year for forty openings, and the foundation, which oversees the entire operation and raises money for research and education. About 1,000 patients a day, from those referred by physicians all over the world to walk-ins, are at the clinic.

With the move toward the Sun Belt, where there is a population boom, particularly among the elderly who need medical treatment, Mayo hopes to be able to add new services and, above all, to be able to balance its flow of patients. "We tend to have a slackening demand for our services in January, February, and March, and then we tend to have more business than we can handle during the summer," Dr. Mayberry said. "In a warm-weather facility, we might have just the reverse so it would allow us some efficiency of operations."

SOURCE: E. R. Shipp, "Mayo Is Going Where the Patients Are." Copyright ©1984 by the New York Times Company. Reprinted by permission.

For an exchange to take place, marketers must be able to make contact directly or indirectly with the target customers. In the case of products, this means among other things that the goods must be physically delivered. For services, it means making the service available when and where the consumer can utilize it. And for social behaviors, it means having a communications vehicle to directly contact target consumers. All of these involve bringing the marketer and the consumer together to complete the transaction. The marketer's task is to create *time and place utility* for the customer.

THE NATURE AND ROLE OF CHANNEL DECISIONS

We shall refer to the aspects of an organization's marketing strategy that deal with creating time and place utilities as channel decisions. We define a channel as follows:

A **channel** is a conduit for bringing together a marketer and a target customer at some place and time for the purpose of facilitating a transaction.

Among the channels a marketer can use are:

- Specific buildings—stores, offices, clinics, and showrooms
- Salespeople—paid or volunteer
- Independent middlemen, such as wholesalers and retailers
- Telephones
- Advertising media
- Direct mail

An example of the set of channels in one industry is given in Exhibit 17-1.

EXHIBIT 17-1. The health care delivery system of the United States

Health care delivery systems are institutions that deliver preventative and curative health services to the public. In the past, Americans obtained health care services in two ways: by visiting a private physician or an emergency room of a local hospital. Some consumers sought out their pharmacists for advice on minor problems such as the common cold.

Today's health care services are available through several channels.

1. *Health maintenance organizations.* A growing number of people obtain their medical care through health maintenance organizations. By joining and paying a monthly fee, they can see staff doctors at any time and also get their hospitalization cost covered.
2. *Neighborhood health clinics.* Consumers in poorer neighborhoods often go to neighborhood health clinics for help. The clinic charges no fee or a low fee and has doctors ready to examine sick patients. The clinic is supported by public money, private money, or both.
3. *Hospital-based ambulatory care units.* Many hospitals have opened clinics in shopping areas or apartment buildings where people pay a fee for service. Since some of these patients need hospital care, these clinics serve as feeder operations to the hospital.
4. *Group practices.* The vast majority of physicians now belong to private group practices, which give them the opportunity to structure their hours better and gain the advantages of having expert colleagues. Patients pay a fee for service every time they visit their physician.
5. *Freestanding specialized service units.* Consumers can directly obtain specific services such as X-rays, blood tests, and minor surgery in specialized units set up for these purposes. They pay fees that in most cases are reimbursed by their health insurance plans.

Careful planning of channel strategy can have important positive pay-offs. Nonprofit organizations are typically deficient in resources, both financial and personnel. The careful use of channels can make programs more *efficient* by sharing costs, achieving economies of scale, and so on, and make them more *effective* by leveraging meager resources, small staffs, cramped facilities, and so on. The National Cancer Institute's antismoking program, for example, was able to have a significant impact with a relatively small budget by enlisting the help of physicians to distribute how-to-quit materials and to carry out "personal selling" with patients who had a history of smoking. NCI was able to obtain the same kind of leveraging for their breast self-examination program by securing the help of major corporations to serve as middlemen for their awareness and training programs.

While potentially very helpful, channel members can sometimes hurt an otherwise effective program. Here is a telling example:

> In 1976, the Treasury decided to reintroduce the Jefferson $2 bill to save on costs of printing and transporting $1 bills. Treasury officials estimated that if one-half of the 1.6 billion $1 bills in circulation were replaced with $2 bills, the country would save $35 million in printing costs within a five-year period. The Treasury commissioned a Harvard Business School survey to see if the public, banks, and retailers would use the new $2 bill. The survey discovered some negative attitudes, but believed that these could be overcome by a substantial advertising campaign. When the $2 bill was introduced, it met with great resistance from merchants as well as consumers. Merchants felt they needed another drawer in their cash registers or else the $2 bill would be confused with the $20 bills. Merchants also expressed fears that if they pushed the new bills on to consumers, many would not want them and so the merchants would lose patronage. Banks were also reluctant to push the bills, claiming the merchants did not want them and that they could be confused with $20 bills. The Treasury, which had planned to spend $300,000 advertising the $2 bill, dropped the idea because of the expense. A Federal Reserve official said, "They could have test-marketed the bill in two big cities for a year, found out their problems, and applied the information to marketing bills in the rest of the country."[1]

If the Treasury had put more effort in advance into studying the perceptions, needs, and wants of these crucial middlemen (rather than focusing most of their market research on the individual consumers), they could have developed more effective strategies for this crucial intermediary market. With hindsight, it seems clear that a subtle combination of education, persuasion, and a touch of political pressure would have removed the bottlenecks that eventually throttled the entire program.

Some nonprofit organizations are not fully aware of their channel problems and possibilities. Organized religion, for example, can be thought of as operating a religious service distribution system. Consider the following example of the Evangelical Covenant Church of America.

The central church office can be seen as the *manufacturer* or originator of the church's products; the regional offices throughout the country can be viewed as the *wholesaler;* and the individual churches, such as Faith Evangelical Covenant Church in Wheaton, might be viewed as the *retail outlets* for the church's services and products. As a "retailer" of the Evangelical Covenant Church of America's services and products, Faith Covenant Church is the part of the organization that comes face to face with the customer or members of the church and potential members. It is the individual "outlet" that can perform many of the critical functions needed to maintain members of the church and in fact, to increase its membership rolls.[2]

A host of other organizations face the problem of locating a set of facilities to optimally serve a spatially distributed population. This can be characterized in the following terms:

> Hospitals must be located . . . to serve the people with complete medical care, and we must build schools close to the children who have to learn. Fire stations must be located to give rapid access to potential conflagrations, and voting booths must be placed so that people can cast their ballots without expending unreasonable amounts of time, effort, or money to reach the polling stations. Many of our states face the problem of locating branch campuses to serve a burgeoning and increasingly well-educated population. In the cities we must create and locate playgrounds for the children. Many overpopulated countries must assign birth control clinics to reach the people with contraceptive and family planning information.[3]

CHANNEL STRATEGY

All marketers need conduits to their target consumers, and consumers need access to the marketer's services. The kinds of channels a marketer might use will vary depending on whether goods, services, or communications are the major flows within the channel. There are number of strategic problems, however, that apply to all channel decisions.

1. *Quality of service.* The nonprofit must decide how much place and time utility to offer as part of its offer mix.
2. *Direct versus indirect marketing.* The nonprofit must decide whether to carry out channel activities within its own organization, and if so, which ones.
3. *Length and breadth of channel structure.* The nonprofit must decide on (a) the number of levels to be interposed between the production of the offer and its exchange with consumers (length decisions), and (b) the total number of different channels or the number of elements to be included at each level of the channel (breadth decisions).
4. *Allocation of functions.* The nonprofit needs to decide who will handle the several channel flows (for example, information, goods, and money) in the channel.
5. *Recruiting channel members.* The nonprofit needs to know how to recruit and help motivate channel members.

6. *Coordination and control.* The nonprofit must develop systems for coordinating and controlling various channel members in the system.[4]

In considering these complex issues, we will use *efficiency* and *effectiveness* as our principal criteria. We define these as follows:

Efficiency is the extent to which a system achieves a given level of performance at the least possible cost in financial, time, and personnel resources; or achieves the maximum performance for a given level of resource cost.

Effectiveness is the extent to which a system achieves its objectives.

QUALITY OF CUSTOMER SERVICE

The first decision the marketer has to make is to determine the level and quality of service to offer to the target market. Each organization can visualize a maximum level of service that could be offered. Here are some examples:

- A public welfare department must distribute thousands of checks a year to people on public relief. The maximum level of service would be to mail checks daily to their homes or even to deliver the checks personally to avoid mail theft.
- A public library could render the maximum amount of service if it stood ready to receive calls for books and to deliver them within a few hours to the person's home.
- A city health department could dispatch doctors to the homes of sick patients upon call.
- A university could send a lecturer to any home or site upon request.

These solutions are oriented toward maximum consumer convenience. They are not practical because consumers would probably not pay for the extra convenience and the supplying organization could not afford the cost. Organizations have to find solutions that offer less consumer convenience in order to keep down the cost of distribution. Libraries and health departments, for example, can bring down their costs by offering their services in only a few locations and leaving the cost of travel to the consumers. They can cut down their costs still further by running an efficient organization in which waiting time is borne mainly by customers instead of becoming idle time borne by the staff. If a health clinic had five doctors instead of ten, the doctors would be continuously busy while the patients would absorb the cost of waiting. Thus, we see that organizations must begin their channel planning with a concept of the level and quality of place utility they will offer.

A second issue that determines the quality of service is the design of the channel facilities. Nonprofit organizations have to make decisions on the "look" of their facilities, because the look can affect customers' attitudes and behavior and their level of satisfaction. Consider how the "atmosphere" of a hospital can affect patients. Many older hospitals have an institutional look, with long narrow corridors, drab wall colors, and badly worn furniture, all of which contribute a depressed feeling to patients who are already depressed about their own condition. Newer hospitals are designed with colors, textures, furnishings, and layouts that reinforce positive patient feelings. They have circular or rectangular layouts with the nursing station in the center, permitting nurses to monitor patients better. Single-care units are replacing the traditional semiprivate rooms, based on the overwhelming preference for single-care units by both patients and physicians.

One of the most dramatic changeovers in atmosphere has occurred in abortion clinics.[5] When abortions were performed illegally, women would enter a depressing office with a single table on which the abortion would be performed. The sight of the office contributed to the patient's feeling of risk and sense of guilt and shame. Today's abortion clinics resemble normal doctor's offices with a comfortable waiting room and a competent receptionist who shows great understanding in dealing with the patient's needs and fears. The patient feels that she is being professionally supported in this difficult moment in her life.

Marketing planners in the future will use atmospherics as consciously and skillfully as they now use price, advertising, personal selling, public relations, and other tools of marketing *Atmospherics* describes the conscious designing of space to create or reinforce specific effects on buyers, such as feelings of well-being, safety, intimacy, or awe.[6]

An organization that is designing a service facility for the first time faces four major design decisions. Suppose a city wishes to build a public art museum. The four decisions are as follows:

1. *What should the building look like on the outside?* The building can look like a Greek temple (as many museums have looked in the past), a villa, a glass skyscraper, or another genre. It can look awe-inspiring, ordinary, or intimate. The decision will be influenced by the type of art collection and the message that the museum wants to convey about art in general.
2. *What should be the functional and flow characteristics of the building?* The planners have to consider whether the museum should consist of a few large rooms or many small ones. They also have to consider whether the major exhibits and best-known art works should be located near the entrance or at the other end of the building. The rooms and corridors must be designed in a way to handle capacity crowds so that people do not have to wait in long lines and experience congestion.
3. *What should the museum feel like on the inside?* Every building conveys a feeling, whether intended or unplanned. The planners have to consider whether the museum should feel awesome and somber, bright and modern, or

warm and intimate. Each feeling will have a different effect on the visitors and their overall satisfaction with the museum.

4. *What materials would best support the desired feeling of the building?* The feeling of a building is conveyed by visual cues (color, brightness, size, shapes), aural cues (volume, pitch), olfactory cues (scent, freshness), and tactile cues (softness, smoothness, temperature). The museum's planners have to choose colors, fabrics, and furnishings that create or reinforce the desired feeling.

The same questions arise for other organizations such as a post office, social service agency, unemployment office, college science building, city police station, and so on. Each facility will have a look that may add or detract from consumer satisfaction and employee performance. The latter point deserves special emphasis. Since the employees work in the facility all day long, the facility should be designed to support them in performing their work with ease and cheerfulness. Granted, many nonprofit organizations are financially weak and cannot afford the facilities that would be desired in principle. But the organization should pay attention to small details of the present facility and take even minor steps to improve the comfort or effectiveness of the facility. Every facility conveys something to the users about the service provider's attitudes toward them. It has been argued that a major reason for the ineffectiveness of YMCAs in attracting fitness-conscious consumers has been the antiquated and excessively spartan facilities they have in many locations.

DIRECT VS. INDIRECT CHANNELS

Other things being equal, organizations normally prefer to deal with their consumers directly. There are a number of advantages to such an approach:

1. Any revenue from the transaction does not have to be shared with other organizations or individuals.
2. All channel activities are controlled by the marketer.
3. Direct contact with customers provides the marketer with a better understanding of their needs and wants.
4. Direct contact with customers means quicker awareness of any problems with programs and products.
5. Responses to changes in the marketplace (for example, to new competitor initiatives) can be more rapid.
6. Opportunities for experimentation with alternative ways of reaching consumers are available.
7. More attention can be given to the marketer's offering than would be possible if it were only one of many carried by middlemen.
8. Strategies aimed at various consumer segments can be precisely tailored.

Given all of these advantages, why would an organization give up control at all? One reason we have already noted is that many organizations lack the financial resources to carry out a full program of direct marketing themselves. Consider the following example.

> The government of India adopted family planning as an official cause and set up a department to disseminate birth control information and contraceptives. The department's goal was to make contraceptives available to the smallest, remotest villages of a vast nation.[7] The solution took the form of engaging the distribution services of some of the largest packaged-goods companies in India because of their reach into the remotest corners of India. For example, the government used the intricate distribution system of Lever Brothers of India and saved itself the tremendous cost of building its own pipeline to the final markets. In choosing types of retailers, their objective was to make contraceptives maximally available and accessible to target users. They eventually elected to work with the following retailers: health clinics, barbers, field workers, retail stores, and vending machines. By placing contraceptives in these channels, the Indian government felt that potential users would have no difficulty finding the product.

Even if an organization has the funds to build its own channel to the final markets, it might not be able to do so as cheaply as through using an existing system. The cost of distributing contraceptives throughout India is low because the middlemen carry many other products that share in the cost of the distribution network. In a one-product distribution system, all the cost would be borne by that product.

Nor should the organization build its own distribution system if it can put its funds to better use. Thus, the number of births averted might be higher if the Indian government spent its funds to advertise family planning nationwide rather than using all its money to set up efficient distribution.

The case for using middlemen often rests on their superior efficiency and effectiveness in the performance of basic marketing tasks and functions. Marketing intermediaries, through their experience, specialization, contacts, and scale, offer the producing organization more than it can usually achieve on its own.

LENGTH VS. BREADTH

Once a nonprofit decides that it would be efficient to use middlemen, decisions must be made as to how many levels to have and how many units to have at each level. These are often referred to as length and breadth decisions, and they usually are not independent decisions. Consider first the breadth decision.

The organization that decides to retail its service rather than directly deliver it has the further decision of how many retail outlets to operate. The most economical decision is to open a single outlet. By having one large library in a major city, duplication of books, staff, and building costs are avoided. Citizens gain in that they will find an extensive collection of books.

They pay the price, however, of having to travel a longer distance. A system consisting of many library branches would attract more users. Most major cities compromise by building a central library and several branch libraries for the convenience of consumers. Some go further and operate bookmobiles, which are mobile libraries that park in different neighborhoods on different days and make books available to consumers.

The cost of running a state university is normally minimized by operating a single campus. Years ago, the University of California was located in Berkeley, California, and the University of Wisconsin was located in Madison, Wisconsin. Gradually these universities opened additional branches, partly to offer more convenience to residents in other parts of the state and partly to keep a single campus from becoming overly large and impersonal. Today the State University of New York (SUNY) operates sixty-four campuses! Once these universities decided to distribute their product throughout the state, they encountered all the classic distribution problems faced by business firms: how many branch locations to establish, how large should they be, where should they be located, and what specialization should take place at each branch.

At the retail level, breadth decisions are often dictated by consumers. Certain offerings must be mass distributed because consumers will not go out of their way to acquire them. These offerings are called *convenience goods.* In retailing, they usually involve offerings that are not particularly distinctive. For example, men will normally not go far out of their way to acquire condoms for birth control. Similarly, messages designed to change social behavior must be broadly distributed. Consumers do not seek out messages about 55 mile-per-hour speed limits or the use of seat belts. Many target consumers actively avoid channels that might influence them in ways they do not really want to be influenced. Alcohol and drug addicts may stop visiting doctors or attending church for fear of inadvertently encountering social marketing messages designed to change their behavior. Marketers must be persistent and innovative to reach these aversive consumers.

Where some offers and messages must be made very convenient for consumers, other offers may be such that consumers will undertake some effort to find and evaluate them. In retailing, these are referred to as *shopping goods,* since consumers believe they would gain something by looking around. Thus, consumers will go a moderate distance to secure the best emergency care service or smoking-cessation clinic. They will go some distance to see a good museum or watch a good play. In such cases, channel breadth becomes less important.

The final class of offerings is usually referred to as *specialty goods.* These are offers that consumers find so special that they will make a strong effort to seek them out. Further, these offers are perceived to be sufficiently unique that consumers will typically not accept substitutes. This status of being a specialty offering is one that many nonprofit marketers covet. The

Mayo Clinic, for example, is clearly a "specialty institution" for well-off consumers with unusual afflictions. The King Tut traveling exhibit was a "specialty good" consumers would go long distances and endure long lines to see. Harvard does not need branch campuses because students consider it a special privilege to study there. On the other hand, the State University of New York (SUNY) needs many branch campuses because students will not travel very far to attend a SUNY institution when nearby substitutes are available.

If a nonprofit organization determines that its customers require a broad distribution system, the next channel strategy question is, "How long should the channel be?" For nonprofits that manufacture a product (like the Sierra Club or the U.S. Treasury), two-, three-, and four-level channels are possible, as suggested in Figure 17-1. In general, the *broader* the distribution at the retail level, the *longer* the channel has to be. That is, if a nonprofit marketer wanted only *exclusive distribution* in a few major locations, a two-step channel (manufacturer to retailer to consumer) would be perfectly adequate. On the other hand, if a *selective distribution* system is chosen, with, say, half a dozen retailers handling the manufacturer's line in each of the largest 250 Standard Metropolitan Statistical Areas in the United States,

FIGURE 17-1

Alternative Channel Structures
for a Hypothetical Nonprofit Manufacturer

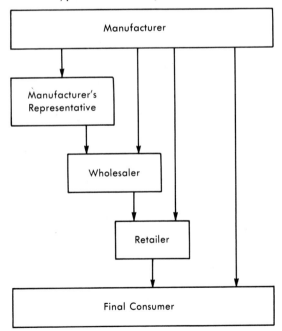

then several regional wholesalers may be needed to provide coverage. And, if the manufacturer wishes to have *mass distribution* in every nook and cranny of the country, then a manufacturer's representative may be needed to contact the hundreds of wholesalers required to service such a broad market.

Finally, note that strategic decisions about the length and breadth of a channel and whether the channel should be owned by the nonprofit marketer are independent decisions. That is, a marketer could choose a three-tiered system but set up its own wholesaling functions. This tactic would be known as *forward integration.* An environmental lobbying organization that produced its own books and calendars, for example, could use wholesalers to market them to recreation areas, book chains, university bookstores, and the like. But later, it could decide that recreation areas were underserved and that it could do better by handling its own product lines and even those of other manufacturers seeking better representation in recreation areas.

Nonprofit organizations can also undertake *backward integration.* Nonprofits such as museums and hospitals have active retail operations for which they contract with one or more wholesalers for merchandise. Many service-based nonprofits, such as nursing homes and religious organizations, acquire substantial amounts of supplies from wholesalers to carry out their operations. Some of these organizations could use available investment capital to integrate backwards in their channel by buying out or setting up a wholesale operation of their own. Again, the prime consideration in such a move should be whether it would result in important efficiencies, better service, or new revenues.

ALLOCATIONS OF FUNCTIONS

Channels exist to perform a number of functions. Consider the distribution channel for an environmental organization's books. For transactions to take place, the following functions would typically have to be performed:

1. *Physical transportation* of the books from the manufacturer to point of sale.
2. *Financing* of the various transactions between channel members, including the final customer.
3. *Transfer of title* from the manufacturer through to the consumer.
4. *Physical storage* of books at different channel levels.
5. *Determining elements of the offer,* including price, channel, discounts, packaging, and so forth.
6. *Communicating* with others about the availability and terms of the offering.
7. *Conducting market research* to learn what consumers want and whether they are satisfied with the present offering.
8. *Providing after-sale service,* such as repairing or replacing damaged merchandise.

Assuming a three-step channel involving a manufacturer, wholesaler, retailer, and final consumer, several alternative allocations of these functions are possible. The standard allocation of functions would be as follows. The manufacturer would determine all pricing and design issues. Books would be delivered to the wholesaler, who delivers to the retailer, to whom the consumer comes to browse and purchase. Each middleman would take title as the merchandise is received, and each would hold some inventory. The manufacturer would carry out some advertising to retailers and wholesalers, and sometimes, in cooperation with the retailer, to final consumers. The book publisher might also have salespeople who would travel to selected retail outlets promoting books and securing orders to be passed on to the wholesalers. "Market research" could be conducted by the retailers, mostly by observing and talking with book buyers. The retailers would pass the information back, either through the wholesaler to the manufacturer or directly to the manufacturer's salespeople. After-sale exchanges and replacements would be handled by the retailer.

But a number of alternative allocations are possible:

1. The manufacturer could retain title to the goods until they are sold to final consumers. This approach, called consignment selling, would put the entire risk of losses of unsold books with the manufacturer. On the other hand, by retaining ownership, the manufacturer could be assured that the retailer (or wholesaler) would not price the books lower or higher than the manufacturer believed was ideal.

2. The wholesaler could not hold inventory except to service its smallest retail customers. These wholesalers would take title, but the goods destined for large retailers would stay at the manufacturer's until the retailers placed an order.

3. Retailers could carry only a browsing copy. Orders would be sent to the manufacturer, who would ship directly by mail to consumers.

4. The manufacturer could delegate pricing and promotion decisions to wholesalers, who are closer to their market and better able to tailor the offer to the particular marketplace.

5. The manufacturer might decide that the books are receiving inadequate attention at the retail level and station its own salespeople in larger retail outlets to communicate with customers, secure feedback, and directly sell merchandise.

Each of these rearrangements could potentially improve the overall system's efficiency or effectiveness. Consider the second example above, in which the manufacturer shipped directly to the retailer. This could increase *efficiency* if (1) the manufacturer's carrying costs (for example, warehouse rental and interest on working capital) were lower than wholesaler's; (2) the manufacturer could more precisely predict consumer demand and smooth out production runs; and (3) the wholesalers would have no returns of unsold books (only retailers would have returns), so total inventory at any time in the system would be less and the costs of the actual paperwork and shipping of returns would be lower. The move could also improve *effectiveness* if (1) these cost savings permitted a reduction in prices to consumers that brought sales closer to desired levels; and (2) closer contact with retailers more quickly revealed spurts or declines in sales to final consumers, allowing faster manufacturer response (for example, price cuts) to changes in demand or new competitors' strategies.

ATTRACTING CHANNEL RESOURCES

Most nonprofits lack the resources to carry out many of the programs they are mandated to achieve. Thus, they must attract the help of others. In some cases, the problem is how to create channels that do not yet exist. Often this means getting other organizations to help out, as occurred when the American College of Physicians helped with the National Cancer Institute's (NCI) antismoking program; AT&T, Alcoa, Xerox, Pillsbury, and Honeywell contributed significantly to NCI's smoking and breast cancer programs; and FAFCO Solar Heating Systems helped distribute a brochure for the President's Council on Physical Fitness and Sports (see Figure 17-2).

Securing corporate sponsorship of programs in the workplace can be particularly effective, especially with respect to health care issues. As Novelli and Siska point out, "The worksite, where millions of Americans spend roughly one-third of their average day, may be the most promising environment for health behavior change." They note that Kimberley-Clark and Metropolitan Life Insurance both maintain extensive health promotion programs for their staff. Metropolitan's program includes nutrition education and special cafeteria meals as well as fitness, smoking-cessation, breast self-examination, and stress management programs. The director of Metropolitan's Center for Health Help offers the company's rationale for such programs: "People are our company's single biggest asset. It makes good business sense to invest wisely in our employees' good health."[8] New York Telephone claims that its health promotion programs saved it a minimum of $2.7 million in 1981, not considering the possible benefits of more positive employee attitudes and feelings.[9] Many companies would respond very favorably to the kinds of promotions indicated in Figures 17-3 and 17-4.

The organization can secure help by showing that the cooperating organizations can benefit in two ways. First, their participation can improve *public goodwill.* Many consumers, for example, feel more favorable toward the 7-Eleven Convenience Store chain for helping out with the annual Muscular Dystrophy campaign. Many businesses are impressed with advertising agencies that contribute free help to public service campaigns for the Advertising Council.

Second, their participation can confer *political advantages.* This was clearly a major incentive for five multinational convenience goods marketers who were willing to help the government of India in the early stages of its Nirodh contraceptive marketing program. A major problem for any contraceptive program in a developing country is distributing the product in the most distant regions of the market. The fact that marketers like Unilever and Brooke Bond Tea Company had extensive networks of trucks and peddlers on horseback reaching these remote areas provided major leverage for the Indian program. These foreign-owned companies rely on the government for their import licenses and other assistance. This was undoubtedly in their minds when they agreed to assist the government in its Nirodh program.

FIGURE 17-2

Private-Sector Distribution of a Nonprofit Marketer's Offer

THIS BOOKLET IS YOURS FREE!

DISCOVER 63 WAYS TO SHAPE UP AND HAVE FUN IN YOUR POOL!

PUT MORE LIFE IN YOUR LIFE!

Did you know that swimming is one of the best forms of exercise?

Truth is, swimming can help improve your physical condition, strength and circulation with *less effort* and in *less time* than other types of exercise. That means you'll have more time to enjoy the benefits. Namely, looking better and feeling younger.

SEE HOW EASY IT CAN BE.

To get you started, we're offering this free booklet, *Aqua Dynamics*. In it you'll find more than 60 exercises you

can do in your pool.

Start with the easy ones like Elementary Bobbing, Toe Bouncing and the Standing Crawl. Within weeks you'll be ready for the more daring Double Leg Raiser Twist... and many others.

The booklet is yours free—just for finding out

about solar heating for your pool!

FAFCO CAN HELP YOU WARM UP.

With a FAFCO solar heating system, you'll be swimming earlier in the year, and be able to keep on exercising in your pool well into the "off" season. Which means you'll not only get more for your investment, you'll get more out of life.

So fill in the reply card and mail it today, and start swimming for your health, energy ...and your life! This offer is limited to the first 1000 pool owners who respond, so act now.

SOURCE: With Permission of FAFCO, Inc.

There are many examples of *goodwill-based* private-sector assistance in carrying out nonprofit programs. Examples include the following:

- Major corporations permit payroll deductions for charitable contributions, which provide a significant proportion of United Way's annual collections of more than $3 billion.
- Various media companies contribute substantial amounts of free time and space for public service announcements.

FIGURE 17-3

Advertisement Asking for Private-Sector Support

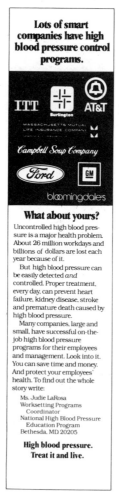

SOURCE: Needham Porter Novelli. Reprinted with permission.

- General Motors contributes to the seat-belt usage drive by offering a $10,000 insurance payout to the beneficiary of anyone killed in a G.M. car while wearing a seat belt.
- Many small retail stores are willing to display containers soliciting donations for charities such as the Kiwanis Club.
- Several milk companies have been putting photographs of lost children on their milk cartons, and selected utilities send out such pictures with their monthly bills.

FIGURE 17-4
Advertisement Asking for Private-Sector Support

SOURCE: Needham Porter Novelli. Reprinted with permission.

EXHIBIT 17-2. Using middlemen to promote mass transit

Robert Prowda of the Portland, Oregon, Transit System recently listed a wide range of possibilities that have been tried or proposed for securing middlemen help in promoting mass transit. He grouped these into three categories: fare or service subsidies, cooperative promotional, and institutional.

A. FARE or SERVICE SUBSIDIES

1. Employers purchase tickets or passes and sell them at a discount to employees. The Southern California Rapid Transit District sells 5,100 passes per month to twenty major employers in the Los Angeles area under such a program.
2. A shopping center, city, or merchants' association may subsidize fares for shoppers coming to their markets. In 1984, for example, SCRTD sold 53,000 tokens to the city of Downey to encourage shopping in their city.
3. Level-of-use guarantees can be made by employers in several cities for special schedules and routes to bring workers to their offices and factories.
4. Sponsors of special recreation, sporting, and cultural events can provide fare subsidies and cooperation on promotion for special transit service to their events.
5. A company or group may subsidize a bus or the entire transit system for a day, night, or weekend for the publicity or advertising benefits. In Champaign, Illinois, a local supermarket chain subsidizes a "generic bus." In another American city, a firm has subsidized all transit fares on New Year's Eve to reduce accidents.
6. Firms or organizations can erect bus shelters or transit information displays on their property or provide space for a park-and-ride lot.

B. COOPERATIVE PROMOTION

1. Employers can sponsor contests, drawings, and the like in which the prizes are passes or reduced fares on public transit.
2. Radio stations can sponsor contests for listeners offering public transit prizes.
3. The Southern California RTD has programs for distributing discount coupons on buses good at selected Pizza Hut and El Pollo Loco locations in Los Angeles.

C. INSTITUTIONAL

1. Efforts can be made to change public incentives to ride the transit system. The Duluth Transit Authority has proposed that bus riders receive a credit on their Minnesota income tax.
2. The Massachusetts Bay Transportation Authority obtained an agreement with the state insurance commission for transit users to receive a 10 percent reduction on their automobile insurance.

EXHIBIT 17-2. (continued)

3. State agencies reimbursing citizens for any transportation costs could be encouraged to include bus transit. It was discovered, for example, that the state of Oregon was paying jurors 15 cents a mile for auto travel but nothing for use of public transit.

4. If work contracts provide parking subsidies for employees, they should also include subsidies for public transit.

SOURCE: Adapted from Robert M. Prowda, "Leveraging Marketing Efforts Through Third Parties," in Richard K. Robinson and Christopher H. Lovelock, eds., *Marketing Public Transportation* (Chicago: American Marketing Association, 1981), pp. 81–86.

In late 1985, E. F. Hutton agreed to prepare in-house ads for the American Red Cross's emergency disaster relief campaign. It spent an additional $500,000 on placement of the ads on ABC's "Monday Night Football" and in eighty-five newspapers. Seven thousand Hutton brokers and corporate officers also made telephone solicitations just before the Christmas holidays. *Advertising Age* suggests that Hutton's motives may be mixed: "The effort should add some luster to Hutton's image as the company continues to feel aftershocks of its check float problems."[10]

Alternative possibilities for using middlemen to promote mass transit systems are outlined in Exhibit 17-2.

ACHIEVING COORDINATION AND CONTROL

Whether a nonprofit marketer is the "captain" of a channel system or a member of someone else's system, a crucial set of issues involves the day-to-day management of the system. In a mature marketing system, it is usually extremely important not only to have the right intermediaries performing the right function, but to make sure that they are carrying out those functions *when* and exactly in the *form* that is in the best interests of the overall system.

For many reasons, coordination and cooperation is difficult to achieve in nonprofit organizations. Among the impediments are the following:

- Competition for limited funds from either federal sources or third sector agencies like the United Way may make organizations reluctant to help out present or possible future rivals. Cooperation may be viewed as helping another agency grow, possibly at the expense of one's own agency.
- The insecurities of nonprofit leaders or staff may lead to the perception of cooperation as potential meddling, as a waste of time, or as a distraction from an insecure job.
- Territoriality can be a problem if one agency is unwilling to be subservient to another in an area in which the first agency believes it should be in charge.
- Differences in goals and values can often be a very serious problem when marketing "rears its ugly head." Those who have a social service orientation may feel that involvement with another agency that is an aggressive marketer will be "unprofessional" or will otherwise taint the potential channel member.

- Excessive time and energy costs may occur. If the channel is not well managed, much time might be spent in meeting, planning, and "coordinating." Besides delaying action, this can drive away more action-oriented participants. It has discouraged more than one private-sector marketer from cooperating in a non-profit program.
- Personality clashes are not unusual. Early in their organizational life cycle, many nonprofits are small and dominated by strong-willed, charismatic executives. In the struggling years of the enterprise, rivalries with other equally strong-willed leaders may develop. These can be very acrimonious and for many years stand in the way of needed cooperation.

THE BASIC PROBLEM[11]

The fundamental issue in achieving coordination and control is that another, separate organization with different perceptions, goals, and skills must undertake tasks that will help the organization achieve its goals. Yet the "channels problem" is not really different from the problem involved in marketing to final consumers. The problem is still one of *achieving exchanges with target markets,* in this case, key middlemen. As such, the steps involved in developing an effective middleman marketing strategy are clear:

1. Identify all potential middlemen segments.
2. Evaluate potential segments and select the best subset for detailed investigation.
3. Identify the basic needs and wants of these target middlemen.
4. Ascertain their current perceptions of the organization as to the *costs* and *benefits* of compliance as well as noncompliance in the proposed exchanges.
5. Develop strategies to increase the perceived benefits and reduce the perceived costs of participation.
6. Evaluate the probable costs and payoffs of each strategy and select, for the given planning period, those that will best achieve the organization's objectives.
7. Determine optimal strategies for *maintaining* the desired relationships.

Implicit in this approach are a number of marketing principles that we have already emphasized:

- The best marketing strategy *begins with the customer* (the middleman) rather than the organization.
- It is the target customer's needs, wants, and perceptions that are crucial to success, not those of the organization.
- Since these needs, wants, and perceptions are subjective phenomena, the marketer cannot *know* them and so must resort to formal or informal research to ascertain them.
- The number of exchanges *increases* if and only if the cost/benefit ratios perceived by selected target audiences are *changed* in a favorable direction.

- Since *change* in cost/benefit ratios is crucial, the key research issue is how will target audience perceptions *change* as a result of alternative marketing strategy choices?

- Strategies must be developed not only to create first-time trials, but also to ensure *continued* usage by trial participants, to *increase* usage by present or trial participants, or both.

- Finally, the selection of optimum short- and long-run strategies is not merely a matter of increasing *effectiveness* in creating exchanges, the selection must also take into account the costs to the organization of creating exchanges (the *efficiency* issue).

THE PLACE of POWER

Some channel strategies focus only on achieving one-time trials. Examples would include getting middlemen to secure donations to a specific university endowment fund, getting people to put up posters for a given charity event, or obtaining sponsorship of a specific educational or persuasion seminar. More frequently, however, nonprofit marketers strive—or ought to strive— to secure some kind of continuing cooperation in the form of repeated exchanges beyond the "trial" period.

How can continuing cooperation be achieved? The "channels literature" in the main has considered the relationships between interinstitutional *power* and organizational *roles* as the key elements in bringing about long-run cooperation. These relationships, in turn, must be explicitly linked to cost/benefit concepts of exchange theory. For practicing managers, the latter linkage is essential if the approaches are to be useful.

COSTS, BENEFITS, POWER, and ROLES

The long-term role that a marketer adopts in a channel relationship is closely related to the type of influence it wishes to exert. The marketer may choose to establish an independent or dependent relationship with the target channel member. Within this relationship, the marketer attempts to exert *influence* over the channel member. Helbert Kelman has suggested that for influence to work, one of three types of responses on the part of the target channel member must have occured: internalization, identification, or compliance.[12] (See Figure 17-5.)

Internalization occurs if the channel member sees that participation in the channel relationship is a rational choice that, whatever the benefits to the channel leader, is clearly in the channel member's own best interests. The channel leader needs to do little but explain the option and the channel member will voluntarily cooperate. This might be the case of businesses choosing to participate in a stress management program sponsored by a local nonprofit hospital. Voluntary relationships, while generating the healthiest, most candid kind of cooperation, involve little loyalty. Although the

FIGURE 17-5

Channel Strategy Possibilities for Nonprofit Marketers

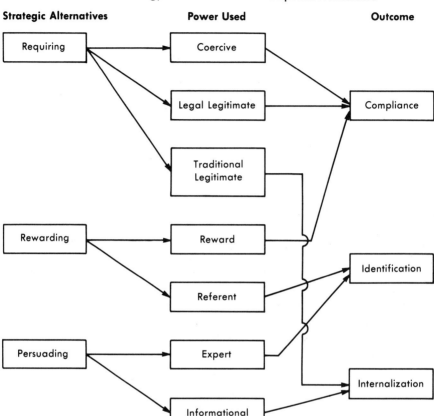

channel member does not feel coerced into the relationship, a better offer elsewhere may lead to a rapid defection. Unless and until that occurs, it is likely that interactions between the parties will be rational and pleasant, not unlike those occurring between two adults carrying out a mutually beneficial task.

Identification, on the other hand, is not a situation in which the channel member feels that he or she has made a rational choice. Participation is largely motivated by wanting to be part of something—to identify with another organization, cause, or event. In such cases, the channel member feels both loyalty to the program and a touch fearful that someday he or she may be dropped from participation. In a sense, it is a relationship more like that that exists between a child (the channel member) and its parent (the channel leader), in which the former participates but is not entirely independent and is perhaps a bit resentful of having to rely on the channel leader for "permission" to participate. One suspects that some of the relationships at the 1984 Summer Olympics were of this character. Needless to say, like many parent-child relationships, there is general goodwill among the parties, but there is also potential for friction because the basic link in the relationship is seen by the channel member as not altogether a matter of free will. And, obviously, if the channel leader becomes tarnished in any fashion, as has occurred with some inner-city social projects and several political campaigns, one might expect channel members to desert the relationship very quickly.

Compliance occurs when the channel member feels that he or she *has* to cooperate, either because the rewards are so desirable or because the punishment for nonparticipation is so undesirable. Thus, a political candidate may suggest that an organization sponsor a campaign dinner because it will bring great favors to the organization when the candidate is elected or because these favors will go to a competitor if sponsorship is not forthcoming. This, too, is a parent-child relationship, but one much more fraught with potential conflict because the channel member feels so dependent on the marketer. The compliant channel member may be very difficult to work with or always be looking for ways to get out of the relationship or even to sabotage it.

To be effective, it is important that the channel leader both understand the responses of different channel members and be prepared for the advantages and problems that each kind of response implies.

STRATEGIES for INVOLVING MIDDLEMEN

The ability to make the channel dependent on the marketer indicates that influence has been exerted. The influence potential, as noted earlier, rests on some form of power. French and Raven have identified seven sources of such power.[13] Each is a *perceived* source of power. To be effective, power never need actually be exerted nor even mentioned (a mob loan enforcer need never *really* break any arms or legs or even *suggest* this to achieve a 100 percent repayment rate). The following are examples of each type of power in nonprofit marketing. (See also Figure 17-7.)

1. *Reward Power:* The ability to offer *rewards.* The Public Broadcasing System can allow corporate sponsors of PBS programs to present "commercials" at the beginning and end of prestigious productions. Weight Watchers and Alcoholics Anonymous can permit successful dieters or abstainers to brag about their accomplishments in public. Federal agencies secure cooperation from local counterparts by suggesting that future contracts or grants will be funded or re-funded. Charities can provide considerable favorable publicity to cooperating businesses and other organizations.

2. *Coercive power:* The ability to impose punishments. Both public and private universities can be threatened with loss of federal grants if they do not meet Department of Education guidelines as to minority and female hiring.

Corporations continuing to pollute the air or water can be threatened by governmental and private groups with significant adverse publicity about their "antisocietal" actions (or *in*actions).

3. *Legal legitimate power:* The ability to legally require desired behaviors. Government contracts can impose requirements for nondiscriminatory behavior on the part of contractors. Contracts for various social change programs can require specific performances, including, for example, evaluation studies at their conclusion (marketing research or a marketing audit).

4. *Traditional legitimate power:* The socially accepted (but not yet legal) ability to require desired behaviors. Although volunteer workers are not contractually bound to the organizations they serve, the latter can dictate dress codes, sales presentations, and sometimes timing and place of work. Contractors in government programs may not be *required* to permit inspection of their programs, but aspects of those programs that don't involve "trade secrets" are generally considered to be open to funders' observations and even participation. Corporations today can be made to feel that local and state officials, by virtue of permitting operations in a given community, have the "right" to dictate certain socially responsible behaviors (specific kinds of waste treatment, job training, and so forth).

5. *Expert power:* The ability to provide expert assistance or guidance. Local chapters of voluntary agencies such as the United Way or the Republican Party can be made to acquiesce to the marketing recommendations of their national organizations because of the latter's presumed greater sophistication. Research contractors new to a topic area can be encouraged to permit heavy editorial guidance for reports aimed at unfamiliar target audiences.

6. *Referent power:* The ability to offer association with a prestigious program or institution. Presumably many liquor manufacturers and beer distributors offer goods and services or funding for charitable events because this increases their goodwill. Commercial researchers may agree to carry out specific methodologies because they wish to include work for a prestigious sponsor in their organizational brochures.

7. *Informational power:* The ability to offer information that will help the target organization achieve its goals. This differs from expert assistance in that no superiority in skills is implied. Thus, the Office of Cancer Communications can offer participating physicians informational kits containing antismoking office posters, pamphlets to give to patients who wish to quit, and so on. Various public service agencies can provide cooperating television stations with commercials, announcements, speakers, or educational films to help the stations meet the requirement that they devote a given percentage of their weekly air time to so-called public service announcements (PSAs).

Kasulis and Spekman have proposed that these seven different types of power can be grouped according to the different responses they will typically receive from channel members:[14]

1. Reward, coercive, and legal legitimate power are associated with *compliance.*
2. Referent and expert power are associated with *identification.*
3. Traditional legitimate and informational power are associated with *internalization.*

Furthermore, they suggest that within the "compliance" group, coercive power yields the lowest level of long-run compliance since this relationship often fosters conflict within the channel. On the other hand, legal legitimate power is seen as the most effective in this group since it may be internalized to some degree. Within the "identification" group, referent power is less effective than expert power in achieving long-run identification because the former is subject to the vagaries of peer and public opinion, which is to some degree outside the marketer's control. Finally, they suggest that in the last group, traditional legitimate power is less effective than informational power in achieving internalization since the latter, by definition, means that participation in the marketer's program fits closely with the middleman's goals.

DEVELOPING MIDDLEMEN COORDINATION STRATEGIES

The nonprofit marketer seeks to choose influence strategies that will secure middlemen participation and cooperation in particular programs. The choice should be based on an analysis of the marketer's power bases. While the choice often yields a mixed strategy, the options can be grouped into three broad strategic categories. These categories can be described as follows:

> 1. *Requiring* middleman cooperation through the use of coercive, traditional legitimate, and legal legitimate power, often in the framework of specific contracts.
> 2. *Rewarding* middlemen cooperation through the manipulation of reward or referent power.
> 3. *Persuading* middlemen to cooperate through the use of expert and informational power (although persuasion, in a sense, is implicit in *all* of these alternatives).

Requiring cooperation. Requiring cooperation is a common form of channel control in both the private and public sectors. It is carried out through the use of formal contracts, which specify in greater or lesser degree the rights and duties of each party. These contracts can cover specific functions, as when an advertising agency agrees to provide copy and execution for a series of ads, place the ads in media, and perhaps evaluate the advertising's effects.

> In Bergen County, New Jersey, the state Division of Youth and Family Services (DYFS) handles responsibilities for group counseling and foster day-care services but contracts out half of its services to private medical practitioners and community-based organizations. For example, in cases involving child abuse, emotional neglect, or sexual molestation, it uses the Family Life Center, a hospital-based therapeutic agency. The Family Life Center (FLC) is compensated on a per case basis as specified in the contract. DYFS maintains

overall case responsibility as it is legally mandated to do. Operational decisions such as treatment method (individual, family, or group) are left to FLC. DYFS assigns a caseworker to each case, who attends FLC case conferences. DYFS has the final say as to whether and when a case is terminated, although it seeks the advice of FLC therapists.[15]

Such contracts can be very beneficial to the nonprofit because it gains the skills and economies of others while having the contract power to insist on performance. An issue here is how tightly to word the contract. In the private sector, contracts are usually very specific and carefully monitored. In the nonprofit sector, contracts sometimes involve voluntary assistance by the contractee at or below market prices. In such cases, the temptation is to write the contract loosely so that the partly-volunteer subcontractor (for example, a research or advertising agency or a broadcasting medium) is not "offended" by "meddling" in their delegated area of responsibility. This loose wording is generally unsatisfactory to both sides. Subcontractors may not know what is expected of them. They may exaggerate their independence and feel abused when the contractor tries to impose its will upon them. The contractor, on the other hand, may feel that it has no clear grounds for making criticisms and that it has lost control of the subcontracted operation. And, of course, if legitimate disputes do arise, the ensuing bickering can destroy a channel relationship that may be the *only* way for a nonprofit contractor to get its job done.

A channel control technique that has become increasingly common in the private sector is *franchising*. For years, there have been territorial agreements in the automobile and beverage industries whereby the number of dealers in an area is regulated. In return for this local partial monopoly, the franchisee is expected to meet certain performance standards (for example, quotas) and to carry on the enterprise in a particular fashion (for example, use certain signs, charge certain prices, engage in so much cooperative advertising, and so on). Recent growth, however, has been in franchise systems with much stronger central control. In the McDonald's, Burger King, Midas Muffler, and other chain franchises, virtually the entire operation of the franchise may be specified by the franchisor down to the size of the dollop of catsup to go on a hamburger or the number of straws in a soft drink. Usually, the franchise is based upon some distinctive trade name or style such that the franchisee is willing to pay for both the expertise and the extra marketplace competitive edge.

Territorial franchises have existed in the nonprofit sector as well. Many charitable organizations give local chapters territorial rights and proscribe other chapters from entering their market. However, franchises of the McDonald's type have been rare, except in the health care area. Recent mergers of hospitals and nursing homes have led to a certain standardization of operating practices, promotions, and physical appearances. Many of the new smaller emergency centers and local clinics may also take on a franchise format.

In Egypt, the franchise concept was recently proposed as a way of standardizing family planning clinics and upgrading their image in the minds of target consumers. The Family of the Future (FOF) social marketing organization has been building a reputation as an efficient and effective marketer of contraceptive products. It has begun four successful clinics of its own. By contrast, other clinics in Egypt, especially in the more rural areas, are in very poor condition, are poorly managed, and suffer very low reputations. It has been proposed that FOF take over the *management* of these clinics and possibly franchise its name to other clinics that are currently private as a way of securing higher, more standardized quality of services. To the extent that such a network could be established, national advertising could be used to make the franchise name attractive to other private clinics or new investors.

Another approach to formal control is the *cooperative.* Some nonprofits band together and contractually establish a central office to carry out or coordinate specific marketing activities on a cooperative basis. For example, various university and community arts centers financially support the Association of College, University, and Community Arts Administrators. ACUCAA provides pooled data, carries on research, and conducts seminars that are designed to benefit the individual centers. The United Way of America in Alexandria, Virginia, provides many of the same functions for 2,200 local United Ways and carries on major programs of national advertising.

The contractual approach ultimately relies on legal authority and the potential imposition of penalties as a means of achieving the nonprofit marketer's ends. As long as the terms are carefully described, are fair to both sides, and there is a sense of shared responsibility for desired social outcomes, a contractual approach can work well, and the use of formal power by the contractor need only be a subtle background issue. On the other hand, if the contractual relationship is unclear and the interaction between the parties discordant, power may be used by the contractor to coerce the contractee into performing the needed channel functions. To the extent that such formal coercive power has to be used, the long-term potential for the channel relationship is not promising.

Rewarding and Persuading Cooperation.   Rather than base channel cooperation on negative incentives, many organizations simply make it worthwhile for others to help them out. They offer specific economic rewards such as commissions or noneconomic rewards such as increased prestige through cooperating with a major social program. In both cases, extensive persuasion may still be needed to convince potential target middlemen that cooperation will benefit both parties.

In deciding which approach to use, the marketer needs to look at the

target middlemen and how they might be influenced to cooperate. The steps
in this process would be as follows:

1. Identify all possible audiences that the nonprofit marketer may be able to
influence using one or more of the seven kinds of power.

2. Ascertain the middleman's perceptions of the organization and the specific
costs and benefits of participating. Forecast what kind of internal response will
be generated. To permit effective use of whatever power leverage is available,
answer the following questions to ascertain the organization's *power potential:*

a. Do the target audiences perceive the organization as able to inflict any
kinds of "punishment" on them? Can the organization withhold vital
resources, add to their costs of operation, or bring about unfavorable publicity if they do not participate? If so, how serious are these potential costs
perceived to be by the target audiences? These questions assess the *coercive
power potential.*

b. Are there direct rewards that the non-profit marketer can offer the middleman for participation? Does the middleman perceive that the nonprofit
marketer can offer favorable publicity? Will there be significant funding
directly available for the middleman or can participation allow them to
seek grants elsewhere (for example, CETA funds)? If so, are target audiences aware of this, and how highly do they value these potential benefits?
These questions assess the *reward power potential.*

c. Do target middlemen perceive that the organization has a legal or
socially supported right to require participation in the proposed programs?
This question assesses *traditional and legal power potentials.*

d. Is the organization or its programs perceived to have high prestige?
What is the nature of this prestige and how can it be enhanced? If prestige
is high, how valuable do target middlemen perceive association with these
programs to be? These questions assess *referent power potential.*

e. Similarly, is the organization perceived to have special competencies,
and if so, how much are target middlemen willing to rely on this expertise?
(Expert power potential.)

f. What assistance can the organization provide in the way of information
about products or services that can be potentially helpful to target middlemen in meeting their objectives? How great are these benefits perceived to
be? *(Informational power potential.)*

3. Assemble an array of possible influence strategies to implement the power
potentials discovered in step 2.

4. Evaluate in detail the probable effectiveness and efficiency of each strategy
for each target middleman group.

5. Select the optimum combination of influence strategies within and across
middleman audiences that will secure initial participation in the program by
middlemen not now involved.

6. Ensure that this combination of power strategies will maintain and increase
participation by middlemen *already* involved in the program.

7. Develop detailed tactics to implement the selected strategies.

8. Where possible, implement programs to systematically test competing
alternatives.

9. Measure performance and adjust strategies and tactics on the basis of
experience.

A concrete example of this method is provided in Exhibit 17-3.

EXHIBIT 17-3. Choosing a channel and influence strategy

Suppose that the Office of Cancer Communications at the National Institute of Health (OCC) is considering two new alternative middlemen to further their programs to get more individuals to quit smoking. The two alternatives are member unions in a specific AFL-CIO union and registered and practical nurses working in hospitals. Assume further that because of the Office's resource constraints—primarily funds and man-power—only one of these middlemen will be recruited. How does the framework described on pp. 000–000 suggest that one proceed?

The first consideration is whether nurses or union representatives would be more effective as "retailers" of OCC programs. Assuming for the moment that the two are judged equally effective, the next step is to develop an array of possible influence strategies based on each kind of power directed at each target group. Such a set of influence strategies could include the following:

An AFL-CIO Union

A. Coercive Power
   1. Threaten to take the program to rival unions, to company management, or to both.
   2. Promote the program directly to union members, telling them to ask their union to participate.
B. Reward Power
   1. Offer to publicize the union's cooperation to the general public thereby improving the unions' public image.
   2. Conduct contests with rewards for union representative securing the most quitting smokers.
   3. Offer exclusive "rights" to program participation.
C. Legal Legitimate Power
   1. Require federally funded training programs conducted by unions in high risk occupations to have an antismoking module.
D. Traditional Legitimate Power
   1. None.
E. Referent Power
   1. Show that participation in the OCC program would permit the union to tell members that the union is concerned about their health and is working with a leader in the health care field to that end.
F. Expert Power
   1. Show that OCC/NIH is an expert in smoking behavior change tools and techniques and offer to provide this exper-tise as part of participation.
   2. Differentiate OCC/NIH by showing that its skills, pro-grams, etc. are superior to rivals (e.g., American Cancer Society).
   3. Offer assistance in setting up demonstration projects.
G. Informational Power
   1. Show how smoking reduction can lengthen the lives of union members especially in high risk occupations and there-fore prolong their participation in the union.

EXHIBIT 17-3. (continued)

2. Show how antismoking propaganda and training should be part of any union's preventive health care benefits for its members.

3. Show how participation in a smoking cessation program can help an individual union compete with a rival in representation fights.

4. Produce sample first quality brochures, films, posters specifically for unions to use with their members. Emphasize unions' care for members' welfare in the brochures.

5. Provide unions with free literature that can be locally tagged to enhance union identification with a "socially good" program.

HOSPITAL NURSES

A. Coercive Power
1. Point out the high smoking rates among nurses compared to rates among physicians and suggest that they have a special responsibility to themselves and their patients to promote quitting.
2. Promote the program directly to patients, telling them to ask their "health professionals" for more information.

B. Reward Power
1. Publicize nurses' contributions to the general public and to other health professionals.
2. Offer specially framed certificates to individual nurses for participation.
3. Conduct contests wtih rewards for nurses who secure the most quitting smokers.
4. Fund demonstration projects with extra pay for nurses who help in the program.

C. Legal and Legitimate Power
1. Require that education in behavior change techniques be part of nursing licensing requirements.

D. Traditional Legitimate Power
1. Tell nurses that it is part of their professional obligation to get people to quit smoking.

E. Referent Power
1. Create a crusadelike atmosphere in which *all* health professionals (including physicians, pharmacists, dentists, *and* nurses) work together on a major health problem.
2. Offer to write letters to each nurse's employer commending his or her cooperation with a federal health effort.
3. Position the program as a research effort in which the nurses can help advance the frontiers of preventive health care.

F. Expert Power
1. Show that OCC/NIH is an expert in smoking behavior-change tools and techniques and offer to provide this expertise as part of participation.
2. Differentiate OCC/NIH by showing that its skills, programs, etc., are superior to those of rivals.

Exhibit 17-3. (continued)

    G. Informational Power

        1. Show how encouraging patients to quit smoking is an expected part of a total patient care role.

        2. Show how learning antismoking behavior change techniques can be useful training for the nurse that can be generalized to other behavior change situations (for example, getting patients to take medicine, diet, exercise, etc.).

        3. Produce sample first-quality brochures, films, and posters for patient education with nurses' cooperation prominently portrayed.

The next step would be to conduct discussions with knowledgeable observers inside and outside of each target group to (1) eliminate obviously ineffective or overly costly strategies; (2) add additional strategies or details of implementation; and (3) begin to calibrate the probable costs and effectiveness of each surviving alternative. The fourth step, then, would involve more precise estimates of the costs and effectiveness of the most promising strategies. This step might well require field interviewing of samples of target audience members.

The next steps would require selecting the target middleman and a set of influence strategies for implementation, followed by implementation and control.

In this example, nurses appear to show the most promise as middlemen since more influence strategies seem to be available to recruit them. Further, since OCC's experience with other health professionals could be used to evaluate the various alternatives, choices among future strategies and tactics ought to be relatively easier for nurses than for the union target market.

SOURCE: Alan R. Andreasen, "A Power Potential Approach to Middleman Strategies in Social Marketing," *European Journal of Marketing* Vol. 18, No. 4 (1984), pp. 56–71.

SUMMARY

Exchanges require physical contact between the marketer and target audiences. Often, this requires the services of other agencies (who can provide warehouse and transportation facilities) and careful coordination of complex interacting systems. While channels may simply be means to facilitate consumers' time and place utilities, they have the potential to either significantly augment or effectively sabotage carefully designed marketing programs.

To achieve an effective and efficient channel strategy, the nonprofit marketer must decide what quality of service to offer and whether marketing will be direct or indirect. Then, the marketer must determine the length and breadth of the channel, recruit channel members, and assign functions. Finally, the marketer should put systems for effective coordination and control among the channel members in place.

Coordination and control are best achieved by judicious use of the power potentially available to the nonprofit marketer. This power can be based on rewards, coercion, law, social norms, expertise, prestige, or control of critical information. In general, power strategies that rely on simple compliance on the part of middlemen (for example, those based on coercion or the law) are less effective in the long run than strategies that encourage middlemen to identify with and internalize the non-profit organization's goals.

QUESTIONS

1. A nonprofit hospital in a small town would like corporations to serve as middlemen in distributing materials on proper diet and other behaviors that would reduce the risk of heart attacks. What corporations would be the best candidates for participating in this program based on the types of power the hospital might be able to exert over them?

2. A museum sells its posters, calendars, and reproductions through the mail and at a gift shop in the museum itself. Should it also market through local department stores, smaller gift shops in local malls, or both? What gains or losses in effectiveness and efficiency would ensue from these choices?

3. In what ways can a branch library change the atmospherics to increase demand for its offerings?

4. What distribution functions are performed in offering opportunities for individuals to give to the American Cancer Society? How might these functions be reallocated to make the Society more effective, more efficient, or both?

5. In securing applications for its executive programs, UCLA seeks the assistance of former alumni. What coordination problems are there in using such middlemen? How can UCLA achieve the desired actions from these "independent" agents?

NOTES

1. Michael B. Anspaugh, "Americans Continue to Ignore the $2 Bill," *Flint Journal,* November 7, 1978, reprinted in Christopher H. Lovelock and Charles B. Weinberg, eds., *Readings in Public and Nonprofit Marketing,* (Palo Alto, Calif.: Scientific Press, 1978), pp. 222–23; and "Numismatic Ms.," *Time,* July 9, 1979, p. 54.

2. Quoted from an unpublished term paper on the Faith Covenant Church of Wheaton written by Mark F. Pufundt at Northwestern University, 1980.

3. Ronald Abler, John S. Adams, and Peter Gould, *Spatial Organization* (Englewood Cliffs, N.J.: Prentice-Hall, 1971), pp. 531–32.

4. An excellent introduction to these issues is found in Louis W. Stern and Adel I. Ansary, *Marketing Channels,* 2d ed. (Englewood Cliffs, N.J.: Prentice-Hall, 1982).

5. Donald W. Ball, "An Abortion Clinic Ethnography," in William J. Filstead, ed., *Qualitative Methodology* (Chicago: Markham, 1970).

6. For more details, see Philip Kotler, "Atmospherics as a Marketing Tool," *Journal of Retailing,* Winter 1973–74, pp. 48–64.

7. Nicholas J. Demerath, "Organization and Management Needs of a National Family Planning Program: The Case of India," *Journal of Social Issues,* No. 4 (1967), pp. 179–93.

8. This and the Novelli and Siska quote above are from William D. Novelli and Deborah Ziska, "Health Promotion in the Workplace: An Overview," *Health Education Quarterly,* Vol. 9, Special Supplement, 1982, pp. 20–26.

9. "Health Program Savings Cited," *American Medical News,* September 4, 1981.

10. Brian Moran, "Hutton Aids Red Cross Plea," *Advertising Age,* December 9, 1985, p. 67.

11. The material in the following section is adapted from Alan R. Andreasen, "A Power Potential Approach to Middlemen Strategies in Social Marketing," *European Journal of Marketing,* Vol 18, No. 4 (1984), pp. 56–71.

12. Herbert C. Kelman, "Processes of Opinion Change," *Public Opinion Quarterly,* 25 (1961), p. 57ff.

13. John R. French and Bertram Raven, "The Bases of Social Power," in D. Cartwright, ed., *Studies in Social Power* (Ann Arbor: University of Michigan Press, 1959).

14. Jack Kasulis and Robert Spekman, "A Framework for the Use of Power," *European Journal of Marketing,* October 1980, pp. 70–78.

15. Adell P. Fine and Seymour H. Fine, "Distribution Channels in Marketing Social Work," *Social Casework,* 67 (April 1986), p. 231.

CHAPTER 18

Formulating Communication Strategies for Influencing Behavior

Should advertising ever make people uncomfortable? That's a question Vinyard & Lee & Partners of St. Louis ran up against in creating advertising for the Diabetes Treatment Center of America, a division of American Health Corporation of Nashville, Tennessee.

Yes, say the company and the agency. When the question is health, it's sometimes necessary to shock people into action. Of the 12 million diabetics in this country, half don't know that they have the disease, and many who do have the disease prefer to ignore some of its ramifications.

But some TV and radio stations refuse to air commercials that offend viewers or scare them. In fact, all three TV networks have rejected certain DTCA commercials, which describe the negative effects of letting diabetes go unchecked. CBS told the agency, "We don't want to discuss the possible harmful consequences of wrong treatment of diabetes. . . . We consider this scare copy." ABC called one commercial "scare copy" and unacceptable.

DTCA's most controversial TV spot shows a man taking off his shoes and socks. It includes one shot of a leg prosthesis being removed. The announcer says, "If you give diabetes an inch, it'll take a foot."

Allan Gordon, senior vice-president and account supervisor at Vinyard & Lee, admits that some of the DTCA information is frightening. But he said it's meant to be.

"We talked to people in the centers and found that they'd often gone through years of self-denial," even when they suffered the ravages of the disease, he said. "This is a justifiable approach to get people off the fence. We may be saving lives."

Vinyard & Lee has created two separate campaigns for the center and tested both. The first one takes a positive approach. It says, in effect, that you can learn to live with diabetes with a little help from the treatment center.

The second conveys the message that "if you have diabetes, you damn well better take care of it," said Stephen Puckett, Vinyard & Lee senior vice-president and creative director.

Both were shown to focus groups made up of people who have the disease. Most respondents apparently preferred the positive approach, but follow-up research indicated that the negative commercials generated higher recall.

The psychologist who conducted the follow-up interviews believed that "the positive campaign gave those people a chance to deny the problems of their disease," said Mr. Puckett. "The negative one didn't. It spurred them to action."

That, he said, may explain why DTCA records indicate that the "foot" commercial outpulls the positive message three to one.

SOURCE: Adapted from Lori Kesler, "Diabetes Ads are too Scarey [sic] for Some." Reprinted with permission from *Advertising Age,* October 29, 1984, p. 66w. Copyright 1984 by Crain Communications, Inc.

In Chapter 1, we defined marketing as a philosophy, process, and set of strategies and tactics for influencing behavior—either changing behavior or preventing it from changing (for example, keeping teenagers from taking up smoking). In the immediately preceding chapters, we considered the offer, price, and place components of the marketing mix and saw that these components must be in place before any program can be successful. We have also seen that these components can influence behaviors directly by providing incentives for action or reducing disincentives. But in the vast majority of nonprofit marketing strategies, influencing behavior is largely a matter of *communication.* It is a matter of *informing* target audiences about the alternatives for action, the positive consequences of choosing a particular one, and the motivations for acting (and often *continuing* to act) in a particular way.

Communication is not something that nonprofits can ignore. Everything about an organization—its products, employees, facilities, and actions—communicates something. Each organization should examine its communication style, needs, and opportunities and develop a communication program that is influential and cost-effective. The organization's communications responsibilities go beyond communicating to target consumers. The organization must communicate effectively with external publics such as the press, government agencies, and the financial community. It must communicate effectively with its internal publics, particularly its board members, middle management, and professional and clerical employees. The organization must know how to communicate about itself to various groups in order to gain their support and goodwill.

An organization may use a great many communications vehicles to inform and motivate target publics. These include

- Space and time advertising
- Loudspeaker advertising
- Mailings
- Speeches
- Sales presentations
- Demonstrations
- Word of mouth
- Posters and show cards

- Point-of-sales displays
- Sales literature
- Catalogs
- Films
- Trade exhibits
- Sales conferences
- Packaging
- Packaging inserts

- House-organ publications
- Offer publicity
- Corporate publicity
- Corporate identification programs
- Endorsements
- Special events
- Promotional giveaways

Different institutions have evolved distinct communications tools to serve their needs. Fundraising organizations make heavy use of benefit dinners and dances, auctions, bazaars, concerts, telethons, walkathons, door-to-door campaigns, plate-passing, and direct mail to raise money. Summer camps make heavy use of camp brochures, get-acquainted parties, T-shirts displaying the camp name, camp movies, and direct mail.

THE COMMUNICATIONS PROCESS

Any communication process involves a message *sender* and a message *receiver* (a target audience). The sender has an *intended message,* but whether or not the *received message* is in most respects indentical to it is determined by the extent to which the communications process is relatively noise-free and the sender and receiver share the same *cultural codes.* This process is outlined in Figure 18-1.

A *sender* (the Los Angeles Philharmonic, for example) formulates an *intended message* ("A new conductor, André Previn, brings fresh, new excitement to Los Angeles Philharmonic concerts"). The *encoder* (an advertising agency) translates this intended message into an *encoded message* (a picture of an energetic André Previn, a headline: "Musical Excitement Comes to L.A.," and four paragraphs describing Previn's past connections with Los Angeles and his rave reviews as conductor of the London Philharmonic and Pittsburgh Symphony. The paragraphs also describe the diversity of his background in classical, popular, and jazz idioms and his own thoughts on his plans for Los Angeles).

FIGURE 18-1

Elements in the Communication Process

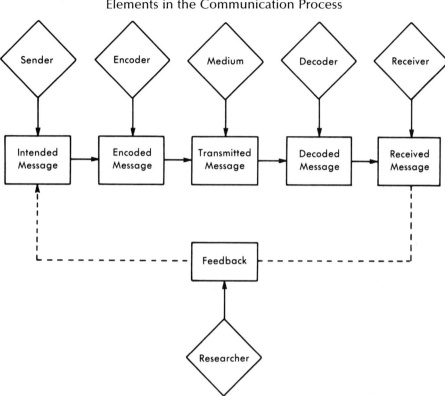

This message gets transmitted through such *media* as regional editions of *Time* and *Newsweek* magazines, which the ad agency believes will add an aura of "seriousness" to the encoded message. The *decoders* may be a young couple glancing at the magazine in a doctor's office, discussing between themselves the direct and implied content of the ad ("Gee, his hair is long. I wonder if he's one of these far-out Los Angeles types?") Finally, each *receiver* member of the couple retains traces of the more memorable parts of the message and its associations (for example, the long hair and Previn's quotes), which can be assessed by a market *researcher* checking for *feedback* in a posttest telephone survey.

In many actual situations, the roles portrayed in Figure 18-1 may be combined. For example, there can be two-party communication involving (1) the sender-encoder-medium-researcher, and (2) the decoder-receiver. This would be the case in many kinds of personal selling situations. The salesperson would decide what message to get across, encode it into a "sales pitch," transmit it verbally, and watch for or inquire about the customer's response. The customer would decode the salesperson's sales pitch and store whatever was personally meaningful in it.

Even in this relatively simple two-party situation, a number of kinds of "noise" can creep in:

1. *Encoding.* The salesperson may choose the wrong wording to convey key concepts. A donor solicitation specialist for a nonprofit foundation, for example, may intend to make it clear that the donor can be anonymous, but by making frequent references to *possible* forms of recognition, leave the overall impression that the donor cannot escape publicity.

2. *Transmitting.* Vocal inflections or body language in the delivery of the message can change its meaning. For example, if a person seeking a donation for a hospital adopts too "serious" a tone of voice when speaking about the scientific quality of the research work being done at the hospital, he or she may unintentionally convey the impression that the scientists are pessimistic about possible outcomes. In another example, if a flip-chart is used to outline the possible types of funding sought and possible uses of those funds, the speed with which the chart is physically "flipped" may unintentionally tell a potential donor which areas the hospital *really* thinks are important.

3. *Decoding.* The target audience can mishear what is said. A 73 percent success rate for a health care facility may be heard as 17 percent. A distracted decoder may miss important benefits. The meaning given to heard statements can also vary greatly, depending on what experiences the decoder brings to the message.[1] A potential donor with queasy personal reactions to the sight of blood may not really "see" flip-chart pictures or slides showing or implying "bloody" events. A racially prejudiced potential donor may "decide" that an agency is not well run if "too many" blacks or Hispanics are portrayed. The target audience member may not like the salesperson and so tend to discount his or her opinions or assertions.

4. *Researching.* Salespeople vary greatly in their ability to read the responses of target customers. Indeed, as noted below, an important characteristic of a good salesperson is "empathy," the ability to put oneself in another's shoes. Thus, noise is added to the communications process if the salesperson interprets a potential donor's silence as signaling a lack of interest when it actually means that the donor is reflecting carefully on the merits of a proposal. Alternatively, a salesperson might decide that the cause of a potential donor's indifference is stinginess when in fact it is caused by the donor's irritation at the salesperson's manner of presentation. Finally, it is possible that the target consumer may encode his or her own feelings with some distortion. Indeed, feedback is really another communications process with the target consumer as the sender and the marketing organization as the receiver.

Of course, in a great many communications situations, the process involves several agencies or individuals acting in one or more of the roles indicated in Figure 18-1. The potential for "noise" is enhanced

1. *Encoding.* Salespeople may be designated as agents for communicating top management's sense of mission for the hospital—and can get the message wrong or distort it. Alternatively, an advertising agency or public relations firm may be given the task of encoding the organization's *intended* message but may

produce words or images that distort or inflate management's intentions. Thus, too-slick graphics or a "with it" ad layout for a symphony orchestra may suggest that the orchestra is not a solid, well-trained ensemble or that its repertoire is too avant-garde for most tastes. Every time another player is added to the communication process, he or she brings to it his or her own interests, values, goals, and perceptions. Some advertising or public relations agencies direct their messages at least partly towards their fellow advertising or PR colleagues. Sometimes their main goal seems to be to attempt to dazzle their peers with the style and drama of a message's "encoding." The advertising community is replete with stories of award-winning campaigns (such as Alka Selzer's "spicy meatball" ads of the 1970s) that were later abandoned by the advertiser because they were ineffective in generating sales.

2. *Transmitting.* The vehicle through which you say something can enhance or distort a message. Many advertisers believe that putting an ad in a particular medium (for example, *The New Yorker* or *Town and Country*) adds a sense of "class" to their presentation. Or they may choose a spokesperson (a Cliff Robertson, John Houseman, or Bill Cosby) who will bring his or her own prestige or charisma to the nonprofit agency's message. But sometime the spokesperson can be inappropriate, can be seen as "doing it for the money" or as having little in common with the target audience.

Other media can also be inappropriate. Radio ads on a rock station may be wrong for a "serious" hospital, and a classical music station may be wrong for a hospital trying to position itself as being "for everyone." Print ads in *Playboy* may get high readership but convey the wrong impression about a clinic's therapeutic massage and exercise therapy program. A symphony that wants to seem more elite should avoid *U.S. News and World Report,* while a political candidate might find this magazine a very appropriate vehicle for adding to his or her "stature."

3. *Decoding.* Depending on how they are viewed by potential customers, channel members and their agents may serve as decoders for consumers. Thus, a physician may be asked by a patient to interpret the latest publicity release on smoking or high blood pressure or by a young woman to explain what a new low-dose contraceptive pill will really do for her (or *to* her, in the case of side effects). In a similar fashion, critics may "decode" a symphony or theatre's offering. The Consumers Union may evaluate products, services, and even advertising themes. Reporters and political analysts play the same role for voters. In all of these cases, what the marketer wants to say may take on very different meaning once it is filtered through these "helpful" role players.

4. *Researching.* Outside agencies can be hired by the marketer to directly assess the target audience's present moods, opinions, or specific responses to the marketer's messages. To the extent that this intervention involves the perceptions, judgments, empathy, *and* communications skills of these other agents, there is significant potential for distortion.

Most problematic is the case where "independent" third parties take on the role of providing feedback to the marketer. Examples would include the self-appointed spokesperson for the oppressed who tells marketers "the truth" about how the group has been mistreated and the respected opinion polls that tell the government how the public is reacting to particular ongoing programs or new proposals. There are also many respected associations that claim to offer feedback about what their members think and feel as well as thoughtful newspaper, magazine, and television commentators who are well attuned to the public opinions of special subgroups.

The major implication of this view of the communication process is that in any given situation the probability is very high that the *received message* will be different from the *intended message*. Two corollaries of this conclusion are:

1. The more role players there are in the communications process, the greater the chance for distortion.
2. The less control the marketer has over the role players in the communications process, the greater the chance for distortion.

This has several implications for marketing strategy:

1. The nonprofit communicator should *never* assume that the target audience is "receiving" what the communicator thinks is being "sent."
2. If communication strategy is to be improved, it is essential that the marketer know what is being received.
3. If knowing what is received is crucial, careful attention must be paid to the quality of the *feedback* link in the system.
4. If quality feedback is desired, the marketer should carefully control the feedback process, at the very least conducting formal research before or after the message is transmitted.
5. If formal feedback research is carried out before the launch of the message or a message campaign, pretesting should simulate the *entire* communication process. For example, if a program of patient hypertension education is to be conducted by slide presentations and brochures that physicians pass along to patients, simply testing physicians' responses or patients' responses to the materials alone would be inadequate. The marketer must test *both* steps in either a laboratory or a test market setting to see (a) how the physicians perceive the materials, (b) how often and with what advice they pass them on to the patients, and (c) how patients decode and store what the physicians tell them.
6. If communications are distorted at the receiving end, it is important to trace the source of the distortion to its roots. In the preceding example, the hypertension message could be inaccurately received because:
    (a) it was poorly encoded by the marketer in the first place (that is, the brochures and slides were poorly designed);
    (b) it was well encoded, but physicians often added their own embellishments, verbal cues, or body language, which changed the content;
    (c) the typical receiver was sufficiently misinformed about the disease *before* hearing the message that parts that seemed frightening were simply not "heard" at any important level.
The changes needed in the communications program would vary significantly depending on which of these problems was the primary source of message noise.
7. If a message *must* be received undistorted (for example, instructions about what a mother should do when her child is in a life-threatening situation), and it must be the same for all targeted customers, perfectly clear written communications *directly delivered* to the consumer are obviously superior.

8. On the other hand, if a message must be carefully adjusted to individual consumers (for example, how a person should change personal diet and exercise patterns), then a flexible, personally delivered message strategy is preferable because of its potential for ongoing feedback. (The one proviso here is that the personal salesperson be one who is naturally empathetic or is carefully trained in *undistorted listening* techniques.)

MAJOR STEPS IN DEVELOPING EFFECTIVE COMMUNICATIONS

We shall now consider the major steps in developing effective communications. The steps include (1) setting communication objectives, (2) generating possible messages, (3) overcoming selective attention, (4) overcoming perceptual distortion, (5) choosing a medium, and (6) evaluating and selecting messages.

SETTING COMMUNICATION OBJECTIVES

The first step calls for the marketer to define carefully the objective or objectives of the communications program. Possible objectives include

1. Making target consumers aware of a product, service, or social behavior.
2. Educating consumers about the offer or changes in the offer.
3. Changing beliefs about the negative and positive consequences of taking a particular action.
4. Changing the relative importance of particular consequences.
5. Enlisting the support of middlemen agencies (for example, securing shelf space).
6. Recruiting, motivating, or rewarding employers or volunteers.
7. Changing perceptions about the sponsoring organization.
8. Influencing governing agencies, review boards, commissions, and the like.
9. Preventing discontinuation of behaviors.
10. "Proving" superiority over competitors.
11. Combating injurious rumors.
12. Influencing funding agencies.

GENERATING POSSIBLE MESSAGES

Once the nonprofit marketer has determined a broad objective for the communications program, the next step is to encode it in *specific* messages. Message generation involves developing a number of alternative messages (appeals, themes, motifs, ideas) from which the best one can be chosen.

Messages can be generated in a number of ways. One approach is to talk with members of the target market and other influential parties to determine how they see the product or service, talk about it, and express their desires about it. A second approach is to hold a brainstorming meeting with key personnel in the organization to generate several ideas. A third method is to use some formal deductive framework to tease out possible advertising messages. We will discuss three deductive frameworks.

Rational, Emotional, Moral Framework.   One framework identifies three types of messages that can be generated: rational, emotional, and moral.

> 1. *Rational messages* aim at passing on information, serving the audience's self-interest, or both. They attempt to show that the service will yield the expected functional benefits. Examples would be messages discussing a service's quality, economy, value, or performance.
>
> 2. *Emotional messages* are designed to stir up some negative or positive emotion that will motivate the desired behavior. Communicators have worked with fear, guilt, and shame appeals, especially in connection with getting people to start doing things they should do (for example, brush their teeth, have an annual health checkup) or stop doing things they shouldn't do (for example, smoke, overimbibe, abuse drugs, overeat, or bring illegal fruit across the border). (See Figure 18-2.) Advertisers have found that fear appeals work up to a point, but if there is too much fear the audience will ignore the message.[2] Communicators have also used positive emotional appeals such as love, humor, pride, and joy. Evidence has not, however, established that a humorous message, for example, is necessarily more effective than a straight version of the same message.
>
> 3. *Moral messages* are directed to the audience's sense of what is right and proper. They are often used in messages exhorting people to support such social causes as a cleaner environment, better race relations, equal rights for women, and aiding the disadvantaged. An example is the March of Dimes appeal: "God made you whole. Give to help those He didn't." Moral appeals are less often used in connection with everyday products.

Reward/Situation Framework.   Maloney proposed another deductive framework. He suggested that buyers may expect any of four types of reward from an offering: a *rational, sensory, social,* or *ego satisfaction* reward. And they may visualize these rewards from *results-of-use experience, product-or-service-in-use experience,* or *incidental-to-use experience.* Crossing the four types of rewards with the three types of situations generates twelve types of advertising messages.[3] (See Table 18-1.)

Attitude Change Theory Framework.   A third way to generate possible messages is to work through an attitude change framework. Consider the communications problem of the marketing director of St. Anthony's Hospital, Axel Arneson, who is seeking to persuade a specific physician, Dr. Laura Goldman, to admit more of her patients to the hospital's oncology ward instead of to a competitor, the Downtown Medical Center. Suppose that from conversations with Dr. Goldman, Mr. Arneson has determined that there are four key consequences that Dr. Goldman considers when deciding where to admit a patient. These consequences are:

> 1. The extent to which the nursing staff is well trained enough to competently administer Dr. Goldman's treatment plan and to make sensible judgments on

FIGURE 18-2
Example of "Shame" Appeal

IF YOU FORGET TO HAVE YOUR FRUIT INSPECTED, YOU'RE NO LONGER A TOURIST. YOU'RE A SMUGGLER.

Having incoming fruit inspected isn't a suggestion—it's a law. A law that's absolutely vital to protecting the agricultural industry in California.

In 1980, somebody broke that law. And as a result, cost themselves and you over 100 million in tax dollars to eradicate the Medfly in California.

The crisis was resolved: the problem was not. Because there is no end to the risk of reoccurrence.

All it takes is one careless tourist bringing home one little piece of fruit with one small cluster of Medfly eggs hidden inside it, and boom—we're right back where we started. Spending millions of dollars, putting thousands of people out of work, and destroying the crops grown in the state that supplies more fruit and vegetables to this country than anyone else in the world.

Don't you be that careless tourist.

DON'T BUG ME

Have incoming fruit inspected...please.

County of Los Angeles ©1983

SOURCE: Reproduced with permission. Foote Cone & Belding, Chicago, IL.

occasions when the plan doesn't apply and Dr. Goldman is unavailable for consultation.

2. The extent to which other physicians affiliated with the hospital (especially those in oncology) can provide good advice and share in patient treatment.

3. The extent to which Dr. Goldman will have access to the latest testing and treatment equipment and other patient care facilities.

4. The extent to which Dr. Goldman will have her wishes respected and carried out regarding admissions, treatment, office space, fees, and billing.

Table 18-1

EXAMPLE OF REWARDS/SITUATIONS MESSAGES FOR A HOSPITAL
OBSTETRICS PROGRAM
Situations

Rewards	Results-of-Use	Product-or-Service-in-Use	Incidental-to-Use
Rational	You pay less at our hospital.	You make the major decisions about the birth at our hospital.	We bill your insurance company directly.
Sensory	We videotape the birth so you can relive the wonder of the birth.	Husbands share the emotions of the birth.	We have great food and wine.
Social	Husbands and wives will feel they shared something important.	Husbands can help in the delivery.	We allow your children to visit.
Ego Satisfaction	You will be assured that you have given your new baby the best start on life.	First-time mothers will feel really in control of our program.	You can tell your friends you were among the first to use our new service.

Mr. Arneson has estimated her beliefs about the likelihood of achieving these consequences from each of the rival hospitals as follows:

	St. Anthony's	Downtown Medical Center
Good nursing care	.8	.7
Access to knowledgeable colleagues	.9	.6
Access to best facilities	.5	.7
Respected	.4	.8

From his conversation, Mr. Arneson judges that Dr. Goldman gives weightings of 20 percent, 30 percent, 30 percent, and 20 percent, respectively, to the four consequences. Mr. Arneson further believes that Dr. Goldman's attitude toward the two institutions is very similar to those of a sizable contingent of other physicians in the area. Finally, Mr. Arneson believes that his hospital's low ratings on the "facilities" and "respect" consequences stem from the relative age and overcrowded appearance of his physical plant.

Now let's apply the attitude framework to Mr. Arneson's problem. Given the definition of attitude in Chapter 3 as an overall evaluation of the consequences of taking action, attitudes can be changed in three ways:

- Changing the importance of one or more consequences
- Changing beliefs about one or more consequences
- Adding new (presumably positive) consequences

CHANGING IMPORTANCE WEIGHTS. The first possibility open to Mr. Arneson is to attempt to change the importance weightings that Dr. Goldman and those like her attach to the four consequences. Thus, he might attempt to increase the weighting given to "access to knowledgeable colleagues" (on which his hospital scores well) and reduce that given to "access to best facilities" by arguing as follows:

"Many physicians think that the kind of hospital they want to work in is the one with the very best equipment and testing facilities. We know that's important. But the best equipment is only as good as the people who make it work and who help draw the most from its results. It is one thing to have the latest CAT scanner, quite another to be around colleagues who know just when to use it and how to wring the last ounce of meaning out of its readouts. We think that is *really* the kind of institution you want to be affiliated with, one that has the most up-to-date facilities but, even more, that has the staff and colleagues who are on the leading edge of research and diagnoses using these new technical wonders."

Notice that this attempt at attitude change made no mention of St. Anthony's or its rivals. Mr. Arneson knew that St. Anthony's scored well on "colleagues" and not so well on "facilities." He knows that if he can switch the weightings from 30 to 40 percent on "colleagues" and 30 to 20 percent on "facilities," St. Anthony's would be the favored institution, not Downtown Hospital.

CHANGING BELIEFS. Should Arneson decide that changing the weightings is too difficult or too risky to attempt, he has another option, trying to change beliefs. Here, he can make use of suggestive social science frameworks, such as dissonance and assimilation/contrast theories.

Dissonance theory. One characteristic of human beings is we prefer order and meaning. We like things to fit well together. We don't take kindly to messages that run counter to our present cognitions. When we encounter such dissonant messages, if the issue is involving, we will attempt to reassert order in our cognitive structure, our view of the world. That is, we will attempt to restore consonance.[4] We adopt several strategies to cope with dissonance.

Suppose that Dr. Goldman heard a rumor that several Downtown Medical internists and laboratory technicians had serious drug abuse problems. This would be dissonant with her view that Downtown had reasonably good colleagues (and, of course, with any interest in sending her patients there). Dr. Goldman could restore consonance in several ways:

1. *Denial.* She could convince herself that the rumors "couldn't be true" (for example, that they were the work of "enemies" of DMC).

2. *Search for disconfirmation.* She could seek information from administrators at DMC that would counter the rumors.

3. *Reduce the importance of the issue.* We can all live with some amount of dissonance provided it isn't perceived to be related to an issue in which we are highly involved. Thus, Dr. Goldman might decide that although the rumor may be true, it isn't really a very serious matter because (a) the people in question probably don't work in highly technical areas like hers; (b) even if they did, she could personally spot them and avoid them; (c) hospital administrators would certainly take care of the problem; or (d) even if the problem can't be entirely dealt with, it would be no better anywhere else (for example, at St. Anthony's).

4. *Change prior beliefs.* Dr. Goldman may judge the rumors to be true and change her belief about DMC's staff and her own decision to send patients there.

The last-mentioned is, of course, an instance of *changed beliefs.* It is a case in which new information caused a negative result from DMC's standpoint but a positive one where St. Anthony's is concerned. While one would not expect Mr. Arneson to resort to spreading unsubstantiated rumors about a rival institution, one can see that the introduction of dissonant information can change beliefs. Thus, Mr. Arneson could seek to offer facts about St. Anthony's or about Downtown Medical Center that he believed Dr. Goldman would find dissonant. It is crucial that the facts chosen (a) be so convincing that they could not easily be denied, (b) concern some highly involving area not likely to be minimized by Dr. Goldman, and (c) be difficult to counter by other facts.

Assimilation/contrast theory. A danger that Mr. Arneson risks in presenting potentially dissonant information is that it may fail a plausibility test even before Dr. Goldman considers it. Sherif, Sherif, and Nebergill have proposed that each individual has a position on a given belief dimension.[5] Thus, we noted that Dr. Goldman's best estimate of the likelihood that she will receive respectful treatment at St. Anthony's is currently .4. If one were to probe Dr. Goldman's beliefs further, we might discover that given additional information she might revise this probability downward as low as .2 or upward as high as .7. Sherif, Sherif, and Nebergill refer to this range as Dr. Goldman's *latitude of acceptance.* By contrast, if for some reason Mr. Arneson tried to maximize Dr. Goldman's dissonance by suggesting that the true probability would be .9 or 1.0 (in sharpest contrast with .4), Dr. Goldman would just find the assertion implausible. In such a case, dissonance would not occur and no attitude change would ensue. The region in which implausible statements would fall is labeled by the Sherifs as the *latitude of rejection.* (Beliefs falling into neither range are said to be in the *latitude of indifference.*)

To get the maximum attitude change, the Sherifs would recommend that Mr. Arneson try to bring information to bear that would seem likely to bring Dr. Goldman's belief to the .7 level. Thus, he should *not* promise her a large, immaculately furnished office and instant response to requests for laboratory tests. Rather, he should indicate, for example, that she would have a recently redecorated if modest-sized office equal to that of other senior staff members and that her laboratory requests would be given rapid attention as befits a senior staffer (providing she was judicious in the number of rush requests). That is, he should suggest that the "respect" and "facilities" consequences of affiliating with St. Anthony's would be at the believable level of .7 rather than the unbelievable 1.0 level. In general, as suggested in Figure 18-3, it is best to bring individuals to the farthest and most desirable point *within* their latitude of acceptance. Further, the theory suggests that, as the target audience adjusts to this new belief, their latitude of acceptance will also shift and new communciation strategies can be designed to move them even further along. By this process, they may eventually be brought to the point advocated by the dissonance theorists in the first case.

Of course, not everyone will have either the same beginning beliefs or the same range of acceptable positions. Indeed, one measure of the firmness of a person's beliefs is the ratio of the latitude of acceptance to the latitude

FIGURE 18-3

Hypothetical Beliefs of Two Individuals about the Consequences of Electing Ronald Reagan President in 1984

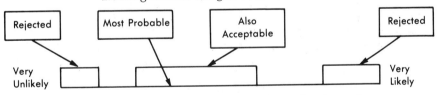

A. "Electing Ronald Reagan will lead to war within 4 years."

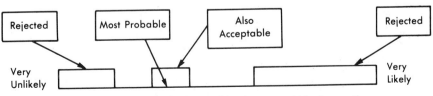

B. "Electing Ronald Reagan will lead to war within 4 years."

of rejection. The individual in Figure 18-3a is clearly much more fixed in beliefs than the individual in Figure 18-3b. The former is described as being much more *dogmatic* or narrow-minded.

ADDING CONSEQUENCES.   A third alternative available to Mr. Arneson is to add one or more new, positive beliefs. Indeed, this is a common strategy in the profit sector for differentiating a brand in a highly competitive market environment or rescusitating a brand in the decline phase of its life cycle. Potential customers are told about a new consequence of using the product or service or engaging in a behavior. Sometimes, these new consequences only require imagination and not a fundamental change in the offering. Thus, a marketer may point out to those not swayed by arguments about the positive health consequences of participating in a stop-smoking clinic that participation may also lead to making new friends. Or new parents may be encouraged to use a library not only for information about parenting, but also to learn about library services that their new child could appreciate or learn to use, such as weekly storytelling hours or children's record rentals.

Sometimes, however, the marketer may wish to fundamentally or marginally change the offer by adding one or more new consequences. This, of course, is the intended effect when marketers offer premiums or bonuses for purchases or attendance. Thus, a symphony orchestra could entice more new attenders by having the conductor or soloist on a particular evening agree to autograph album covers before a performance. Or the Peace Corps could offer to photograph participants in the field and to write reference letters to impress future employers.

In Mr. Arneson's case, he may discover "perks" that might appeal to Dr. Goldman. This could be an augmentation to the basic offering such as a special parking location, an advanced dictation system for patient reports, or first perusal of the library's copies of key journals in her field. Alternatively (or in addition), Mr. Arneson may simply point out additional existing features of St. Anthony's and its staff, such as the publication record of attending physicians, which would indicate that both typing facilities and knowledgeable colleagues would be available for whatever writing ambitions Dr. Goldman might harbor.

Assuming that Mr. Arneson wishes to improve Dr. Goldman's belief about the "respect" consequences of sending her patients to St. Anthony's, he can only do so *moderately.* There are other problems he must also overcome. These are customers' tendencies to selectively attend to messages and to distort perceptually what they see.

OVERCOMING SELECTIVE ATTENTION

Mr. Arneson must recognize that people are constantly bombarded with promotional messages. Some estimates suggest that we are exposed to as many as 1,400 messages in a day. But, of course, we perceive far fewer. We selectively attend to the information environment around us. This is often called "the cocktail party effect."[6] It helps us simplify and manage our lives. We attend to subjects, themes, or images that interest us and ignore others that don't. Thus, women will notice ads with babies, men will notice ads with dogs. Hypochondriacs catch ads for over-the-counter drugs and business people seldom ignore computer ads.

On the other hand, we tend to avoid messages that don't interest us or that in some way frighten us. This is a particular problem with fear appeals. Many nonprofit organizations involved in social or health issues find it tempting to use fear appeals. For example, the Metropolitan Energy Council, a group of New York fuel dealers, tried to compete with gas suppliers with an ad in the *New York Times* that depicted a young mother saying: "Gas comes from a big utility. They don't know my family. If you need prompt service from them, you have to say, 'I smell gas.' That's what scares me most. I think gas heat is dangerous . . . too dangerous for my home, my kids."[7]

Fear is not always effective. Researchers in Ontario, Canada, reviewed past studies of seat-belt usage and determined that an appeal based on the fear of being injured *but not killed* in a car crash could be potentially quite powerful. A test set of six messages was constructed (see Table 18-2) and run 943 times over nine consecutive months on one cable network of a dual cable system in Ontario. Seat-belt usage of a random sample of drivers was unobtrusively observed before, during, and after the study by using license plates to learn which cable network each driver was exposed to. After correcting for the effects of weather (seat belts are less often used with bulky clothes in Canadian winters), the researchers concluded that the television campaign was a failure and that only coercion would work, either laws or mandatory passive restraint systems like air bags or automatic seat belting systems.[8]

The researchers may have been too pessimistic about persuasive approaches in general. The level of invoked fear may have been too great! Ray and Wilkie point out that fear can have both motivating and inhibiting effects.[9] Fear has the potential to motivate use *if* we (1) attend to the message, and (2) are scared by it. But the greater the fear level, the more our selective attention mechanisms will be invoked, and the fear appeal will never get the *chance* to motivate us. Thus, Wilkie and Ray argue that fear effects may well be curvilinear. The ideal level will also vary by topic and individual involvement. Those who wish to use fear, therefore, must pretest their message to assess just what amount of fear is optimal in their particular setting or for a particular audience. Burnett and Wilkes, for example, found that while high-fear appeals were more effective in changing attitudes toward a health maintenance organization (HMO) than low-, medium-, or no-fear approaches, this result held only for three segments: older blue-collar whites, older blue-collar blacks, and older liberals.[10]

Table 18-2

1. A father is shown lifting his teenaged son from a wheelchair into a car. As they ride along, safety belts obviously fastened, the father's thoughts are voiced off-camera intermixed with the son's on-camera expressions of excitement at going to a football game. The father expresses guilt for not having encouraged his son to use safety belts before the crash in which he was injured. An analogy to the protection that the son wore when he played football is drawn.

2. A teenaged girl is shown sitting in a rocking chair looking out a window. She says, "I'm not sick or anything. I could go out more but since the car crash, I just don't . . . The crash wasn't Dad's fault. I go for walks with my father after dark . . . that way I don't get, you know, stared at." She turns enough to reveal a large scar on what was the hidden side of her face. She continues, "It doesn't hurt anymore." An announcer says off camera, "Car crashes kill two ways: right away and little by little. Wear your safety belts and live!"

3. A woman whose face cannot be seen is shown in front of a mirror applying makeup. A full-face picture on her dressing table shows her as a beautiful woman. Her husband enters the scene and suggests that they go to a party. She asks him not to look at her without makeup as she turns to reveal a scarred face. An off-camera announcer describes a crash in which the wife was driving slowly and carefully. The announcer continues, as the picture on the table is shown, "Terry would still look like this if she had been wearing seat belts." Safety belts are shown through a shattered windshield. Announcer: "It's much easier to wear safety belts than to hear your husband say, 'Honey, I love you anyway.'"

4. A father and mother are shown riding in the front seat of a car, their eight-year-old daughter seated between them. The father must brake hard to avoid another car entering from a side road. The daughter bumps her head as she is thrown into the dashboard and begins to cry. A policeman walks up to the car and the father angrily says: "Did you see what that guy just did? That jerk. I had to jam on my brakes. My little girl hit her head." The policeman asks the father why the child wasn't wearing safety belts. Over the father's protestations about the other driver, the policeman emphasizes the father's responsibility to protect his child. The scene closes with the policeman walking away saying "When are people gonna learn?" and the announcer following with "It doesn't take brains to wear safety belts. But it sure is stupid not to."

5. Two physicians and a nurse are shown ordering coffee. The nurse asks: "Trouble?" A doctor replies: "Another guy driving

Table 18.2 (continued)

home not wearing his safety belts." Nurse: "Gonna live?" Doctor: "Guess you could call it living." Nurse: "You've had a lot of car crash cases lately." Doctor: "Yeah, and I'm getting sick of it. They've got safety belts in the cars. Why . . . why in the name of God don't they put 'em on?" Waitress: "Do safety belts really make a difference?" The doctor shows her how a thermometer case can be hit and the thermometer inside not broken, but it shatters when hit out of the case. The waitress expresses further doubt and the doctor says: "How many times do you have to tell 'em?"

6. A car is shown in a driveway. From a puff of smoke steps a witch who announces: "Ha, ha, ha. I'm the Wicked Car Witch. Your Mommy and Daddy cannot see me but I make them drive without their safety belts. That's how they get hurt in car crashes." The mother gets into the car and the witch hides some belts in the seat and tangles others. A Good Car Fairy appears and says: "Children! I am the Good Car Fairy. When your Mommy and Daddy get in the car, say 'Mommy! Daddy! If you love me, wear your safety belts!'" The Wicked Witch and the Good Fairy argue as the father enters the car. A little girl calls from the porch: "Mommy! Daddy! Wear your safety belts." The parents fasten the belts, the Wicked Witch disappears in a puff of smoke, and the Good Fairy again admonishes the children to urge their parents to demonstrate their love by wearing their safety belts.

SOURCE: Leon S. Robertson, Albert B. Kelley, Brian O'Neill, Charles W. Wixom, Richard S. Eiswirth, and William Haddon, Jr., "A Controlled Study of the Effect of Television Messages on Safety Belt Use," *American Journal of Public Health*, Vol. 64, November 1974, p. 1074. Reprinted with permission of the American Public Health Association.

The existence of the selective attention phenomenon should alert Mr. Arneson to the possibility that Dr. Goldman may simply not hear what he says or see what he might send her in the mail. If she has determined that she is simply not interested in St. Anthony's, she may not really notice his messages. He may need to invoke some unusual or humorous pretext to introduce the topic, perhaps catching her off guard. If he has a potentially scary piece of information about Downtown Medical, he should first consider whether it may be too fear-provoking for Dr. Goldman to pay attention.

Overcoming the selective attention problem is the responsibility of the creative specialists on the nonprofit communication team (in-house or at the advertising or public relations agency). These specialists have several variables at their command in designing an effective message. They need to find a *style, tone, wording, order,* and *format* to make the message effective.

Any message can be put across in different *execution styles.* Suppose the YMCAs around the country are planning to launch an early-morning jogging program (6:30 A.M.) and want to develop a thirty-second television commercial to motivate people to sign up for this program. Here are some major advertising execution styles they can consider:

1. *Slice-of-life.* A wife says to her tired husband that he might enjoy jogging at the Y in the early morning. He agrees, and the next frame shows him coming home at 7:45 A.M. feeling refreshed and invigorated.

2. *Life-style.* A thirty-year-old man pops out of bed when his alarm rings at 6:00 A.M., races to the bathroom, races to the closet, races to his car, races to the Y, and then starts racing with his companions with a "big kid" look on his face.

3. *Fantasy.* A jogger runs along a path and suddenly imagines seeing her friends on the sidelines cheering her on.

4. *Mood.* A jogger runs in a residential neighborhood on a beautiful spring day, passing nice homes, noticing flowers beginning to bloom and neighbors waving to him. This ad creates a mood of beauty and harmony between the jogger and his world.

5. *Musical.* Four young joggers run side by side wearing YMCA T-shirts. A specially written pulsating rock melody fills the background.

6. *Personality symbol.* A well-known sports hero is shown jogging at the Y with a smile on his face.

7. *Technical expertise.* Several Y athletic directors are shown discussing the best time, place, and running style that will give the greatest benefit to joggers. (For an example of a technical expert dealing with water safety, see Figure 18-4.)

8. *Scientific evidence.* A physician tells about a study of two matched groups of men, one following a jogging program and the other not, and the greater health and energy felt by the jogging group after a few weeks.

9. *Testimonial evidence.* The ad shows three members of the Y jogging group telling how beneficial the program has been.

The communicator must also choose a *tone* for the message. The message could be deadly serious (as in an antismoking ad), chatty (as in a message on weight control), humorous (as in a zoo ad), and so on. The tone must be appropriate to the target audience and target response desired.

Words that are memorable and attention-getting must be found. This is nowhere more apparent than in the development of headlines and slogans to lead the reader into the message. There are six basic types of headlines: *news* ("New Boom and More Inflation Ahead . . . and What You Can Do about It"); *questions* ("Have You Had It Lately?"); *narrative* ("They Laughed When I Sat Down at the Piano, But When I Started to Play . . .!"); *command* ("Save water—shower with a friend"); *1–2–3 ways* ("12 Ways to Save on Your Income Tax"); and *how-what-why* ("Why They Can't Stop Buying").

A symphony orchestra such as the Toronto Symphony Orchestra (TSO) might develop headlines for its season-ticket mailings using each of these styles:

FIGURE 18-4

Using a Technical Expert

DIVING SAFETY

Presented by the National Swimming Pool Foundation

:30 Second PSA

(Background sounds)

"Jamie, Jamie!" Learning how to dive the right way. . .

can prevent a serious injury.

I'm Greg Louganis and I'd like to pass along these tips.

Always know the depth of the water before you dive...

don't dive deep, plan your dive path...

keep your hands in front of your face at all times.

And don't clown around or showboat. They cause more accidents than anything.

Diving is a great sport...let's do it right!

SOURCE: Needham Porter Novelli. Reprinted with permission.

1. *News:* "The TSO's new conductor has received rave reviews from international music critics. Just listen to these glowing reports . . . "
2. *Questions:* "Why are this famous football player . . . this executive secretary . . . and this twenty-five-year-old rock star attending a TSO concert?"
3. *Narrative:* "At the flash of the downbeat, the orchestra was galvanized into a dynamic performance of the Carmen Suite and I found my head spinning in wonderment."

4. *Command:* "You've always said you wanted to 'get into' classical music. Well, do it now while our season ticket discounts make it so easy."

5. *1–2–3 ways:* "Our seventeen combinations of season concert packages let you design a music season to *your* taste and *your* schedule."

6. *How-what-why:* "Designing your very own music season is as easy as connecting the dots when you were a kid. Let us show you the way."

Once the headline and the themes are determined, the communicator must consider the ordering of the ideas. There are three issues: conclusion drawing, one- or two-sided arguments, and order of presentation.

The first is the question of *conclusion drawing,* the extent to which the ad should draw a definite conclusion for the audience, such as telling them to "give their fair share." Experimental research seems to indicate that explicit conclusion-drawing is more persuasive than leaving it to the audience to draw their own conclusions. There are exceptions, however, such as when the communicator is seen as untrustworthy or the audience is highly intelligent and annoyed at the attempt to influence them.

The second is the question of the *one- or two-sided argument*—that is, whether the message will be more effective if one side or both sides of the argument are presented. Two-sided arguments are of two types. First, there is the approach that admits that the offering has some defects. The classic example of this approach is the series of ads for the Volkswagen Beetle that admitted it was homely and that it didn't change its looks every model year, but that otherwise it was a marvelously sensible purchase! In the nonprofit sector, there are many situations in which the target audience will *know* there is a negative side to a requested behavior:

- Potential blood donors *know* the needle will hurt and that they may feel a little faint.
- Alcoholics, smokers, and drug addicts *know* that quitting or cutting down will be agonizing and require very strong willpower.
- Older persons *know* that investigating a retirement home means admitting negative things about their own competence.
- Young people *know* that not drinking or smoking in some cases may subject them to the teasing of friends and classmates.
- Symphony, theatre, and museum goers *know* that a great many of the events they could attend will have elements they don't understand.

The other kind of two-sided argument recognizes the fact that there are other alternatives. The burger and cola "wars" are message compaigns fully recognizing that there are tough competitors "out there." In the nonprofit sector, there are many parallel situations:

- Going to the theatre or symphony means not going to a movie or nightclub or just staying home to watch TV.

- Having a medical checkup or practicing breast self-examination means giving up the "bliss of ignorance."
- Giving to the United Way means not giving to the American Cancer Fund or a university's alumni fund.
- Choosing UCLA means not choosing Stanford, Northwestern, and Harvard.
- Choosing to vacation in Jamaica or Southeast Asia means not vacationing in Sun Valley or Paris.
- Practicing birth control means not having the economic and psychic pleasures of an additional child.

One-sided presentations are common in both the profit and nonprofit sectors. They are often synonymous with what many would call a "hard-sell" approach. Yet social science research suggests that one-sided approaches may be relatively more effective in three situations: (1) when the audience is less educated; (2) when the audience already favors the message's central proposition; and (3) when the audience is not likely to be exposed later to counterpropaganda. Two-sided messages are said to be more effective when the opposite is true.

There is another, perhaps more compelling factor that should influence whether two-sided messages are used: it is the degree of the audience's involvement in the behavior that the marketer is attempting to influence. In general, we would argue the following: the higher the audience's involvement in the behavior, the more frequently the nonprofit marketer should use two-sided messages.

There are several reasons for this. In high-involvement situations, target audience members are more likely to

- be very concerned about the *costs* of the behavior (see Chapter 16);
- be opposed to the action advocated, if it means change;
- be aware of very attractive alternatives.

In high-involvement situations, the target audience will engage in extensive internal cognitive activity, which will include considering costs and alternatives. They will engage in an extensive external search that will make available to them the "other side" of the argument. The marketer should seize the initiative and deal with the other side of the issue rather than leave it to the individual or to competitors. A useful concept in this regard is what is called *inoculation theory*. If a communicator knows that a target audience member will *later* be exposed to counterpropaganda (the "other side"), a more favorable outcome will be achieved if the marketer deals with the counterarguments in advance, in effect "inoculating" the target audience against the later influence attempts.

Finally, it must be reemphasized that in situations in which a two-sided strategy would be appropriate, the nonprofit communicator must go to great lengths to understand what *the target audience* perceives to be the key costs of the behavior and what *they* consider to be the reasonable alternatives. Only with a solid research base can an effective two-sided strategy be developed.

In the case of St. Anthony's Hospital, Mr. Arneson should recognize that Dr. Goldman will be exposed to counterpropaganda from DMC at some later point. Thus, the two-sided inoculation concept indicates that Arneson must say things like "I know you'll hear people say that St. Anthony's is overcrowded. Let me set the record straight right now." If at all possible, Arneson should seek to have Dr. Goldman agree with St. Anthony's arguments. Internalizing a position makes it more likely that an individual will adhere to it even after other information is received.

A third issue for the marketer in cases where several ideas are to be conveyed is the best *order of presentation.* Social scientists have found that, other things being equal, people tend to remember the items in a message stream presented first (the primacy effect) and last (the recency effect). There are arguments for putting one's strongest statements in either position. Where one is using a two-sided message, the case is more complex. However, the following approach appears reasonable:[11]

> 1. If the audience is likely to attend to the message under most circumstances (that is, not filter it out), it is probably best to place the message about the "other side" in the middle of the message where it is more likely to be forgotten and the arguments for one's own position in the first and last positions.
>
> 2. If the audience is opposed to the message and likely to screen it out, then beginning with the other side of the issue or with the other alternative may disarm the audience into "hearing" the marketer's message. Thus, a symphony marketer might say, "A night at home with the family watching TV by a warm fire would be great this winter. But the Toronto Symphony Orchestra has some good reasons for you to consider other pleasures."

Format elements can make a difference in an ad's impact, as well as in its cost. If the message is to be carried in a print ad, the communicator has to develop the elements of headline, copy, illustration, and color. Advertisers are adept at using such attention-getting devices as *novelty, contrast, arresting pictures,* and *movement.* Large ads, for example, gain more attention, and so do four-color ads, and this must be weighed against their higher costs. If the message is to be carried over the radio, the communicator has to carefully choose words, voice qualities (speech rate, rhythm, pitch, articulation), and vocalizations (pauses, sighs, yawns). If the message is to be carried on television or given in person, then all of these elements plus body language (nonverbal clues) have to be planned. Presenters have to pay attention to their facial expressions, gestures, dress, posture, and hairstyle.

As we have already noted, individuals have a substantial background of experiences, categorization schemes, prejudices, associations, needs, wants, and fears that can markedly affect what they "see" or "hear" in the message. Thus, poor children will draw foreign coins that they have seen larger than will children who are economically better off. Pessimists will see half-empty glasses, optimists half-full ones.

This potential for distortion can work to the communicator's advantage. Messages can be relatively economical in what they say by using associations that they know people will bring to a symbol, a word, or an example. For example, readers need to see only *one* of these symbols depicted in an ad to know that a restaurant is *not* a fast-food outlet: a tablecloth, flowers on the table, silverware, a waiter taking an order, candles or subdued lighting, upholstered chairs, wine glasses, or china. Someone sipping wine is assumed to be of a higher social class than someone who has a beer mug. Someone with glasses is supposed to be smarter than someone without them. Colors have symbolism. White is pure, gold is rich, blue is soothing, pastels are "modern," and so on.[12]

This is a major advantage to communicators. The problem, of course, is to choose the right symbols and to be assured that your audience sees them as you do. Mr. Arneson may make an important mistake by assuming, for example, that Dr. Goldman would associate formica furnishings with high-quality office decor. While Mr. Arneson should carefully plan his choice of associations, one advantage of personal communication is that a sensitive communicator can secure feedback on how the message is actually perceived and fine-tune it so that it is perceived as intended.

Even if a message is perceived in an appropriate fashion, this does not guarantee that it will be retained or, more importantly, recalled at the moment it is "needed" to influence a particular behavior. One technique to reduce this possibility is, of course, repetition. Krugman and others have suggested that up to three repetitions will improve the probability of retention under high-involvement conditions.[13] Thus, Mr. Arneson might mention the hospital's superior accounting and scheduling services several times in a conversation or over a series of conversations to increase the likelihood that the information will be permanently retained. Another technique is to link the new information to existing cognitions. Individuals are more likely to recall things that they can assimilate well.

Choosing a Medium

The message the marketer decides to use will be transmitted to the target consumer through some medium or a combination of media. The medium chosen can be *personal,* as when the organization's own salesperson is used, or *impersonal,* as when a poster, a brochure, a magazine or newspaper advertisement, a product container, a shopping bag, or the side of a truck is used. The medium can be perceived by the customer as an *advocate* for the offering or as *independent.* Thus, there are four possibilities, as suggested in Table 18-3.

We consider the use of conventional advocate media in the following two chapters. We turn to the possibilities of using independent media—to the extent that they can be influenced—in Chapter 21. Here, we consider the problem of choosing spokespeople.

In many situations involving either paid or unpaid advocacy of a nonprofit organization and its product, service, or cause, the marketing manager will wish to use some person to deliver the message. Whom to choose and what to have the person say are crucial questions. *Balance theory* is useful here.

Balance theory starts with a fundamental assumption similar to that of dissonance theory, that is, that individuals like to have balance in their cognitive structures. They like things to "fit." And when they come across a piece of information that is not consistent with their present cognitions, they exert some effort to restore balance. The level of effort is proportional to the degree of imbalance and the importance of the subject. For example, executives of Coca-Cola in mid-1985 were convinced that New Coke would be a successful substitute for Old Coke. The evidence to the contrary that emerged after the introduction presumably took a long time to sink in, in part because it was so different from what management expected and because the subject was so important to them. Presumably, the readers of this book did not find the less-than-spectacular introduction of New Coke so difficult to accept.

Balance theory helps explain the problem facing the marketing manager in choosing a spokesperson. Consider the diagram in Figure 18-5. Here we see a situation in which the marketer wishes to use a spokesperson (S)

Table 18-3
ALTERNATIVE MEDIA

	Personal	Impersonal
Advocate	Salesperson	Brochure
	Political supporter	Advertisement
	"Friend of the Arts"	Billboard
Independent	Newscaster	*Wall Street Journal*
	Independent researcher	Government study
	Noted physician	*Consumer Reports*

FIGURE 18-5

Hypothetical Balance Theory Diagram

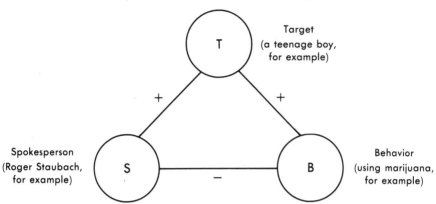

to advocate a behavior (B) to a target consumer (T). (The target, of course, could be a corporation, a political body, or the nonprofit's own employees.)

The three sides of the triangle in Figure 18-5 can be seen as having algebraic signs—plus or minus. The system is in balance whenever the multiplication of the signs is *positive*. Thus, if the target hated the spokesperson or did not wish to perform the behavior the spokesperson advocated, the system would be in balance, just as it would be if the target's views of the three links were all positive. (Remember that the signs are all in the target consumer's head. This is where the spokesperson will "do battle.")

If the system is out of balance and the issue is important enough to the target consumer, he or she will seek to restore balance. Presumably, change will take place at the weakest link of the system portrayed in Figure 18-5. In the typical case, the target consumer is presented with a spokesperson's message advocating a behavior that the target does not wish to perform. For example, a teenager hears a message discouraging marijuana use, which he or she likes or feels the need to engage in because of peer pressure. In such cases, the T-B link is negative and the S-B link is positive. Now, suppose further that, as the nonprofit marketer hopes, the T-S link is positive. What will happen? Obviously, there are four possibilities:

    1. The target changes his or her attitude toward the advocated behavior. The target says, "I guess that person is right, I should give up the behavior." T-B becomes positive.

    2. The target changes his or her attitude toward the spokesperson. The target says, in effect, "I guess I was wrong about the person. How can he be against such a great behavior?" T-S becomes negative.

    3. The target distorts his or her perception of what the spokesperson is saying. The target says, in effect, "That person really mustn't mean that. He must have been paid a lot to say that." S-B becomes negative.

4. The target simply diminishes the importance of the issue ("Oh, it's no big deal!") and lives with the imbalance.

Obviously, the marketer wishes the first outcome to take place. The obvious solution, as advocated by Figure 18-5, is to make sure that the T-B link is the *weakest* in the system. Therefore, to make sure that the T-S link is as strong as possible, the nonprofit marketer must be very careful in the selection of spokespersons. It is critical that the spokesperson have as strong a positive connection with the target consumer as possible.

Spokespersons tend to be viewed positively for one of two reasons.[14] First, they may be respected as *credible experts* on a particular topic. This would be the case where a teenage former drug user or a noted medical expert is the spokesperson for the advocated behavior. The other case is where the person is not an expert but is considered by the target audience to be highly *trustworthy*. Thus, the nonprofit might use Roger Staubach or President Reagan to advocate a drug-free life. The target may reason that although the spokesperson doesn't necessarily know anything about the subject, he or she can be counted on to tell the truth or advise one wisely. Betty Ford, when speaking about drugs, is presumably both a credible and a trustworthy person.

Choosing the ideal spokesperson is not easy. Of course, the appropriate choice will depend on both the topic and the issue. One possibility is to hedge one's bets by using multiple spokespeople as has the Boy Scouts of America. (For one example see Figure 18-6.) In all cases, it is important that the nonprofit marketer research the credibility and trustworthiness of the proposed spokespersons with the target audience. It is seldom a good idea to use someone who is very famous but who may seem to be so lacking in expertness that his or her credibility is low. Thus, in the private sector, John Houseman may have been an excellent spokesperson for a stockbrokerage, but he threatened his credibility when he was hired to speak for a fast-food chain.

Once the spokesperson is chosen, the last link, S-B, must also be constructed as firmly as possible. Half the battle will be won if the right spokesperson is chosen. Still, alternative messages must be carefully pretested to ensure that there is little possibility that the target audience could believe that the spokesperson somehow really didn't mean it.

MESSAGE EVALUATION AND SELECTION

Now the marketer must select the best message from the set of alternatives. This calls for evaluation criteria. Twedt has suggested that contending messages be rated on three scales: *desirability, exclusiveness,* and *believability*.[15] He believes that the communication potency of a message is the product of these three factors because if any of the three has a low rating, the message's communication potency is greatly reduced.

FIGURE 18-6

Use of a Spokesperson in a Nonprofit Advertisement

SOURCE: Reproduced with permission, Foote Cone & Belding, Chicago, IL.

The message must first say something desirable or interesting about the product. This is not enough, however, since many brands will be making the same claim. Therefore the message must also say something exclusive or distinctive that does not apply to every brand in the product category. Finally, the message must be believable or provable. By asking consumers to rate different messages on desirability, exclusiveness, and believability, these messages can be evaluated for their communication potency.

For example, the March of Dimes was searching for an advertising theme to raise money for its fight against birth defects.[16] A brainstorming session led to over twenty possible messages. A group of young parents were asked to rate each message for interest, distinctiveness, and believability, assigning up to 100 points for each. The message "Seven hundred children are born each day with a birth defect," for example, scored 70, 60, and 80 on interest, distinctiveness, and believability, while "Your next baby could be born with a birth defect" scored 58, 50, and 70 (see Figure 18-7). The first message outperforms the second and would be preferred for advertising purposes. The best overall message was "The March of Dimes has given you: polio vaccine, German measles vaccine, 110 birth defects' counseling centers" (70, 80, and 90).

FIGURE 18-7

Advertising Message Evaluation

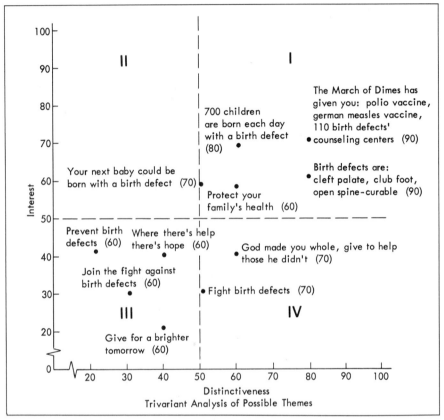

SOURCE: William A. Mindak and H. Malcolm Bybee, "Marketing's Application to Fund Raising." *Journal of Marketing,* July 1971, pp. 13–18.

MODIFYING BEHAVIOR DIRECTLY

The approaches offered for communications strategies to this point have been based on a model of the attitude-behavior relationship that assumes that attitude change must be obtained *before* behavior change. Indeed, the traditional persuasion approach required that attitudes be changed in order for behavior to change. This position has been challenged by a number of scientists on both theoretical and empirical grounds. They argue that we often adjust our attitudes to fit our behavior rather than vice versa. We observed in the Ontario seat-belt study that it is often very difficult to get behavior to change by first changing beliefs. This is more true the more involved the individual is in the behavior to be changed, that is, the more central the behavior is to the person's self-concept. Thus, a teenager

who believes smoking is "absolutely necessary" to the image of a self-pos-
sessed young person may be virtually impermeable to attitude-change-based
persuasion strategies. Or the older person who sees herself as perfectly self-
sufficient may selectively screen out or distort any messages attempting to
lead her to enter a "retirement home" or to have professional helpers routinely come to her home.

In such circumstances, a more cost-effective communication strategy
may be to seek behavior change directly rather than worrying about attitude
change at all. One approach is through legal sanctions, although this has had
mixed results.[17] Another approach is known variously as *instrumental conditioning* or *behavioral modification* and is most closely associated with the
name of B. F. Skinner.[18]

The approach is grounded in the view of consumer behavior that we
have used throughout this volume. We have argued that consumers take
particular courses of action because of the anticipated consequences. The
persuasion approach to behavior change seeks to modify consumer's *antic-
ipations* about possible consequences. Behavior modification attempts *to
modify the consequences themselves.* By teaching the target individual that
a particular action will lead to a desired reward, the probability of the action
is increased. Thus, if a consumer finds an unanticipated coupon at the bottom of a box of cereal or a jar of instant coffee, behavior modification theory
predicts that the chances are increased that the consumer will buy the product again. The coupons in this case are referred to as *reinforcers.* Cracker
Jack has successfully used modest prizes for years as just such reinforcers.

There are many kinds of reinforcers, including:

- *Economic:* Coupons, trading stamps, prizes, rebates, chances in a contest, free
goods.
- *Social:* Praise, commendation, affection, conversation, attention.
- *Other:* Food, candy, feedback on achievement.

Social scientists have documented that children who are given more
attention and praise after eating unfamiliar foods are more likely to repeat
this behavior (and subsequently to "like" the foods) than those who are not.
Simple feedback on household energy consumption has led to a reduction
in energy use. Reductions in home oil usage, for example, were induced by
rewarding householders with a window sticker saying "We Are Saving Oil."

A great many companies are using economic incentives to get their
employees to take better care of their health. At Johnson & Johnson, for
example, employees can earn "Live-for-Life Dollars" to be exchanged for
sweat suits, socks, or fire extinguishers for attending smoking or stress workshops, exercising for twenty minutes, wearing seat belts, or installing home
smoke detectors. Intermatic, Inc. gives employees who quit cigarettes for a
year a trip for two to Las Vegas. Hospital Corporation of America pays

workers twenty-four cents for each mile walked or run, each quarter mile swum, or each four miles bicycled. The government of Bellevue, Washington, and firms like the Berol Corporation and King Broadcasting in Seattle give rewards negatively related to the amount of health insurance claims an employee files. Speedcall Corporation gives a $7 bonus for each week an employee doesn't smoke on the job. In four years, the number of smokers in the company fell 65 percent and the number of health insurance claims by quitters fell 50 percent.[19]

Examples of incentives and disincentives that have been used around the world to promote smaller families are reported in Exhibit 18-1.

There is some controversy about what patterns of reinforcement should be used. In general, *constant reinforcement* (rewarding every instance of the desired behavior) yields the fastest rate of learning but also the fastest extinction of the behavior when the reinforcements are stopped. On the other hand, *random reinforcement* yields slower rates of initial learning but also slower extinction. The reasons offered for this finding are that during the reinforcement period, the subject is initially not sure which behavior (if any) is being rewarded. This accounts for the slower rate of initial learning. Then, when rewards *are* linked to the behavior, the subject must interpolate his or her own rewards on those occasions when the externally manipulated rewards are absent.

In a recent study, Deslauriers and Everett found that offering 10-cent tokens to bus riders had a positive effect on bus usage. However, they found that variable reinforcement (every third passenger) was just as effective as continuing reinforcement and, of course, much more economical.[20]

For this type of behavioral modification to work, certain simple conditions must be present:

1. The desired behavior must be under the individual's control (thus, it is not particularly effective with physical drug dependency).
2. There must be a clear link between the behavior and the reinforcement, although this need not always be apparent to the subject; the closer the reward is in time to the behavior, the greater the effect (thus, praising someone two days after a desired behavior—for example, cutting out certain smoking occasions—is less effective than immediate praise).
3. The reinforcer must constitute a reward for the individual (thus, praise from a feared autocratic school teacher would not be as reinforcing for a schoolchild as praise from a peer).

SHAPING

The approach just described presumes that there is a specific behavior that is rewarded and that the probability of its recurrence is affected by the manipulation of reinforcements. There are some behavioral outcomes that can be approached, not in one step, but by successive approximations. This

EXHIBIT 18-1. Worldwide small family incentives and disincentives

1. Villages in Indonesia are passing resolutions to have not more than two children per family. Each year, the provincial governors award certificates of acclamation to those villages that have been successful in achieving the two-child goal.

2. In China, a collective decision is made at the community level as to who will have children during a specific year. Parents are encouraged, often through peer pressure, to have only one child.

3. In Korea, Mothers Clubs are formed to give support to couples who have one and two children. The clubs have given health, education, and financial assistance to those members who are committed to small families.

4. In Bangladesh and India, Green Cards are being issued to couples who have only one or two children. The cards give the holder priority health and educational opportunities.

5. In Taiwan, family planning field-workers are asking couples to register their intent to have a child. The government is better able to provide for the educational, health, and social services for those communities where all births are planned and wanted.

6. In Singapore, couples with three or more children are taxed more, are not eligible for governmental housing, and the third child cannot go to the same school as his or her siblings.

7. In some religious ceremonies, couples are being asked to decide on how many children they want and when they want them. Some marriage vows include commitments to having only one or two children.

8. In Thailand and Indonesia, community awards that help employ women are being given by banks and cooperatives when the prevalence of contraceptive use leads to a level of reproduction that keeps the population from growing.

9. In Indonesia, successful family planners are given awards by President Suharto. These awards give the bearer status within the community. Awards are also given to those individuals who come up with the most innovative incentive and disincentive proposals.

10. In some Chinese villages "Certificates of Praise" are placed on the doors of couples who have only one child.

11. In Kerala State, India, nonpregant women receive money deposits every six months. After three years, they can withdraw the funds.

12. In Gujarat, India, a bag of cement is given to the village councils for every vasectomy performed in the villages.

SOURCE: Robert W. Gillespie, *A Review of Incentives and Disincentives in Developing Countries.* Working paper, Population Communications, Inc., Pasadena, California, November 1985. Reproduced with permission.

is known as "shaping" behavior. A good example of this technique is in securing smoking cessation. The ultimate goal of complete cessation is set initially and the smoker is asked to observe his or her own smoking behavior, noting two things: the occasions on which a cigarette is smoked, and the relative importance of the smoking behavior on each occasion. The smoker then determines his or her own schedule of cutting down (shaping) the smoking behavior. The smoker starts by eliminating the least important smoking occasions and then works up to the most important. Smokers are trained to either reward themselves directly or to report their successes to a smoking cessation group or an individual therapist for attention, praise, and affectional reinforcement.

Several variations on personal reinforcement have been devised. One technique is simply selecting a desired reward (for example, a weekend vacation, dinner in a fancy restaurant, or a manicure) after a certain number of behavior change "points" have been accumulated. Another approach is to set aside a significant sum of money to go to a disliked organization or cause (for example, a pro- or antiabortion group, the Ku Klux Klan, or the Communist Party). Then a specific amount of money may be withdrawn from the amount set aside with the passage of each milestone.

Two variations on the concept of shaping behavior are the so-called "foot-in-the-door" and "door-in-the-face" techniques.

The Foot-in-the-Door Technique.   The "foot-in-the-door" technique is based on a finding that if you can get target audience members to take a small step in a desired direction, they are much more likely to take a major step later. This effect is explainable by self-perception theory, which says that we all tend to behave in ways that we feel are consistent with our views of ourselves. What is alleged to happen in the foot-in-the-door situation is that compliance with the initial modest request changes target persons' self-perceptions. They now see themselves as "the kind of person" who helps out in these situations. This makes them much more likely to comply with a later, more demanding request.

Scott tested this foot-in-the-door technique in the context of a recycling campaign.[21] Residents were assigned experimentally to different treatment conditions, and all but one group was asked to place a small sign in their windows promoting recycling. Some were given small incentives ($1.00 or $3.00) to take the initial small step. These incentives had no effect on whether a person complied with the initial request.

Two weeks later, *all* subjects were asked to perform a more substantial helping behavior. Half were asked to address twenty-five envelopes to be used in the recycling campaign and half were asked to address seventy-five envelopes. Those who received no incentive but did place the sign in the window were four times as likely to agree to a request to address twenty-five envelopes as were those who were not asked to display the sign. Further, when the first behavior was prompted by financial rewards, the rate of behavioral compliance to the second request declined. This is consistent with self-perception theory, which would suggest that, in the latter cases, individuals would be saying to themselves (at least in part), "I helped with the sign because I could use the reward. I perceive myself as someone who does things for a reward. I didn't get a reward the second time." Those who got no reward would be assumed to ask themselves "Why did I help out? It wasn't for money. It must be because I am someone who helps out in this cause." It should be noted that the findings for the larger request are in the expected direction but are not statistically significant. This led Scott to conclude that the foot-in-the-door technique will work when:

- The behavior is not too large. In practice this would not appear to be a serious restriction. Rather, it indicates that change may be achieved through a series of foot-in-the-door operations, each requiring a larger change in behavior than the one before (that is, shaping). What constitutes a "large" behavior, of course, may depend on a number of factors, including the nature of the task itself.
- The requests are made in person. Mere repetition of contact did not affect subsequent behavior (that is, those who did not comply with the initial request were no more likely to comply with the second request than control subjects); thus, personal communication may be needed to ensure initial compliance. Some initial evidence exists, however, which suggests that foot-in-the-door and other attribution-based messages may be more effective than traditional persuasive appeals in mass communication settings where personal contact is not possible.[22]

Mr. Arneson might wish to try the foot-in-the-door technique. He could suggest to Dr. Goldman that she "try out" St. Anthony's by bringing two outpatients for some particular test. The hope would be that Dr. Goldman would begin to perceive herself as "someone who sends patients to St. Anthony's." As Scott suggests, it may be necessary to gradually increase the suggested behaviors before Dr. Goldman would send *all* of her patients there.

The Door-in-the-Face Technique.   This technique is just the opposite of foot-in-the-door, but, surprisingly, it is based on the same theory. The door-in-the-face technique requires that the communicator begin with an *initial* request that is so large that it is sure to be turned down. Assuming that the behavior involves a socially desirable end, it may be expected that when a later, more modest request is made, the target audience member who had earlier slammed the door "in the face" of the requester will say "I'm not the kind of person who is unwilling to help with these causes. I should change my behavior to fit my self-perception. I'll help out this time." Empirical research using this technique has yielded mixed results.[23]

In Mr. Arneson's case, the "door-in-the-face" technique might suggest first asking Dr. Goldman to assign all her patients to St. Anthony's and then, after this is refused, asking her to assign a few patients initially.

SUMMARY

Every contact a nonprofit has with its many publics directly or indirectly is an occasion for influence. These contacts may be carried out by many different departments or people using diverse vehicles ranging all the way from standard paid and unpaid media to package designs, corporate publicity releases, personal sales presentations, and even promotional "gimmicks" like shopping bags and T-shirts. The chapters to follow will consider detailed influence strategies involving advertising, sales promotion, public relations, and personal selling. For programs to be effective, however, they must be grounded in a clear understanding of influence processes.

Influence typically involves persuasion. This requires the preparation and transmittal of specific messages. Messages must be encoded by the marketer, communicated through media, and then decoded by the receiver. At each of these stages, considerable noise can be introduced into the communications process such that the accumulated effect of the received message is very different from what was intended. In general, the more parties involved in the communications system and the less control the marketer has over them, the greater the chance for miscommunication. Marketers use formal and informal feedback to track these effects. Where communication is face to face, feedback can be easily obtained. Where it is not, as in media campaigns, pre- and posttests of message strategies must always be carried out.

Six steps are involved in developing effective messages. First, the communication objectives must be determined. Second, messages must be generated. These can be rational, emotional, or moral, or they can be generated from a rewards/situations framework. Third, thought must be given to how these communications can overcome consumers' tendencies to selectively expose themselves or attend to messages in which they are interested. The style, tone, wording, order, and format of the messages are all critical to getting a message noticed. Fourth, thought must be given to constructing the communications to overcome perceptual distortion, the tendency to add to and reinterpret what is actually in the message based on the audience member's own past experience, motives, and biases. Fifth, a medium must be chosen to convey the message to achieve maximum impact. Often, in the nonprofit sector, this means choosing a spokesperson. If a spokesperson is used, the marketer must assure that he or she is credible and trustworthy and that their message is so clear that it cannot be distorted by a target audience. Sixth, the marketers must evaluate all the possible messages and select the ones that are most desirable, exclusive, and believable.

The marketer must recognize that strategies to influence behavior need not rely only on persuasion; that is, on first changing cognitions in order to change behavior. Other strategies, such as behavior modification, can simply manipulate rewards. These strategies (such as shaping and the foot-in-the-door and door-in-the-face techniques) rely on a different model, in which it is assumed that changing behavior is an adequate goal in itself and that, once behavior is changed, attitudes and other cognitions may also change.

QUESTIONS

1. The National Cancer Institute wishes to tell pregnant women that smoking can injure their fetuses. Focus group interviews show that members of the target audience frequently misunderstand what NCI is telling them. What are some possible explanations for this?

2. How could the National Cancer Institute design warnings on cigarette packages to get past smokers' selective attention bias against the messages?

3. Who would be good spokespeople for family planning programs in the United States, and why? How would you go about learning who the best spokespeople would be in a foreign country and whether spokespeople would be effective at all?

4. List the communciations goals that a rapid transit district in a medium-sized community might have for an annual strategic plan.

5. Suggest how a headline to introduce a new children's wing at a library might be written using each of the nine execution styles outlined in this chapter.

6. How could behavior modification techniques be used to get college students to become more active recruiters of future enrollees from their hometowns?

NOTES

1. See, for example, Peter L. Wright, "The Cognitive Processes Mediating Acceptance of Advertising," *Journal of Marketing Research,* February 1973, pp. 53–62.

2. See Michael L. Ray and William L. Wilkie, "Fear: The Potential of an Appeal Neglected by Marketing," *Journal of Marketing,* January 1970, pp. 55–56; and Brian Sternthal and C. Samuel Craig, "Fear Appeals Revisited and Revised," *Journal of Consumer Research,* December 1974, pp. 22–34.

3. See John C. Maloney, "Marketing Decisions and Attitude Research," in George L. Baker, Jr., ed., *Effecting Marketing Coordination* (Chicago: American Marketing Association, 1961).

4. The classic work in this field is Leon Festinger, *A Theory of Cognitive Dissonance* (Evanston, Ill.: Row, Peterson, 1957). See also J. W. Brehm and A. R. Cohen, *Explorations in Cognitive Dissonance* (New York: John Wiley, 1962). For an example showing consumers' willingness to live with dissonance in a nonprofit context, see M. T. O'Keefe, "The Anti-Smoking Commercials: A Study of Television's Impact on Behavior," *Public Opinion Quarterly,* 1971, pp. 242–248.

5. Carolyn W. Sherif, Muzafer Sherif, and Ronald Nebergill, *Attitude and Attitude Change* (New Haven, Conn.: Yale University Press, 1961).

6. See J. T. Bertrand, "Selective Avoidance on Health Topics: A Field Test," *Communications Research,* July 1979, pp. 271–294. Also, Wolfgang

Schaefer, "Selective Perception in Operation," *Journal of Advertising Research,* February 1979, pp. 59–60.

7. "Death Turns Up the Thermostat," *Newsweek,* October 15, 1984.

8. Leon S. Robertson, Albert B. Kelley, Brian O'Neill, Charles W. Wixom, Richard S. Eiswirth and William Haddon, Jr., "A Controlled Study of the Effect of Television Messages on Safety Belt Use," *American Journal of Public Health,* November 1974, p. 1070 ff.

9. Ray and Wilkie, "Fear: The Potential."

10. John J. Burnett and Robert E. Wilkes, "Fear Appeals to Segments Only," *Journal of Advertising Research,* Vol. 20, No. 5, October 1980, pp. 21–24.

11. There is some debate over order effects with two-sided messages. See James F. Engel and Roger Blackwell, *Consumer Behavior,* 4th ed. (Chicago: Dryden Press, 1982), pp. 479–481.

12. See, for example, A. L. Edwards, "Political Frames of Reference as a Factor Influencing Recognition," *Journal of Abnormal and Social Psychology,* Vol. 36, 1941, pp. 34–50.

13. Herbert E. Krugman, "Why Three Exposures May be Enough," *Journal of Advertising Research,* December 1972, pp. 11–15.

14. See Brian Sternthal, R. R. Dholakia, and Clark Leavitt, "The Persuasive Effect of Source Credibility: Test of Cognitive Response," *Journal of Consumer Research,* 4 (1978), pp. 252–260; and C. Samuel Craig and John M. McCann, "Assessing Communications Effects on Energy Conservation," *Journal of Consumer Research,* 5, September 1978, pp. 82–88.

15. Dik Warren Twedt, "How to Plan New Products, Improve Old Ones, and Create Better Advertising," *Journal of Marketing,* January 1969, pp. 53–57.

16. See William A. Mindak and H. Malcolm Bybee, "Marketing's Application to Fund Raising," *Journal of Marketing,* July 1971, pp. 13–18.

17. See, for example, Stanley I. Ornstein and Dominique M. Hanssens, "Alcohol Control Laws and the Consumption of Distilled Spirits and Beer," *Journal of Consumer Research,* Vol. 12, No. 2, September, 1985, pp. 200–213.

18. Michael Rothschild and William C. Gaidis, "Behavioral Learning Theory: Its Relevance to Marketing and Promotions," *Journal of Marketing,* Spring 1981, pp. 70–78.

19. "Giving Goodies to the Good," *Time,* November 18, 1985, p. 98.

20. Brian C. Deslauriers and Peter B. Everett, "Effects of Intermittent and Continuing Token Reinforcement on Bus Ridership," *Journal of Applied Psychology,* 62, 4, 1977, pp. 369–375.

21. Carol A. Scott, "Modifying Socially-Conscious Behavior: The Foot-In-The-Door Technique," *Journal of Consumer Research,* 1977, pp. 156–164.

22. Although the foot-in-the-door approach appears promising here, two researchers were unsuccessful in applying it to blood donations behavior; see R. B. Cialdini and K. Assam, "Test of a Concession Procedure for Inducing Verbal, Behavioral, and Further Compliance with a Request to Give Blood," *Journal of Applied Psychology,* 1976, pp. 295–300.

23. Peter H. Reingen, "On Inducing Compliance with Requests," *Journal of Consumer Research,* September 1978, pp. 96–102; John Morwen and Robert Cialdini, "On Implementing Door-In-The-Face Compliance Techniques in a Business Context," *Journal of Marketing Research,* May 1980, pp. 253–258.

CHAPTER 19

Managing Advertising and Sales Promotion

At first glance it looks like a cigarette ad.

The macho model with his shirt open stands defiantly, cigarette pack in hand.

But something strange is going on here. A cigarette is stuck in the model's nose. And the message reads, "I smoke for smell."

The ad is one of a series designed to promote good health by satirizing the ads used to sell cigarettes, liquor, and other products linked with bad health. Perhaps even more unusual than the ads is that their writers and producers come from a group of physicians called DOC—Doctors Ought to Care.

Why are physicians trading in their white lab coats for grey flannel suits?

"DOC feels that advertising is a powerful tool that can be used to change people's life-styles," said Dr. Alan Blum, a thirty-two-year-old Chicago family practitioner who helped found the 1,000-member organization three years ago. "Though some doctors think it isn't dignified to advertise, DOC's philosophy is that it is incumbent upon doctors to do everything they can, including advertising, to prevent illness."

Dr. Blum maintains that medical science is years behind advertising science in learning how to motivate people. "DOC is saying that medicine is as much communications as pills and prescriptions," he added.

DOC points to the precedent set in the late 1960s by antismoking campaigns on television as an indication of the potential impact health promotion advertising can have. "Cigarette sales in the U.S. may have fallen as much as 25 percent below expected levels in the late 1960s because of counteradvertising," said Dr. Blum.

However, unlike past counteradvertising campaigns, which were run as public service announcements, DOC pays for media time and space. The group, which is funded through donations from physicians and some small grants, has spent only $30,000 for ads on bus benches, outdoor boards, local radio, and in newspapers. "DOC hopes someday to have ads on television. As a matter of fact, we have them in the can," said Dr. Blum, who recently completed a journalism fellowship for the *Journal of the American Medical Association*. "But, we'd rather not run them as PSAs. Personally, I'd rather have one paid spot than ten PSAs at 3:00 in the morning."

SOURCE: Howard Wolinsky, "Doctors Try Satire to Sell Health," reprinted with permission from *Advertising Age*, December 15, 1984. Copyright 1984 by Crain Communications, Inc.

The nonprofit marketer has a large number of tools available for carrying a message to a target audience. There are five main tools, and each differs in the coding and encoding problems it presents to managers.[1]

- *Paid Advertising: Any paid form of nonpersonal presentation and promotion of an offer by an identified sponsor through a formal communications medium.* Paid advertising permits total control over encoded message content and over the nature of the medium, plus substantial control of the scheduling of the message (and therefore its specific environment). On the other hand, paid advertising permits no control over message decoding by the audience and little (or, at best, lagged) feedback on the received message.
- *Unpaid (public service) advertising: Any form of advertising in which space or time for the placement of the advertisment is free.* Marketer control is similar to that with paid advertising except that there is very little control over the scheduling of the message. Many public service radio or television advertisements appear after midnight or on Sunday mornings when the audience is small and the media have unsold spots.
- *Sales promotion: Short-term incentives to encourage purchase or sales of a product or service or the performance of a behavior.* Marketer control is substantial, although the decoding of specific promotions by the receiver is not controllable.
- *Publicity: Nonpersonal stimulation of demand for an offering by securing the reporting of commercially significant news about the offer in a published medium or on radio, television, or the stage that is not paid for by the sponsor.* Here, the marketer's control over message encoding and the medium varies depending on whether journalists will use and revise the message. Some feedback is possible from journalists or from selected target audiences.
- *Personal selling: Oral presentation of information about an offering in a con-*

versation with one or more prospective target audience members for the purpose of securing a desired transaction. In personal selling, the organization has less control over encoding, that is, what the salesperson actually says. The salesperson, however, has excellent opportunities to secure feedback on how the message is being received.

In this chapter, we will consider specific issues relevant to advertising and sales promotion. The next two chapters will deal with public relations and personal selling, respectively.

ADVERTISING

Advertising consists of nonpersonal forms of communication conducted through paid media under clear sponsorship. It involves such varied media as magazines and newspapers; radio and television; outdoor media (posters, signs, and skywriting); novelties (matchboxes, calendars); cards (car, bus); catalogs; directories and references; programs and menus; circulars; and direct mail. It can be carried out for such diverse purposes as long-term buildup of the organization's name (institutional advertising), long-term buildup of a particular product (product advertising) or brand (brand advertising), information dissemination about a sale, service, or event (classified advertising), announcement of a special sale (sales advertising), and so on.

Total advertising in the United States was estimated to be $95.1 billion in 1985, with worldwide advertising totaling $159.2 billion. It was also estimated that, of the U.S. total, 56 percent comprised national advertising and 44 percent local.[2] Advertising is coming into increasing use by nonprofit organizations public and private. The major categories of nonprofit organization advertising are as follows:

1. *Political advertising.* Political advertising has skyrocketed in recent elections. The presidential candidates alone spent $47 million in paid political advertising in the 1984 election.[3] Various state and local candidates spent many tens of millions more.

2. *Social cause advertising.* For many years, the Advertising Council, Inc., a nonprofit organization financed by American industry, has used advertising to promote social causes such as brotherhood, safe driving, aid to education, religious faith, forest fire prevention, and so on. It accepts a number of causes each year and solicits donated services from advertising agencies and media to prepare and broadcast this advertising. The estimated value of these services in 1979 was $563 million. It tends to avoid controversial causes. Social cause organizations such as ecology groups, family planners, and women's liberation organizations have also stepped up their advertising budgets to get their messages out to the public.[4]

3. *Charitable advertising.* Charitable advertising is specifically directed toward raising donations on a regular or emergency basis; the money is used to help the needy, unfortunate, or sick. Examples include the paid or donated advertising done by the Red Cross, United Way, Easter Seal Society, and so on. Much charitable advertising takes the form of direct mail solicitation.

4. *Government advertising.* Various government units are frequent advertisers. Municipalities and states spend considerable sums to attract new residents, tourists, and industrial developers. Park and recreation departments advertise outdoor recreational facilities. Police departments issue messages to the general public on safety issues. The federal government has used paid advertising to sell products (U.S. postage stamps), services (Amtrak train travel), and ideas (energy conservation). Its largest advertising expenditures are on military recruitment; it budgeted $65 million on Army recruiting and $20 million on Navy recruiting in 1985.[5] And it arranged for $38 million of donated advertising (courtesy of the Advertising Council) to encourage people, especially blacks and Hispanics, to cooperate with the census takers in the 1980 census.

5. *Private nonprofit advertising.* Colleges, museums, symphonies, hosptials, and religious organizations all have strong communication programs and develop annual reports, direct mailings, classified ads, broadcast messages, and other forms of advertising. Various professionals whose ethical codes formerly banned advertising—social workers, psychologists, etc.—have been free to advertise ever since the Federal Trade Commission ruled that the American Medical Association could not prevent physician members from advertising.

6. *Association advertising.* Professional and trade associations have substantially increased their use of paid advertising. The American Bankers Association, the American Dental Association, and the National Association of Realtors spend several million dollars annually on television and print advertising. Their objective is to improve their public image and also the public's knowledge of their services. Public service advertising programs have recently been undertaken by associations representing lawyers, accountants, engineers, and nurses.

In developing an advertising program, marketing management must make five major decisions (see Figure 19-1). We considered message issues in the preceding chapter and will discuss the remaining four in the following sections.

FIGURE 19-1

Major Decisions in Advertising Management

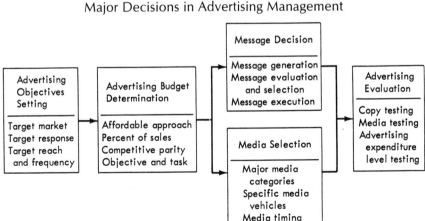

ADVERTISING OBJECTIVE-SETTING

Before an advertising program and budget can be developed, advertising objectives must be set. These objectives must flow from prior decision-making on the target market, market positioning, and marketing mix. The marketing strategy defines advertising's job in the total marketing mix.

Developing advertising objectives calls for defining the target market, target response, and target reach and frequency.

TARGET MARKET SELECTION

A marketing communicator must start with a clear target audience in mind. The audience may be potential buyers of the organization's services, current users, deciders, or influencers. The audience may consist of individuals, groups, particular publics, or the general public. The target audience has a crucial influence on the communicator's decisions on *what* to say, *how* to say it, *when* to say it, *where* to say it, and *who* should say it.

Consider this in terms of a small private college in Iowa called Pottsville. Suppose it is seeking applicants from Nebraska, and it estimates that there are 30,000 graduating high school seniors in Nebraska who might be interested in Pottsville College. The college must decide whether to aim its communications primarily at high school counselors in Nebraska high schools or at the high school students themselves. Beyond this, it may want to develop communications to reach parents and other people who are influential in the college decision process. Each target market would warrant a different advertising campaign.

TARGET RESPONSE

Once the target audience is identified, the marketing communicator must define the target response that is sought. The ultimate response, of course, is purchase behavior. But purchase behavior is the end result of a consumer decision-making process. The marketing communicator needs to know the current state of the target audience and which state it should be moved to next.

Any member of the target audience may be in one of six *buyer readiness states* with respect to the service or organization. These states—*awareness, knowledge, liking, preference, conviction,* and *action*—are described in the following paragraphs:[6]

1. *Awareness.* The first thing to establish is how aware the target audience is of the object (service, organization, etc.). The audience may be completely unaware of the object, know only its name, or know one or two things about it. If most of the target audience is unaware, the communicator's task is to build awareness, perhaps just name recognition. This calls for simple messages

repeating the name. Even then, building awareness takes time. Pottsville College has no name recognition among high school seniors in Nebraska. The college might set as its objective making 70 percent of these students aware of Pottsville's name within one year.

2. *Knowledge.* The target audience may be aware of the object but may not know much about it. In this case the communicator's goal is to transmit some key information. Thus, Pottsville College may want its target audience to know that it is a private four-year college in eastern Iowa that has distinguished programs in ornithology and thanatology. Following its advertising campaign, Pottsville can sample the target audience to measure whether they have little, some, or much knowledge of Pottsville College and to assess the content of their knowledge. The particular set of beliefs that makes up the audience's picture of an object is called the *image.* Organizations must periodically assess their public images as a basis for developing communication objectives.

3. *Liking.* If the target audience members know the object, the next question is, how do they feel about it? We can image a scale covering a range of responses such as *dislike very much, dislike somewhat, indifferent, like somewhat,* and *like very much.* If the audience has an unfavorable view of Pottsville College, the communicator has to find out why and then develop a communications program to build up favorable feeling. If the unfavorable view is rooted in real inadequacies of the college, then a communications campaign would not do the job. The college would have to first improve and then communicate its quality. Good marketing calls for "good deeds followed by good words."

4. *Preference.* The target audience may like the object but may not prefer it over others. It may be one of several acceptable objects. In this case the communicator's job is to build consumer preference. The communicator will have to tout its quality, value, performance, and other attributes. The communicator can check on the success of the campaign by subsequently surveying the audience to see if their preference has grown stronger.

5. *Conviction.* A target audience may prefer a particular object but may not develop a conviction about buying it. Thus, some high school seniors may prefer Pottsville to other colleges but may not be sure they want to go to college. The communicator's job is to build the conviction that going to college is the right thing to do. Building conviction that a person should buy a particular object is a challenging communications task.

6. *Action.* Some target audience members may have conviction but not act. They may be waiting for additional information, may plan to act later, and so on. In this situation, a communicator must lead the consumer to take the final step, which is called "closing the sale." Among the action-producing devices used are offering a low price if the object is bought now, offering a premium, offering an opportunity to try the object on a limited basis, and indicating that the object will soon become unavailable.

This model assumes that buyers pass through a hierarchy of states on the way to purchase. The communicator's task is to identify the stage that most of the target audience is in and develop a communication message or campaign that will move them to the next stage. It would be nice if one message could move the audience through all stages, but this rarely happens. Most communicators seek a cost-effective communication approach to move the target audience one stage at a time. The critical thing is to know where the main audience is and what the next feasible stage is.

This hierarchical model was elaborated recently in a proposed social marketing approach for the Egyptian government's family planning program. It was suggested that a totally uninformed man or woman would have to pass through eleven steps to become what the Egyptian government seeks—a *continuous correct user* of some effective family planning method. The steps comprise a *contraceptive social behavior change model* and are outlined in Figure 19-2. The eleven steps are grouped into five broad sets of tasks for management:

1. *Basic education.* To become a family planner, an individual must have some rudimentary understanding of the nature of reproduction and contraception.

2. *Value change.* The individual must believe that family planning is an *acceptable* practice. Furthermore, the individual must come to see that family planning is something potentially relevant to his or her own life. These steps may require modification of religious or moral values and a breaking away from the influences of family, peers, village elders, and other significant figures in the individual's community.

3. *Attitude change.* The individual must learn of the existence of at least one specific method and believe that the benefits of using it exceed the costs.

4. *Motivation to act.* The individual must have access to and learn where and how to acquire the preferred method. Furthermore, the individual must be propelled to try the method.

5. *Training and reinforcement.* Once the consumer undertakes a trial of a method, the process is almost completed. At that point, the individual must know proper usage and be sufficiently satisfied to continue using contraceptive methods.

A key feature of this contraceptive social behavior change model is that each target consumer can be categorized as being at one of the eleven steps at any point in time. The fact that target consumers can be assigned to unique stages in this process has several uses:

1. The model can be used to measure the overall progress of a program in a country or to compare one country to another.

2. It can be used to segment the market into groups requiring different messages.

3. It can be used to set communication goals, such as moving 100,000 households from stage 2 to stage 3.

The hierarchical model leads to many specific communications objectives for advertising. Colley distinguished fifty-two possible advertising objectives in his *Defining Advertising Goals for Measured Advertising Results* (DAGMAR). The various advertising objectives can be categorized on the basis of whether their aim is to inform, persuade, or remind.[7]

The *inform* category includes such advertising objectives as telling the market about a new service, suggesting new uses for a product, pointing out

FIGURE 19-2

Contraceptive Social Behavior Change Model

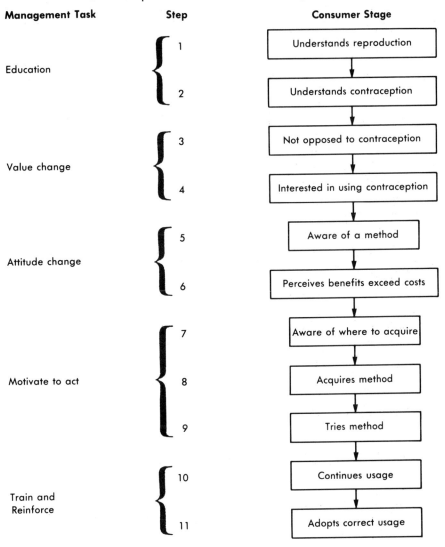

Management Task	**Step**	**Consumer Stage**
Education	1	Understands reproduction
	2	Understands contraception
Value change	3	Not opposed to contraception
	4	Interested in using contraception
Attitude change	5	Aware of a method
	6	Perceives benefits exceed costs
Motivate to act	7	Aware of where to acquire
	8	Acquires method
	9	Tries method
Train and Reinforce	10	Continues usage
	11	Adopts correct usage

the benefits of a different health behavior, informing the market of a price change, explaining how a service works, describing various available services (say, at a museum or college), correcting false impressions, reducing consumers' fears, and building an organizational image.

The *persuade* category includes such advertising objectives as building preference for an organization's offering, encouraging switching to the advertiser's brand or institution, trying to change the customer's perception of the importance of different behavior attributes, persuading the customer to act now, and persuading the customer to receive a sales call.

The *remind* category includes such advertising objectives as reminding consumers that the service might be needed in the future, reminding them

EXHIBIT 19-1. Demarketing John Wayne Airport

It is an odd assignment by any standard. The advertiser wishes to discourage customers and refer them to a competitor.

The advertiser in this case is Orange County's John Wayne International Airport. Stretched to capacity and unable to expand, the beleaguered commercial airport has hired an agency to help it steer some of the local airline passengers to nearby Ontario International Airport in Los Angeles County. Also a self-supporting public facility, Ontario Airport says it welcomes growth but it is concerned that a vigorous ad campaign simply will transfer the overcrowding problem over the county line.

Basso & Associates, Newport Beach, won a contract last summer to develop the creative concept for an overall awareness program to urge residents of the northeast quadrant of Orange County to consider using Ontario rather than John Wayne.

Basso's recommendation, awaiting approval from a special Orange County Airport task force, calls for a comprehensive $150,000 to $300,000 radio, print, and outdoor campaign.

If the recommendation meets with the approval of both the airport commission and the county board of supervisors, agencies will bid on the execution of the recommendation.

As the only commercial airport in Orange County, John Wayne has suffered from overcrowding since its terminal building was dedicated in the late 1960s. It now accommodates about 10 million passengers annually. Residents in nearby Newport Beach—directly under the airport's flight path—have blocked an increase in the number of commercial flights allowed to enter or leave the airport. They are also unwilling to have the airport extend its hours.

Twenty-five miles away in Los Angeles County, Ontario International Airport, which was acquired by the County in 1967, handles about 3 million passengers annually, although the facility was designed ultimately to accommodate 12 million.

While Ontario Airport has no plans to combat John Wayne Airport's advertising campaign if it passes the various boards, it has adopted a policy of "noncooperation," according to a spokesman.

"We'd rather see slow, steady growth," the spokesman said. "We don't want to see ourselves as a convenient area for Orange County's spillover."

SOURCE: Cleveland Horton, "John Wayne Airport Steers Traffic to Reluctant Rival." Reprinted with permission from *Advertising Age,* November 5, 1984, p. 72w. Copyright 1984 by Crain Communications, Inc.

where to obtain it, pointing out other ways to enjoy the service or event next time, and keeping it in their minds during off-seasons.

And, as we noted in Chapter 1, not every marketing objective involves building demand. Sometimes nonprofits have to demarket a product or service, as was the case at Orange County Airport in 1984. (See Exhibit 19-1).

TARGET REACH AND FREQUENCY

The third decision a nonprofit manager must make is determining the optimal *target reach and frequency* of the advertising. Funds for advertising are rarely so abundant that everyone in the target audience can be reached, and reached with sufficient frequency. Marketing management must decide what percentage of the audience to reach with what exposure frequency per period. Pottsville College, for example, might decide to use direct mail and buy 20,000 advertising exposures. This leaves a wide choice available concerning target reach and frequency. Pottsville could send one letter to 20,000 different students, or it could send two different letters a week apart to 10,000 students, and so on. The issue is how many exposures are needed to create the desired response, given the market's state of readiness. One exposure could be enough to convert students from being unaware to being aware. It would not be enough to convert students from awareness to preference.

ADVERTISING BUDGET DETERMINATION

In Chapter 12, we reviewed the major ways that organizations set their marketing budgets: the affordable method, percentage-of-sales method, competitive basis method, and objective-and-task method. We prefer the last method. Suppose that Pottsville College wants to send two letters to each of 10,000 students. The gross number of exposures would be 20,000. Suppose that the average mailing piece will cost $2 to design and mail. Then Pottsville College will need a rough advertising budget of $40,000 to accomplish its objectives.

In addition to estimating the total size of the required advertising budget, a determination must be made of how the budget should be allocated over different market segments, geographical areas, and time periods. In practice, advertising budgets are allocated to segments of demand according to their respective populations or sales levels or in accordance with some other indicator of market potential. It is common to spend twice as much advertising money in segment B as in segment A if segment B has twice the level of some indicator of market potential. In principle, the budget should be allocated to different segments according to their expected marginal response to advertising. A budget is well allocated when it is not possible to shift dollars from one segment to another and increase total market response.

Many nonprofit organizations, especially charities, have avoided *paid advertising,* even though they acknowledge its potential value. They are the beneficiaries of *donated advertising,* which they fear will be withdrawn if they started to do paid advertising. The American Red Cross, for example, has its advertising copy produced by a volunteering advertising agency (through the Advertising Council of America), and public service time and space are donated by the media. Unfortunately, the Red Cross has no control over the time when their ads are aired, and it is rarely prime time. Yet the Red Cross fears that if it started to buy media time, it would lose all its free media time.

MEDIA SELECTION

Once the advertising budget is set for a given market segment, region, and time period, the next step is to allocate this budget across media categories and vehicles. Presumably, some thought will already have been given to this problem, since the selection of a target segment inevitably leads to the use of the medium to which the segment is most frequently exposed. Also, the medium chosen will affect one's thinking about the size of the overall budget; a television campaign is much more costly than a radio campaign. Finally, the medium affects the kind of message one can use.

There are three basic steps in the media selection process: choosing among major media categories, choosing among specific media vehicles, and timing.

CHOOSING AMONG MAJOR MEDIA CATEGORIES

The first step calls for allocating the advertising budget to the major *media categories.* These categories must be examined for their capacity to deliver reach, frequency, and impact. Table 19-1 presents profiles of the major advertising media. In order of their advertising volume, they are newspapers, television, direct mail, radio, magazines, and outdoor. Marketers choose among these major media categories by considering the following variables:

1. *Target audience media habits.* For example, radio and television are the most effective media for reaching teenagers.
2. *Product or service.* Media categories have different potentialities for demonstration, visualization, explanation, believability, and color. Television, for example, is the most effective medium for demonstrating how a product or service works, while magazines are ideal for accurately reproducing the appearance of food products or home decorating ideas.

3. *Message.* A message announcing an emergency blood drive tomorrow requires radio or newspapers. A message containing a great deal of technical data might require specialized magazines or direct mailings. Messages that would benefit from consumers adding their own images and fantasies might be most effective on the radio.

4. *Cost.* Television is very expensive, and newspaper advertising is inexpensive. What counts, of course, is the cost per thousand exposures rather than the total cost.

On the basis of these characteristics, the marketer has to decide how to allocate the given budget to the major media categories. The U.S. Army Recruiting Command, for example, might decide to allocate $14 million to evening television spots, $4 million to male-oriented magazines, and $2 million to daily newspapers.

SELECTING SPECIFIC MEDIA VEHICLES

The next step is to choose the specific media vehicles within each media category that would produce the desired response in the most cost-effective way. Consider the category of male-oriented magazines, which includes *Playboy, Penthouse, Home Mechanics, Esquire, Motorcycle,* and so on. The media planner turns to several volumes put out by Standard Rate and Data that provide circulation and cost data for different ad sizes, color options, ad positions, and quantities of insertions. Beyond this, the media planner evaluates the different magazines on qualitative characteristics such as credibility, prestige, geographical editioning, occupational editioning, reproduction quality, editorial climate, lead time, and psychological impact. The media planner makes a final judgment as to which specific vehicles will deliver the best reach, frequency, and impact for the money.

Media planners normally calculate the *cost per thousand persons* reached by a particular vehicle. If a full-page, four-color advertisement in *Newsweek* costs $73,710 and *Newsweek*'s estimated readership is 3 million persons, then the cost of reaching each one thousand persons is $24.57. The same advertisement in *Business Week* may cost $18,000 but reach only 763,000 persons, at a cost per thousand of $23.59. The media planner would rank the various magazines according to cost per thousand. The next step would be to adjust these rankings for impact. One simple procedure would be to assign an impact score of 1.0 to the best vehicle and values from 0 to 1 for the remainder. Each vehicle cost per thousand could then be divided by the impact index to yield an impact-adjusted cost per thousand, which would then guide media allocation.

In situations where media allocation decisions are to be made repeatedly (as in an advertising agency), it may be desirable to computerize the process. Vast quantities of data can be stored in modern computers and

Table 19-1

PROFILES OF MAJOR MEDIA CATEGORIES

Medium	Volume in Billions (1983)	Percentage (1983)	Example of Cost (1984)	Advantages	Limitations
Newspapers	$20.6	27.1	$20,974 one-page, weekday Chicago Tribune	Flexibility; timeliness; good local market coverage; broad acceptance; high believability	Short life; poor reproduction quality; small "pass-along" audience
Television	16.1	21.2	$6,000 for 30 seconds of prime time in Chicago	Combines sight, sound, and motion; appealing to the senses; high attention; high reach	High absolute cost; high clutter; fleeting exposure; less audience selectivity
Direct mail	11.8	15.5	$1,280 for the names and addresses of 19,000 veterinarians	Audience selectivity; flexibility; no ad competition within the same medium; personalization	Relatively high cost; "junk mail" image

			Cost Example	Advantages	Limitations
Radio	5.2	5.8	$500 for one minute of prime time in Chicago	Mass use; high geographical and demographic selectivity; low cost	Audio presentation only; lower attention than television; non-standardized rate structures; fleeting exposure
Magazines	4.2	5.6	$73,710 one-page four color in *Newsweek*	High geographical and demographic selectivity, credibility, and prestige; high-quality reproduction; long life; good pass-along readership	Long ad purchase lead time; some waste circulation; no guarantee of position
Outdoor	0.8	1.1	$21,960 per month for 71 billboards in metropolitan Chicago	Flexibility; high repeat exposure; low cost; low competition	No audience selectivity; creative limitations
Others	17.2	22.7			
Total	$75.9	100.0			

SOURCE: Columns 2 and 3 are from *Advertising Age*, May 28, 1984, p. 50. Reprinted with permission. Copyright 1984, Crain Communications, Inc.

updated frequently. Mathematical models can then be used for actual media selection. Four kinds of sophisticated models that have been used in recent years are described in Exhibit 19-2.

A medium increasingly being used by nonprofits, particularly arts and health care organizations and charities, is direct mail. Novelli has suggested that direct mail has seven important advantages for nonprofit marketers:[8]

1. It tends to be very focused: it can achieve maximum impact on a specific target market.
2. It can be private and confidential, a major advantage for charities and programs dealing with venereal disease, child abuse, and family planning.
3. Purchase of direct mail services is not forbidden to government agencies, whereas purchase of broadcast, newspaper, magazine, outdoor, and other media sometimes is forbidden.
4. Cost per contact and cost per response can often be very low, which is an important appeal to impoverished nonprofits.
5. Results are quite often clearly measurable, and this can help make nonprofit marketing programs more accountable. The American Heart Association may not know their effect on cholesterol levels, but they can calculate how many responded to a specific mail promotion of a low-cholesterol cookbook and what cost they incurred per inquiry.
6. Small-scale tests of proposed strategies are very feasible with direct mail. In fact, direct mail is an ideal field-test vehicle. A number of marketing factors can be varied over several mailings and the results compared to baseline measures. In tests of other media, it is often difficult to link a specific surge in sales to, say, a flight of radio advertisements. By contrast, if more cookbook requests come in from those who receive a mailing with a message about cholesterol involving a medium level of fear than from those who get a high-fear or low-fear treatment, it is hard not to conclude that a medium-fear message works best.
7. The effectiveness of direct mail can be assessed directly in terms of *behavior* (for example, orders, requests, and inquiries), whereas other media assessments usually require attitude and awareness indicators which, as discussed earlier, are fraught with measurement problems.

There are several steps in establishing a strategically effective mail order operation.

1. *Determine the objectives* of mail-order programs carefully in advance. Is the program to produce sales, create awareness, change attitudes, or make contacts to be followed up through other media? In some cases, a phased strategy is appropriate in which earlier mailers are used to develop awareness and later mailers for direct action.
2. *Determine the target audience.* Some groups are more responsive to direct mail than others. According to Herb Bell of NLT Computer Services Corporation, charities should target "women, 49 to 79 years old, as they are more likely to be touched by emotional appeals and more likely to have disposable

EXHIBIT 19-2. Media mix models

Linear programming can be used to select the media mix that will maximize the number of effective exposures subject to a set of constraints. Here is a linear-programming statement of the media-selection problem:

$$\text{Maximize: } E = 3{,}100X_1 + 2{,}000X_2 + 2{,}400X_3$$

$$
\begin{aligned}
\text{Subject to: } \quad & 15{,}000X_1 + 4{,}000X_2 + 5{,}000X_3 \leq 500{,}000 \\
& 15{,}000X_1 \geq 250{,}000 \\
& X_1 \geq 0 \\
& X_1 \geq 52 \\
& X_2 \geq 1 \\
& X_2 \leq 8 \\
& X_3 \geq 6 \\
& X_3 \leq 12
\end{aligned}
$$

There are three media vehicles, X_1, X_2, and X_3. Vehicle 1 gives 3,100 (in thousands) effective exposures per issue, vehicle 2 gives 2,000, and vehicle 3 gives 2,400. The media planner will seek to buy the number of issues of each vehicle that will maximize the total number of effective exposures, E. The media planner has an advertising budget of $500,000, which cannot be exceeded. Vehicle 1 costs $15,000 per issue, vehicle 2, $4,000, and vehicle 3, $5,000. Furthermore, the media planner wants to spend at least $250,000 on vehicle 1. Vehicle 1 puts out fifty-two issues a year, vehicle 2, eight issues, and vehicle 3, twelve issues. The media planner wants to buy at least one issue of vehicle 2 and six issues of vehicle 3.

A mathematical-solution technique is used to find the media mix. The limitations of this model are (1) linear programming assumes that repeat exposures have a constant marginal effect; (2) it assumes that media costs are constant (no discounts); (3) it cannot handle the problem of audience duplication; and (4) it does not schedule the ads.

This model selects media sequentially rather than simultaneously. The model selects the single best buy the first week. The remaining media choices are reevaluated to take into account audience duplication and potential media discounts. A second selection is made for the same week if the exposure rate for the week is below the *optimal* rate. The latter is a function of several marketing and media variables. This process continues until the optimal exposure rate for the week is reached, at which point new media choices are considered for the following week. This cycling process continues until the year's schedule is completed.

The sequential procedure has the following advantages: (1) it develops a schedule simultaneously with the selection of media; (2) it handles

EXHIBIT 19-2. (continued)

the audience duplication problem; (3) it handles media discount problems; and (4) it incorporates important variables such as brand-switching rates and multiple-exposure coefficients.

SIMULATION MODEL

A simulation model estimates the exposure value of any given media plan. The Simulmatics media model, for example, consists of 2,944 make-believe media users representing a cross-section of the American population by sex, age, type of community, employment status, and education. Each person's media choices are determined probabilistically as a function of the person's socioeconomic characteristics and location. A particular media schedule is exposed to all the persons in this hypothetical population. The computer tabulates the number and types of people exposed. Summary graphs and tables are prepared at the end of the hypothetical year's run, and they supply a picture of the schedule's probable impact. The advertiser decides whether the audience profile and the reach and frequency characteristics of the proposed media schedule are satisfactory.

Simulation complements rather than competes with the preceding models. Its major limitations are (1) simulation normally does not include an overall effectiveness function; (2) it lacks a procedure for finding better schedules; and (3) the representativeness of the hypothetical population can be questioned.

MEDIAC

Little and Lodish created a model called MEDIAC. MEDIAC handles in an analytical fashion a large number of marketing and advertising variables in the real media problem, such as marketing segments, sales potentials, exposure probabilities, diminishing marginal response rates, forgetting, seasonality, and cost discounts. MEDIAC asks questions, and the user supplies data and receives in a matter of seconds an optimal media schedule. The user can change the data inputs and note how this affects the media schedule.

Computerized media selection is an aid, not a substitute, for executive judgment. The plan is only a starting point, because the model cannot capture all the variables. The final media plan should be the joint product of the machine's ultralogical mind and people's imagination and judgment.

SOURCE: For more information on the linear program technique, see James F. Engle and Martin R. Warshaw, "Allocating Advertising Dollars by Linear Programming," *Journal of Advertising Research,* September 1964, pp. 41–48. For an example of heuristic programming, see William T. Moran, "Practical Media Decisions and the Computer," *Journal of Marketing,* July 1963, pp. 26–30. The MEDIAC model is described in John D. C. Little and Leonard M. Lodish, "A Media Planning Calculus," *Operations Research,* January-February 1969, pp. 1–35.

income. Women usually open the mail and pay the bills. Older women are less likely to be supporting children. They are looking for meaningful ways to perpetuate themselves through charity."[9]

3. *Develop mail lists.* Outside services can be the source of highly tailored prospect lists defined by schooling; occupation; area of the country; socioeconomic status of the neighborhood; ownership of certain credit cards; patronage of particular products, services, or outlets; and so on. Whenever time permits, new rented lists should be tested with small mailings to see if they are productive before a modest budget is committed to an unknown target list. The best lists, however, are always those containing the addresses of people with whom the organization *already* has some form of contact. Thus, one's best prospects are those who have responded to past mailings, who have made enquiries in some other fashion, or who are past or present supporters of the organization.

4. *Develop effective copy.* Investment in effective graphics and compelling messages is seldom wasted. Direct mail pieces are meeting more and more competition every day in the "mail box arena," and one needs powerful messages and compelling visual images to stand out. Attention must be paid to envelope design (to get the message exposed), the cover letter (to get it read), and motivational themes (to get it acted on). Many mailings fail because they are not consciously directed towards stimulating responses.

5. *Pretest each mailer.* This can be done inexpensively and, if sample target audience members are used, can both indicate probable successes and point up potential problems.

6. *Schedule mailings carefully.* Some mailings have predetermined timings (for example, for particular events). In those cases, the mailing should arrive just as the evaluation stage of consumer decision-making is taking place. Thus, mailings for arts events are best sent six to eight weeks before the event. They are seldom effective in the last week unless targeted to an impulse-purchase audience. When the timing of mailings is discretionary, the marketer should carefully test different patterns, for example, with mailings bunched together in *flights* or spread out over time.

7. *Use responses as feedback.* The savvy direct mailer learns from each mailing what works or doesn't work in the mailing design itself. If a systematic program of experimentation is used over the years, much can be learned about effective tactics for particular audiences. Mail responses can also tell something about the responder. As Tom McCabe of International Marketing Group notes: "You know exactly who responds and why. . . . Every time someone responds to a mailing, you learn something about that person. Direct marketing is very efficient because eventually you will be able to know what kind of return to expect on every marketing dollar you spend."[10]

DECIDING ON MEDIA TIMING

The third step in media selection is *timing.* It breaks down into a macro problem and a micro problem. The macro problem is that of *seasonal timing.* For most products and services, audience size and interest vary at different times of the year. There is not much interest in Senator X until his reelection comes up or much interest in university affairs during the summer. Most marketers do not advertise when there is little interest, spending the bulk of their advertising budgets just as natural interest in the product class begins to increase and when it peaks. Counterseasonal advertising is still rare in practice.

The other problem is more of a micro problem, that of the *short-run timing* of advertising. How should advertising be spaced during a short period of, say, one week? Consider three possible patterns. The first is called *burst advertising* and consists of concentrating all the exposures in a very short period of time, say all in one day. Presumably, this will attract maximum attention and interest, and if recall is good, the effect will last for a while. The second pattern is *continuous advertising,* in which the exposures appear evenly throughout the period. This may be most effective when the audience buys or uses the product frequently and needs to be continuously

EXHIBIT 19-3. Sequenced strategy at Royce Hall

The performing arts program at UCLA's Royce Hall has been highly successful because it attracts high-quality performers. Recent attendance has been further enhanced by the careful development of well-thought-out marketing strategies. One feature is the careful *sequencing* of communications for each season. In a recent year, it carried out the following eight steps:

1. First, announcements were sent to past program subscribers to give them first chance at the best seats for season subscriptions and, not incidentally, to make them feel that they were receiving special attention.
2. After a suitable delay, full-page advertisements in local papers announced the entire program to the general public and solicited season ticket subscriptions.
3. Once season ticket subscription orders plateaued, single ticket availability was announced to past subscribers by mail and then to the general public.
4. At this point, attention was shifted to recapturing past season ticket subscribers who had not renewed through relatively high cost telephone marketing (telemarketing).
5. Just before the season started, mailers were sent to subscribers, nonsubscribers, and others, and newspaper ads were placed reintroducing the fall portion of the schedule.
6. Radio ads, both paid and public service, and quarter-page newspaper ads then promoted the first (and each subsequent) performance.
7. Flyers were sent to those who subscribed to or bought single tickets for one specific series promoting *other* similar events in which they might be interested.
8. Finally, on the night of the performances, posters were hung on campus and ads were placed in programs promoting related events, presumably catching concertgoers at the moment when they are most in the spirit of "going out to the theatre."

reminded. The third pattern is *intermittent advertising,* in which intermittent small bursts of advertising appear with no advertising in between. This pattern is able to create a little more attention than continuous advertising, yet it has some of the reminder advantage of continuous advertising.

Timing decisions should take three factors into consideration. *Audience turnover* is the rate at which the target audience changes between two periods. The greater the turnover, the more continuous the advertising should be. *Behavior frequency* is the number of times the target audience takes the action one is trying to influence (for example, smoking, not wearing seat belts). The more frequent the behavior, the more the advertising should be continuous. The *forgetting rate* is the rate at which a given message will be forgotten or a given behavior change extinguished. Again, the faster the forgetting, the more continuous the advertising should be.

A related issue is the sequencing of various types of advertising in an overall strategic program. An example of such a program is shown in Exhibit 19-3.

ADVERTISING EVALUATION

The final step in the effective use of advertising is *advertising evaluation.* The most important components are copy testing, media testing, and expenditure-level testing.

Copy testing can occur both before an ad is put into actual media (copy pretesting) and after it has been printed or broadcast (copy posttesting). The purpose of *ad pretesting* is to make improvements in the advertising copy to the fullest extent prior to its release. There are several methods of ad pretesting:

1. *Comprehension testing.* A critical prerequisite for any advertisement is that it be comprehensible. This can be a major problem when dealing with less educated or even illiterate audiences. When words are used in the advertisement, a marketing staff member can apply one or more readability formulas to predict comprehension. These formulas measure the length of sentences and the number of polysyllabic words. One popular measure called SMOG is used by the Office of Cancer Communications of the National Cancer Institute to test public and patient education health materials.

2. *Direct mailings.* Here a panel of target consumers or of advertising experts examines alternative ads and fills out rating questionnaires. Sometimes a single question is raised, such as "Which of these ads do you think would influence you most to buy the service?" Or a more elaborate form consisting of several rating scales may be used, such as the one shown in Table 19-2. Here the person evaluates the ad's attention strength, read-through strength, cognitive strength, affective strength, and behavioral strength, assigning a number of points (up to a maximum) in each case. The underlying theory is that an effective ad must score high on all these properties if it is ultimately to stimulate buying action. Too often ads are evaluated only for their attention-getting or comprehension-creating abilities. At the same time, direct rating methods

Table 19-2

RATING SHEET FOR ADS

Attention: How well does the ad catch the reader's attention?	_____(20)
Read-through strength: How well does the ad lead the reader to read further?	_____(20)
Cognitive strength: How clear is the central message or benefit?	_____(20)
Affective strength: How effective is the particular appeal?	_____(20)
Behavioral strength: How well does the ad suggest follow-through action?	_____(20)

0	20	40	60	80	100
Poor ad	Mediocre ad	Average ad	Good ad	Great ad	

_____Total

are judgmental and less reliable than harder evidence of an ad's actual impact on target consumers. Direct rating scales help primarily to screen out poor ads rather than to identify great ads.

3. *Portfolio recall tests.* Here respondents are asked to read a dummy portfolio of ads. After putting them down, the respondents are asked to recall the ads they saw—unaided or aided by the interviewer—and to describe as much as they can about each ad. The results are taken to indicate an ad's ability to stand out and its intended message's ability to be understood.

4. *Physiological tests.* Some researchers assess the potential effect of an ad by measuring physiological reactions—heartbeat, blood pressure, pupil dilation, perspiration—using such equipment as galvanometers, tachistoscopes, size-distance tunnels, and pupil dilation measuring equipment. These physiological tests at best measure the attention-getting and arousing power of an ad rather than any higher state of consciousness that the ad might produce.

5. *Focus-group interviews.* Since advertisments are often viewed in a group setting, pretests with groups can often indicate both how a message is perceived and how it might be passed along. As noted in Chapter 6, the focus-group technique also has the advantages that (a) its synergism can generate more reactions than a one-on-one session, (b) it is more efficient in that it gathers data from eight to twelve people at once, and (c) it can yield data relatively quickly.

6. *Self-administered questionnaires.* This approach can be valuable in reaching hard-to-get-at target audiences like politicians, doctors, or influential community figures. Since response rates can be a problem with this technique, oversampling and follow-up calls are necessary to yield a representative sample.

7. *Health Message Testing Service* (HMTS). Nonprofit organizations that produce radio and television and certain print materials have a unique pretesting opportunity. In the late 1970s, the Office of Cancer Communications established a free standardized system for pretesting health messages. The system is designed to evaluate rough presentations of messages prior to final production. The HMTS staff takes the rough materials and mails them to 300 respondents recruited in three areas. Norms are available and preliminary results are available in two weeks. The kinds of questions used in the HMTS are indicated on Exhibit 19-4. Cost estimates made in 1980 by HMTS for various pretesting methods using commercial research services are reported in Exhibit 19-5.

EXHIBIT 19-4. Standard questions used by the Health Message Testing Service

In pretesting radio and television public service announcements or printed materials such as booklets, the Health Message Testing Service uses a standard set of core questions to assess main idea communication, believability, personal relevance, and other target audience reactions. These standard questions are listed below to assist program planners in developing pretest questionnaires. The questions can be modified by changing the words in parentheses to fit the particular item that is being pretested.

1. *Main Idea Communication/Comprehension.* What was the *main idea* this (message) was trying to get across to you?

_____

_____

What does this (message) ask you to do?

_____

_____

What action, if any, is the (message) recommending that people take? (Probe: What other actions?)

_____

_____

In your opinion, was there anything in the (message) that was confusing?

_____

_____

Which of these phrases best describes the (message)?
    Easy to understand
    Hard to understand
2. In your opinion, was there anything in particular that was worth remembering about the (message)?

_____

_____

What, if anything, did you particularly like about the (message)?

_____

_____

Was there anything in the (message) that you particularly disliked or that bothered you? If yes, what?

_____

_____

3. *Believability.* In your opinion, was there anything in the (message) that was hard to believe? If yes, what?

_____

_____

EXHIBIT 19-4. (continued)

Which of these words or phrases best describes how you feel about the (message)?
Believable
Not believable

4. *Personal Relevance/Interest.* In your opinion, what type of person was this (message) talking to?
Was it talking to . . .
Someone like me
Someone else, not me
Was it talking to . . .
All people
All people, but especially (the target audience)
Only (the target audience)
Which of these words or phrases best describes how you feel about the (message)?
Interesting
Not interesting
Informative
Not informative
Did you learn anything new about (health subject) from this (message)? If yes, what?

_____

_____

5. *Other Target Audience Reactions.* Target audience reactions to pretest materials can be assessed using pairs of words or phrases or using a five-point scale. The following is an example of how this is done:

Listed on this sheet of paper are several pairs of words or phrases with the numbers 1 to 5 between them. I'd like you to indicate which number best describes how you feel about the (message). The higher the number, the more you think the phrase on the right describes it. The lower the number, the more you think the phrase on the left describes it. You could also pick any number in between. Now, let's go through each set of words. Please tell me which number best describes your reaction to the (message).

Practical	1	2	3	4	5	Not practical
Too short	1	2	3	4	5	Too long
Discouraging	1	2	3	4	5	Encouraging
Comforting	1	2	3	4	5	Alarming
Well done	1	2	3	4	5	Poorly done
Not informative	1	2	3	4	5	Informative

6. *For Assessing Artwork.* Just looking at the drawing (or picture), what do you think it says?

_____

_____

EXHIBIT 19-4. (continued)

> Is there anything in this drawing (or picture) that would bother or offend people you know?
>
> _____
>
> _____

SOURCE: *Pretesting in Health Communications*, Bethesda, Md.: National Cancer Institute, National Institutes of Health, 1981. Reproduced with permission.

EXHIBIT 19-5. Estimated direct costs for pretests using commercial research firms (1980)

The following tables indicate approximate costs for conducting pretests *with the assistance of commercial research firms.* Costs vary by region and by supplier, so it can pay to request bids from several companies. Also, savings are possible by using existing facilities and staff. Like any other assessment from which judgments will be drawn, however, it is important not to operate on so low a budget that the results may be compromised.

Focus Group Interviews (estimated for one group of 10 respondents)

a. Recruitment (general audience)	$150–300
b. Respondents' fees (not always necessary)	100–150
c. Facilities, audio taping, miscellaneous	75–175
d. Moderator	100–250
e. Moderator's analysis and report	200–400
	$625–1,275

In-depth Interviews (estimated for 25 interviews)

a. In-home interviews	$500–1,125
b. Clinic or other single-site interviews	250–625
c. Tabulation, analysis, and report	250–1,625
	$750–2,250

Central Location Intercept (estimated for 100 interviews)

a. Facilities (for example, renting space in a shopping mall)	$50–100
b. Recruit respondents and conduct interviews	1,000–2,500
c. Tabulation, analysis, and report	1,000–2,500
	$2,050–5,100

Self-Administered Questionnaire (estimated for 20 respondents)

a. Questionnaire and booklet reproduction and mailing	$50–150
b. Tabulation, analysis, and report	150–500
	$200–650

SOURCE: *Pretesting in Health Communications*, Bethesda, Md.: National Cancer Institute, National Institutes of Health, 1981. Reproduced with permission.

There are three popular *ad posttesting methods,* whose purpose is to assess if the desired impact is achieved or what the possible ad weaknesses are:

1. *Recall tests.* These involve finding persons who are regular users of the media vehicle and asking them to recall advertisers and products contained in the issue under study. They are asked to recall or play back everything they can remember. The administrator may or may not aid them in their recall. Recall scores are prepared on the basis of their responses and used to indicate the ad's power to be noted and remembered.

2. *Recognition tests.* Recognition tests call for sampling the readers of a given issue of the vehicle, say a magazine, and asking them to point out what they recognize as having seen or read before. For each ad, three different Starch readership scores (named after Daniel Starch, who developed the leading service) are prepared from the recognition data.

- *Noted.* The percentage of readers of the magazine who say they had previously seen the advertisement in the particular magazine.
- *Seen/associated.* The percentage of readers who say they have seen or read any part of the ad that clearly indicates the names of the product (or service) of the advertiser.
- *Read most.* The percent of readers who not only looked at the advertisement, but who say that they read more than half of the total written material in the ad.

The Starch organization also furnishes Adnorms—that is, average scores for each product class for the year—and separate scores for men and women for each magazine, to enable advertisers to evaluate their ads in relation to competitors' ads.

3. *Direct response.* The preceding techniques measure *communication outcomes* of advertising. But favorable communication outcomes may not translate into *behavioral* outcomes! Behavioral responses can be solicited by a message, however, and the results directly measured. Direct mail, of course, is very often designed expressly for this purpose. The effectiveness of alternative messages or media in influencing behavior can be tracked as follows:

a. Placing mailback coupons with a code number or P.O. box in the advertisement that varies by message and medium.

b. Asking target audience members to mention or bring in an advertisement in order to receive special treatment (for example, a price discount or free parking).

c. Setting up an 800 number and asking individuals to call for further information (on which occasion they can be asked where they saw the ad, what they remember, and so on).

d. Staggering the placement of ads so that this week's attendance or sales can be attributed to ad A while next week's can be attributed to ad B. This is also an effective method for assessing alternative expenditure levels.

As mentioned in Chapter 6, marketers can learn a great deal about the effectiveness of alternative message and media strategies by designing experiments coupled with careful posttest measures.

SALES PROMOTION

Many direct mail or advertising campaigns are built around sales promotion strategies. Sales promotion comprises a wide variety of tactical promotional tools of a short-term incentive nature designed to stimulate earlier or stronger target market response. These tools can be subclassified into tools for *consumer promotion* (for example, samples, coupons, money refund offers, prices off, gifts, contests, trading stamps, demonstrations), *middleman promotion* (for example, free goods, merchandise allowances, cooperative advertising, push money, dealer sales contests), and *sales force promotions* (for example, bonuses, contests, sales rallies). While usually used to stimulate *sales* of goods and services, promotion tools can also be designed to affect social behaviors such as blood donations, applying to college, joining the armed forces, and so on.

Although sales promotion tools are a motley collection, they have two distinctive qualities:

1. *Insistent presence.* Many sales promotion tools have an attention-getting, sometimes urgent, quality that can break through habits of individual inertia toward a particular offering. They tell the target audiences of a chance to get something special. This appeals to a broad spectrum of people, particularly to the economy-minded, but there is the disadvantage that those who respond to special promotions tend to be less loyal in the long run.

2. *Offer demotion.* Some of these tools suggest that the marketer is anxious for the transaction. If they are used too frequently or carelessly, they may lead audience members to wonder whether the offer is desirable or reasonably priced.

Sales promotion tools are used by a large variety of nonprofit organizations. Some colleges in recent years have passed out frisbees with their names on them on the beaches of Fort Lauderdale, sent up scholarship balloons, offered finder's fees, sponsored all-expense-paid college weekends for high school counselors and prospective students, and so on. Some hospitals have sponsored filet mignon candlelight dinners for new mothers, televised bingo games for patients, and provided country club memberships for new doctors joining their staff. And family planners in many parts of the world have offered incentives—transistor radios, cookware, costume jewelry, free bank accounts, and so on—to potential adopters of birth control measures.

Sales promotion expenditures have grown faster in recent years than advertising expenditures. Various factors have contributed to the rapid growth of sales promotion. The internal factors include the following: (1) promotion has become more acceptable to management as an effective means to stimulate sales, (2) more managers are qualified to use sales promotion tools, and (3) managers are under greater pressure to obtain a quick sales response. External factors include the following: (1) the number of brands has increased, (2) competitors have become more promotion-minded, (3) inflation and recession have made consumers more incentive-oriented, and (4) there is a belief that advertising efficiency has declined due to costs, media clutter, and government constraints on messages.

No single purpose can be ascribed to sales promotion tools, since they are so varied in form. Overall, sales promotion tools make three contributions: (1) *communication*—they gain attention and usually provide information that will, it is hoped, lead to trying the product; (2) *incentive*—they incorporate some concession, inducement, or contribution that is designed to represent value to the receiver; and (3) *invitation*—they include a distinct invitation to engage in the transaction now.

We will define an *incentive* as *something of financial or symbolic value added to an offer to encourage some overt behavioral response.*[11] The decision by an organization to use incentives as part of its promotional plan calls for seven distinct steps.

The first step is to specify *the objective* for which the incentive is undertaken. Three objectives can be distinguished. Sometimes incentives are offered to create an immediate behavioral response because the organization has excess capacity or inventory. A local YMCA lacking sufficient enrollment may offer a low-cost trial membership plan. Incentives may also be offered to promote trial of a product or service by groups that normally would not try it. Thus, a museum might give away free art posters to adolescents attending a new exhibit. Finally, incentives may be offered to win goodwill toward the organization, as when an organization offers to match its employees' contributions to a particular charity.

The second step is to determine the *inclusiveness of the incentive*—that is, whether it will be offered to individuals or to the groups to which the target individuals belong. Most incentives are offered to individuals for their direct benefit. The case of an incentive that is offered to a group is exemplified in communities that offer to provide free blood to all persons in the community if 4 percent or more of the community's residents make blood donations. Another is the case in Thailand where villages get economic development money in proportion to the extent that the village as a whole practices family planning.

The third step is to specify the *recipient* of the incentive—that is, whether incentives will go to consumers, suppliers, or sales agents. Incentives to promote vasectomies, for example, may be offered to the consumer, to the doctor, or to the canvasser who recruits prospects. At one time, canvassers for vasectomies in India received such incentives to find prospects that they brought in men who were too young to know better and men who were too old for it to matter!

The fourth step is to determine the *direction of the incentive*—that is, whether it should be positive (rewarding) or negative (punishing). Commercial organizations normally work with incentives rather than disincentives in promoting their offer. Governments work with both. They offer subsidies and special advantages to encourage certain types of behavior and impose taxes or costs on other types of behavior. In any particular problem area, either option may be available. Nations wishing to expand the birthrate offer family allowances as an incentive. Nations wishing to contract the birthrate reduce family allowances or disproportionately tax large families.

The fifth step is to determine the *form of the incentive*—that is, whether it will consist of money or items of nonmonetary value, such as food, free education, health care, lottery tickets, or old age security. The form of the incentive must be carefully researched because its nuances may offend the target group. Although cash is a very tangible incentive, for example, it may be viewed as a corrupt consideration if it is used to influence decisions on how many children to have. An offer of better housing may be received more favorably.

The sixth step is to determine the *amount of incentive.* Too small an incentive is ineffective and an overly large one is wasteful. If the incentive is nongraduated, the amount may seem too small for those in higher income brackets and too much for those in lower income brackets. This has led to interest in graduated incentives whereby the amount offered varies with the consumer's economic circumstances or interest in the offer. Public television stations, for example, vary the premiums offered based on how much one gives.

The seventh step is the *time of payment of the incentives.* Most incentives are paid immediately upon the adoption of the target behavior. Thus, in the family planning area, the adoption of sterilization is usually immediately followed by payment. But the agreement to use birth control pills may not be rewarded except on the basis of results each year.

In summary, incentives are an important means of promotion but they require research and analysis. Commercial companies tend to learn over time which incentives work best and what amounts and timing are optimal. As noted in Chapter 18, several propositions are emerging about incentives and their effective use. Knowledge is also accumulating on the effectiveness of incentives in other health-related areas, such as nutrition, immunization, and self-medication practice. The outlook is for increasing use of incentives in social and organizational marketing.

SUMMARY

Advertising, nonpersonal communication conducted through paid media under clear sponsorship, must be planned strategically like any other element of the marketing mix. Objectives must be set, budgets determined, messages defined, media selected, and a system of evaluation established.

Advertising objectives must fit with prior decisions about the target market, offer positioning, and the nature of the remainder of the marketing mix. It must be clear what response from the target audience is sought. Typically, the response is movement forward among the six buyer readiness states: awareness, knowledge, liking, preference, conviction, and action.

Budgets can be set by affordable, percent-of-sales, or competitive methods, but the objective-and-task method is best. Budgets must be both set in total and allocated among different market segments, geographical areas, and time periods. Budgets must also be allocated across media categories and to specific media vehicles. Choices here depend on the marketer's objectives, the intended target audience, the planned message, and media costs. Various mathematical media mix models are available to help with this task.

Managers must also decide on media timing. Ads should be scheduled seasonally to parallel changes in audience interest. Within seasons, decisions must be made on short-run timing. The major options are to advertise continuously, intermittently, or in preplanned bursts. These choices should be based on audience turnover, the frequency of the behavior to be influenced, and forgetting rates.

Evaluation schemes involve pretesting and posttesting advertising. Pretesting can incorporate comprehension studies, direct mailings, portfolio recall tests, physiological tests, focus-group interviews, self-administered questionnaires, or the use of the Health Message Testing Service. Posttests are usually based on recall, recognition, or some direct behavioral response such as inquiries or sales.

Sales promotion involves a wide range of incentives designed to have short-term effects on specific behaviors of consumers, middlemen, or the sales force. There are two features of sales promotions that the manager must keep in mind when planning to use them. First, they are typically perceived as urgent requests for action and so can break through habitual patterns. On the other hand, the same urgency may imply that there is some negative reason for the urgency, which may tend to diminish the offer's image.

QUESTIONS

1. Under what circumstances should a nonprofit pay for its own advertising time on radio or television rather than accept free public service slots offered by the media but scheduled at the latter's convenience? How can this approach be justified in terms of costs?

2. Six buyer-readiness states are outlined in this chapter. Develop magazine advertising headings for each of the stages leading a target consumer toward wearing seat belts routinely.

3. Develop a set of ten opening sentences for a direct mail letter for the Los Angeles Symphony Orchestra that you believe would get a thirty-five-year-old female labor lawyer to read the rest of a subscription solicitation proposal. Which of these headlines would you *not* use if your target was a thirty-five-year-old male branch office manager for a life insurance company? How would you test your ten sentences?

4. Select three print ads for nonprofit hospitals appearing in your local newspaper. First, make an overall judgment as to which is best. Subject them to the message-testing questionnaire in Exhibit 19-4. In your opinion, which is superior and why? How did the questionnaire affect your judgment, if at all?

5. It is argued that giving promotional incentives such as tokens or gifts only teaches target audiences to take the desired action (for example, practice birth control) to gain the promotional incentive. When the incentive is discontinued, the behavior stops. How would you design a population control incentive program to reduce this possibility?

NOTES

1. These definitions, with the exception of the one for sales promotion, came from *Marketing Definitions: A Glossary of Marketing Terms* (Chicago: American Marketing Association, 1960).

2. Stewart Alter, "Ad Spending to Top $100 Billion in '86?" *Advertising Age,* December 16, 1985, p. 10.

3. "Reagan, Fritz Use Whips at Wire," *Advertising Age,* November 5, 1984, p. 3.

4. See John A. Zeigler, "Social Change Through Issue Advertising," *Sociological Inquiry,* Winter 1970, pp. 159–65.

5. "For the Record," *Advertising Age,* March 25, 1985, p. 113.

6. There are several models of buyer readiness states. See, for example, Robert J. Lavidge and Gary A. Steiner, "A Model for Predictive Measurements of Advertising Effectiveness," *Journal of Marketing,* October 1961, pp. 59–62. For another approach, see Geraldine Fennell, "Persuasion as Behavioral Science in Business and Nonbusiness Contexts," in Russell W. Belk, ed., *Advances in Nonprofit Marketing,* Vol. 1 (Greenwich, Conn.: JAI Press, 1985), pp. 95–160.

7. See Russell H. Colley, *Defining Advertising Goals for Measured Advertising Results* (New York: Association of National Advertisers, 1961).

8. William D. Novelli, "Social Issues and Direct Marketing: What's the Connection?" presentation to the Annual Conference of the Direct Mail/Marketing Association, Los Angeles, Calif., March 12, 1981.

9. Belinda Hulin-Salkin, "Strategies of Charities," *Advertising Age,* January 19, 1981, pp. 528–531.

10. *Ibid.,* p. 529.

11. This definition and the following discussion rely largely on two sources: Edward Pohlman, *Incentives and Compensation in Birth Planning* (Chapel Hill: Carolina Population Center, University of North Carolina, 1971); and Everett M. Rogers, "Effects of Incentives on the Diffusion of Innovations: The Case of Family Planning in Asia," a chapter in Gerald Zaltman, ed., *Processes and Phenomena of Social Change* (New York: John Wiley, 1973).

C H A P T E R   2 0

Managing Public Relations

A seven-member team of heart surgeons, anesthesiologists, and nurses hovers over a patient on the operating table at Memorial Medical Center, Springfield, Illinois. It's the grand opening of the hospital's new cardiology and cardiac surgery facility. A crowd of people shuffles by and local media roll their cameras, but the medical specialists never flinch.

They can't. They are lifeless mannequins borrowed from a local department store to simulate open-heart surgery.

This is just one of the innovative techniques hospitals are using to market their capabilities and services to the public.

Four or five years ago, the traditional hospital public relations department was content to produce a house organ and a press release here and there. Today, in response to the rapidly changing health care industry, hospitals are adding marketing personnel, hiring outside communications specialists, and launching aggressive, multimedia consumer ad campaigns.

Recent evidence suggests that this fledgling trend is beginning to gain momentum.

Today, more than three-quarters of all metropolitan hospitals have a marketing department or person responsible for marketing, according to a recent survey by MarketPlus Measurement Systems, a management information service of Walker Research, Indianapolis.

USA Today reports that 60 percent of hospitals have hired marketing specialists. One consultant estimates that hospitals are spending $1 billion a year promoting their services.

Perhaps the biggest contributing factor is the nation's overabundance of hospitals.

Faced with what may be a widespread hospital "recession," hospital administrators must break out of their traditional not-for-profit orientations and take a long, hard look at the advantages of marketing.

"Hospitals are faced with the exact same marketing challenges as General Foods is—they just don't know it," says Susan Anthony, senior account supervisor for Silverman Mower, a full-service agency in Syracuse, New York. Ms. Anthony directs the marketing program for United Health Services, a not-for-profit operator of three hospitals in Johnson City, New York.

Because everyone needs health care at some point, the industry always has been very consumer-oriented, says Ron Watt, a Cleveland-based health care specialist and president of Hesselbart & Mitten/Watt, a full-service marketing company. He says health care "is the highest form of consumerism—but no one realized it until all the competition arose."

SOURCE: M. Lynn Folse, "Marketing Staffs Give Hospitals a Shot in the Arm." Reprinted with permission from *Advertising Age,* November 8, 1984. Copyright 1984 Crain Communications, Inc.

The basic mission of nonprofit and public sector organizations who incorporate marketing into their strategic planning is to influence the behavior of one or more target audiences. To carry out this mission, they need the active support of many diverse publics and at least the tolerance of a number of others. In Chapter 5, we noted four basic types of publics: *input publics* (donors, suppliers, regulators), *internal publics* (management, staff, volunteers, board), *intermediary publics* (merchants, agents, facilitators, marketing firms), and *consuming publics* (clients, local residents, the general public, activists, media). These publics can be further divided into (1) those that are actively involved in carrying out the organization's mission, either directly or indirectly (for example, donors, suppliers, internal and intermediary publics), and (2) those whose goodwill and tolerance are needed for the organization to exist and to carry out its mission as efficiently and effectively as possible. These two groups can be designated the *active* and *passive* publics, respectively.

The local community, news media, bankers, local politicians, government officials, social action groups—all may take an active or reactive interest in the organization's activities. Of course, the organization's general managers can attempt to influence these publics in the course of carrying out their other duties. But sooner or later the organization recognizes the advantages of consolidating or coordinating these activities through a *public relations manager.* In employing a public relations manager, the organization can gain several advantages: (1) better anticipation of potential problems, (2) better handling of these problems, (3) consistent public-oriented policies and strategies, and (4) more professional written and oral communications.

The public relations function will be of high or low influence in the organization, depending on the board's and chief executive officer's attitude toward the function. In some organizations, the public relations manager is a vice-president and sits in on all meetings involving information and actions that might affect public perceptions of the organization. He or she not only puts out fires but also counsels management on actions that will avoid starting fires. In other organizations, public relations is a middle-management function charged with getting out publications and handling news and special events. The public relations people are not involved in policy or strategy formulation, only in tactics.

The recent emergence of marketing as a "hot topic" in nonprofit circles has raised a major question in the minds of chief administrators and public relations managers as to the relations between marketing and public relations in a nonprofit organization. Clearly, the two functions work well together in business firms, with marketing focusing on the development of plans to market the company's products to consumers, while public relations takes care of relations with the other publics. In nonprofit organizations, the relationship between the public relations and marketing departments has been marked by tension and lack of clearly defined areas of responsibility. The tension is mainly a historical artifact. In many institutions, the public relations function was already well established when marketing was introduced. In such cases, three factors tended to create friction between the two areas. First, the marketing department was often assigned functions that were "taken away" from public relations. Second, public relations directors often felt that they should have been given the new, often more prestigious and better-paying position of marketing director in the new organization. Third, many public relations executives felt that marketing ought properly to be a division within their department or that marketing as a separate function was not needed at all.

These frictions were often exacerbated by lack of clearly specified separate roles for the two functions and a clear understanding of how they were to be coordinated with each other. Both are boundary functions concerned with achieving certain results with various internal and external publics. Are the two functions redundant? Is one more important or comprehensive than the other? Do they play equal but different roles?

This chapter advances the thesis that public relations is most effective when viewed and conducted as part of the marketing mix being used by the organization to pursue its marketing objectives. We will look at the following questions:

1. How did the public relations function evolve?
2. What is the relation between public relations and marketing in nonprofit organizations?
3. What are the main tools of the public relations practitioner?

THE HISTORICAL EVOLUTION OF PUBLIC RELATIONS

Public relations, like marketing, is a relatively new corporate function, although its roots go back into ancient history.[1] Edward L. Bernays, one of the fathers of modern public relations, posited that the three main elements of public relations are as old as society: informing people, persuading people, and integrating people with people.[2] Bernays traced public relations from primitive society, in which leaders controlled by force, intimidation, and persuasion, to Babylonia, where kings commissioned historians to paint favorable images of them. The Renaissance and Reformation freed people's minds from established dogmas, thus leading institutions to develop more subtle means of influencing people. In America, historical milestones for "public relations" include:

- Samuel Adams's use of the press to unite the colonists against the British.
- The abolitionist movement's use of public relations as a political tool to rally support for blacks in the North, including the publication of *Uncle Tom's Cabin.*
- P. T. Barnum's use of public relations to generate newsworthiness about an event—the arrival of his circus—by placing articles in newspapers.

Corporate public relations first emerged in the late nineteenth century and passed through the five stages shown in Figure 20-1. In the first stage, corporations established a *contact* function to influence legislators and newspapers to support positions favorable to business. The legislative contact function became known as *lobbying,* and the newspaper contact function became known as *press agentry.* George Westinghouse is credited with formally establishing public relations when he hired two men in 1889 to fight the advocates of direct current electricity and to promote instead alternating current.[3]

The next stage occurred when companies began to recognize the positive value of planned *publicity* in creating customer interest in the company

FIGURE 20-1

Historical Evolution of Public Relations

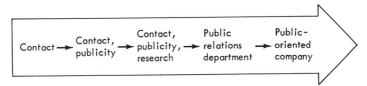

and its products. Publicity entailed finding or creating events, preparing
company- or product-slanted news stories, and trying to interest the press
in using them. Companies recognized that special skills are needed to
develop publicity and began to add publicists to their ranks.

Somewhat later, public relations practitioners began to recognize the
value of conducting *research* into public opinion prior to developing and
launching public relations campaigns. The emerging sciences of public opinion measurement and mass communication theory permitted more sophistication in the conduct of public relations. Forward-looking firms added specialists who could research public opinion.

These functions—contact, publicity, and research—were uncoordi-
nated in the typical firm. The organization's lobbyists had little to do with
the organization's publicists and the publicists had little to do with the
researchers. This led finally to the concept of a *public relations department*,
which integrated the work going on to cultivate the goodwill of the company's different publics. In larger organizations, public relations departments
grew to encompass subspecialties to deal with each public (stockholders,
neighbors, employees, customers, government agencies) and each tool (publications, press relations, research, and so on).

The establishment of a public relations department did not ensure that
the organization as a whole acted like a *public-oriented company*. The vice-
president of public relations had limited influence over other departments
and needed the backing of top management to press for public-oriented
actions by all departments. Organizations were facing growing challenges in
the form of consumerism, environmentalism, energy conservation, inflation, shortages, employment discrimination, and safety. Public relations
people wanted a more active role in counseling the organization and its
departments on how to act as public citizens. PR practitioners emphasize
that their job is not just to produce "good words" but to produce "good
deeds followed by good words." Unless they can get the organization to act
like a good citizen, good words alone will not be enough.

THE RELATIONSHIP BETWEEN PUBLIC RELATIONS AND MARKETING

Public relations is often confused with one of its subfunctions, such as
press agentry, company publications, lobbying, fire-fighting, and so forth.
Yet it is a more inclusive concept. The most frequently quoted definition of
PR is the following:

Public relations is the management function that evaluates the attitudes of important publics, identifies the policies and procedures of
an individual or an organization with the public interest, and executes
a program of action to earn understanding and acceptance by these
publics.[4]

Sometimes a short definition is given, which says that PR stands for *performance* (P) plus *recognition* (R).

Most of today's public relations people have come out of English departments and journalism schools. Management thinks of PR as essentially a communication tool. Journalism training adds the advantage that the PR person knows how the press thinks and probably knows many press people, thus assuring greater access to the media.

We see the following differences between public relations and marketing:

1. Public relations is primarily a communication tool, whereas marketing also includes need assessment, product development, pricing, and distribution.
2. Public relations seeks to influence attitudes, whereas marketing tries to influence specific behaviors, such as purchasing, joining, voting, and so on.
3. Public relations does not define the goals of the organization, whereas marketing is intimately involved in defining the business's mission, customers, and services.

On the other hand, the mission of public relations is one that can benefit from the kind of strategic marketing planning that we have stressed throughout this book. For the public relations function, we have simplified the strategic planning process to the six steps outlined in Figure 20-2.

FIGURE 20-2

The Public Relations Strategic Planning Process

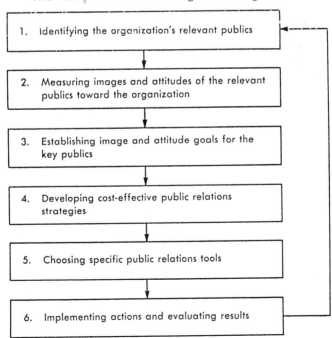

THE PUBLIC RELATIONS STRATEGIC PLANNING PROCESS

We cannot emphasize strongly enough the need for careful long-range and annual planning of the public relations function. It has been our experience that in many organizations, public relations is mainly (or *only*) *reactive*. It gets out press releases as needed, fights "brush fires" as they emerge, and copes with individual and group complaints. This reactive stance has many negative consequences:

1. The environment rather than the organization sets the public relations agenda.
2. The organization's image is defined only by its response to special situations rather than by the creation of a set of carefully designed messages over a long period of time.
3. The organization's responses to crises are not guided by a long-term strategy.

The *active* public relations stance avoids these problems and assures that the organization has control over how others see it. We now examine the six steps in the public relations planning cycle necessary to implement such a *strategic* approach. (See Figure 20-2.)

Identifying the Organization's Relevant Publics

An organization would like to have the goodwill of every public that it affects or is affected by. Given limited public relations resources, however, the organization will have to concentrate more of its attention on some publics than on others.

An organization's primary publics are those that it relates to actively and continuously, such as its clients, employees, directors, and the community. The clients receive the services of the organization. The employees provide the services. The directors govern the organization. And the community provides the setting and location in which the organization carries on its activities. If the goodwill of any of these groups disappears—if clients stop coming, employees start quitting, directors lose their interest, or the community becomes hostile—the organization is in deep trouble.

An organization also faces secondary publics that it must monitor and relate to on a fairly continuous basis—suppliers, dealers, government groups, and competitors. Suppliers provide the organization with its equipment, office materials, fuel, and other inputs needed to carry on the organization's daily operations. Dealers carry the organization's goods and services to the final clients, who may be scattered widely. The government groups are the legislators, jurists, and agency heads who provide services, define and enforce the law, and collect taxes. Competitors are those groups who represent direct and indirect alternative sources for the same goods, services, or satisfactions provided by the organization.

Finally, an organization has to deal with various tertiary publics from time to time. General purpose groups are those that seek to advance the interests of their members, such as labor unions, churches, clubs, and associations. Special purpose groups are those that exist to carry out some purpose outside of themselves, such as charitable organizations and social action groups. The organization contributes time or money to a number of these groups because their causes are worthwhile (charitable groups) or because it benefits the organization directly (for example, trade associations). Other tertiary groups may take on a confrontation role toward the organization (for example, a hostile labor union or social action group), and the organization must choose between appeasement and counterattack.

The various publics are related not only to the organization, but also to each other in many important ways. A particular public may have great influence on other publics. Consider a college whose students are highly satisfied. Their enthusiasm will be transmitted to their parents and to friends back home who might be potential students. Their enthusiasm will have a reinforcing effect on the faculty, who will feel that their teaching is effective. Their enthusiasm will affect the future level of support they give to the school as alumni. Thus, the satisfaction felt by students will influence the attitudes and behavior of other university publics. These dynamics are outlined in Figure 20-3.

Likewise, the dissatisfaction of a particular public will affect the attitudes of other publics. Suppose that current students are highly dissatisfied with the college over some policy. If the students choose to act, Figure 20-3 suggests they have several recourses. First, they may go directly to the college (administration, trustees, faculty) and try to negotiate a better policy.

FIGURE 20-3

Dynamic Relations between a University and Its Publics

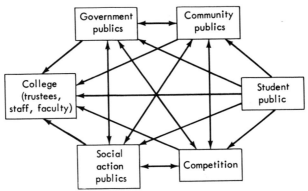

Second, they may attempt to win community support to bring pressure to bear on the college. Third, they may attempt to get the government to intervene. Fourth, they may solicit the support of various social action groups. Fifth, they might give up, leave the college, and transfer to other colleges. Thus, publics that are passive in one period might suddenly erupt into action because of sympathy with the grievance of a particular public.

It is important for the organization to set up relations that produce satisfaction with its valued publics. The organization must consider what benefits to offer its valued publics in exchange for their resources and support. Once an organization begins to think about cultivating the support of a public, it is beginning to think of that public as a *market,* a group to whom it will offer benefits in exchange for valued resources.

MEASURING IMAGES AND ATTITUDES OF THE RELEVANT PUBLICS

Once the organization has identified its key publics, it needs to find out how each public thinks and feels about the organization. Management will have some ideas of each public's attitude simply through its regular contacts with that public. But impressions based on casual contact cannot necessarily be trusted. Recently, a college wanted to rent its stadium facilities to a professional football team for five Sundays as a way of raising more revenue. The college's administrators thought that most local residents and city council members would approve. When it sought a favorable city council vote, however, a group of local citizens attacked the college, calling it insensitive and arrogant. They complained that the football crowd would use up parking spaces, leave litter, walk on lawns, and be rowdy. A large number of citizens, including city council members, revealed deep-seated hostile attitudes toward the college that only needed an issue to flare up. Even in this case, the college's administration dismissed the community spokesman as a minority. Needless to say, the vote went against the college, to its surprise.

To know a public's attitudes well enough to use them as a solid basis for its strategic planning, the organization needs to undertake some formal marketing research. A good start is to organize focus groups of publics annually to probe their knowledge and feelings about the organization. While the observations of these focus groups are not necessarily representative, they normally contribute perspectives and raise interesting questions that the organization will want to explore more systematically. Most importantly, they will alert management to key problems as they emerge. Eventually, the organization may find it worthwhile to conduct formal field surveys on a regular basis. It can track awareness, knowledge, interest, and attitudes toward the organization. Exhibit 20-1 describes the highlights of a public opinion survey conducted for the American Red Cross.

EXHIBIT 20-1 Public opinion research for the American Red Cross

The public opinion polling firm of Louis Harris conducts periodic surveys of public opinion toward the American Red Cross. Here is a sample of the questions asked in the 1976 survey.

WHAT DOES THE PUBLIC KNOW ABOUT RED CROSS SERVICES?

1. What comes to mind first when you hear the words "American Red Cross"?
2. What other kinds of activities is the Red Cross engaged in?
3. For each activity, please say which statement on the list describes how important you feel that activity is (extremely important, very important, quite important, rather important, not too important, not at all important).
4. For each activity, please mention which one or more organizations provide that service.
5. Which one of these activities do you think the American Red Cross spends the most money on?

HOW IMPORTANT IS THE WORK OF THE RED CROSS AND HOW WELL DOES IT DO ITS JOB?

1. These organizations serve the American community. Which one do you personally feel does the *most* important work? Which does the *next* most important work? Which does the *third* most important work?
2. For each organization, would you say its performance is extremely good, very good, good, just fair, or poor?
3. Is there anything you don't especially like about the American Red Cross?

WHERE DOES THE RED CROSS GET ITS FUNDS?

1. Do any of the United Way contributions get distributed to the American Red Cross or not?
2. If yes, about what percent of the money raised by the United Way would you guess *is* distributed by it to the American Red Cross?
3. Which one of these statements best describes your feeling about the amount of money the Red Cross has available? It has more than it really needs. It has enough money to do the job. It doesn't have quite enough money to do its job. It has a serious lack of funds. Not sure.

The 1976 poll yielded a number of important findings: (1) The Red Cross is perceived almost exclusively as a disaster relief organization, its other services being less well known. (2) There is a vague antipathy toward the Red Cross. (3) Red Cross performance is perceived to be not as good as that of other organizations. (4) Perception of Red Cross need for funds is relatively low.

SOURCE: 1976 National Public Opinion Research Concerning the American National Red Cross.

By periodically researching its key publics, the organization develops hard data on how these publics view the organization. To translate this information into a strategic plan, the organization must evaluate each key public in terms of the probability that they have a negative attitude toward the organization and the degree of impact they can have on the organization if they act on their negative attitude.

Suppose the public relations manager for a hospital rates twenty key publics in terms of these two factors. (See Table 20-1.) She concludes that there are five groups that have a *high* probability of being unfavorably disposed toward the hospital in the next year. However, the competitve nature of the hospital market and the relatively weak position of unions in this particular state have led her to conclude that the negative attitudes of two publics, competitors and labor unions, will have little impact on the hospital. Local politicians are seen as hostile, but no legislation is presently pending. If politicians do decide to act, however, they can be troublesome, so the hospital must pay some attention to them. Technicians and insurers are a more serious problem. Technicians are upset about the hospital's recent decision not to buy certain state-of-the-art equipment to replace older equipment. Insurers are rankled by the hospital's antiquated billing procedures and higher-than-average charges for certain exotic surgical procedures. Both groups should receive considerable attention in the upcoming year.

Physicians, patients, and media should also receive close attention. All are concerned about a recent scandal at the hospital in which two physicians

Table 20-1

A PORTFOLIO OF PUBLICS FOR ST. ANTHONY'S HOSPITAL

Probability of Negative Attitude	Potential Impact		
	Low	Medium	High
Low	Suppliers	Nursing Schools Volunteers	Board Nurses Regional Health Agency Charities
Medium	General Public Non-medical Staff	Medical Schools Research Foundations	Physicians TV/Radio Newspapers Patients
High	Competitors Labor Unions	Local Politicians	Technicians Insurers

were discovered abusing drugs. The same issue has caused a potential problem for the groups in the medium-probability, medium- and high-impact cells of the matrix. Informal soundings indicate that all six publics in these two cells are concerned about the hospital's medical staff and control systems. Medical schools and research foundations must be satisfied, since negative attitudes on the part of these publics have the potential for affecting future recruitment of physicians and winning of research grants. The upper right cell is a discretionary target. The administrator may devote time, if any is available, to the board, nurses, regional health agencies, and charitable organizations. Their interests and concerns, however, might be met by programs directed at other target publics.

As for the cells in the upper left corner of the matrix, the analysis suggests that the public relations manager can pay relatively little attention to suppliers, nursing schools, volunteers, the general public, and nonmedical staff in the upcoming year. She should continue, however, to monitor their attitudes over the year to make sure that her initial assessment is correct and that they do not "migrate" to other, more potentially damaging categories.

Once the public relations manager has determined the amount of effort to direct to each key public in the matrix, specific communication goals must be set for each segment. The manager might specify, for example, that "90 percent of TV and radio news directors and city editors within a fifty-mile radius of the hospital should know within six months the full details of the hospital's internal policing system. Seventy-five percent should have full confidence in the hospital by the end of that period." These specific goals naturally suggest the means for their achievement and indicate what results should be measured later to evaluate the success of the strategic plan.

DEVELOPING COST EFFECTIVE PR STRATEGIES

An organization usually has many options in trying to improve the attitudes of a particular public. Its first task is to understand why the attitudes have arisen so that the causal factors can be appropriately addressed. Consider the case of the college that found it had weak community support when it wanted to rent its stadium to a professional football team. In digging deeper into the negative citizen attitudes, the college discovered that many citizens harbored a history of resentment against the college for reasons including (1) the college never consults citizen groups before taking actions, (2) the college discriminates against local high school students, preferring to draw students from other parts of the country, (3) the college does not actively inform the local community about campus events and programs, and (4) the college owns local property that goes tax-free and thereby raises the taxes of the citizens. Essentially, the community feels neglected and exploited by the college.

The diagnosis suggests that the college needs to change its ways and establish stronger ties with the community. It needs to develop a *community relations program* as part of its public relations strategy. Here are some of the steps it might take:

1. Identify the local opinion leaders (prominent business people, news editors, city council members, heads of civic organizations, school officials) and build better relationships by inviting them to campus events, consulting with them on college issues that will affect the community, and sponsoring luncheons and dinners.
2. Encourage the college's faculty and staff to join local organizations and participate in community campaigns such as the United Way and American Red Cross Blood Bank programs.
3. Develop a speakers' bureau to provide speakers to local groups such as the Kiwanis, Rotary, and so on.
4. Make the college's facilities and programs more available to the community. Classrooms and halls can be offered to local organizations for meetings.
5. Arrange open houses and campus tours for the local community.
6. Participate in community special events such as parades, holiday observances, and so on.
7. Establish an advisory board of community leaders to act as a sounding board for issues facing the college and the community.

Each project involves money and time. The organization will need to estimate the amount of expected attitude improvement for each project to arrive at the best mix of cost-effective actions.

Choosing Specific Public Relations Tools

Here, we want to examine in more detail the major public relations media and tools to be used in implementation. They are (1) written material, (2) audiovisual material, (3) corporate identity media, (4) news, (5) interviews, (6) public service announcements, (7) events, (8) speeches, and (9) telephone information services.

Written Material.   Organizations rely extensively on written material to communicate with their target publics. A public library, for example, uses such written material as an annual report, catalogues, employee newsletters, informational flyers, and posters.

In preparing each publication, the public relations department must consider *function, aesthetics,* and *cost.* The function of an annual report is to inform interested publics about the organization's accomplishments during the year and about its financial status, with the ultimate purpose of generating confidence in the organization and its leaders. Aesthetics enter in because the annual report should be readable, interesting, and professional. If the annual report is published in mimeograph form, it suggests a poor, amateur-type organization. If the annual report is extremely fancy, the public may raise questions as to why a nonprofit organization is spending so much money on graphics instead of needed services. Cost acts as a constraint in that the organization will allocate a limited amount of money to each publication. The public relations department has to reconcile considerations of function, aesthetics, and cost in developing each publication.

Audiovisual Material.   Audiovisual materials such as films, slides, and audio and video cassettes are coming into increasing use as communication tools. In the old days, college recruiters would visit different campuses and present a talk, answer questions, and pass out some written materials to the high school seniors gathered to hear about the college. The students had to concentrate hard on the recruiter's words. Today's recruiter, in contrast, delivers a high-impact audiovisual presentation about the college. A recruiter from the University of Richmond, for example, shows a 16 mm, full-color, twelve-minute film dramatizing life on the University of Richmond's campus. The film cost $13,000 to produce and has apparently paid for itself many times over in improved recruitment effectiveness. Other colleges use a combination of slides and recorded campus sounds that can be very effective. In all cases, the visual materials should be put together with some care. One of the authors witnessed a college recruiter make a presentation involving 100 slides showing mostly campus buildings, in no particular order, with several slides upside down. The whole presentation bored the high school seniors, and few applications came in.

Corporate Identity Media.   Normally, an organization's separate materials lack a uniform look, which not only creates confusion but also misses an opportunity to create and reinforce a *corporate identity.* In an overcommunicated society, organizations compete for attention. They should try to create a visual identity that the public immediately recognizes. Visual identity is conveyed through logos, stationery, brochures, signs, business forms, call cards, buildings, uniforms, and rolling stock.

The corporate identity media become a marketing tool when they are attractive, memorable, and distinctive. The task of creating a coordinated visual identity is not easy. The organization should select a good graphic design consultant. The consultant will try to get management to identify the essence of the organization, and will then try to turn it into a big idea backed by strong visual symbols. The symbols are adapted to the various organizational media to create immediate brand recognition in the minds of various publics.

News.   One of the major tasks of a public relations department is to find or create favorable news about the organization and market it to the appropriate media. The appeal of publicity to many organizations is that it is "free advertising"—that is, it represents exposures at no cost. As someone once said, "Publicity is sent to a medium and prayed for while advertising is sent to a medium and paid for." Publicity is far from free, however, because special skills are required to write good publicity and to "reach" the press. Good publicists cost money.

Publicity has three qualities that make it a worthwhile investment. First, it may have *higher veracity* than advertising because it appears as normal news and not as sponsored information. Second, it tends to catch people *off guard* who might otherwise avoid sponsored messages. Third, it has high potential for *dramatization* in that it arouses attention, coming as it does in the guise of a noteworthy event.

Getting news items in the local press or on television or radio is itself a marketing task. As such, the publicist must start with the immediate audience. One must ask what the media are looking for in a news story. Among the prime characteristics they will have in mind are:

1. The interest of the subject to their audience.
2. The possibility for dramatization through pictures, live interviews, and so forth.
3. The clarity and exhaustiveness of the press release (for example, including supporting materials, statistics, etc.).
4. Limited need for further "digging."
5. The possibility of "exclusive" coverage—for either the entire story or for a specific "angle."

Long-term cultivation of media gatekeepers helps get news items reported and insures full and accurate coverage. To this end, publishers or the presidents of TV or radio stations can be added to the organization's board of directors. Favorable attitudes on the part of these gatekeepers can be particularly valuable when a crisis arises or a "scandal" is uncovered.

The publicist must remember a key marketing principle outlined in Chapter 2. Publicity must *not* be selling the organization's story. Don't tell the media what *you* want them to hear. Respond to what *they* want to hear. Customer-centeredness is as critical to public relations strategy as it is to any other marketing operation.

Finally, the publicist must learn to think strategically. A clear, continuing program of releases and stories should be developed for each planning period. These should be tailored to end the period with specific communications objectives achieved for specific audiences. Not all stories that are interesting to the publicist or the organization's administrators should be brought out if they do not help promote the organization's long-term interests.

Interviews.   An often-effective vehicle for publicity is the media interview. It was recently reported that there are 4,250 local news and talk shows on 988 TV stations in the United States. On these shows, 10,200 guests appear annually.[5] Often these guests are not celebrities or especially news-worthy individuals. They are simply experts on some subject or people with a simple story to tell. Nonprofits can usually provide a number of subjects and guests over a year's time to meet the voracious need for program material. An attractive, articulate veterinarian from a zoo can tell of the special problems of dealing with large animals. A college recruitment director can talk about the new competition for students or offer advice on how to get one's son or daughter into their college of choice. Visiting artists at theatres or music performances are always in demand. Anything offbeat generally has a much better chance of getting time or space to tell the organization's story than a subject that has already been worn out in the media.

Public Service Announcements.   In addition to their need for guests, TV and radio stations (and networks) are usually quite willing—even eager—to give air time to public service announcements (PSAs). There was a time when they were required to do so by the Federal Communications Commission. They no longer have this requirement, but most still wish to include PSAs as part of their programming. This is in part because they need to fill otherwise empty air time with interesting material, but more so because the stations simply wish to be good community citizens. At the same time, many local and national advertising agencies and production houses are willing to donate some or all of their services to developing such PSAs. The program of the Advertising Council is perhaps the most prominent in this regard.

A recent survey indicated that TV stations were most apt to use PSAs under the following conditions:[6]

1. PSAs of differing length are offered.
2. One of the following subjects is dealt with: health, safety, alcohol and drug abuse, child abuse and molestation, family and social relations, education, crime prevention, and drunk driving.
3. There is a possibility for a local tie-in (respondents said they broadcast 56 percent of PSAs for local organizations and 44 percent for national issues).
4. The target audience is children, the elderly, the handicapped, or minorities.

A recent study by the Health Message Testing Service (mentioned in Chapter 19) showed that effective PSAs on health issues had the following characteristics:

- They emphasized both the health problem and the solution in the PSA.
- They used a person typical of the target audience when presenting a testimonial.
- They visualized a reward from practicing the recommended healthful behavior.

- They communicated the psychological benefits of practicing the healthful behavior.
- They used an approach other than humor.
- They demonstrated the healthful behavior (if possible).
- They used a high or moderate emotional appeal.[7]

Events.   The organization can increase its newsworthiness by creating events that attract the attention of target publics. Thus, a hospital seeking more public attention can host major research symposia, feature well-known speakers and celebrities, celebrate anniversaries of important events in the history of the institution, and hold news conferences. Each well-run event not only impresses the immediate participants, but also serves as an opportunity to develop a multitude of stories directed to relevant media vehicles and audiences.

Event creation and management is a particularly important skill in running fundraising drives for nonprofit organizations. Fundraisers have developed a large repertoire of special events, including anniversary celebrations, art exhibits, auctions, benefit evenings, bingo games, book sales, cake sales, contests, dances, dinners, fairs, fashion shows, parties in unusual places, phonothons, rummage sales, tours, and walkathons. The American Cancer Society, for example, distributes a brochure to local units in which they outline the following ideas for special events:

> Dramatic special events attract attention to the American Cancer Society. They bring color, excitement, and glamor to the program. Well planned, they will get excellent coverage in newspapers, on radio and TV, and in newsreels. . . . A Lights-On-Drive, a one-afternoon or one-night House-to-House program have such dramatic appeal that they stir excitement and enthusiasm . . . keep in mind the value of bursts of sound such as fire sirens sounding, loudspeaker trucks, fife and drum corps. . . . A most useful special event is the ringing of church bells to add a solemn, dedicated note to the launching of a drive or education project. This should be organized on a division or community basis, and the church bell ringing may be the signal to begin a House-to-House canvass. Rehearsals of bell ringing, community leaders tugging at ropes, offer good picture possibilities.[8]

Speeches.   Speeches are another tool through which the organization can communicate with target publics. The public relations director will look for effective spokespersons for the organization and will try to arrange speaking engagements. If a college's president is articulate and attractive, the public relations director will try to line up appearances on national and local talk shows and at major convention meetings. The president's impact will be further enhanced by engaging a good speech writer and coach. Articulate faculty can also be lined up for speaking engagements and news conferences. The public relations director can set up a speakers' bureau to deliver appropriate talks to community organizations.

Telephone Information Service.   A relatively new public relations tool is a telephone number through which members of the public can get information about the organization. Triton Community College, for example, set up a telephone number which gives prerecorded information about the college, registration times, and costs. Various health organizations have set up telephone numbers that provide health messages about specific symptoms and diseases. The American Cancer Society has set up a national network of offices, called Cancer Information Services Offices, to take calls. Going further, drug abuse centers have set up "hot lines" to take emergency calls. These telephone services suggest that the organization cares about the public and is ready to serve them.

IMPLEMENTING ACTIONS AND EVALUATING EVENTS

The actions to be taken have to be assigned to responsible individuals within the organization along with concrete objectives, time frames, and budgets. The public relations department should oversee the results. Evaluating the results of public relations activities, however, is not easy, since it occurs in conjunction with other marketing activities and its contribution is hard to separate.

Consider the problem of measuring the value of the organization's publicity efforts. Publicity is designed with certain audience-response objectives in mind, and these objectives form the basis of what is measured. The major response measures are exposures, awareness/comprehension/attitude change, and sales.

The easiest and most common measure of publicity effectiveness is the number of *exposures* created in the media. Most publicists supply the client with a "clippings book" showing all the media that carried news about the organization and a summary statement such as the following:

> Media coverage included 3,500 column inches of news and photographs in 350 publications with a combined circulation of 79.4 million; 2,500 minutes of air time on 290 radio stations and an estimated audience of 65 million; and 660 minutes of air time on 160 television stations with an estimated audience of 91 million. If this time and space had been purchased at advertising rates, it would have amounted to $1,047,000.[9]

The purpose of citing the equivalent advertising cost is to make a case for publicity's cost-effectiveness, since the total publicity effort must have cost less than $1,047,000. Furthermore, publicity usually creates more reading and believing than ads.

Still, this exposure measure is not very satisfying. There is no indication of how many people actually read, saw, or heard the message, and what they thought afterward. Furthermore, there is no information on the net audience reached, since publications have overlapping readership. Indeed, there is the very real danger that the organization will attempt to maximize *what it can measure.* Success is measured by brochures passed out, articles written, and so on. Distributing more brochures in 1986 than in 1985 is considered great progress.

A better measure calls for finding out what change in public *awareness/ comprehension/attitude* occurred as a result of the publicity campaign (after allowing for the impact of other promotional tools). This requires the use of survey methodology to measure the *before* and *after* levels of these variables. The best measure is sales and profit impact.

Certain PR activities will be found to be too costly in relation to their impact and might be dropped. Or the PR goals might be recognized as too ambitious and require modification. Furthermore, new problems will arise with certain publics and require redirection of the public relations resources. As the public relations department implements these actions and measures the results, it will be in a position to return to the earlier steps and take a new reading of where the organization stands in the mind of specific publics and what improvements in public attitudes it needs to pursue. Thus the public relations process is continually recycling, as shown in Figure 20-2.

SUMMARY

Public relations is a well-established function in profit and nonprofit organizations. The recent introduction of marketing into nonprofit organizations has raised the question of marketing's relation to public relations.

There are five views on the subject. Public relations and marketing are seen by various people (1) as separate but equal functions; (2) as equal and overlapping functions; (3) with marketing as the dominant function; (4) with public relations as the dominant function; or (5) with public relations and marketing as the same function. This book assumes that public relations is a tool used to advance the marketing purposes of the organization. As such, it can benefit from careful strategic planning.

The task of public relations is to form, maintain, or change public attitudes toward the organization or its products. The process of public relations consists of six steps: (1) identifying the organization's relevant publics, (2) measuring the images and attitudes held by these publics, (3) establishing image and attitude goals for the key publics, (4) developing cost-effective public relations strategies, (5) carefully choosing specific public relations tools, such as written material, audiovisual material, corporate identity media, news, events, speeches, and telephone information services, and (6) implementing actions and evaluating results.

QUESTIONS

1. A Midwestern hospital was the site at which a doctor, on her own volition, decided to withhold nourishment from her own severely deformed child. Which publics are likely to be influenced by the highly negative publicity from this event? Develop a brief statement of strategic public relations objectives for each key public.

2. It is argued that, since public relations always affects the organization's image, it should be placed under a senior general manager rather than under marketing. What are the pros and cons of having public relations *outside* of marketing?

3. Develop a public relations portfolio for the city in which you live.

4. The Southern California Rapid Transit District wishes to obtain the support of key representatives and senators for a large-scale mass transit system in Los Angeles. How would it develop a customer-oriented marketing approach to a specific representative from a district in *Northern* California? What could it offer the representative in exchange for support for the desired appropriation?

5. The Whitney Museum of Contemporary Art has chosen a very daring design for the construction of new facilities on its site, in part because it wishes to change its image to that of an institution supporting very contemporary work. Critics claim the new design overwhelms the classic Marcel Breuer building the Museum now inhabits. As the debate continues, what public relations benchmarks should the Whitney establish to monitor the success or failure of its new design and the PR campaign surrounding it?

NOTES

1. Some of the material in this chapter is adapted from Philip Kotler and William Mindak, "Marketing and Public Relations," *Journal of Marketing,* October 1978, pp. 13–20.

2. Edward L. Bernays, *Public Relations* (Norman: University of Oklahoma Press, 1952).

3. Scott M. Cutlip, "The Beginning of PR Counseling," *Editor and Publisher,* November 26, 1950, p. 16.

4. *Public Relations News,* October 27, 1947.

5. Timothy G. Manners, "TV Talk Show Tour Extends Marketing Reach," *Marketing News,* August 16, 1985, p. 1.

6. "Free TV Time Abounds For Public Service Messages," *Marketing News,* August 16, 1985, p. 7.

7. "Study Identifies Qualities of Effective Health Public Service Announcements," *Marketing News,* April 3, 1981, p. 7.

8. *Public Information Guide* (New York: American Cancer Society, 1965), p. 19.

9. Arthur M. Merims, "Marketing's Stepchild: Product Publicity," *Harvard Business Review,* November-December 1972, pp. 111–112.

CHAPTER 21

Managing Personal Selling

In January, 1982, St. Elizabeth's Medical Center in Dayton, Ohio, faced problems not unlike many other hospitals. Most serious was the increased competition for both patients and physicians. In response to this situation, Joan Thomas, St. Elizabeth's marketing director, developed a unique method of in-home personal communication by the hospital that effectively meets patients' needs for better health care information, physicians' needs to build their practices, and the Medical Center's own needs to attract more new patients and improve its community image.

The new approach is an adaptation of home sales parties developed in the private sector by Tupperware and others. In early focus group interviews among women, Thomas found that although they read a good deal about health care, most wanted information "delivered in a personalized manner."* The women were uncomfortable discussing certain medical subjects and often withheld important diagnostic information from physicians. Thomas conceived of the idea of BodyCues™ home health parties to meet this consumer need. They are expressly designed to help women learn in face-to-face conversations and discussions more about their bodies and the "cues" they are sending and more about how to deal openly and confidently with the medical community.

Home health parties were first tested on St. Elizabeth's hospital employees in January of 1984. The approach is relatively straightforward. Hostesses in neighborhoods, churches, or other organizations (including businesses) first send out twenty to thirty invitations. The invitations and other party-game prizes and materials are provided by St. Elizabeth's. The hostess provides the location and the refreshments. The two-hour party is led by a physician or a nurse. It begins with a game called "The Doctor's Bag" in which guests pull instruments from a doctor's bag and try to guess what they are for. The hilarity provoked by many of the answers makes the game an excellent icebreaker. As the "party" proceeds, the leader discusses various topics with the guests. She explains what goes on in a routine physical examination, what the various procedures attempt to do, and what is going through the doctor's mind as she works. Current topics such as breast cancer and osteoporosis are brought up, and the attending women are taught to practice breast self-examination. The session ends with a question-and-answer period. Pamela Blumensheid, director of the program, has found that during the question period, young women tend to ask more about children and childbirth while older women are more concerned about menopause.

The parties have proved to be a great success for all concerned. After an initial trial period and some favorable media coverage, St. Elizabeth's now finds that it can schedule at least one party a week. It is training nurses to handle the leadership role to permit further expansion. Word of mouth is excellent, and the participants are obviously very pleased with the experience. They indicate that they not only learn a great deal of information, but they become much more comfortable talking with physicians and other health practitioners.

For their part, although many physicians (and others) were initially skeptical about the approach, they now see the parties as helping to train patients to be better partners in the health care process. More directly, physicians who have participated have found the parties to be good sources of new patients. Although the parties are explicitly designed not to encourage "doctor-switching," one participating doctor claims she now gets one new patient a week from the parties. A second physician is also seeing women from the parties, and a resident has received requests for her services once she enters private practice. Young physicians seem especially pleased with the opportunity for exposure that the parties provide.

St. Elizabeth's itself is very pleased with the program. The parties cost very little. Organization and leadership time as well as space and refreshments are donated. The brochures and invitations cost St. Elizabeth's very little, and much of the other literature is provided free by the American Cancer Society. An evaluative survey of 200 participants showed that 62 percent saw their doctor within a few months of the party, and 72 percent said they felt more comfortable and self-confident in talking with the physicians about their health problems. Thirty-four percent claimed they were now checking their breasts more than before the parties. Although only 38 percent had been to St. Elizabeth's before the parties, a recent monitoring check showed that up to four party participants were admitted to the hospital each month. The parties and the attendant publicity have been good for the institution's image. And, finally, information generated during the parties themselves has proven to consititute an excellent source of ideas for developing new programs.

St. Elizabeth's has found BodyCues™ so successful that they have copyrighted the name and materials and are beginning to promote the program to other hospitals nationally.

*Joan Thomas, "How a Hit Program Was Developed," *Healthcare Marketeer*, Vol. 1, No. 3 (March 1986), p. 1.

SOURCE: The St. Elizabeth Corporation, Dayton, Ohio, with permission.

It has been our experience that the marketing tool that nonprofit marketers are most often reluctant to employ vigorously is personal selling. This reticent posture seems to follow from two attitudes. First, nonprofit managers typically believe that their offering is inherently good and needs simply to be made available to be happily embraced by a grateful public. Second, they often believe that personal selling is synonymous with manipulation and is therefore unethical to a greater or lesser degree. This is less a problem when the selling situation involves an economic transaction such as occurs in museum gift shops. But, when it is suggested that the nonprofit's workers personally persuade people to donate to a charity, attend a college, or join a political party, library, or church, resistance to using a planned, vigorous approach is quite common.

Not only is personal selling resisted when clear opportunities exist for its use, it is often neglected in more general situations. The best-run for-profit service organizations and many retailers long ago recognized that *every time* a member of the organization and a member of a key public interact, there is an opportunity to further or weaken progress toward the organization's marketing goals. How often have our favorable feelings about a hospital been destroyed by the perfunctory attitude of the admissions officer! What nonprofit marketers have to recognize is that almost everyone in their organization is at one point or another a *boundary person*. Their personal communication style will affect the organization's success. It is better to manage these communications than just to let them happen.

In this chapter, we want to look at strategic management problems involving boundary personnel. These boundary personnel fall within two groups. The first are salespeople, whose job it is to actively influence the behavior of others. Major examples of such personnel are:

- *recruiters* (college recruiters, military recruiters, job recruiters)
- *fundraisers* (development officers, door-to-door callers, telephone solicitors)
- *change agents* (agricultural extension agents, outreach workers, family planners, community organizers)
- *vote-seekers* (politicians, lobbyists)

The second group consists of *service personnel,* those who provide the organization's services to members of the public. The group includes:

- *operators* (bus drivers, librarians, U.S. income tax advisors, ticket takers, museum guards)
- *protective personnel* (police officers, firefighters)
- *repair personnel*
- *receptionists*

Although the job of service personnel is service, they too should train to be client-oriented. In this chapter, however, we will concentrate on sales personnel and the problems of running an effective sales force.

PERSONAL SELLING

We shall use the term *personal selling* to refer to *all attempts at using personal influence to affect target audience behavior.* Personal selling is the most effective tool at certain stages of the consumer decision process, particularly in building up preference, conviction, and action on the part of buyers. This is because personal selling has three distinctive qualities in comparison to advertising:[1]

1. *Personal confrontation.* Personal selling involves a living, immediate, and interactive relationship between two or more persons. Each party is able to observe the others' needs and characteristics at close hand and make immediate adjustments.

2. *Cultivation.* Personal selling permits all kinds of relationships to spring up, ranging from a matter-of-fact selling relationship to a deep personal friendship. In most cases, the sales representative artfully woos the target audience. The sales representative is at times tempted to apply pressure to induce an action, but he or she normally keeps the customer's long-run interests at heart.

3. *Response.* Personal selling makes the target audience member feel under some obligation for having listened to the sales talk or for taking up the sales representative's time. He or she has a greater need to attend and respond, even if the response is a polite "thank you."

These distinctive qualities come at a cost. Personal selling is the organization's most expensive customer contact tool, costing organizations an average of $102 a sales call in 1984.[2] Even when the sales force consists of

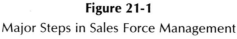

Figure 21-1

Major Steps in Sales Force Management

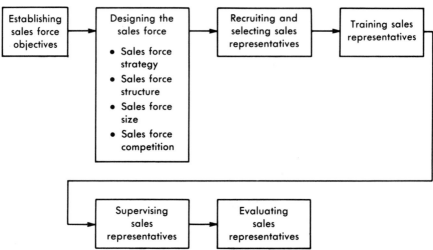

volunteers, there is a cost for recruiting, training, and motivating them, and their time should be used wisely.

We will examine the major decisions in building and managing an effective sales force as part of the total marketing mix. These steps are shown in Figure 21-1 and examined in the following sections.

ESTABLISHING SALES FORCE OBJECTIVES

Personal communication is part of the marketing mix, and as such is capable of achieving certain marketing objectives better than other tools in the marketing mix. Sales representatives can perform as many as six tasks for their organization:

1. *Prospecting.* Sales representatives can find and cultivate new customers.
2. *Communicating.* Sales representatives can communicate useful information about the organization.
3. *Selling.* Sales representatives can be effective in the art of "salesmanship"—approaching, presenting, answering objections, and inducing action.
4. *Servicing.* Sales representatives can provide various services to customers—counsulting on their problems, rendering technical assistance, and expediting service times.
5. *Information-gathering.* Sales representatives can supply the organization with useful market research and intelligence.
6. *Allocating.* Sales representatives can advise the organization on how to allocate scarce goods and services to customers in times of shortages.

The organization has to decide the relative importance of these different tasks and coach their sales representatives accordingly. College recruiters, for example, spend most of their time in prospecting, communicating, and selling. Lobbyists, on the other hand, tend to emphasize communicating, servicing, and information-gathering. Each organization normally gets its representatives to set spectific goals for each of their activities so that their performance against these goals can be measured.

DESIGNING THE SALES FORCE

Given the objectives, the organization has to make basic decisions on (1) sales force strategy, (2) sales force structure, (3) sales force size, and (4) sales force compensation.

SALES FORCE STRATEGY

Sales force strategy deals with determining how best to reach prospects and customers, given the marketing objectives. Suppose a social action program is seeking to increase its grants from the Ford Foundation. It wants to (1) "sell" the Ford Foundation on funding some immediate proposals, and (2) build up a stronger relationship with the Ford Foundation for the future. The program can use one or more of six sales force strategies to meet its objectives:

1. *Sales representative to buyer.* Here, a program officer talks to a Ford Foundation officer in person or over the telephone.
2. *Sales representative to buyer group.* Here, a program officer makes a sales presentation to a group of Ford Foundation executives.
3. *Sales team to buyer group.* Here, a team of people from the program (president, controller, researcher) makes a sales presentation to a group of Ford Foundation executives.
4. *Conference selling.* Here, a program officer arranges a meeting between people at the program center and Ford Foundation executives to discuss mutual problems and opportunities.
5. *Seminar selling.* Here, a team of experts from the program presents an educational seminar to Ford Foundation executives about recent state-of-the-art developments. The program provides the free seminar to improve relations with the foundation.
   We see that the sales representative does not always do the whole selling job. The sales representative may act as the "account manager" who initiates and facilitates interactions between various people in the two organizations. Selling is increasingly becoming a matter of teamwork, requiring the support of other personnel. *Top management* (such as the president) is increasingly getting involved in the sales process, especially when *major sales* are at stake. *Technical people* (such as researchers) often work with the sales representatives to supply expert information needed by the customer before, during, or after

the purchase. *Service representatives* provide information, clerical work, and other services to the customer.

6. *Telemarketing.* Telephone sales solicitation has become an increasingly successful personal selling technique in nonprofit marketing. It has the advantages of relatively low cost as compared to face-to-face selling, yet it provides the same opportunity to respond immediately to target audience concerns (for example, to the interests they show or the objections they raise). The development of automatic dialing systems, independently run telephone marketing services, and low-cost WATS calling systems has rapidly extended the potential and the range of telemarketing.

Two of the nonprofit categories in which telemarketing is used most extensively are the performing arts and fund-raising. In the arts, two examples of successful use were by the St. Paul Symphony Orchestra and the Old Globe Theatre in San Diego.

- The St. Paul Symphony had a subscription renewal rate of 50 percent in the 1980–81 season. By using telemarketing to contact those who hadn't resubscribed, the Symphony raised this rate to 68 percent in just two years. Two calls were used. One was made two weeks before the deadline for renewing subscriptions. On this occasion, nonsubscribers had the option to renew on the spot using a credit card, or if they said they needed more time, they were guaranteed their old seats for an extended two-week period after the deadline. A second last-chance call went to those who were still not responding one week before the season. St. Paul also used a 15,000-name prospect list derived from single-event purchasers and from lists of those attending other arts events in the area. Callers reached 8,000 to 10,000 of those on this list, producing 14 percent of new subscriptions in the 1982-83 season.[3]
- The Old Globe began contacting nonrenewers to its theatre season by telephone seven to ten working days after its new season mailer. Between October, 1982, and June, 1984, the Old Globe's telemarketing department was able to generate $750,000 in annual ticket sales and increase season ticket sales by 20,000. Most importantly, the Old Globe's marketing director claimed that the telemarketing program was *more cost-effective* than direct mail. He stated that it costs 15 percent of sales for telemarketing versus 30 percent for direct mail. This was due in part to the fact that the Old Globe only called those with a known interest in the theatre. They did not make cold calls or buy lists. The Old Globe found that telemarketing worked in part because it allowed nonrenewers to voice some of their concerns. Once they had gotten their gripes out of their systems, they were more predisposed toward renewing. Finally, through experimentation, the Old Globe staff found that volunteers were not as effective at telemarketing as were professional salespeople. They experimented with five professionals and five actors and found that the actors "could talk about the theatre but couldn't close the sale." The Old Globe now uses only professional salespeople.[4]

Like the Old Globe, once an organization has clarified the type of selling it needs, it must choose between using (1) paid employees, (2) volunteers, and (3) temporary paid help. All three may be used to advantage. Thus, Stanford University's Office of Development consists of a small employee staff of professional fundraisers who raise money directly; a very large group of alumni who volunteer their services in fundraising drives; and temporary help as needed to make phone calls, stuff envelopes, and so on.

SALES FORCE STRUCTURE

Part of sales force strategy is how to structure the organization's sales force to achieve maximum market coverage and effectiveness. This is relatively simple if the organization provides only one service to one type of customer who is found in many locations. The answer would be a territorial-structured sales force. If the organization sells many different services to many types of customers, it might have to develop product-structured or customer-structured sales forces. We shall review here these alternative sales force structures.

Territorial-structured Sales Force.   In the simplest sales organization, each sales representative is assigned a territory in which to sell the organization's services. Thus, the U.S. Army operates army recruiting stations in different cities, and each station is responsible for planning and attracting enlistments in its area. Likewise, the Easter Seal Society raises money through regional, state, and local organizations, each responsible for fundraising in its respective territory.

A territorially structured sales force has a number of advantages. First, it results in a very clear definition of the salesperson's responsibilities. As the only salesperson working the territory, he or she bears the credit or blame for area sales to the extent that personal selling effort makes a difference. This tends to encourage a high level of effort, especially when management is able to gauge fairly accurately the area's sales potential. Second, responsibility for a definite territory increases the sales representative's incentive to cultivate local customers and personal ties. These ties tend to improve the quality of the sales representatives selling effectiveness and personal life. Third, travel expenses are likely to be relatively small, since each sales representative's travel takes place within the bounds of a small geographical territory.

Along with this structure goes a hierarchy of sales management positions. Several territories will be supervised by a district sales manager, several districts will be supervised by a regional sales manager, and the several regions will be supervised by a national sales manager or sales vice-president. Each higher level sales manager takes on increasing marketing and administrative work in relation to the time available for selling. In fact, sales managers are paid for their management rather than selling skills.

Product-Structured Sales Force.   Organizations that produce a large number of products and services often prefer to organize the selling activity by product line. Harvard University, for example, allows each of its major schools—business, law, medicine, and so on—to do its own fundraising and and recruitment. Personnel within each school can do a good job of representing it to prospects and customers. Specialization of the sales force by product is warranted where the organization's products are technically complex, highly unrelated, numerous, or some combination of these.

The major disadvantage is that of higher travel costs and possible sales redundancy. Thus, instead of Harvard sending one development officer to the Ford Foundation to represent all of the proposals submitted by Harvard, several development officers from Harvard's different schools will converge on the Ford Foundation. Each will come with more knowledge of the relevant proposals at the cost of high sales force expense. At some point, higher level coordination of such activities is necessary.

Customer-Structured Sales Force.   Organizations often specialize their sales forces according to customer type. Cornell University fundraisers, for example, are specialized by donor category: foundations, corporations, government agencies, alumni, and wealthy donors. By working full-time to raise money from, say, corporations, the corporate fundraiser has a clear incentive to know as much as possible about them collectively and individually and to use his or her time more effectively. Furthermore, the person needed for this job may be recruited directly from the ranks of those to be influenced. The major disadvantage of customer-structured sales forces arises if the various types of customers are scattered evenly throughout the country. This means an overlapping coverage of territories, which is always more expensive.

Complex Sales Force Structures.   When an organization sells a wide variety of products to many types of customers over a broad geographical area, it often combines several principles of sales force structure. Thus, the University of Chicago has a fundraising staff with personnel specialized by territory, type of school, and type of donor. Each fundraiser has a line of dotted-line reporting relationship to the development office and various other parts of the university.

SALES FORCE SIZE

Once the organization clarifies its sales force strategy and structure, it is ready to consider the question of sales force size. Sales representatives are among the most productive and expensive assets in a company. Increasing their number increases both sales and costs.

Most organizations use the *workload approach* to establish the size of their sales force.[5] The method consists of the following steps:

1. Customers are grouped into segments according to their sales potential.
2. The desirable call levels (number of days on an account per year) are established for each segment. Both existing and *potential* sales levels are considered.

3. The number of accounts in each segment are multiplied by the corresponding call level to arrive at the total workload in sales calls per year.
4. The average number of call days a sales representative has per year is determined, allowing for other tasks, holidays, and so on.
5. The number of sales representatives needed is determined by dividing the total number of call days required by the average annual number of calls a sales representative can make.

To illustrate, suppose a college recruiting office determines that the recruitment target will require calling on 100 class A high schools, 80 class B high schools, and 40 class C high schools each year. To be effective, a recruiter will have to spend two days at a class A high school, one day at a class B high school, and one half day at a class C high school. Furthermore, each recruiter has only sixty days available per year. Thus, the high schools will require 300 call days (100 × 2 + 80 × 1 + 40 × ½), and the college will require a staff of five recruiters (300 ÷ 60).

In the case of college fundraising, a similar analysis can be undertaken. Given the campaign sales target and the potential of different donor groups, the college can figure out how many fundraisers it needs. Most colleges tend to hire too few fundraisers rather than too many; an additional competent fundraiser can usually add more money to the college's coffers than he or she costs.

SALES FORCE COMPENSATION

The sales force may comprise volunteers, as in many charities or other fundraising activities. Where paid sales representatives are to be used, the organization has to develop an attractive compensation plan. Sales representatives would like a plan that provides income regularity, reward for above-average performance, and fair payment for experience and longevity. An ideal compensation plan from management's point of view would emphasize control, economy, and simplicity.

Management must determine the level and components of an effective compensation plan. The *level of compensation* must bear some relation to the "going market price" for the type of sales job and type of organization. Nonprofit organizations tend to pay less than business firms, and this may result in attracting less skilled people and achieving lower results. Yet nonprofits feel that they can attract good people who are motivated by nonmonetary considerations and a belief in the value of their work. In the authors' judgment, this is usually a mistake. First, nonprofit salespersons who feel they are making a personal sacrifice to work for the organization may be less willing to take direction from management. They may be less efficient and may interfere with management's carefully engineered marketing strategy. Second, underpaid workers who "believe" in their cause may not have a customer-centered attitude. Because they "believe," they may feel that the customer should also believe, and they may be hostile to signs of customer reluctance. Well-paid professionals seldom have either of these problems.

The organization must also determine the *components of compensation*—a fixed amount, a variable amount, expenses, and fringe benefits. The *fixed amount,* which might be salary or a drawing account, is intended to satisfy the sales representatives' need for some stability of income. The *variable amount,* which might be commissions, bonuses, or sales contests, is intended to stimulate and reward greater effort. *Expense allowances* are intended to enable the sales representatives to undertake necessary selling costs, such as travel, taking prospects to lunch, and so on. And *fringe benefits* such as paid vacations, sickness or accident benefits, pensions, and life insurance, are intended to provide security and job satisfaction.

Fixed and variable compensation, taken alone, give rise to three basic types of sales force compensation plans—straight salary, straight commission, and combination salary and commission. In industry, most plans are combination salary and commission, with 70 percent going to salary. In nonprofit organizations, most salespeople are on straight salary. Army recruiters who are especially effective, for example, tend to be rewarded with badges and recognition rather than extra money.

In general, the more a compensation scheme is oriented toward salary over commission or bonus,

- the more management can ask the salesforce to do routine but necessary tasks like market research or prospecting that don't have an immediate payoff.
- the more the salesperson is likely to be farsighted in approaching customers, recognizing that missing a sale (and bonus) now may be desirable so as not to sour a good, building relationship.
- the more difficult it will be to judge performance.
- the less clear it will be to salespersons how they are doing, and the more management will have to develop alternative feedback systems.

RECRUITING AND SELECTING SALES REPRESENTATIVES

Having established the strategy, structure, size, and compensation of the sales force, the organization has to manage the steps of recruiting and selecting, training, supervising, and evaluating sales representatives.

IMPORTANCE OF CAREFUL SELECTION

At the heart of a successful sales force operation is the selection of effective sales representatives. The performance levels of an average and a top sales representative are quite different. A survey of over five hundred companies revealed that 27 percent of the sales force brought in over 52 percent of the sales.[6] Beyond the differences in sales productivity is the great wasted cost in hiring the wrong persons. Of the 16,000 sales representatives who were hired by the surveyed companies, only 68 percent still worked for their company at the end of the year, and only 50 percent were expected to remain through the following year.

The financial loss due to turnover is only part of the total cost. The new sales representative who remains with the organization receives a direct income averaging around half of the direct selling outlay. If he or she receives $25,000 a year, another $25,000 may go into fringe benefits, expenses for travel and entertainment, supervision, office space, supplies, and secretarial assistance. Consequently, the new sales representative should be capable of creating sales on which the amount left after other expenses at least covers the selling expenses of $50,000.

WHAT MAKES A GOOD SALES REPRESENTATIVE?

Selecting sales representatives would not be such a problem if one knew the characteristics of an ideal salesperson. If ideal salespersons are out-going, aggressive, and energetic, it would not be too difficult to check for these characteristics in applicants. But a review of the most successful sales representatives in any company is likely to reveal a good number who are introverted, mild-mannered, and far from energetic. The successful group will also include men and women who are tall and short, articulate and inar-ticulate, well-groomed and slovenly.

Nevertheless, the search for the magic combination of traits that spells surefire sales ability continues unabated. The number of lists that have been drawn up is countless. Most of them recite the same qualities. McMurry wrote:

> It is my conviction that the possessor of *effective* sales personality is *a habitual "wooer," an individual who has a compulsive need to win and hold the affection of others.* . . . His wooing, however, is not based on a sincere desire for love because, in my opinion, he is convinced at heart that no one will ever love him. Therefore, his wooing is primarily exploitative . . . his relationships tend to be transient, superficial and evanescent.[7]

McMurry went on to list five additional traits of the super salesperson: a high level of energy, abounding self-confidence, a chronic hunger for money, a well-established habit of industry, and a state of mind that regards each objection, resistance, or obstacle as a challenge.[8]

Mayer and Greenberg offered one of the shortest lists of traits exhib-ited by effective sales representatives.[9] Their seven years of fieldwork led them to conclude that the effective sales person has at least two basic qual-ities: (1) *empathy,* the ability to feel as the customer does, and (2) *ego drive,* a strong personal need to make the sale. Using these two traits, they were able to make fairly good predictions of the subsequent performance of applicants for sales positions in three different industries.

It may be true that certain basic traits may make a person effective in any line of selling. From the viewpoint of a particular organization, however, these basic traits are rarely enough. Each selling job is characterized by a unique set of duties and challenges. One only has to think about college recruiting, corporate fundraising, and congressional lobbying to realize the different educational, intellectual, and personality requirements that would be sought in the respective sales representatives.

How can an organization determine the characteristics that its prospective sales representatives should "ideally" possess? The particular duties of the job suggest some of the characteristics to look for in applicants. Is the job mostly order-taking, or must a lot of "influencing" be carried out? Is there a lot of paperwork? Does the job call for much travel? Will the salesperson confront a high proportion of refusals? Is creativity necessary? Will the sales person be closely supervised or be expected to use a lot of initiative? In addition, the traits of the company's most successful sales representatives suggest additional qualities to look for. Some organizations compare the standing of their best versus their poorest sales representatives to see which characteristics differentiate the two groups.

RECRUITMENT PROCEDURES

After management develops general criteria for its sales personnel, it has to attract a sufficient number of applicants. Recruiting is turned over to the personnel department, which seeks applicants through various means, including soliciting names from current sales representatives, using employment agencies, placing job ads, and contacting college students.

TRAINING SALES REPRESENTATIVES

Not too long ago many organizations sent their new salespeople into the field almost immediately after hiring them. Nowadays a new sales representative can expect to spend from a few days to a few months in training. Training has the following objectives:

1. The sales representative should know the organization's history and mission and identify with it.
2. The sales representative should know the organization's products.
3. The sales representative should know customers' and competitors' characteristics.
4. The sales representative should know how to make effective sales presentations.
5. The sales representative should know the organization's systems and procedures.

One of the major objectives of sales training programs is to train sales personnel in the art of selling. The sales training industry today involves expenditures of hundreds of millions of dollars in training programs, books, cassettes, and other materials. Almost a million copies of books on selling are purchased every year, bearing such provocative titles as *How to Outsell the Born Salesman, How to Sell Anything to Anybody, The Power of Enthusiastic Selling, How Power Selling Brought Me Success in 6 Hours, Where Do You Go From No. 1,* and *1000 Ways a Salesman Can Increase His Sales.* One of the most enduring books is Dale Carnegie's *How to Win Friends and Influence People.*

All of the sales training approaches are designed to convert a salesperson from being a passive *order taker* to a more active *order getter. Order takers* operate on the following assumptions: (1) customers are aware of their own needs, (2) they cannot be influenced or would resent any attempt at influence, and (3) they prefer salespersons who are courteous and self-effacing. An example of an order-taking mentality would be a college fundraiser who phones alumni and asks if they would like to give any money.

As we have noted, nonprofit salespeople are much more likely to be order takers, but order *getters* are needed. In training salespersons to be order getters, there are two basic approaches—a sales-oriented approach and a customer-oriented approach. The first one trains the salesperson to be adept in the use of *hard sell techniques* such as those used in selling encyclopedias or military service. The techniques include overstating the product's merits, criticizing competitive products, using a slick canned presentation, selling yourself, and offering some concession to make the sale on the spot. The assumptions behind this form of selling are that (1) the customers are not likely to buy except under pressure, (2) they are influenced by a slick presentation and ingratiating manners, and (3) they won't regret the purchase, or if they do, it doesn't matter.

The other approach attempts to train sales personnel in *customer need satisfaction.* Here the salesperson studies the customers' needs and wants and tailors a proposal to meet these needs. An example would be a museum fundraiser who senses that a wealthy shoe manufacturer has a strong ego and need for recognition as a supporter of the arts. The fundraiser could propose building and naming a new room at the art gallery after this person. The assumptions behind this approach are that (1) the customers have latent needs that constitute opportunities for the sales representative, (2) they appreciate good suggestions, and (3) they will be responsive to sales representatives who have their long-term interests at heart. Within a customer-oriented marketing framework, the need satisfier is certainly a more appropriate image for the salesperson than the image of the hard seller or order taker. It is also one with which nonprofit salespersons will feel comfortable.

FIGURE 21-2

Major Steps in Effective Selling

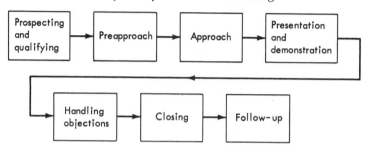

Most sales training programs view the selling process as consisting of a set of steps, each involving certain skills. These steps are shown in Figure 21-2 and discussed in the following sections.[10]

Prospecting and Qualifying.   The first step in the sales process is to identify prospects. A hospital fundraiser, for example, could obtain the names of wealthy people in the following ways: (1) asking current wealthy donors for the names of other potential donors, (2) asking friendly referral sources, such as lawyers, accountants, and bankers, (3) joining organizations such as country clubs, where there is a high probability of meeting wealthy people, (4) giving speeches or writing articles of interest to wealthy people that are likely to increase the salesperson's visibility, (5) examining various data sources (newspapers, directories) in search of names, and (6) using the telephone and mail to track down leads.

Sales representatives also need to know how to screen the leads to avoid wasting valuable time on poor leads. Prospects can be qualified by examining their financial ability, giving history, personality, and location. The salesperson may use the phone or mail to qualify the prospects further.

Preapproach.   This step involves the salesperson in learning as much as possible about each good prospect. The salesperson can consult reference sources, acquaintances, and others. The salesperson should determine *call objectives,* which may be to make an introduction, gather information, or make an immediate sale. Another task is to decide on the best *approach,* which might be a personal visit (possibly with a respected intermediary), phone call, or letter. The best *timing* should be thought out because many prospects are especially busy at certain times of the year. Finally, the salesperson should give thought to an *overall strategy* to use in the approach stage.

Approach.   This stage involves the salesperson knowing how to meet and greet the prospect to get the relationship off to a good start. It consists of how the salesperson looks, opening lines, and follow-up remarks. The salesperson's looks include his or her appearance, manner, and mannerisms. The salesperson is encouraged to wear clothes similar to what the prospect usually wears, such as an open shirt and no tie in Texas; to show courtesy and attention to the prospect; and to avoid distracting mannerisms such as pacing the floor or staring. In general, it has been found that the more like the prospect the change agent is perceived to be, the more effective he or she will be. The opening line should be positive, pleasant, and start with the *customer's* interests, such as, "Mr. Smith, I am Bill Jones from St. Luke's Hospital. My hospital and I appreciate your willingness to see me. I will be brief and do my best to make this visit worthwhile to you."

Presentation and Demonstration.   After this introduction, the salesperson can make a brief statement about the organization and the purpose of the call. The salesperson will follow the AIDA formula: get *attention,* hold *interest,* arouse *desire,* and obtain *action.*

There are three contrasting styles of sales presentation. The oldest is the *canned approach,* which is a memorized sales talk covering the main points deemed important by the organization. It is based on stimulus-response thinking, which assumes that the buyer is passive and can be moved to purchase by the use of the right stimulus words, pictures, terms, and actions. Thus, a museum fundraiser might describe the museum's capital campaign as a "once-in-a-lifetime giving opportunity" and show some beautiful four-color pages of pictures on the present collection, hoping that these will trigger an irresistible desire for giving on the part of the prospect. Canned presentations are used primarily in door-to-door and telephone canvassing and have been pretty much abandoned by other organizations in favor of more flexible approaches.

The *formulated approach* is also based on stimulus-response thinking, but it attempts to draw the prospect into the discussion in a way that will indicate the prospect's needs and attitudes. As these are discovered, the salesperson moves into a formulated presentation that is appropriate to that prospect and shows how the transaction will satisfy that particular prospect's needs. It is not canned but follows a previously thought-out plan.

The *need satisfaction approach* does not start with a prepared presentation designed to sell the prospect, but with a search for the prospect's real needs. The prospect is encouraged to do most of the talking so that the salesperson can really grasp the prospect's real needs and respond accordingly. This is the most customer-centered approach, but it calls for good listening and problem-solving skills.

Sales presentations can be improved considerably with various demonstration aids, such as booklets, flip-charts, slides, movies, and samples. To the extent that the prospect can participate by seeing or handling the offer, he or she will better remember its features and benefits.

Handling Objections.   Prospects almost always pose objections during the presentation or when asked to sign up. Their sales resistance could take a psychological or logical form. *Psychological resistance* can include[11] (1) resistance to interference, (2) preference for established habits, (3) apathy, (4) reluctance to giving up something, (5) unpleasant associations with the other person, (6) tendency to resist domination, (7) predetermined ideas, (8) dislike of making decisions, and (9) neurotic attitude toward money. *Logical resistance* might consist of objections to the terms or organization of the proposal. To handle these objections, the salesperson uses such techniques as maintaining a positive approach, trying to have the prospect clarify and define the objections, questioning the prospect in such a way that the prospect has to answer his or her own objections, denying the validity of the objections, and turning the objection into a reason for buying. The salesperson needs training in the broader skills of negotiation, of which handling objections is a part.[12]

Closing.   In this stage, the salesperson attempts to induce action. Some salespeople never get to this stage or do not do it well. They lack confidence in themselves, their organization, or their product; they feel guilty about asking for the action; or they do not recognize the right psychological moment to ask for action. Salespersons have to be trained in recognizing specific closing signals from the prospect, including physical actions, statements or comments, and questions signaling a possible readiness to close. Salespersons can then use one of several closing techniques. They can ask the prospect to act; recapitulate the points of agreement; offer to help write up an agreement; ask whether the prospect wants A or B; get the prospect to make minor choices among possible variations; or indicate what the prospect will lose if the transaction is not completed now. The salesperson may offer the prospect specific inducements to close, such as a concession or gift item.

Follow-up.   This last stage is necessary if the salesperson wants to assure customer satisfaction and repeat business. Immediately after closing, the salesperson should attempt to complete any necessary details. The salesperson should consider scheduling a follow-up call to make sure everything has gone smoothly. This call is designed to detect any problems, to assure the buyer of the salesman's interest and service, and to reduce any cognitive dissonance that might have arisen.

Indeed, dissonance theory suggests that the postdecision phase is the time during which customers most actively seek information to justify their choices. This is especially true under two conditions: (1) the choice was personally involving for the decision-maker, and (2) the alternatives under consideration were quite similar.

SUPERVISING SALES REPRESENTATIVES

The new sales representative is given more than an assignment, a compensation package, and training—he or she is given supervision. Supervision is the fate of everyone who works for someone else. It is the expression of the employers' natural and continuous interest in the activities of their agents. Through supervision, employers hope to direct and motivate the sales force to do a better job.

DIRECTING SALES REPRESENTATIVES

Organizations undertake a number of activities to improve their sales representatives' performances:

Developing Customer and Prospect Call Levels.   Many organizations classify their customers into account types, such as A, B, and C, reflecting present sales and the growth potential of the different accounts. Army recruiters, for example, may classify different high schools into these groups. They establish a certain desired call level per period that their recruiters should make to each account type. The call levels that are set depend upon competitive call norms and expected account responses.

Organizations also like to specify how much time to spend prospecting for new accounts. Organizations like to set a minimum requirement for the canvassing of new accounts because salespeople, if left alone, spend most of their time with current customers, especially if they are rewarded mainly by the number of sales achieved in the current period. Current customers are better-known quantities. The sales representatives can depend upon them for some business, whereas a prospect may never deliver any business or deliver it only after many months of effort.

Using Sales Time Efficiently.   The sales representatives should know how to schedule planned sales calls and use their time efficiently. One tool is the preparation of an *annual call schedule,* showing which customers and prospects to call on in which months and which ancillary activities to carry out. The other tool is *time-and-duty analysis* to determine how to use sales call time more efficiently. The sales representative's time is spent in the following ways:

1. *Travel.* Travel time is the time spent in travel between rising in the morning and arriving at lodgings in the evening. It can amount in some jobs to as much as 50 percent of total time. Travel time can be cut down by substituting faster for slower means of transportation, recognizing, however, that this will increase costs. More organizations are encouraging air travel for their sales force in order to increase their ratio of selling to total time.

2. *Food and breaks.* Some portion of the sales force's workday is spent in eating and breaks. If this involves dining with a prospect, it will be classified as selling time, otherwise, as food and breaks.

3. *Waiting.* Waiting consists of time spent in the outer office of the prospect. This is dead time unless the sales representative uses it to plan or fill out reports.

4. *Selling.* Selling is the time spent with the prospect in person or on the

phone. It breaks down into "social talk," which is the time spent discussing other things, and "selling talk," which is the time spent on the offer.

5. *Administration.* This is a miscellaneous category consisting of the time spent in report writing, attending sales meetings, and talking to other departments in the organization.

No wonder actual selling time may amount in some companies to as little as 15 percent of total working time! If it could be raised from 15 percent to 20 percent, this would be a 33 percent improvement. Organizations are constantly seeking ways to help their sales representatives use their time more efficiently. This takes the form of training them in the effective use of the telephone ("phone power"), simplifying the record-keeping forms, using the computer to develop call and routing plans, and supplying them with marketing research information on the prospect or customer.

Motivating Sales Representatives

A small percentage of sales representatives in any sales force can be expected to do their best without any special prompting from management. To them, selling is the most fascinating job in the world. They are ambitious and self-starters. But the majority of sales representatives on nearly every sales force require personal encouragement and special incentives to work at their best level. This is especially true for creative field selling, for the following reasons:

1. *The nature of the job.* The selling job is one of frequent frustration. Sales representatives usually work alone, the hours are irregular, and they are often away from home. They confront aggressive competing sales representatives; they have an inferior status relative to the buyer; they often do not have the authority to do what is necessary to win an account; they lose important sales that they have worked hard to obtain. They often feel that a lost sale is really a case of personal rejection.

2. *Human nature.* Most people operate below capacity in the absence of special incentives. They won't "kill themselves" without some prospect of financial gain or social recognition.

3. *Personal problems.* The sales representative, like everyone else, is occasionally preoccupied with personal problems, such as sickness in the family, marital discord, or debt.

Management can affect the morale and performance of the sales force through its organizational climate, sales quotas, and positive incentives.

Organizational Climate. Organizational climate describes the feeling that the sales force gets from their organization regarding their opportunities, value, and rewards for a good performance. Some organizations treat their recruiters, fund-raisers, and others as being of minor importance. Others treat them as highly critical to the organization's success. The company's attitude toward its sales representatives acts as a self-fulfilling prophecy. If they are held in low esteem, there is much turnover and poor performance; if they are held in high esteem, there is less turnover and high performance.

The quality of personal treatment from the sales representative's immediate superior is an important aspect of the organizational climate. An effective sales manager keeps in touch with the members of the sales force through regular correspondence and phone calls, personal visits in the field, and evaluation sessions at headquarters. At different times the sales manager is the sales representative's boss, companion, coach, and confessor.

Sales Quotas.   Many organizations set sales quotas for their sales representatives specifying sales objectives for the period. Thus, a U.S. Navy recruiter is expected to produce five enlistees each month. Sales quotas are developed in the process of developing the annual marketing plan. The organization first decides on a sales forecast that is reasonably achievable. This becomes the basis of planning production, work force size, and financial requirements. Then management establishes sales quotas for all of its regions and territories, which typically add up to more than the sales forecast. Sales quotas are set higher than the sales forecast in order to stretch the sales managers and salespeople to their best effort. If they fail to make their quotas, the organization nevertheless may make its sales forecast.

Each sales manager takes the assigned quota and divides it among the sales representatives. Actually, there are three schools of thought on quota setting. The *high-quota school* sets quotas that are above what most sales representatives will achieve but that are possible for all. They are of the opinion that high quotas spur extra effort. The *modest-quota school* sets quotas that a majority of the sales force can achieve. They feel that the sales force will accept the quotas as fair, attain them, and gain confidence from attaining them. Finally, the *variable-quota school* thinks that individual differences among sales representatives warrant high quotas for some, modest quotas for others.

In all cases, care must be taken that quotas are never set at unrealistic levels. This can lead to counterproductive, sometimes unethical behavior just to meet the quota. Several years ago, military recruiters faced with poorly qualified candidates but high quotas bent the test requirements, or in some cases helped recruits fill in answers.

Positive Incentives.   Organizations use a number of positive motivators to stimulate sales force effort. Periodic *sales meetings* provide a social occasion, a break from routine, a chance to meet and talk with the organization's leaders, a chance to air feelings and to identify with a larger group. Organizations also sponsor *sales contests,* with the best performers winning a product or a trip somewhere. Indeed, an entire industry has grown up in recent years whose goal it is to provide organizations with creative and attractive special employee incentive schemes.

EVALUATING SALES REPRESENTATIVES

We have been describing the *feedforward* aspects of sales supervision—the efforts of management to communicate to the sales representatives what they should be doing and to motivate them to do it. But good feedforward requires good feedback. And good feedback means getting regular information from and about sales representatives to evaluate their performance.

Sources of Information

Management gains information about its sales representatives in a number of ways. Probably the most important source of information is the sales representative's periodic reports. Additional information comes through personal observation, through customers' letters and complaints, and through conversations with other sales representatives.

Much of this information can now be computerized by issuing portable personal computers to salespeople, and sales and expense data can be recorded on desk top PCs in central offices. Those data bases can then be analyzed by imaginative salespeople with only limited training. It has been the experience of many organizations that once salespeople discover that they can use all of the day-to-day data that management insists they record, the reporting task changes from a resented imposition to a task eagerly carried out for the benefits it can give the *salesperson* as well as management.

Formal Evaluation of Performance

The sales force's reports, along with other reports from the field and the manager's personal observations, supply the raw materials for formally evaluating members of the sales force. Formal evaluation procedures lead to at least three benefits. First, they lead management to develop specific and uniform standards for judging sales performance. Second, they lead management to draw together all its information and impressions about individual sales representatives and make more systematic, point-by-point evaluations. Third, they tend to have a constructive effect on the performance of sales representatives. The constructive effect comes about because the sales representatives know that they will have to sit down one morning with the sales manager and explain certain facets of their routing or sales call decisions or their failure to secure or maintain certain accounts.

Salesperson-to-Salesperson Comparisons. One type of evaluation frequently made is to compare and rank the sales performance of the various sales representatives. Such comparisons, however, must be done with care. Relative sales performances are meaningful only if there are no variations among sales assignments in market potential, workload, degree of competition, promotional effort, and so forth. Furthermore, sales are not the only measure of achievement. Management should be interested in how much each sales representative contributed to net surplus. And this cannot be known until the sales representatives' sales mix and sales expenses are examined. A possible ranking criterion would be the sales representative's *actual contribution to surplus as a ratio to his or her estimated potential surplus.* A ratio of 1.00 would mean that the sales representative delivered the potential sales in his or her market segment. The lower a sales representative's ratio, the more supervision and counseling he or she needs.

Current-to-Past-Sales Comparisons.   A second common type of evaluation is to compare a sales representative's current performance with past performance. Each salesperson is expected to improve along certain lines, such as producing more sales, bringing down costs, opening new accounts, and so on. His or her progress can be measured and a judgment made about whether there is enough improvement, and if not, what the problem is.

Qualitative Evaluation of Sales Representatives.   The evaluation usually extends to the salesperson's knowledge of the organization, products, customers, competitors, territory, and responsibilities. Personality characteristics can be rated, such as general manner, appearance, speech, and temperament. The sales manager can also consider any problems in motivation or compliance. Since an almost endless number of qualitative factors might be included, each company must decide which will contribute most to organizational performance. Then, these factors should be objectified as much as possible and routinely fed back to the salesperson. Only when they know the criteria against which they are to be judged can salespeople make efforts to improve in the ways that management wishes.

SUMMARY

Many organizations utilize sales representatives and assign them a pivotal role in the creation of sales. The high cost of the sales resource calls for effective sales management, consisting of six steps: (1) establishing sales force objectives, (2) designing sales force strategy, structure, size, and compensation, (3) recruiting and selecting, (4) training, (5) supervising, and (6) evaluating.

As an element of the marketing mix, the sales force is capable of achieving certain marketing objectives effectively. The organization has to decide on the proper mix of the following sales activities: prospecting, communicating, selling and servicing, information gathering, and allocating.

Given the sales force objectives, the sales force is then designed to answer the question of what sales force strategy would be most effective (individual selling, team selling, etc.), what type of sales force structure would work best (territorial-, product-, or customer-structured), how large a sales force is needed, and how the sales force should be compensated.

Sales representatives must be recruited and selected carefully to avoid the high costs of hiring the wrong persons. Their training should familiarize them with the organization's history, products and policies, customer and competitor characteristics, and the art of selling. The art of selling itself calls for training in a seven-step sales process: prospecting and qualifying, preapproach, approach, presentation and demonstration, handling objections, closing, and follow-up. The salesperson needs supervision and continuous encouragement because he or she must make a large number of decisions and is subject to many frustrations. Periodically, the person's performance must be formally evaluated to help him or her do a better job.

QUESTIONS

1. Assume you are a fraternity president seeking to persuade members to sign up for a blood drive. What would be the advantages of using a sales team, telemarketing, or seminar-selling approach to this task?

2. List all of the boundary personnel in a hospital and, for each, indicate at least one personal selling technique in which they could be trained in order to improve hospital "sales."

3. The U.S. Army uses a territorially structured sales force. What would (a) a customer-structured sales force or (b) a product-structured sales force for the Army look like, and what advantages would each have?

4. A charity is considering paying a modest commission to the volunteers it recruits to solicit contributions, since the volunteers are the very same poor people the charity benefits and they could use the money. Is this a good idea? If they went ahead, are there dangers they should guard against?

5. Design a seminar-selling presentation for the fraternity president in question 1 using the principles of effective salesmanship described in this chapter.

NOTES

1. See Sidney J. Levy, *Promotional Behavior* (Glenview, Ill.: Scott, Foresman, 1971), pp. 65–69.

2. *Sales and Marketing Management 1985 Survey of Selling Costs,* Vol. 134, No. 3, February 18, 1985, p. 33.

3. "The Trend Toward Telemarketing," *The Cultural Post,* VIII, No. 7, March-April 1983, p. 13.

4. Kevin Higgins, "Theatre Groups Discovering the Power of Telemarketing," *Marketing News,* June 22, 1984, p. 1.

5. Walter J. Talley, "How to Design Sales Territories," *Journal of Marketing,* January 1961, pp. 7–13.

6. The survey was conducted by the Sales Executives Club of New York and was reported in *Business Week,* February 1, 1964, p. 52.

7. Robert N. McMurry, "The Mystique of Super-Salesmanship," *Harvard Business Review,* March-April 1961, p. 117.

8. *Ibid.,* p. 118.

9. David Mayer and Herbert M. Greenberg, "What Makes a Good Salesman?" *Harvard Business Review,* July-August 1964, pp. 119–125.

10. The following discussion is drawn in part from W. J. E. Crissy, William H. Cunningham, and Isabella C. M. Cunningham, *Selling: The Personal Force in Marketing* (New York: John Wiley, 1977), pp. 119–129.

11. *Ibid.,* pp. 289–294.

12. See Gerald I. Nierenberg, *The Art of Negotiation* (New York: Hawthorn Books, 1968); and Chester L. Karrass, *The Negotiating Game* (Cleveland: World, 1970).

Marketing Evaluation and Control

Of all the issues facing the U.S. Army in the next decade, none is as nettlesome as the looming demographic black hole.

Having studied the market as thoroughly as any sales force in America, the Army knows that the number of U.S. males aged seventeen to twenty-one will drop from 10.4 million in 1983 to 9.2 million in 1990. After culling out high school dropouts, college students, and those unqualified physically or morally, the Pentagon will be left at decade's end with a target group of 1.3 million to divvy up between the four armed services and nonmilitary employers.

Despite the best recruiting year ever in 1984, there are darker portents, including a sharp drop in the number of recruits signed up in the Army's delayed entry program in 1985. Among the strategies now contemplated to overcome the shortfall is an intensified appeal to older recruits, junior college graduates, and college dropouts.

The Army also has an advertising agency in San Antonio churning out recruiting pitches in Spanish, aimed in part at the parents and priests of potential Hispanic volunteers. Although Hispanics are the fastest-growing segment of the U.S. population, they make up only 4 percent of the Army, roughly half their proportion of the nation's population.

★   ★   ★

Ray Hessler hailed from a North Florida family of fourteen, poor enough to smash the water meter in an effort to forestall the bill collector. He joined the Army eleven years ago for the proffered $1,500 bonus—enough of a grubstake to get married—and made a living jumping out of airplanes. When he arrived as the sole Army representative in the DeLand, Florida, recruiting office, he found file cabinets crammed with old C rations, recruiting brochures from the 1960s, and a parachute. He painted the walls and posted the recruiter's code of ethics, which reminded him in bold type that his failure "could place in danger the American way of life and the sacred cause of human freedom."

He resisted emulating the Marine office in nearby Daytona, where a sign urges recruits to "give a communist the gift that lasts—death." In the main, he went by the book. He scoped out the high school like an infantry scout reconnoitering an enemy bunker. He made regular entries in a monthly log, such as this notation for July 1983: "July was a bad month to go out to the high school. The school had a shakedown in the chain of command. Too much going on as far as drugs [among students] and other uncanny things. The principal down to the teachers are being relieved."

He kept a "smart board," a detailed map of the 365 square miles in his recruiting district. Each recruit was charted by zip code with appropriately colored dots: purple for females, green for males in a high mental category, green with an X for dumber males. And once a month he phoned headquarters with his "enemy report," a summary of what the other three services were doing to recruit in DeLand.

Some volunteers were lured with cash, including college funds of $10,000 or more. Others were wooed with a thick list of Army job openings—362 military occupational specialties (MOSs) for men, 301 for women—such as 19 Delta (cavalry scout), 55 Golf (nuclear weapons maintenance specialist), 71 Quebec (journalist), or 57 Foxtrot (graves registration specialist).

From Army surveys, Hessler knew that nearly half of Army enlistments come from those who once had said they were disinclined to join the service. Thus, he took to heart the recruiters' unspoken motto: "Don't take no for an answer." For those who assented he kept $20,000 in Greyhound bus tickets locked in the desk for trips to the military processing station in Jacksonville. Behind it all, there was the endless paperwork and the bromide that for any task there was the right way, the wrong way, and the Army way.

At the end of every month, Hessler had met or exceeded his quota. But at the beginning of each subsequent month there was a new quota. Failure meant a black smudge on the record and potential career damage. Even in the golden age of recruiting, the pressure from higher authority was unremitting, as in the message last year for the brigade colonel: if a recruiter "fails to achieve mission," the message warned, "then the station commander will use the Recruiter Evaluation Checklist (USAREC Form 661) to identify the recruiter's deficiencies and conduct hands-on training to correct them. . . . Good judgment dictates the retention of quality recruiters and the elimination of those who do not measure up to acceptable standards. We must work hard to make every recruiter a winner."

Eventually, Hessler felt his life begin to unravel. His wife left him for eight months, fed up with his sixteen-hour workdays and the pressure from a company commander who seemed to endorse the old adage that "if the Army wanted you to have a wife they would have issued you one." Last April, unnerved by the emotional collapse of his recruiting buddy, who threatened to shoot the captain, Hessler decided to return to his earlier career in a dental clinic when his tour ended in the summer.

"They've got a good product, but I don't believe they need to put it in a pressure cooker. Now we're starting to fall short [of the quotas] and the pressure's starting to really come back," he said. "We will have another 1978 [a repeat of the pressure-induced recruiting scandals]. I don't know when. It may be five or ten years down the road, but it's coming."

SOURCE: Adapted from "Sgt. Hessler Markets the Army," *The Washington Post,* December 10, 1984, pp. A1, ff. Reproduced with permission.

Strategic planning in marketing is crucial in setting the nonprofit organization off in the proper direction, whether for a year's activities or for an entirely new venture. But pushing an enterprise into the stream of competition by no means assures that it will either get to its desired goal or get there as quickly and efficiently as possible. To assure that strategic marketing achieves its goals in a timely and efficient manner, the nonprofit manager must develop and put in place effective control systems for strategic plans and, where necessary, take corrective action.

In this chapter, we will distinguish between two kinds of assessments the nonprofit marketer will wish to put in place. First, there is a need for more or less continual monitoring of program performance for purposes of day-to-day fine-tuning of the strategic plan to correct for undesirable performance. We shall call such regular monitoring and corrective action *marketing control.* We shall investigate several considerations in designing marketing control systems and look at several measures that could be included for specific institutions. In particular, we shall look at the problem of measuring customer satisfaction, since this is (or ought to be) the primary goal of most nonprofits and since more obvious measures like sales may not be relevant or available. We shall also look at the concept of image-tracking as a technique for monitoring the nonprofit organization's progress in the eyes of other publics whose interests it also serves.

A second form of strategic adjustment involves periodic assessment of various aspects of the organization's performance. Since these assessments are not performed on a regular timetable, we shall describe them as *strategic evaluations*. We shall specifically discuss a tool increasingly used by non-profit organizations, the *marketing audit*.

We shall conclude the chapter by describing how to put in place a comprehensive *marketing information system* designed to acquire the necessary control information and make it available to management in a usable fashion.

MARKETING CONTROL

The purpose of marketing control is to maximize the probability that the organization will achieve its short-run and long-run objectives in the marketplace. Many surprises are likely to occur during the plan's execution that will call for new responses or adjustments. Marketing control systems are an intrinsic part of the marketing planning process since they permit such crucial and timely adjustments.

As indicated in Figure 22-1, the control process is in reality a cybernetic system that will ideally function not unlike a thermostat regulating a building's temperature. Management sets a goal (the desired temperature) and puts in place a device or system for detecting deviations from the goal (a thermometer) and ascertaining causes of the deviations (above or below ideal temperature because the space has warmed or cooled). The loop in the system is then closed by a device or subsystem that makes the necessary corrections (a trip-switch that restarts the furnace or turns on the air conditioning). Control systems in nonprofit organizations, of course, can differ greatly in complexity, timeliness, and precision. A library can simply monitor its total circulation and periodically smooth out irregularities or stimulate increased book usage through radio ads, newspaper articles, or direct mail. Or it can look periodically at the circulation of each of its departments during different parts of the day or week and seek corrective actions that would boost lagging departments or increase patronage in particular depart-

FIGURE 22-1

The Control Process

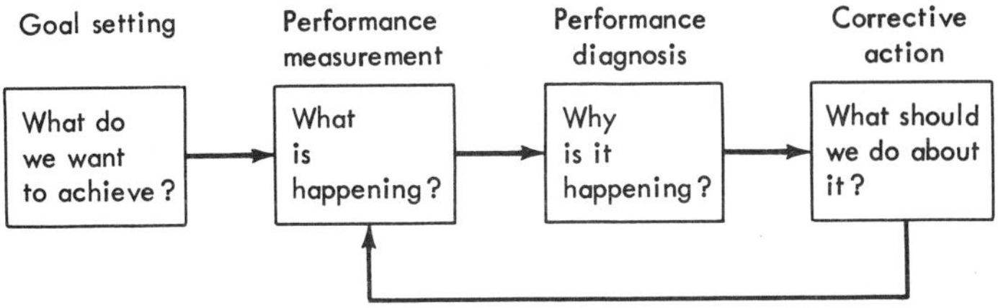

ments during off-peak hours or days. At a more complex level, it could attempt to look, not just at circulation, but at *who* was taking out books and develop control procedures that would, say, bring the number of elderly or teenagers coming to the library up to goal levels.

Control systems can also vary as to timeliness. The library can measure its performance daily, weekly, monthly, quarterly, or even annually. Obviously, the faster an organization's environment changes and the more competitive activity that takes place, the more frequently the system should be "read." Thus, libraries can get by with relatively infrequent measures compared to hospitals in major urban centers. In very volatile situations, daily monitoring may be necessary.

TYPES OF CONTROL TOOLS

Setting in place a control system like that described in Figure 22-1 is called *management by objectives.* Top management starts the process by developing the "sales," "profit," and other aggregate goals for the planning period. These goals are broken down into subgoals for lower levels of management. During the relevant period, managers receive reports that allow them to follow whether their subordinates are reaching their goals, and if they are not, to take the necessary corrective actions.

What are the control tools used by management to check on the progress of their subordinates in reaching their goals? In nonprofit organizations that have some sort of sales objective, the three main control tools are sales analysis, market-share analysis, and marketing expense-to-sales analysis. The first two measures assess effectiveness, the latter efficiency. For nonprofits without sales or revenue outcomes, other measures are necessary.

Sales Analysis.   *Sales analysis* is the effort to measure and evaluate the actual sales being achieved in relation to the sales goals set for different managers. Thus, the management of a concert hall would compare actual to expected sales of tickets by season, audience type, specific performance, and so on, to understand audience behavior and preferences. If too few students are attending the concert series, if certain areas of the city are underrepresented, or if a certain type of music is not well attended, the reasons should be sought out. Management should avoid jumping to conclusions without some research. Too few students attending the Performing Arts Series could be due to any number of causes: (1) high ticket prices, (2) low interest in this season's performers, (3) many competing social events on the same nights, (4) increased academic pressure for grades, and so on. The proper corrective actions would vary with each cause.

Many nonprofits use sales or attendance figures as a key measure of effectiveness. There are good reasons for this. First, strategic decisions about allocating resources are often made in terms of sales figures. Assuming that sales is a good measure of consumer interest in particular offerings, then more effort should be expended on programs that are in high demand or are growing. Thus, sales data would help in assessing activities involving specific good and services, such as museum gift shops, Sierra Club book and calendar marketing and so on. Second, sales figures are politically appealing. Nonprofits must typically market their programs to customers and to other diverse publics. Among the latter, regulators, oversight committees, and even donors will find sales figures easy to understand. If they are high or growing, the activity they reflect will be thought deserving of continued or increased support and perhaps reduced outside interference. Mass transit systems that serve more citizens (for example, more voters) are likely to be well rewarded and actively praised. Obviously, systems with declining sales usually find themselves with reduced budgets and more outside meddling in their day-to-day management.

The "objectivity" of sales data also minimizes charges of bias by groups or factions who might otherwise argue that their constituencies are being slighted. Social service agency directors need only point to usage data to show who is or is not using the organization's offerings and therefore deserving of attention and funding. Finally, there is the "default argument." It is suggested that most alternative methods of assessing nonprofit performance (like those suggested below) are fraught with measurement problems and possible biases. Isn't it safer, then, to measure sales or attendance than something as amorphous and subjective as customer satisfaction?

There are, however, a number of problems with "sales" or usage data. Where no cash changes hands, for example, "sales" measures may be subject to bias. That is, if measurement of park attendance is left to staff members, they may make subjective judgments that favor their own performance. Even where mechanical devices are used, like hand-held counters, turnstiles, or traffic electronic eyes, unethical staff members can manipulate results by turning equipment off and on at will or tripping the system to count themselves as often as is necessary to achieve desired figures.

A more difficult problem is whether attendance or sales is a true measure of organization performance. Assume for the moment that more attendance is sought by an organization. Those who attend may be those who have already been marketed to, or, more likely, who don't need marketing to at all. For many programs to be really successful, nonprofit marketers need to reach those who are *not* attending or *not* buying the offering. And if past resource allocations have been based on sales, the cycle will be self-reinforcing: those who attend will be allocated more marketing effort, which gets more of them to attend. At the same time, budgets and possibly interest are shifted away from other groups who may be no less interested but who come to be ignored as a result of a fixation on past sales as a control measure. Sales will look good, but this scenario suggests that management is really misallocating its effort and wasting scarce resources.

A related problem is that past sales to individuals may not be a good predictor of future sales to the same individuals. An institution can survive for a long time and even grow if it keeps attracting new "triers." But if it gets few repeat sales, its long-term prospects are bleak indeed. This is why many of the more sophisticated profit-centered organizations monitor *repeat* sales or, more frequently, attempt to directly assess customer attitudes or satisfaction with the offering.

Even more compelling is the criticism that sales may not be—ought not to be—the organization's ultimate goal. For example, museum or art gallery attendance is, indeed, important. But many museum directors might reasonably argue that simply processing "bodies" through the institution is not enough. It is the *quality* of the experience that is important. Busing hundreds of disadvantaged kids to a violin concert may increase an organization's "body count," but may well have little or no lasting effect on the "bodies" themselves, and indeed might create a negative image of concerts. Such a criticism would seem to be equally valid for the performing arts, recreation sites, and even libraries and educational institutions. In such cases, there is a very real danger that sales or attendance figures, because of their "objectivity" and ready accessibility, may simply substitute for what the nonprofit should *really* be striving for.

Finally, many nonprofit marketing programs simply do not have easily measured sales or attendance figures. We said earlier that the goal of nonprofit programs is ultimately to affect behavior. Thus, in theory, one ought to be able to develop a measure of that behavior. Unfortunately, in practice this may be very difficult to do, for three reasons. First, the behavior may be personal and private and very difficult to "observe" objectively. An obvious example of private behavior would be families' birth control practices. One can measure *contraceptive* sales, but major assumptions must be made to translate these into estimates of family planning behavior. Second, the behavior may involve a lifelong change that is economically impossible to track. Such would be the case for high-blood-pressure medication, which in most cases must be taken for the rest of a sufferer's life. Finally, there are cases in which the impact of a marketing program may stretch over a long period and even then may be difficult to trace to the marketer's strategies. Thus, an antismoking campaign designed to acquaint smokers with quitting techniques may help break down a smoker's lack of confidence in his or her ability to quit. Then, later—perhaps months or years later—he or she may be encouraged by a friend to enter a quitting program that is only partly effective. Still later, a physician may offer a warning about a worsening heart, a child may nag, and a favorite TV star may mention that he or she has quit. This combination finally leads to permanent quitting. Clearly, for a nonprofit manager to effectively manage strategies aimed at this ultimate behavior, some other interim measure must be attempted.

Market Share.   Organizations should periodically review whether they are gaining or losing ground relative to their competition. Zoo attendance continues to rise for many zoos, for example, yet zoos are declining in their share of the recreational dollar. They are losing ground relative to theme parks such as Disneyworld and Great America. The Chicago Lung Association continues to raise more money each year but is slipping in its share of the total medical charity dollar and also in relation to specific competitors such as the American Heart Association and the American Cancer Society Market share is a much better indicator of marketing effectiveness than total sales. It must, however, be used cautiously. The organization must correctly identify its real competitors. Beloit College, for example, should not measure its enrollment performance against the large state universities or the elite private universities. Instead, it should measure its enrollment performance against the other colleges to which Beloit applicants also apply. A "perfect competitor" would be another college that students applying to Beloit see as equally desirable.

Marketing Expense-to-Sales Analysis.   Annual plan control also requires checking on various marketing expenses as a ratio to sales to make sure that the organization is not overspending to achieve its sales goals. The ratios to watch are *total marketing expense-to-sales, sales force expense-to-sales, advertising-to-sales, sales promotion-to-sales, marketing research-to-sales,* and *sales administration-to-sales.* The organization should continuously check whether these ratios are appropriate and whether shifting from one marketing tool to another could bring down its total cost of sales. Management has to keep an eye on other performance ratios that say something about the efficiency of marketing effort. An experienced fundraising director, for example, periodically checks the following ratios: revenue per fundraiser, number of prospects contacted per fundraiser per day, number of minutes per contact, revenue per contact hour, percentage of closure per contact, percentage of potential contributors covered, and number of lost contributors.

IMAGE TRACKING

One useful measure that nonprofit organizations may wish to develop is a measure of how the organization and its offerings are perceived. Image-tracking can be a very effective control device for monitoring programs aimed at final customers. As we noted in Chapter 3, perceptions about an offering are prime indicators of ultimate behavior (or behavioral intent). Thus, if one cannot monitor sales or behavior change itself, it is most helpful to have measures of whether or not one is improving performance in terms of customer perceptions (which should lead to "sales").

But tracking organizational image can have a broader function. One of the significant features of nonprofit organizations is that they often serve multiple publics. Thus, to insure strong public support, favorable legislation, tax breaks, steadily increasing outside funding, and a substantial supply of eager volunteers, the nonprofit should also track its performance with these other publics. Image-tracking can be an excellent device for this.

Definition of Image.   The term "image" came into popular use in the 1950s. It is currently used in a variety of contexts: organization image, corporate image, national image, brand image, public image, self-image, and so on. Its wide use has tended to blur its meaning. Our definition of image is:

> An **image** is the sum of beliefs, ideas, and impressions that a person has of an object.

This definition enables us to distinguish an image from similar-sounding concepts such as *beliefs, attitudes,* and *stereotypes.*

An image is more than a simple belief. The belief that the American Medical Association (AMA) is more interested in serving doctors than serving society would be only one element of a larger image that might be held about the AMA. An image is a whole set of beliefs about an object.

On the other hand, people's images of an object do not necessarily reveal their attitudes toward that object. Two persons may hold the same image of the AMA and yet have different attitudes toward it because of different weights they place on the beliefs.

How does an image differ from a stereotype? A stereotype suggests a widely held image that is highly distorted and simplistic and that carries a favorable or unfavorable attitude toward the object. An image, on the other hand, is a more personal perception of an object that can vary greatly from person to person.

Image Measurement.   Many methods have been proposed for measuring images. We will describe a two-step approach: first, measuring how familiar and favorable the organization's image is, and second, measuring the organization's image along major relevant dimensions.

FAMILIARITY-FAVORABILITY MEASUREMENT.   The first step is to establish, for each public being studied, how familiar they are with the organization and how favorable they feel toward it. To establish familiarity, respondents are asked to check one of the following:

Never heard of	Heard of	Know a little bit	Know a fair amount	Know very well

The results indicate the public's awareness of the organization. If most of the respondents place the organization in the first two or three categories, then the organization has an awareness problem.

Those respondents who have some familiarity with the organization are then asked to describe how favorable they feel toward it by checking one of the following:

Very unfavorable	Somewhat unfavorable	Indifferent	Somewhat favorable	Very favorable

If most of the respondents check the first two or three categories, then the organization has a serious image problem.

To illustrate these scales, suppose the residents of an area are asked to rate four local hospitals, A, B, C, and D. Their responses are averaged and the results displayed in Figure 22-2. Hospital A has the strongest image: most people know it and like it. Hospital B is less familiar to most people, but those who know it like it. Hospital C is negatively viewed by the people who know it, but fortunately not too many people know it. Hospital D is in the weakest position: it is seen as a poor hospital and everyone knows it.

Clearly, each hospital faces a different task. Hospital A must work at maintaining its good reputation and high community awareness. Hospital B must bring itself to the attention of more people since those who know it find it to be a good hospital. Hospital C needs to find out why people dislike the hospital and take steps to mend its ways, while keeping a low profile.

FIGURE 22-2

Familiarity-Favorability Analysis

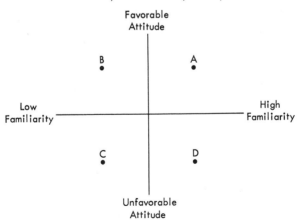

Hospital D would be well advised to lower its profile (avoid news), mend its ways, and when it is a better hospital, start seeking public attention again.

SEMANTIC DIFFERENTIAL. Each hospital needs to go further and research the content of its image. One of the most popular tools for this is the semantic differential.[1] It involves the following steps:

1. *Developing a set of relevant dimensions.* The researcher first asks people to identify the dimensions they would use in thinking about the object. People could be asked: "What things do you think of when you consider a hospital?" If someone suggests "quality of medical care," this would be turned into a bipolar adjective scale—say, "inferior medical care" at one end and "superior medical care" at the other. This could be rendered as a five- or seven-point scale. A set of additional relevant dimensions for a hospital is shown in Figure 22-3.

2. *Reducing the set of relevant dimensions.* The number of dimensions should be kept small to avoid respondent fatigue in having to rate n organizations on m scales. Osgood and his coworkers feel that there are essentially three types of scales:

- evaluation scales (good-bad qualities)
- potency scales (strong-weak qualities)
- activity scales (active-passive qualities)

Using these scales as a guide, or performing a factor analysis, the researcher can remove redundant scales that fail to add much information.

3. *Administering the instrument to a sample of respondents.* The respondents are asked to rate one organization at a time. The bipolar adjectives should be arranged so as not to load all of the poor adjectives on one side.

4. *Averaging the results.* Figure 22-3 shows the results of averaging the respondents' pictures of hospitals A, B, and C. Each hospital's image is represented by a vertical "line of means" that summarizes how the average respondent sees that institution. Thus Hospital A is seen as a large, modern, friendly, and superior hospital. Hospital C, on the other hand, is seen as a small, dated, impersonal, and inferior hospital.

FIGURE 22-3

Images of Three Hospitals (Semantic Differential)

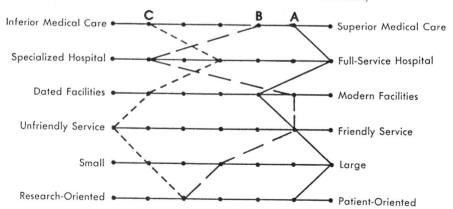

5. *Checking on the image variance.* Since each image profile is a line of means, it does not reveal how variable the image actually is. If there were 100 respondents, did they all see Hospital B, for example, exactly as shown, or was there considerable variation? In the first case, we would say that the image is highly *specific* and in the second case that the image is highly *diffused.* An institution may or may not want a very specific image. Some organizations prefer a diffused image so that different groups can project their needs onto this organization. The organization will want to analyze whether a variable image is really the result of different subgroups rating the organization with each subgroup having a highly specific image.

ATTITUDE MEASUREMENT. An alternative to the semantic differential is the use of the expectancy-value attitude model described in Chapter 3. This approach involves developing an image measure that comprises:

1. Beliefs about the positive and negative consequences of taking an action with respect to the attitude object (actions like entering a hospital, giving the hospital money, offering the hospital a tax break)
2. Weights attached subjectively to each of the consequences.

The advantage of the expectancy-value attitude measurement approach is that it focuses on *behavior,* which is usually what is critical to the nonprofit. The semantic differential more often focuses on an object or institution. The attitude measure also indicates weighting differences on the beliefs held by different critical publics. Since the latter reflect these publics' goals and values, such control information can prove very valuable to the nonprofit manager when the time comes to try to *change* the organization's image.

Both the semantic differential and the expectancy-value model are flexible image-measuring tools that can provide the following useful information:

1. *The organization can discover how a particular public views the organization and its major competitors.* It can learn its image strengths and weaknesses along with those of the competitors and take remedial steps that are warranted.
2. *The organization can discover how different publics and market segments view the organization.* One can imagine that the image profiles in Figure 22-3 represent the images of one organization held by three different publics. The organization would then consider taking steps to improve its image among those publics who view the organization most unfavorably.
3. *The organization can monitor changes in its image over time.* By repeating the image study periodically, the organization can detect any significant image slippage or improvement. Image slippage signals that the organization is doing something wrong. Image improvement, on the other hand, verifies that the organization is performing better as a result of some steps it has taken.

Image Modification.   The leaders of an organization are often surprised and disturbed by the measured image. Thus the chief administrator of Hospital C (see Figure 22-3) might be upset that the public sees the hospital as dated, impersonal, and of low quality. Management's immediate reaction is to disbelieve the results by complaining that the sample is too small or unrepresentative. But if the results can be defended as reliable, management must consider what it ought to do about this image problem.

The first step is for management to develop a picture of the *desired image* that they want to have in the general public's mind, in contrast to the *current image.* Suppose the management of Hospital C wants an image closer to that of Hospital A. Hospital C would like the general public to have a more favorable view of the quality of its medical care, facilities, friendliness, and so on. It is not aiming for perfection because the hospital recognizes its limitations. The desired image must be feasible in terms of the organization's present reality and resources.

The second step is for management to decide which image gaps it wants to work on initially. Is it more desirable to improve the hospital's image of friendliness (through staff training programs, etc.) or the look of its facilities (through renovation)? Each image dimension should be separately reviewed in terms of the following questions:

1. What contribution to the organization's overall favorable image would be made by closing that particular image gap to the extent shown? (Here, weighting data could be very useful.)
2. What strategy (combination of real changes and communication changes) would be used to close the particular image gap?
3. What would be the cost of closing that image gap?
4. How long would it take to close that image gap?

Management might decide, for example, that it would be more effective, swifter, and less costly to improve the hospital's image of friendliness than to improve the physical facilities of the hospital. An overall image modification plan would involve planning the sequence of steps through which the organization would go to transform its current image into its desired image.

An organization seeking to change its image must have great patience. Images tend to be "sticky" and last long after the reality of the organization has changed. Thus, the quality of medical care might have deteriorated at a major hospital, yet the center may continue to be highly regarded in the public mind. Image persistence is explained by the fact that once people have a certain image of an object, they tend to be selective perceivers of further data. Their perceptions are oriented toward seeking what they expect to see. It will take highly disconfirming stimuli to raise doubts and open them to new information. Thus an image enjoys a life of its own for a while, especially when people are not likely to have new first-hand experiences with the changed object.

CONSUMER SATISFACTION

Since responsive nonprofit organizations ultimately aim to create satisfaction rather than mere sales or usage, it is very valuable to track customers' satisfaction as part of the day-to-day control system. First it is necessary to define the term "satisfaction." Our definition is:

> **Satisfaction** is a state felt by a person who has experienced a *performance* (or outcome) that has fulfilled his or her *expectations*.

Thus, satisfaction is a function of the relative levels of expectations and perceived performance.[2] A person will experience one of three states of satisfaction. If the results exceed the person's expectations, the person is highly satisfied. If the results match the expectations, the person is satisfied. If the results fall short of the expectations, the person is dissatisfied.

In this case, the amount of dissatisfaction depends upon the consumer's method of handling the gap between expectations and performance. Some consumers try to *minimize* the felt dissonance by seeing more results than there really are or thinking that they set their expectations too high. Other consumers exaggerate the perceived performance gap because of their disappointment. They are more prone to reduce or end their contacts with the organization.

Thus, to understand satisfaction, we must understand how people form their expectations. Expectations are formed on the basis of people's past experience with the same or similar situations, statements made by friends and other associates, and statements made by the supplying organizations. Thus, the supplying organization influences satisfaction not only through its performance but also through the expectations it creates. If it overclaims, it is likely to create subsequent dissatisfaction; if it underclaims, it might create high satisfaction. The safest course for the nonprofit organization is to plan to deliver a certain level of performance and communicate this level to its consumers.

Consumer satisfaction, in spite of its central importance, is difficult to measure. Organizations use various methods to infer how much consumer satisfaction they are creating.

Complaint and Suggestion Systems.   One possible approach is complaint and suggestion systems. A responsive organization makes it easy for its clients to complain if they are disappointed in some ways with the service they have received. Management will want complaints to surface on the theory that clients who are not given an opportunity to complain might reduce their business with the organization, bad-mouth it, or abandon it completely. Not collecting complaints represents a loss of valuable information that the organization could have used to improve its service.

How can complaints be facilitated? The first step is for management to accept the seemingly contrary notion that more complaining is better and to communicate this perception up and down the organization. Complaints should be seen as customer-volunteered marketing research data to be actively sought, not as information to be squelched for fear that complaints will lead only to reprimands. Once this crucial atmosphere is established,

FIGURE 22-4

A Hospital Comment Card

You are a VERY IMPORTANT PERSON!

Will you let us know how we did?

We strive to provide the best possible hospital care to the patients who come to us. Please take a couple of minutes to complete this questionnaire, there is space on the back for additional comments, which will help us improve our service and continue Memorial's tradition of excellent patient care.

When completed drop it in the mail. It is addressed and the postage is paid.

Thank you for your valuable assistance.

Robert M. Magnuson
Robert M. Magnuson
President

Your room number _____

From _____ To _____

Male _____ Female _____

Your name, if you wish _____

A. Your admission: Yes No

   Were you courteously received and processed by the admitting office?   __ __

   Were you admitted to the hospital from the Emergency Department?   __ __

B. Your room:

   Was it ready for you?   __ __

   Was it attractive?   __ __

   Was it kept clean during your stay?   __ __

Cat No 193540

	Yes	No
Was the proper temperature maintained?	__	__
Were lighting and ventilation facilities adequate?	__	__
Was your room quiet enough for you to sleep and rest?	__	__

C. Your meals:

   Was the food well-prepared and appetizing, considering your diet?   __ __

   Were you satisfied with the portions?   __ __

   Did hot food arrive hot at your bedside?   __ __

   Was your food served attractively?   __ __

   Overall, were you pleased with the food service during your stay?   __ __

D. Nursing service:

   In your opinion were the nurses skilled in the performance of their duties?   __ __

   Were they attentive to your needs and did they explain reasons for medications, treatments, and diagnostic procedures?   __ __

   Was your call for assistance answered with reasonable promptness?   __ __

E. Were you satisfied with the services given by:

   X-ray technicians?   __ __

   Laboratory technicians?   __ __

	Yes	No
Housekeeping personnel?	__	__
Nursing assistants, orderlies and other nursing personnel?	__	__
Volunteers?	__	__
Telephone operators?	__	__
Admitting clerks?	__	__
Other personnel?	__	__

F. Were you informed about tests and treatments ordered by your physician?   __ __

G. Was your schedule arranged so that you could get enough rest?   __ __

H. Personal:

   Were your visitors courteously received?   __ __

   Were visiting hours satisfactory?   __ __

   Were services such as delivery of mail, flowers and packages satisfactory?   __ __

I. Business office:

   Was the cashier courteous and helpful?   __ __

J. Overall, are you satisfied with your care at Memorial Hospital?   __ __

K. Overall, are you satisfied with the information given you about your health, your treatments, and follow-up care?   __ __

L. Would you recommend our Hospital to family members, friends and neighbors?   __ __

the organization can set up systems that make it easy for dissatisfied customers (or satisfied customers) to express their feelings to the organization. Several devices can be used in this connection. A hospital, for example, could place suggestion boxes in the corridors. It could supply exiting patients with a comment card that can be easily checked off (see Figure 22-4). It can establish a patient advocate or ombudsman system to hear patient grievances and seek remedies. It can establish a nurse grievance committee to review nurse complaints.

An organization can then identify the major categories of complaints. Thus, a hospital might count the number of complaints about food, nursing care, and room cleanliness and focus its corrective actions on those categories showing high frequency, high seriousness, and high remediability.

A good complaint management system provides much valuable information for improving the organization's performance. At the same time, it should be recognized that a complaint system tends to understate the amount of real dissatisfaction felt by customers. The reasons are:

1. Many people who are disappointed may choose not to complain, either feeling too angry or feeling that complaining would do no good.
2. Some people overcomplain (the chronic complainers), and this introduces a bias into the data.

Some critics have argued that complaint systems do more harm than good. People who have an opportunity—indeed, an incentive—to complain are more likely to feel dissatisfied. Instead of ignoring their disappointment, they are asked to spell it out, and they are also led to expect redress. If the latter is not forthcoming, they will be more dissatisfied. Although this might happen, it is our view that the value of the information gathered by soliciting complaints far exceeds the cost of possibly overstimulating dissatisfaction. Further, a study by Andreasen and Best found that in many categories as many as 75 percent of all those who had a problem with a product or service felt that the problem had not been solved satisfactorily. Such a group can play significant havoc with the carefully nurtured operation of any nonprofit organization.

Consumer Satisfaction Surveys.   A major problem with volunteered complaints as noted in the Andreasen and Best study is that they are unrepresentative of both the types of complaints and the frequency of complaints. Thus, consumers are more likely to volunteer complaints about problems in which high costs (economic, social, and psychological) are involved or in which they are seriously inconvenienced. Further, they are more likely to complain if they think the nonprofit organization is to blame and they did not contribute to the problem themselves. Finally, they are more likely to complain if the nature of the problem and its source are manifest—that is, if the existence of a problem is not really a matter of individual judgment. For these reasons, a nonprofit is more likely to receive complaints about issues involving large monetary and time costs on the part of clients. Problems involving broken items, delayed services, and discourteous employees are more likely to surface than problems in which, say, medical care just is a bit impersonal or in which the staff of an educational seminar seems underprepared and the seminar is not taught very well.[3] Yet it is just these more minor kinds of unreported feelings of dissatisfaction that management would like to know about. The obvious bad features of any program usually quickly become apparent without much management research. The subtle things that can truly sink a basically good program or institution through poor word-of-mouth, lack of repeat behavior, and perhaps worse still, just plain apathy, are the very things that don't get volunteered by dissatisfied consumers. People must be asked.

People must also be asked because not all of them will speak up. To voice a complaint, one must not only have a problem or a dissatisfaction, but one has to understand where and how to complain and have the skills to do so and the gumption to speak up. Not everyone has these qualities. Indeed, research has consistently shown that vocal complainers are much more likely to be socially upscale and have higher incomes and better educations. They are also likely to be relatively young. Yet many nonprofit programs, such as those in social work or those requiring long-term behavioral change like stopping smoking or practicing family planning, have *downscale* audiences as their primary targets. Hearing from these people is essential to program success, but they are the least likely to volunteer information about their dissatisfaction.

Finally, the voicing of complaints is sometimes inhibited by the institution itself. Unless the circumstances are right and the nonprofit marketer sets the right tone, people are relatively unlikely to complain about their church, their doctor, or even their lawyer or accountant. The Andreasen and Best study reported the following dissatisfaction experience rates for medical and dental services compared with rates for all services and all products.[4]

	Medical/Dental	All Services	All Products
Percentage reporting problems	14.9%	20.9%	20.0%
Percentage with problem voicing a complaint to marketer	32.7%	42.3%	40.2%
Percentage who complained who were not satisfied with marketer response	46.4%	28.7%	23.6%

While patients perceived fewer problems with their medical and dental care than with other services or products, they were significantly less likely to speak up about them. And when they did, they found the medical and dental community much less responsive than other product and service marketers in resolving their complaints. Only one in six of those who had a serious dissatisfaction felt bold enough to speak up about it and were lucky enough to have it handled satisfactorily.

There are many reasons why doctors might not encourage complaints, several of which do not reflect well on the customer orientation of the medical community. Some of these inhibiting perspectives could be described in medical jargon as "syndromes."[5]

1. *The Holier-than-Thou Syndrome.* Many physicians believe that patients do not really know what is in fact in their own best interests. Patients find illness threatening and so have a distorted perception of their true needs. Further, they simply lack the physician's technical knowledge and thus cannot judge what is needed and what is not. Physicians can therefore ignore their complaints.

2. *The They're-Not-Paying-For-It-Anyway Syndrome.* Since third-party insurers frequently bear much of the cost of medical care, patients can (and should) be scheduled for tests, medication, or return office visits that may have only

marginal value. The costs to patients in terms of time and inconvenience are ignored, as are their complaints about excessive tests and medicines and about medical costs in general.

3. *The Higher-Opportunity-Cost Syndrome.* Since physicians perceive themselves to be in the business of saving lives, they frequently assume that their time is much more valuable than that of their patients. Patients therefore should not complain about accommodating to the physician's convenience or paying high fees for his or her services.

4. *The I-Want-to-Be-Alone Syndrome.* Four out of five physicians practice alone. Many do so because they cherish the independence that makes them immune to the peer pressures upon which medical community control largely relies.

5. *The They're-Out-to-Get-Me Syndrome.* Many physicians seem to behave as if all patients have a lawyer friend or relative ready to bring a malpractice suit at the drop of a suture. Such physicians schedule excessive self-protective tests and procedures and tend by demeanor to discourage any consumer inquiries about their medical care that might escalate into a malpractice claim.

6. *The Mystique-of-Omnipotence Syndrome.* Since a positive patient attitude toward the illness and its cure is often an important contributor to the cure itself, many physicians believe that unswerving faith in the physician is essential to a positive outcome. Creating a mystique of omnipotence requires that the physician brook no questioning of his or her methods and outcomes.

As a result of these types of factors, the better, more responsive nonprofits supplement the devices described earlier with direct periodic surveys of consumer satisfaction. They send questionnaires or make telephone calls to a random sample of past users to find out how much they like the service. In this way, they avoid the possible biases of complaints systems on the one hand and consumer panels on the other.

Consumer satisfaction can be measured in a number of ways, three of which will be described here. We will illustrate them in a university setting.

DIRECTLY REPORTED SATISFACTION.   A university can distribute a questionnaire to a representative sample of students, asking them to state their satisfaction with the university as a whole and with specific components. The questionnaire would be distributed on a periodic basis either in person, in the mail, or through a telephone inquiry.

The questionnaire would contain questions of the following form:

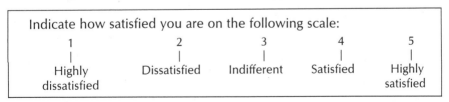

Here five intervals are used, although some scales use only three intervals and others as many as eleven. The numbers assigned to the intervals are arbitrary, except that each succeeding number is higher than the previous one. There is no implication that these are unit distances. When the results are in, a histogram can be prepared showing the percentage of students who fall into each group. Of course, students within any group—such as the highly dissatisfied group—may have really quite different intensities of dissatisfaction ranging from mild feelings of disappointment with the university to intense feelings of anger. Unfortunately, there is no way to make interpersonal comparisons of utility and we can only rely on the self-reported feelings of the respondents.

If the histogram is highly skewed to the left, then the university is in deep trouble. If the histogram is bell-shaped, then it has the usual number of dissatisfied, indifferent, and satisfied students. If the histogram is highly skewed to the right, the university can be very satisfied that it is a responsive organization meeting its goal of delivering high satisfaction to the majority of its consumers. It is necessary to repeat this survey at regular intervals to spot any significant changes in the distribution. Furthermore, the respondents should check similar scales for the significant components of the university, such as its academic program, extracurricular program, housing, and the like. It would help to know how the various components of satisfaction relate to overall satisfaction.

DERIVED DISSATISFACTION. The second method of satisfaction measurement is based on the premise that a particular student's satisfaction is influenced by the perceived state of the object and his expectations. He is asked two questions about each component of the university; for example:

The quality of the academic program:								
a. How much is there now?								
(min)	1	2	3	4	5	6	7	(max)
b. How much should there be?								
(min)	1	2	3	4	5	6	7	(max)

Suppose he circles 2 for part a and 5 for part b. We can then derive a "performance deficiency" score by subtracting the answer for part a from part b, here 3. The greater the performance deficiency score, the greater his degree of dissatisfaction (or the smaller his degree of satisfaction).

This method provides more useful information than the previous method. By averaging the scores of all the respondents to part a, the researcher learns the average perceived level of that attribute of the object. The dispersion around the average shows how much agreement there is. If all students see the academic program of the university at approximately 2 on a 7-point scale, this means the program is pretty bad. If students hold widely differing perceptions of the program's actual quality, further analysis is needed of why the perceptions differ so much and what individual or group factors it might be related to.

It is also useful to average the scores of all the respondents to part b. This reveals the average student's view of how much quality is expected in the academic program. The measure of dispersion shows how much spread there is in student opinion about the desirable level of quality.

By finding the deficiency score for each component of the university's offering, the administration will have a good diagnostic tool to understand current student moods and to make necessary changes. By repeating this survey at regular intervals, the university can detect new performance deficiencies as they arise and take timely steps to remedy them.

Importance/Performance Ratings.   Another satisfaction-measuring device is to ask consumers to rate several services provided by the organization in terms of (1) the importance of each service, and (2) how well the organization performs each service. Figure 22-5 shows how fourteen services of a college were rated by students. The importance of a service was rated on a four-point scale of "extremely important," "important," "slightly important," and "not important." The college's performance was rated on a four-point scale of "excellent," "good," "fair," and "poor." The first service, for example, "academic program," received a mean importance rating of 3.83 and a mean performance rating of 2.63, indicating that students felt it was highly important, although not being performed that well. The ratings of all fourteen services are displayed in Figure 22-5B. The figure is divided into four sections. Quadrant A shows important services that are not being offered at the desired performance levels. The college should concentrate on

FIGURE 22-5

Importance and Performance Ratings for Several College Services

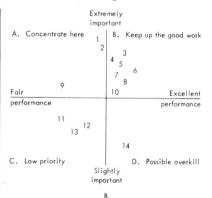

Service	Service description	Mean importance rating[a]	Mean performance rating[b]
1	Academic program	3.83	2.63
2	Housing quality	3.63	2.73
3	Food quality	3.60	3.15
4	Athletic facilities	3.56	3.00
5	Social activities	3.41	3.05
6	Faculty availability	3.41	3.29
7	" "	3.38	3.03
8	" "	3.37	3.11
9	" "	3.29	2.00
10	" "	3.27	3.02
11	" "	2.52	2.25
12	" "	2.43	2.49
13	" "	2.37	2.35
14	" "	2.05	3.33

[a]Ratings obtained from a four-point scale of "extremely important," "important," "slightly important," and "not important."

[b]Ratings obtained from a four-point scale of "excellent," "good," "fair," and "poor." A "no basis for judgment" category was also provided.

A.

B.

improving these services. Quadrant B shows important services that the college is performing well; its job is to maintain the high performance. Quadrant C shows minor services that are being delivered in a mediocre way, but that do not need any attention since they are not very important. Quadrant D shows a minor service that is being performed in an excellent manner, a case of possible "overkill." This rating of services according to their perceived importance and performance provides the college with guidelines as to where it should concentrate its efforts.

Consumer Panels.   Another approach used by some organizations is to set up a consumer panel to keep informed of consumer satisfaction. A consumer panel consists of a small group of customers who have been selected to make up a panel that will be sampled from time to time about its feelings toward the organization or any of its services. Thus, a hospital may set up a doctor panel that would be sampled periodically for its reactions or suggestions. A university may set up a student panel that would be sampled periodically for its reactions to current services.

Consumer panel members may volunteer or they may be paid for their time. Some provision is usually made to rotate membership on the panel to get fresh views from new people. The panel is typically a source of valuable information to the organization. At the same time, the information may not be completely trustworthy. The panel's representativeness can be called into question. People who do not like to be members of panels are not represented. Those who join the panel may be more loyal to the organization and thus less likely to see its faults.

RELATION BETWEEN CONSUMER SATISFACTION AND OTHER GOALS OF THE ORGANIZATION

Many people believe that the marketing concept calls upon an organization to *maximize* the satisfaction of its consumers. This, however, is not realistic and it would be better to interpret the marketing concept as saying that the organization should strive to create a high level of satisfaction in its consumers, though not necessarily the maximum level. The reasons for this are explained below.

First, consumer satisfaction can always be increased by accepting additional cost. Thus, a university might hire better faculty and build better facilities and charge lower tuition to increase the satisfaction of its students. But obviously a university faces a cost constraint in trying to maximize the satisfaction of a particular public.

Second, the organization has to satisfy many publics. Increasing the satisfaction of one public might reduce the satisfaction available to another public. The organization owes each of its publics some specific level of satisfaction. Ultimately, the organization must operate on the philosophy that it is trying to satisfy the needs of different groups at levels that are acceptable to these groups within the constraints of its total resources. This is why the organization must systematically measure the levels of satisfaction expected by its different constituent publics and the current amounts they are, in fact, receiving.

The organization hopes to derive a number of benefits as a result of creating high satisfaction in its publics. First, the members of the organization will work with a better sense of purpose and pride. Second, the organization creates loyal publics and this reduces the costs of market turnover. Third, the loyal publics say good things to others about the organization and this attracts new consumers without requiring as much direct effort on the part of the organization.

EFFICIENCY

The measures just described of sales, attitudes, and satisfaction are all designed to monitor the *effectiveness* of nonprofit programs. Equally important is the need to measure the *efficiency* of those programs. As we pointed out in Chapter 1, nonprofits are notorious for having very limited budgets—both in dollars and personnel. An effective control system therefor also ought to track costs and relate them to the returns from the program elements on which they are spent. Where the returns are dollar revenues, this evaluation is usually referred to as *profitability analysis*. Where the returns involve other measures of satisfaction or attitude change, the evaluation is usually referred to by the more general term, *cost/benefit analysis*. These issues were considered in further detail in Chapter 12 on marketing programming and budgeting.

STRATEGIC CONTROL

We have emphasized that the hallmark of an effective mature nonprofit marketing program is its attention to *strategic* issues. Thus, while an essential ingredient for effective management is a first-rate control system for day-to-day and month-to-month monitoring of *existing* strategies, there is also a critical need for the organization to reassess its strategic position on a periodic basis. The marketing audit is often used for this purpose.

THE MARKETING AUDIT

Marketing is one of the major areas in which rapid obsolescence of objects, policies, strategies, and programs is a constant possibility.

A major tool in this connection is in the marketing audit. Organizations are increasingly turning to marketing audits to assess their marketing opportunities and operations. A marketing audit is defined as follows:[6]

> A **marketing audit** is a *comprehensive, systematic, independent,* and *periodic* examination of an organization's marketing environment, objectives, strategies, and activities with a view of determining problem areas and opportunities and recommending a plan of action to improve the organization's strategic marketing performance.

The four characteristics of a marketing audit are expanded upon in the following paragraphs:

1. *Comprehensive.* The marketing audit covers all of the major marketing issues facing an organization, and not only one or a few marketing trouble spots. The latter would be called a functional audit if it covered only the sales force, or pricing, or some other marketing activity.
2. *Systematic.* The marketing audit involves an orderly sequence of diagnostic steps covering the organization's marketing environment, internal marketing system, and specific marketing activities. The diagnosis is followed by a corrective action plan involving both short-run and long-run proposals to improve the organization's overall marketing effectiveness.
3. *Independent.* The marketing audit is normally conducted by an inside or outside party who has sufficient independence from the marketing department to attain top management's confidence and the needed objectivity.
4. *Periodic.* The marketing audit should normally be carried out periodically instead of only when there is a crisis. It promises benefits for the organization that is seemingly successful, as well as the one that is in deep trouble.

A marketing audit is carried out by an auditor who gathers information that is critical to evaluating the organization's marketing performance. The auditor collects secondary data and also interviews managers, customers, dealers, salespeople, and others who might throw light on the organization's marketing performance. The auditor cannot rely only on internal management opinion, and must seek the opinions and evaluations of outsiders regarding the organization. Often the findings are a surprise, and sometimes a shock, to management.

Table 22-1 is a guide to the kinds of questions that the marketing auditor will raise. Not all the questions are important in every situation. The instrument will be modified depending on whether the organization is a museum, college, social service agency, government agency, and so on.[7] However, the sequence of topics should be maintained.

Table 22-1

MARKETING AUDIT GUIDE

Part I. Marketing Environment Audit

Macroenvironment

A. DEMOGRAPHIC

1. What major demographic developments and trends pose opportunities or threats for this organization?
2. What actions has the organization taken in response to these developments?

B. ECONOMIC

1. What major developments and trends in income, prices, savings, and credit have an impact on the organization?
2. What actions has the organization taken in response to these developments and trends?

C. ECOLOGICAL

1. What is the outlook for the cost and availability of natural resources and energy needed by the organization?
2. What concerns have been expressed about the organization's role in conservation and what steps has the organization taken?

D. TECHNOLOGICAL

1. What major changes are occurring in relevant product, service, and process technology? What is the organization's position in these technologies?
2. What major generic substitutes might replace this product or service?

E. POLITICAL

1. What new legislation could affect this organization? What federal, state, and local agency actions should be watched?
2. What actions has the organization taken in response to these developments?

F. CULTURAL

1. What changes are occurring in consumer life-styles and values that might affect this organization?
2. What actions has the organization taken in response to these developments?

Task Environment

A. MARKETS

1. What is happening to market size, growth, and geographical distribution?
2. What are the major market segments? What are their expected rates of growth? Which are high-opportunity and low-opportunity segments?

B. CUSTOMERS

1. How do current customers and prospects rate the organization and its competitors, particularly with respect to reputation, product quality, service, sales force, and price?

Table 22-1 (continued)

2. How do different classes of customers make their buying decisions?

3. What are the evolving needs and satisfactions being sought by consumers in this market?

C. COMPETITORS

1. Who are the major competitors? What are the objectives and strategy of each major competitor? What are their strengths and weaknesses? What are the sizes and trends in market shares?

2. What trends can be foreseen in future competition and substitutes for this product?

D. DISTRIBUTION AND DEALERS

1. What are the main distribution channels bringing products to customers?

2. What are the efficiency levels and growth potentials of the different distribution channels?

E. SUPPLIERS

1. What is the outlook for the availability of different key resources used in production?

2. What trends are occurring among suppliers in their pattern of selling?

F. FACILITATORS AND MARKETING FIRMS

1. What is the outlook for the cost and availability of transportation services?

2. What is the outlook for the cost and availability of warehousing facilities?

3. What is the outlook for the cost and availability of financial resources?

4. How effectively is the advertising agency performing?

G. PUBLICS

1. What publics (financial, media, government, citizen, local, general, and internal) represent particular opportunities or problems for the company?

2. What steps has the company taken to deal effectively with its key publics?

Part II. Marketing Objectives and Strategy Audit

A. ORGANIZATION'S OBJECTIVES

1. Is the mission of the organization clearly stated in market-oriented terms? Is the mission feasible in terms of the organization's opportunities and resources?

2. Are the organization's various objectives clearly stated so that they lead logically to the marketing objectives?

3. Are the marketing objectives appropriate, given the organization's competitive position, resources, and opportunities?

B. MARKETING STRATEGY

1. What is the core marketing strategy for achieving the objectives? Is it a sound marketing strategy?

2. Are enough resources (or too many resources) budgeted to accomplish the marketing objectives?

3. Are the marketing resources allocated optimally to prime market segments, territories, and products of the organization?

4. Are the marketing resources allocated optimally to the major elements of the marketing mix, that is, offer quality, service, sales force, advertising, promotion, and distribution?

Table 22-1 (continued)

Part III. Marketing Organization Audit

A. FORMAL STRUCTURE

1. Is there a high-level marketing officer with adequate authority and responsibility over those organizational activities that affect the customer's satisfaction?
2. Are the marketing responsibilities optimally structured along functional, product, end user, and territorial lines?

B. FUNCTIONAL EFFICIENCY

1. Are there good communication and working relations between marketing and sales?
2. Is the product management system working effectively? Are the product managers able to plan profits or only sales volume?
3. Are there any groups in marketing that need more training, motivation, supervision, or evaluation?

C. INTERFACE EFFICIENCY

1. Are there any problems between marketing and operations that need attention?
2. What about marketing and R&D?
3. What about marketing and financial management?
4. What about marketing and purchasing?

Part IV. Marketing Systems Audit

A. MARKETING INFORMATION SYSTEM

1. Is the marketing intelligence system producing accurate, sufficient, and timely information about developments in the marketplace?
2. Is marketing research being adequately used by managers?

B. MARKETING PLANNING SYSTEM

1. Is the marketing planning system well conceived and effective?
2. Is sales forecasting and market potential measurement soundly carried out?
3. Are sales quotas set on a proper basis?

C. MARKETING CONTROL SYSTEM

1. Are the control procedures (monthly, quarterly, etc.) adequate to ensure that the annual plan objectives are being achieved?
2. Is provision made to analyze periodically the profitability of different products, markets, territories, and channels of distribution?
3. Is provision made to periodically examine and validate various marketing costs?

D. NEW-PRODUCT DEVELOPMENT SYSTEM

1. Is the organization well organized to gather, generate, and screen new product ideas?
2. Does the organization do adequate concept research and business analysis before investing heavily in a new idea?
3. Does the organization carry out adequate product and market testing before launching a new product?

Table 22-1 (continued)

Part V. Marketing Productivity Audit

A. PROFITABILITY ANALYSIS

1. What is the profitability of the organization's different products, customer markets, territories, and channels of distribution?
2. Should the organization enter, expand, contract, or withdraw from any market segments, and what would be the short- and long-run profit consequences?

B. COST-EFFECTIVENESS ANALYSIS

1. Do any marketing activities seem to have excessive costs? Are these costs valid? Can cost-reducing steps be taken?

Part VI. Marketing Function Audits

A. PRODUCTS

1. What are the product line objectives? Are these objectives sound? Is the current product line meeting these objectives?
2. Are there particular products that should be phased out?
3. Are there new products that are worth adding?
4. Are any products able to benefit from quality, feature, or style improvements?

B. PRICE

1. What are the pricing objectives, policies, strategies, and procedures? To what extent are prices set on sound cost, demand, and competitive criteria?
2. Do the customers see the organization's prices as being in line or out of line with the perceived value of its offer?
3. Does the organization use promotional pricing effectively?

C. DISTRIBUTION

1. What are the distribution objectives and strategies?
2. Is there adequate market coverage and service?
3. Should the organization consider changing its degree of reliance on distributors, sales reps, and direct selling?

D. ADVERTISING, SALES PROMOTION, AND PUBLIC RELATIONS

1. What are the organization's advertising objectives? Are they sound?
2. Is the right amount being spent on advertising? How is the budget determined?
3. Are the ad themes and copy effective? What do customers and the public think about the advertising?
4. Are the advertising media well chosen?
5. Is sales promotion used effectively?
6. Is there a well-conceived public relations program?

E. SALES FORCE

1. What are the organization's sales force objectives?
2. Is the sales force large enough to accomplish the organization's objectives?
3. Is the sales force organized along the proper principle(s) of specialization (territory, market, product)?

Table 22-1 (continued)

> 4. Does the sales force show high morale, ability, and effort? Are they sufficiently trained and incentivized?
> 5. Are the procedures adequate for setting quotas and evaulating performances?
> 6. How is the organization's sales force perceived in relation to competitors' sales forces?

Criteria of Audit Success.   The marks of a good marketing audit are the following:[8]

- *Comprehensiveness.* Have all the key dimensions of the organization's marketing program been investigated?
- *Objectivity.* To what extent have the evaluations been
  Quantified?
  Based on valid internal or external secondary data?
  (If subjective) replicated or cross-checked with other observers?
  (If original research) based on a valid, reliable research methodology?
- *Timeliness.* Was the examination based on up-to-date inputs and information?
- *Usefulness.* Was the report delivered in time to meet management decision-making needs? Were the recommendations relevant, affordable, and otherwise feasible?
- *Well Communicated.* Was the final report
  Simply, clearly written?
  Prefaced by an executive summary?
  Illustrated with forceful, necessary graphics?
  Concise and understandable?
  Supplemented by necessary documentation and appendices?

Marketing Audit Procedure.   A marketing audit is sometimes requested by a funding agency or a governing body. More often the management of the organization itself will request a marketing audit. The actual task of carrying out an audit for the first time can be divided into ten stages[9] (see Figure 22-6). Several stages can be modified or eliminated in subsequent audits. Although these stages are typically carried out in sequence, it is often necessary to return to earlier stages as later stages suggest new avenues of investigation. (On-site interviews, for example, may reveal new secondary sources to be reviewed which, in turn, may suggest additional questions for later interviews.) Some key issues to be addressed in several of these steps are listed below.

BACKGROUNDING AND INITIAL MANAGEMENT CONTACT. The auditor should begin by reviewing any previous studies of the organization that are available, including past marketing audits. Discussions should be held with those who requested the audit to ascertain their expectations for the audit's outcomes. At this stage, tentative final deadlines should be specified.

FIGURE 22-6

Steps in a Marketing Audit

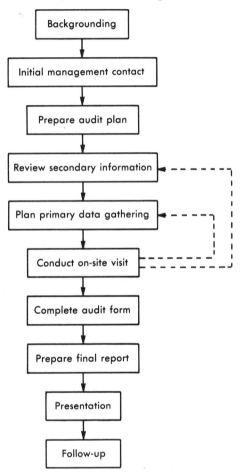

The auditor should next meet with the management of the organization audited in order to

1. Assure management that the audit is designed to assist management in developing a better marketing organization and better marketing strategies. Management must know and accept that the audit is *not* at all like an accounting audit, which looks for errors, deceptions, or other evidence of mismanagement. Instead, the marketing audit is a *forward-looking* document indicating to management what can and should be the focus of their strategic efforts in the coming months and years.

2. Introduce the auditor (or the auditing team) to management and explain to management that the audit will be based on hardheaded practical considerations that take full recognition of local conditions. A marketing audit is not an ivory-tower exercise that outlines ideal strategies or evaluates programs according to unrealistic standards. Rather, it is a down-to-earth set of guidelines to point the organization in directions consistent with the best marketing wisdom and experience.

3. Ascertain management's wishes and expectations for the audit's outcomes. It is important that the audit meet not only the needs of those individuals who initiate or pay for the audit, but also those of management.

4. Describe the audit procedure and review with management the specific audit instrument.

5. Present a formal request for archival information to learn from management what required information is available and when and how it can be obtained. A checklist of the basic information to be requested should be prepared in advance.

6. Begin planning a site visit (or several visits) for first-hand observation and interviews with staff and knowledgeable outsiders.

7. Establish a procedure to keep management informed of insights secured during the audit, and test the feasibility of (and management's receptivity to) various courses of action that could be proposed. If the audit's recommendations are to be implemented, it is critical that they not come as surprises to management.

DATA GATHERING.   Background information to be obtained from the organization is not always available on the dates indicated by management. Some will turn out not to exist, some will be received late, and some will have to be secured from other sources. A bibliography of the material used in the audit, both internal and external to the organization, should be appended to the final report.

Secondary data must usually be supplemented by original research. This research might include

- Interviews with key staff.
- Review of documents not previously available.
- Observation of sales training meetings, sales calls, press briefings, and trade exhibits.
- Visits to outlets.
- Observation of advertisements, brochures, and point-of-purchase materials for the subject organization.
- Observation of competitors' products, packaging, advertisements, and point-of-purchase materials.

A specific audit form should be used to record the data from these investigations. This standardized document will facilitate comparisons from audit to audit and across units within a single audit.

FINAL REPORT AND PRESENTATION. The audit form itself contains the raw material and detailed recommendations that will feed into the final report. The final report must contain three additional elements:

- An executive summary
- A presentation of recommendations
- An appendix

The appendix will contain exhibits, reports, questionnaires, tables, or sample materials to back up the audit report itself. Some of these may be original documents prepared by the auditor.

The first and second additional elements are more critical. The recommendations section should summarize and prioritize the audit's major recommendations, pointing out clearly how the results of the next audit should differ from the current one. The executive summary should briefly present the audit's major findings and recommendations.

The audit is valuable only if it is used. The auditor, therefore, has primary responsibility to make sure that the final report is clearly and thoroughly understood. This means not only that the report should be stated in the simplest, most direct, and most compelling language, but that it should also be discussed in person with all interested parties. Such discussion will ensure that major ambiguities are cleared up, that there is no misunderstanding of the auditor's major recommendations, and that management understands what is required of them to implement necessary changes. Finally, face-to-face presentation offers one additional opportunity to secure feedback about the report that may or may not necessitate revision.

FOLLOW-UP. As already noted, the audit must be very explicit about *what the organization must do to carry out the report's recommendations.* In this regard, it is important that the date of the next audit be set, at least at the point of the final presentation, so that management can develop a timetable to achieve the goals implied by the audit. It may also be useful for management or the organization sponsoring the audit to identify interim benchmarks that would permit it, as well as the implementing organization, to make sure the goals of the audit will be achieved on schedule.[10]

MARKETING INFORMATION SYSTEMS

As we have seen, nonprofit managers need timely, accurate, and adequate market information as a basis for making sound marketing decisions. We shall use the term *marketing information system* (MIS) to describe the organization's system for gathering, analyzing, storing, and disseminating relevant marketing information. More formally:

A **marketing information system** is a continuing and interacting structure of people, equipment, and procedures designed to gather, sort, analyze, evaluate and distribute pertinent, timely, and accurate information for use by marketing decision-makers to improve their marketing planning, execution, and control.[11]

The role and major subsystems of an MIS are illustrated in Figure 22-7. At the left is shown the marketing environment that marketing managers must monitor—specifically, target markets, marketing channels, competitors, publics, and macroenvironmental forces. Developments and trends in the marketing environment are picked up in the company through one of four subsystems making up the marketing information system—the internal reports system, the marketing intelligence system, the marketing research system, and the analytical marketing system. The information then flows to the appropriate marketing managers to help them in their marketing planning, execution, and control. The resulting decisions and communications then flow back to the marketing environment.

We will now expand on the four major subsystems of the organization's MIS.

INTERNAL RECORDS SYSTEM

The oldest and most basic information system used by managers is the internal records system. Every organization accumulates information in the regular course of its operations.

A hospital will keep records on its patients, including their names, addresses, ages, illnesses, lengths of stay, supplies and room charges, attending physicians, complaints, and so on. From these patient records, the hospital can develop statistics on the number of daily admissions, average length of patient stay, average patient charge, frequency distribution of different illnesses, and so on. The hospital will also have records on their physicians, nurses, costs, billings, assets, and liabilities, all of which is indispensable information for making management decisions.

A museum will keep several record systems. Its contributor file will list the names, addresses, past contributions, and other data of its contributors. Its campaign progress file will show the amount raised to date from each major source, such as individuals, foundations, corporations, and government grants. Its cost file will show how much money has been spent on direct mail, newspaper advertising, brochures, salaries, consultant fees, and so on.

Every internal records system can be improved in its speed, comprehensiveness, and accuracy. Periodically, an organization should survey its managers for possible improvements in the internal records system. The

FIGURE 22-7

The Marketing Information System

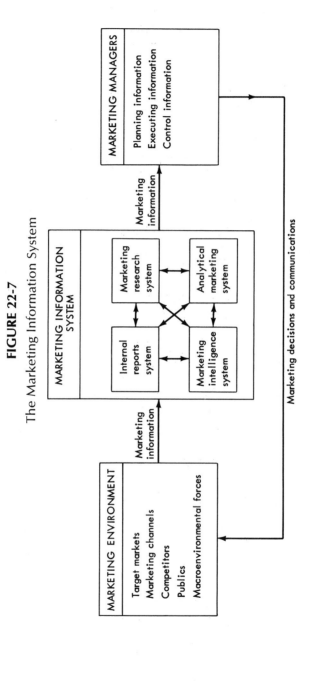

goal is not to design the most elegant system, but one that is cost-effective in meeting the manager's information needs. A cross-section of managers should be queried as to their information needs. Table 22-2 shows the major questions that can be put to them. Once their opinions are gathered, the information system designers can design an internal records system that reconciles (1) what managers think they need, (2) what managers really need, and (3) what is economically feasible.

MARKETING INTELLIGENCE SYSTEM

Whereas the internal reports system supplies executives with *results data,* the marketing intelligence system supplies executives with *happenings data.* Our definition is:

> The **marketing intelligence system** is the set of sources and procedures by which marketing executives obtain their everyday information about developments in the external marketing environment.

Managers carry on marketing intelligence mostly on their own by reading newspapers and trade publications and talking to various people inside and outside the organization. In this way, they are able to spot important developments. At the same time, their casual approach to gathering marketing intelligence can also result in missing or learning too late of some other important developments, such as a fund-raising opportunity with an

Table 22-2

QUESTIONNAIRE FOR DETERMINING MARKETING INFORMATION NEEDS
OF MANAGERS

1. What types of decisions are you regularly called upon to make?
2. What types of information do you need to make these decisions?
3. What types of information do you regularly get?
4. What types of special studies do you periodically request?
5. What types of information would you like to get that you are not now getting?
6. What information would you want daily? weekly? monthly? yearly?
7. What magazines and reports would you like to see routed to you on a regular basis?
8. What specific topics would you like to be kept informed of?
9. What types of data analysis programs would you like to see made available?
10. What do you think would be the four most helpful improvements that could be made in the present marketing information system?

important donor or a new law that might hurt the organization's nonprofit status.

An organization can take some concrete steps to improve the quality of the marketing intelligence available to its managers. First, the organization must "sell" its managers and staff on the importance of gathering marketing intelligence and passing it on to others in the organization. Their intelligence responsibilities can be facilitated by designing information forms that are easy to fill out and circulate. Managers should know the kind of information that would be useful to other managers.

Second, the organization should encourage outside parties with whom it deals—advertising agencies, professional associations, lawyers, accountants—to pass on any useful bits of information. A museum's lawyer, for example, may hear about a wealthy donor who is revising his will, and this information can be useful to the development office of the museum.

Third, the organization could hire people to carry on specialized intelligence-gathering activities. Many organizations hire "mystery shoppers" to canvass their own organization and competitors' organizations. A mystery shopper might visit the admissions offices of several colleges and report back on the quality of their "customer handling." In one case, the "bogus student" reported receiving widely different receptions, some of which were absolute "turnoffs" and others of which were highly effective. Mystery shopping is also an important means for learning whether the organization's own staff is really practicing a customer orientation in its dealings with the public.

Fourth, the organization can establish an office that is specifically responsible for gathering and disseminating marketing intelligence. The staff would perform a number of services. It would scan major publications, abstract the relevant news, and disseminate the news to appropriate managers. It would install suggestion and complaint systems so that clients and others would have an opportunity to express their attitudes toward the organization. It would develop a master index so that all the past and current information could be easily retrieved. The staff would assist managers in evaluating the reliability of different pieces of information. These and other services would greatly enhance the quality of the information available to marketing managers.

Marketing Research System

From time to time, managers need to commission specific marketing research studies in order to have adequate information to make pending decisions. Administrators of nonprofit organizations are increasingly finding that they need marketing research, such as when a hospital wants to know whether people in its service area have a positive attitude toward the hospital, when a college wants to determine what kind of image it has among high school counselors, or when a political organization wants to find out what voters think of its candidate and other candidates. Many studies could prove worthwhile to an organization, but in the face of a limited budget, the organization must have know-how to choose marketing research projects carefully, design them efficiently, and implement the results effectively. Because of its growing importance in nonprofit marketing, we have treated marketing research in more detail in Chapter 6.

ANALYTICAL MARKETING SYSTEM

The marketing information system contains a fourth subsystem called the analytical marketing system. The analytical marketing system consists of a set of advanced techniques for analyzing marketing data and marketing problems. These systems are able to produce more findings and conclusions than can be gained by only commonsense manipulation of the data. Large organizations tend to make extensive use of analytical marketing systems. In smaller organizations, managers resist these approaches as too technical or expensive.

An analytical marketing system consists of two sets of tools known as the statistical bank and the model bank (see Figure 22-8). The *statistical bank* is a collection of advanced statistical procedures for learning more about the relationships within a set of data and their statistical reliability. They allow management to go beyond the frequency distributions, means, and standard deviations in the data.

Managers often want answers to such questions as:

- What are the most important variables affecting my performance, and how important is each one?
- If I raise my price 10 percent and increase my advertising expenditures by 20 percent, what will happen to sales?

FIGURE 22-8

Analytical Marketing System

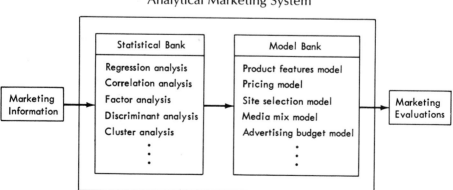

- What are the most discriminating predictors of which persons are likely to change their behavior in response to my marketing strategy?
- What are the best variables for segmenting my market, and how many segments should be created?

The statistical techniques are somewhat technical, and the reader is advised to consult other sources for understanding and using them.[12]

The *model bank* is a collection of models that will help marketers make better marketing decisions. Each model consists of a set of interrelated variables that represent some real system, process, or outcome. These models can help answer "what if?" and "which is best?" questions. In the last twenty years, marketing scientists have developed a great number of models to help marketing executives do a better job of pricing, designing sales territories and sales call plans, selecting sites for outlets, developing optimal advertising media mixes, developing optimal size advertising budgets, and forecasting new product sales.[13]

This concludes our review of the nature of a marketing information system and its main subsystems—internal reports, marketing intelligence, marketing research, and analytical marketing. All of these are essential to effective evaluation and control of soundly conceived strategic marketing plans.

SUMMARY

For strategic planning to be successful, it must be supported by effective control systems. We distinguish between two kinds of control systems. *Marketing control systems* routinely monitor marketing performance and suggest corrective action for fine-tuning of strategic plans. *Strategic evaluations* involve periodic assessments of various aspects of the marketing program. A major tool here is the marketing audit. Both marketing control and strategic evaluations should be incorporated as essential elements in a marketing intelligence support system that will also include the marketing research function.

Organizations exercise at least three types of marketing control. Annual plan control consists of monitoring the current marketing performance to be sure that the annual sales and profit goals are being achieved. The main tools are sales analysis, market-share analysis, marketing expense-to-sales analysis, and market attitude tracking. If underperformance is detected, the organization can implement a variety of corrective measures. Profitability control consists of determining the actual profitability of different marketing entities, such as the organization's products, territories, market segments, and distribution channels. Marketing profitability analysis reveals the weaker marketing entities, although it does not indicate whether the weaker units should be bolstered or phased out. Strategic control consists of making sure that the organization's marketing objectives, strategies, and systems are optimally adapted to the current and forecasted marketing environment. It uses the tool known as the marketing audit, which is a comprehensive, systematic, independent, and periodic examination of the organization's marketing environment, objectives, strategies, and activities. The purpose of the marketing audit is to determine marketing problem areas and recommend corrective short-run and long-run actions to improve the organization's overall marketing effectiveness.

To carry out effective control, the organization also needs timely, accurate, and adequate information. Four systems make up the organization's marketing information system.

The first, the internal records system, consists of all the information that the organization gathers in the regular course of its operations. It includes sales and cost information by product, customer, territory, and so on. Many useful questions can be answered by analyzing the information in the internal records system.

The second, the marketing intelligence system, describes the set of sources and procedures by which executives obtain their everyday information about developments in the marketplace. An organization can improve the quality of its marketing intelligence by motivating its managers to scan the environment and report useful information to others, and hiring intelligence specialists to find and disseminate important information.

The third, the marketing research system, consists of the systematic design, collection, analysis, and reporting of data and findings relevant to a specific marketing situation or problem facing an organization. The marketing research process consists of five steps: developing the research objectives and problem definition; exploratory research; formal survey and/or experimental research; fieldwork; and data analysis and report presentation.

The fourth, the analytical marketing system, consists of two sets of advanced tools for analyzing marketing data and marketing problems. One set of tools is the statistical bank, which is a collection of statistical procedures for analyzing the relationships within a set of data and their statistical reliability. The other is the model bank, which is a collection of mathematical models that will help marketers make better marketing decisions.

QUESTIONS

1.   Describe a set of quantitative indicators that could be used by a municipal rapid transit system to indicate when its marketing programs are and are not succeeding.

2.   Data on the number of patient-days achieved by hospitals in specific health care regions for various treatment specialties are available to most hospital marketing managers. These data can be translated into market shares. Evaluate the worth of such measures in guiding marketing programs for a specific hospital.

3.   Outline a set of semantic differential dimensions that could be used to measure the image of careers in the U.S. Coast Guard. Classify the dimensions as to whether they measure evaluation, potency, or activity.

4.   A public television station in a major metropolitan area routinely catalogues and summarizes "complaints and kudos" sent or telephoned into the station by its listeners. Staff consider these data to be extremely good measures of how well the station is doing. Criticize the value of such measures.

5. A charitable organization has available to it a number of free or low-cost services, including volunteer labor for some activities, donated local air time for commercials, preparation of advertising at cost by a local advertising agency, and so on. The organization wishes to evaluate the cost-effectiveness of various marketing programs it has developed. The programs vary significantly, however, in the extent to which they are able to utilize donated goods and services. How might the agency proceed to make such programs comparable for control purposes?

NOTES

1. C. E. Osgood, G. J. Suci, and P. H. Tannenbaum, *The Measurement of Meaning* (Urbana: University of Illinois Press, 1957). Other image-measuring tools exist, such as *object-sorting* (see W. A. Scott, "A Structure of Natural Cognitions," *Journal of Personality and Social Psychology*, Vol. 12, No. 4, 1969, pp. 261–278), *multidimensional scaling* (see Paul E. Green and Vithala R. Rao, *Applied Multidimensional Scaling* (New York: Holt, Rinehart and Winston, Inc. 1972), and *item lists* (see John W. Riley, Jr., ed., *The Corporation and Its Public* (New York: John Wiley, 1963), pp. 51–62.

2. See Ralph E. Anderson, "Consumer Dissatisfaction: The Effect of Disconfirmed Expectancy on Perceived Product Performance," *Journal of Marketing Research*, February 1973, pp. 38–44.

3. See Alan R. Andreasen and Arthur Best, "Consumers Complain—Does Business Respond?" *Harvard Business Review*, (July–August 1977), pp. 93–101.

4. *Ibid.*

5. Alan R. Andreasen, "Consumer Behavior in Loose Monopolies: The Case of Medical Care," in Ronald F. Bush and Shelby D. Hunt, eds., *Marketing Theory: Philosophy of Science Perspectives* (Chicago: American Marketing Association, 1982).

6. For details, see Philip Kotler, William Gregor, and William Rodgers, "The Marketing Audit Comes of Age," *Sloan Management Review*, Winter 1977, pp. 25–43.

7. For a marketing audit guide for social service organizations, see Douglas B. Herron, "Developing a Marketing Audit for Social Service Organizations," in Charles B. Weinberg and Christopher H. Lovelock, eds., *Reading in Public and Nonprofit Marketing* (Palo Alto, Calif.: Scientific Press, 1978), pp. 269–271. For arts organizations, see Tom Horwitz, *Arts Administration* (Chicago: Review Press, 1978), pp. 81–85. For hospitals, see Eric N. Berkowitz and William A. Flexner, "The Marketing Audit: A Tool for Health Service Organizations," *HCM Review*, Fall 1978, pp. 55–56.

8. Alan A. Andreasen, *Problems in Practical Application of a Standardized Marketing Audit*, (Washington, D.C.: The Futures Group, 1983).

9. Alan R. Andreasen, *A Marketing Audit Model for Contraceptive Social Marketing Programs*, (Washington, D.C.: The Futures Group, 1983).

10. *Ibid.*

11. The definition is adapted from Samuel V. Smith, Richard L. Brien, and James E. Stafford, "Marketing Information Systems: An Introductory Overview," in their *Readings in Marketing Information Systems* (Boston: Houghton Mifflin, 1968), p. 7. See also Lee G. Cooper and Daniel Jacobs, "Marketing Information Systems for the Profession and Science of Arts Management," *The Journal of Arts Management and the Law,* Vol. 14, No. 1, Spring 1984, pp. 77–89.

12. See David A. Aaker, ed., *Multivariate Analysis in Marketing: Theory and Applications* (Belmont, Calif.: Wadsworth, 1971).

13. Various models are described in Gary L. Lilien and Philip Kotler, *Marketing Decision Making—A Model Building Approach,* 2d ed., (New York: Harper and Row, 1983).

Indexes

NAME INDEX

ORGANIZATIONS INDEX

SUBJECT INDEX

Abortion clinics, 477
Adopter categories, 402–6
Advertising, 21, 124, 372–73, 445, 542–57, 642
    agencies, 310
    association, 545
    budget determination, 551–52
    burst, 560
    charitable, 544
    continuous, 560
    donated, 552
    evaluation, 561–66
    government, 545
    intermittent, 561
    management, 545
    objective-setting, 546–51
    paid, 543, 552
    political, 544
    pretesting, 561–65
    private nonprofit, 545
    social cause, 544
    unpaid, 543
Advertising Age, 397
Age, and market segmentation, 54, 122, 127
Agents, 171–72
AIDA sales formula, 607
Alumni associations, 62
Analytical marketing system, 651–52
Annual call schedule, 609
Aquariums, 52
Arts administration, 5
Arts institutions, 29, 50
Assimilation/contrast theory, 516
Association advertising, 545
Atmospherics, 477
Attitude change theory, 512–18
Attitude measurement, 223, 627
Audience
    forecasting, 250–51
    potential, 260
    profile, 67
Automobile clubs, 14
Average revenue, 453

Backward integration, 482
Balance theory, 528–30
Behavior modification, 532–38
Benefit segmentation, 146–48
Benefit/cost analysis, 211, 213–18, 353–57, 491, 637
    implementation, 213–18
    problems in, 356–57
    theory of, 354–56
Bias
    frame, 230
    interviewer, 231
    nonresponse, 231
    processing, 231
    questionnaire, 231
    respondent, 231
    selection, 230
    systematic, 229–30
Blood banks, 48–49, 52, 103, 106–7, 148–49, 174, 409, 584
Board of directors, 229

Boston Consulting Group Portfolio approach, 182–84
Boundary person, 594–95
Brainstorming, 385
Brand name, 424, 426
Breakeven analysis, 462–64
Budget maximization, 359
Budgeting, 124
    advertising, 551–52
    affordable, 211
    competitive matching, 211
    cost/benefit approach, 211, 213–18
    historical increment, 211
    marketing planning, 270
    percent of revenues, 211
Business analysis, 390
Business firms, 313–17
Buyclasses, 110
Buyer behavior
    family life cycle and, 131–32
    stages of readiness, 148, 372–73
    see also Consumers; Customer; Donor markets
Buyer intentions surveys, 248–49

Campaign, 200, 343, 344
Camps, 457–58, 462–63
Channel *see* Marketing channel
Charitable advertising, 544
Charitable giving *see* Donor markets
Charities, 29, 36, 62, 171, 180, 325, 429, 493, 496
Charity campaigns, 316–17
Cheaper goods strategy, 412
Child welfare organizations, 10
Churches, 10, 25, 162–64, 171, 342, 361–62, 429, 430, 474–75
Cognitive dissonance theory, 100–1
Colleges and universities, 2, 9, 29, 39, 50, 59–61, 86–102, 104–6, 143, 146–47, 165–73, 186–96, 236–40, 248, 253, 259, 261, 265–71, 273–74, 276, 278, 280, 294–95, 307, 317, 327, 330, 333–38, 343, 345, 362–63, 367–71, 381–82, 386–91, 414–15, 426, 429, 431, 449–50, 476, 480, 493, 497, 546–47, 579–80, 583–85, 599–601, 633–36
    see also Education
Comment card, 630
Commercial organizations, 12, 29, 310–13
Commercialization, 391–92
Communication
    choosing a medium, 527–30
    definition, 505
    developing effective execution styles, 511–32
    format elements, 526
    message evaluation and selection, 530–32
    objectives, 511
    one-/two-sided arguments, 524–26
    order of presentation, 526
    perceptual distortion, 527
    process, 506–11
    vehicles, 506
    see also Message
Communication strategies, 504–41
    and marketing strategy, 510–11
Communications manager, 286
Community relations program, 584